UMI ANNUAL SUNC O M M

PRECEPTS
FOR
LIVING

2002-2003

International Sunday School Lessons

published by

URBAN MINISTRIES, INC.

A. Okechukwu Ogbonnaya, Ph.D., *Editor*
Melvin E. Banks, Sr., Litt.D., *Founder and Chairman*

VOLUME 5

Urban Ministries, Inc.

CONTRIBUTORS

Editor
A. Okechukwu Ogbonnaya, Ph.D.

Layout & Design
Larry Taylor,
Vice President, Creative Services

Bible Illustrations
Fred Carter

Editorial Staff
Kathryn Hall, Managing Editor
Shawan Brand, Production Manager
Kim Brooks, Publications Assistant
Cheryl Wilson, Publications Assistant

Contributing Writers
Essays
Deborah Branker-Harrod
Dr. Jacquelyn Donald-Mimms
Overseer Terry S. Goodlow
Jennifer King
Dr. Leonard Lovett
Dr. Clyde Oden
A. Okechukwu Ogbonnaya, Ph.D.
Dr. Jean Porter
Dr. Robert Scott
Judith St.Clair Hull, Ph.D.

Bible Study Guides
Minister Terry Brock
Moussa Coulibaly, Ph.D.
Dr. Jacquelyn Donald-Mimms
Rev. Robert Dulin
Melody Goodwin
Crystal Green
Pastor Wilkins O. Jones
Jennifer King
Rev. Fred Thomas
Rev. Alajemba Reuben Unagebu
Karen F. Williams

More Light On The Text
Dr. Aye Adewuya
Moussa Coulibaly, Ph.D.
Dr. Jacquelyn Donald-Mimms
Rev. Robert Dulin
Melody Goodwin
A. Okechukwu Ogbonnaya, Ph.D.
Rev. Fred Thomas
Rev. Alajemba Reuben Unaegbu

Unless otherwise indicated, all Scripture references are taken from the authorized King James Version of the Bible.

A LETTER FROM THE EDITOR

Dear Brothers and Sisters in Christ,

We here at UMI are in the business of spreading the Gospel of Jesus Christ and equipping the church for an effective ministry in the world. We are especially concerned with providing relevant tools to the church, making her Divine witness to the Lord among God's children of African descent more effective. We believe that it is through the knowledge of the Word—that God's people can be healed and restored to their true place in the heart of God.

PRECEPTS FOR LIVING is one of the tools that we believe will help Christians become more effective communicators of the Word of God. This is the first Sunday School Lesson Commentary written from an African American perspective. In this, we continue the UMI tradition of giving relevant gifts to the body of Christ as it seeks to reach the people of African descent for our Lord.

The unique contribution of this work is that it is written from an African American Christian perspective, providing deep analysis of scriptural passages in both the IN DEPTH section and in the section entitled MORE LIGHT ON THE TEXT. The latter is a linguistic and cultural exposition of the text. It takes the passages verse by verse and comments on them from the perspective of the original language and culture. The TEACHING TIPS section preceding each lesson is important for those in the church who teach Sunday School and Bible studies. It gives direction and suggests activities that may help you as you teach God's Word. This volume also includes a CD ROM version of *PRECEPTS FOR LIVING* with the King James Version of the Bible and Strong's Concordance reference numbers.

PRECEPTS FOR LIVING is a useful tool for pastors in sermon preparation and Bible study, Church School teachers, Sunday School superintendents, and all Christians who are interested in a deeper understanding of the Word of God. At UMI we have put much prayer into this Sunday School Annual. We know that God will use it to bless you in your walk.

Peace be with you,

A. Okechukwu Ogbonnaya, Ph.D.

TABLE OF CONTENTS

Fall Quarter, 2002

Winter Quarter, 2002, 2003

v

CYCLE OF 1998-2004

Arrangement of Quarters According to the

Church School Year, September through August

	1998 - 1999	1999 - 2000	2000 - 2001	2001- 2002	2002- 2003	2003- 2004
Sep Oct Nov	God Calls a People to Faithful Living (Old Testament Survey) (13)	From Slavery to Conquest (Exodus, Leviticus, Numbers, Deuteronomy, Joshua) (13)	The Emerging Nation (Judges, 1,2, Samuel [1 Chronicles], 1 Kings 1-11 [2 Chronicles 1-9]) (13)	Jesus' Ministry (Parables, Miracles Sermon on the Mount) (13)	Judgment and Exile (2 Kings 18-25 [2 Chronicles 29-36] Jeremiah, Lamentations, Ezekiel, Habakkuk, Zephaniah) (13)	Faith Faces the World (James, 1,2, 2 Peter, 1,2,3, John, Jude) (13)
Dec Jan Feb	God Calls Anew in Jesus Christ (New Testament Survey) Christmas Sun. (12/20) (13)	Emmanuel: God with Us (Gospel of Matthew) Christmas Sun. (12/19) (13)	Good News of Jesus (Gospel of Luke) Christmas Sun. (12/24) (13)	Light for All People (Isaiah 9:1-7, 11:1-9; 40-66; Ruth, Jonah, Naham) Christmas Sun. (12/23) (13)	Portraits of Faith (Personalities in the New Testament) Christmas Sun. (12/22) (13)	A Child is Given (4) (Samuel, John the Baptist, Jesus [2]) Lessons from Life (9) (Esther, Job, Ecclesiastes, Song of Solomon) Christmas Sun. (12/21)
Mar Apr May	That You May Believe (Gospel of John) Easter (4/4) (13	Helping a Church Confront Crisis (1, 2 Corinthians) Easter (4/23) (13)	Continuing Jesus's Work (Acts) Easter (4/15) (13)	The Power of the Gospel (Romans, Galatians) Easter (3/31) (13)	Jesus: God's Power in Action (Gospel of Mark) Easter (4/20) (13)	Jesus Fulfills His Mission (6) (Passion Narratives) Living Expectantly (7) (1,2 Thessalonians, Revelation) Easter (4/11)
Jun Jul Aug	Genesis: Beginnings (Genesis) (13)	New Life in Christ (Ephesians, Philippians, Colossians, Philemon) (13)	Division and Decline (1 Kings 1-17, [2 Chroni-cles 10-28], Isaiah 1-39, Amos, Hosea, Micah) (13)	Worship and Wisdom for Living (Psalms, Proverbs) (13)	God Restores a Remnant (Ezra, Nehemiah, Daniel, Joel, Obadiah, Haggai, Zechariah, Malachi) (14)	Hold Fast to the Faith (8) (Hebrews) Guidelines for the Church's Ministry (5) (1,2 Timothy, Titus)

* Parenthetical numerals indicate number of sessions.

For My People

Calm, calm, calm
the eye of the storm
propelling the movement of the wind
discerning the rising tides' ebb and flow
overturning a faithless ease and lax
envisioning a new world in the vanishing terrain
ne'er has it been more clear
divine newness arises out of the ash

Peace, peace, peace
in the center of the tumult
echoes the Master's soothing voice
sweeter than Helena's siren song
blanket of blue ice over the restless sea
undulating promise of splendor
ne'er has it been more clear
a crystal fountain rises here

Strength, valor and confidence
holding back the rising flood
in the flow of the divine blood
as the Spirit in power broods
to undo hell's nimbus shroud
mahogany, tis not mere wood that
builds heaven's gate
ne'er has it been so clear,
a great mighty oak grows here

Rock, stone, rock
the waters of the ages beat
Rock, stone, rock
firmly planted in the Master's heart
Stone, though small and rough
yet, hid within the Rock of ages
ne'er has it been more clear
within the Rock a Jewel is formed.

A. Okechukwu Ogbonnaya

INTRODUCTION TO THE SEPTEMBER 2002 QUARTER

The Quarter at-a-Glance

JUDGMENT AND EXILE

Studies this quarter deal with the historical period beginning with the reign of King Hezekiah and ending with the fall of Jerusalem in 587-586 B.C. This era has been described as a time of struggle between sin and obedience. It is marked by the rejection of God's law, impending judgment, signs of God's anger, and calls to repentance. At the same time, God's steadfast love and the possibility of renewing a right relationship with God are manifested in the leadership of certain kings and in the messages of true prophets.

UNIT 1. CHALLENGED TO CHANGE

This unit recreates the periods of reform promoted by some of Judah's kings and the messages of the prophets encouraging the nation to live in obedience to God. The unit includes passages from 2 Chronicles and the prophets Zephaniah and Jeremiah. Although there were periodic rejections of the covenant, both the kings and the prophets expressed hope that a change would be possible.

LESSON 1: September 1
Repentance and Renewal
2 Chronicles 30:1-6, 8-12

The biblical content emphasized in this lesson is grounded in the story of Hezekiah. Hezekiah, the king of Judah, invited all Israel and Judah to come to the temple in Jerusalem to celebrate the Passover in the second month because the Passover had not been observed at the proper time (vv. 1-3). The king and the Jerusalem assembly jointly issued the proclamation throughout all Israel and Judah, sending letters inviting the people to return to God (vv. 4-6). The letters urged the people not to be like their obstinate and faithless ancestors, but to yield themselves to God, come to the temple, and serve God (v. 8). The king hoped that through this act of repentance, God would forgive the people and would cause the nation's enemies to treat them with compassion (v. 9).

People in Israel responded poorly, but in Judah they were positive (vv. 10-12). This lesson teaches us the necessity of repentance. Our renewal—like that of Israel—is grounded in repentance and a heart-felt return to the Most High God. Repentance has within it the seed of hope. For here we see that although Hezekiah has heard the judgment of God, he still proceeds to call the people to repentance. There is no theological crisis of fatalism in the acts of the people of Judah and their king. Repentance is our way out when we have hedged ourselves in through sin. Repentance is that human-divine reasoning that prepares our heart to receive the latter rain of the Lord. Although we may not get everything we seek, repentance gives us the opportunity to seek out God once more.

LESSON 2: September 8
God Restores a Sinner
2 Chronicles 33:1-13

This lesson continues the emphasis of the previous lesson but with a different narrative periscope. Here we meet Manasseh, the son of King Hezekiah, who was crowned king as a child and had a long but evil reign in Jerusalem (vv. 1-2). Manasseh was the son of a righteous king. His reign was evil by virtue of the reestablishment of idol worship, which led the people into sinful practices (vv. 3-9). Manasseh and his people—unlike his father and the people of Judah—ignored God's warnings. Since there was no repentance, God sent the Assyrian army, which captured Manasseh and took him to Babylon (vv. 10-11). The text ends by telling us that in distress Manasseh prayed to God for help, and God listened and restored Manasseh to Jerusalem and to his kingdom. This divine favor led Manasseh to the knowledge of the Lord, the God of his father (v. 13).

From our human perspective, we have difficulty understanding how people like Manasseh can be forgiven, let alone restored to the favor of God. This lesson vivifies the idea of God's sovereignty in dealing with human beings. Manasseh is the extreme example of the fallen sinner, yet we find that even this villain receives forgiveness from the Lord when he repents. How far have you gone? How deep have you sunk? How dead are you in your iniquity? If you will only call on His name, He will be there to set you free. God's mercy is waiting for you. If God is able to restore someone like Manasseh, God can restore you, too.

LESSON 3: September 15
Present and Future
Zephaniah 1:12; 3:1-5, 11-13

The passage of Scripture that forms the basis of this lesson begins with Zephaniah the prophet declaring that the Lord would search Jerusalem and punish the complacent (1:12). This judgment is the result of the rebellion of the people of Jerusalem against God's laws. Moreover, they were acting as if they only had to answer to themselves and could ignore God completely (3:1-2). Zephaniah reminds the cynics who were equating the corrupt political officials with God that while the political, judicial, and religious leaders of Jerusalem violated their offices and abused the people, God remained righteous and just (vv. 3-5). The passage ends by telling us that in the time of God's judgment, the haughty leaders would be removed, and the humble, righteous people would be justified and safe (vv. 11-13).

In this lesson, we see another dimension of the nature of God's dealing with His people. While repentance does lead to renewal and restoration, this lesson teaches us that obstinacy in the present assures a future of futility. Our present actions will produce punishment from the Lord if we fail to turn in repentance to God. However, in this lesson, more than individual or personal actions were being judged. The whole social agenda of the leaders—political, judicial, and religious—was being brought under divine judgment.

LESSON 4: September 22
A New Beginning
2 Chronicles 34:1-3, 21, 29-33

Josiah, who became king of Judah when he was 8 years old, did what was right in God's eyes and began to remove all elements of idol worship (vv. 1-3). The heart of this king is revealed by his actions. When a book of the law was discovered in the temple, Josiah wanted to find out what God's law required (v. 21). The king gathered all the people of Judah and Jerusalem and read the book of the covenant to them (vv. 29-30). Josiah made a covenant with God to keep the words of the book; then he made all present in Jerusalem and in Benjamin swear to it (vv. 31-32). To show that his commitment was complete, Josiah removed all the idols from the territory, and for the rest of his life the people followed God (v. 33).

God gives us opportunities to redirect our paths. In this lesson, we see the providence of the Lord as the people of Judah once again discover the ways of the Lord. Here we see the fruits of repentance in action. First, there is a discovery of the divine decree; that is, there is a revelation of the divine standard. Next, there is a commitment to change in light of God's standard to act differently. But this commitment to act differently is not based solely on human will. It's a covenantal act that acknowledges the fact that without God any such commitment falls flat. In addition, we see that a leader may commit to obey God, but the people also need to understand this commitment and to buy into it for themselves. Josiah got the people to commit to this covenant, thus making sure that evil manners did not corrupt the good intention. This created accountability. Finally, there was the actual removal of the idols. This lesson shows us the steps we must take as we seek to move from the possibility of judgment to the blessing of restoration.

LESSON 5: September 29
Rebellion and Judgment
Jeremiah 6:16-21, 26-28

The book of Jeremiah focuses on the sins of the people and the coming judgment of God If the people failed to repent. In the Scripture passage for this lesson, God commanded the people to return to the ancient covenant and sent prophets to lead them, but the people refused to obey (vv. 16-17). Because the people rejected God's teaching, God pronounced disaster on them (vv. 18-19). God also rejected their offerings and set obstacles in their paths (vv. 20-21). As Jeremiah saw the destruction of the people drawing near, he called the people to contrition and began to lament (v. 26). The passage tells us that God even called Jeremiah to test the people to see if there were any faithfulness in them, but they were all found to be rebellious (vv. 27-28).

This lesson addresses the human tendency to rebel against God. It focuses on the fact that rebellion against God will ultimately lead to destruction. The lesson also shows that God never stops calling us to repentance, even when judgment is being pronounced. If we listen to God and repent, we can avoid many dangers. If you have been in rebellion, repent—turn around today and live.

UNIT 2. A LIMITED HOPE

This unit deals with a period of despair as the maneuvers of the political powers around Judah made clear that the end of independence was near. Passages from 2 Chronicles, Jeremiah, and Habakkuk are included in the lessons. The messages from the prophets suggest that the time for the fulfillment of their words was coming soon.

LESSON 6: October 6
Another Strong Warning
Jeremiah 25:1-7; 26:12-13

This passage from Jeremiah continues the biblical emphasis of the previous lesson. We read how the Lord spoke again through Jeremiah the prophet to all the people living in Judah and Jerusalem in the fourth year of the reign of King Jehoiakim (25:1-2). Although the word of the Lord had come persistently to the people, they had not listened (vv. 3-4). In this text, the prophet's declaration has moved from God's warning to divine anger. Because the people refused to listen and turn away from their sin, the Lord was provoked to anger (vv. 5-7). So that they would not attribute injustice to God, Jeremiah reminded all the officials and all the people that God had sent him to warn them (26:12). But even in this moment of divine judgment, Jeremiah told the people again to mend their ways and obey God's commands so that God would not bring upon them the judgment He had pronounced against them (v. 13).

What an awesome God—the Lord God of

Israel—must be! How extensive is His mercy! How deep is His compassion! How may times do we provoke God when we anger Him with our actions and our refusal to repent? Yet, just as He continued to show mercy to the people of Judah, God keeps showing His mercy to us. God is always hoping that before the judgment we will come to our senses and embrace His kindness. Have you responded to the call of God to repent? There is still a chance for you. Even in the midst of your punishment, God is still waiting for you with mercy.

LESSON 7: October 13
God Demands a Just Society
Jeremiah 22:13-17, 21-23

In this lesson, God condemns the descendants of Josiah, who were unrighteous and unjust, did not pay their workers fairly, and gloried in opulence (vv. 13-14). Jeremiah declared that Josiah, as a true king, worked through justice (vv. 15-16). In contrast, unlike Josiah, the current king was greedy and oppressive (v. 17). The text ends by declaring that because the leaders trusted prosperity more than God, they would suffer shame under God's judgment to come (vv. 21-23).

The demand to work for justice is unequivocal in Scripture. This lesson points us directly to the consequences that attend injustice. We are called here to do justice because the God whom we serve delights in justice.

LESSON 8: October 20
Hope for the Future
Jeremiah 31:23-34

God promised to restore Israel and Judah to their lands and homes after the Exile. Just as God watched over Israel and Judah to break them down, God promised to build them up again (vv. 27-28). God's promise of a new day did not include blame for the sins of their ancestors but involved personal accountability for one's own sins (vv. 29-30). The Lord would make a new covenant, unlike any covenant that had come before, for the law would be put into the people's hearts (vv. 31-33). In this new covenant, all the people would know God, and He would forgive their iniquity and remember their sin no more (v. 34).

Although several of this quarter's lessons speak of God's judgment, these declarations of God's judgment are always accompanied by the possibility of divine mercy. No matter how far we have gone, as long as there is life we can turn to God. In this lesson, we see God promising a future to the people of Israel. Divine restoration is possible. Are you currently paying for your sins? Are the consequences of your action overwhelming you? There is good news. Even in the midst of judgment, God can remember mercy, and restoration is still possible. Notice that this promise is made even before Israel repents. It is based solely on the mercy of God.

LESSON 9: October 27
Living in Faith
Habakkuk 3:2-6, 17-19

The biblical content for this lesson is from the book of Habakkuk. In this passage, the prophet praises God's wondrous works and prays that God will act in the desperate situation that the people of God currently face (vv. 2-3). Habakkuk describes the coming of the Lord to judge the world (vv. 4-6). He further declares that he will praise God as Lord and Savior, even if the land were to become desolate and barren (vv. 17-18). Habakkuk affirms that God was the strength that made him secure in the midst of troubles (v. 19).

This lesson teaches us the power of living faith. Here we see a prophet who, although he finds himself in a situation of death and barrenness, still believes that God is able to bring life out of death. This lesson calls us to affirm the possibilities that are in God. Though the world may be in constant tumult, yet we shall trust in the Lord. Though success as defined by the world eludes us now, yet we will rejoice in the Lord. Though the nation fails to hear our plea for help, yet we shall rejoice in the Lord our God. This lesson calls us to possess a living faith that acknowledges God as the source of strength. If in fact God is our strength, we know that we will have the ultimate victory.

UNIT 3. FALL AND EXILE

Unit 3 focuses on the fall of Jerusalem and analyzes the painful experience of exile. A story from 2 Chronicles and the messages of Ezekiel and Lamentations provide the biblical background for understanding the emotions associated with the Exile.

LESSON 10: November 3
The Fall of Jerusalem
2 Chronicles 36:11-21

This final chapter of Judah's history before the Exile chronicles how Zedekiah the king disregarded Jeremiah and the word of the Lord that Jeremiah sought to deliver (vv. 11-12). Zedekiah continued to resist God by rebelling against Nebuchadnezzar (v. 13). However, it was not just the king who had a problem; the people and leading priests were also unfaithful and desecrated the temple (v. 14). Then God, out of steadfast love, sent messenger after messenger to speak His word; but the people rejected the messengers and God's word (vv. 15-16). As a result, the destruction of Jerusalem is executed by the Babylonians. They destroyed the temple and took the people into captivity (vv. 17-21).

This lesson describes the result of the sins of the people. They have sown the wind; now they reap the whirlwind. They have walked in their own way, disregarding the direction of the Lord; now they face people who care not for the Lord and know not of His compassion. They have refused to hear the cry of the poor; now they cry and no one shows them compassion. The fall of Jerusalem teaches us not to take for granted the warnings of the Lord. If God let His chosen city of Jerusalem be destroyed, we also ought to be careful lest the same thing happen to us. Right now God's warning against rebellion is going out to us. Are we going to hear? We ought to hear and heed it so we can live.

LESSON 11: November 10
Grief and Hope
Lamentations 1:12-16; 3:22-24, 31-33

This lesson describes Jerusalem's sorrowful plight and attributes it to God's judgment (1:12-15). Because Judah had ignored the word of God, no comfort or comforter was available for Judah; its courage was gone, and its enemies had prevailed (v. 16). Notwithstanding this, Jeremiah declares God's steadfast and never-ending love (3:22). The prophet sees God as a source of hope

(vv. 23-24). Although God's judgment is painful, God continues and will continue to act out of compassion (vv. 31-33).

Yes, there is always hope. The same God who disciplines also embraces those who turn to Him. In the midst of our grief—even that grief which comes from the hand of God—there is still a ray of hope if we look to Him. For as the Scripture says, "The steadfast love of the Lord never ceases" (v. 22, RSV). As you study this lesson, be of good courage and remember that God is waiting to show mercy to you.

LESSON 12: November 17
Who is to Blame?
Ezekiel 18:1-4, 20-21, 25-32

Biblically, the source of this lesson is Ezekiel's criticism of the false theology of Israel, which implied a refusal of responsibility. Ezekiel, speaking on God's behalf, rejected an old proverb that implied children would inherit the sins of their parents (vv. 1-4). The Lord informed the exiles that each person would be held accountable for his or her own righteousness or wickedness (v. 20). The people were offered the opportunity to repent of their ways, do right, and live (v. 21). Those who did not want to be accountable for their wickedness claimed that God was unfair, but God declared they were the ones who were unfair (vv. 25-29). The people of Israel would be judged according to how they lived, and they still had opportunity to change and find the life that God desired for them (vv. 30-32).

Accountability to God is not always pleasant. From the time of Adam and Eve until today, people have had a problem accepting their part in the consequences that befall them. The people of Israel were no different. While in exile, they felt that they were guiltless and were suffering mainly because of the sins of their ancestors. Hence the proverb: "The fathers have eaten sour grapes and the children's teeth are set on edge." But we are all accountable for our own actions. By quoting this proverb, the people of Israel suggested that God was unjust. But God answers their charge and makes it clear that people suffer as a consequence of their own actions. The Israelites who were in exile had the opportunity to change the direction of the nation, but they failed to do so because of a lack of repentance. In contrast, we learn that we are all responsible and accountable to God.

LESSON 13: November 24
A Look to the Future
Ezekiel 36:22-32

Ezekiel delivered the word that God would act, not for Israel's sake, but for the sake of His name, which Israel had defiled before other nations (vv. 22-23, 32). God promised to return the people of Israel to their own land from all other countries and to cleanse Israel from its sinfulness and idolatry (vv. 24-25). He promised to put within the people a new spirit that would lead them to be faithful (vv. 26-27). He would restore the people to the land of their ancestors, give them abundance, and save them from their uncleanness (vv. 28-30). God's future blessings would cause Israel to be ashamed of their former sins and evil ways (vv. 31-32).

In this lesson, we are reminded to take courage and to know that in God there is always the hope of a better future for us. A look toward the future will help us through times of grief, brokenness, and struggle. Even when we feel like exiles, we can look to the future because God has given us a promise that will not fail. God promised that He would raise his people up. Though they were beaten down by Babylon, the Lord would return them to the place of promise.

EDUCATING AFRICAN AMERICANS FOR HEALTH

Dr. Clyde W. Oden

Many African Americans are in poor health for reasons that are preventable, or at least manageable. The problem is that we have chosen toxic lifestyles over therapeutic lifestyles. We are living to die, rather than living to live. The goal of this essay is not to bemoan our difficulties but to point out options available to us today if we choose to follow a TLC: Therapeutic Lifestyle for Christians.

In a radio address on February 21, 1998, President Bill Clinton committed the United States of America to an ambitious goal of eliminating the disparities in health status experienced by racial and ethnic minority populations by the year 2010. The United States Department of Health and Human Services (DHHS) selected six focus areas in which racial and ethnic minorities experience significant disparities in health access and outcomes. As reported by the DHHS, a snapshot of African Americans in the six focus areas reveals the following:

1. Infant Mortality. African American babies are dying at birth and within the first 28 days of birth at a rate that is twice that of White babies.
2. Heart Disease. Coronary heart disease (CHD) kills more Americans than nearly all other diseases combined.
3. Cancers. Cancer is the second leading cause of death, but for African Americans the incidence of many forms of cancer is much higher than for nearly every other ethnic group living in America.
4. Diabetes. According to the National Diabetes Information Clearinghouse report issued on September 20, 1998, diabetes is a very serious problem in the African American community. This report reveals the following: In 1998, of 35 million African Americans, about 1.5 million have been diagnosed with diabetes. This is

almost four times the number known to have diabetes in 1968. About 730,000 African Americans have diabetes but do not know they have the disease. Identifying undiagnosed cases and providing additional clinical care and treatment for diabetes is a major challenge for the health care community. For every six White Americans who have diabetes, ten African Americans have diabetes. Diabetes is particularly common among middle-aged and older adults and among African American women. Among African Americans aged 50 years or older, 19% of men and 28% of women have diabetes. African Americans with diabetes are more likely to develop complications from the disease and to experience greater disability than White Americans with diabetes. Death rates for people with diabetes are 27% higher for Blacks than for Whites.

5. Immunizations. In a report issued on April 17, 2000, Donna Shalala, Secretary for the Department of Health and Human Services reported that while 83% of White children (19 to 35 months old) have received the most commonly recommended series of vaccinations by age 2, only 74% of Black children and 77% of Hispanic children are fully vaccinated. For adults, the African Americans' rate was less than half the targeted goal for those 65 years and older.

6. HIV Infections/AIDS. According to the United States Government Centers of Disease Control, HIV and AIDS is a particularly serious problem among African Americans. Representing only an estimated 12% of the total U.S. population,

African Americans make up almost 37% of all AIDS cases reported in this country.

When we look at these statistics for African Americans, we begin to understand the analogy of the "pool at Bethesda." If Jesus were walking near the pool at Bethesda today, He would find this group of African Americans lying around the pool looking for a miracle, and I believe that he would look deep into our souls and ask the question: "Do you want to be well?" In response, we must answer and take action. Jesus commanded the invalid man who had been at the pool for 38 years to get up and do something positive about his life. As the Scripture reports in John 5:8, "Then Jesus said to him, 'Get up! Pick up your mat and walk.'" Briefly, here are the steps that are involved in obeying Jesus' command today:

1. Know your current health status. Get a regular comprehensive health check-up to establish a baseline to which everything can be compared as you monitor your health in subsequent years. It is disgraceful that nearly 20% of all African Americans in this nation do not have any form of health insurance. However, there are 80% who *do* have coverage. Find out what is going on with your body. Ignorance is a sin! (See 1 Corinthians 6:19.)

2. Follow the instructions given to you by your healthcare professional. If you don't agree with him/her, find another qualified healthcare professional and follow that person's instructions. Whatever you do, don't replace their opinion with that of your hairdresser, barber, baker, local shopping mall clerk, health food store employee, or any other person who tells you what you want to hear. Take your medications, follow the regimen given to you, and if you have problems or questions, ask your doctor.

3. Start living a healthful life by avoiding harmful and sinful habits, behaviors, and choices. For example, Jesus would never authorize His followers to smoke cigarettes, cigars, pipes, marijuana, crack cocaine, heroin, or any other substance that needs to be lit and then sucked into your lungs. We were created to breathe clean air.

Similarly, the sin of sex outside of marriage is destroying our families and our lives. The consequences of this behavior are also evident in the statis-tics. A majority of our infants are born to unmarried parents. We have some of the highest rates of sexually transmitted diseases of any people in the United States. The percentage of African American women being infected by the HIV virus is greater than that of any other ethnic group in this country. These are just a few of the results of having sex outside of marriage or having sex with people who have multiple sexual partners. There are no acceptable explanations for polluting our bodies with harmful chemicals or destroying our health through poor lifestyle choices. Doing so is a sin before God! (See James 4:17.)

4. Change to a lifestyle of therapeutic eating habits. We are killing ourselves in our kitchens, in our dining rooms, and in those convenient fast food places in our neighborhoods. We eat too much animal fat, too many fried foods, too few vegetables, too little fruit, and too much snack food. One of our gifts as a people is that we have developed the skill to make fatty meat taste good. We call it "barbecue." The problem is that we no longer eat this food sparingly and in moderation. Barbecue is okay to eat four times a year or at holiday gatherings, but it is deadly when we are eating it every week.

Our diet, along with our failure to monitor our health, keep our blood pressure low, and check our cholesterol levels, produces a toxic lifestyle. Jesus asked the question, "Do you want to be well?" We as a people must eat properly in order to be well. We must eat to live, not to die. Soul food is good in moderation, but it is vitally important that we significantly reduce our intake of fatty meats, cheeses, dairy products, and eggs and increase our daily intake of vegetables, fruits, water, and grains.

5. Exercise to live longer. African Americans have been blessed with wonderful bodies. Our physiques, our shapes, and our musculature are the envy of the world. But we must "use it or lose it." The fact of the matter is that many of our people are grossly overweight and out of shape. As a result, we are "lying around the pool of Bethesda" with our stomachs larger than our chests and bodies shaped more like pears than traditional Coke bottles, and these are all physical indications that we are not exercising enough. Exercise can be simple and inexpensive. All that is needed is a 20-30 minute walk in the neigh-

borhood (if necessary, with a stick to keep the dogs away). Encourage others to take action. Walk in pairs or in groups of three or four. Walk with your children, especially those who are also overweight. Our toxic lifestyle keeps us in front of the television or lying down on the couch. If we want to be well, we will get up and exercise.

6. Take control of our neighborhoods and communities. Instead of waiting for the miracle, we must understand that we have been given the power to change the world, starting with our own houses and neighborhoods. It is unhealthy to sit around and complain about what "they" aren't doing to make "your" community safer, cleaner, or a better place in which to live. We must use the empowerment that is available through the Holy Spirit to let our lights shine in the communities in which we live. Don't stand (or lie) passively by and think the politicians are going to do it for you and your family. We must speak out, act out, and get out and make a difference in our communities.

7. Pray and meditate regularly. Prayer and meditation are essential for healthy living. There are some things that your doctor and your healthcare professionals cannot do for you. Prayer is powerful, yet personal. You have to spend time with God; it is unhealthy and downright antithetical to Christian living not to have a healthy relationship with the Lord. A personal relationship with God and communication with Him in prayer allows one with health problems to talk to God about them. As the song "I Once Was Lost in Sin," written by Clevant Derricks and traditionally sung during worship, says in the refrain: "Have a little talk with Jesus, Tell Him

all about your trouble, Hear our faintest cry and He will answer by and by . . . ."

8. Finally, participate regularly in expressive praise and worship. Too many Christians are in poor health today because they fail to take advantage of the therapeutic environment found in the worship experience. This is something that cannot be achieved by listening to the radio or watching television. In order to get the full therapeutic value of praise and worship, one has to *be there*. Not only must one be present, but there must also be some involvement by the individual. It is healthy every now and then to give out a shout for the Lord.

The Lord is calling His people to live healthier lives. Yes, everyone in this country should have available, accessible, affordable, and high-quality health care. Yes, there should be qualified healthcare professionals in every neighborhood, town, and city in this nation. Yes, America's health care system can be much improved. But there is no excuse for the disparities in health now experienced by African Americans. In general, our health is governed more by the choices we make, than by the resources that are currently unavailable to us. As Christians, we can make a difference, individually and collectively, in the health status of African Americans. We must determine to get up and take action. We can begin to make a difference by adopting a TLC: a Therapeutic Lifestyle for Christians.

Dr. Clyde W. Oden is President and CEO of WATTSHealth Systems, Inc. He is also the Senior Pastor of Holy Trinity A. M. E. Church in North Long Beach, California and has gained six earned degrees.

RELIGIOUS EDUCATION AS A TOOL TO MOVE FROM MEMBERSHIP TO DISCIPLESHIP

by Dr. Robert Scott

There are those who would agree that within the context and framework of the African American church, preaching is central. It has the tendency to be the focal point of the worship experience and the propensity to perpetuate and promote numerical growth. While preaching is central, if the African American church is going to be a relevant institution in the new millennium, there must be a greater emphasis on the teaching component of our churches, with an Afro-focal insight and a Christocentric perspective. There must be an intentional critique of and challenge to those who pass the portals of our hallowed doors to do more and be more for Christ.

The problem in many churches is they are filled with more members than disciples. I define a member as a person who really does not make much of a commitment. However, a disciple is a learner/follower who pursues emulation and excellence. If we are going to transform the landscape of our communities and provide a balance to preaching and teaching, perhaps we need to change the way that we in the church refer to ourselves. It is my contention that we need to intentionally refer to ourselves as disciples and make a move from membership to discipleship. Language is important because it can make the abstract concrete and help us to see (both understand and envision) what we hear.

Sunday after Sunday, congregants gather in sanctuaries across the land in droves to worship God. However, they trickle into Sunday School, Bible Study, or any other teaching ministry. Dr. John Kinney, Dean of the Samuel D. Proctor School of Theology (Richmond, VA), once said, "People who are shouting ought to get some learning and people who have learning ought to be shouting."[1]

The lack of knowledge and religious understanding is pervasive in many churches, especially in Black church culture. It is a sad testimony and a terrible indicator for the future of our churches in a highly technological age in which information is the new currency. And, if information is the new currency, then from a religious perspective, our churches should serve as repositories for the tools needed to make it in this postmodern, semi-agnostic culture. The majority of persons who attend worship do not attend teaching ministries. Thus, it is rather difficult to engage in authentic worship without understanding *who* is being worshiped and why.

If the African American church is going to be relevant in the new millennium, there must be a commitment to making religious education a high priority. This education must be undergirded by a liberation motif and not just a certification mantra. Dr. Mack King Carter states in his book, *A Quest for Freedom: An African American Odyssey,* "However, in the midst of oppression, learning to read can be a path to liberation, or further enslavement by the oppressor's Eurocentricity, which casts aspersions on anything having to do with Africa."[2] In various teaching ministries, we must empower, enhance, and enrich the attendees with the tools and resources to love God, appreciate self, and serve humanity.

Dr. Carlyle Stewart asserts in his book *African American Church Growth: Twelve Principles for Prophetic Ministry* that "the basic tasks of the educational ministry in the growing prophetic church are to raise critical consciousness, help people develop a pragmatic and viable faith, and assist them in the acquisition of spiritual principles, through the development and implementation of meaningful programs." Our churches must be on the cutting edge because we must instill within the disciples inspiration and education. Thus, in all preaching there should be some teaching, and in teaching there must be some preaching.

Nevertheless, it is important for the pastor to be at the forefront of this charge. Since the pastor is the key leader in most churches, the pastor must rise to the challenge and push the educational component of the ministry. Religious education must be the heart of the church's ministry. Jesus declared in the Great Commission, "Go ye therefore, and teach all nations, baptizing them in the name of the Father, and of the Son, and of the Holy Ghost: teaching them to observe all things whatsoever I have commanded you: and, lo, I am with you alway, even unto the end of the world" (Matthew 28:19-20, KJV). The Master emphasized that disciples are made through teaching. The church cannot neglect or negate the necessity of religious education that goes beyond memorizing Bible verses and telling Bible stories. Disciples must be taught life application components that will empower them to become agents of transformation and bring God's kingdom here on earth. In *The Prophethood of Black Believers*, the idea that theologian J. Deotis Roberts affirms "the goal of the Christian life includes concern from the liberation of an oppressed people."[3] Thus, Christian education goes beyond the Eurocentric motif of spiritual salvation and stresses the importance of holistically addressing the concerns of humanity.

The education of disciples cannot be stressed enough. In the world and in our churches, there are too many people perplexed and not cognizant of the full Gospel message for living, and they suffer for a lack of knowledge because the church is not taking religious education seriously. This is why there is a shift from the mainline Protestant churches to "Word churches," where there seems to be a greater emphasis on teaching rather than the traditional mode of preaching. There is a thirst for knowledge. However, some of the material being fed to congregations is somewhat antithetical to the Scriptures and perverts the teachings of the biblical Christ. While our preaching is rousing and elevating, without adequate and proper teaching, it becomes like "clanging brass and tinkling cymbals." Pastors must stress the synergism between teaching and preaching in order to move our churches from membership to discipleship.

Therefore, if the Black church wants to impact this postmodern generation, we must pursue the application of information that comes through religious education and nurturing. If our churches are going to have an impact on our homes, our communities, our cities, and this world, we must share information that has the ability to transform individuals into disciples and empower them to live in this present age. The Bible says, "For my people are destroyed for a lack of knowledge" (Hosea 4:6a, KJV). Let's stop the destruction.

Reverend Dr. Robert Charles Scott is Pastor of the historic Central Baptist Church in St. Louis, Missouri. He has earned a B. A. in Political Science, A Masters of Divinity, and a doctoral degree from the United Theological Seminary in Dayton, Ohio.

1. John Kinney, *Lecture at Hampton University Minister's Conference* (Hampton, VA:, 1999).
2. Mack King Carter, *A Quest for Freedom: An African American Odyssey* (Winter Park, Fl: Four-G Publishers, 1993), p. 118.
3. J. Deotis Roberts, *The Prophethood of Black Believers* (Louisville, KY: Westminster/John Knox Press, 1994), p. 42.

THEMATIC ESSAY

JUDGMENT AND EXILE

Jennifer D. King

One has to wonder how Israel, a nation that began with God's promise to establish David's throne forever (2 Samuel 7:16), ended up with God thrusting them from His presence (2 Kings 24:20). Time and time again, God lavished His chosen people with blessings. Under Solomon, Israel enjoyed a period of immense peace and prosperity. Israel's area was almost tripled; the great temple was erected in Jerusalem. The cause of God's judgment was a broken promise accompanied by an unrepentant spirit. The split of the kingdom and the subsequent fall of Judah was precipitated by a succession of wicked kings and marked by a cycle of sin and forgiveness, rejection and restoration, and finally, the inevitable judgment of God.

Beginning with Judah's thirteenth king, Hezekiah, the future appeared promising for the small southern nation. Hezekiah was a true adherent to God who zealously promoted true worship in Judah and the surrounding territory. Upon his succession to the throne, Hezekiah's first order of business was the renovation and reopening of the temple that had been desecrated and looted by his father, King Ahaz. The young king made a covenant of faithfulness with God in the hope that if Judah was reconciled to God, then His wrath would be turned away (2 Chronicles 29:10). Following the dedication of the temple, there were sin offerings for the kingdom, the sanctuary, and the people (2 Chronicles 29:20-29).

Hezekiah's restoration efforts were followed by a call for national revival. He sent letters throughout Judah and portions of Israel calling for people to return to God and celebrate the Passover at the Temple in Jerusalem. Hezekiah's revival was more than just a transient emotional gathering. Before they returned home, the celebrants had been moved to tear down the altars and high places of worship throughout the kingdom, signaling their willingness to return to the one true God (2 Chronicles 31:1). Hezekiah himself crushed the copper serpent crafted by Moses, because the people had made it an idol and had begun to worship it (2 Kings 18:4).

After the death of King Hezekiah, his 12-year-old son, Manasseh, was enthroned. No two men could have been more different. Manasseh proved to be one of Judah's most corrupt and iniquitous leaders. Whereas Hezekiah heralded a period of spiritual enlightenment and a return to worship of the one true God by destroying the idols and reviving worship throughout the kingdom, Manasseh desecrated Solomon's temple by building false religious altars in two of the temple courtyards. Manasseh participated in some of the vilest acts against God and the people in his charge. He practiced divination, promoted witchcraft, and sacrificed his children by having them pass through the fire in the valley of the son of Hinnom (2 Chronicles 33:3-6). Despite the warnings of the prophets to cease his evil practices, Manasseh continued to shed innocent blood (2 Kings 21:10-12, 16). Manasseh ranks as one of the most evil kings of Judah, as he seduced the people to do worse than the nations that God had annihilated during Israel's earlier history (2 Kings 21:2).

On the political front, Manasseh foolishly

adhered to his father's policy of antagonism toward Assyria. Consequently, the capital city of Jerusalem was besieged, and Manasseh was shackled and carried off to Babylon. While in captivity, Manasseh repented, humbled himself, and prayed to God. God heard Mannaseh's prayer and restored him to the throne (2 Chronicles 33:10-13). Following his return to Jerusalem, Manasseh built an outer wall for the city, removed the idol images from the temple, tore down the idol altars, and commanded the people to serve the Lord God of Israel. However, the people continued to worship at the pagan shrines, while still worshiping the Lord their God. As a result, while Judah made sacrifices to God, they continued to make those sacrifices in the wrong place, thus intermingling godly worship with pagan religious practices.

The people of Judah yielded again to these pagan influences under the reign of Amon, Manasseh's son. Though his reign was brief (a mere two years), it was marked by a repetition of his father's earlier idolatrous ways. Amon's ignoble rule was cut short when his servants assassinated him. Josiah, Amon's 8-year-old son, succeeded him to the throne.

In spite of his father, Josiah proved to be one of Judah's most admirable kings, turning to the Lord with all his heart, soul, and might (2 Kings 23:25). With a fervor that rivaled that of his great-grand-father Hezekiah, during the 12th year of his reign Josiah began a six-year campaign against idol worship. The detestable altars of Baal were purged, not only from Judah, but even from the desolated area that had once been Israel.

No doubt Josiah's awareness of the need to eradicate idol worship from his kingdom was heightened by the young prophet Zephaniah, who admonished the people that God would execute vengeance upon unrepentant wrongdoers. God, he prophesied, was the embodiment of righteousness, and while He would provide opportunities for repentance, He would not allow the idolatry and violence that marked Judah prior to Josiah's

reforms to go unchecked and unpunished. The prophet warned that God was incensed by Judah's unfaithfulness and duplicity. The people that God had chosen as His elect were swearing allegiance to Him and yet were bowing down and worshiping the pagan gods of the Canaanites from their rooftops (Zephaniah 1:4-5). The people of Judah foolishly believed they could practice astrology and worship God at the same time.

Josiah attempted to heed the prophet's call and lead his people in a national atonement for their sins before the Lord's fierce anger was visited upon them (Zephaniah 2:2-3). In addition to cleansing the land of idols, Josiah began repairing the temple. During the restoration work, the high priest Hilkiah found the book of the Law of Moses. When the book was read to Josiah, the young king was so horrified when he learned how far from God the people had strayed that he ripped his garments and cried. Josiah immediately sent a five-man delegation to the prophetess Huldah. Her response was chilling. Calamities would be visited on Judah. However, because of his tenderheartedness and humility, Josiah would not live to see his kingdom subjugated (2 Chronicles 34:18-28).

Josiah's love and concern for his people prompted him to intensify his campaign against idolatry. He assembled all of the people and read the law to them and made a covenant of faithfulness to God. Josiah backed up his words with action. The priests of foreign gods dwelling in Judah were expelled, and the Levite priests who were improperly worshiping were stripped of their priestly privileges. Most importantly, the high places built during Solomon's reign were destroyed. Josiah pulled down and burned the altar built by Israel's King Jeroboam at Bethel (2 Kings 23:12-15).

The Passover celebration arranged by Josiah during the 18th year of his reign was more splendid than any observed since the days of Samuel. Josiah's 31-year reign was ended when he disregarded the words of God spoken by Pharaoh

Necho. Josiah was fatally wounded by an archer's arrow in a vain attempt to come against the Egyptian forces in the Valley of Megiddo (2 Chronicles 35:20-23). Although three of his sons (Jehoahaz, Jehoiakim, Zedekiah) and one grandson (Jehoiakim) ruled as king, none of them followed Josiah's example of turning to God with their whole hearts, souls, and minds. The failure of the people of Judah to fully embrace God with a whole heart resulted in Josiah's religious reforms being forgotten and the people quickly returning to their idolatrous ways.

The prophecies of Zephaniah and Jeremiah came to fruition in 586 B.C. when Babylon completely destroyed Jerusalem and deported her people. As prophesied, the Prophet Jeremiah, descendants of Jonadab, and a few other faithful ones who kept the precepts of God were spared from the wrath of God (Jeremiah 35:18-19; 39:11-12, 15-18). Because the kings and the people refused to honor their covenant with God and turned their backs on Him in favor of idol gods, refusing to heed God's efforts to discipline them, the City of David would lie in desolation for the next 70 years.

The heartbreaking account of Judah's continual pattern of sin, judgment, and exile provides a chilling confirmation of God's righteous nature. He honors His covenants and expects nothing less from His people. Although He is quick to forgive and pardon, God will visit judgment on those who fail to repent and remain unresponsive to His message.

The 21st century Christian must be careful to learn from the experience of Judah. God still demands that we honor Him by worshiping and serving Him with our whole hearts, minds, and souls. Unfortunately, Judah did not learn from Israel's fatal mistakes. Instead of separating themselves from their wicked neighbors, they adopted their sinful practices and tried to intermingle them with worship. We should avoid any attempts to comingle true worship with new-age idolatry. Our devotion to and worship of God must be pure and untainted. We would do well to search our hearts for any "high places" and altars to false gods in our lives today. Yielding to the temptation to indulge in astrology, seeking counsel from television psychics, or viewing Internet pornography are as detestable to God as Judah's penchant for consulting mediums and offering human sacrifices. These high places must be torn down, crushed, and destroyed if we are to honor our covenant with God and serve Him alone.

Jennifer D. King is Superintendent of Sunday School for Bay Area Christian Connection. She holds a B. A. with honors in English and is currently working toward a Masters of Arts degree.

BLACK PERSONALITY

MAHALIA JACKSON

(1911-1972) • *Queen of the Gospel Song*

The day was October 4, 1950. The hush that descended upon Carnegie Hall was almost palpable. The New York City audience was enthralled by the rich, vibrant contralto of Mahalia Jackson. Her powerful voice gave simple, honest interpretation to each gospel song, and throughout her program, most of the eyes in the packed house were filled with tears. Such was the ability of the "Queen of the Gospel Song" to touch people's hearts as she ministered through her music.

Sixteen years later, she expressed delight that White American and European audiences of various religious persuasions received her singing with enthusiasm. Throughout her life, Mahalia Jackson believed in the power of gospel music to reaffirm faith and inspire hope and consolation in all people.

Mahalia was born in 1911 in New Orleans, Louisiana. Her parents were poor, with six children to care for. Her father was a preacher, barber, and longshoreman. Her mother was a devout Baptist who took care of the children and the house. To get wood for the stove, she picked up scrap pieces of wood and driftwood that had washed up on the shore. When Mahalia was four years old, Mrs. Jackson died.

Mahalia began to sing in her father's church choir. Athough familiar with the music of New Orleans, her deeply religious parents allowed nothing but church music in their home. Later, Mahalia felt God wanted her to sing gospel songs only, and she vowed to do so. After her popularity had increased, she was offered large sums of money to sing in nightclubs and Las Vegas. Even when some club owners promised not to serve whiskey while Mahalia sang, she still refused their lucrative offers.

When she turned 16, Mahalia wanted to become a nurse, and she went to Chicago to live with her aunt Hannah. With only an eighth-grade education, she washed White people's clothes for one dollar a day. She also worked as a hotel maid and eventually saved enough money to open her own beauty salon.

Mahalia joined her aunt's church, the Greater Salem Baptist Church. There, she became a soloist in the choir and also sang with the Johnson Singers. In 1934, she recorded her first song, "God's Gonna Separate the Wheat from the Tares."

In 1939, Jackson started touring with the gospel great, Thomas A. Dorsey. While performing at churches and gospel tents around the country, her reputation as singer and interpreter of gospel songs grew. Having a strong sense of entrepreneurship, she next opened a flower shop. In 1946, she recorded the song, "Move On Up a Little Higher." This recording sold 100,000 copies overnight and quickly passed the one million mark. While touring in the segregated South, she equipped her large car to allow her to sleep and to have a store of food to eat in order to avoid the embarrassment of being refused or relegated to the colored section in segregated facilities.

Mahalia participated in the Montgomery, Alabama bus boycott. In 1963, at the March on Washington ceremony, she sang, "I Been 'Buked and I Been Scorned" as a prelude to Dr. King's "I Have A Dream" speech. During the Civil Rights movement of the 1960's, she inspired many with her song, "We Shall Overcome." She recorded albums and songs such as "Even Me" and "Silent Night." She was featured in films such as *Imitation of Life* and *The Best Man*. Many books have been written about her, and she coauthored her own autobiography, *Movin' On Up*. She held concerts around the United States and throughout Europe. She was the first gospel singer to have a radio show. One of her most memorable experiences was when she held a concert in Israel, singing to Jews, Christians, and Muslims.

When Mahalia Jackson died in 1972, over 6,000 people attended her funeral. Ella Fitzgerald, a famous jazz/pop singer, called Mahalia "one of our greatest ambassadors of love."

Mahalia Jackson was a gifted gospel singer, an intelligent business-woman in spite of a limited education, a civil rights activist, a writer, and a woman who tried to live the life she sang about.

Marshall Cavendish Corp., *1993. The African American Encyclopedia:* North Bellmore, N.Y.

Barbara Bigelow, editor, *1994. Contemporary Black Biography:* Detroit, MI.

TEACHING TIPS

September 1
Bible Study Guide 1

1. Words You Should Know

A. Passover (2 Chronicles 30:1); Hebrew *Pehsak*—Commemoration of God's sparing the lives of Israel's firstborn sons in Egypt.

B. Princes (v. 2); Hebrew *sar*—Officers, ambassadors, head official, or captain.

C. Posts (v. 6); Hebrew *ruwts*—To run; a runner with a message.

D. Yield (v. 8); Hebrew *nathan*—Obeying God with our bodies; to give over to God.

E. Sanctuary (v. 8); Hebrew *miqdash*—A consecrated place or thing; a place set apart for the worship of God.

F. Sanctification (v. 8); Hebrew *qadash*—Purified and made holy by God; to make clean, dedicate, or hallow.

2. Teacher Preparation

A. Familiarize yourself with the lessons for this quarter by reading the INTRODUCTION TO THE SEPTEMBER 2002 QUARTER and the Thematic Essay.

B. Begin your study by reading all of the background Scriptures to understand the national revival that was undertaken by King Hezekiah. Take note of the extraordinary lengths to which Hezekiah goes to restore true worship to his kingdom.

C. Review the key words for this week's passages.

3. Starting the Lesson

A. Introduce the students to the new quarter. Ask for volunteers to read the Thematic Essay and general introduction, "Judgment and Exile," and then have someone else read the paragraph under "Unit 1. Challenged to Change" from the QUARTER-AT-A-GLANCE.

B. Encourage your students to discuss the sinful condition of Judah prior to Hezekiah's reign. Talk about the relationship between Judah and Israel. Also discuss reasons for Judah's apparent rejection of the one true God.

4. Getting into the Lesson

A. Read the LESSON AIM and the KEEP IN MIND Scripture.

B. Discuss some modern leaders who were responsible for significant renewal or reconstruction projects and the keys to their success.

C. Ask for volunteers to read the FOCAL VERSES. Talk about the significance of Hezekiah's restoring the Passover celebration.

D. What do we learn about Hezekiah's dedication to God and the people of Judah? Discuss the significance of Hezekiah's including the nation of Israel in the Passover celebration.

5. Relating the Lesson to Life

A. Have a volunteer read IN FOCUS and allow 7 to 10 minutes for discussion.

B. Give the students an opportunity to answer the questions in SEARCH THE SCRIPTURES. Also focus on THE PEOPLE, PLACES, AND TIMES section.

6. Arousing Action

A. Assign students to read and answer the DISCUSS THE MEANING questions to prompt them to apply the lesson to their own lives.

B. Close the class with a prayer.

WORSHIP GUIDE

For the Superintendent or Teacher
Theme: Repentance and Renewal
Theme Song: "Lord Prepare Me to Be a Sanctuary"
Scripture: Psalm 122:1-9
Song: "I'll Go All the Way"
Meditation: Dear God, we thank You for our covenant through Your Son Jesus Christ. Guide us that we might continue to please You in our thoughts, words, and deeds.
Amen.

REPENTANCE AND RENEWAL

Bible Background • 2 CHRONICLES 29—30; 2 KINGS 18—20
Printed Text • 2 CHRONICLES 30:1-6, 8-12
Devotional Reading • PSALM 122:1-9

LESSON AIM

After studying today's lesson, students should be able to describe King Hezekiah's national reform and evaluate whether it was genuine and sincere. Students should also be able to analyze the events that lead to Judah's restoration, repentance, obedience, and commitment and realize that their personal renewal must begin with obedience to God.

KEEP IN MIND

"The LORD your God is gracious and merciful, and will not turn away his face from you, if ye return unto him" (2 Chronicles 30:9b).

FOCAL VERSES

2 Chronicles 30:1 And Hezekiah sent to all Israel and Judah, and wrote letters also to Ephraim and Manasseh, that they should come to the house of the LORD at Jerusalem, to keep the passover unto the LORD God of Israel.

2 For the king had taken counsel, and his princes, and all the congregation in Jerusalem, to keep the passover in the second month.

3 For they could not keep it at that time, because the priests had not sanctified themselves sufficiently, neither had the people gathered themselves together to Jerusalem.

4 And the thing pleased the king and all the congregation.

5 So they established a decree to make proclamation throughout all Israel, from Beer-sheba even to Dan, that they should come to keep the passover unto the LORD God of Israel at Jerusalem: for they had not done it of a long time in such sort as it was written.

LESSON OVERVIEW

LESSON AIM
KEEP IN MIND
FOCAL VERSES
IN FOCUS
THE PEOPLE, PLACES, AND TIMES
BACKGROUND
AT-A-GLANCE
IN DEPTH
SEARCH THE SCRIPTURES
DISCUSS THE MEANING
LESSON IN OUR SOCIETY
MAKE IT HAPPEN
FOLLOW THE SPIRIT
REMEMBER YOUR THOUGHTS
MORE LIGHT ON THE TEXT
DAILY BIBLE READINGS

6 So the posts went with the letters from the king and his princes throughout all Israel and Judah, and according to the commandment of the king, saying, Ye children of Israel, turn again unto the LORD God of Abraham, Isaac, and Israel, and he will return to the remnant of you, that are escaped out of the hand of the kings of Assyria.

30:8 Now be ye not stiffnecked, as your fathers were, but yield yourselves unto the LORD, and enter into his sanctuary, which he hath sanctified for ever: and serve the LORD your God, that the fierceness of his wrath may turn away from you.

9 For if ye turn again unto the LORD, your brethren and your children shall find compassion before them that lead them captive, so that they shall come again into this land: for the LORD your God is gracious and merciful, and will not turn away his face from you, if ye return unto him.

10 So the posts passed from city to city through the country of Ephraim and Manasseh even unto Zebulun: but they laughed them to scorn, and mocked them.

11 Nevertheless divers of Asher and Manasseh and of Zebulun humbled themselves, and came to Jerusalem.

12 Also in Judah the hand of God was to give them one heart to do the commandment of the king and of the princes, by the word of the LORD.

IN FOCUS

Karen cleared her desk, locked the file cabinets,

and hurried out of the office. Earlier she had over-heard her boss talking to one of the division managers about Fred, one of her co-workers. The boss said that he thought someone should take a closer look into Fred's sales records. Karen was especially upset because of her own statement earlier that week. When her boss was telling other staff members about how high Fred's sales were, she had made an ugly remark and implied that she had "heard" that not all of Fred's sales were legitimate.

Karen knew that jealousy had made her say such a thing. She couldn't seem to help it, even though no one had ever implied that Fred was anything but an honest and hardworking salesman. People were always remarking about how well-dressed and how personable Fred was. Karen's desk was next to Fred's, so she knew he really was a go-getter and pursued all sales leads. However, since Fred's arrival, her performance as the unit's top salesperson had been eclipsed.

While leaving the building, Karen passed Fred in the hallway. He smiled and spoke to her, complimenting her on a recent report she had prepared. Karen was too ashamed to do anything except mumble a word of thanks and scramble from the building. Her hands shook as she started her car. She knew that by tomorrow morning the entire staff would be talking. Fred was being investigated because she had made a careless and false remark in anger.

An investigation of Fred's sales could cause a lot of problems. Charges of sales mismanagement were taken seriously in her company. Even if Fred were cleared, the fact that he had been investigated would be a matter of record. Maybe, Karen thought, when she got home, she could send her boss an e-mail, explaining that her remark had been just a joke. Maybe that would make everything all right.

THE PEOPLE, PLACES, AND TIMES

King Hezekiah. Hezekiah was the thirteenth king of the southern kingdom of Judah. He succeeded his father Ahaz to the throne at age 25. He began his reign in about 715 B.C. Hezekiah reigned during the Prophet Isaiah's ministry.

Manasseh and Ephraim. Two sons of Joseph by his Egyptian wife, Asenath (Genesis 41:45).

Although many Israelites were Black, these two tribes had specific ties to Africa through Asenath.

Passover. This memorial celebration of Israel's transition from slavery to nationhood is the centerpiece of Jewish worship. Passover is a seven-day celebration. The highlight is the main feast on the first night, the *seder* (pronounced **SAY-duhr**). This event recalls the final meal eaten by the Jews during their captivity in Egypt. Participants are reminded that the blood of an unblemished lamb was smeared on the doorposts of Jewish households, and the "passing over" of their firstborn took place when God destroyed the firstborn children of Egypt. This event foreshadowed the sacrifice of Jesus Christ and the shedding of His innocent blood that mankind might be delivered from the slavery of sin and death. Jesus observed the Passover meal on the evening before He was put to death.

Based on information from Illustrated Manners and Customs of the Bible, J. I. Packer and M. C. Tenney, editors (Nashville: Thomas Nelson Publishers, 1980). pp. 467.
African insight: Sacrifice and communal participation in a ritual meal is a significant part of African culture.

BACKGROUND

Following the reign of King Solomon and the division of the United Kingdom into the northern nation of Israel and the southern kingdom of Judah, the latter had been ruled by a succession of both godly and evil kings. King Ahaz had committed atrocious acts before God, including sacrificing his own sons to the idol god, Molech. Idol worship was rampant in Judah under Ahaz, and under his direction, the temple was looted and shut down. As a result, God permitted Judah to suffer at the hands of her enemies, particularly Assyria, the rising world power during this time. Ahaz's son, Hezekiah, was the complete opposite of his father. Hezekiah proved to be one of Judah's most outstanding kings, a man who was committed to following God's commandments, reviving true worship, and restoring his people to God's favor.

From the beginning of his reign, Hezekiah promoted true worship in Judah and Israel by reopening and cleansing the temple and reestablishing public worship of the LORD. Hezekiah's restoration was both external and internal. He also organized the daily temple services, organizing the Levites in their service and reestablishing the arrangement of the musical instruments and praise singing.

With equal enthusiasm and energy, Hezekiah began the work of restoring the hearts of the people. He called for a national celebration of the Passover in Jerusalem. Hezekiah's commitment to the LORD extended beyond his own kingdom. He insisted that the northern kingdom of Israel be included in the celebration as well. In spite of the nation's idolatrous and sinful past, King Hezekiah was determined to lead his people into spiritual revival.

> ### AT-A-GLANCE
>
> **1. Hezekiah's Urgent Call**
> **(2 Chronicles 30:1-5)**
> **2. Urged to Return to Faithfulness**
> **(vv. 6-9)**
> **3. The Response and Hope (vv. 10-12)**

IN DEPTH

1. Hezekiah's Urgent Call (2 Chronicles 30:1-5)

Among all of Judah's kings, Hezekiah is distinguished because he "did . . . right in the sight of the LORD" (2 Chronicles 29:2). Immediately after he came to the throne of Judah, Hezekiah began a national program of religious restoration of the worship of the true God. He began by reopening and restoring the temple. He organized the priests and the Levites, and supervised cleansing the temple of the wicked influences of his father, King Ahaz.

Throughout Judah, the altars were torn down and the pagan idols were removed. Under Hezekiah's leadership, public worship of the LORD was reestablished and music was again brought into the worship. The singing and instrumental music that had been introduced by David were restored.

This commitment to the spiritual revival of the nation was further demonstrated in the planning of a national celebration of the Passover at the temple in Jerusalem. This feast was organized by Hezekiah, along with the priests and princes of Judah. The word "prince" is derived from the Hebrew verb *sar*, meaning to exercise dominion. Though it is often translated "prince," it does not necessarily apply only to the son of a king. An army chief or a tribal head was also referred to as *sar*, meaning ruler, captain, or official.

Passover was normally celebrated during Nisan (within the months of March—April). However, the impurity of the people and the uncleanness of the temple had prevented the celebration of Passover at the regular time. Hezekiah very shrewdly took advantage of the law that allowed for the unclean to celebrate the Passover a month later (Numbers 9:10-11). Hezekiah sent letters of invitation, not only to the people of Judah, but to the neighboring kingdom of Israel, to come to Jerusalem to celebrate the Passover, the Jewish feast of redemption.

These letters were sent by runners from Beersheba to Dan (the southernmost and northernmost parts of the kingdom). The tribal territories of Ephraim and Manasseh, two tribes in the northern kingdom that were descended from Joseph's two sons, were also singled out. As the most prominent and influential tribe of the northern kingdom, Ephraim came to stand for the entire kingdom of Israel. The spiritual reforms undertaken many years earlier by King Asa prompted many Manassehites to desert the northern kingdom of Israel. Although inter-tribal conflicts had existed between Ephraim and Manasseh, both tribes were generally united in their opposition to Judah (Isaiah 9:20-21). Hezekiah's inclusion of Israel points to his sincerity in seeking to restore a right relationship with God for the entire kingdom. The northern 10-tribe kingdom of Israel was in even worse shape than Judah. Because of her gross sins against God, Israel had become a tributary to Assyria, and many of her people had been carried away to foreign lands. Under his father's (King Ahaz's) reign, the relationship between Judah and Israel was openly hostile.

Hezekiah did not let this strained past deter him. His invitation was extended to the remnant that remained in the land. He was convinced that the hearts of all of God's people needed renewing.

2. Urged to Return to Faithfulness (vv. 6-9)

The cleansing of the temple was merely the beginning. Under Hezekiah's direction, Judah sought to ask God's forgiveness and restore their relationship with Him by offering both sin and peace offerings at the temple. Hezekiah urged the people not to be obstinate or "stiff-necked" like their fathers, whose stubborn refusal to adhere to true worship had landed them in this condition. It was their fathers who had joined with the unbelievers living in the land and had adopted their abominable practices of idol worship, divination, and even child sacrifice. Hezekiah appeals to them to renew their covenant relationship with God and obey Him. The appeal to enter into "his sanctuary" implies more than simply returning to the temple in Jerusalem. The "sanctuary," it can be argued, need not refer to a special building, but rather to Judah and Israel's position as God's chosen people. God had promised that He Himself would become a "sanctuary" for His people (Ezekiel 11:16). Similarly, Hezekiah's request included a special appeal to the nation of Israel. If they yielded themselves, obeyed wholeheartedly, returned to Jerusalem, and were reconciled with God, then "the fierceness of his wrath" or anger would be abated.

No doubt, Hezekiah was aware that the people could have reverted to their former idolatrous ways. In order for this revival to bring about a lasting change, there had to be reformation! Revival begins with the admission of guilt; reformation begins with the actual repentance relating to the acts that caused the guilt. Under Ahaz's wicked leadership, Judah had turned their backs on the LORD. Yet in a relatively short period of time, Hezekiah sought to lead his people in a tremendous swing back to the LORD.

3. The Response and Hope (vv. 10-12)

The word went out by courier to the various tribes, calling all Israel to come participate. The reaction was mixed. The people of the tribes of Ephraim, Manasseh, and Zebulun were said to laugh and mock the messengers to scorn. But there were a few who humbled themselves and went to Jerusalem, including people from the tribe of Asher. The Chronicler paints a picture of a nation that is split in its loyalties—until he mentions Judah. Judah is said to be given "one heart to do the commandment of the king and of the princes, by the word of the LORD." Judah reacts to the summons with one heart, one mind, and one purpose. While the rest of the tribes are divided in their loyalties, Judah, under

the leadership of King Hezekiah, seeks to do the will of God.

Like Judah and Israel, many of us have become rebellious or stiff-necked, and we seem to have forgotten the source of our blessings and provisions. Our values are no longer grounded in the Word of God, and in our rejection of biblical values we seem to have lost our moral center. We have pushed God out of our classrooms, our businesses, and our courtrooms. All one has to do is turn on the radio or television to hear the message that there is no correct opinion, no absolute authority, no right and wrong; therefore, anything goes. It is amazing how closely America's moral condition parallels that of Israel and Judah.

Just as rebellion brings judgment, Christians are reminded that repentance and obedience will bring restoration and blessings. God still sits in judgment of our sins, both private and corporate. Yet in His infinite goodness and mercy, He does not sentence us to life without hope. Our hope for restoration lies in the righteousness of His Son, Jesus Christ. It is only through Christ that we can find salvation and restoration. Just as He did with Judah, God is still calling His people to renewal. He wants us to value the lives of people who were saved by his Son's sacrificial death and to reflect that value in our everyday living. His call is for our total commitment to Him.

SEARCH THE SCRIPTURES

1. To whom did Hezekiah send the letter of invitation to the Passover? (v. 1)

2. Where was the Passover to be celebrated? (v. 1)

3. Who had reached an agreement to keep the Passover? (v. 2)

4. Why couldn't the Passover be celebrated at the regular time? (v. 3)

5. If the people returned to the LORD God, what did Hezekiah tell them they could expect in return? (vv. 6, 8)

6. What was the result of the stiff-necked reaction of the "fathers"? (v. 8)

DISCUSS THE MEANING

1. Think about why it was so important to Hezekiah that the entire nation come to Jerusalem to celebrate the Passover. What similarities might we

observe between Judah's present condition and that of the Jews during the Egyptian captivity?

2. Hezekiah sent his letter throughout Judah and to the neighboring nation of Israel as well. How did the people of Israel receive this invitation? What does this act tell us about Hezekiah's character and motivation?

3. We hear a lot of discussion these days about the importance of working together, and we frequently salute "team players" on our jobs. How was cooperation evidenced in Hezekiah's attempt to rally the nation?

LESSON IN OUR SOCIETY

The need for revival in the lives of the men and women of God is just as great today as it was in Hezekiah's time. Over the last 30 years, violent crime increased by 560%, the divorce rate quadrupled, illegitimate births increased 400%, single-parent homes tripled, and teenage suicide rose by 200%. It is hard to remember that America is a country that was supposedly founded on biblical principles and Judeo-Christian values. So what happened?

MAKE IT HAPPEN

Before personal revival can begin, the temple must be restored. Today Christians are the temples of the Holy Spirit, both individually (1 Cor. 6:19), and collectively as the Church (1 Cor. 6:16). Restoration to God means that unholiness must be cleansed from our temple. Pray and then make a list of the unholy thoughts or habits that need to be removed from the temple of your body and life in order for your revival to begin.

FOLLOW THE SPIRIT

What God wants me to do:

_____

_____

REMEMBER YOUR THOUGHTS

Special insights you have learned:

_____

_____

MORE LIGHT ON THE TEXT
2 Chronicles 30:1-6, 8-12

Job once asked, "Who can bring a clean thing out of an unclean?" (Job 14:4). Similarly, in utter desperation, the Prophet Jeremiah said that the Children of Israel who practiced evil would only be able to do good if it were possible for the leopard to change its spots (Jeremiah 13:23). Is there such a thing as hope for the hopeless or renewal for the recreant? Our study this week shows that God renews and restores all (personally or collectively) who come to Him with a desire for renewal and with repentant hearts. Yet it is clear that in the case of a group, church, family, or nation, renewal must begin with leadership—from the top down! That's how Judah's renewal began. It started with a leader whose heart was fully committed to God and whose eyes were open to see the need for renewal. Hezekiah knew that it was time to decide to follow God and do that which pleases Him. Revival or renewal typically begins with the leaders of God's people having a heart to obey God.

In this chapter, we see that renewal spread from the leadership to the people of God as they responded to the letter that Hezekiah sent out to call them to celebrate the Passover. Motivated by a zeal for God and upon consultation with his nobles, Hezekiah decided to observe the Passover in the second month. Having so determined, he sent messengers throughout Israel and Judah to inform them. God placed the desire in the heart of Hezekiah to celebrate the Passover because He was going to use that time to restore the people.

In this story, we see an appeal of love issued to God's people through King Hezekiah. This appeal is summed up in one verse. God said to them: "Return to me, and I will return to you!" (2 Chronicles 30:6, paraphrased). It is so simple that it's profound! In spite of Judah's unfaithfulness to God and their idol worship, God reassured them of His love by pleading for their return. God wants Judah back, notwithstanding all her waywardness! God says to come home! What was the response? It was mixed. On the one hand, some people mocked the king's messengers and laughed them to scorn. Thus, one can see that pride is a barrier to renewal and revival. It is a sobering thought that suffering and threatened destruction do not always drive people to God.

However, many of God's people were cut to the heart by God's appeal to return to Him, and they responded in earnest. If our hearts are truly repentant, we will respond in much the same way as they did! We will be humbled before Almighty God and admit our need for renewal. We will "rend our hearts and not our garments" (Joel 2:13).

2 Chronicles 30:1 And Hezekiah sent to all Israel and Judah, and wrote letters also to Ephraim and Manasseh, that they should come to the house of the LORD at Jerusalem, to keep the passover unto the LORD God of Israel.

Hezekiah wasted no time in doing what he knew was right. Although the two kingdoms had long been separated, Hezekiah saw a unique opportunity to bring the two kingdoms back together. Hence, Hezekiah invited all Israel and Judah, "and he wrote letters also to Ephraim and Manasseh," the two chief tribes of the northern kingdom. He sent the invitation to all of Israel (the 10 tribes). Hezekiah's vision was a broad one. It was inclusive, embracing the breakaway tribe and reaching the limits of the land (30:1-5). Hezekiah's message to the 10 tribes was to remind them of their prescribed duty to God and encourage them to return to the LORD as commanded in His law (cf. Deuteronomy 16:1). The door was open, and there should be no divisions.

2 For the king had taken counsel, and his princes, and all the congregation in Jerusalem, to keep the passover in the second month.

"The king took counsel" is translated in Hebrew as *wayiwaa'ats hamelek wasaraavw.* The Hebrew verb *ya'ats,* translated "to counsel," generally means to advise, counsel, or consult. It is translated by the Greek word *bouleuo* (**bool-YOO-oh**) several times in the Septuagint (Greek Old Testament, also known as LXX). It means to deliberate or take advice. Moreover, in a reflexive sense, *eboulusato* (pronounced **eh-bool-YOOSE-ah-toh**) as it is used here in the Septuagint (LXX) means to resolve, determine, or purpose. Thus, it sometimes expresses the idea of "decision." For example, in Isaiah 23:9, "The LORD of hosts hath purposed it" (RSV, NEB, NASB, "planned it"), a decision is expressed. The use of the term in our text underscores the determination of Hezekiah and his leaders to have the Passover cele-

brated. One must not fail to notice the need for cooperation among leaders in order to effect any meaningful and lasting change as Hezekiah shares his vision with his princes. The decision to celebrate the Passover, although broached by the king, was communicated to the elders of the assembly, who in turn endorsed it before its transmission to the populace.

The fact that the king took counsel also suggests that there was a comradery between the king and his counselors. Unlike his predecessors, who were tyrants, Hezekiah saw the princes as co-regents and accepted their input. Further along in the verse we read, "all the congregation in Jerusalem," which indicates that the decision included the people of God. Three levels were involved in the conversation: the king, the princes, and the people. The inclusive nature of the conversation assured that all the people understood their participation in the problems of Israel. Note also that this conversation did not focus on the evil of Israel but instead on the celebration of the act of God in delivering Israel from bondage. They agreed to keep the Passover. Why the Passover? Why not just call the people to repent? To keep the Passover recalls Moses' word to Israel as they prepared to move from the realm of slavery to the realm of freedom that was divinely provided. Every move toward repentance must focus on the act of God for the people.

3 For they could not keep it at the time, because the priests had not sanctified themselves sufficiently, neither had the people gathered themselves together to Jerusalem.

The Passover could not be celebrated at the appointed time for two reasons. First, a sufficient number of the priests were not sanctified or prepared to slay all the Passover lambs the people who came to the feast would want. Second, the notice was short. Since the custom which mandated that all the males should appear at Jerusalem for the feast had been abandoned for years, time was needed to reeducate the people and to reacquaint them with the meaning of the Passover celebration.

Verse 3 serves as a retreat from verse 2. They wanted to, they declared it, but verse 3 says "they could not keep it" (Hebrew *Kiy lo'yak luw lasotow* pronounced **kee LOW yak-loo la-SO-tow**). This phrase conveys a lack of ability and absence of moral warrant. Although they proclaimed this Passover and intended to act on it, they had lost their right to act.

The inability to carry out their counsel is not permanent, but temporary. This temporary inability is underscored by the use of the phrase "at that time" (Hebrew *ba 'et hahi*, pronounced **ba-et ha HEE**). This temporary setback to renewal was due to two things. First, "the priests had not sanctified themselves," (Hebrew *kiy hakohaniym lo hitqadshuw lamaday*, pronounced **KEE ha-KO hamin HIT-kad-shoe la-MA day**). Note how the plight of the people is shown here. None of the priests had taken the time to sanctify themselves according to the law. The Hebrew term *hitqadshuw* used here underscores the need for the priests to be holy. Another revealing aspect is the use of the word "sufficiently" (Hebrew *lamaday*, pronounced **la-MA-day**). The implication is that they were not fulfilling their purpose as priests because they had failed to fulfill their moral duty. It is not that they did not do good things, but this was insufficient. The second setback to renewal was that the people had not "gathered to Jerusalem." There could be several reasons for this. The journey was long; but the non-gathering may also have been a result of the long lethargy of the people. The reader must recall that according to the Chronicles this inability was temporary; the inability was just for "that time."

4 And the thing pleased the king and all the congregation.

Here is an important step to renewal. Both the leader and his followers not only unanimously agreed as to what should be done, but they also determined that it should be done. This is the import of the Hebrew word *yashar* (**yah-SHARR**), rendered by the word "please." Both the king and the congregation found the Passover a pleasant thing to do. It is wise to strike while the iron is hot and to motivate people while they are in a good frame of mind.

5 So they established a decree to make proclamation throughout all Israel, from Beer-sheba even to Dan, that they should come to keep the passover unto the LORD God of Israel at

Jerusalem: for they had not done it of a long time in such sort as it was written.

The word was established based on the counsel of the king and the people to make a proclamation. The word "decree" or *dabar* (**daw bar**) is used here, meaning a word or a matter. Consider its use in conjunction with the word "proclamation" (*gowl*, pronounced **kole**). This usage points to the fact that the *dabar* or "decree" was made in the secret chambers, but "proclamation" (*gowl*) refers to giving voice or sound to what is being considered in rational deliberation.

Heralds were appointed and sent to proclaim it throughout the land, that all might know, and none plead ignorance. Some translations (e.g., NIV, NASB) contain the phrase "it had not been celebrated in large numbers according to what was written" (v. 5), referencing a multitude of persons who had been very deficient in their observance of this ordinance rather than to the length of time. Hence, it reads, "they had not kept it in full numbers, as it was written," i.e., "they (the Israelites of the northern kingdom) had not (for some while) kept the Passover in full numbers, as the law required." This agrees more with the tenor of the entire event. The 10 tribes had not observed the Passover from the time of the schism of Jeroboam (931 B.C.), and many in the kingdom of Judah had also neglected it, or at least had not kept it as the law required.

The people of Dan and Beersheba were not there when counsel was taken, but they could only come to the knowledge of the divine when it was given voice. This could mean that this counsel was now to be thunderously expounded openly. What was to be proclaimed? First, that the people were to come: "They should come." The tense here confirms that, although the counsel included all the people of Jerusalem, this was now an imperative: "They should come." This calls for an approach toward a location with the intent of being counted for the cause to which one has been invited. They were being asked to draw near, not just to one another, but to their God.

Second, they were to "keep the Passover unto the LORD God of Israel." This was not a social call; it was a divine mandate; hence the imperative "come."

The phrase "to keep" is translated from the Hebrew word *la'asowt, which is* rooted in the word *asah* meaning to fashion, accomplish, or make. They were not just supposed to appear and celebrate; this involved work! They were to keep the Passover in ritual form. Since the Passover required self- and communal purification, keeping it required working on themselves. It required sacrifice and putting things in divine order before celebrating.

They were proclaiming that Israel must do the work of God. Note that Israel was not asked to celebrate the Passover, but to "keep it." All these acts were targeted, not to show allegiance to the king of Judah, but to the "LORD God of Israel." Another aspect of the decree is that all those who were willing to keep the Passover must do so in Jerusalem. It was to be done unto God, on God's terms, at the place of God's own choosing. These demands explain why they had not kept the Passover for a very long time because of the way it was written. Also note that it is not that they had not "kept" the Passover, but that they had "kept" it as they chose—unto themselves, on their own terms, and at the place of their choosing.

6 So the posts went with the letters from the king and his princes throughout all Israel and Judah, and according to the commandment of the king, saying, Ye children of Israel, turn again unto the LORD God of Abraham, Isaac, and Israel, and he will return to the remnant of you, that are escaped out of the hand of the kings of Assyria.

This verse tells us the message was sent by "posts" (Hebrew *ruwts*, pronounced **roots**), meaning to run or rush.

The purpose of the Passover celebration was well stated by the king. It was not to be a mere ritual but an avenue of returning to God. It was to be a means of renewing their covenant with God. This is underscored by the words added to the invitation, "turn again unto the LORD God of Abraham, Isaac, and Israel, and he will return to the remnant of you." The Hebrew word *shuv* (**shoov**), translated "turn again," means to turn back, suggesting the idea of returning back to the starting point. Thus, the mention of Abraham, Isaac, and Israel accentuates the significance of the covenant to the Chronicler. The Israelites were to return to the covenant that God had made with their forefathers.

30:8 Now be ye not stiffnecked, as your fathers were, but yield yourselves unto the LORD, and enter into his sanctuary, which he hath sanctified for ever: and serve the LORD your God, that the fierceness of his wrath may turn away from you.

The heart of Hezekiah's appeal is for Israel not to be stiff-necked (Hebrew *qashah,* **kah-SHAH'**, i.e., hard-hearted). This is a clear reference to those carried away by Tiglath and Shalmaneser, as the previous verse suggests. Instead, Israel was to yield to the LORD and "worship him." The word "yield," from the Hebrew word *tachat* (meaning to submit or be humble), denotes the giving of the hand as a pledge of fidelity, as in 2 Kings 10:15; Ezra 10:19; Ezekiel 17:18. Coupled with the renewal of the covenant, Israel was to enter the LORD's sanctuary. God wanted His people to return to Him and seek Him face-to-face so He would not have to forsake them permanently. Israel was to be subject unto Him, enter into covenant with Him, and in so doing avoid His wrath.

9 For if ye turn again unto the lord, your brethren and your children shall find compassion before them that lead them captive, so that they shall come again into this land: for the LORD your God is gracious and merciful, and will not turn away his face from you, if ye return unto him.

Hezekiah gives an important reason for the celebration of the Passover. It was to enable the Children of Israel to turn to the LORD and thereby find compassion. The Hebrew word *shuv* (**shoov**) means to turn back (hence, away). As used here, it is equivalent to the Greek word *epistrepho* (**ep ee streff o**), which in a moral sense designates primarily the fulfilment of religious conversion. It means to revert (literally, figuratively, or morally), come again, convert, or (re)turn (about, again). This underscores the necessity of repentance in order to be forgiven. God is a compassionate God. However, what the backslider or sinner needs to do is to return to the LORD. In turn, God will keep His promises (cf. Exodus 34:6). He will not only preserve those who return, but through their repentance will restore their brethren, who because of their sins He gave into the hands of the enemies. Moreover, when Israel turns, God will not turn (Hebrew *suwr* (**soor**) or withdraw from them.

10 So the posts passed from city to city through the country of Ephraim and Manasseh even unto Zebulun: but they laughed them to scorn, and mocked them.

The king's message got a mixed reception. Some mocked, while others were moved and accepted it (v. 11). The former obviously despised the contents and paid no regard to it. Instead, they laughed at the messengers and ridiculed the invitation. The bearers appeared to these people to be jesting (cf. Genesis 19:14). When people become entrenched in sin because of years of sinful activity, they do not readily see a need for change. They think that serving God cannot make a difference. This is also true in our day. Having lived in sin and a morally polluted society for so long, people reject the suggestion that worshiping God can make a difference. The sin in their lives has caused such moral depravity that they wouldn't want to change things even if they thought it was possible. However, just a handful of changed people can make a difference in a church or in a nation. And we see that in this example.

11 Nevertheless divers of Asher and Manasseh and of Zebulun humbled themselves, and came to Jerusalem.

It is important to note what it says in these verses. Even though many people scorned and ridiculed the couriers, "nevertheless, some men of Asher, Manasseh and Zebulun humbled themselves and went to Jerusalem" (2 Chronicles 30:11, NIV). In the worst of times, God still has a remnant; so He had here. Many from the tribes of Asher, Manasseh, and Zebulun humbled themselves and came to Jerusalem. In other words, they were sorry for their sins and submitted themselves to God.

The Hebrew word *kana'* (**kah-NAH**), which means to bend the knee—hence, to humiliate, vanquish, or humble (oneself)—is employed here. The emphasis is on a proud and independent spirit abasing itself. There were indeed some who put away their pride, their indignation, and their sense of superiority over the people of the south. Many of God's people were cut to the heart by God's appeal to return to Him, and they responded in earnest. Pride keeps people from yielding themselves to the LORD. It's when that pride is brought down that the work is done.

12 Also in Judah the hand of God was to give them one heart to do the commandment of the king and of the princes, by the word of the LORD.

The people of Judah unanimously obeyed the command to attend this solemn assembly. They did it with one heart, were all of a mind in it, and the hand (Hebrew *yad*, which indicates power, means, direction, etc.) of God gave them that "one heart," for it is in the day of power that God's subjects are made willing.

When God's people come together and put away divisions, they are moving toward renewal and revival. The hand of God—God by the power of His grace—inclined their hearts to unanimous compliance with God's and the king's will. And this is mentioned as the reason for the wonderful change wrought in these people, who had lately been given to idolatry. Here is a case of God working in the lives of the people, both to will and to do. Whenever people manifest an unexpected boldness to do that which is good, we must acknowledge the hand of God in it.

TEACHING TIPS

September 8
Bible Study Guide 2

1. Words You Should Know

A. Baalim (2 Chronicles 33:3); Hebrew *Baal*—From a Phonecian diety.

B. High places (v. 3); Hebrew *Bamah*—An elevated place used for idol worship by Israel.

C. Valley of Hinnom (v. 6)—A valley near Jerusalem where pagan sacrifices occurred.

D. Fetters (v.11); Hebrew *nechoshei*—A handcuff made of bronze or copper; shackles or manacles.

E. Supplication (v. 13); Hebrew *Tekhinnaw*—Entreat; ask for grace or favor; a prayerful petition.

2. Teacher Preparation

Read all the background Scriptures and today's lesson text. Consider the impact of wicked leadership that immediately follows godly leadership.

3. Starting the Lesson

A. Begin the class with a prayer. Thank God that in His sight there is no sin we can commit that disqualifies us from redemption and restoration.

B. Ask for volunteers to define the following words: revival, redemption, repentance, and restoration.

4. Getting into the Lesson

As you begin the lesson, remind your students that the lesson's focus is on God restoring the sinner. Point out that while God stands ready to forgive those who repent and turn away from their past sins, the consequences of those sins may remain indefinitely.

In today's lesson, we will see Manasseh commit atrocious sins and ask for God's forgiveness. Even though he is forgiven and fully restored, the consequences of his past sins are visited upon an entire nation.

5. Relating the Lesson to Life

A. Review the information presented in THE PEOPLE, PLACES, AND TIMES section.

B. Ask your students to identify examples of current attempts to mingle ungodly practices with true worship.

C. Give students the opportunity to answer the questions in the SEARCH THE SCRIPTURES section.

D. LESSON IN OUR SOCIETY deals with people who think that their past is too bad to be forgiven. Have your students find other Scriptures that address this opinion. Then have them discuss how they can minister to someone who expresses this particular concern.

6. Arousing Action

A. Read the questions in the MAKE IT HAPPEN section. Challenge the students to examine their hearts.

B. Allow students to share what God spoke to them as they went through the lesson.

C. Close the class with prayer.

GOD RESTORES A SINNER

Bible Background • 2 CHRONICLES 33:1-20; 2 KINGS 21
Printed Text • 2 CHRONICLES 33:1-13
Devotional Reading • 2 CHRONICLES 6:36-42

**SEPT
8TH**

LESSON AIM

After studying today's lesson, students will understand that in spite of the nature and gravity of our sins, God will forgive them and restore us when we truly repent. Additionally, students will discover that very often our sins affect not only ourselves but many other people as well.

KEEP IN MIND

"And he was intreated of him, and heard his supplication, and brought him again to Jerusalem into his kingdom. Then Manasseh knew that the LORD was God" (2 Chronicles 33:13).

FOCAL VERSES

2 Chronicles 33:1 Manasseh was twelve years old when he began to reign, and he reigned fifty and five years in Jerusalem.

2 But did that which was evil in the sight of the LORD, like unto the abominations of the heathen, whom the LORD had cast out before the children of Israel.

3 For he built again the high places which Hezekiah his father had broken down, and he reared up altars for Baalim, and made groves, and worshipped all the host of heaven, and served them.

4 Also he built altars in the house of the LORD, whereof the LORD had said, In Jerusalem shall my name be for ever.

5 And he built altars for all the host of heaven in two courts of the house of the LORD.

6 And he caused his children to pass through the fire in the valley of the son of Hinnom: also he observed times, and used enchantments, and used

LESSON OVERVIEW

LESSON AIM
KEEP IN MIND
FOCAL VERSES
IN FOCUS
THE PEOPLE, PLACES,
AND TIMES
BACKGROUND
AT-A-GLANCE
IN DEPTH
SEARCH THE SCRIPTURES
DISCUSS THE MEANING
LESSON IN OUR SOCIETY
MAKE IT HAPPEN
FOLLOW THE SPIRIT
REMEMBER YOUR THOUGHTS
MORE LIGHT ON THE TEXT
DAILY BIBLE READINGS

witchcraft, and dealt with a familiar spirit, and with wizards: he wrought much evil in the sight of the LORD to provoke him to anger,

7 And he set a carved image, the idol which he had made, in the house of God, of which God had said to David and to Solomon his son, In this house, and in Jerusalem, which I have chosen before all tribes of Israel, will I put my name for ever:

8 Neither will I any more remove the foot of Israel from out of the land which I have appointed for your fathers; so that they will take heed to do all that I have commanded them, according to the whole law and the statutes and the ordinances by the hand of Moses.

9 So Manasseh made Judah and the inhabitants of Jerusalem to err, and to do worse than the heathen, whom the LORD had destroyed before the children of Israel.

10 And the LORD spake to Manasseh, and to his people: but they would not hearken.

11 Wherefore the LORD brought upon them the captains of the host of the king of Assyria, which took Manasseh among the thorns, and bound him with fetters, and carried him to Babylon.

12 And when he was in affliction, he besought the LORD his God, and humbled himself greatly before the God of his fathers,

13 And prayed unto him: and he was intreated of him, and heard his supplication, and brought him again to Jerusalem into his kingdom. Then Manasseh knew that the LORD he was God.

IN FOCUS

The members of the senior high Sunday School class were eager to get to their class on time. Having Earlene in the class always made the sessions more enjoyable. She came to class well prepared and anxious to participate. Earlene's contributions to class discussions were thoughtful and insightful. She could always be counted on to have read all of the background Scriptures beforehand and would often point out interesting highlights of each lesson. In addition to her Sunday School participation, Earlene led the group of young people that made monthly visits to the local convalescent hospital. What a changed person she was from five years ago.

People remembered Earlene as the rebellious only child of one of their deacons. Shortly after entering high school, Earlene's grades began to fall, and she started drinking and hanging out with a rough crowd of teenagers. Earlene stopped coming to church altogether and according to her father would frequently break her curfew and take the car without his permission. By the eleventh grade, Earlene had been arrested several times for drunkenness and disorderly conduct. No one was really surprised to hear that Earlene had become pregnant during the summer before her senior year.

During her fourth month of pregnancy, Earlene came back to the church and re-dedicated her life to Christ. Earlene regularly attended Alcoholics Anonymous meetings for teens, and she enrolled in an alternative school and began course work that would enable her to receive her diploma.

Although Earlene's baby was later born with fetal alcohol syndrome, she knew that God had forgiven her.

THE PEOPLE, PLACES, AND TIMES

Valley of the Son of Hinnom. Also called the Valley of Hinnom, this deep, narrow ravine was a site of pagan worship located to the south and southwest of ancient Jerusalem. One section of the valley was called "Tophet," or fire stove. It was here that Manasseh's grandfather, King Ahaz, sacrificed, burned incense, and burned his sons as an offering to the pagan god Molech (2 Chronicles 28:1-3).

After their return from the Babylonian exile, the Jews turned this valley into the city dump, where garbage and anything deemed unclean (including the bodies of executed criminals) was incinerated. For this reason, a fire was constantly burning. In Nehemiah's time, the Valley of Hinnom marked the northern limits of the settlements of the sons of Judah. By the first century, the constantly burning Valley of Hinnom was also known as the Valley of Gehenna, depicting hell.

Child sacrifices. The most detestable of all the pagan practices was that of child sacrifice. Despite God's law to Israel that prescribed the death penalty for anyone who sacrificed his offspring to pagan gods, apostate Israelites—both in Judah and in Israel—indulged in this sinful practice and passed their children through the fires of Molech. With the impetus to child sacrifice given by Ahaz and Manasseh, the practice apparently became entrenched (2 Kings 16:3; 21:6; Jeremiah 7:31; 32:35; Ezekiel 20:26).

Manasseh's grandson, King Josiah, would try to put an end to this horrible practice by defiling the place, making it unfit for worship. But this did not totally eradicate the practice. Ezekiel, who began prophesying 16 years after Josiah's death, mentions it as occurring during his lifetime (Ezekiel 20:31).

Based on information from Illustrated Manners and Customs of the Bible, J. I. Packer and M.C. Tenney, editors (Nashville: Thomas Nelson Publishers, 1980), pp. 206, 635, 705.

BACKGROUND

The extraordinary revival efforts undertaken by Judah's King Hezekiah resulted in a change of heart for his people. The northern kingdom of Israel had recently been attacked by Assyria and the people deported. Hezekiah extended his appeal to Judah and to the few remaining Israelites to celebrate the Passover in Jerusalem. Although it was initially met with derision and skepticism by some, the opportunity to gather and worship in Jerusalem was embraced by others. There had been no Passover celebration to equal this one since the time of Solomon. The rejoicing was so tremendous, in fact, that the celebration lasted an extra week. Following Hezekiah's example, the people were eager to return to true worship and renew their covenant relationship with God.

Despite the change of heart of the people, the threat of military invasion loomed heavy over the land. There may have been two invasions of Judah by

Assyria's King Sennacherib. On both occasions, God used Hezekiah to protect his beloved city. Most of the land around Jerusalem was devastated, and all of the fortified cities were destroyed. Under the powerful spiritual influence of Hezekiah and the Prophet Isaiah, and the protective hand of God, the capital city of Jerusalem was preserved.

AT-A-GLANCE

1. Manasseh's Evil Reign
(2 Chronicles 33:1-6)
2. Manasseh Ignores God's Warning
(vv. 10-11)
3. Manasseh Prays to God for Help
(v. 12)
4. God Hears and Restores a Sinner
(v. 13)

IN DEPTH

1. Manasseh's Evil Reign (2 Chronicles 33:1-6)

The time of the kings in Judah is marked by a cycle of godly kings followed by evil kings. Such was the case with Judah's King Manasseh. His grandfather, Ahaz, turned his back on the LORD and wallowed in idol worship, but his father, King Hezekiah, was a powerful spiritual force in Judah. Manasseh's name gives us a key to his poor performance as a ruler of God's people. His name means "one who makes to forget." Manasseh did indeed seem to forget God, and he influenced his people to be forgetful as well. Under his father's leadership and no doubt due to the influence of the Prophet Isaiah, idolatry had been purged from the nation. Although the Assyrians had devastated much of Judah, God had used Hezekiah to miraculously deliver the capital city of Jerusalem and spare her people from direct assault. Under Manasseh, pagan worship would be reinstated on a monumental scale.

Although Manasseh came to the throne at age 12, he co-reigned with his father. When Manasseh was about 25, his father died and sole control of the kingdom was in his hands. Despite the godly demeanor and influences of his father, Manasseh turned his back on God and "did evil in the sight of the LORD"

in much the same way as the Canaanite nations that were expelled by Joshua and the Israelites when they first entered the Promised Land. Manasseh rebuilt the groves on the tops of hills (or "high places") that had been built by his grandfather Ahaz and destroyed by his father. He erected altars for Baal (the chief pagan deity) and Asherah (the female goddess of sex and fertility).

Judah was initially introduced to these high places when King Jehoram made high altars in the hill country of Judah and led the inhabitants of Jerusalem into unfaithfulness (2 Chronicles 21:11). It could be argued that the high places themselves did not represent idolatry because the people initially worshiped God there. The problem was that it was not the prescribed place of worship. God had sanctified the temple as the only place of worship and sacrifice, and Judah was worshiping in the high hills because that was where they saw their pagan neighbors worshiping. This disobedience and lowering of God's standards was the first step that led to their decline into full-blown pagan worship.

Manasseh's worshiping of the "host of heaven" implies that he worshiped the sun, moon, and planets and was apparently a practitioner of astrology. Manasseh added to his catalog of sins by defiling the temple itself by placing altars to foreign gods in the temple and the outer courts. The temple was now defiled by the presence of idol images, astrologers, and wizards, all sanctioned by the king. This rebellious son was undoing the hard work that his father had put into cleansing the temple. This willful disregard for family is reflected in Manasseh's willingness to participate in the abominable practice of child sacrifice. The "pass[ing] through the fire in the Valley of the son of Hinnom" has been regarded by some biblical scholars as signifying a purification ritual in which children were dedicated to pagan gods. However, the parallel Scripture in 2 Kings 16:3 indicates that "passing through fire" is synonymous with sacrificing. Ezekiel 16:20-21 implies that the children were sometimes killed first, rather than being burned alive.

2. Manasseh Ignores God's Warning (vv. 10-11)

Manasseh completely abandoned the worship of God. The idols and altars he erected and the spiritualistic practices he indulged in were selected from all the cultures surrounding the nation of Judah: the Canaanites, the Philistines, and the Amorites. Yet he excluded the worship of the one true God. Manasseh actually outdid the heathen Canaanite nations in his wickedness. God held him personally responsible for seducing Judah "to err and to do worse" (33:9) than the nations God had destroyed before the Israelites took possession of the land.

Yet in spite of Manasseh's wickedness, the LORD undertook steps to reclaim him and bring him out of his rebellion. The parallel Scriptures in 2 Kings 21 confirm that God, through His prophets, warned Manasseh that Jerusalem belonged to Him. God had sanctified the temple and promised David and Solomon that He had placed His name there forever. Manasseh was reminded of the promises of God, both positive and negative: promises of blessings for obedience and of judgment for disobedience. Finally, God's warning about the fate of Judah if Mannasseh continued was chilling: Judah would be delivered into the hands of their enemies.

We should note the impact of Manasseh's leadership. His ungodly example had led the people to sin, and God's punishment of Manasseh would be visited on the entire nation. Leaders have a responsibility to set godly standards for those whom God has entrusted to them. In the account of Manasseh, it is clear that the shortcomings and sins of a leader often affect not only the leader himself, but those who follow him.

We see that God took extraordinary steps to turn Manasseh around and prevent him from following his fateful course. He kept trying to reach Manasseh, using His prophets as intermediaries. Manasseh was so determined to silence the voice of God that he silenced the voice of His messengers by killing them. In 2 Kings 21:16, we see that Manasseh shed "innocent blood . . . till he had filled Jerusalem from one end to another." Both Jewish and Christian tradition relate that it was during this time that Manasseh put the prophet Isaiah in a hollow oak tree and had him sawn in two. This may account for the reference in Hebrews 11:37 to men of faith, some of whom were "sawn asunder."

While Manasseh may have been able to silence the message of God, he could do nothing to stop God's sentence. Just as God had pronounced, the army of Assyria invaded Jerusalem, and the arrogant

Manasseh, with chains on his hands and feet, was dragged off to a Babylonian dungeon. Between 652 and 648 B.C., the Assyrians had crushed a coup by the city of Babylon. The Assyrians may have suspected that Manasseh was behind this insurrection; therefore, he was taken to Babylon rather than to Nineveh, the capital city of Assyria. Manasseh's confinement in Babylon is backed by archeological confirmation. An inscription was found that dates from the reign of Esarhaddon, son of the Assyrian king Sennacherib. The inscription describes the invasion and 22 kings being summoned to the king prior to deportation. One of the kings mentioned by name is Manasseh, king of Judah. The tragedy is that Manasseh could have averted divine judgment and the destruction of so many lives by turning to God.

3. Manasseh Prays To God for Help (v. 12)

The truth that every knee shall bow and every tongue confess that Jesus is LORD is a reality. However, the question then becomes, "When?" When will sinners call on the name of the LORD? Will they do it prior to judgment, so that they may save their lives and possibly the lives of many others, or will their confession come after judgment and devastation?

Manasseh had steadfastly refused to heed the warning of God and now found himself languishing in a Babylonian prison. It was during this time that he "besought the LORD his God" and "humbled himself greatly." Notice that Manasseh had lost his title as king, yet he had not lost his ability to turn to God. Now that he had hit rock bottom, he turned to the LORD. Perhaps Manasseh came to realize that he had no one to blame but himself, and more importantly, no hope of help but God. Manasseh had every advantage in life, having been reared in a royal and godly household. Similarly, he had been given every opportunity to change his ways: God had sent the prophets. The problem had been Manasseh's own rebellious heart. Now that he found himself stripped of everything, he was finally willing to humble himself and submit to God.

4. God Restores Manasseh (v. 13)

God frequently chastens, but only those whom He loves. God, because He is just and righteous, had to chasten Manasseh, but he never stopped loving him. When Manasseh humbled himself and prayed, the LORD "heard his supplication" and restored him to his place of authority. Manasseh didn't have to prove that he was worthy of being king again. God, in his forgiveness of Manasseh, fully restored him. This Scripture reminds us of New Testament assurances that in Jesus believers have complete redemption through His blood, including complete forgiveness for our past sins and restoration to a place of authority in Christ Jesus!

Manasseh's very name takes on new meaning. The sins of the "one who makes to forget" are forgiven and forgotten as promised in Hebrews 10:17 ("and their sins and iniquities will I remember no more"). What a painful and protracted process Manasseh had to go through to finally acknowledge that the LORD was God. God redeemed Manasseh and used his despicable sins to show him that God, not the idols, was the one true God.

This is not as much the saga of Manasseh as it is the odyssey of divine mercy and compassion. If God can instantly forgive Manasseh, we can surmise that no matter how low a sinner may get, God's mercy still reaches out.

SEARCH THE SCRIPTURES

1. How long was Manasseh's reign in Judah? (v. 1)

2. What type of sinful practices did Manasseh indulge in during his reign? (vv. 3-6)

3. Where did Manasseh erect carved idol images? (v. 3)

4. What was the effect of Manasseh's evil on the people of Judah? (v. 9)

5. What was the reaction of Manasseh and the people when the LORD spoke to them concerning their evildoing? (v. 10)

6. Who did the LORD use to humble Manasseh? (v. 11)

7. What effect did imprisonment have on Manasseh? (v. 12)

8. How did God respond to Manasseh's prayer of repentance? (v. 13)

DISCUSS THE MEANING

1. Many of us know of fine Christian parents who have children who are rebellious or out of the will of God. How do such situations compare to the case of Hezekiah's son, Manasseh?

2. Manasseh was perhaps the most wicked king that ever reigned in Judah, yet his reign lasted 55 years. What might be some of the reasons that God allowed Manasseh to reign longer than any of Judah's other kings? What does this tell us about God's unwillingness that anyone should perish?

3. Manasseh's evil ways influenced his people. In what ways can we see examples of poor leadership influencing the lives of people today?

LESSON IN OUR SOCIETY

We often encounter friends or family members who won't come to church because they are ashamed of things they may have done in the past. It is heartbreaking to listen to these people as they try to convince us of how unworthy they are. They honestly, though mistakenly, believe that their past behavior precludes a relationship with God.

It is our responsibility to continue to witness to them and assure them that God intends for each of us to live in victory over every circumstance of our lives. Let them know that through Jesus Christ they can be fully forgiven and restored.

MAKE IT HAPPEN

It is easy for us to compare ourselves to King Manasseh and judge him. Surely none of us has ever worshiped Baal or Asherah, but we certainly have worshiped other things. We should examine ourselves to see what idols we have set up in our lives. Have we worshiped or do we still worship our jobs, our homes, or some man or woman? Are we perhaps just as guilty as Manasseh? Are our spiritual ears attuned to the still small voice of God? Can we hear Him speaking quietly to us? Do we hear Him reminding us that we are His elect, His chosen? Are we attuned to the Holy Spirit witnessing to our spirit? Perhaps we are just as stubborn as Manasseh. If so, we need to ask ourselves just how far God must go to get our attention.

FOLLOW THE SPIRIT

What God wants me to do:

_____

_____

REMEMBER YOUR THOUGHTS

Special insights you have learned:

_____

_____

MORE LIGHT ON THE TEXT
2 Chronicles 33:1-13

He could have become a preacher of righteousness, but he became a perpetrator of evil and wickedness. He detested his father's ways, and he would have none of his piety. For a period of 55 years, this terrible king ruled Judah. His name was Manasseh, and his rebellion against God led to some of the worst atrocities imaginable. Manasseh was born three years after his father Hezekiah's memorable sickness. Manasseh's name signified "forgetfulness." Manasseh lived up to his name. Not only did he forget his father's ways, but he forsook God's ways as well. Second Chronicles tells us that he sacrificed sons in the fire (33:6), set up altars to Baal (v. 3), and "worshiped the stars" (v. 3). Manasseh thought it better to go with the times, worship Baal and Asherah, and make friendly alliances with nations holding other creeds. Manasseh's sin was deep and grievous. Not only did he disdain the ways of his father, he undid all the good work his father began. Also, Manasseh's sin was aggravated by the fact that he chose to follow the very worst of examples.

Would God still have anything to do with a man like Manasseh? One might think that God would write him off. Amazingly, God didn't give up on him! Manasseh had spent years building a brutal legacy of crimes against God and humanity, yet he found forgiveness.

The Assyrians (not known for extending charity to conquered kings) took Manasseh prisoner and carted him off to Babylon. The judgment that God executed upon the land was of such magnitude and intensity that it made the ears of those who heard it tingle. The king must, in no small way, have experienced some indescribable afflictions at the hands of the tyrant, Assyria. He must have been wretched to the last degree: his crown gone, his kingdom devastated, his subjects put to unheard of miseries. In his awful despair and deep abasement, Manasseh prayed. Faced with unmitigated torture and possible death, Manasseh "humbled himself greatly before the God of his fathers" (v. 12). What was God's response? As soon as God saw him broken down and confessing his wrong, He took pity on him. God

heard and answered his prayer. God blotted out his sins like a cloud and his transgressions like a thick cloud. God allowed Manasseh to return to his home in Jerusalem (v. 13).

2 Chronicles 33:1 Manasseh was twelve years old when he began to reign, and he reigned fifty and five years in Jerusalem: 2 But did that which was evil in the sight of the LORD, like unto the abominations of the heathen, whom the LORD had cast out before the children of Israel.

Of special note is the young age at which Manasseh began to reign; he was one of the longest-reigning kings in Israel. The fact that he was 12 years old tells us that he was at an age at which he understood the requirements of the LORD. Furthermore, by reminding us of his reign in Jerusalem, the writer prepares us for the depth of Manasseh's apostasy. He had learned the law and he was at the center of Israelite worship and faith. Verse 2 begins with a contrast, _waya'as_, which could be understood to read, "Although he began to reign at the age of 12 and reigned 55 years in Jerusalem, he did that which was evil."

Note that the word for "evil" used here is from the word _baarah_, rooted in _ra_, which suggests the embodiment of evil, as opposed to _owlaah_, which suggests the intention of evil with the possibility of changing. Here the idea is that mischief dwelt at the very core of Manasseh's being. He was bent on creating misery and making people wretched. Note that the text reads, "in the sight of the LORD." This phrase may communicate the idea that Jerusalem was the seat of God's presence. Evil done in Jerusalem carried peculiar weight. As king, Manasseh was God's anointed, so he was in the presence of God by virtue of his anointing. As king, he was in the sight of God by being at the place of God's sanctuary. His evil deeds were literally and figuratively in the sight of the LORD. Manasseh did the same evil deeds that caused the LORD to remove the Canaanites from the land.

The writer uses the word "abomination" from the Hebrew _batoebot_ to describe the action of Manasseh. He acted abhorrently in the face of his God. Rather than follow the ritual prescribed by the God of Israel, he replaced them with the demonic rituals of the unclean nations around him. The writer reminds us of what befell this nation: "The LORD cast them out." The words "cast out" imply a loss of occupancy, a seizure of that which once belonged to another. It can also mean that God impoverished them because of this act. They were disinherited by the LORD. The writer, of course, wants us to know that Manasseh, at this time, did not care that he was leading Israel down the wrong path.

Manasseh had the privilege of leading God's people from a young age. However, this foolish young king, in contrast to the good example of his father, yielded himself to all impiety. He imported the abominations of the heathen into his kingdom. He abandoned the religion of his father for pagan practices. He committed idolatry in imitation of heathen nations. Even an awareness of the judgment of God upon those nations did not provide sufficient incentive for him to stop his wicked ways.

3 For he built again the high places which Hezekiah his father had broken down, and he reared up altars for Baalim, and made groves, and worshipped all the host of heaven, and served them.

The emphasis on Manasseh's undoing of his father's good works is shown by the word "again." The Hebrew word *shuv* (**shoov**) means to return or turn back (hence, away). It indicates a retreat or return. What Manasseh's father had painfully accomplished, he unraveled as fast as he could. What the father built up for God, the son pulled down; and what the father had destroyed because it was evil, he immediately proceeded to reconstruct. The story of Manasseh here compares with that of Ahaz (cf. 2 Chronicles 33:2-6 with 28:2-4, 25). Choosing a wrong model was the undoing of this young king. Although he had in his father one of the best examples of purity and devotion, that would not do. Instead, he chose other role models: Ahab and Ahaz, kings who had been judged by God for their wickedness.

The high places were not necessarily places of idol worship. They were places where Israel worshiped until the building of the temple, but very often they became places of idolatry. The problem was not the fact that he "built up the high places," but what he did after building them. Manasseh could have made them a place of Yahweh's memorial, but instead he proceeded to create an abode and to confirm and raise up Baal. This is more than just

building an altar; he actually built up gods, which suggests the actual creation of these gods. He proceeded to "make" (*waya'as*) "groves" (Hebrew *asherah*). Actually this is a sort of tree or pole used to carry the female counterpart of Baal. He created a male and a female god and placed them up on mountains. If he had just created them and left them, they could be considered art, but the next phrase convicts him. The writer says "and worshiped," meaning he prostrated himself and bowed down to these idols. Having worshiped what he had made, he also began worshiping the host of heaven. Everything he did contradicted the first commandment; Manasseh worshiped and served everything but God.

4 Also he built altars in the house of the LORD, whereof the LORD had said, In Jerusalem shall my name be for ever. 5 And he built altars for all the host of heaven in the two courts of the house of the LORD.

Manasseh went a step further than Ahab, who worshiped idols but did not go so far as to erect them in God's sanctuary. Manasseh's preoccupation with pagan religion is seen in his worship of the "host of heaven" (*tseba' hashamayim*, pronounced **tsuh-VAH-ha-shah-MY-yim**). This expression, although used in the Old Testament to refer to stars as witnesses in their number, order, and splendor and to the majesty and providential rule and care of Yahweh (Isaiah 34:4; 40:26; 45:12), is more frequently employed to denote the stars as objects of idolatry (Deuteronomy 4:19; 17:3; 2 Kings 17:16; 21:3, 5; 23:4ff; Jeremiah 8:2; 19:13; Zephaniah 1:5). Although star worship seems to have been an enticement to Israel at first (Deuteronomy 4:19; 17:3; Amos 5:26), it attained special prominence in the days of the later kings of Judah. The name of Manasseh is particularly connected with it. This king built altars for "all the host of heaven" in the courts of the temple (2 Kings 21:3, 5). Not only did he erect an altar in the outer court of the congregation, but he also went so far as to erect one in the inner sanctuary, which was meant for the priests!

6 And he caused his children to pass through the fire in the valley of the son of Hinnom: also he observed times, and used enchantments, and used witchcraft, and dealt with a familiar spirit, and with

wizards: he wrought much evil in the sight of the LORD, to provoke him to anger.

Manasseh's actions directly violated God's instructions in Deuteronomy 18:9-13. What God expressly condemned, he cherished and practiced. He made his children pass through fire—by way of oblation, so as to be consumed for a burnt offering. He dedicated his children to Molech and made the devil's lying oracles his guides and counselors. He "observed times"; that is, he practiced divination by observing the clouds, noting their course at particular times, the different kinds, the contrary directions, etc. He used "enchantments" (*nachash*, pronounced **nah-KAHSH**); that is, he used incantations, spells, and charms. He dealt with familiar spirits (*'owb*, pronounced **ohv**); hence, he became a necromancer. He also consulted wizards. All these things were clearly forbidden in Leviticus 19:26-31. Yet the king committed these abominations with impunity, provoking the LORD to anger. The judgment that later followed should have surprised no one.

7 And he set a carved image, the idol which he had made, in the house of God, of which God had said to David and to Solomon his son, In this house, and in Jerusalem, which I have chosen before all the tribes of Israel, will I put my name for ever:

Manasseh set up a carved image, probably in the likeness of himself, in the sanctuary. As if going into idolatry were not enough, Manasseh carved an idol and set it up in the sanctuary. What great defiance of God! We must also learn that sin is progressive. One sin, unrepented of, leads to another.

8 Neither will I any more remove the foot of Israel from out of the land which I have appointed for your fathers; so that they will take heed to do all that I have commanded them, according to the whole law and the statutes and the ordinances by the hand of Moses.

If only Manasseh had taken time to ponder and reflect upon the just dealings of God as well as the fair terms he stood upon with God, he would have quickly retraced his steps and repented. God promised security and peace to Israel as long as they walked in His ways and obeyed His commandments. Had they been faithful to God's testimonies, they never would have gone into captivity, and should even at this day have been in possession of the Promised Land.

9 So Manasseh made Judah and the inhabitants of Jerusalem to err, and to do worse than the heathen, whom the LORD had destroyed before the children of Israel.

Under the leadership of Manasseh, the people of Judah exceeded even the heathen in their wickedness. Although it is not stated that he forced them, yet it is written that he "made [them] to err, and to do worse than the heathen." This is the power of influence. It is true that in most cases, the direction in which the leader moves is the one in which the followers tread. In disdain of God's choice of Zion to be His rest forever and of Israel to be His covenant people, Manasseh set up other gods, profaned God's chosen temple, and corrupted His chosen people. A family, church, group, or nation will never rise above its leadership.

10 And the LORD spake to Manasseh, and to his people: but they would not hearken.

The proper way for a sinner to be reconciled to God is for God to speak to him or her and for that person to listen. This He did to Manasseh, who had refused to come that way. In other words, what aggravated the sin of Manasseh was that God spoke to him and his people by the prophets, but they would not hearken. Here is God's grace displayed. Despite their obstinacy in turning a deaf ear to Him, He spoke. Although they hated to be reformed, their wickedness did not prevent Him from showing forth His goodness—still God waited to be gracious. When people's hearts are set on evil, no warning is taken seriously. Instead, the prophet always seems like one who is mocked.

11 Wherefore the LORD brought upon them the captains of the host of the king of Assyria, which took Manasseh among the thorns, and bound him with fetters, and carried him to Babylon.

Because Manasseh refused to heed God's words, God got his attention through harder means. The Assyrians took multitudes of captives, including the king himself, as prisoners. They bound him with fetters and carried him to Babylon. The Hebrew word rendered "fetters" denotes two chains of bronze. The humiliating state in which Manasseh appeared before the Assyrian monarch goes beyond description. Manasseh was taken among the thorns. This may mean, as is commonly supposed, that he had hid himself among a thicket of briers and brambles since it was not uncommon for the Hebrews to take refuge from their enemies in thickets (cf. 1 Samuel 13:6). But instead of the Hebrew *bacochim* (**bah-koh-KEEM**), "among the thorns," some versions read *bechayim* (**Buh-KAI-yim**), "among the living," and so the passage could read "took him alive." The Assyrians bound him with fetters and carried him to Babylon. This is indeed a free fall "from grace to grass." How terrible the consequences of sin can be!

12 And when he was in affliction, he besought the LORD his God, and humbled himself greatly before the God of his fathers,

Manasseh was afflicted by his captors. The Hebrew word *tsarar* (pronounced **tsah-RAHR**), translated "affliction," means to be shut up, be in distress, be in pangs, or to be in a strait (trouble). It shows the difficult situation in which Manasseh found himself as a result of his sins. It would appear that Manasseh had probably never thought of his God except to despise His prerogative and offend against His laws, until he was incarcerated in that dungeon. In the loneliness of exile and imprisonment, Manasseh finally had time for reflection. By now, he must have realized that his present condition was due to his awful and unprecedented apostasy (2 Chronicles 33:7) from the God of his fathers. So Manasseh "besought" (Hebrew *chalah*, pronounced **kah-LAH**) the LORD his God. The word not only suggests that he was sorry, but also that he entreated God with the intensity of a woman in travail. Furthermore, he "humbled" himself (Hebrew *kana'*, pronounced **kah-NAH**), repented, and prayed for forgiveness.

It is interesting to see the manner of the captive king's self-humiliation. Our text says that he did so "very greatly." Here we find the Hebrew word *meod* (**meh-ODE**), translated "very," a word that is often used with other words to intensify them. By implication, it means the self-humiliation of Manasseh is not only to be seen as complete, but also as being diligently and speedily carried out. There seems to be a deliberate contrast between Manasseh and Ahaz, his

model. While in his affliction Manasseh besought the LORD, Ahaz did not do so in similar circumstances (2 Chronicles 28:22). It is not surprising therefore, that the latter did not find God's favor. Like Manasseh, sinners ought to humble themselves before God, whom they have offended.

13 And prayed unto him: and he was intreated of him, and heard his supplication, and brought him again to Jerusalem into his kingdom. Then Manasseh knew that the LORD he was God.

Manasseh's prayer was heard, for his conqueror not only released him, but after two years' exile, restored him—with honor and the full exercise of royal power—to a tributary and dependent kingdom. Perhaps the Assyrian king was motivated by some political reason to restore Manasseh—most probably to have the kingdom of Judah serve as a buffer between Egypt and his Assyrian dominions. But God overruled this measure for higher purposes. The Hebrew word *yada`* (**yah-DAH**), meaning to know, although used in a variety of senses, here suggests an acknowledgment, acquaintance, or comprehension. Manasseh knew that the LORD is God.

DAILY BIBLE READINGS

M: Manasseh Did Much Evil
2 Chronicles 33:1-6

T: Manasseh Repents and Is Restored
2 Chronicles 33:7-13

W: Solomon's Prayer
2 Chronicles 6:36-42

T: If My People Will Pray
2 Chronicles 7:11-16

F: Manasseh Sacrifices to God
2 Chronicles 33:14-20

S: A Publican's Prayer Is Heard
Luke 18:9-14

S: Repentance That Leads to Salvation
2 Corinthians 7:5-13a

TEACHING TIPS

September 15
Bible Study Guide 3

1. Words You Should Know

A. Lees (Zephaniah 1:12); Hebrew *shemer*—Sediment or dregs of wine.

B. Polluted (3:1); Hebrew *gaal*—Implies freedom to have things one's own way; desecrating the things of God.

C. Light and treacherous (v. 4); Hebrew *pachaz bogedowth*—To bubble up with no substance; prone to betrayal with intent to harm.

D. Iniquity (v. 5);Hebrew *avel*—Refers to moral evil; unrighteousness.

2. Teacher Preparation

Read all the background Scriptures and the FOCAL VERSES. Think about the concept of people taking a proactive course of action in a situation as opposed to having a reactive response. Prepare to discuss the need for Christians to be proactive regarding sin and disobedience to the Word of God, rather than waiting for situations to arise that call for a reactive response.

3. Starting the Lesson

Open the class by having students discuss situations in their own lives when they clearly understood that there were consequences for taking or not taking a particular course of action, yet they chose not to take the necessary preliminary steps.

4. Getting into the Lesson

A. Open a discussion by reminding the students of the old adage, "An ounce of prevention is worth a pound of cure." Encourage students to discuss our responsibility to warn others that there is always a consequence to sin and that God has warned us that He will execute judgment on those who sin against Him.

B. Read today's IN FOCUS story. Discuss Marvin's and his wife's complacent attitude toward his brother's illegal activities. The stolen merchandise is in Marvin's house. Although Marvin did not steal anything, he still may have to face charges and try to clear himself. Is Marvin legally or morally innocent?

5. Relating the Lesson to Life

A. Review the concepts described in THE PEOPLE, PLACES, AND TIMES article.

B. Ask your students to identify current examples of attempts to mingle ungodly practices with true worship.

C. Give students the opportunity to answer the questions in SEARCH THE SCRIPTURES.

6. Arousing Action

Have a volunteer read aloud the LESSONS IN OUR SOCIETY section. Follow this with a discussion of examples of arrogance and complacency among many believers. Have the students discuss what the Word of God says about the results of ungodly behavior and practices by His people. Ask the students if they can support their answers with Scripture.

WORSHIP GUIDE

For the Superintendent or Teacher
Theme: Present and Future
Theme Song: "Search Me, Lord"
Scripture: Isaiah 55:6-11
Song: "I Have Decided to Follow Jesus"
Meditation: Lord, we realize that we have not always been faithful and kept our covenant with you. We thank You for Your darling Son Jesus, the provision by which we may be forgiven and fully restored to You. Amen.

PRESENT AND FUTURE

Bible Background • ZEPHANIAH
Printed Text • ZEPHANIAH 1:12; 3:1-5, 11-13
Devotional Reading • ISAIAH 55:6-11

SEPT 15TH

LESSON AIM

After studying today's lesson, students will be able to describe how God's love is related to His justice and righteousness. In so doing, students will choose to turn away from transgressions and be led specifically to stop acts that offend the love of God.

KEEP IN MIND

"The just LORD is in the midst therof; he will not do iniquity: every morning doth he bring his judgment to light, he faileth not; but the unjust knoweth no shame" (Zephaniah 3:5).

FOCAL VERSES

Zephaniah 1:12 And it shall come to pass at that time, that I will search Jerusalem with candles, and punish the men that are settled on their lees: that say in their heart, The LORD will not do good, neither will he do evil.

3:1 Woe to her that is filthy and polluted, to the oppressing city!

2 She obeyed not the voice; she received not correction; she trusted not in the LORD; she drew not near to her God.

3 Her princes within her are roaring lions; her judges are evening wolves; they gnaw not the bones till the morrow.

4 Her prophets are light and treacherous persons: her priests have polluted the sanctuary, they have done violence to the law.

5 The just LORD is in the midst therof; he will not do iniquity: every morning doth he bring his judgment to light, he faileth not; but the unjust knoweth no shame.

LESSON OVERVIEW

LESSON AIM
KEEP IN MIND
FOCAL VERSES
IN FOCUS
THE PEOPLE, PLACES, AND TIMES
BACKGROUND
AT-A-GLANCE
IN DEPTH
SEARCH THE SCRIPTURES
DISCUSS THE MEANING
LESSON IN OUR SOCIETY
MAKE IT HAPPEN
FOLLOW THE SPIRIT
REMEMBER YOUR THOUGHTS
MORE LIGHT ON THE TEXT
DAILY BIBLE READINGS

3:11 In that day shalt thou not be ashamed for all thy doings, wherein thou hast transgressed against me: for then I will take away out of the midst of thee them that rejoice in thy pride, and thou shalt no more be haughty because of my holy mountain.

12 I will also leave in the midst of thee an afflicted and poor people, and they shall trust in the name of the LORD.

13 The remnant of Israel shall not do iniquity, nor speak lies; neither shall a deceitful tongue be found in their mouth: for they shall feed and lie down, and none shall make them afraid.

IN FOCUS

Marvin couldn't recall ever having felt so humiliated. He stood in his hallway, helplessly looking on as police officers searched through their bedroom bureau drawers, searched through the closets, and shoved their furniture aside. They had a search warrant and had told him they were looking for "possible" stolen merchandise in the house.

Marvin's brother Timothy had been staying with Marvin and his family for several months. Marvin knew that Timothy was unemployed and that the boxes of merchandise that he brought into the house late in the evenings were probably stolen; yet he had never confronted Timothy about it. Timothy had always been lazy and irresponsible. Marvin had often had to pay his bills and get him out of trouble in the past. When Timothy told him that he had lost his last job, Marvin had invited him to come and stay with his family until he got back on his feet.

The children had been excited when their Uncle Timothy had presented them with a brand new color television last Monday. Marvin and his wife had their doubts about allowing the kids to keep the television, but after discussing it, they had agreed to just keep quiet and not get involved in the "details." Just this morning Timothy had assured Marvin that he would be moving out in the next few weeks.

As Marvin looked on, the police loaded boxes from his garage into a van. Some of his neighbors were standing on their porches watching too. He checked his watch and realized that there was no way he was going to be able to get to work on time this evening. He groaned as he wondered what possible excuse he could give his boss and what he would tell his children.

THE PEOPLE, PLACES, AND TIMES

Zephaniah. This prophet of Judah traces his lineage back to royalty and may have been the great-grandson of King Hezekiah. Because he mentions the presence of pagan priests, the worship of Baal, and the practice of astrology in Judah, Zephaniah's ministry probably began prior to the religious reforms undertaken by King Josiah in 621 B.C. His position among other prophets is unique in that he prophesied during a period of revival. Zephaniah's message is clear: Judah's indifference and stubborn refusal to obey God would bring His wrathful judgment. This judgment would be three-fold and would involve purifying, purging, and restoration. Zephaniah was a contemporary of Jeremiah and was one of the last prophets before the captivity.

Based on information from Eerdman's Handbook to the Bible, David Alexander and Pat Alexander, editors (Oxford: Lion Publishing, 1983), p 454.

Josiah's Revival. In the eighteenth year of Josiah's reign, he ordered the cleaning and repair of the temple. During the cleaning, the high priest Hilkiah found "a book of the law of the LORD given by Moses" (2 Chronicles 34:14). This book, probably the original copy of Deuteronomy, was then read to the young king. After he heard God's Word, Josiah ripped his clothes and commissioned a five-man delegation to inquire of God on behalf of his people. A prophetess foretold that because the people had dis-

obeyed, disaster was impending. However, because of Josiah's repentant spirit, he would not live to see the calamity that would befall his kingdom. Josiah's aim to turn his people back to true worship was so intense that he and the entire kingdom renewed their covenant with God. His purging of evil influences from the land was so complete that the high places of idol worship that had been built centuries earlier by King Solomon were made unfit for any future worship. Josiah was zealous in his attempts to rid Judah of all vestiges of idolatry.

BACKGROUND

The reign of King Manasseh was followed by the wicked but relatively short reign of his son, Amon. Unlike his father, Amon never repented or turned away from idol worship. After two years on the throne, he was assassinated by his servants. He was succeeded by his son, Josiah. Like his great-grandfather Hezekiah, Josiah "did that which was right in the sight of the LORD" (2 Chronicles 34:2). During the twelfth year of his reign, Josiah began a campaign of revival throughout Judah. The pagan altars were torn down and desecrated, and the idols erected by his father were ground to powder. Josiah assembled the entire kingdom, including priests and prophets, and read aloud to them from the book of the law. Josiah was so fervent in his intent to hear the Word of God and follow it that he renewed the covenant of obedience with God. Also, he made everyone present do the same. Josiah began a second campaign against idolatry that was more intensive than the first. He wanted people to turn away from their wicked past and return to true worship.

AT-A-GLANCE

1. Zephaniah Predicts Impending Punishment (Zephaniah 1:12)
2. Judah Rebels Against God (3:1-2)
3. Political, Judicial, and Religious Leaders Fail to Uphold the Laws (vv. 3-5)
4. Prophecy of Judgment and Justification (vv. 11-13)

IN DEPTH

1. Zephaniah Predicts Impending Punishment (Zephaniah 1:12)

The opening verses of the first chapter of Zephaniah should ring a bell with parents. If we see our toddlers headed into oncoming traffic, we don't pause, sigh, and begin a lecture about the dangers of wandering into the street. We cry out. Divine predictions are always meant as warnings, which if heeded may save our lives. Zephaniah had witnessed the foolish attempt by the people to try to worship God alongside of Molech and other idol gods. He was aware of the proliferation of pagan priests and saw the people worshiping the hosts of heaven, the moon, and the stars from their rooftops.

The prophet of God cried out to the people of Judah. Zephaniah warned them, "God has told you what to do, yet you refuse to do it. Now you're headed for destruction!" The prophet got right to the point. Judah was headed for destruction because of her sinful practices. This prediction is based on the people's refusal to repent. It is not the prediction that destroys them, but their sinful acts and stubborn refusal to repent that seals their doom.

Because they would not search their hearts and follow the commandments of God, Zephaniah warns that God intends to uncover their sins by searching them out with a "candle" or a light. God never punishes people without clear warning. How long did Judah think they could continue to disobey God and ignore divine precepts before they came under judgment?

2. Judah Rebels Against God (3:1-2)

The divine love that God had continually shown the people of Jerusalem was easily forgotten by them. Many of them professed to worship the one true God, yet they adopted many customs of their pagan neighbors, or as Zephaniah relates, they would "swear oaths by the LORD" (Zephaniah 1:5) and simultaneously swear to the pagan god Molech. This immoral conduct was far reaching. Zephaniah tells us that even the princes' and king's children were dressing in the foreign apparel of the pagans (Zephaniah 1:8). This mingling of cultures and religious practices was expressly prohibited, yet the people in Jerusalem shamelessly participated in them and ignored God.

The seriousness of playing with God cannot be overemphasized. The attempt to serve two masters also brings a stern warning from our LORD (Luke 16:12). They mixed the holy with the unholy, and they equated the true God with a false god. This speaks directly to the issue of faith. They sought a relationship with the god of the heathen just in case their God failed them. This divided allegiance of faith was their undoing. There are believers today who think that they can follow Jesus and the God of Israel whom He proclaimed and still believe in the salvific efficacy (power to save) of other religions and remain Christians. As sure as there is one God, there is only one way to Him—through Christ Jesus. Any refusal to stand on this fact places us under judgment.

3. Political, Judicial, and Religious Leaders Fail to Uphold the Laws (vv. 3-5)

Many historical events confirm that the fall of great nations or empires has often been precipitated by the fall of its officials. In the case of Jerusalem, this was painfully true as well. The evil in Jerusalem was so widespread and deeply imbedded that there was no likelihood of correction from within. The religious corruption in Jerusalem permeated every sector of society. Instead of setting godly examples, the princes, officers, tribal elders, and other officials callously disregarded the commandments and participated in spreading polluting influences throughout the city. Zephaniah refers to them as "roaring lions." Normally lions roar only when they are attempting to frighten other animals, causing them to stampede and leave the safety of a flock or herd. By adopting these pagan practices, the princes were causing the people to leave the protection and safety provided by obedience to God's commandments.

Similarly, the judges were compared to "evening wolves." Rather than upholding the law, their unscrupulous actions endangered the people. Under the auspices of their office, they were greedy in their dealings and devoured rather than served the people.

The princes used the double-mindedness of the people as a gateway for their avarice and greed. One of the reasons why people play both sides or run a double game is because they need insurance in case of danger—it grows out of fear. Rather than assure the people that single-minded devotion is the key to their security, the princes used the possibility of the pagan gods as a means to keep the people in bondage. The reading of the prophets suggests that they sold charms and idol amulets. The irony in this scenario is that the people wanted to secure a future for themselves but ended up destroying their future by sacrificing their children. But the truth they could not see is that only God, who had preserved them thus far, could save them and secure their future.

Also included in this indictment is the religious leadership. The prophets played a vital role in promoting and maintaining true worship. Their activities often served as a check and balance on the behavior of the kings and priests. The prophets were expected to boldly declare God's judgments against wickedness. However, as indicated in verse 4, the prophets had failed miserably in their responsibilities. Rather than reproving erring ways, these false prophets were rendering prophecies that were not in harmony with God's revealed Word or His commandments and definitely were not promoting true worship. Like the priests, they were little more than religious frauds and racketeers. The pollution of the temple may refer to the introduction of idols, or perhaps to disrespect of the temple caused by ungodly practices held within the temple walls. By failing to teach the Word of God, the priests had "done violence to the law."

The danger in any generation is that prophets become silent because they are afraid for their lives or their livelihood. The prophets themselves had become infected with materialism. Money and power had become the object of prophecy; justice and righteousness are even ignored.

While the prophets and priests may have failed in upholding justice, Zephaniah is clear that God will not fail (v. 5). The fact that God had not acted against them did not mean that He was not present and aware of their iniquities. Unlike the religious leaders, God would not pervert His own word. He would not do evil or "iniquity" by not punishing the wicked. He was there "in the midst" and at the appointed time He would move in judgment against them.

4. Prophecy of Judgment and Justification (vv. 11-13)

Included in the charges against the leaders of Jerusalem were haughtiness and pride. They expressed no shame for their gross immorality and no remorse for their vile acts. Zephaniah is clear that the pride of these people would result in disaster. In the day of reckoning God would "utterly consume all things from off the land" (Zephaniah 1:2). These haughty leaders would be removed in the cataclysmic destruction that would ensue.

With corrupt leaders and faithless prophets and priests, it appears that Jerusalem was hopeless and helpless, just awaiting judgment. The Word of God, as proclaimed by Zephaniah, provided relief for those who were suffering, "I will also leave in the midst of thee an afflicted and poor people" (Zephaniah 3:12). The self-righteous and arrogant leaders would be replaced with a *remnant*, or remainder, of the humble and meek believers who had remained faithful to God.

Zephaniah's message included judgment and hope. Following the darkness and the slaughter, God would bring redemption. There was joyful hope that God would fully restore the righteous people who had heeded and obeyed. God's word of judgment in Scripture always leaves room for hope. No matter how deep into judgment you may have gone, there is a word of hope from God.

SEARCH THE SCRIPTURES

1. What falsehood would be punished by God? (Zephaniah 1:12)

2. How had the people responded to the corrections of the prophets? (3:2)

3. What were the charges made against the prophets? (v. 3)

4. What were the charges made against the priests? (v. 4)

5. What was the prevailing sentiment of the unjust? (v. 5)

6. Who would be removed from the midst of the people? (v. 11)

7. Who would remain? (v. 12)

8. What would be the character and attitude of the remnant? (v. 13)

DISCUSS THE MEANING

1. How might Zephaniah's prophecies have been a motivating factor in the revival that would take place under King Josiah?

2. Zephaniah is issuing a dire warning against complacency on the part of the people of God. How does that tie in with the foolish claims made by some that "the LORD will not do good, neither will he do evil"? (1:12)

3. Much of Zephaniah's prophecy seems harsh and cruel, yet it can be argued that there is an undertone of love throughout. Explain.

4. In what ways do popular culture, literature, and media contribute to our difficulty in associating love with the judgment of God?

LESSON IN OUR SOCIETY

The sinking of the Titanic was one of maritime history's greatest disasters. While the exact cause of the disaster continues to be a topic of ongoing research and debate, this much is clear: On the evening of April 14, 1912, the RMS Titanic hit an iceberg and sank. Of the 2,228 men, women, and children aboard, 711 made it onto lifeboats and survived.

The storm of controversy surrounding this disaster still rages. Fault and blame has shifted from human error to mechanical flaws and failures. The question still remains why the most luxurious ocean liner in the world (at that time) was only outfitted with 20 lifeboats—enough to carry less than half her passengers to safety in the event of an emergency. After the Titanic began to sink, why, out of the 20 lifeboats that were available, were only 18 ever launched? The lifeboats were capable of holding 65 people each, yet only four of them were filled to capacity. Many of the lifeboats that were launched contained fewer than 30 people. In short, on the lifeboats that were deployed, there was room for about 500 more passengers.

Just as surely as the designers of the Titanic were reckless in their regard for human life by failing to provide enough lifeboats for all of her passengers, the leaders of Jerusalem failed to provide a godly example for the people to follow. Zephaniah faced the difficult task of rendering God's message of judgment on a city that was filled with arrogant and complacent people. God had heretofore guarded and protected Jerusalem, and they foolishly believed they could sin against Him and still enjoy His protection. Just as many did not believe the Titanic could sink, the people of Jerusalem didn't believe that the day would come when God would exact a terrible price for their disobedience.

MAKE IT HAPPEN

Zephaniah points out two major obligations for believers. First, the Church is to go out and offer salvation and forgiveness through Christ to nonbelievers who have fallen deeply into sin. Second, the Church must reach out and warn the believer who has fallen into sin.

Oftentimes parents try to warn young people about the pitfalls of ungodly behavior before they are forced to face the bitter consequences. This week make an attempt to identify someone who may be falling into sin or exhibiting ungodly behavior. Make a point of going before the LORD in prayer for that person. Allow God to speak, and then commit to follow and obey what He shares with you.

FOLLOW THE SPIRIT

What God wants me to do:

_____
_____

REMEMBER YOUR THOUGHTS

Special insights you have learned:

_____
_____

MORE LIGHT ON THE TEXT
Zephaniah 1:12; 3:1-5; 11-13

Christians are in danger of contracting a dangerous disease—one that affects millions of people who focus on their privileges and forget their responsibilities. This disease is called complacency. Complacency is killing Christians. G. A. Smith in his classic commentary has rightly stated that "the great causes of God and humanity are not defeated by the hot assaults of the devil, but by the slow, crushing, glacier-like mass of thousands and thousands of indifferent nobodies. God's causes are never destroyed by being blown up, but by being sat upon" (G. A. Smith, "Zephaniah," *The Expositor's Bible*, 1896;54). In our study this week, we shall see

Zephaniah's condemnation of spiritual complacency. In general, Zephaniah's prophecies focused on God's judgment on both Jews and Gentiles for their sins, and on His goodness to both godly Jews and Gentiles. His prophecies were designed to warn Judah that unless they repented and submitted to God, judgment would certainly come. At the same time, he sought to convey a message of encouragement to the godly, particularly regarding the hope of final and complete restoration under the Messiah.

In Zephaniah 1:12, we see what has been described as the "criminal apathy of the well-to-do classes sunk in ease and religious indifference." While the Israelites do not theoretically deny the existence of God, they deny His activity and involvement, both on a social and pragmatic level. Judah was spiritually stupefied by security. ("God is not involved in the nation's life, either for good or bad.") Neither blessings nor grief can be attributed to Him. Theirs was an absentee God. This is nothing but practical atheism.

Those who ought to have been leaders were relaxed and leading a selfish, idle existence, doing nothing about the situation in the land. There was no concern whatever for justice and righteousness. Complacency is an insidious foe, and overcoming it is a great challenge. We must realize that the attitude, "it won't happen to me and mine," will never work. The killer stalks the homes of those who bury their heads in the sand to steal ideals, values, and morals and eventually to destroy the family, church, and nation. Complacency is the problem of resistance to change. People become accustomed to the patterns of their lives, seeing no need for a change. The complacent must be jolted in order to wake up from their stupor.

In Zephaniah's denunciation of Judah, he revealed that God would not leave the godly without a ray of hope. He assured them of the possibility of being preserved in the day of judgment (Zephaniah 2:3), a dwelling place for the remnant, divine visitation and a turning away from the prophesied activity (2:7), the purging of Judah (3:11-13), and above all, the future glory of Israel under the Messiah.

God is of purer eyes than to behold evil, and He cannot look on iniquity. His holiness and justice demand that sin be punished wherever it is found. Judah was engrossed in various sins. Morally, the nation was filthy and polluted. The prophets became shallow and treacherous, while the priests polluted the sanctuary and did violence to the law. The unjust were haughty and shameless. Against this background, God had to bring down His judgment. Nonetheless, God does not judge without sufficient warnings.

Zephaniah 1:12 And it shall come to pass at that time, that I will search Jerusalem with candles, and punish the men that are settled on their lees: that say in their heart, The LORD will not do good, neither will he do evil.

God promises to search for the iniquity of the people in dark places. He will fully uncover and punish sin, however concealed from the eyes of others it is thought to be. Nothing is hidden from God. Although people may think their sins are hidden, being privately and secretly committed, all will be made manifest sooner or later—if not now, then at the day of judgment. For Judah, it was to be "at that time"—a time appointed by God. The people's false security is described by the prophet as men being "settled on their lees," a phrase that alludes to liquor and suggests thickness and foulness. The image is of wine that becomes sour if allowed to remain on the lees without being removed.

Jeremiah uses this same metaphor: "Moab hath been at ease from his youth, and he hath settled on his lees, and hath not been emptied from vessel to vessel, neither hath he gone into captivity: therefore his taste remained in him, and his scent is not changed" (Jeremiah 48:11). The inhabitants of Judah had not only become careless, satisfied with the goods of this life; they had also trusted in their riches and become completely irreligious. Quiet and undisturbed, abounding in wealth and riches, they had totally shut God out of their thoughts. They denied His providence and became fearless and thoughtless of His judgments. But God promised that He would visit them.

In the opening verses of chapter 3, the prophet reproves Jerusalem and all her guides and rulers for their obstinate perseverance in impiety, notwithstanding all the warnings and corrections they had received from God. The hardness, impenitence, and shamelessness of this people is exposed and aggravated by the presence of the LORD among them, who, by His example and commandments taught them otherwise; yet they were not convicted or made ashamed (Zephaniah 3:5). They neither received instruction nor took warning from the judgments of God on other nations. However, they are encouraged to look for mercy and restoration after they have been chastised for and cured of their idolatry.

3:1 Woe to her that is filthy and polluted, to the oppressing city!

In pronouncing judgment on Judah, the prophet describes her situation with three words. First, it is filthy (Hebrew *mara'*, pronounced **maw-RAH**), a word that is better translated as rebellious. It is the picture of an ostrich that lashes itself with its wings while running. Second, Jerusalem is described with the word *ga'al* (pronounced **gah-AHL**), translated as "polluted." It means blood-stained and is so translated in Isaiah 59:3.

Hence, here it refers to Jerusalem's inward moral pollution, in spite of her outward ceremonial purity. The word *mara* combined in a sentence with *ga'al* suggests they have become haughty through bitterness and their own arrogance has now removed them from their unique place as priests of God. Both words underscore each other here; the idea is that they have no intention of removing the filth.

Third, the prophet describes Jerusalem as an oppressing city by using the Hebrew word *yanah* (pronounced **yah-NAH**), a word that means to rage or be violent. By implication, it means to suppress, to maltreat, destroy, or thrust out by oppression. This is what Jerusalem and its leaders did to the poor, the weak, and the widows, orphans, and strangers (cf. Jeremiah 22:3). The final part of the passage literally reads "city to the oppressing." The priests themselves have become polluted; they have no problem providing refuge for the oppressors. Their allegiance lies with those who oppose the program of God's people.

2 She obeyed not the voice; she received not correction; she trusted not in the LORD; she drew not near to her God.

The city of Jerusalem—rather than being God's faithful covenant city and a joy of the whole earth, in contrast to her pagan neighbors—had instead become like one of them in her sinfulness and unfaithfulness. She was morally rotten. This verse gives us a description of the fundamental nature of sin: a refusal to obey God's voice, failure to heed His warnings through His messengers, and self-idolatry. "She obeyed not the voice" of conscience, of God, or of His prophets. "She received not correction"—Jerusalem is incurable, obstinately rejecting salutary admonition and refusing to be reformed by "correction" (Jeremiah 5:3). She was uneasy and ill-tempered under her afflictions and derived no manner of good from these chastisements. "She trusted not in the LORD"—did not consider God as the fountain from whence all help and salvation comes.

Rather, she sought for support elsewhere by turning from God. "She drew not near to her God"—did not worship Him, did not walk in His ways, did not make prayer and supplication to Him. Though God was near to her (Deuteronomy 4:7) as her God, she drew not near to Him, but gratuitously estranged herself from Him. Our text alleges perfidy, or faithlessness, toward God. Sinners refuse to trust in the LORD but instead move far away from God by not serving and worshiping Him as they should. It was a state of dreadful impiety. This is the conduct pursued by multitudes today who only look to human prudence and prowess.

3 Her princes within her are roaring lions; her judges are evening wolves; they gnaw not the bones till the morrow.

Her princes (Hebrew *sar*, pronounced **tsar**), that is, persons of principal place and authority, were supposed to protect the city from the inside. In Joshua 5:14, the term refers to the captain of the LORD's army. When the people are attacked by destructive forces, they should be able to go to the *sar* or principalities. But what can the people do when those who should defend them are the very ones who are inside their wall of safety undermining their security? (Micah 3; Habakkuk 1:8) Instead of protecting the people, the princes became like lions and wolves in shepherd's clothing. Note that it was the princes who were "roaring." The ferocity that was to be their weapon against evil has been turned against the sheep and used to terrorize the people.

If the princes were to protect the people, the judges were to give them justice, but the text indicates that the "judges are wolves" (Hebrew *shopatey-*

haa Zeebee, pronounced **shaw-FAT zeh-ABE**). The combination of the words shows the problem: the shepherd dog is now bloodthirsty. But the prophet makes it more ominous by saying these are not just wolves but "evening wolves" (*ereb zeeb*). They are never satisfied; they want the people dead. Could it be that, contrary to the law, these judges pass judgment in the night and leave the victims of their injustice to be killed in the morning? Judges were supposed to be transparent, but these judges were working in darkness. They inflicted punishment in the open, but their judgment was shrouded in darkness. Thus the phrase, "gnaw not . . . till the morrow." Look at the process: the princes caused the spirit of the people to faint by their constant roaring; the judges took away their hope and then killed them.

The civil leaders of Israel were guilty of behaviors and actions that betrayed the trust that was reposed in them. Their actions were incompatible with their positions. They are described as lions that are roaring for prey (Proverbs 28:15; Amos 3:4; Micah 3:2) and evening wolves that are most ravenous at evening after suffering hunger all day due to lack of food (Ezekiel 22:27; Jeremiah 5:6, Habakkuk 1:8). Their greed, viciousness, and ruthlessness are vividly portrayed in the phrase, "gnaw not the bones till the morrow." They cannot wait until the following day before gnawing the bones. Instead, they devour all at once, bones and flesh.

4 Her prophets are light and treacherous persons: her priests have polluted the sanctuary, they have done violence to the law.

The spiritual leaders of Judah, namely the prophets and the priests, failed in their duties. The prophets are "light" (Hebrew *pachaz*, pronounced **pah-KHAHZ**), which signifies bubbling or frothing, as soap lather. There was no truth, gravity, or steadiness in their life or teaching. The prophets were treacherous men who could not be trusted. Instead of God's revelations, they deceitfully dished out their own imaginations, passing them off as the former. They were false to the LORD, yet they professed to be His prophets (Jeremiah 23:32; Ezekiel 22:28).

In the phrase, the "priests have polluted the sanctuary," the word *qodesh* (pronounced **KOH-desh**), translated "sanctuary," may mean a consecrated, dedicated thing or a sacred place. The point is that

the primary task of the priests was to be the guardians of holiness. Instead, they themselves become agents of pollution, caught up in worldliness and consequently unable to distinguish between the holy and profane. They did "violence to the law" by refusing to teach it as they should have. They added false interpretations of it and made it void.

In verse 4, Zephaniah turns the prophetic spotlight on the prophets. They are described as "light and treacherous" (Hebrew *pachaz . . . bog edowth*). The idea implied by the word *pachaz* (pronounced **paw-KHAZ**) is that they look at things in a superficial way. Here are the people who are supposed to hear the heart of God, but instead they look at things "lightly." This attitude means that they are insolent toward God. Because they make light of God and His Word, they have no problem being treacherous. They cover up things that should be brought into the open by making light of the Word of God. This implies that they used deceit as a means of pillaging the people. They spoke what God had not said in order to line their own pockets at the expense of the people's blood and sweat.

Zepheniah picks up the theme that he begins in verse 1: identifying the root of this pollution that has infected the entire city and all levels of political and religious leadership. The priests, those who should teach the people the difference between the holy and the unholy, have done two things. They have polluted the holy things and the holy places. The King James Version says "sanctuary," but it could simply read "holy." The idea here is that they have created a wedge between God and His people. Also, in so doing, they have removed the hedge of protection surrounding the people.

However, their bent to pollution is not grounded in the neglect of the law, but "in doing violence to the law" (Hebrew *chamac towrah* pronounced, **khaw-MAS to-RAW**). They have shaken off the burden of the law. The idea here is that they have wrongfully imagined the law apart from God. The law was now reformed by their own warped imagination, which has already been polluted by their lifestyle. They were forcing the law to fit into their lifestyle and not letting the law stand in judgment over their actions.

5 The just LORD is in the midst thereof; he will not do iniquity: every morning doth he bring his judgment to light, he faileth not; but the unjust knoweth no shame.

How can God in justice overlook these corrupt practices? The fact that the just LORD is in the midst (Hebrew *qereb*, pronounced **KEH'-rev**) makes their conduct even more reprehensible. He sees, marks down, and will punish all wickedness. The false prophets were probably denying this aspect of God's nature. Moreover, "He will not do iniquity" by leaving their sins unpunished (cf. Deuteronomy 32:4). "Every morning (literally, "morning by morning") doth he bring his judgment to light." The meaning is that not a day passes that we do not see instances of God's faithfulness in the laws of nature. He is just and faithful in the administration of His moral laws, showing His goodness to the righteous and pouring His vengeance on the wicked. But nothing seems to move the unjust, calloused Israelites. They know no shame.

Speaking more specifically to Jerusalem and its inhabitants, God offers them hope in spite of their sin. He would remove impure elements from the nation (cf. v. 9) so that a righteous remnant would remain.

The beginning of verse 5 says, "the just LORD is in the midst thereof," in direct contrast to verse 3, in which the princes and judges were "in the midst." Here, the "just LORD" *(tsadaq Yahweh)* is contrasted to the "unjust princes." Unlike them, God "will not do iniquity" *(aseh evel)*. While the judges worked in darkness and paraded in the day for show, every morning God brought His judgment to light.

The idea here is that God is going to shine a greater light on the people. There is comparison of divine light with the light of injustice and contrast between their purposes. Since God is the light, He will not fail to bring to light the failure of all the leaders. They may have fooled the people, but their lives are open before God. At the end of the verse we read, "but the unjust knoweth no shame." Here is the indictment: even though God exposes them, they refuse to be shamed into justice. That is the reason for the terrible judgment they face.

11 In that day shalt thou not be ashamed for all thy doings, wherein thou hast transgressed against

me: for then I will take away out of the midst of thee them that rejoice in thy pride, and thou shalt no more be haughty because of my holy mountain.

Although they refuse to be ashamed because they are still under the illusion that their guilt is hidden, the prophecy says, "in that day." The idea is that the dawning of the light of justice in that day is closely tied with "the day of the LORD." Several things will happen in that day. First, "Shalt thou not be ashamed for all thy doings?" The question here implies that they know what they have been doing. In fact, that is why they perform their deeds away from the light and play with the Word of God, to keep their shame hidden. "Shall you not be ashamed of all your doing" is a rhetorical phrase indicating that surely they shall be ashamed, but it is not merely because they did something; rather, it is because of the nature of what they did. They were raised up to protect, but they killed and maimed; they were appointed to do justice and show mercy to the poor, but they betrayed them instead.

Prophets were to speak for God, but they spoke for themselves. Priests were to uphold holiness, but they prohibited holy things. Of their sinful acts, God says, "thou hast transgressed against me." They broke away from God. No matter what they may pretend to be, they were in fact quarrelling with God by their actions. In that day, something will happen to them because God will do certain things. God says, "I will take away out of the midst of my people those who rejoice in their own pride." All of those who *gaawaatue* (**ga'vanah**), that is avail themselves of the position and power that God's city affords, will be removed. The next part of the verse suggests that the haughty projected arrogance in the presence of God. God says, "they are haughty because of my holy mountain." They boasted in the holy place of God, but they themselves refused to be holy.

In contrast to verse 5, where the "unjust knoweth no shame," the remnant will have no need of shame. There will be no cause to be ashamed because, God says, "I will take away out of the midst of thee them that rejoice in thy pride." Sin, the source of shame, has been removed. So, although that day would bring punishment and shame due to the people's sins, it was also going to be a day of help, hope, and comfort. That's because God would secure the safety of the remnant by removing the proud and the haughty who had been in their midst.

What is the antidote to spiritual complacency? God's part is to awaken the one who is so infected by administering whatever punishment He may deem appropriate. Pride must be purged and humility imbibed. Those who had become great because of the LORD but refused to honor Him would suffer removal.

12 I will also leave in the midst of thee an afflicted and poor people, and they shall trust in the name of the LORD.

Here again we see the word for "in the midst," *beqirbbek.* The idea here of "leave" suggests a coming up—a reservation. The afflicted are those who have been oppressed by their circumstances, as well as by the princes, judges, prophets, and priests. The poor are those who are needy in Israel, without property and dangling on the economic edge while the rich feed on the best. Why will they rise? The prophet gives us the answer: "They shall trust in the name of LORD." If in fact those afflicted and poor have been depressed, deprived, distressed, and dismissed from the face of human justice, to whom will they turn? The Word suggests that they have hoped in the LORD. Having no place to hide from injustice, they have sought the LORD as their refuge. The circumstances have led them to trust in the name of Yahweh.

Instead of being boastful and proud, the remnant would share the characteristics of God. Unlike the haughty (cf. 3:2) who refused to trust in their God, the remnant will be humble and will trust in the name of the LORD. This is a crucial step in overcoming spiritual complacency. Self-idolatry must be done away with, and God must be trusted unreservedly.

13 The remnant of Israel shall not do iniquity, nor speak lies; neither shall a deceitful tongue be found in their mouth: for they shall feed and lie down, and none shall make them afraid.

Verse 13 says something even more profound. These groups of the poor and afflicted are in complete contrast to those who are being removed. First, they "shall not do iniquity." The word here for "iniquity" is *avlah,* which represents an intentional moral. It is not so much that the people will not err, but that

their error can truly be attributed to ignorance. Second, the prophet says, they shall not speak lies (Hebrew *Walo dabar kazab*). The idea here is that of bearing false witness. Note that this is perhaps the condemnation of the judges of Judah. Third, the prophet says, "Neither shall a deceitful tongue be found in their mouth." This is just another way of speaking of how the tongue is used. The final part of the verse, "for they shall feed and be down and none shall make them afraid," seems to imply that their sins grow out of hunger, insecurity, and fear. But God promises to remove all of these so as to purify their actions.

A great change will take place. Iniquity, lying, and deceit shall not be found among them! They shall indeed be God's holy people. Instead of the false security that they once had, they will now enjoy the true security that is provided by their God, "for they shall feed and lie down, and none shall make them afraid." In Eaton's words, "They are set in a transfigured world which lies beyond the devastation of the old order, and they themselves are made so pure and perfect before God that without exaggeration they could be termed new creatures" (J. H. Eaton, *Obadiah, Nahum, Habakkuk and Zephaniah,* 1961:147).

DAILY BIBLE READINGS

M: Seek the Lord
Zephaniah 1:15 2:3
T: Wait for the Lord to Work
Zephaniah 3:1-10
W: The Remnant Will Find Refuge
Zephaniah 3:11-20
T: Plans for a Future
Jeremiah 29:10-14
F: Surely There Is a Future
Proverbs 23:15-23
S: A New Thing
Isaiah 43:14-21
S: Hope in the Lord
Psalm 130:1-8

TEACHING TIPS

September 22
Bible Study Guide 4

1. Words You Should Know

A. Molten (2 Chronicles 34:3); Hebrew *mac-cekah*—Melted and cast.

B. The Book (v. 21); Hebrew *hespher*—Refers to the law of Moses; Torah.

C. Statues (v. 31); Hebrew *wakukdyn*—Formally established and recorded rules.

D. Stand to it (v. 32); Hebrew *yemed*—Pledge or take an oath.

2. Teacher Preparation

Read all the background Scriptures and FOCAL VERSES to gain information on the character and spiritual qualities of King Josiah that enabled him to enact his zealous campaign of reform throughout the kingdom.

3. Starting the Lesson

A. Have class members discuss the very real difficulty Josiah must have faced in attempting to lead this obstinate nation back to God.

B. Ask class members to look at Josiah's background and the zeal with which he made efforts to lead the nation into revival.

4. Getting into the Lesson

A. Begin the lesson by reminding students of the old adage: "The fruit does not fall far from the tree." Have class members explain its meaning and discuss why it did not apply to the life of Josiah. Guide the discussion so that it focuses on children of ungodly parents being able to make a fresh start and take a different course of action in their lives.

B. As you discuss today's lesson, draw attention to Josiah's devotion to the Lord at such an early age. We often disregard the religious inclinations of small children, yet in this situation we see that the seed of godliness was evident in Josiah quite early and remained with him throughout his life.

5. Relating the Lesson to Life

A. Ask for a volunteer to read THE PEOPLE, PLACES, AND TIMES section aloud.

B. Ask students to explain whether they believe that our nation is ready for a revival. Allow 10 minutes for them to discuss this.

SEPT 22ND

C. Give students the opportunity to answer the questions in SEARCH THE SCRIPTURES.

6. Arousing Action

A. Have students list various types of close and intimate relationships (e.g. husband/wife, parent/child, sibling/sibling). Have them discuss how these relationships are nurtured and maintained (e.g., through trust, communication, faithfulness, etc.). Remind students that our relationship with the Lord requires our continued faithfulness, trust, communication, and obedience. Challenge your students to evaluate their personal relationship with the Lord to see that, like Josiah, their commitment to faithfulness is to grow as they grow older.

B. Ask a student to lead the closing prayer, focusing on the KEEP IN MIND Scripture.

WORSHIP GUIDE

For the Superintendent or Teacher
Theme: A New Beginning
Theme Song: "Have Thine Own Way Lord"
Scripture: Psalm 119:1-8
Song: "I Surrender All"
Meditation: Lord, we want to hear Your voice and yield to Your Word. Direct our ways so that we may recognize and reject anything that offends You and keeps us from glorifying You. Amen.

A NEW BEGINNING

Bible Background • 2 CHRONICLES 34—35; 2 KINGS 22—23
Printed Text • 2 CHRONICLES 34:1-3, 21, 29-33
Devotional Reading • PSALM 119:1-8

LESSON AIM

After today's lesson, students will be able to narrate the events surrounding Josiah's revival, assess King Josiah's response to the Word of God, and examine and determine their own response to God's Word today.

KEEP IN MIND

"Because thine heart was tender, and thou didst humble thyself before God, when thou heardest his words . . . I have even heard thee also, saith the LORD" (2 Chronicles 34:27).

FOCAL VERSES

2 Chronicles 34:1 Josiah was eight years old when he began to reign, and he reigned in Jerusalem one and thirty years.

2 And he did that which was right in the sight of the LORD, and walked in the ways of David, his father, and declined neither to the right hand, nor to the left.

3 For in the eighth year of his reign, while he was yet young, he began to seek after the God of David his father: and in the twelfth year he began to purge Judah and Jerusalem from the high places, and the groves, and the carved images, and the molten images.

34:21 Go, inquire of the LORD for me, and for them that are left in Israel and in Judah, concerning the words of the book that is found: for great is the wrath of the LORD that is poured out upon us, because our fathers have not kept the word of the LORD, to do after all that is written in this book.

34:29 Then the king sent and gathered together all the elders of Judah and Jerusalem.

30 Then the king went up into the house of the

LESSON OVERVIEW

LESSON AIM
KEEP IN MIND
FOCAL VERSES
IN FOCUS
THE PEOPLE, PLACES, AND TIMES
BACKGROUND
AT-A-GLANCE
IN DEPTH
SEARCH THE SCRIPTURES
DISCUSS THE MEANING
LESSON IN OUR SOCIETY
MAKE IT HAPPEN
FOLLOW THE SPIRIT
REMEMBER YOUR THOUGHTS
MORE LIGHT ON THE TEXT
DAILY BIBLE READINGS

LORD, and all the men of Judah and the inhabitants of Jerusalem, and the priests, and the Levites, and all the people, great and small: and he read in their ears all the words of the book of the covenant that was found in the house of the LORD.

31 And the king stood in his place, and made a covenant before the LORD, to walk after the LORD, and to keep his commandments, and his testimonies, and his statutes, with all his heart, and with all his soul, to perform the words of the covenant which are written in this book.

32 And he caused all that were present in Jerusalem and Benjamin to stand to it. And the inhabitants of Jerusalem did according to the covenant of God, the God of their fathers.

33 And Josiah took away all the abominations out of all the countries that pertained to the children of Israel, and made all that were present in Israel to serve, even to serve the LORD their God. And all his days they departed not from following the LORD, the God of their fathers.

IN FOCUS

As Kat waited for her friend Patricia to come out of the house and get into the car, she marveled at Patricia's situation. Patricia called Kat every Saturday evening and asked her for a ride to church. Kat knew that both of Patricia's parents owned cars, and they frequently sent Patricia on errands for them or grocery shopping, but they would not allow Patricia to drive either of the cars to church. Kat had never met

Patricia's parents. They never came to church; and when members went to visit Patricia at her home, they were rudely received by her parents, who openly ridiculed Patricia for trying to be what they called a "do-gooder."

Several of the older ladies in the church gave Patricia gifts of clothing, aware that she was ashamed of the raggedy and worn condition of her own. Just last week, Patricia's Sunday School teacher had noticed a large bruise on the girl's arm and expressed her concern that someone might be abusing Patricia. When asked about her parents, Patricia would only smile and say that they needed prayer.

THE PEOPLE, PLACES, AND TIMES

The Great Religious Revivals. The great revival undertaken by King Josiah is the fifth and final revival for the nation before they are taken into captivity. In each case, revival began as a personal matter for the king, although they were probably inspired greatly by the prophets. Other elements of national revival include an attempt by the people to reform or to return to the Word of God and repent of their past sins. The other four great revivals were led by King Asa, King Jehoshaphat, King Joash, and King Hezekiah. This last great revival under King Josiah occurred during the last hours of Judah's history; yet God allowed the revival to occur, letting us know that there is always hope.

Prophetesses. When King Josiah heard the reading of the book of the law found by Hilkiah (the high priest) during the repair of the temple, he sent a delegation to "inquire of the LORD" what the nation should do. These men sought out Huldah, the prophetess. Women served as prophetesses, or spokespersons for the LORD. Miriam is the first woman designated a prophetess in the Bible. God conveyed messages through her (Exodus 15:20-21). In the period of the Judges, Deborah served as a source of information from God and conveyed His instructions to Barak (Judges 4:4-7, 14-16). Isaiah refers to his wife as a prophetess (Isaiah 8:3). The prophecy of Joel 2:18 foretold of sons and daughters prophesying. In the New Testament, the aged and faithful Anna served as a prophetess (Luke 2:36-38). In the newly formed Christian congregation, certain Christian women, such as Philip's four virgin daughters, prophesied under the influence of the Holy Spirit (Acts 21:9; 1 Corinthians 12:4, 10).

BACKGROUND

Judah was once again under the leadership of a godly king. The hearts of the people had no doubt been pricked by the dire message of God delivered by the Prophet Zephaniah. You must remember that the people of Judah were notoriously stubborn. The fact that altars had to be torn down and images ground up lets us know that these vestiges of immorality remained throughout the kingdom despite the intensive efforts of King Hezekiah. Now that they have heard the Word of God from the man of God, their hearts are ready to be revived.

AT-A-GLANCE

1. Prelude to a Revival (2 Chronicles 34:1-3)
2. The Rediscovery of the Law (v. 21)
3. The Revelation (vv. 29-30)
4. The Renewal of the Covenant with God (vv. 31-33)

IN DEPTH

1. Prelude to Revival (2 Chronicles 34:1-3)

Josiah's reign started off on a positive note. As a very young boy, he did the right thing "in the sight of the LORD." Josiah was obedient and did what God said was the right thing to do. No doubt the young king had the assistance of godly advisors to guide him. In the eighth year of his reign, when he was about 16, we are told that he began to seek the LORD. Josiah must have expressed an intense interest in matters of faith. It is not surprising, then, that in just four years—by the time he was 20—he began reforms that would lead his nation in a great revival.

The heart of the young man had been watered by the divine wisdom of the elders. How important it is for those who have known God's way to pass it on to the new generation.

Even before the revival hit, Josiah was working on cleansing the people from idolatry, but it would seem that these actions were taken based solely on the feeling that they were wrong. Moral consciousness is the prelude to genuine revival. Also, the king and the priests had repentant hearts, which served to prepare them for revival.

Josiah's efforts extended far beyond the borders of his own territory. Josiah was determined that widespread immorality bc put away not only in Judah, but in all the kingdom of God. This selfless act of inclusion allows us to recognize Josiah's reformation and revival efforts as the greatest of them all. Josiah went about cleaning up the kingdom and removing all the carved and metal images of false gods that were kept by the disobedient residents. The groves once used for pagan worship were cleared and all pagan influences removed.

2. The Rediscovery of the Law (v. 21)

So far everyone had done what was right in their own eyes; every god was okay. The people rejected absolutes in religion and morality. But to be renewed, they had to rediscover divine absolutes. The rediscovery of the law must be accompanied by genuine acceptance of its weight. But this book could not be discovered while the temple was in shambles.

The second act of reformation undertaken by Josiah was the clearing and renovation of the temple. Under King Manasseh, his grandfather, and King Amon, his father, the temple had fallen into disrepair. During the cleaning, the high priest Hilkiah "found a book of the law of the LORD given by Moses" (v. 14). This book (possibly the original copy of Deuteronomy) had been lost for many years.

When Josiah had the law read to him, his reaction was extraordinary. He tore his clothes, symbolizing how strongly he was grieved by what he had heard. Upon hearing the exact commandments of God, the king was distressed when he realized how far his people had strayed from God. The Word of God had a profound impact on the king because it revealed the sins of the people with absolute clarity.

The rediscovery of the law must lead us beyond fear of what may happen to us personally. It must lead us back to the Lawgiver. Josiah knew this, so he desired an audience with the God whose laws had been breached. Josiah immediately commissioned a delegation of religious officials to "inquire of the LORD." In other words, Josiah wanted to know what God wanted him to do about the situation. Josiah expressed his certainty that because the people had

strayed so far from God's commandments, the "wrath of God" was forthcoming. Now that he had heard the Word of the LORD, he was ready to take action and do the right thing.

3. The Revelation (vv. 29-30)

Genuine revival must not only include the rediscovery of absolutes; it must move on to revelation. Revelation implies an opening of the law to all so that its spirit is grasped and lives are changed. True revelation leads to humility before God.

Josiah sent a delegation to consult with Huldah the prophetess. Huldah's prophecy to the delegation revealed that Judah would be punished for her iniquities. However, the fact that Josiah had a tender heart and was humbled by the Word of God had not gone unnoticed by God (v. 27). God graciously designed that Josiah would be spared from seeing his beloved city destroyed.

Josiah could have breathed a sigh of relief and become complacent about the whole matter, but he did not. Instead, his heart was moved to ensure that all of his people heard the Law. Perhaps he hoped that they would be similarly convicted by the Word and moved to repent and change. Josiah gathered all of the elders and the people "great and small," and he read aloud to them from the Word of God.

4. The Renewal of the Covenant with God (vv. 31-33)

Finally, this revival ended with renewal of commitment. A revival cannot be a revival unless there is a renewal of the relationship between God and the people. But it must also result in the renewal of godly relationships between God's people. Josiah entered into a covenant with God to obey His commandments and rules with his entire being. Josiah was not just giving feeble lip service; he knew that true worship of God had to be genuine and heartfelt. He compelled everyone present to enter into this same covenant. Again we see Josiah's unselfish devotion to and care for his people. Josiah had much more than a king's title; he apparently had a king's heart.

Such renewal of relationships empowered Josiah to ensure that the covenant made by the people of Judah was honored. He embarked on an intensive campaign against idolatry. The pagan priests were expelled, and Jewish priests who had conspired to participate in pagan worship were stripped of their privileges to serve at God's altar (see 2 Kings 10).

Under Josiah's courageous leadership, Huldah's prophecy was fulfilled. For the duration of Josiah's life, the people of Judah obeyed the Word of God. They heard the Word of God, repented, heeded the commandments, reformed their ways, and changed. They expressed their commitment to faithfulness by becoming not only hearers of the Word, but doers of the Word.

SEARCH THE SCRIPTURES

1. How old was Josiah when he became king? How long did he reign as king in Judah? (v. 1)

2. What great king did he imitate? (v. 2)

3. When did he begin to seek after the LORD? (v. 3)

4. Why did Josiah believe the wrath of God was about to be poured out? (v. 21)

5. When the king had gathered all of the people, what did he do publicly? (v. 30)

6. What covenant did Josiah make with the LORD? (v. 31)

7. Who else did Josiah compel to pledge the covenant? (v. 32)

8. How did Josiah go about cleansing the land of pagan influences? (v. 33)

DISCUSS THE MEANING

1. Despite the poor influences in Josiah's life shown by his father (Amon) and grandfather (Manasseh), what were some of the positive influences?

2. What do we learn about the character of God from the prophecy by Huldah that Josiah would not live to see the destruction of his people?

3. Look closely at the areas cleansed by Josiah. What does this tell us about his desire that reformation take place throughout the land?

LESSON IN OUR SOCIETY

Despite the efforts of godly kings like Hezekiah and Josiah, the nation of Judah was doomed. The root of the problem appeared to be the unwillingness of the people to yield to the will of God. While many cry out for a revival in this time, believers must remember that we are not going to be able to get God to move on our behalf when our own lives are not right in God's sight.

There is nothing in the Word of God that precludes a great revival from occurring in our day. In matters of spiritual revival, God is still sovereign. As hopeless as our present situation may appear to many, there is always hope.

MAKE IT HAPPEN

How can believers stir the flames of revival in our churches, homes, and communities?

FOLLOW THE SPIRIT

What God wants me to do:

_____

_____

REMEMBER YOUR THOUGHTS

Special insights you have learned:

_____

_____

MORE LIGHT ON THE TEXT
2 Chronicles 34:1-3, 21, 29-33

These were dark times in Judah; the law was lost and ignorance of God's will prevailed. The scene took place during one of the lowest points in Israel's history. King Manasseh had already been in power for 55 long years, during which time he had led Judah into the worst condition of paganism and idol worship they had ever experienced. Not only did he do all manner of evil—which the LORD called an abomination in His sight—he led Judah into all manner of sin such as child sacrifice, witchcraft, and divination, as well as several kinds of sexually perverse idol worship (2 Kings 21). His wickedness was unprecedented. Both Josiah's grandfather, Manasseh, and his father, Amon, were wicked. From this wicked heritage came Josiah, who typically would have followed in the footsteps of his father and grandfather. Instead, Josiah went against the tide of the popular culture of his day and became one of the great kings of Judah, carrying out a major reformation in his own time. "For in the eighth year of his reign, while he was still young, he began to seek after the God of David his father" (2 Chronicles 34:3).

From Josiah we learn that achievements and accomplishments, both physical and spiritual, are not solely determined by circumstances of life. Josiah faced a unique set of circumstances. He started off on top of the heap. Unlike David who rose on sheer ability and charisma, Josiah had leadership thrust upon him. Josiah's story provides us important keys to personal or group reformation. First, Josiah sought the LORD (34:3). Second, he returned to "the Book of the Law" (vv. 14-19). Previously ignorant of the wrath of God that hung over the head of Judah, Josiah rediscovered "the Book" and it changed his life. He responded to what he knew by removing idols and leading the way in the restoration of the temple. It caused him to reevaluate the traditions of the day and go back to the patterns and purposes of God. He reached back to the biblical pattern in God's Word and God's pattern of worship. Therefore, true reformation took place throughout his realm. Josiah began to serve God by responding to what he knew. Third, Josiah refused to condone compromise, sin, and wickedness. Instead, he declared war against all forms of ungodliness in his domain. Fourth, Josiah acted prayerfully (v. 21). Last, Josiah called for commitment. He led the people in making a commitment to the "God of their fathers" (v. 32), who thus became "their God" (v. 33). The king discovered the "Book of the Law," personally read it to all the people, and then led them in making a covenant to keep the words of God's law.

1 Josiah was eight years old when he began to reign, and he reigned in Jerusalem one and thirty years.

To have been entrusted with such a great responsibility at such a tender age was no small matter. Yet, as his history would show, even without much experience to bank on, Josiah succeeded in what he set his hands to do.

2 And he did that which was right in the sight of the LORD, and walked in the ways of David his father, and declined neither to the right hand, nor to the left.

Josiah's history started on a positive note. Of him, it is recorded that he did that which was right in the sight of the LORD. The Hebrew word `asah (pronounced as-SAH'), translated as "did," suggests that Josiah's acts were calculated and entailed a commitment on his part to achieve his aim. He declined neither to the right hand, nor to the left. He didn't follow the example of his father before him, who was corrupt and evil, but followed the example of his

ancestor David. He followed David in all the ways David had followed the LORD. The Hebrew reads *wayeebek bador kesy daawyd*, translated "and walked in the ways of David his father." The idea here is that he remained in the flow of the stream that David had started; he carried on the legacy of David. It also carries with it the idea of pursuing a particular course of action. He pursued the ideal of his father David. The text adds "declined neither to the right hand, nor to the left" (Hebrew *walo caar yaamiyn usmowt*). This indicates determination informed by godly idealism. The suggestion implied may be that there was enough to distract, but he chose the path laid down by the ancients. The Hebrew word *derek* (DEH-reck), translated as "way" in the text, may mean way or journey; more often it refers to human behaviors, whether wicked (Psalm 1:6) or righteous (Genesis18:19; 1 Kings 2:3). Josiah chose the path he would follow. He never swerved from God and truth; he never neglected what he knew to be his duty to God and his kingdom. He carried on his reformation with a steady hand; he was neither timid nor overzealous.

3 For in the eighth year of his reign, while he was yet young, he began to seek after the God of David his father: and in the twelfth year he began to purge Judah and Jerusalem from the high places, and the groves, and the carved images, and the molten images.

One could play with the numerical significance of the number eight, but we may be sure that the significance of the eighth and twelfth years was not lost on the writer. At the age of 12, Josiah would be expected to be a man of the law. The text says "he began to seek after God," or he turned himself to the proper serious pursuit of God. The idea implied here is that he began to tread the path of God on a frequent basis. Wherever he could catch a glimpse of God's work, he pursued God; he searched for God in genuine worship. This intense search culminated in the purging of the flesh. The text says "he began to purge." The idea here is that of transparency or brightness, as represented by the use of the word *latahlean*, from *taler* (pronounced **tawlence**). Finding God and embracing Him was a goal of God's people, and it became for Josiah an all-consuming passion. The many evidences of idolatry are often repeated in the Josiah narratives to emphasize the depth of the people's idolatry and their damaged and distant relationship to God.

King Josiah stands as an example for all Christians today. He didn't follow the example of his father before him, who was corrupt and evil, but followed the example of his ancestor, King David. He chose the path he would follow. One is not destined to be exactly like anybody else. A person chooses who and what he/she will become. You cannot blame your parents or teachers or anyone else, you must choose. At the age of 16, Josiah began to seek the LORD with all his heart. His was not a half-hearted religion or mere church attendance in order to ease his conscience, nor was he going just to satisfy his parents. He certainly had a heart for God, and that is what made the difference. When he was but 16 years old, he showed himself zealous for God's glory. At 21 years old, he abolished idolatry and restored the true religion. He pulled down all carved and molten images that had been made in the time of Manasseh and restored in the reign of Manasseh's son, Amon. Josiah purged the land from these by destroying them when he was 21 years of age.

34:21 Go, enquire of the LORD for me, and for them that are left in Israel and in Judah, concerning the words of the book that is found: for great is the wrath of the LORD that is poured out upon us, because our fathers have not kept the word of the LORD, to do after all that is written in this book.

In this verse, we see Josiah's response upon meeting God in God's law. Watch the sequence of the words here. The word "go" carries with it an imperial imperative. Josiah was saying to his people, "Carry yourself toward this direction." First, they are to move from their present location, second, they are to go into an arena where God can be heard.

The king says "enquire of the LORD. In verse 3, we are told that the king began to "seek"; the same Hebrew word is translated "enquire" in the King James Version. This time it was with a specific question that the LORD was being sought. This was to be a diligent searching out of God's mind and purpose based on what had been revealed to them in the law. Notice the content of the inquiry: "concerning the words of the book that is found." This very mode of inquiry points to the fact that they had departed far away from

the LORD. The text implies that if this book is true, then from the king's perspective, there was great wrath already poured out upon them. How awful that they were under judgment but did not know it. The king does not allude to the future, but states as an accomplished fact that wrath was upon them.

Another key insight from the king is that he realizes his immediate ancestors had not kept the Word of the LORD. The use of the plural "our fathers" (*abowteeyaus*) points to this as a generational problem. The law was not "kept" (*sharamarus*); that is, they have not tended the Law of God as one would tend a garden with precious flowers. They were supposed to tend the Law as one would tend a garden, but they had allowed all sorts of seed-destroying acts to enter in and corrupt it. They had not protected or obeyed the law of the LORD. Also, the text says they failed "to do after all that is written." They did some things as they chose, but failed in the essentials.

For Josiah, ignorance was not an option. He sought to know what was contained in God's law. He came to know the gravity of God's judgment that hung over their heads, and as a result the king lamented the sins of his fathers. Thus, Josiah is part of a godly heritage. For example, Nehemiah and Daniel not only lamented their own sins, but also those of their predecessors.

In verses 29-33, we have an account of the progress of Josiah as he sought to reform his kingdom through the impact of the law as well as the message from God through the prophetess. Josiah personally instructed the people in the law of God before engaging their services. Although the account in the book of Jeremiah (Jeremiah 3:6, 10-11; 25:3-7) would show that not all embraced the reform by Josiah, it is to his credit that for the rest of his life, all the people followed the LORD.

34:29 Then the king sent and gathered all the elders of Judah and Jerusalem.

The idea of the Hebrew word *acaph* (pronounced **aw saf**), translated as "gathered," is to come together with a purpose in order to receive and take away something that hopefully may restore one's spiritual state. Those who were gathered were to be consumed by the passion that had set their king ablaze for God.

He called all the people together, great and small, young and old, rich and poor, high and low. Recognizing the absolute sway of the law over everyone, Josiah read the law to all alike. Just as none could be exempt from its blessings if obeyed, neither young nor old could be exempt from the curses that are the consequences of transgression.

30 And the king went up to the house of the LORD, and all the men of Judah, and the inhabitants of Jerusalem, and the priests, and the Levites, and all the people, great and small: and he read in their ears all the words of the book of the covenant that was found in the house of the LORD.

The king was the lead reformer. Although there were priests and Levites present, the king himself read the book to the people and must have done so in such manner as to show that he was himself affected by it. In turn, that would be a means of affecting the hearers. This would no doubt have given honor and weight to the service and engaged the people's attention more.

31 And the king stood in his place, and made a covenant before the LORD, to walk after the LORD, and to keep his commandments, and his testimonies, and his statutes with all his heart, and all his soul, to perform the words of the covenant which are written in this book.

The king in his place covenanted to keep God's commandments with all his heart and soul, according to what was written in the book (v. 31). He urged the people to declare their consent and to solemnly promise that they would faithfully perform everything that was to be done according to this covenant. This they did; they could not for shame do otherwise. When the articles of agreement between God and Israel had been read so that they might intelligently covenant with God, both the king and the people with great solemnity subscribed to the articles.

32 And he caused all that were present in Jerusalem and Benjamin to stand to it. And the inhabitants of Jerusalem did according to the covenant of God, the God of their fathers.

Josiah probably made all the people "rise" (Hebrew *waya`amed*, pronounced **vy-yah ah-MED**) when he read the terms of the covenant. In so doing, they testified to their acceptance of the covenant itself and to their resolution to live true to it. They pledged to observe it faithfully and perseveringly.

Thus, Josiah caused them to promise on oath that they would observe the laws of God, as his predecessors had done and as those earlier had been obliged to do.

33 And Josiah took away all the abominations out of all the countries that pertained to the children of Israel, and made all that were present in Israel to serve, even to serve the LORD their God. And all his days they departed not from following the LORD, the God of their fathers.

Josiah reestablished the rule of God through his righteous rule. He achieved his aims to engage the people for God and to have them diligently serve Him. By the abolition of idolatry, Josiah compelled not only his own subjects, but all who belonged to Israel, to serve God and worship Yahweh in accordance with the covenant. The concluding words of the verse, "all his days they departed not from following the LORD, the God of their fathers," signified that for as long as Josiah lived, he allowed no open idolatry, but externally maintained the worship of Yahweh. It was to his honor and credit that he could sustain the reformation while he lived. He retained a strong influence over the people and prevented them from going back into idolatry.

DAILY BIBLE READINGS

M: Josiah Does Right
2 Chronicles 34:1-7
T: Hilkiah Finds the Law Book
2 Chronicles 34:8-18
W: The Words Grieve Josiah
2 Chronicles 34:19-28
T: Josiah Makes a Covenant
2 Chronicles 34:29-33
F: Josiah Keeps the Passover
2 Chronicles 35:1-10
S: No King Like Him
2 Kings 23:24-50
S: Be Renewed
Ephesians 4:17-24

TEACHING TIPS

1. Words You Should Know

A. Watchmen (Jeremiah 6:17)—A guard or sentry.

B. Sheba (v. 20)—A wealthy kingdom in southwestern Arabia renowned for perfumes and incense.

C. Stumblingblocks (v. 21)—Obstacles or instruments of ruin.

D. Lamentation (v. 26)—Mournful poems for the dead.

E. Sackcloth (v. 26)—Garment of mourning.

F. Wallow (v. 26)—To roll around.

G. Grievous revolters (v. 28)—Hard-hearted rebels.

2. Teacher Preparation

A. Read today's FOCAL VERSES and the background Scriptures.

B. Review the WORDS YOU SHOULD KNOW.

C. Recall a time in your life when you rebelled against authority or refused to follow instructions. Then think about how you would have felt if someone had explained to you the consequences of your rebellion and just how you were going to be disciplined or punished. Now consider the effect that Jeremiah's message might have had on the people of Judah who had rebelled so often.

3. Starting the Lesson

A. Begin the class with a prayer. Thank God for sending believers who will love us and care enough about us to warn us, inform us, and, if necessary, rebuke us when we are walking outside of the will of God.

B. Ask a volunteer to read aloud the KEEP IN MIND Scripture.

C. Ask students to share their experiences (either in the home or in the workplace) of when rules were repeatedly broken. Discuss the problems this caused and the result.

4. Getting into the Lesson

A. Read the LESSON AIM.

B. Have students review the cycle of sin, repentance, revival, and reformation that characterized Judah during this period. Ask them to give specific examples.

C. Have volunteers read the FOCAL VERSES aloud.

5. Relating the Lesson to Life

A. Have a volunteer read the IN FOCUS story and allow 7 to 10 minutes for a discussion.

B. Give the students an opportunity to answer the questions in SEARCH THE SCRIPTURES.

SEPT 29TH

6. Arousing Action

A. Have students read the LESSONS IN OUR SOCIETY section. Encourage a discussion focusing on the role, duty, and obligation of the believer in the face of sin. Stress the importance of being "watchmen" for the Lord and speaking out when we witness wrongdoing, rather than ignoring it and keeping quiet.

B. Challenge the students to read the DAILY BIBLE READINGS and incorporate the key points into their lives.

C. Close the class with prayer, using the KEEP IN MIND Scripture as the focus.

WORSHIP GUIDE

For the Superintendent or Teacher
Theme: Rebellion and Judgment
Theme Song: "It Is Well with My Soul"
Scripture: Psalm 16:5-11
Song: "Just A Closer Walk with Thee"
Meditation: We thank, You, Lord for new beginnings. We thank You for the new mercy You show us each and every day. We pray that in times of trouble You will lead us so that we will select the right roads and walk "wherein is the good way," that we may glorify You and find rest for our souls. Amen.

REBELLION AND JUDGMENT

Bible Background • JEREMIAH 6
Printed Text • JEREMIAH 6:16-21, 26-28
Devotional Reading • PSALM 16:5-11

LESSON AIM

After studying today's lesson, students will know the characteristics of a godly ruler, understand that prophetic warnings against sinful practices are a God-given chance for repentance, and resolve to practice repentance in the presence of God.

KEEP IN MIND

"Thus saith the LORD, Stand ye in the ways, and see, and ask for the old paths, where is the good way, and walk therein, and ye shall find rest for your soul" (Jeremiah 6:16).

FOCAL VERSES

Jeremiah 6:16 Thus saith the LORD, Stand ye in the ways, and see, and ask for the old paths, where is the good way, and walk therein, and ye shall find rest for your souls. But they said, We will not walk therein.

17 Also I set watchmen over you saying, Hearken to the sound of the trumpet. But they said, We will not hearken.

18 Therefore hear, ye nations, and know, O congregation, what is among them.

19 Hear, O earth: behold, I will bring evil upon this people, even the fruit of their thoughts, because they have not hearkened unto my words, not to my law, but rejected it.

20 To what purpose cometh there to me incense from Sheba, and the sweet cane from a far country? Your burnt offerings are not acceptable, nor your sacrifices sweet unto me.

21 Therefore thus saith the LORD, Behold I will

LESSON OVERVIEW

LESSON AIM
KEEP IN MIND
FOCAL VERSES
IN FOCUS
THE PEOPLE, PLACES,
AND TIMES
BACKGROUND
AT-A-GLANCE
IN DEPTH
SEARCH THE SCRIPTURES
DISCUSS THE MEANING
LESSON IN OUR SOCIETY
MAKE IT HAPPEN
FOLLOW THE SPIRIT
REMEMBER YOUR THOUGHTS
MORE LIGHT ON THE TEXT
DAILY BIBLE READINGS

lay stumblingblocks before this people, and the fathers and the sons together shall fall upon them; the neighbour and his friend shall perish.

26 O daughter of my people, gird thee with sackcloth, and wallow thyself in ashes: make thee mourning, as for an only son, most bitter lamentation: for the spoiler shall suddenly come upon us.

27 I have set thee for a tower and a fortress among my people, that thou mayest know and try their way.

28 They are all grievous revolters, walking with slanders: they are brass and iron; they are all corrupters.

IN FOCUS

Sharon was nervous as she waited for her husband to arrive from work. She sat down and re-read the letter from the Department of Motor Vehicles. John's driving privileges were being revoked. On several occasions, he had driven while intoxicated and been stopped by the police. Although she had talked with him, begging him to get counseling for his drinking problem, he had shrugged it off. His drinking, John declared, was only for relaxation, and he angrily announced that he didn't have a drinking problem. Sharon had even cut out a newspaper article describing how the Department of Motor Vehicles was going to rigidly enforce the laws about drunk driving and issue more severe punishment to repeat offenders. She had shown the article to John. After reading it, he tore it up and threw it in her face. Now Sharon was close to tears. John was a driver for a newspaper company. If he couldn't drive, he would lose his job. Where would that leave her and the children?

THE PEOPLE, PLACES, AND TIMES

The Exile. Exile is a forcible expulsion from one's homeland. Israel and Judah underwent periods when they were removed from the land that God had given them and deported into foreign lands. Consequently, the Jews were scattered throughout the known world, where they became known as the *Diaspora* (**di-AS-pur-ruh**), which is the Greek word for "scattering." Israel and Judah were told that God would lead the nations away into exile if they became unfaithful to the covenant He made with them through Moses (Deuteronomy 28:36-37, 64; 29:28). Since God was the authority, He allowed the armies of other nations to be His instruments. The northern kingdom of Israel was conquered by the Assyrians in 722 B.C. Judah was also conquered three times by the Babylonians. In 605, King Nebuchadnezzar took the royal court and the ablest men of Judah into Babylon. He returned again in 597 B.C. and again in 586 B.C. At the fall of Jerusalem to Babylon in 586 B.C. the city was burned, and the remaining people of Judah were deported, from which only a remnant returned 70 years later. The phrase "the Exile" is most often associated with the 70-year Babylonian captivity of Judah. The lasting effects of exile were profound. Aside from the stress of being removed from their homes and loved ones, while in captivity they had the status of slaves, were unfamiliar with the language, and were sometimes required to worship idols (Daniel 3:4-7).

Based on information from Illustrated Manners and Customs of the Bible, J. I. Packer and M.C. Tenney, editors (Nashville: Thomas Nelson Publishers, 1980), pp. 36-43, 500-501.

BACKGROUND

Jeremiah was called to be a reformer in a time of spiritual crisis and impending judgment. With deep love for his people, Jeremiah sought to cooperate with his LORD in calling the people of Judah to repent and return to God that they might not be destroyed. Jeremiah's prophetic ministry was heartbreaking and dangerous life-

work. Ultimately, it was his job to declare God's complaint against a stiff-necked people.

> ### AT-A-GLANCE
>
> 1. Jeremiah Warns Judah to Return to God
> (Jeremiah 6:16-17)
> 2. God Pronounces Judgment (vv. 18-19)
> 3. God Rejects Judah's Offerings (vv. 20-21)
> 4. Call to Lament (v. 26)
> 5. Judah Is Tested for Faithfulness
> (vv. 27-28)

IN DEPTH

1. Jeremiah Warns Judah to Return to God (Jeremiah 6:16-17)

To clarify the message from God that the people of Judah return to Him and obey the covenant, Jeremiah presented a vivid example. He asked them to imagine themselves as travelers who have lost their way. The lost travelers needed to stop and "inquire"(ask) the way back to the right path. Like the traveler, Judah had once been on the right path, but through disobedience they had wandered away from that path. Now mired in sin and apostasy, they were traveling the wrong way. The "old paths" no doubt allude to the covenant with God, made in ancient times under Abraham and Moses. Obedience to the covenant had brought the people innumerable blessings: a land of their own, victory over their enemies, extended periods of peace, and their special position as God's chosen people. Their half-hearted attempts to comingle true worship with idolatry, aside from dishonoring God, brought them no peace or contentment. Only true allegiance to God, the prophet urged, would give their souls rest.

Jeremiah reminded the people that God had provided them with "watchmen." Again, Jeremiah uses an example that all the people would understand. As their name implies, the watchmen stood in the towers to provide a protective watch for the inhabitants. One of the responsibilities of the watchmen was to sound an alarm or blow the trumpet if they spied impending danger. Upon hearing the alarm, the people could seek protective shelter, and the military would gather to take a defensive position. God had provided prophets and priests as the spiritual watchmen for His people. Jeremiah was one of these watchmen. He had tried to lead the people to repentance, warning them that a terrible day of accounting was coming because of their continued wickedness. Jeremiah's message fell on deaf ears. The people would not listen to the man of God and continued in their sinful ways.

2. God Pronounces Judgment (vv. 18-19)

Judah was all that remained after the Assyrians devastated the kingdom of Israel and carried off her inhabitants. Jerusalem was miraculously saved, but God would not save it against the Babylonian invasion. In the preceding verses, Jeremiah had painstakingly spelled out the specific sins Judah had committed against God. Instead of being repentant and turning away from their sins, Jeremiah declared that "they were not ashamed" of their sinful behavior; "neither could they blush" (v. 15). God's chosen people had lost their sense of shame and grief for sin. They no longer felt God's hatred of sin. In rejecting God's law, they had rejected God.

God speaks to the entire nation through Jeremiah. Judah had heard and rejected the law of the LORD and willfully broken their covenant with God. Jeremiah invites his listeners to be a witness to the great perversity of Judah. He is certain that Judah deserves the severe punishment about to be inflicted upon her.

3. God Rejects Judah's Offerings (vv. 20-21)

The people of Judah were so numbed by their sin that their entire lives had become superficial. The offering that Jeremiah referred to was insincere. God would not accept external services without heartfelt obedience to Him. God did not require incense or burnt offerings; He demanded their faithfulness.

4. Call to Lament (v. 26)

Because the people refused to heed his warnings, the sad task of declaring the impending judgment fell to Jeremiah. The spiritual death of Judah would soon be followed by the nation's physical death. Coarse sackcloth was a traditional garment of mourning. The prophet tells them to prepare themselves for great suffering and anguish by dressing in mourning garb. They were to put on sackcloth and then wallow, or roll around, in ashes as a symbol of mourning and repentance.

Here we see the depth of the mourning that is to be expressed. Usually they would only place ashes upon the head. However, being told to cover themselves with ashes indicates how sorrowful they should appear. The combination of sackcloth and ashes further symbolizes the national humiliation Judah would undergo. The prophet likened the sorrow they would feel to that of a woman who had lost her only son. Custom dictated that it was the duty of a son to provide for and protect his widowed mother. The loss of one's only son exposed a woman to dire circumstances. The loss of the covenant relationship with God would mean the loss of Judah's Provider and Protector. The LORD would not intercede and stop the utter destruction that was coming their way.

5. Judah Is Tested for Faithfulness (vv. 27-28)

In these final verses, it would appear that God and Jeremiah are speaking to one another. God had appointed Jeremiah as an assayer (or tester of metal) of the faithfulness of His people. Jeremiah was in a position where he could not only preach to them, but also observe them and be an eyewitness to their wickedness and stubborn refusal to obey God. Having tried and tested them, Jeremiah knew them to be unfaithful and no longer worthy of God's benevolent protection.

SEARCH THE SCRIPTURES

1. Which paths did Jeremiah urge the people to take? (v. 16)

2. What would be the result if they chose the good way? (v. 16)

3. Who had God placed over the people? (v. 17)

4. How had the people reacted to the words and the law of the LORD? (v. 19)

5. What offerings and sacrifices did God reject? (v. 20)

6. As a result of Judah's unfaithfulness, how would they be hindered? (v. 21)

7. How did Jeremiah tell the people to prepare themselves for destruction? (v. 26)

8. To what did Jeremiah compare the anguish that would come on Judah? (v. 27)

DISCUSS THE MEANING

1. Jeremiah goes to great lengths to paint vivid pictures of the depth of Judah's sinfulness. What might he have hoped this would accomplish? What does this tell us about Jeremiah's concern for the people?

2. The incense and offerings of the people are soundly rejected by God. In your opinion, what was the purpose of these offerings? What does this attempt on their part tell us of their character and motivation? What are the modern counterparts of incense and burnt offerings we see today?

3. While God forgives us of our sins, we quite often have to face the consequences of those sins. What choices had Judah made about its covenant relationship with God? What were the consequences that Judah now had to face for those choices?

4. Compare the spiritual condition of Judah with the apparent spiritual condition of America in our time. What are the similarities? Who are the "watchmen" today? Is their message being heeded? What is the role of believers in our present-day situation?

LESSON IN OUR SOCIETY

It would be so easy for the 21st century believers to read about and harshly judge the moral decay of Judah—their steady decline into apostasy, their brazen sinful practices, and their steadfast refusal to heed the warnings delivered by the prophets. Surely that could never happen again; or could it? The people of Judah had become so wicked that Jeremiah declared: "Were they ashamed when they had committed abomination? Nay . . . ." In fact, "neither could they blush" (v. 15). The same people who had once delighted

in the Word of the LORD had grown weary of rebuke and no longer took pleasure in it. Before we judge Judah too harshly, we must ask: How different are we?

A study of Jeremiah presents us with an object lesson on rejecting the Word of God. In spite of the tremendous blessings Judah had enjoyed, God brought judgment on them. Today, America is no longer a nation that prides itself on being a nation under God. By rejecting God's Word as our standard, do we bring judgment upon this land?

Habitual sin hardens our heart to the Word of God and hardens our ability to receive correction. Eventually we will begin to live as though the wrong path is all right. We will come to a place in our lives where we no longer "blush." Our special relationship with God requires that, like Him, we feel wounded, devastated, and ashamed in the presence of sin. God's warning to Judah holds true today: "Be thou instructed, O Jerusalem, lest my soul depart from thee" (Jeremiah 6:8). Dire predictions of global warming, nuclear holocausts, and world wars all pale in comparison to the possibility that God would allow His soul to depart from our nation.

MAKE IT HAPPEN

Many people seem to think that because God does not immediately punish them for wrongdoing they have escaped His judgment. Jeremiah's message makes it clear that God is always watching. He is recording our sins, and one day we will be judged. Now is a good time to take a spiritual inventory of your life and assess your faithfulness to God. Are there any unconfessed, rebellious, or sinful acts you have committed? Are there any idols you have placed before the LORD?

FOLLOW THE SPIRIT

What God wants me to do:

_____

_____

REMEMBER YOUR THOUGHTS

Special insights you have learned:

_____

of which may be disastrous if we make a wrong choice. Judah had a decision to make. Judah was obsessed with sin. Will she heed God's call to return to Him, renew her covenant relationship with Yahweh, and live? Or, would God's people rather continue in their idolatrous ways, shun God's call, and face the inevitable judgment from God? In a clear manner and with a yearning heart, Jeremiah—in an uncompromising prophetic fashion— prescribes a remedy for the sins of Israel, making them know that all hope was not lost but that there was a way out of the darkness in which they groped. They were just to "ask for the old paths, where is the good way, and walk therein." If they did, Jeremiah told them, "ye shall find rest for your souls."

Will Judah consider? Will the enjoyment of sin prevent the people of God from seeing their folly? It seems the old ways are just not acceptable anymore. Jeremiah sees the result of the people's rebellion coming. God's prophet cries out for the people to put on their mourning robes, for the day that is fast approaching is one of great lamentation. "Wallow thyself in ashes and make bitter lamentation . . . for the spoiler shall suddenly come upon us" (v. 26). It is not difficult to feel the throb of the pain in the heart of the prophet as he conveys to them the impending doom and disaster. Yet Judah will not change. She, therefore, must be tested and be made to pass through a refining process, failing which the LORD would reject them. Let us seek for the direction of the LORD. When He shows us the path we have forsaken, the one to which He wants us to return, we must heed

MORE LIGHT ON THE TEXT
Jeremiah 6:16-21, 26-28

Choices and consequences, decisions and destiny, actions and reactions—these are as inseparable as Siamese twins whose lives depend on each other. In the final analysis, life both present and future all boils down to the decisions we have to make. All of us, no matter what our situation in life, are confronted with choices big and small every day. We must also be prepared to live with the consequences of our decisions, pleasant or otherwise. Like Judah in our text, some of us may come to a major decision point, the consequence

His voice, knowing that our blessings depend on our obedience to Him.

In this passage, the Prophet Jeremiah clearly shows the emptiness of ceremonial religion. Through the prophet, the LORD calls His people to look for the "old paths" and to walk in them, but they refuse. He calls them back to the first principle of their faith through the trumpets of their watchmen, but they will not heed. Therefore, the LORD tells the nations and His people that they will reap the fruit of their devices.

16 Thus saith the LORD, Stand ye in the ways, and see, and ask for the old paths, where is the good way, and walk therein, and ye shall find rest for your souls. But they said, We will not walk therein.

The prophet demands that Israel should do three things. First, Israel was to "stand" (Hebrew `amad, pronounced **ah-MAHD**), that is, to arise in order to be able to examine their choices. There were many courses of action open. Jeremiah has described several: materialism, licentiousness, idolatry, ceremonialism, and true faith. Second, Israel was to "see" (Hebrew ra'ah, pronounced **rah-AH),** that is, to look, consider, and more importantly, discern. Third, having stood and seen the ways in which they were treading, Israel was to "ask" (Hebrew sha'al, pronounced **shah-AHL**; or shael, pronounced **shah-ALE**).

17 Also I set watchmen over you, saying, Hearken to the sound of the trumpet. But they said, We will not hearken.

God never leaves His people without a witness. He has set watchmen over His people. Those were the prophets, of whom Jeremiah was one (Ezekiel 3:17). The watchmen were those who stood on the wall of the city and warned the people when danger threatened. They did not create the danger; they faithfully sounded the alarm and blew the trumpet of God's judgment, delivering messages of warning, but they were ignored. Ephraim treated the watchmen, that is, the true prophets, as if they were the danger, rather than friends who were trying to stave off the disaster. Despite the prophet's plea and reminder to

Judah of previous warnings from God, the people continued to rebel, saying, "We will not hearken."

18 Therefore hear, ye nations, and know, O congregation, what is among them. 19 Hear, O earth: behold, I will bring evil upon this people, even the fruit of their thoughts, because they have not hearkened unto my words, nor to my law, but rejected it.

The nations, the congregation of Israel, and the earth are called to witness the judgment that would fall upon rebellious Judah. The threefold call serves to show the justice of God in executing judgment. This might also serve as a warning to other nations not to rebel. If God did not spare Judah, neither would He spare other nations that go the same way.

20 To what purpose cometh there to me incense from Sheba, and the sweet cane from a far country? your burnt offerings are not acceptable, nor your sacrifices sweet unto me.

What's in materialism, idolatry, lying, defrauding, living loosely, playing church, looking for something for nothing, and stepping on anyone who gets in our way to success? Yet in the midst of these, as this verse shows, Judah remained deeply and formally religious, multiplying rituals and offerings with abandon. But such would not please God. He abhors sacrifices, offerings, activities, and religious ceremony when they are not accompanied by righteous living. God would not accept the offerings of Judah because the people sinned with impunity. Like Samuel, Jeremiah made clear that ritual performances divorced from an attitude of obedience and faith were of no value in God's sight. Activities will never be a substitute for a dynamic relationship with the living God.

21 Therefore thus saith the lord, Behold, I will lay stumblingblocks before this people, and the fathers and the sons together shall fall upon them; the neighbour and his friend shall perish.

With the same tone of finality and determination with which Judah said, "We will not," God says, "I will." God will lay stumbling blocks (Hebrew mikshowl, pronounced **mick-SHOWL**), that is, obstacles along their way. God was determined to judge their rebellion. God would place stumbling blocks in their path (6:21), and they would never achieve the goal for which they strove. This is the natural consequence of their conduct. "This people," He says, "shall stumble and perish." Despite divine entreaty and warning, the people continue down a road littered with stumbling blocks. They will stumble. In laying stumbling blocks before the people, God makes the way of sinners hard, not for the fun of afflicting or punishing them, but in order to turn them from sin. The idea of totality is realized by individual cases in "fathers and . . . sons, . . . neighbour and his friend." None will be spared from the impending judgment.

26 O daughter of my people, gird thee with sackcloth, and wallow thyself in ashes: make thee mourning, as for an only son, most bitter lamentation: for the spoiler shall suddenly come upon us. 27 I have set thee for a tower and a fortress among my people, that thou mayest know and try their way.

By a metaphor from metallurgy in Jeremiah 6:27-30, Yahweh in conclusion confirms the prophet in his office. Jeremiah was set as *bachown'* (**bah-KONE**), an assayer of metals (see RSV), rather than "tower," as translated in the King James Version. His call for Judah to repent or face judgment was sent to test Judah and see if there were some faithful and repentant people among them. The impending judgment is described in terms of a severe refining process as Judah is put to the test.

28 They are all grievous revolters, walking with slanders: they are brass and iron; they are all corrupters.

The assayer gives his reports in metallurgical terms: he finds the people are brass and iron; in spiritual terms, they are stubbornly rebellious, slanderous, and corrupt. Basically, the verse is descriptive of the moral character of the people. "Grievous revolters," or literally, "revolters of revolters," is a Hebrew mode of expressing a superlative. The Hebrew root word *sarar* (pronounced **sah-RAHIZ** and translated "revolters") means "to be refractory; stubborn" and is used of rebellious animals (Hosea 4:16) or a son who disobeys his parents

(Deuteronomy 21:18). Joined this description is the figurative expression with "brass and iron." These ignoble, baser and harder metals are in contrast with gold and silver (cf. Ezekiel 22:18). To this analogy is added that they are all corrupters.

These descriptions were used by the prophet to express the debased and obdurate character of the people (Isaiah 48:4; 60:17). It is clear that Jeremiah's prophetic "fire" was unable to remove the impurities from Judah. Unlike metal ore from the earth, they have a will of their own, and as a result could decide whether to cooperate with God or not. Judah must either take God's commandments or take the consequences. The evil habits and dispositions of the Israelites were so ingrained that they would not yield to either the ordinary or extraordinary means of salvation. Therefore, God gave them up as incorrigible, and their adversaries prevailed against them. The passage is concluded in verse 30 by a statement of the Lord's rejection of Judah. What an important and timely warning to other nations, and indeed to the Christian church; for if God did not spare the natural branches, neither will He spare these.

DAILY BIBLE READINGS

M: Look for the Good Way
Jeremiah 6:16-21
T: People Tested as Silver
Jeremiah 6:22-30
W: Amend Your Ways
Jeremiah 7:1-7
T: People Will Not Listen
Jeremiah 7:16-28
F: Return and Rest
Isaiah 30:15-19
S: Those Who Enter God's Rest
Hebrews 4:1-11
S: Christ Will Give Rest
Matthew 11:25-30

TEACHING TIPS

October 6
Bible Study Guide 6

1. Words You Should Know

A. Hearken (Jeremiah 25:3-4, 7); Hebrew *shama* (**shah-MAH**)—To hear with the intention of obeying. Often translated directly as "to obey."

B. Amend (Jeremiah 26:13); Hebrew *yatab* (**yah-TAHV**)—Root meaning to make well or healthy.

2. Teacher Preparation

A. Find a quiet place and time for prayer. Ask the Holy Spirit to help you understand the Scripture, the lesson, and its relevance for your students.

B. Study the Devotional Reading (Proverbs 4:20-27) and the background Scripture (Jeremiah 25-26; 2 Chronicles 36).

C. Read the BACKGROUND and THE PEOPLE, PLACES, AND TIMES sections.

D. Carefully read the FOCAL VERSES several times. Read the FOCAL VERSES at least once in another Bible translation if you have one available. Review the AT-A-GLANCE outline and read the FOCAL VERSES again, paying attention to the structure of the passage.

E. Gather materials needed for your class: medicine bottle, empty pack of cigarettes, or some other item that has a warning on it.

3. Starting the Lesson

A. Ask a student to lead the class in prayer.

B. Introduce the lesson by holding up the item that you brought to class with the warning label. Ask students why the manufacturer put a warning label on the item. Ask students if they can think of other warning labels that they come across in their daily life. Point out that most warning labels list possible consequences that can occur if the warning is ignored.

C. Have one student read the IN FOCUS story out loud to the class.

4. Getting into the Lesson

A. Review the AT-A-GLANCE outline with the students.

B. Have different students read the FOCAL VERSES aloud for each section of the outline.

C. Summarize for the class the life and role of Jeremiah, God's prophet.

5. Relating the Lesson to Life

A. Ask the students to think about the first DISCUSS THE MEANING question. Spend about five minutes getting student responses.

OCT 6TH

B. Have a class discussion on LESSON IN OUR SOCIETY.

6. Arousing Action

A. Lead students in reciting together the KEEP IN MIND verse (Jeremiah 26:13).

B. Encourage students to read the DAILY BIBLE READINGS each day.

C. Close the class with prayer.

WORSHIP GUIDE

For the Superintendent or Teacher
Theme: Another Strong Warning
Theme Song: "Trust and Obey"
Scripture: Matthew 7:21-27
Song: "I Have Decided to Follow Jesus"
Devotional Thought: Lord, help me to listen to and obey Your Word daily that I might walk in the newness of life.

ANOTHER STRONG WARNING

Bible Background • JEREMIAH 25—26; 2 CHRONICLES 36
Printed Text • JEREMIAH 25:1-7; 26:12-13
Devotional Reading • PROVERBS 4:20-27

LESSON AIM

By the end of the lesson, students will decide to heed God's warnings and walk in obedience, understanding that by this they can experience His blessings instead of His judgments.

KEEP IN MIND

"Therefore now amend your ways and your doings, and obey the voice of the LORD your God; and the LORD will repent him of the evil that he hath pronounced against you" (Jeremiah 26:13).

FOCAL VERSES

Jeremiah 25:1 The word that came to Jeremiah concerning all the people of Judah in the fourth year of Jehoiakim the son of Josiah king of Judah, that was the first year of Nebuchadrezzar king of Babylon;

2 The which Jeremiah the prophet spake unto all the people of Judah and to all the inhabitants of Jerusalem, saying,

3 From the thirteenth year of Josiah the son of Amon king of Judah, even unto this day, that is the three and twentieth year, the word of the LORD hath come unto me, and I have spoken unto you, rising early and speaking; but ye have not hearkened.

4 And the LORD hath sent unto you all his servants the prophets, rising early and sending them; but ye have not hearkened, nor inclined your ear to hear.

5 They said, Turn ye again now every one from his evil way, and from the evil of your doings, and

LESSON OVERVIEW

LESSON AIM
KEEP IN MIND
FOCAL VERSES
IN FOCUS
THE PEOPLE, PLACES,
AND TIMES
BACKGROUND
AT-A-GLANCE
IN DEPTH
SEARCH THE SCRIPTURES
DISCUSS THE MEANING
LESSON IN OUR SOCIETY
MAKE IT HAPPEN
FOLLOW THE SPIRIT
REMEMBER YOUR THOUGHTS
MORE LIGHT ON THE TEXT
DAILY BIBLE READINGS

dwell in the land that the lord hath given unto you and to your fathers for ever and ever:

6 And go not after other gods to serve them, and to worship them, and provoke me not to anger with the works of your hands; and I will do you no hurt.

7 Yet ye have not hearkened unto me, saith the LORD; that ye might provoke me to anger with the works of your hands to your own hurt.

26:12 Then spake Jeremiah unto all the princes and to all the people, saying, the LORD sent me to prophesy against this house and against this city all the words that ye have heard.

13 Therefore now amend your ways and your doings, and obey the voice of the LORD our God; and the LORD will repent him of the evil that he hath pronounced against you.

IN FOCUS

Andre was a 28-year old accountant who worked for the Environmental Protection Agency making $40,000 a year with an opportunity to advance further in his career. He had all the trappings of success: a new car, an upscale apartment, and the clothes that made him look like the young Black professional that he was. Andre was a Christian and had even been faithful in church attendance during his college years when many other young people dropped out. But in the last year or so, he had begun associating with a group of people for whom spiritual things were of no importance. Over time, he began adopting the ways of some of his "friends," including using cocaine. It wasn't too long before his attendance at work suffered and the quality of his work dropped. He was warned about his conduct twice by his supervisor. After a third warning and Andre's failure to change, he was fired. The 28-year old accountant was stunned. He couldn't believe it; he had been fired from his secure government job.

In today's lesson, we'll see how God sent His prophet Jeremiah to warn His people that because of their disobedience, they were on a collision course with His judgment.

THE PEOPLE, PLACES, AND TIMES

Jeremiah. Jeremiah is one of the giants of Old Testament prophecy. The son of a priest, he was born in Anathoth, a village three miles northeast of Jerusalem. Jeremiah received his calling as a prophet in 626 B.C. during the thirteenth year of King Josiah's reign. The Book of Jeremiah reveals a lot about the inner turmoil and conflict out of which Jeremiah delivered his prophetic burden. Jeremiah's life demonstrates the hardships that sometime accompany the task of bringing God's word to His people. Perhaps anticipating the difficulties of being a prophet, Jeremiah resisted his call to prophetic ministry, citing his youth as an obstacle (Jeremiah 1:6-9). But God's will cannot be resisted. Jeremiah followed his calling faithfully, but the road was hard. He was rejected by his people (Jeremiah 15:10). He was frustrated by their hardheartedness (Jeremiah 5:3). And he was cut off from the normal joys and pleasures of life (Jeremiah 16:9). In spite of all of the difficulties that Jeremiah experienced, he found that he could not resist God's call to prophesy. He had to declare the word of the LORD as the LORD had directed him. It was a compulsion. It was a dynamic, powerful inner motivation that made him prophesy. "Then I said, I will not make mention of him, nor speak any more in his name. But his word was in mine heart as a burning fire shut up in my bones, and I was weary with forbearing, and I could not stay" (Jeremiah 20:9).

BACKGROUND

Jeremiah uttered the prophecies recorded in Jeremiah 25:1-13 during the time when Babylonia had gained prominence as the most powerful nation in what is known today as the Middle East. King Josiah, the last of the good kings of Judah, was killed in battle against the Egyptians in 609 B.C. at the Pass of Megiddo. During his reign, he instituted a major religious reformation in Judah. With his death came the end of Judah's political independence as a nation and the end of the spiritual and godly leadership that Josiah had provided his country. For a brief period, Egypt held sway over the fortunes of Judah, but at the battle of Carchemish in 605 B.C., the Babylonians defeated the Egyptians and became the superpower of the region. Jeremiah prophesied that if the people of Judah did not change their ways, God was going to use Babylon as His instrument of judgment to punish the nation for its wickedness. In the Scripture passage for today's lesson, Jeremiah tries one last time to get the people of Judah to turn away from evil and turn toward God.

AT-A-GLANCE

1. Past Warnings Have Gone Unheeded (Jeremiah 25:1-4)
2. God Is Angry with His People (vv. 5-7)
3. Another Strong Warning and Call to Obedience (26:12-13)

IN DEPTH

1. Past Warnings Have Gone Unheeded (Jeremiah 25:1-4)

Jeremiah has prophesied to the people of Judah for 23 years. Yet his message has gone unheeded. And not only did his own message go unheeded, but the messages of God's other prophets went unheeded as well. Whether it's Jeremiah or Jesus giving the warning, people who are straying from the pathway of righteousness seem to have difficulty in responding appropriately. A certain bumper sticker reads, "God Allows U-Turns." Indeed, He does. The fact that God gives us time and space to reverse course and to

as an outdated Old Testament concept. In fact, God, who does not change, is a God of love who can and does become angry with His people when they are unfaithful to Him. God's reproof for sin and call for obedience is an act of love, just as loving parents discipline their disobedient children. The failure to discipline when a child is disobedient is not a mark of love, but of apathy and unconcern. Likewise, God's willingness to discipline us is a mark of our sonship (Hebrews 12:6-7).

The actions of the Judeans that had angered God can be put into two basic categories: idolatry and unrighteous living. The first leads to the second. As soon as Josiah died, the people of Judah returned to their old ways. They offered incense to Baal, and the women kneaded dough to make cakes for the queen of heaven. The first commandment says, "Thou shalt have no other gods before me" (Exodus 20:3). By worshiping the works of their hands—gods that they had created—the people of Judah had provoked God to anger. Whenever our focus of worship moves away from God, we're headed for trouble. When the Judeans exchanged the worship of the true God for the worship of Baal, they ceased to live out the ethical dimensions of their covenantal relationship with God. They began to live unrighteous lives. Lying, stealing, murder, and adultery became the order of the day (Jeremiah 7:9). Yet God's people consoled themselves with the fact that they went to the temple (Jeremiah 7:4). While the Word clearly tells us to forsake not the assembling of ourselves together, God won't let us use our attendance at church as a coverup for a lifestyle that is not Christian.

go in the right direction with our lives is in itself an act of God's love and grace.

Perhaps part of the difficulty with God's people is that we refuse to really hear what is being said to us and about us in the Word. Instead, our own ideas about what God likes and doesn't like and what kind of "person" we think God is lure us into a false sense of security. Too often, we fail to realize that there is a difference between being a "hearer of the word" and being a "doer of the word" (James 1:22). Sitting in the pew on Sunday does not automatically mean that we live better, more faithful Christian lives.

2. God Is Angry with His People (vv. 5-7)

In our age, it is unpopular to talk about God being angry. We find comfort in the love of God and sometimes dismiss the idea of an angry God

3. Another Strong Warning and Call to Obedience (26:12-13)

Jeremiah 26:12-13 is part of a sermon that Jeremiah preached in the court of the temple (beginning with verse 1). He makes it clear that this is a message the LORD has given to him. Announcing that his message is intended for this house and this city, he addresses the priests and prophets (the house) and the political leaders (the city). God is calling on the religious leaders and well-to-do citizens of Judah—as well as the common man—to turn from their wicked ways. To avoid God's judgment, they will have to demonstrate their sincerity by showing real change. At this point, Jeremiah is saying there is still time: "You can still avoid disaster if you just change." God did this very thing with the city of Nineveh. He had intended to destroy the city because of its wickedness. But after Jonah preached to the people, the Bible says, "God saw their works, that they turned from their evil way; and God repented of the evil, that he had said that he would do unto them; and he did it not" (Jonah 3:10).

There is no substitute for obedience in the Christian life. It is what God requires of us. Our failure to heed the warnings that God gives us through His preachers and teachers or directly from his Word usually brings heartaches and difficulties that we could otherwise avoid.

SEARCH THE SCRIPTURES

1. Who was the king of Judah during the first year of the reign of Nebuchadnezzar, king of Babylon? (Jeremiah 25:1)

2. For how many years did Jeremiah say he had prophesied to the people of Judah and Jerusalem? (v. 3)

3. What did the people of Judah do that angered God? (v. 6)

4. Who did Jeremiah specifically mention he was prophesying against? (26:12)

DISCUSS THE MEANING

1. Why do people tend to ignore the warnings that God puts in their lives?

2. Why does the Scripture say that "obedience is better than sacrifice"?

LESSON IN OUR SOCIETY

Warning labels, signs, and messages abound in our society. Yet many people ignore them without thinking of the consequences. Discuss the value of heeding God's warnings. What negative consequences can we avoid? What positive consequences may result?

MAKE IT HAPPEN

Take inventory of your life and identify those areas in which you need to "amend your ways and doings." Ask God to forgive you for your disobedience. Ask the Holy Spirit to help you to turn away from sin and turn toward God.

FOLLOW THE SPIRIT

What God wants me to do:

_____

_____

REMEMBER YOUR THOUGHTS

Special insights you have learned.

_____

_____

MORE LIGHT ON THE TEXT
Jeremiah 25:1-7; 26:12-13

The message of the Prophet Jeremiah, generally known as the "weeping prophet," covers the period that can be described as the darkest days in the kingdom of Judah, from the reign of Josiah (the last of the good kings) until the exile in Babylon and beyond. The passage under review, including the whole section (Chapters 25—29), contains Jeremiah's warnings and predictions of divine judgment. Here, Jeremiah warns the people of their stubbornness and the consequences of their rebellion, which include the overthrow of Jerusalem and 70 years of captivity that was imminent. In verses 1-7, Jeremiah accuses both Judah and Jerusalem of not listening to God's words and caution. Then he calls on them to amend their evil ways in order to avoid God's judgment against them.

25:1 The word that came to Jeremiah concerning all the people of Judah in the fourth year of Jehoiakim the son of Josiah king of Judah, that

was the first year of Nebuchadrezzar king of Babylon; 2 The which Jeremiah the prophet spake unto all the people of Judah, and to all the inhabitants of Jerusalem, saying,

Verses 1 and 2 give the precise period in the history of Judah when Jeremiah delivered the oracle to the people. Important events in the history of Israel/Judah are usually marked and dated by the period when the kings reigned. Specifying the time period tends to authenticate the historical accuracy of the event. "The word . . . came to Jeremiah concerning all the people of Judah" during the fourth year of the reign of Jehoiakim, the son of Josiah.

Jehoiakim came to power after the defeat of Judah by Egypt. After the death of Josiah, the people made Jehoahaz his son king. Jehoahaz reigned for three months but was defeated by the Egyptians and carried away into Egypt. The king of Egypt replaced him with his brother Eliakim, whose name the king also changed to Jehoiakim. Jehoiakim reigned for 11 years in Judah, but he rebelled against God and Nebuchadnezzar and was carried away into exile in Babylon (2 Chronicles 36:5-7). It was in the fourth year of Jehoiakim's reign that Jeremiah gave his prophecy warning Judah and all the people of their evil deeds and calling for repentance. It should be noted that Jehoiakim was one of the four kings after the reign of Josiah whose reigns were characterized as "evil" (2 Chronicles 36:5, 9, 12).

Another important event marked this period (i.e., when Jeremiah delivered this particular oracle): Nebuchadnezzar came to power after defeating Egypt. The word or the message that Jeremiah had was for "all the people of Judah, and to all the inhabitants of Jerusalem"— everyone in the land. It was a call of warning and a call for national repentance and turning back to their God.

3 From the thirteenth year of Josiah the son of Amon king of Judah, even unto this day, that is the three and twentieth year, the word of the LORD hath come unto me, and I have spoken unto you, rising early and speaking; but ye have not hearkened. 4 And the LORD hath sent unto you all his servants the prophets, rising early and

sending them; but ye have not hearkened, nor inclined your ear to hear.

Jeremiah begins this section of his message by reminding the people how long he has been warning them and accuses them of stubbornness. From the thirteenth year of the reign of Josiah until "this day" was a total of 23 years. Josiah reigned for 31 years, which means that Jeremiah prophesied for 18 or 19 years during his reign, then during the reign of Jehoahaz, and now four years in the reign of Jehoiakim. For all of these years, Jeremiah contends, he has been speaking to them from the LORD. He uses a familiar Hebrew idiom, "rising early and speaking," which means that he spoke to them "again and again" or "consistently." It can also mean "speaking early and often" or "persistently without interruption" (7:13; 11:7; 32:33) and "taking pains to speak" to them. This persistence in trying to woo them back to God is also seen in verse 4 in the reference to God "rising early and sending" (7:25; 26:4-5; 29:19; 35:15) other servants (i.e., prophets from the past). It demonstrates God's love and grace and His unwillingness that anyone should perish. It shows how far God will go to give us opportunities to amend our evil ways and be reconciled to Him.

In spite of these warnings (proclamations of God's word) and numerous opportunities for change, the people's response had been consistent: total rejection of and disobedience to the Word of God. They refused to *shama`* (pronounced **shah-MAH**), which means to hearken, listen, or hear intelligently with the implication of paying attention and obeying. This refusal to listen and obey is further emphasized by the negative metaphor: "nor inclined your ears to hear." In other words, "they turned a deaf ear" to all the words of the LORD proclaimed to them by prophets of the past and by Jeremiah. The charge of refusing to listen is found more than 30 times in the Book of Jeremiah (e.g., 7:13, 24, 26, 28; 13:11; 35:14)

The exact time period covered by the phrase, "From the thirteenth year of Josiah the son of Amon king of Judah" has been debated. The argument could be made that this was only the third year since the word translated "thirteenth," taken from the word *shaliysh* (pronounced **shaw-leesh'**) or *shalowsh* (**shaw-loshe'**) as in 1 Chronicles 11:11; 12:18 or *shalosh* (**shaw-loshe'**) could mean triple, threefold, or even treble. In a hierarchy, it could also mean third rank. Some have even insisted that the word *shalowsh* represents the primitive number three and the ordinal third. Furthermore, it could mean a multiple. However, what is important is the fact that this word came to Jeremiah in the reign of Josiah early enough so as to warrant a rebuke for the obstinacy of the people from the prophet of the LORD. It was during that time that Jeremiah states, "the word of the LORD came unto me" (*haya dabar YHVH eelaey*). The use of *dabar* here implies a matter spoken of or that came up in a conversation. This is not merely passive speech, but speech that causes or produces a particular mode of action. This "word" has the capacity to set something in motion. It is not a word that can be ignored; it must be responded to. It calls for care. This is a commandment deriving from intimate communion and conference with someone special. This word carries with it power, promise, provision, and purpose. It questions the reason for all the people do. In a sense, it signifies the disposition of the One who speaks to the hearers. The word *dabar* is not just any word, but the word belonging to YHWH. Such a word one ignores to their own peril. The phrase *haya dabar* is literally translated as "existed the word." The word *haya* (pronounced **haw-YAW**) in its rudiments represents the coming into being or existence of something.

The word broke forth into the consciousness of this man named Jeremiah. And for 23 years, he could not keep from responding to its breaking forth from within him. He says, "and I have spoken unto you rising early and speaking; but you have not heard." God spoke, so Jeremiah speaks. The constancy of the word is revealed in the use of temporal descriptions, such as "rising early and speaking." But this is more than constant speech, it includes the idea of warning as it relates to the proximity of danger. One might call it an "early warning system." This early warning contains all the messages given to the people by the prophets before Jeremiah. After this,

Jeremiah indicts them with the phrase, "but ye have not hearkened." The use of the word "hearken" would have taken the hearers back to the words which God spoke in the Decalogue: "Hear, O Israel" (Deuteronomy 6:3-4). The word *shama`* (**shaw-MAH**) means to hear intelligently. It is not merely the auditory function of the physical ear, but to grasp what is being said with obedient attentiveness. There is a certain care and consideration to be given to the content of the declaration. Due diligence and discerning insight are called for. According to the prophet, Judah had not done this. In fact, they had done the exact opposite.

5 They said, Turn ye again now every one from his evil way, and from the evil of your doings, and dwell in the land that the LORD hath given unto you and to your fathers for ever and ever: 6 And go not after other gods to serve them, and to worship them, and provoke me not to anger with the works of your hands; and I will do you no hurt.

The content of the message of the prophets had been the same: a call to return back to God. The Hebrew word translated "turn ye again now" is *shuwb* (pronounced **shoov**), which means to turn back, to retreat, or to change toward a different course than one is traveling on. It is a call to repentance. The call is for everyone (all-inclusive) to turn from his or her evil ways and to return to God. This summons to repentance always precedes a promise. In this case, the promise is that they may "dwell in the land that the LORD hath given unto and to your fathers for ever and ever."

While in verse 5 the summons to repentance and turning to God is stated positively and followed with a positive benefit, the call not to go after other gods and serve them is followed by a negative consequence or threat of harm (v. 6). Here, the sin of the people is exposed: apostasy and idolatry. Turning back to God is tantamount to turning away from other gods and refusing to worship them. The purpose for this call is that they might not provoke God's anger, and so avoid God's fury against them.

In verses 5 and 6, we hear the content of Jeremiah's speech (*dabar*) and the early warning of the prophet of YHWH. First, the call is to "turn ye again now everyone from his evil way." Usually the word *shuwb* (**shoob**) may be followed by a call to return to God, but here it is a call to "turn from" or to turn back to one's primary pathway. They are not being called, in this particular usage, to return to the starting point, but simply to retreat from the danger before them. They must disown their character and disposition of evil. This turning is meant to dislodge the inner embrace of evil. They are to move from rejoicing in their present disposition to an aversion to what they now consider normal. It is hoped that this aversion will bring them back home again. They are to call back their wandering minds and, in a sense, carry themselves back.

In the King James Version we read the phrase, "evil way," but the Hebrew is literally "evil from his ways," or *midrakow haaraa' aah*. The word translated "evil" here is from the word *ra`*, meaning simply bad or natural and/or moral evil. But there is a sense in which the consequence of evil is more inherent in the use of this word than others. It also speaks to the adversity, affliction, calamity, or distress caused by this path that the people have chosen. There is, in fact, a sense in which God is saying to Israel, "You have lost your favour; your joy has been replaced with great grief." Rather than the joyful litheness of spirit which should accompany those who serve God, they now have a heavy, sorrowful spirit. But this is a result of the journey on which they have embarked. Their habitual course of life or mode of action, in national conversation as well as custom and individual manner, was marked by evil.

7 Yet ye have not hearkened unto me, saith the LORD; that ye might provoke me to anger with the works of your hands to your own hurt.

Verse 7 begins with the Hebrew word *shama`* (**shaw-mah'**), which is meant here to remind them of the first commandment. This call to intelligence is directed against the disobedience that has become a part of them. Much more than that, it is a reference to their idolatry. The first commandment, which also begins with the word *shama,* is an injunction against idol worship. The phrase "ye have not hearkened unto me" implies

that they have not been careful to do what God had commanded. Instead, they have consented to other voices and become content to adhere to what is declared by false prophets. They have not given due diligence to the voice of the Most High God. Lack of discernment has caused them to participate in and promote falsehood. This phrase is followed by "saith the LORD." The use of this phrase is unique here because it contains a word that is not usually used to end a divine proclamation. Rather, it is often used to describe the act of going to inquire of the LORD. The Hebrew word used here is *ne'um* (**neh-OOM**), which means an oracle. This word refers to a mystical prognostication of the divine intent.

In spite of these warnings to change and do the right thing—to turn to God and refuse to follow other gods—they would not hearken to the LORD. Instead, they persisted in sin, thereby provoking God to anger, and thereby hurting themselves. The phrase translated "provoke to anger" is the Hebrew verb *marah* (pronounced **mah-RAH**), which means to arouse into indignation or to grieve somebody. They provoked God's anger "with the works of their hands," that is, by serving graven images and idols made with their own hands. By this act, the people continued to break the first and second commandments (Exodus 20:2-5). Note that their choice of continued defiance to God's words and provocation of God's anger would prove to be to their own hurt. In other words, they pronounced punishment on themselves. God punishes (v. 6), but people do things to their own hurt (v. 7); for whatever one sows, that will he reap (Galatians 6:7-8).

26:12 Then spake Jeremiah unto all the princes and to all the people, saying, The LORD sent me to prophesy against this house and against this city all the words that ye have heard. 13 Therefore now amend your ways and your doings, and obey the voice of the LORD your God; and the LORD will repent him of the evil that he hath pronounced against you.

In the previous chapter, Jeremiah preached directly to all the inhabitants of Judah and Jerusalem, probably by going from place to place, or through "evangelical" gatherings. In Chapter

26, Jeremiah speaks specifically to the priests, prophets, and all those who gather at the temple to worship. He warns them of the impending disaster that is coming upon the temple and upon the city unless they amend their ways (vv. 1-7). The priests and (false) prophets reject his message and threaten his life. They invite the princes (i.e., the chief rulers) into the temple to oppose Jeremiah, accuse him of falsehood for predicting judgment against the temple and Jerusalem, and seek approval for his death (vv. 8-11).

In response, Jeremiah defends himself (v. 12ff). The phrasing of his words suggests that he may have been accused of some wrong doing. The use of the word "spake" ('amar pronounced **aw-mar'**) suggests that he answered them according to something previously appointed. They have been speaking about him, and now he must certify what he has been saying.

In addition, Jeremiah challenges them and, at the same time, brings a charge against them in a communal setting. In fact, they have to consider and then declare in his presence what their intent is. He has spoken words of judgment but also of promise. He has published condemnation; however, he has also reported hope. He has spoken of the divine requirement but has presupposed divine mercy. The key here is that he did not speak based on his own feelings about them, but based on a direct communication from the God of Israel. The content of this communication, and the defense which Jeremiah puts forth, is grounded in the divine revelation of God.

The phrase "the LORD sent me to prophesy" communicates that God appointed him to do this. But more than a mere appointment, God brought him to the point of this prophetic action; God had grown him for this specific act about which they now question him. While they were still away from Him, God reached forth and set Jeremiah in prophetic motion. He was like an arrow from the quiver of the Most High shot forth to Israel. Jeremiah implies that he really had no choice in this act of prophecy which he has given to the people. He could not stop even if he so desired. All the people gathered in the temple must understand the authenticity of his message. It is the LORD who inspired him to speak or prophesy against the city and the temple. He cannot deny his prophecy, but maintains God's word against the city and the temple. His message is not about himself or his own glory. They are not called to respect Jeremiah or to acknowledge his gift but to turn to the LORD. That is the heart of the divine communication which so compels this prophet.

Jeremiah offers them another chance for repentance so that the calamity pronounced against the temple and the city can be avoided. He invites them to "amend your ways and your doing, and obey the voice of the LORD your God." If they would hear him and obey, he says, "the LORD will repent him of the evil that he hath pronounced against you." The word "amend" comes from the Hebrew verb *yatab* (pronounced **yah-TAHV**), which means to reform or to correct their ways. The word "repent" used here is the Hebrew *nacham* (pronounced **nah-KAHM**), which means "to be sorry" and, by implication, "to have a change of mind" and, in this case, "to avoid God's proposed plan against the people."

DAILY BIBLE READINGS

M: The Lord Has Spoken Persistently
Jeremiah 25:1-7
T: Jeremiah Speaks the Lord's Warning
Jeremiah 26:1-6
W: The Lord Sent Me to You
Jeremiah 26:7-13
T: Officials Believe Jeremiah
Jeremiah 26:14-19
F: Turn from Evil
Proverbs 4:20-27
S: Listen, Stubborn of Heart
Isaiah 46:8-13
S: People Hear but Do Not Understand
Matthew 13:10-16

TEACHING TIPS

October 13
Bible Study Guide 7

1. Words You Should Know

A. Wide house/large chambers (Jeremiah 22:14); Hebrew *beeyt midowt walyowt*—A house with elaborate ornamentation, possibly a royal residence.

B. Closet thyself in cedar (v. 15)—Symbolizes self-exaltation, false security, and loftiness.

C. Judged (v. 16); Hebrew *mishpat*—Pronouncing a verdict.

D. To shed innocent blood (v. 17); Hebrew *damhamaagiy lish powk*—Condemnation of those who were not guilty of a particular crime.

E. Woman in travail (v. 23); Hebrew *kayoleedaah*—Painful labor pains.

2. Teacher Preparation

A. Begin preparing for this lesson by reading chapters 20 and 21 of Jeremiah to familiarize yourself with the circumstances under which this prophecy was delivered.

B. Read the FOCAL VERSES at least twice and be sure to use a different translation for each reading. If available, refer to Scripture commentaries and footnotes.

3. Starting the Lesson

A. Begin the class with a prayer. Thank God for allowing and inviting us to question Him in prayer, and ask that we listen attentively to His answers.

B. Ask a volunteer to read the KEEP IN MIND Scripture aloud.

4. Getting into the Lesson

A. Read the LESSON AIM.

B. Have students read the entire lesson in detail.

C. Have students review what they know about the Prophet Jeremiah and the spiritual condition of Judah.

D. Remind students to write their ideas in the REMEMBER YOUR THOUGHTS and FOLLOW THE SPIRIT sections.

5. Relating the Lesson to Life

A. Have students break into small groups and work on the DISCUSS THE MEANING questions.

B. Read THE PEOPLE, PLACE, AND TIMES section.

C. Discuss our role as Christians in addressing social inequities.

6. Arousing Action

A. Have students read the LESSON IN OUR SOCIETY article.

B. Ask students to give specifics about how they can complete the MAKE IT HAPPEN section.

C. Close the class with a prayer, using the KEEP IN MIND Scripture as the focus.

WORSHIP GUIDE

For the Superintendent or Teacher
Theme: God Demands a Just Society
Theme Song: "Shine On Me"
Scripture: Ephesians 5:8-17
Song: "Walk in the Light"
Meditation: Father God, we thank You for Your lovingkindness and for Your tender mercies. Father, we ask that You open our hearts and minds so that we might hear and understand all that You are teaching us. Amen.

GOD DEMANDS A JUST SOCIETY

Bible Background • JEREMIAH 22
Printed Text • JEREMIAH 22:13-17, 21-23
Devotional Reading • EPHESIANS 5:8-17

LESSON AIM

After studying today's lesson, students should understand that the Lord used His prophet Jeremiah to warn the people of Judah that He was greatly displeased with the unjust treatment the poor received at the hands of their wealthy neighbors and employers. Jeremiah warns that this injustice is contrary to the will of God and will not go unpunished. Students will decide to treat poor people fairly.

KEEP IN MIND

"I spake unto thee in thy prosperity; but thou saidst, I will not hear" (Jeremiah 22:21a).

FOCAL VERSES

Jeremiah 22:13 Woe unto him that buildeth his house by unrighteousness, and his chambers by wrong; that useth his neighbour's service without wages, and giveth him not for his work;

14 That saith, I will build me a wide house and large chambers, and cutteth him out windows; and it is cieled with cedar, and painted with vermilion.

15 Shalt thou reign, because thou closest thyself in cedar? did not thy father eat and drink, and do judgment and justice, and then it was well with him?

16 He judged the cause of the poor and needy; then it was well with him: was not this to know me? saith the LORD.

17 But thine eyes and thine heart are not but for thy covetousness, and for to shed innocent blood, and for oppression, and for violence, to do it.

22:21 I spake unto thee in thy prosperity; but thou saidst, I will not hear. This hath been thy manner from thy youth, and thou obeyedst not my voice.

22 The wind shall eat up all thy pastors, and thy lovers shall go into captivity: surely then shalt thou be ashamed and confounded for all thy wickedness.

23 O inhabitant of Lebanon, that makest thy nest in the cedars, how gracious shalt thou be when pangs come upon thee, the pain as of a woman in travail!

IN FOCUS

OCT 13TH

Lauren was putting on her coat and preparing to leave her office when the telephone rang. It was Damien, her Sunday School superintendent. He told her that he had just completed the six-month audit of the records and wanted to know if she could come down to the church and meet with him this evening. Damien was not his usual cheerful self and had sounded very serious. As Lauren hung up the telephone, a cold chill went through her. She had no doubt that Damien had discovered that her classes' offering envelopes were missing money. Last Sunday, when no one was looking, Lauren had taken 40 dollars from the envelope with the intention of replacing it. Her checking account was seriously overdrawn, and she didn't even have gas money to get to work on Monday. Lauren really had intended to replace the money. She didn't realize that last Sunday was the end of the quarter or that the superintendent and the secretary would tally all of the offerings. How would she face Damien? Damien had been a friend of Lauren's family for years. He and Lauren had attend-

LESSON OVERVIEW

LESSON AIM
KEEP IN MIND
FOCAL VERSES
IN FOCUS
THE PEOPLE, PLACES, AND TIMES
BACKGROUND
AT-A-GLANCE
IN DEPTH
SEARCH THE SCRIPTURES
DISCUSS THE MEANING
LESSON IN OUR SOCIETY
MAKE IT HAPPEN
FOLLOW THE SPIRIT
REMEMBER YOUR THOUGHTS
MORE LIGHT ON THE TEXT
DAILY BIBLE READINGS

ed high school together, and he was the one responsible for her being placed on the teaching staff. He had always encouraged Lauren, helped her prepare difficult lessons, and constantly praised her for her commitment and dedication to Sunday School and to her students. What would he think when he found out she was a thief?

THE PEOPLE, PLACES, AND TIMES

King Jehoiakim. One of the last kings of Judah, Jehoiakim was the son of godly King Josiah. The Bible discloses that, following a raid by Nebuchadnezzar, king of Babylon, "Jehoiakim became his vassal for three years" (2 Kings 24:1, NIV). In addition to the marauding Babylonians, Egypt was a constant threat to Judah during the period that Jehoiakim ruled. The Egyptian Pharaoh Necho had taken the previous king, Jehoahaz, captive; and it was he who had made the young Jehoiakim king. Although he was originally called Eliakim, his name was later changed by Pharaoh Necho. Jehoiakim was one of Judah's ungodly kings who did "evil in the sight of the LORD" (2 Kings 23:37). Oppression, social injustice, and murder characterized Jehoiakim's 11-year reign.

When Pharaoh Necho imposed heavy fines on the kingdom of Judah, Jehoiakim exacted these fines by heavily taxing his people. He also burdened them with large-scale personal building projects such as an elaborate palace for himself. Throughout his reign, Judah was also under constant threat from the Babylonians and Syrians.

Though it is not clear, many biblical scholars believe that Jehoiakim was killed when Nebuchadnezzer raided Jerusalem. Jehoiakim was succeeded by his son Jehoiachin, who ruled for only three months before he was succeeded by his uncle Zedekiah, one of the remaining sons of Josiah, the weakest of all the kings of Judah and the last of the Davidic line.

Based on information from Illustrated Manners and Customs of the Bible, J. I. Packer, M.C. Tenney, editors, (Nashville: Thomas Nelson Publishers, 1980), pp. 60-61, 135, 324, 329, 489, 644.

BACKGROUND

We often hear Jeremiah referred to as the "weeping prophet." This is understandable, as there was much for the young man to cry about. God had

selected this sensitive man to deliver a harsh message of judgment to the people of Judah. Jeremiah was condemned to watch Judah and his beloved capital city, Jerusalem, in its final death throes. Sadly, it fell on Jeremiah to prophesy at a time when all things in his nation were rushing to a horrible conclusion. Jeremiah had a front row seat and was a witness to all of the violence and corruption that had become commonplace in Judah. Kings, judges, and even priests could not be relied upon to behave honorably.

Jeremiah's ministry begins during the reign of the godly King Josiah. The revival and reformation work that was started with King Josiah would quickly be forgotten after his death. Understandably, Jeremiah is heartbroken to witness the spiritual wickedness practiced by the descendants of such a godly king. In the midst of all of this spiritual darkness, Jeremiah continued to deliver the message of God.

AT-A-GLANCE

1. Descendants of King Josiah Condemned for Their Unrighteousness (Jeremiah 22:13-14)
2. Jeremiah Proclaims the Righteousness of King Josiah (vv. 15-16)
3. Cruelty of King Jehoiakim Condemned (v. 17)
4. Punishment Pronounced for Unfaithful Leaders (vv. 21-23)

IN DEPTH

1. Descendants of King Josiah Condemned for Their Unrighteousness (Jeremiah 22:13-14)

This particular chapter contains one of the harshest judgments that is pronounced on Judah. The situation in the southern kingdom had reached an all-time low spiritually, socially, and morally. In Judah, the rich were getting richer through unethical methods, and their exploitation of the poor was shameless. Jeremiah is commanded to go to the king and talk with him face-to-face. God wanted King Jehoiakim and other leaders to know that He was displeased with the fact that the rich in Judah were becoming wealthier at the expense of their poorer brothers.

These verses also imply that the poor would be hired to perform labor, and then cheated out of their rightful pay. In their arrogance, the wealthy leaders behaved as though God was completely unaware of their behavior. How terribly wrong they were! "Woe unto him" expresses God's dissatisfaction with this sinful behavior. The Word of God has much to say about God's attention to the plight of the poor and needy. This is only one of many examples we find throughout the Old and New Testaments when we see God condemning the rich for the sinful ways in which they obtain their money and the selfish ways they use it.

2. Jeremiah Proclaims the Righteousness of King Josiah (vv. 15-16)

During a time when his nation was bankrupt, King Jehoiakim was selfishly embellishing his own private home. This king cared very little for his people. Judah's treasures had been looted from the temple, and the Babylonian army currently surrounded the city itself. In the midst of this turmoil, an insensitive Jehoiakim makes his subjects build him a royal palace.

Jeremiah demanded to know whether Jehoiakim thought having a grand home or a "house in cedar" was the standard that made him king. He was, in short, questioning the content of Jehoiakim's character, rather than the content of his pocketbook.

Jeremiah goes on to compare this faulty standard to that of "thy father," meaning Jehoiakim's father, King Josiah. Josiah had "judged the cause of the . . . needy" ". . . was not this to know me? saith the LORD." God asks this rhetorical question to point out that Josiah was aware that he could not be a true believer in the living God and not have concern for his needy subjects.

3. Cruelty of King Jehoiakim Condemned (v. 17)

In addition to seeing to the needs of the poor, as their king, Jehoiakim was responsible for ensuring that the courts were kept honest and just. Jeremiah declares, "but thine eyes and thine heart are not but for thy covetousness, and for to shed innocent blood . . . ." This implies that the government in Judah was allowing guilty (wealthy) people to go unpunished,

while innocent people were wrongly punished, and perhaps even killed. Here, the prophet may be referring to Jehoiakim's ordering the murder of the Prophet Urijah (2 Kings 23:35; 24:4).

This had to have been an especially painful message for Jeremiah to deliver. He had begun his ministry during the reign of Jehoiakim's father, King Josiah, and was a mourner at Josiah's funeral (2 Chronicles 35:25). How sad it must have made Jeremiah to see the son of such a godly man stray so far from his father's ways.

4. Punishment Pronounced for Unfaithful Leaders (vv. 21-23)

The rich leaders, Jeremiah declared, would suffer for their sins against the poor. Time and again Judah had failed to heed the Word of God. During the good times (before the Babylonians encamped outside the city gates), the people had steadfastly refused to "hear" or obey God. "This hath been thy manner from thy youth" means that this behavior was not anything new. "Youth" may even refer to the infancy of the people—back when they were delivered from Egyptian bondage.

The prophet now declares that they must pay for this sinful disobedience. The wind would "eat up" or utterly consume the "pastors." Jeremiah is referring to the king here. How ironic that the king, who was responsible for leading his people (or sheep), would himself be led away and fed upon by the conquering Babylonian armies.

"O inhabitant of Lebanon" is a direct reference to the City of Jerusalem, whose exquisite temples and royal palaces were hand-hewed from the precious cedars of Lebanon. Jeremiah is quite graphic in depicting the suffering the sinners will be made to endure. It shall be, he declares, that of a woman in the grip of labor pains. The suffering would be both painful and protracted.

SEARCH THE SCRIPTURES

1. For what wicked practices were the wealthy being condemned? (Jeremiah 22:13)

2. What attitude had the wealthy adopted? (v. 15)

3. How had King Josiah treated the poor? (v. 16)

4. How did the attitude of the wealthy living under King Jehoiakim differ? (v. 17)

5. What had been the reaction of the well-off to

the Word of God? (v. 21)

6. What would be the punishment for the unrighteous behavior of the people? (vv. 22-23)

DISCUSS THE MEANING

A. Reread verses 15-16 and discuss what it means to have your actions changed by the knowledge you have of the God who watches over the needy and the weak.

B. Discuss whether or not you believe that governmental leaders (elected and appointed) are obligated to set examples of righteousness. Read Romans 13 to see what the Word of God has to say.

LESSON IN OUR SOCIETY

Verses 22 and 23 of Jeremiah Chapter 23 explain the fate of Judah's sinful leaders. The Bible is clear that governmental leaders are agents or ministers of God. When elected or appointed officials are guilty of wrongdoing, the effects are intensified. A former president was embroiled in a scandal involving an illicit affair with an aide. For months, details of his extramarital affair were covered on the television and radio. Photos of the attractive aide were plastered on the cover of every major magazine. There was even an attempt to impeach and convict the popular young president. While many said that his affair did not affect the nation, still others rightly reckoned that the conduct of the nation's leader did indeed affect the nation.

God sent Jeremiah to tell Jehoiakim not only what was wrong in the land, but what was wrong in Jehoiakim's life. While we can sympathize with leaders and public officials caught in wrongdoing, they are very much accountable for their actions. They have been entrusted with great trust, and when they fail to uphold that public trust, they introduce dissension into the country.

Likewise, it is a weak and morally bankrupt leader who turns a deaf ear to the poor, helpless, or disenfranchised people among his or her constituents. These leaders have been empowered to protect people of color as well as the White majority to ensure the health, welfare, and legal rights of the wealthy and destitute alike. Wrongdoing by leaders is no small matter. When the lives of our government's leaders are corrupt, our national life is jeopardized.

MAKE IT HAPPEN

How do you personally respond to the poor and needy in your community? Are you merely seeing people in need, shaking your head, and then going on about your business? Ask God to raise your level of compassion and commit to a course of action to assist those in need.

FOLLOW THE SPIRIT

What God wants me to do:

_____

_____

REMEMBER YOUR THOUGHTS

Special insights you have learned:

_____

_____

MORE LIGHT ON THE TEXT
Jeremiah 22:13-17, 21-23

Although the sin of Judah and Israel can be summed up in one word—disobedience— it has several dimensions to it. It includes idolatry and apostasy. However, the sin of injustice to the poor and the needy is one of the greatest sins against God, especially as practiced by the rulers of the people and by the king in particular. Here in Chapter 22, Jeremiah prophetically denounces such practices and warns the kings of the consequences of their actions unless they turn back from their evil ways and obey the LORD their God. The prophecy recorded here is directed to King Jehoiakim, who replaced his brother, Jehoahaz (Shallum), after the latter had been carried away into captivity in Egypt. The prophecy took place in the king's palace.

22:13 Woe unto him that buildeth his house by unrighteousness, and his chambers by wrong; that useth his neighbour's service without wages, and giveth him not for his work;

Jeremiah is instructed to go to the house of the king and confront him (vv. 1-2). The prophet begins his prophecy with a word of condemnation: "Woe unto him that buildeth his house by unrighteousness." The word "woe" (Hebrew *hîy,* used as preparation for a declaration of judgment and condemnation) appears only here in Jeremiah but is found frequently in Isaiah (1:4; 5:8, 11, 18, 20, 21, 22; 10:1).

It is often used in a prophetic oracle to denounce evil or unjust practices that tend to disrupt the social order of the community (e.g., Isaiah 5:8-23; Amos 6:1-6). The charges against Jehoiakim are injustice, pride, arrogance, greed, and oppression of the poor and laborers and the lack of right (reversed) priorities as king. Instead of "knowing God"—which, to Jeremiah and Hosea, seems to be the highest priority (Jeremiah 9:24; Hosea 4:6; 6:6)—demonstrated by love and care for the disadvantaged, Jehoiakim exploited them. He lived for himself at the expense of his subjects. Indeed, Jehoiakim's reign was a reverse of his father Josiah's reign.

Then Jeremiah accuses him of building "his house by unrighteousness, and his chamber by wrong." The word "unrighteousness" comes from the combination of two Hebrew words: *tsedeq* (pronounced **TSEH-deck**) and the particle *lo'* (pronounced **low'**). The word *tsedeq* is usually translated as justice, rightness, and righteousness. It relates to what is right, just, or normal with the idea of rightness or justness as in weights and measures. It is used of kings, judges, and rulers and of God. When combined (suffixed in Hebrew) with the particle *low'*, which can be translated in various ways (without, not, no), the word *tsedeq* has a negative meaning (e.g., injustice, unrighteousness), with the idea of that which is not right, normal, and just. So Jehoiakim's reign is described as unrighteous, wicked, or evil.

14 That saith, I will build me a wide house and large chambers, and cutteth him out windows; and it is cieled with cedar, and painted with vermilion.

The indictment of unrighteous rule and unjust practices is fully developed in verse 14 in the description of the way Jehoiakim builds his house: "by unrighteousness and his chambers by wrong." How? First, by mistreating his neighbors and laborers, as demonstrated by his disregard for proper wages and refusal to pay them. The notion here is that Jehoiakim made forced laborers of his subjects by not paying them what they were worth or by refusing to pay them for their services. Second, he proposed in his heart to live excessively or lavishly, as if all this were the mark of a great king. His pomposity is described in his desire to build for himself a stately palace, "a wide house, and large chambers." He

must cut out windows for himself, probably the latest model; the ceiling must be with cedar, the richest sort of wood, and the walls painted and decorated with vermilion (see Ezekiel 23:14).

The accusation here is not that Jehoiakim built such an elaborate house for himself. There is nothing wrong with kings and great men building and furnishing their houses so as to reflect their position. However, the motive behind the building described here and the method (or practice) by which it is constructed makes it sinful. Note how dictatorial and determined the king is in his resolution. It may be read like this: "I will build myself a wide house . . . I am resolved and I will . . . nothing will change it, and no advice to the contrary will change my mind; I don't care who is hurt or how it is paid for." The question and comparison that follows in the next verse further reveal the evil nature and motive of Jehoiakim's practices.

15 Shalt thou reign, because thou closest thyself in cedar? did not thy father eat and drink, and do judgment and justice, and then it was well with him?

With dual rhetorical questions, Jeremiah exposes the ungodly practices that characterize Jehoiakim's reign and contrast with his father's reign. "Shalt thou reign, because thou closest thyself in cedar?" has been translated and understood in different ways. For instance: "Does it make you a king to have more and more cedar?" (NIV). "Do you think you are a king because you compete in cedar?" (RSV).

These translations are based on the individual understanding of the Hebrew verb *tacharah* (pronounced **takh-ah-RAH**) used here and translated in the KJV as "closest." It can be translated as "close" or "to contend." It comes from the root word *charah* (pronounced **kah-RAH**), which can also mean to glow or grow warm, or to blaze up because of anger, zeal, or jealousy. Since the subject of the prophecy has focused on the king's extravagant housing project, I believe the correct interpretation of this statement would be, "Do you think enclosing yourself with cedar makes you a king?"

Cedar is considered as one of the costliest and strongest woods and "the trademark of royal builders." For Jehoiakim to build such an extravagant cedar-house, which to him is the mark of a king (probably imitating King Solomon), he resorted to extortion of his poor neighbors and subjects, rather than following his father's example of modest living. In other words, the question goes like: "What is your priority as king? Big houses or justice for the poor?" It ought to be noted that at this time, while the people were burdened with heavy taxes the Egyptian pharaoh imposed upon them (2 Kings 23:33-35), the king was building himself a palace at their expense. That is not the type of king the Lord requires.

With another rhetorical question (v. 15b), Jeremiah contrasts Jehoiakim's evil reign with his father's good reign—"did not thy father eat and drink, and do judgment and justice, and then it was well with him?" What does this statement mean? It can be viewed in a number of ways. First, it can mean that his father, as one writer puts it, "enjoyed a balanced life of aesthetic pleasure and the practice of justice." Second, the statement can be seen, based on the NIV translation, to mean that his father lived modestly but focused on doing judgment and justice—ruling rightly.

Third (this is my interpretation), the statement does refer to physical food and drink or living modestly, but that is only part of it. Rather, the statement is proverbial or metaphorical. That is, his father's priority was to "do judgment and justice"; they were his "food" and "drink"—nothing else mattered more to him than to rule in equity and justice. And because of this, "it was well with him." The use of the rhetorical is to remind him of what he already knew and what he had observed his father do.

16 He judged the cause of the poor and needy; then it was well with him: was not this to know me? saith the LORD. 17 But thine eyes and thine heart are not but for thy covetousness, and for to shed innocent blood, and for oppression, and for violence, to do it.

This motif of his father's righteous reign characterized with justice, which translates into the knowledge of God, is further contrasted with Jehoiakim's wicked reign of injustice, covetousness, violence, oppression, and bloodshed. The "he" in verse 16 refers to Josiah (Jehoiakim's father); he "judged the cause of the poor and needy." The word "judged" is from the Hebrew

diyn (pronounced **deen**), which means to contend, defend, or plead. That is to say, Josiah was not influenced by the position of the nobles and princes or the rich. Rather, he defended the poor and needy, and he was properly discriminatory in his judgment. Caring for the disadvantaged is what it means to "know me," the LORD says. Knowledge here is not so much information as it is experience. It is relational. And such was Josiah's priority.

In contrast, Jehoiakim's priority was the opposite (v. 17). Instead of pleading for and defending the cause of the poor and needy, he exploited them. Rather than setting his "eyes" and "heart" on knowing God, he set them on his own selfish ends in covetousness and greed. The words "eye" (*ayin*, pronounced **AAH-yin**) and "heart" (*leb*, pronounced **lave**) are used synonymously here; `ayin refers not to the physical eye, but to mental and spiritual faculty, and *leb* speaks of the mind, the inner man or the thinking faculty. Both refer to the inner desire.

Instead setting his "mind on things above" (Colossians 3:2), he set his heart to "covetousness," shedding of "innocent blood," "oppression" of the poor, and "violence." While "it was well with his father," i.e., God was pleased with Josiah and he was blessed (vv. 15-16), Jehoiakim is condemned."Woe" is pronounced on him, and judgment is passed against him in God's court of law (vv. 18-19).

22:21 I spake unto thee in thy prosperity; but thou saidst, I will not hear. This hath been thy manner from thy youth, that thou obeyedst not my voice.

Although the oracle and the verdict (as we have been discussing above) have been directed personally to King Jehoiakim (vv. 13-19), the following pronouncement is leveled against Judah and Jerusalem. They may not share in the king's evil deeds, but they all (corporately) had wandered away from their God in disobedience and done that which was evil in His sight. The direction of the pronouncement that begins in verse 21 is indicated by the use of the feminine forms, metaphorically referring to a city.

The prophet starts with his case against the

city. The statement, "I spake unto thee in thy prosperity" is better translated, "I warned you when you were at ease" or when "you felt secure." The word "prosperity" is translated from the Hebrew word *shalvah* (pronounced **shal-VAH**), which means security, abundance, or quietness.

The prophet warned them about their sin and the consequences that would follow when things were going well, but they refused to listen or obey and heed the warning. Rather, they said in their heart, "I will not hear." Disobedience, the prophet contends, has been a way of life for the city from their early days (Jeremiah 3:25; Deuteronomy 9:7; Psalm 25:7; Isaiah 54:4).

22 The wind shall eat up all thy pastors, and thy lovers shall go into captivity: surely then shalt thou be ashamed and confounded for all thy wickedness.

As a result of their continued disobedience, the city will be punished, and this punishment will affect everyone; then she will be ashamed and confounded. The punishment is that they will be carried away into captivity. Metaphorically put, "the wind shall eat up all thy pastors" and "thy lovers shall go into captivity." "Pastors," i.e. shepherds (Hebrew *ra`ah*, pronounced **rah-AH**), meaning rulers of all kinds, will be swept or blown away as with the "wind" (Hebrew *ruwach*, pronounced **ROO-ahk**).

This signifies the force and severity of the punishment: all the leaders, including the king, will be carried away; the destruction will be as fierce and total as the force of a hurricane, the statement seems to imply. Their "lovers," which here implies other nations or her allies (e.g., Egypt, whom they trusted and relied on) will also be carried away into captivity. No one will come to her rescue. Judah will be put to shame and "confounded" (*kalam*, pronounced **kah-LAHM**) or ridiculed because of their wicked deeds.

23 O inhabitant of Lebanon, that makest thy nest in the cedars, how gracious shalt thou be when pangs come upon thee, the pain as of a woman in travail!

The verdict of verse 23 seems to revert to Jehoiakim. The word "Lebanon" refers not to the territory north of Palestine (vv. 6, 20) but to the king's palace, which he built with cedar. Lebanon is known for its cedar wood, and because of the amount of cedar used in the ceiling and decoration of the palace (v. 14), Jeremiah refers to Lebanon. When all this—which tends to be the king's glory—is destroyed, Jeremiah sarcastically exclaims: "how gracious shalt thou be when pangs come upon thee, the pain as of a woman in travail!"

The words "pangs" (*chebel* pronounced **KEH-vel**) and "pain" (*chiyl* pronounced **KHEEL**) are used synonymously to describe the pain or agony that the king and the whole nation will go through as a consequence of their sin and wickedness. The agony and pain of the coming desolation, Jeremiah prophesies, will be like the labor pain of a pregnant woman. There will be shrieks and screaming (Jeremiah 13:21; 30:4-6).

DAILY BIBLE READINGS

M: Act with Justice and Righteousness
Jeremiah 22:1-9

T: A House Built by Injustice
Jeremiah 22:13-23

W: The Shepherds Scatter the Sheep
Jeremiah 23:1-6

T: Do Justice
Micah 6:3-8

F: The Faithful Have Disappeared
Micah 7:1-7

S: Judge According to Righteousness
Psalm 7:1-11

S: Righteousness in Christ
1 John 2:28 3:7

TEACHING TIPS

October 20
Bible Study Guide 8

1. Words You Should Know

A. Satiated (Jeremiah 31:25); Hebrew *ravah*—Fully satisfied, being drunk, or to soak oneself.

B. Sow (v. 27); Hebrew *zarah*—To establish or plant for the purpose of growth.

C. Sour grape (v. 29); Hebrew *bocer*—Unripe grape.

D. Teeth set on edge (v. 29); Hebrew *qahah*—Cause to be damaged or dulled so that one is unable to chew.

E. Covenant (v. 31); Hebrew *beriyth*—Oath, contract, or solemn agreement. From the root "to cut," as in the cutting of an animal for sacrifice.

F. Inward parts (v. 33); Hebrew *baqirbaam*—Seat of emotions and thought; the metaphorical center of the human will to act.

2. Teacher Preparation

A. Do some research on the Prophet Jeremiah. You should be able to find plenty of information in your local religious bookstore or library.

B. Read today's FOCAL VERSES and the background Scriptures.

3. Starting the Lesson

A. Begin the class with a prayer. Thank God for His Son, Jesus Christ, and His ability to transform our lives from the inside out.

B. Have students briefly review the spiritual conditions that led to the destruction of Israel and Judah and the captivity of the people.

C. Ask a volunteers to read aloud THE PEOPLE, PLACES AND TIMES and the BACKGROUND information.

4. Getting into the Lesson

A. Read the LESSON AIM.

B. Divide the class in half. Have each group make a list of all of the biblical covenants they can recall. You may wish to start them off by reminding them of the covenant between God and Adam and Eve or the one between God and Noah.

C. Have volunteers read the FOCAL VERSES.

5. Relating the Lesson to Life

A. Encourage students to discuss the various covenants in their personal lives. Discuss what problems they may experience in remaining faithful to those covenants.

B. Give the students an opportunity to answer the questions in SEARCH THE SCRIPTURES.

6. Arousing Action

A. Have students read the IN FOCUS story. Allow 5-7 minutes for a discussion.

B. Close the class with a prayer, using the KEEP IN MIND Scripture as the focus.

HOPE FOR THE FUTURE

Bible Background • JEREMIAH 30—31
Printed Text • JEREMIAH 31:23-34
Devotional Reading • HEBREWS 10:11-18

LESSON AIM

After studying today's lesson, students should understand that what we could not do on our own, God, in His infinite love and mercy, elected to do for us. We no longer have to depend upon our ability alone to do the right thing. God came personally into our world and rescued us from sin and gave the Holy Spirit to dwell within us and transform us.

KEEP IN MIND

"But this shall be the covenant that I will make with the house of Israel; After those days, saith the LORD, I will put my law in their inward parts, and will write it in their hearts; and will be their God, and they shall be my people" (Jeremiah 31:33).

FOCAL VERSES

Jeremiah 31:23 Thus saith the LORD of hosts, the God of Israel; As yet they shall use this speech in the land of Judah and in the cities thereof, when I shall bring again their captivity; The LORD bless thee, O habitations of justice, and mountain of holiness.

24 And there shall dwell in Judah itself, and in all the cities thereof together, husbandmen, and they that go forth with flocks.

25 For I have satiated the weary soul, and I have replenished every sorrowful soul.

26 Upon this I awaked, and beheld; and my sleep was sweet unto me.

27 Behold, the days come, saith the LORD, that I will sow the house of Israel and the house of Judah with the seed of man, and with the seed of beast.

28 And it shall come to pass, that like as I have watched over them, to pluck up, and to break down, and to throw down, and to destroy, and to afflict; so will I watch over them, to build, and to plant, saith the LORD.

29 In those days they shall say no more, The fathers have eaten a sour grape, and the children's teeth are set on edge.

30 But every one shall die for his own iniquity: every man that eateth the sour grape, his teeth shall be set on edge.

31 Behold, the days come, saith the LORD, that I will make a new covenant with the house of Israel, and with the house of Judah.

32 Not according to the covenant that I made with their fathers in the day that I took them by the hand to bring them out of the land of Egypt; which my covenant they brake, although I was an husband unto them, saith the LORD.

33 But this shall be the covenant that I will make with the house of Israel; After those days, saith the LORD, I will put my law in their inward parts, and write it in their hearts; and will be their God, and they shall be my people.

34 And they shall teach no more every man his neighbour, and every man his brother, saying, Know the LORD: for they shall all know me, from the least of them unto the greatest of them, saith the LORD: for I will forgive their iniquity, and I will remember their sin no more.

LESSON OVERVIEW

LESSON AIM
KEEP IN MIND
FOCAL VERSES
IN FOCUS
THE PEOPLE, PLACES, AND TIMES
BACKGROUND
AT-A-GLANCE
IN DEPTH
SEARCH THE SCRIPTURES
DISCUSS THE MEANING
LESSON IN OUR SOCIETY
MAKE IT HAPPEN
FOLLOW THE SPIRIT
REMEMBER YOUR THOUGHTS
MORE LIGHT ON THE TEXT
DAILY BIBLE READINGS

OCT
20TH

IN FOCUS

Stephanie turned off the engine but made no attempt to get out of the car. She just sat staring up the sidewalk at the house on the corner. Sixteen years ago, she had walked out the front door and had never returned, until today. There were two cars in the driveway, and Stephanie was fairly certain that her parents were at home. What would she say to them after all of these years? Although she had thought of them often, she had never once written or called. She had been so angry when she left home. Her parents had suspected that she was using drugs, and their final confrontation had been terrible. They insisted that Stephanie get help for her drug problem or leave their house—Stephanie left. The first couple of years after she left home she wandered across the country with some friends. When her money ran out, so did her friends. She had been a heavy drug user, and her addiction and the need to support her habit had caused her to do some things that she didn't think she would ever be able to tell anyone about. However, three years ago Stephanie entered a drug rehab program, and through one of the counselors, she had been led to Christ.

Stephanie was married now and had an 11-month-old son. She loved her husband and her son, but she really missed her parents. She and her husband had been in prayer about it all year long. Two days ago, she finally decided to fly home to see her parents. Her husband suggested that she call them first, but she was afraid they might hang up on her. As she opened the car door, she still had no idea what she would say to them. What if they told her to go away?

THE PEOPLE, PLACES, AND TIMES

The Prophet Jeremiah. Jeremiah was born into a priestly family in Anathoth, located right outside of Jerusalem. As a young man, Jeremiah was commissioned as a prophet in the thirteenth year of the reign of King Josiah of Judah. He declared God's message of impending disaster to Judah for more than 40 years during the reigns of Judah's last five kings. Jeremiah was a researcher and a historian as well as a prophet. In addition to the book bearing his name, he is generally credited with writing the Books of 1 and 2 Kings, covering the history of Judah and Israel. Jeremiah's contemporaries were the prophets

Habakkuk, Zephaniah, Ezekiel, and Daniel. The last two were exiled in Babylon. The Prophet Daniel was apparently strengthened by studying Jeremiah's words and was in turn able to offer comfort to the people regarding their 70-year exile and impending release (Daniel 9:1-2). In 586 B.C., King Nebuchadnezzar destroyed Jerusalem and carried off its people. Although Jeremiah was offered a comfortable life in the Babylonian court, he elected instead to remain in Jerusalem, where he continued to preach to the people. Jeremiah was among the group that went to Egypt following the murder of the Babylonian governor in Judah. Jeremiah began to prophesy to the southern kingdom of Judah almost 100 years after Isaiah. Jeremiah's historical background is found in 2 Kings 22-25 and 2 Chronicles 34-36.

Based on information from Eerdman's Handbook to the Bible, David Alexander and Pat Alexander, editors (Oxford: Lion Publishing, 1983), pp. 396-397.

BACKGROUND

Jeremiah's words come in the wake of Judah's darkest hours. The sister kingdom of Israel has been destroyed, and Jeremiah himself has been held captive by the rebellious spirit of the sinful nation. He was arrested and shut up in a courtyard following his conflict seven years earlier with false prophets. These false prophets had predicted that Babylon would be broken, but it was not broken. In fact, the army of the Babylonian King Nebuchadnezzer was camped outside the wall of Jerusalem, preparing to destroy the holy city and reduce the great temple to ashes.

The preceding chapter of Jeremiah emphasizes the "Day of the LORD," opening with a great tribu-

AT-A-GLANCE

1. God Promises to Restore Israel and Judah (Jeremiah 31:23-28)
2. God Will Require Personal Accountability for Sins (vv. 29-30)
3. God Promises a New Covenant (vv. 31-33)
4. Former Sins Will Be Forgiven (v. 34)

lation period. Yet now, God, speaking through His prophet Jeremiah, offers His people hope of restoration.

IN DEPTH

1. God Promises to Restore Israel and Judah (Jeremiah 31:23-28)

Despite the fact that the northern kingdom (Israel) had long ago been ransacked and her people taken into captivity, it is clear that the new covenant God intends to make will include both Israel and Judah. Here God is promising that there will be an ultimate and permanent restoration for all twelve tribes. Because of their sin and rebellion, Judah is in peril now and will suffer greatly in the years to come. Yet God is assuring them through Jeremiah that the day will come when their suffering will end and both the land and the people will again be viewed as "holy."

2. God Will Require Personal Accountability for Sins (vv. 29-30)

God is equally clear that He will hold every man accountable for his actions. In the past, the people of Judah had seriously perverted the law for their own use, rather than God's. Sometimes they would define the law in a way that suited their own sinful purposes. The law said that they should have no other gods. The people foolishly rationalized that it was all right to have idol gods as long as they didn't put them before the LORD God Almighty. God is clear that the people would no longer be able to blame their sins on their parents by hiding behind a popular proverb that implied if the parents ate unripened or "sour" grapes, the effects would become evident in the teeth of their children. By using this proverb, the people had attempted to blame their parents for the situation they were now in. However, responsibility and punishment for sin would rest squarely on the individual.

3. God Promises a New Covenant (vv. 31-33)

The new covenant would be unlike the former covenants God had made with the nation. Israel and Judah had failed to live up to the terms of the old covenant. This should not be surprising if we keep in mind that the old covenant was never intended to bring salvation; rather, it was intended to point the

way to salvation. The old covenant proved that man was a depraved sinner, guilty in the eyes of a holy God and unable to live up to the demands of the perfect law. Yet God so loved humankind that He pursues guilty sinners and ransoms them with the blood of His only Son.

The old covenant is marked by the words "thou shalt" and "thou shalt not." In contrast, God says the words "I will" 15 times in this chapter alone! God's love for these sinful and wicked people is unmistakable. Indeed, God has loved His people with an "everlasting love."

Unlike the old covenant, which was inscribed on stone, God declares that the new law will be imbedded in their minds; the new covenant would be written on their hearts rather than a tablet of stone. This was essential because it was the heart of the people that was the root of their spiritual problem. "The heart," Jeremiah rightly claims, "is deceitful above all things and desperately wicked" (Jeremiah 17:9). Unless their hearts changed, God knew the people would never change. That inner, radical change could only occur with the provision of salvation through Jesus, the Christ.

4. Former Sins Will Be Forgiven (v. 34)

The act of forgiveness is difficult, nearly impossible for many of us. When we have been slighted, hurt, or injured, quite often we can vividly recall all of the details. Like a video camera, our minds replay the painful details over and over. This is because we can't forget it. Here we see God choosing to forget. The operative words here are "I will." It can be argued that nowhere in the Old Testament is God's omnipotent grace and love toward His people more fully revealed than when he says, "For I will forgive their iniquity, and I will remember their sin no more." It is from His position of supreme strength that God makes this promise. It will be through Jesus that God will deal with man's sin. This new covenant is actually His plan of forgiveness for the entire human race. How wonderful it is to know that God's plan for the forgiveness of our guilt fully expresses the nature of His love for each one of us.

SEARCH THE SCRIPTURES

1. With what will the houses of Judah and Israel be sown? (v. 27)

2. What proverb did the people use to assign blame for their sins to their parents? (v. 29)

3. Who did God say would be held accountable for sin? (v. 30)

4. What would be made with Judah and Israel (v. 31)

5. When had an earlier one been made? (v. 32)

6. Where would the law be placed? (v. 33)

7. What would people no longer be able to say? (v. 34)

8. What would God do about humanity's former sins? (v. 34)

DISCUSS THE MEANING

1. God declares that just as he allowed Israel and Judah to be destroyed, He would watch over them as they were restored. What does this reveal to us about the nature of God?

2. The LORD is clear that everyone will be held personally accountable for his own sins. Why is this so important?

3. Read Hebrews 10:5-18. What are the similarities between this passage and Jeremiah 31:23-34? What is more fully explained about Jesus Christ in the passage in Hebrews?

LESSON IN OUR SOCIETY

Several years ago, a newspaper published a survey of American values and morality. Among other things, the survey revealed that while most Americans admitted knowing the Ten Commandments, the majority of people also admitted they did not live by them. The survey's results were clear: Americans knew better—they simply didn't behave as though they knew. This refusal to "do the right thing" is not new. God made a covenant with His people, the Children of Israel. He gave them the Ten Commandments and asked that they keep them. In return, God made them His "special" people; He promised and then gave them a land flowing with milk and honey. He gave them victory over their enemies. Time and time again, He proved His faithfulness to them. Yet God's blessings were not enough to keep them faithful to Him. The people of Judah and Israel were just too stubborn and hard-hearted to obey God and keep His commandments. They lied, cheated, and bowed down to all kinds of idols. In short, they did whatever made them feel

good at the moment. Does that sound like anyone we know today? Over and over, God sent prophets to convict Judah and Israel of their sinful ways. For a time, the people would heed the warnings and make some feeble attempts to behave better, but they couldn't seem to keep it up. Eventually, they went right back to their sinful ways.

God finally resorted to disciplining them by allowing them to be taken into captivity. One would think that He finally had their attention. Now that they had lost their land, their homes, and their families, perhaps they could at last respond to God.

In His infinite wisdom, God knew that even the harsh discipline of defeat and captivity was not enough to change the attitudes of such a stubborn and willful people. God was aware that the people "knew" the old covenant, yet they chose to ignore it. He knew that our inner nature had to be changed so that we could obey Him. His new covenant, God declares to Jeremiah, will be "put within them." The new covenant is how God deals with you and me today. In the new covenant, we do not rely on our own ability to be faithful or righteous. Through His Son, Jesus Christ, God made the law flesh and blood. In Jesus, God's Word became flesh that was broken for us so that we could obtain "new hearts" and become adopted as God's children. Thank God, we do not have to rely on our own efforts to try to please God and become accepted by Him. Under the new covenant, we have God's gracious gift of salvation. We need only believe the Gospel of Jesus Christ and allow God to write His law on our hearts.

MAKE IT HAPPEN

The provision of salvation offered in the new covenant no longer requires us to struggle vainly to obtain righteousness. Salvation is a free gift from God, yet many Christians continue to think that by keeping the law they can "save themselves." They are foolishly trying to become righteous by their own efforts. Can you identify some areas in your own life where you might be trying to save yourself? Take the time to reread today's Scriptures. Pray and ask Jesus to come in. Allow Him to change and save you.

FOLLOW THE SPIRIT

What God wants me to do:

_____

REMEMBER YOUR THOUGHTS
Special insights you have learned:

_____

_____

MORE LIGHT ON THE TEXT
Jeremiah 31:23-34
In spite of the "doom and gloom" that characterize the prophecy of Jeremiah (e.g., his pronouncement of the punishment of exile to Judah and Jerusalem because of their waywardness), there are rays of hope and restoration for the remnant. This hope is detailed in the later part of the Book of Jeremiah, especially Chapters 30-33. In this section, the LORD demonstrates His love, mercy, grace, and faithfulness by His promise and assurance of restoration and forgiveness—even before the people confess their sins. In His anger, God declares a punishment against His people, but in His mercy and grace, He assures them of a bright future. He does this through His prophets, including Jeremiah.

31:23 Thus saith the LORD of hosts, the God of Israel; As yet they shall use this speech in the land of Judah and in the cities thereof, when I shall bring again their captivity; The LORD bless thee, O habitation of justice, and mountain of holiness.

Jeremiah begins this section of his prophecy by declaring its source from "the LORD of hosts, the God of Israel." He uses the personal, proper name of God: *YAH-weh*, which is the Jewish national name for the LORD (found in all capital letters). Jesus considered the name of *YAHWEH* so holy that it could not be verbalized or written with unwashed hands.

Indeed, whenever the copyists or scribes wanted to write the LORD's name, they would wash their hands and use fresh writing material and substitute the other name *Adonai*. Not only does Jeremiah use the proper name of God; he qualifies that name by using one of God's attributes, "LORD of hosts." The word "hosts" is a translation from the Hebrew word *tsaba'* (**tsah-RAH**) or *tseh'ah* (**TSEH-ah**), which literally means a mass of persons or a group organized for war (an army). Therefore, "LORD of hosts" means one who is head and commander in charge of a large army. The NIV translates it using the word

"Almighty," which describes the enormous power and authority that belongs to God. In addition, Jeremiah identifies the source of this prophecy as "the God of Israel" (as opposed to gods of other nations). The invocation of this word "God" is to assure the people of the truthfulness of the prophecy and the conviction that the promise will surely be fulfilled.

The message is that God will surely restore Judah and the rest of the cities by gathering the people back to their land after the exile. The regathering of the people will also bring back worship to the land, justice to the people, and peaceful coexistence among different inhabitants of the land. The people will be able to use the old blessing and pronounce blessing on the land. Jerusalem will be restored to its former glory as the seat of "justice" (Psalm 122:5-8; Isaiah 1:26), a sacred mountain of worship (Zechariah 8:3).

24 And there shall dwell in Judah itself, and in all the cities thereof together, husbandmen, and they that go forth with flocks. 25 For I have satiated the weary soul, and I have replenished every sorrowful soul.

At this time, there will be camaraderie between the farmers (husbandmen) and the shepherds, for both will coexist peacefully in the land (v. 24). The statement that the "husbandmen" (Hebrew *'ikkar*, pronounced **ick-KAHR**), i.e., farmers, and "they that go forth with flocks" (shepherds) dwelling together in Judah, itself signifies the notion of peace and tranquility that will exist in the land when the LORD restores the people to their land. Agronomy and animal rearing were the two main occupations in Judah and Jerusalem. The "husbandmen" and "they that go forth with flocks" represent the entire populace or all the inhabitants of the land. It follows, therefore, that the statement not only signifies the peaceful coexistence the people will enjoy, but the type of peace that characterizes the place. The people will go about their daily business peacefully and without fear of invasion as they had before and during the exile.

At that time, the LORD will refresh the souls of those who are weary with thirst and feed those who languish from hunger (v. 25). The word "satiated" is a translation of the Hebrew verb *ravah* (pronounced rah-VAH), which means to make drunk, to satisfy, to soak, or to water, and the word "replenished" comes from the Hebrew verb *male'* (pronounced **mah-LAY**), meaning to fill or to be full, i.e., to satisfy a hungry soul. The idea here tends to be both physical and spiritual (Psalms 36:8; 63:5; 107:9; Isaiah 55:1; 58:11). In other words, the restoration of the people will bring about transformation of the land: the cultivation of the fields, the shepherding of the flocks, and the restoration and transformation of their "weary soul."

26 Upon this I awaked, and beheld; and my sleep was sweet unto me.

The interpretation of verse 26 poses some difficulty to commentators. However, it seems that the message in this section (vv. 23-25) comes to Jeremiah in a dream. He wakes up and looks around and probably finds that it *is* a dream. The preposition "upon this" or "at this" probably means "at this point of the message, I woke up and looked around." The clause "and my sleep was sweet unto me" seems to refer to the content of the vision. That is the good news of the message: the bright future that waits Judah and its people makes his sleep a sweet one.

27 Behold, the days come, saith the LORD, that I will sow the house of Israel and the house of Judah with the seed of man, and with the seed of beast.

Jeremiah continues his message from the LORD, relating the LORD's promises to the people. Here (vv. 27-34) he quotes the LORD. The phrase, "Behold, the days come" speaks of the event that will come to pass in the future, and the preposition "behold" or *hinneh* (pronounced **hin-NEH** and often translated as lo, see, or look) tends to add emphasis and assurance to what is being said. Here the LORD says to the people through Jeremiah, "Look!" as if calling them to pay attention to what He is about to tell them. The LORD's promise to the people is that

He will repopulate the house of Israel and the house of Judah with both the "seed of man" and the "seed of beast." The LORD uses an agricultural metaphor of sowing seed to describe how He will replenish the land with people and animals (Hosea 2:23). This metaphor is also used to describe scattering the people from their land (Zechariah 10:9).

28 And it shall come to pass, that like as I have watched over them, to pluck up, and to break down, and to throw down, and to destroy, and to afflict; so will I watch over them, to build, and to plant, saith the LORD.

In verse 28, the LORD assures the people of a total reversal of the calamity that hitherto befell them (both Israel and Judah) under the watchful eyes of the LORD. Here, just as in the past when He watched the total annihilation of the people, the LORD will watch over the people to ensure the rebuilding and replanting of the people in their land. In the past, the LORD seemed to supervise the total destruction of the land as described by a number of action verbs: "pluck up . . . break down . . . to destroy, and to afflict." But in the future, He will watch over them "to build and to plant" them again in the land. The terrible past loss of human and animal lives during the invasion of the land and the cities (see Jeremiah 7:20) will be reversed in the future. The horror of the past will be replaced with blessings in the future.

29 In those days they shall say no more, The fathers have eaten a sour grape, and the children's teeth are set on edge. 30 But every one shall die for his own iniquity: every man that eateth the sour grape, his teeth shall be set on edge.

When all these things will come to pass, the people would no more have an occasion to complain or criticize God's righteousness and justice, using the common adage, "The fathers have eaten a sour grape, and the children's teeth are set on edge," which the people used during their suffering and exile. Unlike in the past (Ezekiel 18:1-4, 20-21) when the people complained of being punished because of their fathers' sins, the future will be different. Instead, everyone will be responsible for his or her own acts. No more will the children pay for the sin of their fathers; neither will the fathers bear the brunt of their children's wrongdoing. But anyone who sins will be punished for his own iniquity, for "every man that eateth the sour grape, his teeth shall be set on edge" (Ezekiel 18:25-29; 33:17-20), since every soul belongs to God (Ezekiel 18:4).

31 Behold, the days come, saith the LORD, that I will make a new covenant with the house of Israel, and with the house of Judah: 32 Not according to the covenant that I made with their fathers in the day that I took them by the hand to bring them out of the land of Egypt; which my covenant they brake, although I was an husband unto them, saith the LORD:

The good news of the future is not restricted to improving the physical and spiritual condition of the people. The LORD promises to change the relational condition between Himself and His people. The change in relationship will focus on improving His "covenant" (*berith*, pronounced **buh-REETH**) with "the house of Israel and with the house of Judah." *Berith*, or "covenant," can also be rendered as "an alliance" or "a treaty between two people or a group of people." It is more than an agreement. It is more binding than a mere agreement between two people. The Hebrew verb used for "to make" a covenant is *karath* (pronounced **kah-RATH**), which in its simplest form means to cut. This originally involved cutting flesh (e.g., animals) and passing the pieces. The implication of "cutting" a covenant was that whoever broke the covenant would be cut in pieces just as the animal was. In some traditions, such as that of the Igbo tribe of Nigeria, people made treaties by making a little cut in each person's finger and squeezing their blood into a cup of wine. The cup is then passed around and each person in league drinks from it. It is strongly believed that whoever breaks the covenant will die.

The LORD promises to make a new covenant with the people, which will replace the old one that He made with their forefathers when they left Egypt. The old covenant made with Israel after the Exodus from Egypt refers to "the Sinai covenant," also known as the "Decalogue" or the "Law of Moses." The problem with the old covenant is that the people did not keep it and therefore rendered it ineffective. Hence, the LORD found it necessary to make a new covenant (see Hebrews 8:6-13).

Different interpreters of the Bible have interpreted the phrase "although I was an husband unto them" in a number of ways. The word "husband" comes from the Hebrew word *ba`al* (pronounced **bah-AHL**), which can be rendered as master, one who has dominion, husband, or married spouse. Hence the differences in interpretation (e.g., "though I was LORD over them" or "I had to exert my authority over them"). Others render the last part of this verse: "Because they broke my covenant, I reassert my authority over them." The phrase refers to the breaking of the covenant by the people. The word *ba`al* should therefore be interpreted with the idea of a "loving and caring" attitude of a husband toward his wife. The LORD uses the husband-and-wife metaphor to describe His loving relationship with the Children of Israel (Isaiah 54:5; Jeremiah 3:14, 20; Ezekiel 16:32; Hosea 2:16). Therefore, it makes sense to render this part of the verse (32) as, "Although I was a husband unto them, they broke (or refused to keep) my covenant with them."

33 But this shall be the covenant that I will make with the house of Israel; After those days, saith the LORD, I will put my law in their inward parts, and write it in their hearts; and will be their God, and they shall be my people.

The new covenant will not be the same as the old. There are a number of differences between the two, and each has special features. First, while the old covenant was written on tablets of stone, the new covenant will be written on the tablets of the heart ("put . . . in their inward parts, and written in their hearts"). The important difference between the two lies not in the material they are written on, but in their content. Here it is clearly stated that the new covenant will not be the same as the old covenant God made with Moses: "Not according to the covenant that I made with their fathers in the day that I took them by the hand to bring them out of the land of Egypt . . ." (v. 32).

The new covenant is what has been accomplished through Jesus as found in the New Testament (see Isaiah 42:6; 49:8; 55:3; 59:21; 61:8; Hebrews 8:6-13; 10:16; 12:24; 13:20). This promise points beyond the time of Jeremiah and the house of Israel. It points us to the Gospel of the New Testament and to the Christian Gospel. It is fulfilled in Christ Jesus when He confirms: "This cup is the new covenant in my blood, which is poured out for you" (Luke 22:20, NIV). This covenant is for all those who will come to God through His Son Jesus Christ, both Jews and Gentiles. The new covenant will bring about a relational restoration between the LORD and His people, which hitherto had been severed as a result of breaking the old covenant—"and (I) will be their God, and they shall be my people."

34 And they shall teach no more every man his neighbour, and every man his brother, saying, Know the LORD: for they shall all know me, from the least of them unto the greatest of them, saith the LORD: for I will forgive their iniquity, and I will remember their sin no more.

The second special feature in the new covenant is that "they shall teach no more every man his neighbor, and every man his brother, saying, Know the LORD." Because the law would be written in their hearts, there would no longer be the need for people to teach others to know God. Until now, the priests, scribes, and prophets were the custodians of the law and the "mediators of knowledge," but in the new covenant the law would be internalized in the hearts of God's people (Deuteronomy 30:6; Psalm 37:31).

This divine transformation of human nature will result in the personal knowledge and love of God from the "least of them to the greatest of them." This means there will be no class distinction, and everyone will have equal opportunity and responsibility to know and love God. Consequently, their iniquity will be forgiven and their sin remembered no more. Just as forgiveness was incorporated in the old covenant (Exodus 34:6; Leviticus 4:31, 35), forgiveness would become the "cornerstone of the relationship." This prophecy is now completely fulfilled in Jesus Christ, the God-Man, for generations (Luke 2:20; 1 Corinthians 11:24; Hebrews 8:7-13).

DAILY BIBLE READINGS

M: The Lord Will Restore Jacob
Jeremiah 30:18-22
T: An Everlasting Love
Jeremiah 31:1-6
W: God Will Satisfy
Jeremiah 31:23-30
T: God Will Make a New Covenant
Jeremiah 31:31-37
F: God Will Bring Healing
Jeremiah 33:1-13
S: You Have Made Me Hope
Psalm 119:49-56
S: Eternal Hope
Titus 2:11-15

TEACHING TIPS

October 27
Bible Study Guide 9

1. Words You Should Know

A. Selah (Habakkuk 3:3)—A pause or suspension in the singing of a psalm.

B. Horns (v. 4); Hebrew *qeren* (**keh-ren**)—Refers to the peak of a mountain; rays or radiant beams.

C. Pestilence (v. 5); Hebrew *daber*—Rapidly spreading infectious disease; plague.

D. Meat (v. 17); Hebrew *okel*—Food.

E. Hinds (v. 19); Hebrew *ayalah* (**ah-yaw-law**)—A female deer.

2. Teacher Preparation

A. Read the entire Book of Habakkuk. It is short and will take you less than thirty minutes.

B. Read today's FOCAL VERSES and the background Scriptures.

3. Starting the Lesson

A. Begin the class with prayer. Thank God for allowing and inviting our questions in prayer and ask that we listen attentively to His answers.

B. Ask a volunteer to read the KEEP IN MIND Scripture aloud.

4. Getting into the Lesson

A. Read the LESSON AIM.

B. Have students review the cycle of sin, repentance, revival, and reformation that characterized Judah during this period. Ask them to give specific examples.

C. Have volunteers read the FOCAL VERSES.

5. Relating the Lesson to Life

A. Encourage students to share their last "crisis of faith" with one another. Discuss their problems with God and talk about how they reconciled their doubts and what they learned from their experiences.

B. Give the students an opportunity to answer the questions in the SEARCH THE SCRIPTURES section.

6. Arousing Action

A. Have students read the LESSON IN OUR SOCIETY section. Encourage a discussion by asking your students to explain what it means to "keep our eyes on Christ." What is the alternative? How will this help us to have deeper faith in Him?

B. Challenge the students to read the entire Book of Habakkuk.

C. Close the class with a prayer, using the KEEP IN MIND Scripture as the focus.

OCT 27TH

WORSHIP GUIDE

For the Superintendent or Teacher
Theme: Living in Faith
Theme Song: "Great Is Thy Faithfulness"
Scripture: Hebrews 12:2
Song: "Hold to God's Unchanging Hand"
Meditation: Dear Lord, help us to grow in righteousness and live in faith, that we may say "no" to everything that stands in the way of saying "yes" to You. Amen.

LIVING IN FAITH

Bible Background • HABAKKUK
Printed Text • HABAKKUK 3:2-6, 17-19
Devotional Reading • HEBREWS 11:32—12:2

LESSON AIM

After studying today's lesson, students should understand that the question of why God allows certain things to happen is a universal one. Like Habakkuk, we too must recognize that there are times when we just cannot understand how God is moving. We will learn that the character of God dictates that unrighteousness will not go forever unpunished, nor charity unrewarded.

KEEP IN MIND

"O LORD, I have heard thy speech, and was afraid: O LORD, revive thy work in the midst of the years, in the midst of the years make known; in wrath remember mercy" (Habakkuk 3:2).

FOCAL VERSES

Habakkuk 3:2 O LORD, I have heard thy speech, and was afraid: O LORD, revive thy work in the midst of the years, in the midst of the years make known; in wrath remember mercy.

3 God came from Teman, and the Holy One from mount Paran. Selah. His glory covered the heavens, and the earth was full of his praise.

4 And his brightness was as the light; he had horns coming out of his hand: and there was the hiding of his power.

5 Before him went the pestilence, and burning coals went forth at his feet.

6 He stood, and measured the earth: he beheld, and drove asunder the nations; and the everlasting mountains were scattered, the perpetual hills did bow: his ways are everlasting.

LESSON OVERVIEW

LESSON AIM
KEEP IN MIND
FOCAL VERSES
IN FOCUS
THE PEOPLE, PLACES,
AND TIMES
BACKGROUND
AT-A-GLANCE
IN DEPTH
SEARCH THE SCRIPTURES
DISCUSS THE MEANING
LESSON IN OUR SOCIETY
MAKE IT HAPPEN
FOLLOW THE SPIRIT
REMEMBER YOUR THOUGHTS
MORE LIGHT ON THE TEXT
DAILY BIBLE READINGS

3:17 Although the fig tree shall not blossom, neither shall fruit be in the vines; the labour of the olive shall fail, and the fields shall yield no meat; the flock shall be cut off from the fold, and there shall be no herd in the stalls:

18 Yet I will rejoice in the LORD, I will joy in the God of my salvation.

19 The LORD God is my strength, and he will make my feet like hinds' feet, and he will make me to walk upon mine high places. To the chief singer on my stringed instruments.

IN FOCUS

Terri struggled to keep her car on the road as she sped home from the office. After 13 years with the school district, the administrators had decided to eliminate her position. As she drove, Terri thought bitterly of the hundreds of hours of overtime she had worked and never charged the district for. Her reports were always well prepared and on time. Her supervisors always praised her for her efforts, and she had been named "Employee of the Year" five times.

The worst cut was that Lauren and Crystal were remaining. Neither of those women had been with the district more than four years. Lauren rarely reported to work on time and frequently left early. The reports prepared by Crystal were sloppy and often contained wrong information. Terri had to cover for both of these women countless times, yet the district chose to cut her job. It just didn't seem fair! Since her husband's death three years ago, Terri was the sole supporter of her three sons. How would she make the payments on the house? How soon could she find another job? Terri began crying and wondering why God would allow her efforts to end so terribly.

THE PEOPLE, PLACES, AND TIMES

Habakkuk, the prophet. Other than his writings, we have very little reliable information about Habakkuk. Unlike other prophets, we don't know his father's name or what city he is from. We do know that Habakkuk lived in Judah. To determine the time that he lived and the date for his writings, we must consider that for Habakkuk, the Babylonian overthrow of the Assyrians was in the past and the Babylonian invasion of Judah was in the future. Given the bleak picture he paints of Judah, we can safely assume that Habakkuk probably lived during the period when King Jehoiakim was on the throne. He may have been a contemporary of the prophets Jeremiah and Zephaniah. Because the book ends with what appears to be a note: "To the chief singer on my stringed instruments," many scholars believe that Habakkuk may have been a member of the Levitical choir. His small book is only three chapters long, yet two of the most famous verses in Scripture come from him: "The just shall live by . . . faith," and "the LORD is in his holy temple: let all the earth keep silence."

Based on information from Baker Theological Dictionary of the Bible, Walter A. Elwell, editor (Grand Rapids: Baker Book House, 1996), pp. 320-321.

BACKGROUND

The Prophet Habakkuk was greatly disturbed at the condition of Judah. All around he saw the people living in wickedness and the violence and oppression that permeated the land. Her wicked sister, Israel, has been invaded and the people carted away, and Judah is little better morally. Judah's constant state of debauchery, combined with God's apparent indifference, worries the prophet. Habakkuk knew that God was just, and yet there was injustice all around him. He struggled to reconcile what he knew about God with what he saw going on around him. Because he was a man of God, Habakkuk took his problem directly to God in prayer. In the first chapter of the Book of Habakkuk, the prophet demands to know how long God will allow this sinful condition to go unchallenged. The

second chapter is God's response to Habakkuk. God responds to Habakkuk's accusation that He has remained silent by pointing out that Habakkuk has not known how to recognize His answers. God's response has not come in the way that the prophet expected. God tells Habakkuk that He will use the Babylonians to punish Judah. God also tells Habakkuk to wait and see just what He would do. Habakkuk was astonished by God's response. Rather than a revival, the lawlessness of Judah would be dealt with through an invasion. Habakkuk wonders how God could afflict Judah by an even more evil nation. God assures Habakkuk that Babylon too would be punished. Our lesson focuses on Habakkuk's remarkable prayer when he finally recognizes that God is the author of all history and that He has everything under control. Habakkuk's faith rests in his remembering what God has done in the past and his conviction that God alone can be trusted with the future. Although his book begins in fear, it ends in a marvelous revelation of faith.

AT-A-GLANCE

1. Habakkuk Asks God to Respond to the Crisis (Habakkuk 3:2-3)
2. Habakkuk Describes the Impending Judgment (vv. 4-6)
3. Declaration of Praise in the Face of Destruction (vv. 17-18)
4. Recognition of God as Source of Strength and Comfort (v. 19)

IN DEPTH

1. Habakkuk Asks God to Respond to the Crisis (Habakkuk 3:2-3)

Although Habakkuk had begun his prayer by asking God to do something, now he appears to be asking Him not to do too much. Habakkuk appeals to God to remember mercy in His wrath. God has revealed His plan to the prophet, and the prophet is pleading on behalf of the people. He seems to ask that in the ensuing 70 years of captivity, God would succor His people and show them some compassion.

In prayer, Habakkuk remembers what God has

done in the past. Like Habakkuk, we do not live on blind faith. Rather, we live by faith in a God who has acted in time and space and recorded His will in the progress of all human events. It is God's past performance that convinces Habakkuk that he can continue to trust in God.

Habakkuk identifies God as the God of their fathers who gloriously appeared among his forefathers, full of works that affirmed that God is worthy of all praise. The dazzling light around God was as pure and clear as the sun itself. In other words, God's glory covered him completely. As dazzling as the light was, the prophet acknowledges that it hid more than it revealed. Here, we are reminded that the variety of God's workings is so infinite that our feeble human minds cannot begin to grasp it.

2. Habakkuk Describes the Impending Judgment (vv. 4-6)

Habakkuk remembers that God hid His awesome power, which flashed out in sudden acts of miraculous interventions such as the various plagues He leveled against Egypt. When God was leading the people out of Egyptian captivity, He made the pestilence go before Him to prepare room for the people. While these acts must have been terrifying to those who opposed the LORD, to those who loved Him, they were mighty acts of salvation. God had measured out the earth and lined up the nations of the world according to the way He gave the land to Abraham. Just by looking upon the lands with His frowning countenance, God cast out the people dwelling there and made way for His people.

3. Declaration of Praise in the Face of Destruction (vv. 17-18)

The prophet knew that the destruction of Judah was at hand, yet he finds comfort in recalling the mighty acts of God, perhaps believing that in the midst of the impending horror, the LORD would still save His chosen people. At the end of this book, the prophet begins to give his own personal experience by sharing his physical reaction to all of this. The prophet says that his heart trembled and his lips quivered upon hearing the impending desolation that God threatened against Judah. Habakkuk knew that when God moved in judgment against Judah, the people and the land itself would endure a diffi-

cult time. The prophet laments that there would come a time when there would be no fruit on the trees and the livestock would be gone. God's people, who had once been blessed with a land of milk and honey, would soon suffer starvation. In spite of this, Habakkuk has been strengthened and goes on to render a remarkable testimony of faith and confidence. He declares that "the LORD [Himself] is my strength." In spite of the situation, Habakkuk has recovered his confidence in God. He is now prepared to walk by faith. Habakkuk does not pray that the situation be changed.

4. Recognition of God as Source of Strength and Comfort (v. 19)

He is no longer worried about the situation because he knows that his salvation lies in the LORD. He declares that God will make his feet like those of a hind. This female deer is a slender, graceful creature, renowned for its swiftness and surefootedness, which enables it to escape from its enemies. Habakkuk uses this allusion to demonstrate how he and all the remaining faithful will be able to escape to the refuge of God. The faithful will not only survive the Babylonian disaster; they will overcome it triumphantly. Nothing has changed Habakkuk's situation. Judah is still sinful, and the Babylonians are still going to invade. The change is in Habakkuk! This book begins in the prophet's declaration of fear and ends in a declaration of faith in the nature and character of God. With God as the source of his strength and comfort, Habakkuk is now confident that he can rise above the challenge that faces him.

SEARCH THE SCRIPTURES

1. What was Habakkuk's initial reaction after hearing God's "speech"? (v. 2)

2. In the midst of God's wrath, what virtue did Habakkuk appeal to God to remember? (v. 2)

3. How extensive is the glory and praise of God as described by Habakkuk? (v .3)

4. What afflictions are described by the prophet? (v. 17)

5. How does the prophet declare he will respond in the face of these afflictions? (v. 20)

6. What confidence does the prophet express in the LORD God? (v. 21)

DISCUSS THE MEANING

1. After God revealed His plans to Habakkuk, the prophet said that he "was afraid." Why might he have felt this way, rather than being relieved that God was going to act?

2. Habakkuk declared that he would rejoice in God even though affliction may surround him. How do we respond to God in the midst of a crisis? What do these responses reveal about our level of faith in God?

3. Read Hebrews 10:35 and 12:2. How do faith and perseverance go hand-in-hand?

4. Based on his response in Chapter 3, what do we know of Habakkuk's character?

LESSON IN OUR SOCIETY

We too often forget that God did not promise us peace and prosperity in the days in which we live. He did, however, promise to remain a source of strength and comfort to us. Our inability to understand why God allows things to happen should not hinder our belief that it is He who stands behind all that happens. The creator of the universe knows and understands what we cannot comprehend. God has a divine plan and purpose for each of us—whether we recognize it or not. In the beginning of this book, Habakkuk wants to know why God is allowing such evil to go on in the land. He wants to know why God won't move to stop it. Today, we need only pick up a newspaper and we find ourselves asking the same questions. "Why won't God stop these terrible things?" It often appears to us that God is not moving. However, God brought Habakkuk to the watchtower and revealed that He was indeed moving, but not in the way the prophet expected.

The Apostle Paul provides us with a watchtower revelation when he writes: "And we know that all things work together for good to them that love God, to them who are called according to his purpose. For whom he did foreknow, he also did predestinate to be conformed to the image of his Son, that he might be the firstborn among many brethren" (Romans 8:28-29). In spite of everything going on around us, we must be mindful that it is God's desire that we become more like His Son. This confidence and trust in Christ is only available to us if we have complete faith in Him. It is only when we trust in Christ that He begins to work in us.

It does not matter what our problems are because God is always in control. This fact allows us to move from our fear to faithfulness and truly rejoice in the God of our salvation.

MAKE IT HAPPEN

"I will rejoice in . . . the God of my salvation." This particular verse should speak loudly and boldly to each of us. The God who saved our souls from destruction is the God who can be trusted in all things. Not only will God give His people the ability to face the challenges of life; He will also give us the power to rise above them. Make a list of the perplexing or troubling things in your life. How can you use Habakkuk's example as a model for expressing your faith in the Lord in spite of these situations?

FOLLOW THE SPIRIT

What God wants me to do:

_____

_____

REMEMBER YOUR THOUGHTS

Special insights you have learned:

_____

_____

MORE LIGHT ON THE TEXT

Habakkuk 3:2-6, 17-19

The first two chapters of the Book of Habakkuk contain a dialogue between the writer (Habakkuk) and God. In these chapters, the prophet expresses his concern over the oppression of the poor by the leaders and the deplorable situation in Israel. He asks why God allows the wicked to prosper. Upon receiving an answer from God, the prophet responds with a beautiful prayer (or psalm) of confession, expressing faith in the LORD God (Chapter 3).

Habakkuk 3:2 O LORD, I have heard thy speech, and was afraid: O LORD, revive thy work in the midst of the years, in the midst of the years make known; in wrath remember mercy.

Chapter 3 seems to be the prophet's personal meditation and intercession for his people; this can also be applied to the church. The prophet begins by expressing the marvelous works of the LORD in the past and pleads for His intervention in the present circumstances. Here, the prophet's confidence and assurance that God would answer him is anchored in God's previous acts of deliverance and providence. This confidence is expressed at the opening of this psalm: "O LORD, I have heard thy speech, and was afraid." The word translated "speech" (KJV) is the Hebrew word *shema`* (pronounced **sh'-MAH**), which means something heard (i.e., a sound, rumor, announcement, or report); it also can mean fame or tidings. The prophet, therefore, declares to the LORD reports of His fame; that is, what God had done in the past.

This report is probably more than an abstract rumor, but a tradition of recounting God's goodness had been started by his forefathers and passed down through the generations (see Psalm 44:1).

This report causes the prophet to be "afraid" (Hebrew *yare'*, pronounced **yah-RAY**). The word *yare'* means to fear, to revere, to cause astonishment and awe. The prophet confesses the awe and astonishment he felt when he heard of God's past deeds in Israel. Such a feeling of fear does not seem to be a one-time effect when hearing the story for the first time, but a continuous feeling of awe and reverence toward God whenever the prophet remembers His deeds. Such feeling arouses confidence and faith. Hence, he calls out in desperation, "O LORD, revive thy work in the midst of the years, in the midst of the years make known; in wrath remember mercy." The word "revive" is the Hebrew verb *chayah* (pronounced **kay-YAH**), which among other things means to restore to life or health, to quicken, repair, recover, and to renew.

To renew is used here in the sense of repeating and doing over again. With the parallelism, "in the midst of the years, in the midst of the years make known; in wrath remember mercy," the prophet calls on God to intervene in the present situation. These "years" refer to the years of God's wrath against the house of Israel as described in Chapters 1 and 2, which meant the present. With the phrase "in the midst of the years make known," the prophet seems to ask the LORD to bring about the revival in the present—probably during his own lifetime.

The prophet then calls on God to have "mercy" even though God is angry with His people. The word "mercy" comes from the Hebrew verb *racham* (**rah-KHAM**), which means to love, to love deeply, to be

compassionate, to have tender affection, to have compassion. The LORD promised Israel, "For a small moment have I forsaken thee; but with great mercies will I gather thee. In a little wrath I hid my face from thee for a moment; but with everlasting kindness will I have mercy on thee" (Isaiah 54:7-8). The psalmist says that God's mercy is eternal (Psalms 103:17; 106:1); it is boundless (Psalms 108:4; 119:64); it does not fail and is renewed daily (Lamentations 3:22-23).

3 God came from Teman, and the Holy One from mount Paran. Selah. His glory covered the heavens, and the earth was full of his praise.

In the third stanza of this poem, Habakkuk seems to define or expand the thoughts of verse 2 regarding the report that he heard about God's deeds in the past. Contrary to one view that the prophet (in verses 3-15) is relating a theophany (**thee-ah-feh-nee**), or his own experience of the manifestation of Deity, I believe that the prophet is speaking from the Exodus motif and other of God's subsequent miraculous interventions in Israel. He poetically celebrates God's greatness. The statement, "God came from Teman, and the Holy One from mount Paran" definitely refers to God leading the Children of Israel at Teman and Mount Paran. The word "Teman" literally means south and describes the area that encloses Mount Sinai, where Moses received the Ten Commandments.

The capital of Idumeans to the south of Canaan (Numbers 20:21; Jeremiah 49:7), Paran (cf. Genesis 21:21; Deuteronomy 33:2) is the wilderness area bounded on the north by Palestine, on the west by the wilderness of Etham, on the south by the desert of Sinai, and on the east by the valley of Arabah; the Exodus was through this area, and probably all eighteen stops were in this area. (From *The Online Bible Thayer's Greek Lexicon* and *Brown Driver & Briggs Hebrew Lexicon*, Copyright 1993, Woodside Bible Fellowship, Ontario, Canada. Licensed from the Institute for Creation Research.)

The prophet meditates on God's deliverance and His majestic revelation during the Exodus, especially at Mount Sinai. "His glory covered the heavens," and as a result the people bowed in worship and praise of Him. This speaks of the specific times during the wandering when the LORD manifested His

presence and His "glory" *howd* (**hode**) and splendor were felt all over the land (Exodus 24:17; 40:34), particularly when the Law was given: "there were thunders and lightnings, and a thick cloud upon the mount, and the voice of the trumpet exceeding loud; so that all the people that was in the camp trembled" (Exodus 19:16). As the glory of the lord "covered the heavens the heavens," the earth was filled with His "praise." The word "praise" used here is the Hebrew word *tehillah* (pronounced **teh-hil-LAH**), which also means a song or a hymn of praise, adoration, or thanksgiving (paid to God). It also speaks of the act of general or public praise of God's glory. When the Law was given, the people (at a distance) saw the fire on top of Mount Sinai and

praised God of Israel. The word *tehillah* also carries ideas of fame or glory. Hence, "praise, here, refers not to that which is uttered by earth's inhabitants, but rather to the excellence of God which deserves the praise of all creation" (from The *Wycliffe Bible Commentary*, Electronic Database. Copyright 1962 by Moody Press).

4 And his brightness was as the light; he had horns coming out of his hand: and there was the hiding of his power.

Still contemplating the majesty and greatness of God, Habakkuk declares, "His brightness was as the light; he had horns coming out of his hand." "Horns," or the Hebrew equivalent *qeren* (**KEH-ren**), are figuratively used here to represent power and strength. Therefore, this metaphor signifies the power and strength resident in the hands of God; these "horns" are symbols of power and authority, deliverance, and protection (Isaiah 59:1). The Book of 1 Chronicles asserts, "Both riches and honour come of thee, and thou reignest over all; and in thine hand is power and might; and in thine hand it is to make great, and to give strength unto all" (29:12). Hands and arms represented the strongest parts of a strong man, to execute deliverance as well as vengeance or judgment. The phrase "there was the hiding of his power" suggests that God manifests His power over His people but hides His power from the rest of the world. King David says, "He hath not dealt so with any nation: and as for his judgments, they have not known them" (Psalm 147:20).

5 Before him went the pestilence, and burning coals went forth at his feet. 6 He stood, and measured the earth: he beheld, and drove asunder the nations; and the everlasting mountains were scattered, the perpetual hills did bow: his ways are everlasting.

God's greatness and power are also manifested in His judgment against the nations. In verses 5 and 6, the prophet, reminiscing on God's power and majesty, recalls God's exhibition of His might in executing punishment on His enemies. He states, "Before him went the pestilence, and burning coals went forth at his feet," signifying God's command over all instruments of wrath. Here the various plagues with which God visited Egypt before the Exodus are called to mind. Habakkuk also recalls how God delivered the land of Canaan into the hand of his forefathers by driving the inhabitants out as He had promised them. He succinctly describes when God oversaw the dividing and distribution of the land among the Hebrews and supervised the overthrow of the inhabitants. To measure "the earth," or 'erets (**EH-rets**, i.e., land, country, ground) means that God mapped out the land and shared it among the people (see Deuteronomy 32:8).

Not only were the nations driven out, but "the everlasting mountains were scattered, the perpetual hills did bow." This synonymous parallelism further describes (figuratively expressed as mountains disintegrating and hills succumbing) the awesome great-

ness of God's power. The word "scattered" or the Hebrew verb puwts (**poots**) means to dash in pieces or to disperse; the word "bow" (shachach, **shah-KHAKH**) means to prostrate or be cast down. These speak expressly of God's omnipotence and control and authority over His creation. Contemplating the greatness and might of God, Isaiah declares, "Who hath measured the waters in the hollow of his hand, and meted out heaven with the span, and comprehended the dust of the earth in a measure, and weighed the mountains in scales, and the hills in a balance?" (40:12). God's omnipotence is further brought to bear in the use of two synonymous adjectives that describe the "mountains" and the "hills": "everlasting" ('ad) and "perpetual" ('owlam, pronounced **oh-LAHM**), which speak of permanency and age-enduring. These mountains and hills have had continuous existence, and yet at the watchful eyes of the LORD they crumble and give way. What do "mountains" and "hills" represent? They probably represent strength, false hope, and security, which the nations had before the LORD's intervention (driving the nations away) on behalf of Israel. Matthew Henry writes, ". . . the mighty princes and potentates of Canaan, that seemed as high, as strong, and as firmly fixed, as the mountains and hills, were broken to pieces; they and their kingdoms were totally subdued. Or the power of God was so exerted as to shake the mountains and hills; nay, and Sinai did tremble, and the adjacent hills." (From *Matthew Henry's Commentary on the Whole Bible: New Modern Edition,* Electronic Database. Copyright 1991 by Hendrickson Publishers, Inc.)

The phrase "his ways are everlasting" describes the sovereignty of God. That means God does what He pleases, His counsel is perfect, everlasting, and unchanging. He was in the beginning, He is the same now and will remain the same unto eternity. The psalmist says "As for God, his way is perfect: the word of the LORD is tried: he is a buckler to all those that trust in him" (Psalm 18:30); and "The LORD is righteous in all his ways, and holy in all his works" (145:17). His wisdom is perfect, superhuman (Isaiah 55:9), and His ways are right (Hosea 14:9). Paul exclaims: "O the depth of the riches both of the wisdom and knowledge of God! how unsearchable are his judgments, and his ways past finding out!" (Romans 11:33).

3:17 Although the fig tree shall not blossom, neither shall fruit be in the vines; the labour of the olive shall fail, and the fields shall yield no meat; the flock shall be cut off from the fold, and there shall be no herd in the stalls: 18 Yet I will rejoice in the LORD, I will joy in the God of my salvation.

In spite of the circumstances and difficulties (v. 16), Habakkuk expresses his confidence and faith in the LORD and declares his resolve to praise and worship the God of his fathers. Using the agricultural motif (vv. 17-18), the prophet strongly affirms his faith in the LORD and says that nothing will change his determination or affect his joy in the LORD. The preposition "although," from the Hebrew *kiy* (pronounced **kee**), indicates causal relations of all kinds and is widely used as a relative conjunction or adverb, with a variety of English translations (e.g., since, therefore, if, though, etc.). We can translate it as "even if" here. He says that even if there is a total agricultural failure and great famine in the land, probably caused by the enemy invasion (cf. Jeremiah 5:17) or crop failure as a result of divine judgment or natural disaster, his relationship with the LORD will not be altered. The mention of the fig tree, the vine, olive, farm produce, and the flocks and herds of animals covers the whole scope of agricultural produce, which formed the principal occupation of the people and upon which Israel depended. Such disaster, rather than driving the prophet to despair (see Joel 1:10-12), drives him to faith and trust. This faith is expressed in celebrating the LORD in triumph and rejoicing in the LORD his Savior. Similarly, Job is so confident and resolute about trusting and worshiping the LORD that he declares: "Though he slay me, yet will I trust in him: but I will maintain mine own ways before him" (Job 13:15). Even when everything fails, the prophet is confident that the LORD will not fail him. Why does the prophet express such confidence and faith?

19 The LORD God is my strength, and he will make my feet like hinds' feet, and he will make me to walk upon mine high places.

Habakkuk's confidence is based on his knowledge of and relationship with the LORD. The LORD is his "strength" on whom his faith is anchored even in the midst of troubles—an expression of security. This security is further expressed figuratively as "he will make my feet like hinds' feet." "Hinds' feet" or *'ayalah* (**ah-yah-LAH**) refers to the back feet of the deer, which represent strength and swiftness; they speak of his spiritual strength and faith to overcome all troubles and his ability to escape his pursuers. The LORD will also make him "to walk upon high places." In other words, he is so confident in the LORD that he feels as if he is "walking on air," and so surefooted that no height or trial will be able to daunt his faith in the LORD his Savior (see 2 Samuel 22:34; Psalm 18:33).

The psalmist says in Psalm 46:1-3 (NIV): "God is our refuge and strength, an ever-present help in trouble. Therefore we will not fear, though the earth give way and the mountains fall into the heart of the sea, though its waters roar and foam and the mountains quake with their surging."

The closing remark: "To the chief singer on my stringed instruments" signifies the type of music and its use in the community's worship. It is believed that this prayer was intended to be used by the "Levitical choirs, though the psalm, unlike some others which are found outside the collection, e.g., 2 Samuel 22:2ff., 1 Chronicles 16:8ff., was never put in the Book of Psalms." (From *The Wycliffe Bible Commentary*, Electronic Database. Copyright 1962 by Moody Press.)

DAILY BIBLE READINGS

M: I Stand in Awe
Habakkuk 3:2-6
T: The Lord Is My Strength
Habakkuk 3:8-19
W: My Heart Trusts in God
Psalm 28:1-9
T: I Will Trust in God
Isaiah 12:1-6
F: Trust in God
Isaiah 26:1-6
S: Acknowledge God's Plan
Isaiah 26:7-13
S: The Fight of Faith
1 Timothy 6:11-16

TEACHING TIPS

November 3
Bible Study Guide 10

1. Words You Should Know

A. Humble (2 Chronicles 36:12); Hebrew *kana*—To bend the knee or bring oneself down; to vanquish by submitting to a higher cause.

B. Mock (v. 16); Hebrew *laab*—To make fun of or mimic in sport; to ridicule.

C. Remedy (v. 16); Hebrew *marpe*—Something that corrects, counteracts, or cures.

D. Desolate (v. 21); Hebrew *shamen*—To stupefy; show the effects of abandonment and neglect.

2. Teacher Preparation

A. Read the FOCAL VERSES and the background Scripture to develop a better understanding of today's lesson.

B. Compare 2 Chronicles 36:11-21 with 2 Kings 24:8-24. Focus on how Zedekiah led the people of Judah through his example.

3. Starting the Lesson

Ask students to participate. Blindfold them, and allow one to lead the other. Tell the leaders to walk around the room for two minutes with a follower holding onto their waist. Then remove their blindfolds. Ask all students (participants and non-participants) to explain what they saw or experienced.

4. Getting into the Lesson

A. Make a list of the things Zedekiah did wrong as a leader. Discuss his actions with the students. Ask them what impact these things had on Zedekiah's followers.

B. Talk with the class about the action of the chief of the priests and the people.

C. Ask students if they feel that God's wrath was justified.

5. Relating the Lesson to Life

A. Read the IN FOCUS story about the Douglas family. Express the need for correct vision in the church today. Explain that correct vision can only come from God. Note that while Thomas had a vision, it was a blurred one and therefore incorrect.

B. Ask students if they believe their pastor has a vision. If so, ask them if they know that vision.

6. Arousing Action

A. Give each student a pencil and a sheet of paper and ask them to write down how they fit into the vision of their church.

B. Ask them to explain how their work in the church fits into the vision given by God.

C. Explain that every Christian has a gift to be used for the body of Christ (1 Corinthians 7:7), and that this gift should fit into the vision that God has given the pastor of the church. This exercise will allow them to see the importance of following the pastor as the pastor follows the vision of God for the church.

WORSHIP GUIDE

For the Superintendent or Teacher
Theme: The Fall of Jerusalem
Theme Song: "Have Thine Own Way, Lord"
Scripture: 2 Chronicles 36:11-21
Song: "I Have Decided To Follow Jesus"
Meditation: Thank You, Lord, for Your mercy which endures forever. Since Your ways are perfect, help us to accept Your chastening in time of discipline. Open our hearts to understand the benefits of your chastening, so we may learn from it. In Jesus' name we pray. Amen.

THE FALL OF JERUSALEM

Bible Background • 2 CHRONICLES 36:9-21; 2 KINGS 24:8-25; 26
Printed Text • 2 CHRONICLES 36:11-21
Devotional Reading • PSALM 75

LESSON AIM

After studying today's lesson, students should gain a greater desire to follow God's Word. Students should also have a better understanding of the role of a God-appointed leader and determine to follow such leaders as they follow Christ.

KEEP IN MIND

"And the LORD God of their fathers sent to them by his messengers, rising up betimes, and sending; because he had compassion on his people, and on his dwelling place: But they mocked the messengers of God, and despised his words, and misused his prophets, until the wrath of the LORD arose against his people, till there was no remedy" (2 Chronicles 36:15-16).

FOCAL VERSES

2 Chronicles 36:11 Zedekiah was one and twenty years old when he began to reign, and reigned eleven years in Jerusalem.

12 And he did that which was evil in the sight of the LORD his God, and humbled not himself before Jeremiah the prophet speaking from the mouth of the LORD.

13 And he also rebelled against King Nebuchadnezzar, who had made him swear by God: but he stiffened his neck, and hardened his heart from turning unto the LORD God of Israel.

14 Moreover all the chief of the priests, and the people, transgressed very much after all the abominations of the heathen; and polluted the house of the LORD, which he had hallowed in Jerusalem.

LESSON OVERVIEW

LESSON AIM
KEEP IN MIND
FOCAL VERSES
IN FOCUS
THE PEOPLE, PLACES,
AND TIMES
BACKGROUND
AT-A-GLANCE
IN DEPTH
SEARCH THE SCRIPTURES
DISCUSS THE MEANING
LESSON IN OUR SOCIETY
MAKE IT HAPPEN
FOLLOW THE SPIRIT
REMEMBER YOUR THOUGHTS
MORE LIGHT ON THE TEXT
DAILY BIBLE READINGS

15 And the LORD God of their fathers sent to them by his messengers, rising up betimes, and sending; because he had compassion on his people, and on his dwelling place:

16 But they mocked the messengers of God, and despised his words, and misused his prophets, until the wrath of the LORD arose against his people, till there was no remedy.

17 Therefore he brought upon them the king of the Chaldees, who slew their young men with the sword in the house of their sanctuary, and had no compassion upon young man or maiden, old man, or him that stooped for age: he gave them all into his hand.

18 And all the vessels of the house of God, great and small, and the treasures of the house of the LORD, and the treasures of the king, and of his princes; all these he brought to Babylon.

19 And they burnt the house of God, and brake down the wall of Jerusalem, and burnt all the palaces thereof with fire, and destroyed all the goodly vessels thereof.

20 And them that had escaped from the sword carried he away to Babylon; where they were servants to him and his sons until the reign of the kingdom of Persia:

21 To fulfil the word of the LORD by the mouth of Jeremiah, until the land had enjoyed her sabbaths: for as long as she lay desolate she kept sabbath, to fulfil threescore and ten years.

NOV
3RD

IN FOCUS

The Douglas family loaded their car for a trip to their annual family reunion. Thomas (the father), Brenda (his wife), and their three children (David, Brian, and Marcus) left for their seven-hour trip with great expectation. On previous trips, the children remembered certain landmarks; this time they wanted to take pictures of them. Three hours into the trip, Thomas pulled over to remove his contacts and rest his eyes. In the process, the wind blew dirt on the contacts, soiling them. When Thomas put his contacts on again, he noticed a little discomfort but believed it was minor. As they proceeded down the highway, Brenda began to take a nap. The children were busy taking pictures of the landmarks and the beautiful countryside.

Meanwhile, Thomas was having vision problems. As he looked at the exits, he mistook exit 73 for exit 78. Thirty-five minutes after taking the exit, David asked his father, "Dad, when are we going to pass the huge waterfall?" "In about twenty-five minutes," Thomas replied. Ten minutes later, David asked the same question. "In about fifteen minutes," Thomas replied. Ten minutes later, David and Brian asked the same question. "In five minutes," Thomas replied. After hearing this, Marcus set his stopwatch to a five-minute countdown. As the last five seconds ticked away, all the boys in the car gave their dad the countdown. "5, 4, 3, 2, 1, 0!" Brenda woke up. Then the boys explained that Marcus had set his stopwatch according to the time their father gave them. Still, they did not see the huge waterfall. Instead, they began to see things that they had never seen before on this trip.

The family asked Thomas if they were on the right course. He said "yes" and continued driving down the highway. Ten minutes later, Brenda took out the map and realized they were off course by 75 miles. She questioned Thomas about it, but he said they were on the right course and that he would pull over at the next gas station and ask the attendant to prove it. Three miles later, he pulled into the gas station and asked the clerk which way led to Saint Catherine's, Canada. She informed him to go back to the main expressway and take it to exit 78. She pointed out that after taking that exit they would soon see a waterfall. As Thomas walked back to the car, he realized

that his blurred vision had caused him to turn off at the wrong exit.

THE PEOPLE, PLACES, AND TIMES

Zedekiah, the last king of Judah. Zedekiah was the son of Josiah by his wife Hamutal, and therefore a brother of Jehoahaz. His name meant "Jehovah is righteous." He reigned in Jerusalem for eleven years. It was during his reign that Jerusalem fell. After rebelling against Nebuchadnezzar in the ninth year of his rule, Nebuchadnezzar (king of Babylon) seized Jerusalem. Zedekiah and his family were taken as prisoners. His sons were killed before his eyes, and then his eyes were gouged out. He was shackled with chains and taken to Babylon, where he died.

Based on information from The New Unger's Bible Dictionary, R. K. Harrison, editor (Chicago: Moody Press, 1988), pp. 1382-1383.

Babylon. An ancient city-state founded by Nimrod, son of Cush, in the plain of Shinar derived from *Hurrian papil*. Its name is derived from the Hebrew root word *balal* (pronounced **bah-LAHL**), which means to confound and has reference to the confusion of tongues at the Tower of Babel (Genesis 11:9). About 1830 B.C., the city began its rise to prominence. In the arising struggle with surrounding city-states, Babylon conquered Larsa, and the first dynasty of Babylon was established. The city of Babylon did not reach the height of its glory, however, until the reign of Nebuchadnezzar II (605-562 B.C.). Nebuchadnezzar made the city splendid. Among his contributions to the city was the temple of Bel. This consisted of a tower in the shape of a pyramid, more than eight stories high with a sanctuary on top.

Based on information from The New Unger's Bible Dictionary, R. K. Harrison, editor (Chicago: Moody Press, 1988), pp. 134-135.

BACKGROUND

After 100 days, Jehoiachin (king of Judah) was taken into custody by Nebuchadnezzar (king of Babylon). Jehoiachin was only 18 years old when he came to power. But he did evil in the eyes of the LORD. King Nebuchadnezzar captured approximately 1,700 Israelites, including Jehoiachin's mother, his servants, his wives, his officers, and his princes.

King Nebuchadnezzar left only the poorest people of Judah in the land. He also removed treasures from the temple of the LORD and from the royal palace. After cleaning house, Nebuchadnezzar appointed Mattaniah, Jehoiachin's uncle, as king of Judah. He also changed his name to Zedekiah, which means "Yahweh is righteous."

AT-A-GLANCE

1. Resisting God's Authority
(2 Chronicles 36:11-14)
2. Rejecting God's Love (vv. 15-16)
3. Receiving God's Discipline (vv. 17-21)

IN DEPTH

1. Resisting God's Authority
(2 Chronicles 36:11-14)

King Zedekiah was only 21 when he came to power. He was the king of Judah, which included the tribes of Judah and Benjamin (2 Chronicles 10-11). He reigned only 11 years because he resisted Jeremiah and King Nebuchadnezzar, God's authority. The Bible does not state all of the evil Zedekiah did in the LORD's sight, but it does declare that he did the same evil things Jehoiakim and his fathers had done (2 Kings 23:37; 24:19).

King Zedekiah resisted God's authority again when he failed to humble himself before the Prophet Jeremiah. Jeremiah was called by God to be a prophet unto the nations (Jeremiah 1:5). He was a man who was commanded by God to speak on God's behalf. Simply put, when Jeremiah spoke it was as if God was speaking. As a result, when Zedekiah did not humble himself before Jeremiah, he was refusing to humble himself before God. We, too, must remember to humble ourselves before those men and women whom God has placed in authority over us. If we fail to do so, we are rebelling against God, not man.

King Zedekiah continued to resist King Nebuchadnezzar by rebelling against him. By this time, God had delivered Judah into the hands of King Nebuchadnezzar (Daniel 1:1-2). So when Zedekiah rebelled, he really rebelled against God. We also must remember not to rebel against the gov-

erning authority God has placed over us. If we do, we are saying that we know how to work the Creator's plan better than He does.

It's also important to mention that although Zedekiah was a bad king, all the leaders, priests, and people followed him. We must be prayerful every day that God will grant us wisdom to follow our leaders only as they follow Christ. In today's society, it's easy to be led astray.

2. Rejecting God's Love (vv. 15-16)

In spite of Zedekiah's and the leaders' actions, God continued to extend His hand to His people. Through His messengers and prophets, God tried over and over to reach His people. In return, Judah began to ridicule and scoff at God by mocking His messengers and prophets.

It's vital that we see the transition that has taken place. Notice that King Zedekiah and the other leaders are not mentioned in these verses. At this point, the momentum has shifted from the leaders to the followers. The people are now carrying out the commands of their leaders. By following wrong leadership, they, too, are found to be in error in God's sight. The followers go so far overboard that God sends His wrath because there was no other cure for their actions.

Can you imagine that? It may seem hard to believe that someone's actions go so far overboard that God's wrath would serve as the only solution. To completely understand, we must look at God's plan for all mankind. God's Word declares that He wants none to be lost. However, the reality is that many will end up in eternal destruction. Those who are following the road to destruction are being led by Satan and his fallen angels. They will lead people to hell. Hell was created for Satan and his fallen angels. If we are led by Satan, we will end up at the same destination (hell). So it's important to understand that we must not reject God's love. We must remember who God is and how much He really loves us. In this text, even after Zedekiah and the leaders did wrong, God gave Judah the opportunity to choose Him and His ways. God is very personal, and He cares about us individually. Notice, He only sends His wrath after the people reject Him and choose to follow their wicked leaders.

3. Receiving God's Discipline (vv. 17-21)

After exhausting the remedies, God begins to discipline His children in Judah. He starts by allowing their enemy (king of the Chaldeans or Babylonians) to enter Jerusalem. As we look at verses 17 through 19, we see similarities between the actions of their enemy (the Chaldeans) and our enemy (Satan). In verse 17, their enemy kills their people and their seed. In verse 18, their enemy steals all of the vessels and treasures in the house of God. And in verse 19, their enemy destroys the house of God by burning it with fire and breaking down the wall of Jerusalem. In the same way, our enemy tries to defeat us. According to John 10:10, the thief (Satan) only comes to steal, kill, and destroy. Notice, these things happened only after Judah had totally rejected and refused God and His love. It is vital to understand that God's Word is true. He will chasten, correct, or rebuke us to His satisfaction. For Judah, this time was 70 years.

SEARCH THE SCRIPTURES

1. How old was Zedekiah when he became king? (v. 11)

2. How many years did he reign in Jerusalem (v. 11)

3. What prophet of God did Zedekiah refuse to humble himself before? (v. 12)

4. What king did Zedekiah rebel against? (v. 13)

5. What actions did all the chief priests and the people take? (v. 14)

6. Whom did the LORD send to Judah because of this compassion, and what was Judah's response? (v. 15-16).

7. What did the king of the Chaldeans do to Judah? (vv. 17-20)

8. For how long a period was Judah's desolation as prophesied by Jeremiah? (v. 21)

DISCUSS THE MEANING

1. King Zedekiah was only 21 years old when he became king of Judah. Do you think his youth posed a problem for him in following God? Why or why not?

2. What do you think the king of the Chaldeans was trying to accomplish when he burned the house of God and broke down the wall of Jerusalem?

3. Why do you think the chief priests and the people became unfaithful and did evil in the sight of the Lord?

LESSON IN OUR SOCIETY

The saying, ". . . the blind leading the blind" is a very popular one. It expresses the profound thought that a person who cannot see should not be guiding others who cannot see. When we analyze this saying, we discover how powerful and relevant the truth behind it really is.

The Bible states that "where there is no vision, the people perish" (Proverbs 29:18). Many Christians find it hard to believe that a group could follow a person who has no vision. While this may be true, it's only one aspect of this saying and this Scripture. On the other hand, it's easier to be deceived when the one leading has a vision. The problem is that this person's vision is just that—their vision and not God's.

In today's society, it's easy to get caught up in another person's vision. In some cases, it may be another religion or cult. On the other hand, it may be a leader preaching about another "Jesus." The Word of God warns us of this (2 Corinthians 11:4). As Christians we must understand that we possess the true Word of God in the Bible. And nothing or no one can ever successfully deny it.

MAKE IT HAPPEN

Think about how many sermons you've heard in your lifetime. How many of them have you followed to the letter? How many of them have helped to change your life for the better? Since faith comes by hearing, how many times do you think you have to hear each message before the truth begins to sink in? With this in mind, remember that every time God has allowed you to hear His messengers, He was showing compassion on you.

While many Christians hate to hear the same message over and over again, it sometimes takes longer for some of us to hear (or adhere to) the same word from God. This Sunday, share your testimony with some of your brothers and sisters in Christ and discuss how to activate the Sunday sermon in everyday life. The fewer times your pastor has to repeat his sermons, the more new material you'll go over.

FOLLOW THE SPIRIT

What God wants me to do:

_____

_____

REMEMBER YOUR THOUGHTS

Special insights you have learned:

_____

_____

MORE LIGHT ON THE TEXT

2 Chronicles 36:11-21

In this last chapter of 2 Chronicles, the author gives a brief summary account of the last four kings of Judah before the exile to Babylon. These kings, whose reigns were characterized as "evil" (see vv. 5, 9, 12), ruled during the most unstable and rebellious period in the history of Judah. The last of these kings who "did that which was evil in the sight of the LORD" and made the people to rebel against the LORD their God was Zedekiah. It was under this king that Judah was carried into captivity and Jerusalem destroyed.

36:11 Zedekiah was one and twenty years old when he began to reign, and reigned eleven years in Jerusalem.

Zedekiah came into power through the Babylonian policy. Nebuchadnezzar, the Babylonian king, removed Jehoiachin, Zedekiah's nephew, took him into captivity, and replaced him with Zedekiah as king in Judah (vv. 9, 10; for a detailed account read 2 Kings 24:8-20). Zedekiah started his reign at age 21 and ruled for 11 years before the fall of Jerusalem. Sin, disobedience, rebellion, and weakness marked his reign and ultimately led to his downfall, defeat, and the destruction of Jerusalem.

12 And he did that which was evil in the sight of the LORD his God, and humbled not himself before Jeremiah the prophet speaking from the mouth of the LORD.

Zedekiah's reign is characterized by "evil," for "he did that which was evil in the sight of the LORD his God," following in the footsteps of his predecessors. This clause puts him into the group of kings who were noted for their evil deeds and wicked reigns in the history of Israel. The word "evil" is the Hebrew noun *ra`* (pronounced **rah**), which means bad; It can

also be translated "wicked" and appears 17 times in this book.

The Chronicler records here (vv. 12-13) some of the sins of Zedekiah, which can be summed up by any one of the following words: rebellion, pride, and disobedience. First, he rebelled against Jeremiah because he "humbled not himself before Jeremiah the prophet speaking from the mouth of the LORD." This clause indicates not only that Zedekiah rebelled against Jeremiah and was disobedient to his words, but that his rebellion was precisely against the LORD his God, for Jeremiah was God's spokesman (cf. Jeremiah 27:1-18:17; 34:1-22; 37:1-38:28).

13 And he also rebelled against king Nebuchadnezzar, who had made him swear by God: but he stiffened his neck, and hardened his heart from turning unto the LORD God of Israel.

Not only is he rebellious against God; Zedekiah rebels "against king Nebuchadnezzar" by his unfaithfulness to an oath and covenant he made with the king. His rebellion is described metaphorically in the following phrases: "but he stiffened his neck" and he "hardened his heart from turning unto the LORD . . . ." The phrase "stiffened his neck" (Hebrew *qashah*, pronounced **kah-SHAH**) is synonymous with "hardened his heart" (Hebrew *`amats*, pronounced **aw-MAHTA**). Both words convey the idea of absolute stubbornness and rebellion—refusal to make a change or follow instruction (cf., Exodus 32:9; Deuteronomy 21:20; 1 Samuel 8:19; Jeremiah 32:33; 44:16; etc.). Even after warnings and advice from the prophets, including Jeremiah and perhaps Ezekiel (17:12-17), not to rebel against the king of Babylon or seek outside help from Egypt, Zedekiah "hardened his heart" and disobeyed the word of God.

14 Moreover all the chief of the priests, and the people, transgressed very much after all the abominations of the heathen; and polluted the house of the LORD which he had hallowed in Jerusalem.

It was not only King Zedekiah who was rebellious against God; the nation, including "all" the chief priests and "the people," rebelled against the LORD their God. There was total disobedience and anarchy against the will and ordinances of the LORD. No one was found doing good. The people's sin is described in two ways.

First, they "transgressed very much after all the abominations of the heathen," meaning that the whole nation sinned in the same way as the idolatrous nations, chiefly through apostasy and worship of other gods. They followed the way of the heathen nations by imitating their worship of idols. The word "heathen," or the Hebrew *gowy* (shortened **goy,** which means "nation"), is generally used for non-Hebrew people; it carries the notion of idolatrous nations who are without a relationship with the true and living God.

This act contradicts God's ordinance and warning

to the Children of Israel: "Take heed to thyself that thou be not snared by following them, after that they be destroyed from before thee; and that thou inquire not after their gods, saying, How did these nations serve their gods? even so will I do likewise" (Deuteronomy 12:30).

The second sin of the people, which is a consequence of the first, is that the people "polluted the house of the LORD, which he had hallowed in Jerusalem." To "pollute" here means to defile or dirty a place. Here it is the house of the LORD, the temple, which God hallowed or made holy (*qadash,* **kaw-**

DASH) in Jerusalem that is desecrated. How did the people desecrate the temple?

They probably brought in carved images and idols into the temple, worshiped and sacrificed to them, and did other evil practices (2 Chronicles 33:7; Jeremiah 7:30; Ezekiel 8:16; 44:7; cf. John 2:14). This act means total rejection of the sovereignty of the LORD their God. Jeremiah graphically describes this as he laments, "For my people have committed two evils; they have forsaken me the fountain of living waters, and hewed them out cisterns, broken cisterns, that can hold no water" (Jeremiah 2:13).

15 And the LORD God of their fathers sent to them by his messengers, rising up betimes, and sending; because he had compassion on his people, and on his dwelling place:

In spite of their rebellion, apostasy, and desecration of the temple, the LORD still loves them. He gives them chances to repent and come to back to Him. He sends to them messenger after messenger consistently warning and calling on them to repent from their evil ways. The LORD does this out of "compassion," not only for "His people," but also for His temple—His "dwelling place." The word "compassion" is from the Hebrew word *racham* (**rah-KAHM**), which means to be merciful or to have pity. The word can also be translated "loving-kindness," which is one of God's attributes. The word demonstrates the magnitude of God's patience and longsuffering toward those He loves.

16 But they mocked the messengers of God, and despised his words, and misused his prophets, until the wrath of the LORD arose against his people, till there was no remedy.

Rather than taking advantage of God's mercy and grace, the people continue to be stiff-necked and hardhearted like their king Zedekiah (see v. 13). They refused to listen to the messengers of God. Instead, they "mocked" them, "despised his word," and "misused the prophets." The word "mocked" (Hebrew *la`ab*, **lah-AHV**) means to make jokes about or to deride. To "despise," or its Hebrew equivalent *bazah* (**bah-ZAH**), is also used here. It means to hold in contempt, to disdain, or to disregard.

The people not only disregarded and made jokes about the messengers and their messages (which

means they disregarded God and His words), but they also "misused" the prophets. The word "misuse" is the Hebrew word *ta`a`* (pronounced **tah-AH**), which is synonymous with mocking, but also has the idea of being mistreated, including persecution, physical torture, and imprisonment (2 Chronicles 16:10; 24:21; cf. 1 Kings 19:2; 22:27; Jeremiah 20:2; 32:2; Daniel 3:20). Their continued resistance and rejection required that God execute justice and carry out His punishment of Israel.

It should be noted at this point that the prophets and messengers in these three verses refer to events both before and during the time of Zedekiah and the generation before the fall and exile. Likewise the priests, people, and their sin described in these verses refer to the different generations of Israel, with particular reference to Judah and Jerusalem.

Therefore, it includes the culmination of sin, the desolation of the temple, disobedience, and the rejection of God's words through the messengers, and the mockery, scoffing, and mistreatment of the prophets through many generations. Their behavior "broke the camel's back," and "there was no remedy." The word "remedy," or in Hebrew, *marpe`* (pronounced **marr-PAY**), is used figuratively here and refers to cure or healing. The people had become so callous and "thick-skinned" in their evil that they were beyond repentance. That left God with no other choice than to mete out to them their due punishment.

17 Therefore he brought upon them the king of the Chaldees, who slew their young men with the sword in the house of their sanctuary, and had no compassion upon young man or maiden, old man, or him that stooped for age: he gave them all into his hand.

God's method of punishment was to use the king of the Chaldeans as an instrument to carry out His judgment against the people. Having been pushed to the limit, as it were, the LORD allowed the Babylonians (Chaldeans) to invade Judah and handed them over to their enemies.

The destruction was total. No one was spared—male and female, young and old. Not even the feeblest among them—"him that stooped for age"—was spared by the Babylonian invaders. They were slain with the sword "in the house of their sanctuary," or in Hebrew, *miqdash* (pronounced **mick-DAHSH**), i.e., the temple or the sacred place, which was supposed to be a safe hiding place for them. They could not get protection from the LORD because they had polluted and desecrated the temple. Therefore, God was no longer present with them.

18 And all the vessels of the house of God, great and small, and the treasures of the house of the LORD, and the treasures of the king, and of his princes; all these he brought to Babylon. 19 And they burnt the house of God, and brake down the wall of Jerusalem, and burnt all the palaces thereof with fire, and destroyed all the goodly vessels thereof.

The destruction of Judah was complete. It not only included human life (of all ages and gender), but Babylonian invaders also destroyed the temple. All the furnishings, including all the vessels and the treasures of the temple, were taken. The king's and princes' treasures were all carried away to Babylon. Whatever was left of the temple ("the house of God"), they burned. They broke down the fortified walls of Jerusalem; all the king's palaces and all the "goodly" or treasured (expensive) vessels were also destroyed and burned with fire. This is a fulfillment of God's warning to Solomon at the dedication of the temple (see 1 Kings 9, especially vv. 6-9).

20 And them that had escaped from the sword carried he away to Babylon; where they were servants to him and his sons until the reign of the kingdom of Persia: 21 To fulfil the word of the LORD by the mouth of Jeremiah, until the land had enjoyed her sabbaths: for as long as she lay desolate she kept sabbath, to fulfil threescore and ten years.

Although the destruction was total, there were some who survived and escaped death. They were carried away into exile in Babylon and became slaves to the king of Babylon and his sons until Persia came to power. According to Jeremiah's account of this event, a total of about 4,600 people were carried away into Babylonian captivity (Jeremiah 52:28-30), leaving the land of Judah uninhabited and fallow for 70 years. The mention of "the reign of the kingdom of Persia" in verse 20 and the content of verse 21 give a ray of hope and prepare the way for the Book of Ezra. The account here gives

us optimism that there is a brighter future for Judah after the gloomy news.

Historically, it is believed that the destruction of the temple took place around 587-586 B.C. and that it was restored around 516-515 B.C. This represents 70 years of Sabbath (rest) during which the land remained deserted. Theologically, the Sabbath rest alludes to the Levitical law, which allows the land to lie fallow and rest for seven years for purification and enrichment (Leviticus 26:34-35).

In the same way, the exile is used as a time when the land would have its rest and a time of purification for the people. This fulfills "the word of the LORD by the mouth of Jeremiah": "And this whole land shall be a desolation, and an astonishment; and these nations shall serve the king of Babylon seventy years" (Jeremiah 25:11). Also, "after seventy years be accomplished at Babylon I will visit you, and perform my good word toward you, in causing you to return to this place" (Jeremiah 29:10; cf. Daniel 9:2). By referring to Jeremiah's words here, the Chronicler demonstrates God's faithfulness as a just and loving God, full of love and compassion (Psalm 30:5).

DAILY BIBLE READINGS

M: No Remedy
2 Chronicles 36:9-16
T: Jerusalem Falls
2 Chronicles 36:17-21
W: Weeping over Jerusalem
Psalm 137:1-6
T: How Long, O Lord?
Psalm 79:5-13
F: Will the Lord Keep Silent?
Isaiah 64:6-12
S: Daniel's Prayer
Daniel 9:1-10
S: O Lord, Forgive
Daniel 9:11-19

TEACHING TIPS

November 10
Bible Study Guide 11

1. Words You Should Know

A. Lord (Lamentations 1:12); Hebrew *Yahweh*—Usually read as *Adonai*—God.

B. Afflicted (v. 12); Hebrew *yaga*—To cause grief.

C. Comfort (v. 21); Hebrew *Nacham* (**naw kham**)—Literally, to breathe strongly as after a long race. Also means pity, or to console.

2. Teacher Preparation

A. Ask God to give you an understanding of His Word to direct you in presenting the leson to the class.

B. During your personal devotions, meditate on the Devotional Scripture in Psalm 42:5-11.

C. Read the entire Book of Lamentations to equip you with the background for today's lesson. Focus on the highs and lows of the writer. Think about how you can best explain them to the class.

3. Starting the Lesson

A. Have students write down one thing they've blamed God for.

B. Ask students to consider why they assign blame to God for their circumstances. Explain to them that God does not always prevent unfortunate events to occur in life and we must own up to our misdeeds.

C. Encourage them to begin examining their situations more closely and discover where they themselves may have taken a wrong turn or made a bad decision.

4. Getting into the Lesson

A. Make a list of some of the things for which the writer blames God.

B. Ask students to compare their one thing to the writer's many. Discuss any commonalities they may find.

5. Relating the Lesson to Life

A. Give students an opportunity to answer the questions in the SEARCH THE SCRIPTURES and DISCUSS THE MEANING sections.

B. Ask two volunteers to each read a portion of the LESSON IN OUR SOCIETY. Ask students if they have ever used the famous line, "the devil made me do it." If so, in what case?

6. Arousing Action

A. Challenge students to remember not to blame God for any evil, wicked, unfavorable, or unfortunate things that may have occurred in their lives.

B. Give students an opportunity to reflect on any insights they may have gained and to complete the FOLLOW THE SPIRIT and REMEMBER YOUR THOUGHTS sections.

WORSHIP GUIDE

For the Superintendent or Teacher
Theme: Grief and Hope
Theme Song: "Amazing Grace"
**Scripture: Lamentations 1:12-16;
3:22-24, 31-33**
Song: "Wonderful Grace of Jesus"
**Meditation: O Lord, how excellent are
Your mercies. Thank You for allowing
Your mercies to far exceed our expecta-
tions. In times of need, your mercies
have found us over and again. Lord,
You have proven to be constant in
spite of our sinful ways. At this time,
we pray for ourselves and all who seek
Your mercy. May we all find and under-
stand the height, depth, and volume of
Your love through Your mercy. In Jesus'
name we pray. Amen.**

NOV 10TH

GRIEF AND HOPE

Bible Background • LAMENTATIONS
Printed Text • LAMENTATIONS 1:12-16; 3:22-24, 31-33
Devotional Reading • PSALM 42:5-11

LESSON AIM

By the end of this lesson, students will know the content of Jeremiah's lamentation and grasp the consequence of Israel's action. Students will also learn to act in a way that pleases God, realizing that God's plan is always for our good.

KEEP IN MIND

"It is of the LORD's mercies that we are not consumed, because his compassions fail not. They are new every morning: great is thy faithfulness" (Lamentations 3:22-23).

FOCAL VERSES

Lamentations 1:12 Is it nothing to you, all ye that pass by? behold, and see if there be any sorrow like unto my sorrow, which is done unto me, wherewith the lord hath afflicted me in the day of his fierce anger.

13 From above hath he sent fire into my bones, and it prevaileth against them: he hath spread a net for my feet, he hath turned me back: he hath made me desolate and faint all the day.

14 The yoke of my transgressions is bound by his hand: they are wreathed, and come up upon my neck: he hath made my strength to fall, the lord hath delivered me into their hands, from whom I am not able to rise up.

15 The LORD hath trodden under foot all my mighty men in the midst of me: he hath called an assembly against me to crush my young men: the LORD hath trodden the virgin, the daughter of Judah, as in a winepress.

16 For these things I weep; mine eye, mine eye

LESSON OVERVIEW

LESSON AIM
KEEP IN MIND
FOCAL VERSES
IN FOCUS
THE PEOPLE, PLACES,
AND TIMES
BACKGROUND
AT-A-GLANCE
IN DEPTH
SEARCH THE SCRIPTURES
DISCUSS THE MEANING
LESSON IN OUR SOCIETY
MAKE IT HAPPEN
FOLLOW THE SPIRIT
REMEMBER YOUR THOUGHTS
MORE LIGHT ON THE TEXT
DAILY BIBLE READINGS

runneth down with water, because the comforter that should relieve my soul is far from me: my children are desolate, because the enemy prevailed.

3:22 It is of the lord's mercies that we are not consumed, because his compassions fail not.

23 They are new every morning: great is thy faithfulness.

24 The lord is my portion, saith my soul; therefore will I hope in him.

3:31 For the LORD will not cast off for ever:

32 But though he cause grief, yet will he have compassion according to the multitude of his mercies.

33 For he doth not afflict willingly nor grieve the children of men.

IN FOCUS

Michael is a fourth-generation diabetic. He is also a computer guru. When asked by Benita what contributed to his diabetes, his reply was, "my parents." Michael also said that there was no cure for what his parents had done to him. Michael believes that his parents were completely to blame for his illness.

Benita then asks, "What are you doing to treat your diabetes?" "Nothing," he replied. "Many diabetics with proper treatment live normal lives for many years." "Well, my parents only lived to their mid-40's and I'm 39, so I have only a few years left before my time is up." "Michael, that sounds like a sorry and pitiful excuse; you need to look at this diabetes website," said Benita. "It will explain to you your options for treatments and how you should take better care of yourself." Reluctantly, Michael looked up the website and found out he had many alternatives.

THE PEOPLE, PLACES, AND TIMES

Yoke. A yoke is any frame connecting two other parts, such as a frame fitted to the neck and shoulders of a person for carrying a pair of pails or baskets. A yoke is often referred to as a wooden frame that fastens two oxen together to pull a plow. The yoke served as a guide for the animals to follow. Wherever the yoke turned, the animals would follow it. In biblical times, the word "yoke" referred to a burden. In many passages of Scripture, a yoke was described as a problem—whether physical, mental, emotional, or spiritual. Since the primary function of a yoke was to guide, many believed that when someone had a yoke (or burden), they were being led by it and not by God.

Based on information from The World Book Dictionary, Clarence L. Barnhart & Robert K. Barnhart, general editors (Chicago: William H. Nault Publishers, 1985), p. 2421.

The word "LORD" is the Hebrew word, "Yahweh," which is written in all upper case letters or capitals. The true pronunciation of this name, by which God was known to the Hebrews, has almost been lost. The Jews themselves scrupulously avoided every mention of it and substituted in its stead another Hebrew word, usually the name *Adonai.* They continue to write *YHWH,* but it is read aloud as *Adonai.*

Based on information from The New Unger's Bible Dictionary, R. K. Harrison, editor (Chicago: Moody Press, 1988), p. 781.

BACKGROUND

The Book of Lamentations is a very intriguing one. It emphasizes the grief and hope of God's people. The book starts with a picture of Judah in desolation, and the unknown speaker begins to wail with sorrow (many Bible scholars believe Jeremiah is the author). The events that have led up to this desolation can be summed up in Judah's evil practices. At this point, Judah has followed evil kings, bad priests, and false prophets.

They have also ridiculed and mocked the real messengers and prophets of God.

In this desolation, they have fallen prey to their enemies. To add to this misery, they have begun to fault God for their present state or condition. They have begun to focus more on their many problems and not on their one solution (God).

AT-A-GLANCE

1. Blaming God (Lamentations 1:12-16)
2. A Ray of Hope (3:22-24)
3. Everlasting Love (vv. 31-33)

IN DEPTH

1. Blaming God (Lamentations 1:12-16)

The speaker in this text is not identified, but through his wailing and grief we become aware of his serious, sincere, and honest heart for Judah. He begins to see the problems in Judah and starts to focus on the only one who can deliver him— God. However, when he looks at the deliverer and addresses Him, he does not look for deliverance alone; he also blames Him (God) for Judah's present state. The speaker begins a "woe is me" campaign. He believes that his sufferings are different from everyone else's. He assumes this because he believes his sufferings were afflicted by the LORD, not by a lord. You see, this devout Israelite knows the difference between the two. He believes Yahweh God has afflicted him—not some mere lord, king, or human master of man.

The speaker (Jeremiah?) goes on to count the ways he feels that God has betrayed him or left him to die. He not only faults God, but he also begins to count God's (supposed) faults. He pinpoints the origin of the problem with God when he states in verse 13, "From above had he sent fire into my bones." He points out how he feels God has had a hand in this whole scenario when he states in verse 14 that God has bound his transgressions and delivered him into the hands of his enemies. He continues to "count" by stating that God trampled the daughter of Judah.

2. A Ray of Hope (3:22-24)

After the pity party, the speaker begins to

remember his afflictions in a helpful way. As he begins to remember, a ray of hope develops (v. 21). At this point, he begins to see a glimpse of how God's plan works. In spite of the circumstances, he sees God's great love reaching out to him and to all of Judah. He sees that God's mercies held back all that Judah deserved for their disobedience. His total outlook begins to change. He begins to express who God is to him instead of what (he feels) God has done to him. He also begins to express patience with God.

Oftentimes God's mercies protect us from ourselves. God's mercies are not like man's—they never end. His mercies are so powerful that they keep us from judgment. His mercies are also so numerous that they will endure forever (Psalm 118:29). In addition to His mercies, God is faithful. That simply means you can count on Him over and over again. After realizing this, the speaker begins to speak to himself in verse 24. Sometimes we must encourage ourselves like King David did (1 Samuel 30:6).

3. Everlasting Love (vv. 31-33)

According to Psalm 118:29, God's mercy endures forever. If this is true, it is impossible for God to forever cast off or throw away His children. Those who truly belong to Him cannot be plucked out of His hand (John 10:28). Although in the beginning it sounds as though God had abandoned him, through their relationship God was able to give him correction and revelation. He understands that God is in control of everything. God brings blessings and allows calamities. It's just that simple, because He alone is God.

The speaker also realizes that God does not willingly allow afflictions. He is a wise and loving God who gives us trials to build our faith. Just as a plant needs water and sun to grow, we too need a mixture of both joy and pain to become all He has predestined us to be. We must keep in mind that God's love for us is an everlasting love. He made provisions through Jesus to save you so you could be with Him forever. Remember that a person who wants to be with you forever does nothing to jeopardize your staying with Him forever.

SEARCH THE SCRIPTURES

1. What did the speaker claim he had like no one else? (v. 12)

2. Who did the speaker claim had afflicted him? (v. 12)

3. According to the speaker, where did the fire in his bones come from? (v. 13)

4. According to the speaker, what did the LORD use to bind the yoke of his transgressions on his neck? (v. 14)

5. Why did the speaker's eyes run with water? (v. 16)

6. Why are we not consumed? (v. 22)

7. What did the speaker's soul say? (v. 24)

8. Can the LORD cast off forever? (v. 31)

9. How many mercies does the LORD have? (v. 32)

10. Does the LORD bring affliction willingly? (v. 33)

DISCUSS THE MEANING

1. Why do you think the speaker blamed God for Judah's present state? Have you ever blamed God for things that have happened in your life? If so, what things? Do you still hold God accountable? If so, why? If not, how did you resolve the issue?

2. Do you believe that God has a mercy for everything you do wrong? Can you support your answer with Scripture? How can you apply this truth to your life?

LESSON IN OUR SOCIETY

During the 1970's, a talented and funny comedian named Flip Wilson emerged into the spotlight. He portrayed a character named Geraldine on the show. To portray Geraldine, Wilson had to dress like a woman, talk like a woman, and act like a woman. The television comedy was a big hit. It made people all across the world laugh.

Wilson, who was a longtime stand-up comedian, found a niche on "The Flip Wilson Show." He would do bad things on the show and blame it on the devil. His famous line was, "the devil made me do it." It seems no matter what he did, he faulted the devil. His philosophy was simple; since the devil is the source of all badness, he must have had a hand in what was done.

Millions of fans adopted the line. To Wilson, it was a show. To the fans, it was a scapegoat. The fans' focus was on how they could get out of what they had done.

In this present age, some songs have carried this concept as a hook line or chorus line. The use of this line allows the participants (in these acts) to blame the devil for their actions.

However, Christians must accept the responsibility and consequences for our actions. We cannot blame the devil or anyone else for our actions. We must stand firm on God's Word. We need to really embrace Galatians 6:7, " . . . for whatsoever a man soweth, that shall he also reap."

MAKE IT HAPPEN

No one can ever know all of God's plan. He has assigned us a lifetime to unfold it to us and through us. Along the way, we may experience injustices, trials, and catastrophes that our logic cannot comprehend or understand. But as time goes on, God will begin to unfold the reasons these things occurred in our lives. Can you think of anything that God allowed to happen, but you doubted it in the beginning? What was it? How long did it take you to realize God was still in control? Can you share this thing with another believer to help strengthen his or her walk with God?

FOLLOW THE SPIRIT

What God wants me to do:

_____

_____

REMEMBER YOUR THOUGHTS

Special insights you have learned:

_____

_____

MORE LIGHT ON THE TEXT

Lamentations 1:12-16; 3:22-24, 31-33

The Book of Lamentations has been described by some scholars as the "political funeral song" for the people of Israel, particularly Judah and Jerusalem. The book depicts Jerusalem as a woman in grief, bereaved of her children and husband, one upon whom the wrath of God descended because of her transgression. The

writer describes this grief in poetic form using various imagery to capture the seriousness and awfulness of this agony. Apart from expressing grief, the book serves as confession and penitence for her sin. The overriding theme in this book of lament, however, is the expression of hope and assurance that God will rescue her. Jeremiah is generally accepted as the author of the book, mourning over the destruction and captivity of Judah and Jerusalem during their exile to Babylon (cf. 2 Kings 25:8-12).

1:12 Is it nothing to you, all ye that pass by? behold, and see if there be any sorrow like unto my sorrow, which is done unto me, wherewith the LORD hath afflicted me in the day of his fierce anger.

In the first 11 verses, the writer depicts the city of God mourning over the horrible and desolate situation she finds herself in, with no comforter in sight. However, she realizes that her suffering was a consequence of her sin and a judgment from the LORD. In verse 12, she calls on passers-by to see the magnitude of her sorrow. The opening question of this verse, "Is it nothing to you, all ye that pass by?' is rhetorical and has the idea of soliciting sympathy from the people around. Who are the "all that pass by"? They certainly are her enemies among whom she now dwells, those who carried her into captivity, those who also would mock her (Lamentations 2:15). Of course, they show her no sympathy or comfort, but rather annihilate and enslave her. She has no place to turn other than to call on their conscience and sympathy. She calls on them to appreciate the degree of her sorrow—to look and consider if there is any sorrow as severe as what she is going through. This is typical of anyone in trouble, "there is no trouble like mine." This trouble is, however, an "affliction" from the LORD, His retribution against His people "in the day of his fierce anger." The word "fierce" is the Hebrew word *charown* (pronounced **khaw-RONE'**), which means burning anger or sore displeasure. It is usually used of God. God's burning anger is figuratively described in verse 13 as fire from above "into my bones." This figure of "fire" shut into one's bones is also found in Jeremiah 20:9. It

describes the plight of Jerusalem personified as an individual. The phrase "in the day of his anger" refers to the event that brought about the awful situation.

13 From above hath he sent fire into my bones, and it prevaileth against them: he hath spread a net for my feet, he hath turned me back: he hath made me desolate and faint all the day.

Verse 13 describes God's wrath as "fire" sent into her bones, and "it" (i.e., the fire) has prevailed against them (the bones). To "prevail" (Hebrew *radah*, pronounced **rah-DAH**) means to dominate. Like fire, God's anger is felt all over her and consumes her being. Zion's problem is further described as a net or trap that has been spread on her way to ensnare her. The imagery of God setting a net or trap for men as a form of chastisement is common in the Old Testament (Jeremiah 50:24; Ezekiel 12:13; 17:20; 32:3; Hosea 7:12). The phrase "he hath turned me back" follows naturally the theme of the trap, which sug-

gests being trapped with no way of escape. It also shows that God not only sets the traps, but also watches so that she would not wander away or escape. What we have here is a picture of a hunter who sets a trap for an animal and hides in a corner to watch for his prey so that it cannot escape when it is trapped by the net. Later the poet will describe Yahweh as a "lion or bear lying in wait for its prey" (cf. 3:10-11).

Not only is she trapped, but she also complains that God had made her "desolate and faint all the day." The word "desolate" is the Hebrew word *shamem* (pronounced **shah-MAIM**) and means ruined; the word translated "faint" is the Hebrew word *davah* (pronounced **dah-VAH**) and can also mean sick. The circumstances she finds herself in (the fire burning in the inner recesses of the city of Jerusalem, the trap or net that prevents anyone from escaping, and the idea of fainting) graphically paints a complete picture of a hopeless and demoralized community.

14 The yoke of my transgressions is bound by his hand: they are wreathed, and come up upon my neck: he hath made my strength to fall, the LORD hath delivered me into their hands, from whom I am not able to rise up.

The next verse (14) further describes God's anger and punishment against her (Judah) because of her transgression. This punishment is figuratively portrayed as a yoke of sin bound by God upon Judah, like the plowman binds the yoke upon the neck of a workhorse.

Here Judah feels her plight as a yoke that God has bound around her neck that compels her to bear the punishment of her sins. Judah's sins are like the cord that fastened the yoke to the neck so that it would not fall off or be shaken off. The yoke, so fastened, will diminish one's strength and cause one to faint and even fall under a heavy load. The clause, "the LORD hath delivered me into their hands, from whom I am not able to rise up" speaks further of the intensity of her punishment. The yoke is so heavy and the burden so difficult to bear that she falls and cannot rise up from its weight.

15 The LORD hath trodden under foot all my mighty men in the midst of me: he hath called an assembly against me to crush my young men: the LORD hath trodden the virgin, the daughter of Judah, as in a winepress.

Using an agricultural motif, the author presents how the LORD has used the enemies of Jerusalem (Judah) to destroy her and her people. The LORD, the author says, has "trodden under foot all my mighty men" around her. Like sheaves gathered in the middle of the threshing floor, the LORD has gathered all the mighty men, the virgins, and the daughters of Judah. He then calls on all their enemies, and they crush them; the LORD treads them as one treads the winepress. The people were not only trodden underfoot, but they were "crushed" (Hebrew *shabar,* **shah-VAHR**), i.e., broken or shattered into pieces and crippled. The imagery describes the seriousness of Judah's affliction and humiliation, which they ascribe to God as the perpetrator. The "wine-

press" is a graphic way of expressing how the resistance in Jerusalem is crushed, and how the blood of all defenders of the city, the "young men" and women (daughters of Judah), flows like grape juice out of the barrel.

16 For these things I weep; mine eye, mine eye runneth down with water, because the comforter that should relieve my soul is far from me: my children are desolate, because the enemy prevailed.

In verse 16, the writer gives the reason for Judah's weeping. The phrase "for these . . . I weep" refers to the affliction, punishment, and humiliation the nation is going through, and to the fact that she has no one to comfort her. Her tears are described as water running down her eyes, because "the comforter that should relieve my soul is far from me." Who is the comforter? Definitely the comforter is none other than the LORD Himself, who is also the One meting out the punishment being described here.

The only one who could console her and relieve her agony is far away from her. The word "comforter" is the Hebrew word *nacham* (pronounced **naw-KHAM**), which, among other things, means to console or to pity. Here she feels the absence of God, and consequently her children are left desolate because her enemies prevailed against her and her children. To the Christian, the greatest consolation is the Savior, but to Jerusalem the One who would console her is nowhere to be found in her time of desperation. He has deserted her. This is a picture of complete hopelessness; it makes her plight more distressing.

3:22 It is of the LORD's mercies that we are not consumed, because his compassions fail not. 23 They are new every morning: great is thy faithfulness. 24 The LORD is my portion, saith my soul; therefore will I hope in him.

In spite of all Judah's suffering, agony, and grief, the writer musters hope, reminds her of the immutability of God's character (v. 21), and thus declares the love, mercy, and faithfulness of God toward His people. Although the speaker finds herself in a very deplorable state, she is able to assert the LORD's character and compassion toward her. For it is through God's "mercies" she is still alive and "not consumed." The word translated "mercies" here is the Hebrew word *chesed* (pronounced **KHEH-sed**), which means steadfast love or loyal love. "Consumed" is the Hebrew word *tamam* (pronounced **tah-NAHM**), which means to be complete, finished, or exhausted.

Here the speaker recalls God's compassion which endures. God described Himself to Moses on Mount Sinai as "the LORD God, merciful and gracious, longsuffering, and abundant in goodness and truth" (Exodus 34:6). God's mercies and compassion, the writer asserts, are renewed daily (every morning), which speaks of God's consistency and faithfulness. Based on this assertion and truth, the poet claims the place of God's people and their relationship with God and claims God as their "portion" or "share."

This theme is found in God's allotment of the Promised Land to the Children of Israel. The LORD said that the land would be divided among all the inhabitants of Israel except the priests, to whom the LORD said, "I am your portion" (Numbers 18:20). To the priests, it meant that they would not own anything, but live off the offerings. However, this saying later became a statement of assertion and confidence that when everything else fails, the LORD remains faithful and trustworthy.

Hence, the psalmist declares, "My flesh and my heart may fail, but God is the strength of my heart and my portion forever" (Psalm 73:26, NASB; cf. 16:5; 119:57; 142:5). With this confidence, the writer resolves to hope in the LORD.

3:31 For the LORD will not cast off for ever: 32 But though he cause grief, yet will he have compassion according to the multitude of his mercies. 33 For he doth not afflict willingly nor grieve the children of men.

With this hope and brighter future, coupled with God's constancy in His steadfast love toward His people, and because God is Judah's (Jerusalem's) portion, the poet can confidently proclaim, "The LORD will not cast off for ever." To "cast off" (or the Hebrew *zanach,* pronounced **zah-NACH**) means to forcefully reject someone.

Although at the moment it seems that the people have been rejected by their God, the situation will not be perpetual or "for ever." God will show compassion. The psalmist says "For his anger endureth but a moment; in his favour is life: weeping may endure for a night, but joy cometh in the morning" (Psalm 30:5). The affliction that the people have been going through, although attributed to God, will ultimately pass away. Verse 33 asserts the truth that a father does not willingly afflict his children. While He chastens them, it is usually meant as a corrective measure to bring them back. God's purpose is not to grieve His people.

Even the affliction against Judah is not deliberate on God's part. It is not "from His heart," as the text literally says. For a child of God, it is important to remember that even in the midst of insurmountable circumstances, probably caused by personal sin and disobedience, there is hope, and one needs to trust God's unfailing covenant promises of steadfast love toward His own.

DAILY BIBLE READINGS

M: Comfort Is Far from Me
Lamentations 1:12-16
T: Great Is God's Faithfulness
Lamentations 3:19-24
W: God Will Have Compassion
Lamentations 3:25-33
T: Lift Hearts to Heaven
Lamentations 3:34-41
F: God Heard My Plea
Lamentations 3:49-57
S: Restore Us
Lamentations 5:15-22
S: Sow in Tears, Reap in Joy
Psalm 126:1-6

TEACHING TIPS

November 17
Bible Study Guide 12

1. Words You Should Know

A. Soul (Ezekiel 18:4) Hebrew *nephesh* (**nef-fesh**)—Life, personal desire, emotion; the inner being of a person.

B. Sinneth (v. 4); Hebrew *chata* (**khaw-taw**)—The act of sinning, forfeiting the right to cause harm, offend.

C. Repent (v. 30); Hebrew *shuwb*—To feel sorry for having done wrong; change of mind; to turn back or to weep in grief over an act.

D. Righteousness (v. 20)—The quality or condition of being right and just.

E. Wickedness (v. 20)—The quality of being wicked or a wicked thing or act.

2. Teacher Preparation

A. Pray to God to enlighten you with His word concerning this lesson.

B. Read the background Scriptures and the FOCAL VERSES. Focus on how God made a way of escape for Israel through His Word.

C. Think of as many old sayings, superstitions, or proverbs as you can. Then contrast them with God's Word to distinguish God's truth from man's thoughts.

3. Starting the Lesson

A. After students have named some family traditions, old sayings, or superstitions they believe are true, discuss how they line up with the Word of God.

B. Emphasize to the class that they must allow God's Word to supercede their belief in traditions, old sayings and superstitions.

4. Getting into the Lesson

A. Have volunteers read the Lesson Aim and the FOCAL VERSES.

B. Begin a discussion centered around the old proverb of Israel found in Ezekiel 18:2. Point out that this proverb was passed down from generation to generation.

C. Generate a discussion on how God desires man to live and how he has provided of way of escape from death. Therefore, it is invalid to blame God for our troubles; rather, we should look to God's Word to provide deliverance.

5. Relating the Lesson to Life

A. Read the LESSON IN OUR SOCIETY article. Its focus is relying on God and not on superstitions, old sayings, or traditional things. Summarize the lesson by stressing how God relates to their traditions, superstitions, and old sayings and how it is imperative that we relate to God's Word.

B. Give students an opportunity to answer the questions in the SEARCH THE SCRIPTURES section.

6. Arousing Action

A. Read MAKE IT HAPPEN and charge the class to search the Scriptures to determine whether what we believe really lines up with the Word of God.

B. Close the class with a prayer that includes the LESSON AIM.

WORSHIP GUIDE

For the Superintendent or Teacher
Theme: Who Is to Blame?
Theme Song: "Walk with Me"
Scripture: Ezekiel 18:1-4, 20-21, 25-32
Song: Praise God
Meditation: Lord God, You are the God of all flesh, the Creator of Heaven and Earth. Help us, Your people, to rely on You and to lean not to our own understanding. Amen.

NOV 17TH

WHO IS TO BLAME?

Bible Background • EZEKIEL 18
Printed Text • EZEKIEL 18:1-4, 20-21, 25-32
Devotional Reading • ROMANS 6:17-23

LESSON AIM

By the end of this lesson, students will know the importance of their actions and understand that works done in this life on earth must be accounted for in eternity.

KEEP IN MIND

"Behold, all souls are mine; as the soul of the father, so also the soul of the son is mine: the soul that sinneth, it shall die" (Ezekiel 18:4).

FOCAL VERSES

Ezekiel 18:1 The word of the LORD came unto me again, saying,

2 What mean ye, that ye use this proverb concerning the land of Israel, saying, The fathers have eaten sour grapes, and the children's teeth are set on edge?

3 As I live, saith the LORD God, ye shall not have occasion any more to use this proverb in Israel.

4 Behold, all souls are mine; as the soul of the father, so also the soul of the son is mine: the soul that sinneth, it shall die.

18:20 The soul that sinneth, it shall die. The son shall not bear the iniquity of the father, neither shall the father bear the iniquity of the son: the righteousness of the righteous shall be upon him, and the wickedness of the wicked shall be upon him.

21 But if the wicked will turn from all his sins that he hath committed, and keep all my statutes, and do that which is lawful and right, he shall surely live, he shall not die.

18:25 Yet ye say, The way of the LORD is not equal. Hear now, O house of Israel; Is not my way equal? are not your ways unequal?

LESSON OVERVIEW

LESSON AIM
KEEP IN MIND
FOCAL VERSES
IN FOCUS
THE PEOPLE, PLACES,
AND TIMES
BACKGROUND
AT-A-GLANCE
IN DEPTH
SEARCH THE SCRIPTURES
DISCUSS THE MEANING
LESSON IN OUR SOCIETY
MAKE IT HAPPEN
FOLLOW THE SPIRIT
REMEMBER YOUR THOUGHTS
MORE LIGHT ON THE TEXT
DAILY BIBLE READINGS

26 When a righteous man turneth away from his righteousness, and committeth iniquity, and dieth in them; for his iniquity that he hath done shall he die.

27 Again, when the wicked man turneth away from his wickedness that he hath committed, and doeth that which is lawful and right, he shall save his soul alive.

28 Because he considereth, and turneth away from all his transgressions that he hath committed, he shall surely live, he shall not die.

29 Yet saith the house of Israel, The way of the LORD is not equal. O house of Israel, are not my ways equal? are not your ways unequal?

30 Therefore I will judge you, O house of Israel, every one according to his ways, saith the LORD God. Repent, and turn yourselves from all your transgressions; so iniquity shall not be your ruin.

31 Cast away from you all your transgressions, whereby ye have transgressed; and make you a new heart and a new spirit: for why will ye die, O house of Israel?

32 For I have no pleasure in the death of him that dieth, saith the LORD God: wherefore turn yourselves, and live ye.

IN FOCUS

One Sunday while preaching, Pastor Willow noticed four members excusing themselves from the sanctuary. As he watched them, he noticed each walking out with their index finger raised over their head. At the end of service, Pastor Willow asked each member, "Why did you raise your finger as you excused yourselves?" Two of the members said, "I did so to explain I had to use the washroom." Another explained, " My parents taught me that this was the appropriate way to exit the sanctuary of God during service." The last expressed, "I did it because all the other people in the church do it when they exit to the washroom."

Unsatisfied with these responses, Pastor Willow turned to his 105-year-old great-grandfather (Big-daddy Henry). Big-daddy Henry explained, "My grandfather and many other slaves used the same signal to ask their slave masters for permission to use the washroom during church services. It was also necessary for them to keep their finger up when going to and coming from the washroom. This allowed others to see that they had their master's permission. If a slave failed to do this, he was beaten for being disobedient."

THE PEOPLE, PLACES, AND TIMES

Proverb. A proverb is a short, wise saying used for a long time by many people. The proverbs of the Israelites and other people of the east were primarily and essentially "similitudes."A proverb was a condensed parable or fable that was sometimes presented to clearly teach a lesson. The proverbs and the lessons they taught were passed down from generation to generation. Some proverbs were true, while others were false. The main purpose of a proverb was to help families give instruction to their young.

Many proverbs can be found throughout the Bible. The Book of Proverbs lists many wise sayings of kings and powerful leaders. Most of these are short, compact statements that express truths about human behavior.

Based on information from The New Unger's Bible Dictionary, R. K. Harrison, editor (Chicago: Moody Press, 1988), p. 1046

O House of Israel. This is a phrase used to address the Israelites. It is used throughout the Bible, primarily by the prophets (e. g., Jeremiah, Ezekiel, and Amos). The phrase is often used when the LORD begins to speak to Israel through the prophets. The phrase is normally used as a way of getting the Israelites' attention before speaking to them. Many examples in the Bible support this theory (Jeremiah 3:20; Ezekiel 33:11; Amos 5:25).

Based on information from The New Strong's Exhaustive Concordance of the Bible, Dr. Stanley Morris, editor (Nashville: Thomas Nelson, Inc. 1995), pp. 664-666.

BACKGROUND

The Prophet Ezekiel lived during the Babylonian exile and was active as a prophet for approximately 20 years from 593 B.C. to at least 573 B.C. Ezekiel lived as an exile, according to the title of the book that bears his name (Ezekiel 1:1-2), he was carried away as a captive with Jehoiachin (1:2; 2 Kings 24:14-16) in about 597 B.C. His prophetic call came to him in the fifth year of Jehoiachin's captivity (593 B.C.). Ezekiel held a prominent place among the exiles and was frequently consulted by the elders (Ezekiel 8:1; 11:25; 14:1; 20:1). In the ninth year of his exile, he lost his wife by some sudden and unforeseen tragedy (8:1; 24:1, 18). According to the information in the book's opening, he was the son of the priest Buzi (1:3), and his name in Hebrew meant "God strengthens (this child)," or possibly, "May God strengthen (this person)." Because he was of a priestly family, he probably had a good education, especially in the Law, and his father may even have had some influence in Jerusalem. The time and manner of his death is unknown. Legend says that he is buried in a tomb at al-Kifl near the modern town of Hilla Iraq, not far from the site of ancient Babylon.

AT-A-GLANCE

1. **Rejecting Tradition (Ezekiel 18:1-4)**
2. **Individual Accountability (vv. 20-21)**
3. **Resistance (vv. 25-29)**
4. **Final Declaration (vv. 30-32)**

IN DEPTH

1. Rejecting Tradition (Ezekiel 18:1-4)

Ezekiel receives a challenging word from God. As a spokesman for God, Ezekiel was required to deliver messages from God to His people. But this message was one that Israel would not like because it went against their tradition.

The proverb mentioned here was first stated in Jeremiah 31:29, but the concept may have developed from Exodus 20:5 and 34:7. It was believed among the Israelites that God would punish children for some three to four generations for the sins of their fathers. This was a powerful proverb. On one hand, it persuaded people to live a life pleasing to God because they wanted their children to inherit the least amount of punishment for their sins. On the other hand, it kept children of sinful parents in bondage (some for a lifetime). Imagine that, no matter how good you were, if your parents lived a sinful life, you must reap the harvest for their sinful acts. This was not fair. So in response, God explains that thinking and living by this proverb must end for Israel. He sends Ezekiel with the message and backs it up by expressing that He owns everything—meaning, He's God and He can do this if He wants. Then, through Ezekiel, He begins to reject and tear down Israel's false tradition.

2. Individual Accountability (vv. 20-21)

The words of God have now been proclaimed by the lips of Ezekiel. He begins to explain (in simple detail) a new proverb. He begins to point out how the punishment for sins will be handled. He states that everyone will be held accountable for his/her sins. He expresses that no one will be held accountable for someone's sins, except the one who sinned.

This new proverb is sometimes viewed as the foundation or birthing point for the concept mentioned in Galatians 6:7-8, which states, " . . . for whatsoever a man soweth, that shall he also reap. For he that soweth to the Spirit shall of the Spirit reap life everlasting." Ezekiel continues to explain God's plan of redemption to many sinners, who (after hearing the new proverb) wondered if they could change their views. The plan simply requires that the sinner turn away from all of his sins and keep the decrees of the LORD and do good in His sight. In return for this, God would allow his soul to live. What an awesome reward.

3. Resistance (vv. 25-29)

Traditions are sometimes difficult to end. For many different reasons, people choose to hold on to the things of the past. This explains the response of Israel. Many Israelites believed that God's new plan was unfair. The exact reason why Israel may have felt this way is unclear. However, when one begins to ana-

lyze their situation, some conclusions can be drawn. First, Israel (at this point) is in deep trouble. They believed they were in this state due to the sinful living of their parents. Their parents' sin and the old proverb may have been a crutch they used to explain their bondage. Israel may have felt comfortable in sin and thought it was wrong for God to provide a way out now.

They might expect punishment once for the sins of their parents (for which they were presently receiving punishment) and again for their own sinful acts. In their minds, the new proverb was being added to the old one. Instead of relief from the consequences of the past, with this new proverb, they may have felt that God would punish them twice—and this would be total disaster. Some of Israel may have also felt overcome by sin. It is possible that they may not have believed that they could be free.

4. Final Declaration (vv. 30-32)

Through Ezekiel, God gives His final decree by declaring He will judge everyone according to his/her own sins. The interesting thing here is that God's original plan for accountability had not changed. Regardless of Israel's response, God is still carrying out His will. Once again, He allows the option to be clearly stated (so that there will be no excuses). He demonstrates that He wants the best for the Israelites. He offers a new heart and a new spirit for Israel if they will turn away from their sins. Israel will need them for their new lifestyle. Keep in mind that Israel's lifestyle is one of sin, which consists of wickedness. But the new lifestyle that God will require is one of righteousness. Without a new heart and spirit, it would be impossible to believe God and follow Him. In Romans 10:10, God asks us to believe Him in our heart. He also promises the Holy Spirit will come to lead, guide, and direct us (John 14:26). Therefore, it is vital that Israel receives the new things from God because this will determine how well Israel will walk with God.

SEARCH THE SCRIPTURES

1. What proverb did Israel use concerning the land of Israel? (v. 2)

2. What was God's response to Israel's use of this proverb? (v. 3)

3. According to the new proverb, who would pay

for sins, and what was the punishment? (v. 4)

4. What was God's plan for redemption? (v. 21)

5. What was Israel's response? (v. 25)

6. What happened to the righteous man? (v. 26)

7. What happened to the wicked man? (v. 27)

8. What did God say He would do to Israel? (v. 30)

9. What two new things will God give if Israel turns from sin? (v. 31)

10. Does God take pleasure in death? (v. 32)

DISCUSS THE MEANING

1. What did the old proverb ("the fathers eat sour grapes, and the children's teeth are set on edge") mean? Do you believe that this is a form of a generational curse? Can you think of any punishment for sin you have in your life now that your parents may have passed to you? If so, what can you do about it?

2. Why do you think Ezekiel offered a new heart and spirit for the house of Israel who would repent? In your life, do or did you need a new heart and spirit to serve God? Why or why not?

LESSON IN OUR SOCIETY

Many people are familiar with old superstitious sayings passed down through generations. These may include sayings such as: seven years of bad luck for breaking a mirror; you will go to jail if your foot is swept by a broom; you will have bad luck if a black cat crosses your path; or you will have good luck if you eat black-eyed peas at the start of a new year.

If we live our lives according to these kinds of sayings, we not only keep ourselves in bondage, but we also keep generations of our descendants in bondage, too. As children of God, we must realize that no superstition or old saying is more powerful than God. On the contrary, we must depend totally on God, because He holds our complete destiny in His hand.

MAKE IT HAPPEN

Think about two or three traditional things that you and/or your family currently do. Whether passed down through family or friends, ask your Sunday School teacher if it lines up with God's Word. If it does, ask them to show you the Scripture in the Bible. If it does not, ask them to give you the Scripture in the Bible to back up their point of view. Then, go research the Word of God to evaluate if fol-

lowing the tradition or old saying is biblical. Be honest with yourself. If you find out the tradition goes against God's Word, could you drop it? Who do you think you are trying to please: God or man?

FOLLOW THE SPIRIT

What God wants me to do:

_____

_____

REMEMBER YOUR THOUGHTS

Special insights you have learned:

_____

_____

MORE LIGHT ON THE TEXT
Ezekiel 18:1-4, 20-21, 25-32

The eighteenth chapter of Ezekiel contains a full account of the theme of individual responsibility—God deals with people according to their personal acts of sin or righteousness. The Prophet Ezekiel debunks the idea and the common notion held by the people (Israel) that their suffering or punishment (the exile) is the consequence of their fathers' sin. By holding that idea, they refuse to take responsibility for their actions. Instead, they tend to attribute their present plight to consequences of their fathers' wrongs, thus shifting the blame.

18:1 The word of the LORD came unto me again, saying, 2 What mean ye, that ye use this proverb concerning the land of Israel, saying, The fathers have eaten sour grapes, and the children's teeth are set on edge?

The prophet starts this portion of his prophecy with a word from the LORD. The phrase, "the word of the LORD came unto me" means that he heard from the LORD or that God spoke to him. It is a phrase commonly used among the prophets. Here the LORD calls the prophet's attention to a slogan that seemed to be current among the people during their exile. The LORD, through Ezekiel, questions the people as to what they mean by using the proverb, "the fathers have eaten sour grapes, and the children's teeth are set on edge." Rather than accepting their own faults and repenting from their sins, with this slogan the people accuse God of partiality or bad judgment and of punishing them for what their forefathers had done in the past. By using this slogan, the people also seem to doubt the truth that God is a just and righteous judge.

The idea here is that the hardship that the contemporary generation is going through is the fault of the previous generations. It is as if the forefathers ate unripened grapes that tasted sour and bitter, but instead of their receiving the unpleasant effect, it was transferred to those who never tasted the grapes. This sounds absurd. In their opinion, they are taking the brunt of their ancestors' wrongdoing. Although the early laws in Israel's covenant relationship with the LORD stipulated individual responsibility for wrong behavior (Exodus 20:22—23:33), the people tend to hold only to the heart of the Decalogue, where the LORD threatens to punish the children for the sins of their fathers to the third and fourth generation (Exodus 20:5; Deuteronomy 5:9). This enables the people to shift blame and deny their own sin. Therefore, the LORD says that the slogan will no longer hold.

3 As I live, saith the LORD God, ye shall not have occasion any more to use this proverb in Israel. 4 Behold, all souls are mine; as the soul of the father, so also the soul of the son is mine: the soul that sinneth, it shall die.

The LORD continues His instruction to the prophet that the people's notion of transferred guilt will no longer be used as an excuse for evading responsibility. The proverb that they hitherto have been using (see also Jeremiah 31:29) will no longer apply because all people are equal in His sight. He introduces this correction with the phrase, "As I live," which gives authority and emphasis to what He is about to say. Also the use of "behold" (Hebrew *hen*) often used as an interjection, gives an emphasis to the point He makes; that is, "all souls are mine." He continues, "as the soul of the father, so also the soul of the son is mine: the soul that sinneth, it shall die." That means the son will no more carry the brunt of his father's sin; neither will the father any more take the responsibility for the son's wrong action. Whoever commits sin will have to live with it.

The clause, "the soul that sinneth, it shall die" is consistent with God's order of things in other passages of the Bible (cf. Genesis 2:17; Romans 1:29-32; 5:12-21; 6:14-23; 8:12-13; 1 Corinthians 6:9-11;

Galatians 5:19-21). The emphasis here is that God as the sovereign Creator and sustainer of all things has the absolute right to deal with us as He wills without question. He has the right to hand one over to death, just as He can call another to life. Equally, the LORD can hold the son accountable for his father's deed, just as He can decide to call the father to account regarding the son's misdeeds. Life and death are in His hands, and judgment is His prerogative. No one, not even Israel, has a right to question His judgment, and He is not accountable to anyone. He does what is right in His sight.

18:20 The soul that sinneth, it shall die. The son shall not bear the iniquity of the father, neither shall the father bear the iniquity of the son: the righteousness of the righteous shall be upon him, and the wickedness of the wicked shall be upon him.

The theme of verse 4b (that is, "the soul that sinneth, it shall die") is emphatically repeated here and expanded. Here the prophet deals with moral responsibility. He says that the son shall not be held liable for the iniquity of the father, neither shall the father be held liable for the sin of the son. What this means is that each person, whether the father or the son, shall account for his own deeds. The word "iniquity" is the Hebrew noun `avon (pronounced **ah-VONE**), and means evil, perversity, or mischief. It is also translated as punishment or as a consequence for evil deeds. The use of this word suggests that whoever sins will be held accountable and therefore will face the consequence for his action. The thought here is gleaned from the Deuteronomy passage (24:16). The truth is further emphasized with another set of antitheses in verse 20b concerning the "righteous" and the "wicked." The idea here is that the "righteous" shall be recompensed for his goods deeds, and likewise the wicked shall receive punishment for his own wrongdoing. Again, not only is the guilt or sin of one generation no longer transferable, but the righteousness of one generation cannot transfer to another if that generation does not live according to God's ordinances.

The word "righteous" comes from the Hebrew word *tsaddiq* (pronounced **tsah-DEEK**), which can be translated as just or lawful, i.e., to be just and righteous in conduct or character. It has the idea of being in the right or doing what is right. To be right-

21 But if the wicked will turn from all his sins that he hath committed, and keep all my statutes, and do that which is lawful and right, he shall surely live, he shall not die.

After stating in the previous verse that the sinner will suffer the consequence for his sin (i.e., death), the LORD is quick to make it clear that the sinner does not need to die in his iniquity. Rather, if he repents and amends his ways, he shall live. While in the previous verse, the LORD pronounces a verdict for sins committed (and that is death), here He makes a provision and hopes for the sinner to live. Here God demonstrates His steadfast love, grace, and compassion. He further demonstrates that it is never His will that any should perish in their sin, but that they should repent and live (cf. Ezekiel 23; 2 Peter 3:9).

It is interesting to note that the promise of forgiveness extends to all transgressions the sinner has committed. They will be blotted out; they shall not be mentioned to him or recorded against him (v. 22). With a rhetorical question, the LORD affirms to them that He has no pleasure in the death of a sinner, but He affords the sinner the chance to repent and live. The opposite is stated in verse 24, where the righteous receives his due punishment if he turns from his righteousness and does what is evil.

eous or just is basically having or being in a good relationship with the LORD. The evidence of being righteous or in right relationship with God in the Old Testament was in the keeping of the commandments. To be righteous does not means one is free from doing wrong; rather, it is based on one's commitment to God. It is based on one's relationship with God—trusting and believing Him. Abraham believed God and it was counted to him as righteousness (Romans 4:3). The word "wicked" or "wickedness" comes from the Hebrew *rasha`* (pronounced **rah-SHAH**) and has the idea of being a morally wrong or bad, ungodly person. It has to do with rejection of the LORD by not keeping His statutes and by doing things that contradict God's principles and decrees.

18:25 Yet ye say, The way of the LORD is not equal. Hear now, O house of Israel; Is not my way equal? are not your ways unequal? 26 When a righteous man turneth away from his righteousness, and committeth iniquity, and dieth in them; for his iniquity that he hath done shall he die.

As if in a law court, the LORD seems to defend Himself from the people's accusation of injustice.

Having stated His case and the way He operates, the LORD seems to question their rational basis for the accusation against Him. They complain that "the way of the LORD is not equal"; that is, He is partial and unjust in His judgment. What are the people complaining about? What is God addressing here?

The accusation here is in regard to both their complaint that the LORD holds them responsible for the sin of their fathers (v. 2) and God's statement in verse 24. They probably cannot imagine how a righteous God could punish a person who had been righteous for many years but turns to wickedness and sin. Why should he not continue to live if he had lived more in righteousness than in sin? Why should he die for committing one sin? Why shouldn't his former righteous deeds earn him some reward? God takes issue with this type of reasoning and turns the tables back on them. He tells them that they are the ones whose ways are not equal (or fair).

There is no basis for their accusation because the soul that sins shall die—whether one turns from his righteous deeds to sin or whether one is a sinner and continues in his sin. They both will be rewarded equally—they both shall die. That is God's verdict. This is restated in verse 26. However, that need not be the case, for there is room to change the verdict, and it is open to everyone. God has given everyone the privilege to live and not to die in sin. This is stated again in the next two verses regarding the sinner who turns from his sin.

27 Again, when the wicked man turneth away from his wickedness that he hath committed, and doeth that which is lawful and right, he shall save his soul alive. 28 Because he considereth, and turneth away from all his transgressions that he hath committed, he shall surely live, he shall not die.

The LORD restates His case again in verses 27 and 28 (see also vv. 21-22) and maintains that there is a provision and hope for the sinner who forsakes his sin—he will live and not die. Similarly, if the righteous one forsakes his righteous deeds and does evil, He will die for his unrighteousness and not live. Here, just as in the previous verses cited above, the LORD defends Himself once again and reiterates His divine principle of justice to every-

one. Just as surely as the righteous who commits sin incurs the divine death penalty, when the wicked ceases from his sin and does what is right he shall be rewarded with life. There is no exception to the rule; everyone who sins and everyone who does righteousness will be rewarded accordingly. It is like the civil law. Anyone who breaks the law faces the penalty. The only way to avert the penalty of sin is through genuine repentance and turning away from sin.

The synopsis of this whole passage is that, on one hand, the wicked or sinful person can save his soul when he repents and does what is lawful and right, which is the same as obeying the Gospel. On the other hand, the "righteous" man loses his soul when he turns away from his ways and sins, which is the same as rejecting the Gospel. Living godly is therefore a daily affair; it is a moment-by-moment matter. We cannot live on our past glory, neither can we be judged by our past mistakes after we have repented and accepted the divine mercy and grace God offers to all who come to Him. We need to live by the Spirit daily. Paul makes this clear in his letters (Romans 1:29-32; 6:15-23; 8:14; Galatians 5:19-21).

29 Yet saith the house of Israel, The way of the LORD is not equal. O house of Israel, are not my ways equal? are not your ways unequal?

Again the LORD questions the grounds for their accusation of unfairness against Him. Here, as in verse 25, the LORD seems to ask them, "How can you accuse me of being unfair?" He says to them, "There are no grounds for your accusation. Indeed, you are the ones who are unfair and partial in your dealings." The last segment of this chapter (vv. 30b-32) summarizes the purpose and intent of the whole chapter: a call for a change of heart and repentance.

30 Therefore I will judge you, O house of Israel, every one according to his ways, saith the LORD God. Repent, and turn yourselves from all your transgressions; so iniquity shall not be your ruin.

The LORD then begins this section with a conjunction: "Therefore" (or the Hebrew word *ken*, which means "so," or "in view of what has been said") "I will judge you, O house of Israel, every one according to his ways." Although Israel is punished as a community, God still judges individuals based on their own individual response. Although individual sin can affect the whole community, yet the righteous are usually rewarded for their own righteousness.

Now comes the climax of the passage: "Repent, and turn yourselves from all of your transgressions; so iniquity shall not be your ruin." The word "repent" is a translation of the Hebrew word *shub* (pronounced **shoov**), which means turning, or to turn back, go, or come back. It carries the idea of making a right-about turn, to retreat from a certain direction to another. Here it involves turning from their way of sin (transgression) to the way of righteousness. The word "transgression" is the Hebrew noun *pesha`* (pronounced **peh-SHAH**) derived from the verb *pasha`* (pronounced **pah-SHAH**). It means to break away from authority, to trespass, revolt, rebel or apostatize. Transgression can be against an individual, or nation, or against God. In context, the rebellion is against God and His ordinances. The LORD invites Israel to turn away from sin and to return back to Him so that "iniquity shall not be your ruin." The LORD, through the prophet, calls on the people to turn over a new leaf so that they can live and not die.

31 Cast away from you all your transgressions, whereby ye have transgressed; and make you a new heart and a new spirit: for why will ye die, O house of Israel?

Using a stronger word, the LORD invites them to "cast away" or get rid of their transgression and to cultivate "a new heart and a new spirit" so that they will not face the consequences of their transgression. This is a call to transformation of the inner self. Paul, writing to the Romans, says: "Be not conformed to this world: but be ye transformed by the renewing of your mind, that ye may prove what is that good, and acceptable, and perfect, will of God" (Romans 12:2). To "cast away" is another way of saying that they should turn away from their rebellion and come back to Him. Emphasizing the need for repentance, the LORD appeals to their reasoning. He does this rhetorically—"for why will ye die, O house of

Israel?" In other words, life and death are your two choices. You can choose to repent and live, or continue in your sin and face death. The conditions for salvation are consistent both in the Old Testament and in the New Testament (Mark 1:15; 16:15; Acts 2:38; 3:19; 26:18; Romans 10:9-10; 2 Corinthians 5:17-21; 1 John 1:7).

32 For I have no pleasure in the death of him that dieth, saith the LORD God: wherefore turn yourselves, and live ye.

Concluding this oracle, the LORD reiterates His earlier assertion (v. 23) that He does not take delight in the death of the wicked or in the righteous who turn away from His righteousness. Rather, He calls again for genuine repentance and change of heart—the only criterion for living.

At this point, it is necessary to understand the meaning of "death" or "die" in this passage. What does the word "death" or "to die" (used here about 13 times) mean in the context of the passage? Does it mean physical death? Although physical death can be attributed to sin after the Fall, physical death is not necessarily always the penalty for sin. Death here evidently means spiritual death and separation from God.

DAILY BIBLE READINGS

M: The Righteous Will Live
Ezekiel 18:1-9
T: The Person Who Sins Will Die
Ezekiel 18:19-24
W: Turn and Live
Ezekiel 18:25-32
T: Why Will You Die, Israel?
Ezekiel 33:7-11
F: Without Excuse
Romans 1:16-25
S: God Will Repay
Romans 2:1-8
S: Belief in the Son Brings Life
John 3:16-21

TEACHING TIPS

November 24
Bible Study Guide 13

1. Words You Should Know

A. Sanctify (Ezekiel 36:23)—Holy character or sacredness.

B. Profane (v. 23)—To act with contempt or disregard for God or holy things.

C. Famine (v. 29)—The severe lack of food in a place or a time of starving.

D. Loathe (v. 31)—To hate very much.

2. Teacher Preparation

A. As you begin to prepare the lesson, pray that God will enlighten you with His Word.

B. Read Ezekiel 36 and make a list of things God promised Israel in His prophecy.

C. Make a another list to share with the students of things God has promised you.

3. Starting the Lesson

A. Ask the students to make a list of things they believe God has promised them.

B. Ask them what have they done to receive these things. Emphasize the importance of obedience to God's Word and seeking God's will while in expectation of God's promises.

C. Share from your list with the students and talk about the ways in which you have applied God's Word to this concept..

4. Getting into the Lesson

A. Read the IN FOCUS story and point out that the news reporters and tabloids didn't know Kevin. It was only through intimate conversation that the truth was discovered; it is the same with God.

B. Generate a discussion about how God desires to bless us with spiritual blessings as well as natural blessings.

5. Relating the Lesson to Life

A. Read the LESSON IN OUR SOCIETY sec-

tion. Ask students how they handle situations that could make them return to the world's way of doing things.

B. Allow students to answer questions in the SEARCH THE SCRIPTURES section.

6. Arousing Action

A. Read MAKE IT HAPPEN and solicit answers to the questions.

B. Allow students time to complete the FOLLOW THE SPIRIT and REMEMBER YOUR THOUGHTS sections.

WORSHIP GUIDE

For the Superintendent or Teacher
Theme: A Look to the Future
Theme Song: "He Brought Me Out"
Scripture: Ezekiel 36:22-32.
Song: "All Hail, Immanuel!"
Meditation: O Lord, Your will is perfect.
Thank You for all of our trials, for it is through them that we are made stronger. No one can match your awesome ways of deliverance. Lord, when everything seems to be out of control, You alone give us peace through your grace and your mercy. For this, Lord, we thank You. For we know that in the end You see us victorious, triumphant, conquerors over our present situations. Lord, help our eyes to see. In Jesus' name we pray. Amen.

A LOOK TO THE FUTURE

Bible Background • EZEKIEL 36—37
Printed Text • EZEKIEL 36:22-32
Devotional Reading • JEREMIAH 32:36-41

LESSON AIM

By the end of the lesson, students will know the process of claiming the promises of God and believe that God will perform His Word.

KEEP IN MIND

"A new heart also will I give you, and a new spirit will I put within you: and I will take away the stony heart out of your flesh, and I will give you a heart of flesh" (Ezekiel 36:26).

FOCAL VERSES

Ezekiel 36:22 Therefore say unto the house of Israel, Thus saith the LORD God; I do not this for your sakes, O house of Israel, but for mine holy name's sake, which ye have profaned among the heathen, whither ye went.

23 And I will sanctify my great name, which was profaned among the heathen, which ye have profaned in the midst of them; and the heathen shall know that I am the LORD, saith the LORD God, when I shall be sanctified in you before their eyes.

24 For I will take you from among the heathen, and gather you out of all countries, and will bring you into your own land.

25 Then will I sprinkle clean water upon you, and ye shall be clean: from all your filthiness, and from all your idols, will I cleanse you.

26 A new heart also will I give you, and a new spirit will I put within you: and I will take away the stony heart out of your flesh, and I will give you a heart of flesh.

27 And I will put my spirit within you, and cause you to walk in my statutes, and ye shall keep my judgments, and do them.

LESSON OVERVIEW

LESSON AIM
KEEP IN MIND
FOCAL VERSES
IN FOCUS
THE PEOPLE, PLACES,
AND TIMES
BACKGROUND
AT-A-GLANCE
IN DEPTH
SEARCH THE SCRIPTURES
DISCUSS THE MEANING
LESSON IN OUR SOCIETY
MAKE IT HAPPEN
FOLLOW THE SPIRIT
REMEMBER YOUR THOUGHTS
MORE LIGHT ON THE TEXT
DAILY BIBLE READINGS

28 And ye shall dwell in the land that I gave to your fathers; and ye shall be my people, and I will be your God.

29 I will also save you from all your uncleanness: and I will call for the corn, and will increase it, and lay no famine upon you.

30 And I will multiply the fruit of the tree, and the increase of the field, that ye shall receive no more reproach of famine among the heathen.

31 Then shall ye remember your own evil ways, and your doings that were not good, and shall loathe yourselves in your own sight for your iniquities and for your abominations.

32 Not for your sakes do I this, saith the LORD God, be it known unto you: be ashamed and confounded for your own ways, O house of Israel.

IN FOCUS

Cathy and Sherry have been friends since grammar school. Cathy works for a sports agency that represents over 75 professional athletes. Among these athletes is Kevin, who is considered one of the best players in the National Basketball Association. One day, Sherry meets with Cathy to have lunch. In doing so, she bumps into Kevin in the lobby. Both look at each other with a strong desire to get to know the other better. Then Kevin says, "Excuse me, Miss." "The name is Sherry." she replies. The two talk for about 10 minutes before Cathy interrupts. As the two say goodbye, Sherry gives Kevin her phone number. At lunch, Cathy talks with Sherry about

NOV
24TH

Kevin. "Girl, let me give you the 411 on Kevin. He's a male chauvinist pig. He has a list of groupies from Chicago to California that he has to keep in his Rolodex. And if he calls you, he will treat you just like he treats those other girls." She continues to express what she has read in magazines, that he has four children in four different cities whom he supports.

In spite of Cathy's warning, Sherry begins to date Kevin. After three weeks of dating, Sherry finds out that Cathy's stories are lies and that these reporters and tabloids fabricated them. She discovers Kevin owns a modeling agency with locations in New York, Chicago, and Los Angeles (which explains his Rolodex full of women's names). Sherry also discovers that Kevin has adopted four children—to give back what his adopted parents gave him.

In an intimate conversation with Kevin, Sherry also finds out that he has been celibate for 10 years. Overwhelmed by her new discoveries, Sherry asks Kevin, "Do you know about the lies that are circulating about you?" "Yes, I've heard them," he replied. "But those people have never known me, and I have never met them."

THE PEOPLE, PLACES AND TIMES

Sanctify. In the Old Testament economy, things, places, and times as well as persons were sanctified for holy purposes. Connected with this were the Mosaic rites of purification (see Numbers 6:11; Leviticus 22:16, 32; Hebrews 9:13). However, when applied to persons, these Mosaic rites,were effective only in a ceremonial and legal sense and did not extend to the purification of the moral and spiritual nature. They were symbols intended not only to remind the Israelites of the necessity of spiritual cleansing, but also of the gracious plan of God to actually accomplish the work.

Based on information from The New Unger's Bible Dictionary, R. K. Harrison, editor (Chicago: Moody Press, 1988), p. 1124.

Uncleanness. In the early books of the Old Testament, cleanness and uncleanness are ritual issues; that is, calling a person or thing "unclean" was not a moral judgment. "Unclean" simply meant that a person or thing was unable to participate in Israel's worship of Yahweh. During the time of ceremonial uncleanness, one could not attend any worship cer-

emony or eat meat that had been offered in sacrifice. Under certain circumstances an unclean person must be isolated from others in the community.

Based on information from Expository Dictionary of Bible Words, Lyman Tucker Jr. and Gerald Terpstra, editors (Grand Rapids: The Zondervan Corporation, 1985), p. 169.

BACKGROUND

Israel is currently nearing the end of her exile. The Prophet Jeremiah prophesied this exile almost 70 years earlier. Evil practices in the past led to this exile. During this time, Israel lost evil kings, evil leaders, false prophets, mighty men, young men, young virgins, homes, land, livestock, food, and many other things of necessity. They even lost a zeal to love and serve God by turning from God to the sinful and evil ways of other nations. They also lost the vision of God: to show other nations that Yahweh (the LORD) is God alone and to serve as an example for all nations to follow.

It seems that they lost everything except God. It's amazing that through all of their wicked living, God was still there for them. This is a testament that God truly is faithful. Back in the Book of Genesis, God made a covenant with Abraham, and through this remnant of Israel, He continues to fulfill it.

> ### AT-A-GLANCE
> 1. God's Prophecy (Ezekiel 36:22-23)
> 2. God's Promises (vv. 24-30)
> 3. God's Provision (vv. 31-32)

IN DEPTH
1. God's Prophecy (Ezekiel 36:22-23)

God gives Israel another prophecy through Ezekiel. This prophecy, however, is a little different than some in the past. While other prophecies were given based on Israel's evil actions or behaviors, this one is based on God's righteous actions. God says He will do good things for Israel, not for their sake, but for His (God's) holy name's sake. God shows Israel mercy because He knows they cannot earn what He wants to give them. And because God's name is associated with righteousness, riches, wealth, abundance, and fruitfulness, He set these aside for His people. This is an "in spite of" blessing. Notice, God does not offer Israel the opportunity to receive or reject this blessing. He simply proclaims it as a blessing that will be given for His name's sake.

The purpose of this blessing is threefold. First, God wants to declare His name as holy. Second, God wants all the heathen to know that He is God. And finally, God wants to continue to fulfill the covenant He made with Israel's forefathers—Abraham, Isaac, and Jacob.

2. God's Promises (vv. 24-30)

God's undying love for His people is expressed in His promises. Throughout the Bible, we see the power of His promises. With a promise from God, people find hope that can surpass human understanding. This may be due to the fact that God's promises are a sure thing; they are certain. For He has never made a promise that He cannot fulfill (Titus 1:2: He cannot lie).

The pattern of God's promise is truly awesome. First, He wants to set Israel apart from the heathen. Second, He wants to cleanse them from all unrighteousness with clean water. Third, He wants to give them a new heart and spirit. Fourth, He wants to put His Spirit in them so they can walk in His ways. Fifth, He wants them to dwell in the land where He will govern them. And sixth, He wants to multiply and increase them in every area of their lives. When you analyze this, you can see the similarities of that pattern and God's salvation plan for us.

In God's salvation plan, He first calls us from among the world (heathen); He washes us clean by the blood of the Lamb. Then as new creatures in Christ, we develop a new heart or desire for God and receive a new Spirit to lead us in His ways. God then blesses us to increase and multiply (not necessarily financially) as we seek His will in every area of our lives. As if all of this were not enough, God does all of this for mankind based not on our works, but on His mercy (Titus 3:5).

3. God's Provision (vv. 31-32)

God's plan of redemption does not end after He rescues and blesses Israel. To the contrary, the first thing God promised to do was deliver Israel from the heathen. In order for God's plan to be complete, He

must deliver Israel physically, mentally, and spiritually; otherwise, Israel will fall back into their evil ways.

To accomplish total deliverance, God calls Israel to remember their evil ways. He does this not so they'll go back into sin, but to help them say no to it. God wants their memory of wrongdoing to prevent them from doing the things they used to do. Whenever they think on these evil things, God will allow them to feel ashamed and disgraced by them. This unpleasant memory, may in turn, also help Israel stay in God's will, which is where God desires them to be.

SEARCH THE SCRIPTURES

1. For whose sake did God bless Israel? (v. 22)

2. What did God want to do with His great name? (v. 23)

3. Name five things God prophesied He would do for Israel. (v. 24-30)

4. What was Israel to remember? (v. 31)

5. How did God say Israel would feel about their evil ways? (v. 32)

DISCUSS THE MEANING

1. In what ways do you believe Israel profaned God's name? Have you ever done any of these things? If so, do you believe you have profaned God's name? In what ways can you correct this?

2. Why do you think God wanted Israel to hate their old evil ways? Do you hate your old evil ways? Why or why not? How can this help or hurt you?

LESSON IN OUR SOCIETY

In our society, many people accept sinful acts as right behavior. To a certain extent, some Christians have even adopted a sinner's lifestyle. We see it in Christian-based businesses, movies, TV shows, music, videos, and the like. While we may live in the world, we don't live by the world's rules. It is God's rules and likeness we must focus our attention on and admiration toward. We must daily live a life that will be pleasing in His sight. On every front, we must refuse to adopt the world's ways of doing things. When we do, we are saying that God's ways are not what's best for us—and nothing could be farther from the truth.

MAKE IT HAPPEN

The most powerful story in the world is the story

of how much God loves people. For He loves us "just because," and He proves His love unconditionally everyday. While this story is the greatest, a sadly disturbing one is our love for God. It's most disturbing because many people love God conditionally or based on circumstances, and others don't love Him at all. Through sinful acts, many fail to experience God's love for them. Can you think of someone who does not love God or has not experienced His great salvation? If so, will you ask God to show you how to introduce them to His Son, Jesus?

FOLLOW THE SPIRIT

What God wants me to do:

_____

_____

REMEMBER YOUR THOUGHTS

Special insights you have learned:

_____

_____

MORE LIGHT ON THE TEXT
Ezekiel 36:22-32

In the previous section (vv. 16-21), God describes why He previously poured out His fury against the Children of Israel because of their apostasy but now is having pity on them. Through their acts, they profaned the name of the LORD, but now the LORD is about to deliver them, not because of their own sake, but because of His own name.

Ezekiel 36:22 Therefore say unto the house of Israel, Thus saith the LORD God; I do not this for your sakes, O house of Israel, but for mine holy name's sake, which ye have profaned among the heathen, whither ye went.

Since God is concerned for His name, He commands Ezekiel to prophesy to the people of Israel and tell them of His intention—to deliver them. The main purpose for what He is about to do is to preserve His great name, which the people hitherto had profaned. He therefore asks Ezekiel to announce this to them.

In the previous section (vv. 16-21), we saw the reason God scattered the Israelites and glimpsed how the people lived among the heathen nations. Through their lives, they profaned God's name.

How? First, by their rebellious acts, e.g., shedding of blood and worshiping idols. Second, while in exile, the heathen nations mocked God's people. They looked down on God as powerless to deliver His people (when in fact it was their own gods who were powerless). Therefore, they dishonored the name of the LORD with the intent of blaspheming Him. As a result of this, the LORD decided to act on the Israelites' behalf, just to maintain His name. The word "profaned" with its present tense, which appears over 18 times in Ezekiel, is the Hebrew verb *chalal* (pronounced **hak-LAHL**). It means to defile, to make common, to dishonor, or to desecrate. By implication, profanity is the strongest opposite of holiness or sacredness.

23 And I will sanctify my great name, which was profaned among the heathen, which ye have profaned in the midst of them; and the heathen shall know that I am the LORD, saith the LORD God, when I shall be sanctified in you before their eyes.

So, by their actions and the life they lived among the people during the exile, the people defiled and desecrated the name of the LORD. But now the LORD wants to restore and reclaim His "great name." He says, "I will sanctify my great name." To "sanctify," or its Hebrew equivalent *qadash* (pronounced **kah-DAHSH**), is the opposite of "profane" and means to make holy, to consecrate, hallow, dedicate, or set apart. It also carries the idea of being honored. He will do this among the heathen, in the midst of whom His name is profaned. When He does this, the heathen nations will know that "the LORD (*YAHWEH*)" is greater than their powerless idol gods.

From this passage, we learn how important God's name is to Him; it indicates that God is zealous for His name and His integrity and will do anything to protect His name from being blasphemed or ridiculed. In God's plan of salvation for us, what seems to matter most is the integrity of God's name. He should be given the honor due to Him. It should be recognized in the people's minds and reflected in their actions that He alone is the LORD, and therefore there is no place for idols. The clause, "when I shall be sanctified in you before their eyes" suggests that they are God's vehicle of sanctifying His name. It will be through them (the Israelites), and He will

do it before the eyes of the heathen. The phrase "before their eyes" gives assurance to God's people that the heathen nations cannot do anything to stop Him. It also carries an "in your face" attitude. What is it that God is about to do? The answer is contained in the following verses.

24 For I will take you from among the heathen, and gather you out of all countries, and will bring you into your own land.

The LORD promises to take them from among the heathen; that is, to deliver them from their captivity. This statement begins the theme of salvation and restoration. As we shall soon find out, their deliverance is more than physical deliverance from cap-

tivity, but also involves spiritual restoration. First, the LORD says that He will bring them out of the heathen nations into their own land. The LORD has repeatedly promised that He will gather all Israel—not only Judah or Jerusalem, but all the tribes from among the heathen and bring them back into their own land to live forever. This is the first gathering of Israel from all the nations as seen in Ezra, Nehemiah, Haggai, Zechariah, and Malachi. There are other subsequent returns of Israel before and after the coming of Christ, and there will be the final gathering of the Children of Israel to their land when the Messiah will rule forever (cf. Isaiah 9:6-7; 11:1-12:5). The promise to deliver them from captivity will be followed by spiritual deliverance and cleansing from sin. This theme is developed in verses 25-30.

25 Then will I sprinkle clean water upon you, and ye shall be clean: from all your filthiness, and from all your idols, will I cleanse you.

The use of the word "then" suggests that the "sprinkling" of clean water and the spiritual restoration will follow the regathering of all Israel to their own land. The act of sprinkling with clean water symbolizes the work of inward renewal and cleansing; it is the first of the triple acts of restoration of the people to their God, which also makes obedience to God possible. The word "sprinkle" is the Hebrew verb *zaraq* (pronounced **zah-ROCK**). It means to throw or sprinkle fluid or solid particles or to scatter. The idea here is that of ritual washing for purification such as found in Numbers 19:4ff. (especially vv. 9, 17-21; cf. Exodus 12:22; Leviticus 14:4-7, 51).

The psalmist prays for cleansing when he says, "Purge me with hyssop, and I shall be clean: wash me, and I shall be whiter than snow" (Psalm 51:7). Although in this psalm water is not mentioned, the notion is understood. Therefore, the sprinkling with clean water mentioned in Ezekiel 36:25 does not mean that an actual rite of washing with water is intended. Rather, it gives the assurance of the cleansing that the LORD is about to do. It is a spiritual reality symbolized by the ritual of water.

In many cultures, water plays an important part in initiation and rite of passage. In the Igbo culture of Nigeria, for example, young males are taken to the stream by night for washing as an initiation rite into the "okonko" society. Entry into this group symbolizes maturity or age of accountability.

The word "sprinkling" symbolizes the redemption of the people "from all...filthiness, and from all . . . idols," which God does Himself. It is God's act of bringing back His people who hitherto had rejected Him by disobedience and worship of strange gods. Through the inner washing, the people are cleansed from all sin and accepted back into the fold. Writing regarding the Suffering Servant, Isaiah says that He will sprinkle many nations and relieve them from all guilt and sin (Isaiah52:15). Also, writing to the Corinthians, Paul describes God's act of salvation as embodying washing, sanctification, and justification of sinners in the name of the LORD Jesus and through the work of the Spirit of God (1 Corinthians 6:11), thereby alluding to the chief elements of this passage.

26 A new heart also will I give you, and a new spirit will I put within you: and I will take away the stony heart out of your flesh, and I will give you an heart of flesh. 27 And I will put my spirit within you, and cause you to walk in my statutes, and ye shall keep my judgments, and do them. 28 And ye shall dwell in the land that I gave to your fathers; and ye shall be my people, and I will be your God.

The second act of restoration is the giving of a new heart and putting God's Spirit in the people. This coincides with the parallel passages (Ezekiel 11:19; 18:31), where the people are commanded to cultivate a new heart and a new spirit.

The mention of both heart and spirit side by side shows that they do not mean the same thing. The word "heart" (Hebrew *leb* pronounced **lave**) used here refers to the human will where decisions are made; it is the seat of human emotion, and it reflects the whole human personality. The word "spirit" is the Hebrew noun *ruach* (pronounced **roo'-AKH**), which literally means wind or breath but is used figuratively to mean life and mind. In his definition of the term, Eichrodt writes, " . . . it suggests a man's whole inner life as moved by strong and often overmastering passions, which can easily rob the individual man of his independence and drive him in a certain direction almost as if he had no will of his own" *(Walther Eichrodt, Ezekiel: A Commentary, Philadelphia: The Westminster Press, 1970) p. 499.*

Here the renewal of the heart and spirit is defined by saying that it is brought about by the bestowal of a new will and new attitude of spirit toward things. It should also be noted that God did not promise to amend their old heart and old spirit; instead, He would give them a "brand new" heart and a "brand new" spirit—total renewal of the total person. It is like a total spiritual heart surgery (heart and soul transplant), whereby the old "stony heart"—characterized by sin, rebellion, disobedience, and rejection of Yahweh—is totally removed and replaced with a "heart of flesh" that is pliable and sensitive to the will of God.

When this is done, the people will not only walk in God's statutes, keeping His judgments and doing His will, but they will dwell in the land which the LORD gave to their fathers. They will reclaim their place and relationship with God, for they "shall be my people, and I will be your God" (vv. 27-28). They will not be the same again, a sinful and rebellious generation doing their own things; rather, their actions and attitude will now be governed by the Spirit of the living God.

29 I will also save you from all your uncleannesses: and I will call for the corn, and will increase it, and lay no famine upon you. 30 And I will multiply the fruit of the tree, and the increase of the field, that ye shall receive no more reproach of famine among the heathen.

With the gift of a new heart and new spirit, they also will be saved from all uncleanness. The word "uncleanness" used here is the Hebrew *tum'ah* (pronounced **toom-AH),** which covers all types of impurity including ethical, sexual, and religious. Not only will the LORD restore Israel spiritually and save them from all filthiness; He will reverse His judgment against them and will save their land from the entire curse.

Earlier in the book (Ezekiel 5:16-17; 14:13, 21), we find that famine was the result of God's judgment against the people, but it will now be a thing of the past in the new dispensation. For the LORD will "call for the corn, and will increase it" so there will no longer be famine in the land. He will multiply the fruit of the tree, i.e., the fruit trees will bear fruits in abundance, and the farms will yield their crops bountifully. Israel will no longer suffer reproach or be ridiculed by the other nations as a consequence of their punishment from the LORD.

31 Then shall ye remember your own evil ways, and your doings that were not good, and shall loathe yourselves in your own sight for your iniquities and for your abominations. 32 Not for your sakes do I this, saith the LORD God, be it known unto you: be ashamed and confounded for your own ways, O house of Israel.

With all these blessings of restoration—spiritual and agronomic blessings—the people will realize their former sinful ways and will be ashamed of themselves. The product of a new heart and new spirit—salvation and a new relationship with the LORD—is acknowledging our sinfulness, detesting our former ways, and repenting from them.

Again, the LORD reiterates His former assertion to the people: "not for your sakes do I this" (cf. v. 22). The salvation He extends to corrupt, stiff-necked, and rebellious Israel was not because of their worthiness, but rather for His sake: that His name no more be blasphemed by the heathen nations (vv. 20-21) and to complete His salvation plan for His people. The salvation described in this passage is both contemporary and eschatological (for the end times) in nature. God's desire is to restore His people (not only Israel, but also all peoples) to their original relationship before the Fall. This will be accomplished through Christ Jesus.

DAILY BIBLE READINGS

M: Israel Shall Soon Come Home
Ezekiel 36:8-12
T: The Lord's Holiness
Ezekiel 36:16-23
W: A New Heart
Ezekiel 36:24-28
T: God Will Save from Uncleanness
Ezekiel 36:29-33
F: They Shall Know Who God Is
Ezekiel 36:34-38
S: Can Dry Bones Live?
Ezekiel 37:1-6
S: God's Spirit Within
Ezekiel 37:7-14

NOTES

INTRODUCTION TO THE DECEMBER 2002 QUARTER

This quarter's study focuses on outstanding personalities in the New Testament. The sessions examine the lives of people who were instrumental in Jesus' birth and early years, individuals with whom Jesus interacted in His ministry, and key persons in the early church.

The Quarter at-a-Glance

Portraits of Faith
(New Testament Personalities)

UNIT 1. PERSONALITIES INVOLVED IN MESSIAH'S COMING

In this unit, we study the lives of pious people whom God chose to have significant roles in Jesus' birth and early childhood. Our study is meant to give us insight into God's work with human beings to accomplish His divine purpose. The first session focuses on Elisabeth and Zacharias, the parents of John the Baptist, the forerunner of Christ. The second session looks at Mary's being chosen to be Messiah's mother. The third session examines Joseph's role in Messiah's coming and early years. The fourth session explores Mary's giving birth to Jesus and the visit of the shepherds. The fifth session is a study of John the Baptist, Messiah's forerunner.

LESSON 1: December 1
Elisabeth and Zacharias: Parents of the Forerunner
Luke 1:5-14, 39-45, 57-58

The biblical content of this lesson is taken from the first chapter of Luke. In the selected passages, we see Elisabeth and Zacharias, who were faithful and righteous even though childless in their old age (vv. 5-7). As we move along in the text, we read of Zacharias serving in the temple and encountering an angel of the Lord in the process (vv. 8-11). We further read that Zacharias was afraid, but that the angel told him that he and Elisabeth would have a son, John (vv. 12-

14). Elisabeth's child leaped in her womb when she received a visit from Mary (v. 41a). Filled with the Holy Spirit, Elisabeth blessed Mary and the child she was carrying and acknowledged the child as her Lord (vv. 41b-45).When Elisabeth gave birth to a son, her neighbors and relatives rejoiced with her (vv. 57-58).

In this lesson, we see the response of the priest Zacharias to God's answer to Israel's hope. Here was a man who served daily in the temple, showing in his ministrations the promise of the Messiah to Israel. Yet one cannot help but wonder if he really expected the realization and actualization of his symbolic expression. We sometimes serve in hope but fail to grasp its actualization. But whether we grasp the actualization or not, what God seems to require of us is faithfulness in our service. In this lesson, we learn that God will respond to us if we remain faithful. We also learn that what may seem impossible with us is possible with God. The lesson also shows us that there is a thread which runs through the lives of the people whom God chooses to use. There is a spirit of joy that flows from actualization to actualization as God's promise becomes real in each of our lives. Look at the joy that came through the manifestation of the promise of God. First to Elisabeth, then to Mary, then to the child in the womb, and then to Zacharias and the people at the birth of John. What a God!

LESSON 2: December 8
Mary: Chosen for Blessing
Luke 1:26-38, 46-49

The text today narrates the fact that the angel Gabriel appeared to Mary and announced her favor with God. Upon hearing this, Mary was perplexed (vv. 26-29). The angel reassured her and told her that she would have a son, Jesus, who would be the Son of God and rule an endless kingdom (vv. 30-33). When Mary asked how this could happen, the angel explained that her child would be conceived by the Holy Spirit (vv. 34-35). When the angel explained God's infinite power to Mary, using Elisabeth's conception as an example, she accepted her chosen role (vv. 36-38). Mary burst forth in song, magnifying God for having exalted her lowly status in life by giving her a great role in God's mighty works (vv. 46-49).

In this lesson, we see that Mary was chosen to bear the blessing of God to the world in the person of the child within her. She was favored by God, but not because she did anything to deserve it. In that sense, Mary becomes a paradigm of the grace we all experience. God is able to bring out of you that which can transform the world. Here in this lesson, we see God perform what in the sight of humanity is impossible. God used Mary to be a blessing even though she was of low estate, young, and naive. How marvelous when God reaches down to use clay vessels, such as humans are, for His ultimate purpose. This lesson also calls us to respond—to burst forth into singing as we praise God for His marvelous work in us.

LESSON 3: December 15
Joseph: A Righteous Man
Matthew 1:18-21, 24-25; 2:13-15, 19-21, 23

We read that after Jesus' mother Mary was engaged to Joseph, she was discovered to be with child, so Joseph compassionately resolved to break the engagement quietly (vv. 8-19). Matthew tells us further that an angel appeared to Joseph in a dream and told him to make Mary his wife, since her child, whom he was to name Jesus, was from the Holy Spirit (vv. 20-21). Joseph obeyed the angel and took Mary as his wife but refrained from marital relations with her until after Jesus was born (vv. 24-25). Joseph, having been warned by an angel that Herod wanted to destroy Jesus, took his family to Egypt (2:13-15). After Herod's death, the angel again came to Joseph in a dream and urged him to return with his family to Israel, and again he obeyed (vv. 19-21). Having been alerted to a new danger in Judea, Joseph was encouraged to go instead to Galilee, where he made his home in the town of Nazareth (v. 23).

In this lesson, we learn several things from Joseph. We learn how to respond in divine compassion to those whom we may have the right to condemn. We also learn from Joseph the importance of obedience. His obedience saved two lives, Mary's and that of the child Jesus. Obedience can save lives. We also learn that once we take a divine assignment, our agenda must be set by God; we lose our own agenda. Joseph no longer had his own agenda. He went where the angel of the Lord said to go.

LESSON 4: December 22
Mary: Mother of the Messiah
Luke 2:1, 4-20

The biblical content of this lesson deals with the events that surround the birth of Jesus. After Caesar Augustus decreed that all should be registered, Joseph and Mary traveled to Bethlehem, Joseph's ancestral city (vv. 1, 4-5). Mary gave birth to a son in Bethlehem and placed him in a manger because there was no room in the inn (vv. 6-7). Angels, joyfully announcing the Good News and location of the Saviour's birth, appeared to shepherds in the fields (vv. 8-14). The shepherds went to Bethlehem and found the holy family; then they praised God and told others what they had seen and heard (vv. 15-18, 20). Mary meditated on all that had happened (v. 19).

This lesson shows us how God can use even the faithless, such as Caesar, to fulfill heaven's goal. In this lesson, we also encounter persons of great fidelity who surrounded the birth of the Savior. We see the response of angels to divine orders. We see the response of the despised shepherds as they celebrated the good news. But there is also an enigmatic response in the midst of this jubilation. Mary, who had burst forth into singing, is now somber and pensive. This gives us insight into the character of Mary. Could it be that she is just now beginning to understand the magnitude of the event into which God has drawn her? In this lesson, we look at various reactions to the experiences surrounding the Saviour's birth.

LESSON 5: December 29
John the Baptist: Messiah's Forerunner
Matthew 3:1-11; 11:7-10

In this lesson, we examine the life of John the Baptist. We learn from John the meaning of service to the glory of God. We should also learn from the courage of John the Baptist and from his clear understanding of his role in the scheme of God's redemptive plan. It is important to know what our function is in the work of God and not take upon ourselves what God hasn't allotted to us.

The biblical text shows us John fulfilling his prophetic role as a forerunner for the Messiah as he goes into the Judean wilderness, preaching repentance and the nearness of the kingdom of heaven (Matthew 3:1-3). John attracted many followers who confessed their sins and were then baptized by him in the Jordan (vv. 4-6). John harshly criticized the religious leaders for their hypocrisy and warned them of imminent judgment (vv. 7-10). John explained the differences between his mission and that of the One for whom he was preparing the way (v. 11). Jesus spoke highly of John and his role and praised him as a prophet and a human being (11:7-10).

UNIT 2. PERSONALITIES IN JESUS' LIFE AND MINISTRY

This unit presents people with whom Jesus interacted in the course of completing His mission. The first session focuses on the rich man who asked Jesus what to do to gain eternal life. The second session presents Mary and Martha as Jesus' friends. The third session explores Pilate's encounter and exchanges with Jesus. The fourth session is a study of Peter's denying Jesus and being restored to usefulness.

LESSON 6: January 5
The Rich Man: Wrong Priorities
Mark 10:17-27

In the text for this lesson, a man came to Jesus wanting to know what he must do to inherit eternal life (v. 17). Jesus emphasized the need for the man to look to God and affirmed that the man already knew the commandments of the law (vv. 18-19). The man declared he had kept the commandments (v. 20). When Jesus told the rich man to sell his possessions, give the money to the poor, and follow Him, the rich man went away sad (vv. 21-22). Jesus emphasized the difficulty wealthy people have entering the kingdom of God (vv. 23-25). When the surprised disciples asked, "Who can be saved?" Jesus reminded them that with God all things are possible (vv. 26-27).

We learn from this lesson the need to keep our priorities straight. From the life of this rich man, we discover that even the keeping of rules does not mean that our kingdom priorities are right. What is kingdom-priority? God must be first. It is difficult for those who are preoccupied with wealth to enter the kingdom of God. No matter how difficult, the transformation of our priorities is possible with God's help.

LESSON 7: January 12
Mary and Martha: Friends of Jesus
Luke 10:38 12; John 11:20-27, 30-32

The biblical narrative for this lesson tells us what happened when Jesus visited the home of Mary and Martha. In it, we see the different ways in which they responded to the arrival of their guest and friend Jesus (Luke 10:38-40a). We see the interaction

between these two sisters of Lazarus. Martha, who was busy with preparations, asked Jesus to tell Mary to help her. Instead, Mary was sitting at Jesus' feet listening to Him speak (vv. 39-40b). Jesus chided Martha for being so busy that she missed out on the important thing that Mary had chosen (vv. 41-42).

In the second narrative unit for this lesson, we see Jesus again interacting with the sisters upon the death of their brother Lazarus. When Jesus arrived in Bethany after the death of Lazarus, Martha suggested that if Jesus had been there, Lazarus would not have died (John 11:20-21). In response to Martha's statement of faith, Jesus announced that He is the resurrection and the life (vv. 22-27). The final part of the text tells us that Mary went out to meet Jesus before He went to the tomb (vv. 28-32).

In this lesson, we learn several valuable lessons. We learn that Jesus valued His friends. We also learn that physical business, while important, may sometimes keep us from hearing what Jesus is saying to us. For those of us who are so busy that we cannot find time to sit at the feet of the Master, the Lord's word to Martha should serve as a reminder of what is really important. We learn even more about the profound love which Jesus had for this family. Jesus did not love them because they were perfect, but because He Himself was love incarnate. Mary's statement implied that Jesus was to blame for the demise of her brother Lazarus. Even though Mary mixed faith with unbelief, Jesus answered her prayer. It is not perfect faith that God requires, but faith even as small as a mustard seed will do. Because of her small faith, Mary saw the power of God demonstrated at her brother's grave.

LESSON 8: January 19
Pilate: Judge on Trial
John 18:31-38; 19:12-16a

This biblical narrative describes the trial and crucifixion of Jesus. Here we see Him in the presence of Pilate, the Roman judge. Pilate tried to avoid judging Jesus by allowing the religious authorities to try Him, but they declined because they could not pronounce a death sentence (18:31-32). After Pilate's cross-examination of Jesus, he could find no case against Him (vv. 33-38). Pilate wanted to release Jesus, but he did not because of the religious leaders' threats (19:12). Pilate presented Jesus to the religious leaders as their king, but they denied that He was their king and demanded that He be crucified (vv. 13-15). Pilate yielded to the leaders' wishes (v. 16).

Who was on trial here? That is the real question. While Pilate stood in judgment over Jesus, it was actually he who was being judged. He was being judged for his cowardice. He was being judged for a warped sense of justice. He was being judged for his indecisiveness. How many times have we yielded to the pressure of the opinions of others? How many times have we followed the humanly expedient way and avoided the interior divine mandate? Yes, it is true that Jesus had to die. But if truth be told, Pilate did not have to be a part of it. God had sent an angel to his wife to help him keep his hands clean. For all of this, the judge now sits judged. Furthermore, in this lesson we see the Judge of the universe subjected to the flawed and fallen human idea of justice. The Judge of the universe accepted this injustice clothed in the veneer of justice for our sake.

LESSON 9: January 26
Peter: Restored Leader
Luke 22:31-34, 54-62; John 21:17

The events described in this lesson occur before and after Jesus' death and resurrection. In the Lucan narrative, Jesus indicated that Satan would test each of the disciples. In response to Peter's declaration that he would follow Jesus to death (Luke 22:31-33), Jesus predicted that Peter would deny Him three times before the rooster crowed (v. 34). After Jesus' arrest, Peter followed Him at a distance into the high priest's courtyard (vv. 54-55). Three times Peter was confronted about his association with Jesus, and three times Peter denied that he was a follower of Jesus (vv. 56-60). After the third denial, the rooster crowed, and Peter, remembering the words of Jesus, fled the courtyard, weeping bitterly (vv. 60-62). In a passage from the Johannine Gospel, we see that after the resurrection, Jesus questioned and commissioned Peter (John 21:15-17).

We learn valuable things from the life of Peter in this lesson. How do we respond when the Spirit warns us of an impending temptation? In this case, it was God in the flesh who warned Peter that there was danger around the corner. Do we, like Peter, feel that nothing can harm us? Do we challenge the Spirit or the voice of the Lord? From Peter we learn humility. When temptation lurks, we must turn to the Lord for help. This lesson teaches us the danger of taking on temptation in our own strength. The lesson also teaches us that our downfall should never

be our death. However, we must approach our failure as Peter did, with contrition and brokenness of heart. Most of all, we learn that God is willing to restore us to Himself and to grant us a new commission for the kingdom. With God there is never a down and out as long as we are still in the ring.

UNIT 3. PERSONALITIES IN THE EARLY CHURCH

Unit 3 focuses on prominent people in the church's early days. The first session is a study of Barnabas and his key role as an encourager and enabler. The second session examines Paul's testimony before Agrippa, Bernice, and Festus. The third session presents Timothy as Paul's assistant and consistent contributor to the Gospel's spread. The fourth session explores the key role that Aquila and Priscilla played in the church's missionary efforts.

LESSON 10: February 2
Barnabas: Encourager and Enabler
Acts 4:36-37; 9:26-27; 11:22-26; 15:36-41

Biblically, we traverse four chapters of the Book of Acts to discover gems in the life of Barnabas. Joseph, who was called Barnabas ("one who encourages"), sold a field and gave the proceeds to the apostles (4:36-37). When the apostles were frightened of Saul, Barnabas vouched for his good character (9:26-27). The church in Jerusalem sent Barnabas to check out the situation in Antioch, and he welcomed the new converts with joy (11:22-24). Barnabas sought out Paul to minister with him in Antioch, where believers were first called "Christians" (vv. 25-26).

Barnabas and Paul decided to make a second missionary journey, but instead went their separate ways when Barnabas insisted that Mark go with them (15:36-41). From this lesson, we gain insight into the life of a Christian as manifested by one of the early saints, Barnabas. Here we learn that it is important for us as believers to take the posture of encourager in the life of our brothers and sisters in Christ. Too many of us are critics instead of encouragers. We can also learn from Barnabas's generosity. He could not keep the blessing of the Lord to himself; he had to share it with the people of God. We learn of his outreaching spirit as he makes the first missionary journey with Paul.

LESSON 11: February 9
Paul: Obedient Messenger
Acts 26:12-23, 27-29

The biblical content of this lesson is taken from a passage familiar to those who have been in the church for a while. This is the story of the trial of Paul. In this text, we find Paul standing before Agrippa. While in his presence, Paul tells Agrippa that while he was traveling to Damascus under orders from the chief priests, he saw a blinding light and fell to the ground (vv. 12-14). Paul reports that he heard a voice asking him, "Why are you persecuting me?" Paul responded, "Who are you, Lord?" (vv. 14-15). In response to this query, the Lord identified Himself as Jesus and told Paul to stand up because he was being sent to preach the good news of salvation to the Jews and Gentiles (vv. 15-18). At the end of the selected text, Paul states that he had been obedient to God's call, preaching the coming of the Messiah to Jews and Gentiles as the prophets had foretold (vv. 19-23). In conclusion, Paul urged King Agrippa and all who were listening to believe the Gospel (vv. 27-29).

In this lesson, we revisit the story of the conversion of Paul—this time not in the words of a historical narrator, but in his own words. Here we learn the importance of using our encounter with the Lord as the launching point of our witness. We learn that our encounter must also lead to obedience. For Paul, the encounter led to answering a call to the ministry. Even up to the last moment of his life, this encounter with Christ continued to be the impetus for his witness. We must witness to our encounter with Jesus. We also learn from Agrippa's response. Rather than believing the testimony of God's work through Paul, Agrippa hardened his heart to the message of salvation by seeking to "straddle the fence" (v. 28; also see Hebrews 3:15).

LESSON 12: February 16
Timothy: Valued Helper
Acts 16:1-5; Philippians 2:19-24;
1 Timothy 1:1-3; 2 Timothy 1:3-5

Timothy's value to Paul forms the basis of the biblical emphasis of this lesson. In the first text, we learn that on his second missionary journey Paul went to Lystra, where he met a Christian named Timothy who was the child of a Jewish mother and a Greek father (Acts 16:1). In the second passage, we learn that Timothy was highly recommended by believers, so Paul chose him to go with them; but first Paul had him circumcised because the Jews knew his father was a Gentile (vv. 2-3). With Timothy at Paul's side, the missionaries visited the churches to let them know that the Jerusalem Council had approved the missionaries' work in converting the Gentiles. The churches were strengthened in faith and grew in numbers (vv. 4-5). We also learn of Timothy's value when Paul tells the Philippian church that he hoped soon to send Timothy, a trustworthy servant, to minister to them because he was genuinely concerned about their welfare (Philippians 2:19-24). Paul urged Timothy to remain in Ephesus to help keep the doctrines of the faith pure (1 Timothy 1:1-3). Finally, we see how Paul remembered that Timothy's sincere faith had been passed down from his mother Eunice and his grandmother Lois (2 Timothy 1:3-5).

Therefore, we learn in this lesson the power of a godly upbringing. Timothy's life is a clear example of the power of faith to bridge generational and cultural barriers.

LESSON 13: February 23
Priscilla and Aquila: Partners in the Gospel
Acts 18:1-4, 24-26; Romans 16:3-4;
1 Corinthians 16:19; 2 Timothy 4:19

Paul, Priscilla, and Aquila worked together as tentmakers (Acts 18:1-3). This arrangement allowed Paul to attend the synagogue every Saturday to witness to the Gospel of Jesus Christ (v. 4). Priscilla and Aquila helped Apollos, a great apologist for the messiahship of Jesus, to proclaim the Gospel more completely (vv. 24-26). Paul sent greetings to Priscilla and Aquila, who risked their lives to save his life and earned his thanks and those of all the Gentile churches (Romans 16:3-4). Aquila and Priscilla also hosted a Christian church in their home (1 Corinthians 16:19). Paul instructed Timothy to greet Aquila and Priscilla (2 Timothy 4:19).

SPIRITUAL POWER THEN AND NOW

by Jennifer D. King

Aside from the introduction of the Savior, the hallmark of the New Testament writings is the presence of the Spirit in the lives of the personalities we encounter there. The spiritual power active in the lives of these men and women is the key ingredient that propels the Gospel out of the narrow confines of Judaism and the city of Jerusalem and out to the uttermost parts of the world—all within the span of a single generation.

Twenty centuries later, although Christians continue to meet and recite the Great Commission of Jesus Christ to "go therefore and make disciples of all nations" (Matthew 28:19a, RSV), dwindling memberships and lackluster witness are evidence of a marked absence of the spiritual power that built the first-century church. The answer lies perhaps in the contemporary church's mistaken notion that Christ's intention for the Word to reach the ends of the earth was to be borne on the strength of Christians alone. The very idea that kingdom building for *God* should rest on *human* ability is preposterous. Certainly today's church is still the body of Christ; but our ability to operate effectively, as did the first-century church, has been severely hampered because Christians do not fully utilize the gifts given to them by Christ. Effective ministry is essential and relies on more than our "being saved." We must move beyond salvation and claim the spiritual power God promises us.

From the beginning, the men and women in the first-century church were directed, energized, and empowered through the ministry of the Holy Spirit. On the Day of Pentecost, when the Holy Spirit was poured out on the 120 individuals in the temple courts, they ceased their existence merely as believing individuals and became a single living organism. Specifically, they became the resurrected body of Christ. The same men and women who had witnessed the heart-breaking trauma of Jesus' betrayal, His agonizing crucifixion, and the astonishing fact of

His resurrection were now able, through this confirming transformation, to reach out to the "uttermost parts of the earth"—boldly preaching, witnessing, baptizing, teaching, and building up new believers in such a short period of time.

This direction of the Holy Spirit is evidenced in the life of Philip, a leader of the Greek-speaking Christians in Jerusalem. Philip went to Samaria and began preaching the Gospel. The intensity of his speaking and the power of the Holy Spirit were followed by miracles: "When they believed Philip as he preached the good news of the kingdom of God and the name of Jesus Christ, they were baptized, both men and women" (Acts 8:12). Philip is instructed by the Holy Spirit to leave the great city-wide revival he is conducting in Samaria and "go down to a man in the desert." Surely Philip must have been astonished at this direction. There he was, preaching in pagan territory, and the crowds were not only enthusiastically responding but were receiving Christ. Yet instead of relying on his own understanding, Philip followed the direction of the Spirit, left the crowd in Samaria, and went in search of a single man. Philip encountered the Ethiopian eunuch, who was reading but not understanding a passage from Isaiah 53. The Spirit led Philip to the Ethiopian at just the right time—God's time—and Philip was able to use the very Scripture the Ethiopian was struggling with to teach the African about Jesus and baptize him in the name of Christ. Philip's Spirit-directed evangelism helped spread the Gospel to Africa!

Jesus' birth, death, and resurrection secured for each believer the power of the Holy Spirit. This assurance prompted Paul to declare, "Now unto him that is able to do exceedingly abundantly above all that we ask or think, according to the power that worketh in us . . ." (Ephesians 3:20). One can only imagine what would happen if modern saints allowed the Holy Spirit to direct their evangelistic efforts more fully. How the church would grow if only we prayed earnestly for spiritual direction and left the comfort of the "church crowd" to minister to the men and women we encounter on the roads every day. Sadly, many of us simply lack the faith to receive the power of the risen Lord, in spite of Jesus' promise that it is ours. Instead of responding to the divine promise, "But ye shall receive power, after that the Holy Ghost is come upon you" (Acts 1:8a), we continue to rely instead on the power of the world. It is no wonder that many our churches are weak and lifeless: we are trying to do God's work in our own strength, rather than by His gift of spiritual power.

A close look at the ministry of the tentmaker Aquila and his wife Priscilla also testifies to the Holy Spirit's ability to energize and empower believers. The same Spirit that energized Paul energized this couple, not only to open their home to Paul, but to assist in building up the congregation. While it is not clear when Aquila and Priscilla became Christians, it must have occurred very shortly after their meeting. By the time Paul left Corinth for Ephesus, this husband and wife had become zealous promoters of Christianity. It was undoubtably the Spirit who led them to leave their tentmaking business and travel to Ephesus with Paul to help him with his missionary efforts there. Perhaps more important was their Spirit-led ability to teach the eloquent young preacher, Apollos.

Though Apollos "spake and taught diligently of the things of the Lord," he was only aware "of the baptism of John" (Acts 18:25). Aquila and Priscilla invited the young preacher into their home and led him into a more accurate understanding. With Spirit-led hospitality, they were able to "expound unto him the way of God more perfectly" and thus further the spread of Christianity. Whether in Corinth, Ephesus, or later Rome, the home of Aquila and Pricilla was a place of assembly for believers. Paul acknowledged the immeasurable assistance provided by the couple. In his letter to the Romans, Paul addresses them as "my helpers in Christ Jesus" and goes on to acknowledge that in assisting his ministry efforts the couple had even risked their own lives.

Spiritual power was particularly strong in the church at Philippi, a city of Macedonia in northern Greece. Interestingly, this group was composed primarily of women. Among them was Lydia, a Thyatiran businesswoman. Following her baptism and the baptism of her entire household, her first Spirit-led work was to open her home to Paul and his companions. Similarly, the ministry of Phoebe, as well as of Lois and Eunice (Timothy's grandmother and mother), enabled Paul and other missionaries to continue their efforts without having to concern themselves with lodging, food, and hospitality. It is important to note that these women were not ordained ministers, yet we see that their work was absolutely essential to the growth of the early church. The Holy Spirit equipped and enabled all of the necessary workers. Not only ordained preachers, but lay members—men and women— were equipped by the Holy Spirit and empowered to dedicate their lives and wealth to a single goal: the proclamation of the Gospel of Jesus Christ.

How involved is the laity of the modern-day church in the spreading of the Gospel? Do we think that it is the work of the preacher or perhaps the choir to attract, teach, and convict the unsaved? Do we selfishly pray that the Spirit fall afresh on the pastor to enable him to do all the work of the church? If so, then let's return to the Day of Pentecost. The Holy Spirit filled not only the apostles, but other followers as well. After Peter spoke, more than 3,000 baptisms took place, and the church proceeded to grow rapidly. Certainly this could not have taken place had only Peter and the apostles been equipped for ministry. These men had the support of thousands of members, all of whom were dedicated not only to preaching Christ in Jerusalem, but also to evangelizing the world.

The Holy Spirit, the same power that gave impetus to the first-century Christians, is still available to us today. Our Savior promised, "Lo, I am with you always" (Matthew 28:20). It is not enough that we are saved; it is dangerous to merely content ourselves with "going to church." In order to carry out our Lord's commission, we must be involved in kingdom building that "much people" may again be "added unto the Lord" (Acts 11:24).

Jennifer D. King is Superintendent of Sunday School for Bay Area Christian Connection. She holds a B.A. with honors in English and is currently working toward a Masters of Arts degree.

THE PROPHETIC TASK OF THE AFRICAN AMERICAN CHURCH

Dr. A. Okechukwu Ogbonnaya, Ph.D.

"Our young people have forgotten." You may have heard this complaint. I hear this statement from our elders everywhere I go. My question is, "Whose fault is it?" How can our children learn when we keep telling the story to ourselves? Tell the stories in the church. Tell the stories at prayer meeting. The African American church has been the major prophetic voice in this society and a major reminder of God's work among us. Cyprian, one of the African church fathers, referred to the church as "mother." There is hardly a leader in the African American community who has not learned upon the knees of the Black church. Indeed, the church has been the nurturer of greatness among people. It has been the voice of Africans who are without a voice. God has used the African American church powerfully in history. Therefore, it is not surprising that several major figures who have spoken of liberation and conscience have been African Americans.

It is the duty of those in the Black church today to help our people remember the God who brought us through many troubled times. For example, during the Civil Rights movement, the church was the place where the warriors of right-

> *It is the duty of those in the Black church today to help our people remember the God who brought us through many troubled times.*

eousness and justice found refuge and spiritual renewal. The Black church remains the place where people have waged spiritual warfare with those who seek to deny our humanity and keep us in perpetual servitude. From the days of Bishop Allen (the founder of the African Methodist Episcopal church) to the ministers of today, it has been the place where the untapped potential of people of African descent has been released to soar. While society painted a sordid picture of the African, the church proclaimed hope and preached righteousness through the power of God's love as revealed in Jesus Christ.

The paradigm by which the Black church has confronted unrighteousness perpetrated on her people has become the model for many nations around the world. From St. Petersburg to Johannesburg, Romania to Rhodesia—the songs of freedom by the African American church have been heard. The freedom light that burns within the heart and soul of the African American church is what enables her to clearly see the acts of our society. This may lead to her judgment, but it also allows her to be a powerful intercessor with God and a dynamic advocate for the righteousness and justice of God in this century—yes, even in this millennium.

PORTRAITS OF FAITH

by Judith St.Clair Hull, Ph.D.

Hebrews 11:1 defines faith as "the substance of things hoped for, the evidence of things not seen." No human artist could paint a picture of faith, but it is faith that helps us to see the unseen. In the secular world, people often speak of the importance of faith, but they do not say what that faith is in. Biblical faith is not just an ethereal feeling; biblical faith rests upon actual substance. The Bible gives us a body of truth upon which to base our faith. Although this body of truth cannot be measured or seen, it is more solid and more real than the physical world that surrounds us. And God says that it is impossible to please Him without faith (Hebrews 11:6). Then, Hebrews 11 goes on to give examples of how biblical people demonstrated their faith by the ways that they lived.

This quarter, we take a stroll through an art gallery with portraits of faith displayed. An artist tries to portray more than just the physical likeness. Maybe the artist shows some special objects in the picture: a favorite pet, a picture of the children, or maybe just a mysterious smile like that of the Mona Lisa, which intrigues us but gives only hints as to the character of the woman portrayed. The writers of the New Testament paint pictures of personalities with words, words that mostly describe the things these people did but sometimes directly tell us what they were like. When we read these portraits, Scripture beckons us to see if we see ourselves in these personalities.

Not everyone is the same. We each respond differently to Jesus because our personalities are different. Jesus understands our differences because He created us. The New Testament presents us with a cross-section of people who interacted with Jesus and His ministry. Which one is most like you? Which one would you like to be like? How is God interacting with you in your life? This quarter is

entitled, "Portraits of Faith." Which is your portrait of faith?

The first portrait is of a husband and wife—Elisabeth and Zacharias. Luke paints the picture of two people who were faithful and obedient to the Lord for many years, but Zacharias hesitated and doubted when called upon to make a daring leap of faith. This couple had prayed many years for a child until they were old, and then they gave up. Now an angel was telling Zacharias that soon he and Elisabeth would have a wonderful child, John the Baptist. Zacharias doubted the word of the angel, so the angel Gabriel struck him silent until John was born. Although Gabriel declared that Zacharias was to be mute until the birth of John, God still rewarded the faithfulness of Elisabeth and Zacharias with this wonderful child. Maybe you have been faithfully following the Lord Jesus for many years, with no extraordinary adventures in your spiritual life. But would you take a leap if He called you to?

Elisabeth and Zacharias lived in a town in the hill country of Judah, probably one of a number of Levite cities in that area. For six months, Elisabeth felt the stirrings of new life in her belly. Meanwhile, in Nazareth, about a two- or three-day walk away, Gabriel came to tell Mary, kin to Elisabeth, that she also was going to give birth—to the Son of God! Mary was a young virgin; scholars suppose about fifteen years old. She must have meditated often on Scripture, because her song of praise is so much like Hannah's in the Old Testament, when Hannah praised God for the promised birth of Samuel. Biblical archeologists think that Nazareth was a village founded about two or three hundred years before the birth of Christ. Several small villages were founded in that era by exiles returning to the land because they ardently believed that soon God was going to send

His promised Messiah. In such a community of expectation, Mary was suddenly going to be pregnant. Her neighbors were poor (some even lived in caves in the hills), but they were very religious. How would they respond to the pregnancy of an unwed teen? Perhaps the most stirring verse is from Luke 1:38: "Behold the handmaid of the Lord; be it unto me according to thy word." In godly trust, Mary is ready for whatever God has for her, regardless of the personal cost. Are you filled with youthful trust in the Lord? Are you ready for His call to you, no matter what the circumstances?

Joseph, the carpenter, lived in Nazareth also. He was older, perhaps forty-five years old. He looked at innocent and virtuous Mary. He watched her godly life and desired to marry her. He was not rich, but he had a steady trade. Not only did he saw wood and pound nails; he also made walls of piled-up stone covered with stucco-like mud and carved homes into the caves in the hills. In other words, he was an all-around contractor, doing every part of the work of building. He lived the comfortable life of a bachelor but was willing to trade it in for a marriage to the sweet young Mary. But then he heard the news that his supposedly virtuous fiancée was pregnant. Another man might have reacted in anger and not have been blamed for it. But Joseph was going to divorce her privately (necessary even to break an engagement in those days). Then Gabriel appeared to Joseph and told him that this baby was the Son of God, and this comfortable bachelor became the stepfather of our Lord. Is Jesus calling you out of your comfort zone? Are you ready to follow Him?

John the Baptist was born, grew up, and became a fiery prophet, calling people to turn from their sins and turn to God. He had heard of Jesus, his cousin. When Jesus began His ministry, John was soon convinced that Jesus was the Messiah, the promised Savior. But then John was imprisoned by Herod. Behind those bars, he became discouraged. If Jesus was really the Messiah, why didn't He come and get him out of that prison? Why didn't He rescue His cousin, who was trying to point people to Him? We could hardly blame John for having a lapse of faith. How about you? Are you having struggles that are causing you to waver in your faith?

Then we see a portrait of a rich man. We are not given his name, but he is a very moral person. He says that he has kept all of the commandments, yet when Jesus asks him to give his money to the poor, we see beyond the outward appearance. Inside, he values his riches more than people. He has not enough compassion for the poor to share what he has with them. What about you? Are you just a good "church person"? Or are you ready to show your faith, even with your money?

Next we come to Mary and Martha. The actions and words of these two sisters show how different they were from each other, and yet they both loved Jesus. Martha was the take-charge, get-it-done sister. Mary was the reflective, less aggressive one. When Martha criticized her sister for not being like her, Jesus affirmed Mary's priorities of just listening to Him and loving Him. But Jesus did not say that Martha was wrong to cook and clean for Him. He just wanted her to realize the importance of quietness in the presence of the Lord. What is your approach to life? How would you describe your personality? How do you show your love for the Lord? What is your portrait of faith?

The only ugly portrait in this gallery of faith is that of Pilate, the man who sentenced Jesus to die on the cross. Pilate thought he was putting Jesus on trial, but in reality Jesus was putting Pilate on trial. Pilate knew that Jesus was innocent, but he was too anxious to please the crowd. He thought he could wash his hands of this mess, but he is ever remembered as the man who sentenced Jesus to death. Pilate is the only person portrayed in this quarter who completely failed the test of faith. We hope this is not you.

The Bible gives us many pictures of Peter. We see Peter growing in faith right before our eyes. At first, Peter is impetuous and emotional, always speaking before thinking. He promises Jesus that he would die for him, but Jesus could see that Peter would deny Him within the next twenty-four hours. And so Peter denies Jesus as he suddenly sees Him being led to the cross. Peter runs away, weeping bitterly. Sometimes we have crises in our lives and we do not come through for Jesus. But we can be encouraged with Jesus' response to Peter. Jesus knew that deep inside Peter loved Him, and so, not only did He forgive Peter, but He gave him a great responsibility. Peter went on to be a strong leader in the early church, opening many doors in the name of Christ. If you see yourself in this portrait of Peter denying our Lord, do not be utterly discouraged. God sees your heart, and He is giving you another chance.

Scripture tells us very little about Barnabas, but Barnabas had some wonderful character traits. Barnabas was an encourager. When all the disciples were suspicious of Saul, the former persecutor of the church, Barnabas stood up for him, and so Saul was accepted and became Paul, one of the greatest witnesses for our Lord. When the first non-Jewish church was formed, Barnabas was sent to encourage and teach the new believers. He called for Paul to help him, and thus Paul had an opportunity to grow in his own ministry gifts. But when Paul gave up on John Mark because of his immature faith, Barnabas took John Mark under his wing, and one day Paul was able to appreciate John Mark as a more mature believer. Barnabas had a ministry of encouraging others in their faith. Is this a character trait you are nourishing in yourself?

Barnabas introduced the disciples to Paul, whom Scripture portrays as a man who was bent on discovering followers of Jesus and persecuting them, sometimes even to death; but then he was marvelously, whole-heartedly committed to Jesus.

Paul was a brave preacher, suffering much for Jesus. But Paul was never afraid to witness of what the Lord had done for him. What about you? Does your faith in the Lord drive you to tell others about Jesus?

Timothy was discipled by Paul. He was a young believer when Paul met him. Timothy had already established himself as having great potential as a minister of the Gospel. But as Timothy accompanied Paul, he was ready to play a supportive role. After accompanying Paul in extensive ministry, Timothy was ready to minister on his own. Maybe God has a role for you supporting others in the ministry. Who knows what great role of faith will be next!

Our final portrait is that of a couple, as was our first. Priscilla and Aquila had a very egalitarian ministry as teachers together. They taught, they extended hospitality, and they risked their lives for Paul and for the Gospel. Do you have a ministry with your spouse? How can the two of you demonstrate your faith in the Lord?

Make a quick review of the portraits we have seen. Which one do you identify with? This quarter you will take an in-depth look at some of the Scriptures that reveal the portraits. As you study, you will be encouraged to take a leap of faith for Christ and His ministry.

Dr. Judith St.Clair Hull is the Senior Editor at Urban Ministries, Inc. She holds a Masters of Art degree from Northeastern Illinois University and a Ph.D. from Trinity Evangelical Divinity School in Indiana.

ST. AUGUSTINE OF HIPPO
(354-420 A.D.)

To this day, he is respected as one of the greatest church fathers by all branches of Christianity.

An African Christian from the Berber people, born in Tagaste. He received Christian education at home and at church. His father saw to it that he studied liberal arts. After Augustine graduated from school in Tagaste, his father, through the help of a friend, secured money for him to attend the University of Carthage. At the university he majored in Rhetoric, according to his father's wishes. His father's hope was that Augustine would become a lawyer, thereby raising the fortunes of the family.

In the course of studying at Carthage, Augustine moved completely away from the faith that his mother taught him, developing an interest in philosophy. This interest led Augustine from one religion to another, until he met Ambrose of Milan and was converted to Christianity. He became a Christian in 387 A.D. and was baptized in the city of Cassiacum on the day before Easter. The following year, he and his mother boarded a ship bound for Africa, where they intended to serve the Lord among their African brothers and sisters. However, on their way to Africa, his mother died. St. Augustine started a monastery and a school for Christian thought in his home village of Tagaste.

Augustine was a deeply spiritual man, and his spirituality and gifts were evident to many Christians. St. Augustine's thoughts have influenced much of modern theological thought. To this day, he is respected as one of the greatest church fathers by all branches of Christianity. His spiritual depth reflects the deep spiritual sensibility of our African ancestry and its contribution to the Christian faith.

TEACHING TIPS

December 1
Bible Study Guide 1

1. Words You Should Know

A. Course of Abia (Luke 1:5)—The eighth of twenty-four classes, or divisions, of the Jewish priesthood responsible to service the needs of the temple (see MORE LIGHT ON THE TEXT and read 1 Chronicles 24:1-19 and 2 Chronicles 8:14).

B. Ordinances (v. 6)—From the Greek word *dikaioma*, pronounced **dih-KAI-oh-mah.** It is used here in its Old Testament meaning to refer to the highest ideals of Jewish piety: the requirements, statutes, precepts, judgments, and regulations of the Mosaic Law (cp. Genesis 26:5; Deuteronomy 6:1; 7:11; 30:16).

C. Hill country (v. 39)—Luke's use of the phrase "into the hill country" describes the terrain of Judah and helps the reader to appreciate the considerable distance and duration of Mary's journey. Most students of the New Testament judge the distance to have been about 80 to 100 miles, a three- to four-day's journey.

2. Teacher Preparation

A. Read Isaiah 40:3-11, as well as Luke 1:5-66. These readings will help give you a general feeling and deeper appreciation for the drama of the FOCAL VERSES and their historical relationship to Isaiah's prophecy concerning the coming of Israel's long-awaited Messiah.

B. Read IN FOCUS, THE PEOPLE, PLACES AND TIMES, and BACKGROUND.

C. Using WORDS YOU SHOULD KNOW, IN DEPTH, and MORE LIGHT ON THE TEXT, study the FOCAL VERSES.

D. For this session you will need newsprint or a chalkboard.

3. Starting the Lesson

A. Share the purpose and aim of this session. Have one of your students read the FOCAL VERSES aloud.

B. Divide your students into two groups: female and male. Ask the females to discuss how they might have felt and share the questions they might have asked if they had been in Elisabeth's shoes. Ask the males to discuss the same had they been in Zechariah's shoes. Allow 10 to 12 minutes for this dialog.

4. Getting into the Lesson

A. Reconvene the groups and list some of the feelings and questions discussed in the separate groups. Use some of these stated feelings and questions to spark an in-depth discussion of real-life issues, such as the difficulty many couples have conceiving children.

B. If more information is needed, use some of the questions under DISCUSS THE MEANING.

5. Relating the Lesson to Life

A. Ask students to share any personal experiences —concerning the faithfulness of God in the birthing and rearing of children.

B. Guide the students in praying for those couples who may be struggling with any of the issues discussed. Pray that they might remain faithful to God and to each other.

6. Arousing Action

A. Ask two or three students to summarize how this lesson has helped them.

B. Close the session with some encouraging and affirming words about God's faithfulness toward those who remain faithful.

WORSHIP GUIDE

For the Superintendent or Teacher
Theme: The Faithfulness of God
Theme Song: "Great Is Thy Faithfulness"
Scripture: Lamentations 3:22-23
Song: "Joyful, Joyful, We Adore Thee"
Meditation: We thank You, Lord, for Your faithfulness toward us. Give us courage, O God, to delight ourselves in You and to do Your righteous will while we wait for You to give us the desires of our hearts.

ELISABETH AND ZACHARIAS: PARENTS OF THE FORERUNNER

Bible Background • LUKE 1:5-66
Printed Text • LUKE 1:5-14, 39-45, 57-58
Devotional Reading • ISAIAH 40:3-11

LESSON AIM

Using Elisabeth and Zacharias as models, students will be given an opportunity to learn some of the ways God works in our midst, particularly in our disappointments, to reward us for our faithfulness.

KEEP IN MIND

"But the angel said unto him, Fear not, Zacharias: for thy prayer is heard; and thy wife Elisabeth shall bear thee a son, and thou shalt call his name John" (Luke 1:13).

FOCAL VERSES

Luke 1:5 There was in the days of Herod, the king of Judaea, a certain priest named Zacharias, of the course of Abia: and his wife was of the daughters of Aaron, and her name was Elisabeth.

6 And they were both righteous before God, walking in all the commandments and ordinances of the Lord blameless.

7 And they had no child, because that Elisabeth was barren, and they both were now well stricken in years.

8 And it came to pass, that while he executed the priest's office before God in the order of his course,

9 According to the custom of the priest's office, his lot was to burn incense when he went into the temple of the Lord.

10 And the whole multitude of the people were praying without at the time of incense.

11 And there appeared unto him an angel of

LESSON OVERVIEW

LESSON AIM
KEEP IN MIND
FOCAL VERSES
IN FOCUS
THE PEOPLE, PLACES,
AND TIMES
BACKGROUND
AT-A-GLANCE
IN DEPTH
SEARCH THE SCRIPTURES
DISCUSS THE MEANING
LESSON IN OUR SOCIETY
MAKE IT HAPPEN
FOLLOW THE SPIRIT
REMEMBER YOUR THOUGHTS
MORE LIGHT ON THE TEXT
DAILY BIBLE READINGS

the Lord standing on the right side of the altar of incense.

12 And when Zacharias saw him, he was troubled, and fear fell upon him.

13 But the angel said unto him, Fear not, Zacharias: for thy prayer is heard; and thy wife Elisabeth shall bear thee a son, and thou shalt call his name John.

14 And thou shalt have joy and gladness; and many shall rejoice at his birth.

1:39 And Mary arose in those days, and went into the hill country with haste, into a city of Judah;

40 And entered into the house of Zacharias, and saluted Elisabeth.

41 And it came to pass, that, when Elisabeth heard the salutation of Mary, the babe leaped in her womb; and Elisabeth was filled with the Holy Ghost:

42 And she spake out with a loud voice, and said, Blessed art thou among women, and blessed is the fruit of thy womb.

43 And whence is this to me, that the mother of my Lord should come to me?

44 For, lo, as soon as the voice of thy salutation sounded in mine ears, the babe leaped in my womb for joy.

45 And blessed is she that believed: for there shall be a performance of those things which were told her from the Lord.

1:57 Now Elisabeth's full time came that she should be delivered; and she brought forth a son.

58 And her neighbours and her cousins heard how the Lord had shewed great mercy upon her; and they rejoiced with her.

IN FOCUS

Although science has made available alternatives to conceiving one's own children, these options are pursued in the face of difficult questions, ambivalent feelings, and many known and unknown legal issues.

I remember a few years ago talking with a young couple who tried unsuccessfully to have children of their own. After extended consultation with their physician and several medical tests, the wife's inability to conceive was confirmed. After much prayer and counseling they decided to adopt. Today they are the joyful parents of two adopted children—a boy and a girl.

Another story drawn from my own pastoral experience comes to mind. A young lady wanted desperately to birth her own child. She was in her late thirties and had lost hope of ever getting married. The young lady came to me wanting to know the church's stance with reference to artificial insemination and in vitro fertilization. After extended conversations with me and with others who served as a confidential support group for her, it was ultimately her physician who, because of her health, counseled against her pursuing either method. It was then that she and her support group began to pray and talk about adoption. Today she is the proud and happy mother of an adopted son.

In each case, the church proved to be, and continues to be, a source of encouragement and support to these adoptive parents. Moreover, the parents are finding fulfillment in knowing that they are pursuing God's will for their lives.

Whatever the process or difficulties involved in conceiving one's own children or adopting children, the coming of a child into one's family life is an exciting and challenging experience. When they arrive they come as gifts from God. There is probably no greater way by which to exercise faithfulness and to experience the faithfulness of God than to assume responsibility for rearing children.

The biblical story of Elisabeth and Zacharias provides an opportunity for us to look in on a couple who had difficulty in conceiving children, but whose faithfulness, in time, met with the faithfulness of God. Those who, like Zacharias and Elisabeth, wait patiently on the Lord will be rewarded.

THE PEOPLE, PLACES, AND TIMES

During the days of Elisabeth and Zacharias, bearing children was considered a blessing from the Lord. Having children, particularly male children who would grow up to lead godly lives, helped to assure the continuance of the family name within the community of faith. The psalmist echoes this sentiment: "Lo, children are an heritage of the LORD, and the fruit of the womb is his reward. As arrows are in the hand of a mighty man; so are children of the youth. Happy is the man that hath his quiver full of them: they shall not be ashamed, but they shall speak with the enemies in the gate" (Psalm 127:3-5).

Moreover, having children promised the provision of care in one's old age. Not to have children was a disgrace. It was a family tragedy viewed as a sign of God's punishment.

It is little wonder, then, that Zacharias and his wife Elisabeth lived so faithfully (see Luke 1:6) and prayed so fervently (see v. 13) for a child. Luke records, however, that "they had no child, because that Elisabeth was barren, and they both were now well stricken in years" (v. 7). But even so, they remained faithful, "walking in all the commandments and ordinances of the Lord blameless" (v. 6). Despite their years of disappointment, they continued faithfully to serve God. Their years of disappointment coupled with their years of faithfulness are a clear reminder that faithful people do have disappointments. Our disappointments need not be the occasion for or enticement to unfaithfulness.

After many years of living with disappointment and waiting on the Lord, and at a time least expected by Zacharias, God kept His promise and rewarded their faithfulness; "Elisabeth . . . conceived a son in her old age . . . " (v. 36).

141

BACKGROUND

Zacharias and his wife were old when the angel Gabriel announced that "thy wife Elisabeth shall bear thee a son, and thou shalt call his name John" (Luke 1:13). The announcement came while Zacharias was going about his normal priestly duties in the temple. Zacharias knew that if he and Elisabeth were to have a child at their age, it would require a miracle of divine intervention. Moreover, Zacharias remembered that his wife had been barren all her life. Consequently, his response to the angel's announcement is almost predictable. Upon hearing the angel's promise, Zacharias' response is one of awe, mixed with doubt and disbelief. His question, though understandable, nonetheless begs for proof: "Whereby shall I know this? for I am an old man, and my wife well stricken in years" (v. 18).

Zacharias's response is a reminder that even good and faithful people have doubts. It may be that by the time of their midlife, Zacharias and Elisabeth had stopped praying for a child. But God refused to forget the prayers of their more youthful days and used this faithful couple in His unfolding plan of salvation.

AT-A-GLANCE

1. Faithful and Righteous, but Childless
(Luke 1:5-7)
2. Listening and Responding to an Angel while Serving in the Temple (vv. 8-11)
3. Zacharias and Elisabeth Are Promised a Son (vv. 12-14)
4. Elisabeth Visits Mary (v. 41a)
5. Elisabeth Blesses Mary (vv. 41b-45)
6. A Time to Rejoice (vv. 57-58)

IN DEPTH

1. Faithful and Righteous, but Childless (Luke 1:5-7)

Elisabeth and Zacharias were faithful and righteous in their living, and they were childless in their old age—a perfect situation for the God who keeps promises and works miracles to exercise His creative will.

Zacharias, whose name means "God remembers," along with his wife Elisabeth, whose name carries the flavor of "my God is the absolutely Faithful One," were models of Jewish piety. They were truly and wholly devoted to God and to His service. They lived moral and responsible lives before both their peers and God. "They were both righteous before God, walking in all the commandments and ordinances of the Lord blameless" (v. 6).

Zacharias was doubly distinguished in that he was a priest married to a priest's daughter. Likewise, Elisabeth was doubly distinguished in that she was the proverbial "virtuous woman" (Proverbs 31:10), who in the folklore of that day "deserved to be married to a priest." Obviously, the child envisioned in God's mind would descend from priestly origins.

But hovering over the beauty of Zacharias and Elisabeth's devout life, and God's yet unannounced promise and plan, was the cloud of Elisabeth's barrenness. Although they prayed fervently for a child (v. 13), the couple's advanced age cancelled any dreams they may have had to be the parents or ancestors of the long-awaited Messiah. What a disappointment! For all practical purposes, nature had spoken; Zacharias and Elisabeth were past the age of bearing children.

It is a real stretch of faith to pray for a change in what nature has already declared finished. Zacharias and Elisabeth, aware of their old age, had probably given up on ever having children of their own. Surely their disappointment must have been great. Yet they did not allow their disappointment to become an occasion for bitterness nor a reason to withdraw their service and devotion to God. They remained faithful to God. Zacharias continued to perform his temple service. Elisabeth managed her barrenness with poise and dignity while she fulfilled her vows of being the loyal wife of a busy priest.

2. Listening and Responding to an Angel while Serving in the Temple (vv. 8-11)

While Zacharias was performing his routine duties as a temple priest, an angel of the Lord appeared and spoke to him. The angel appeared and spoke on the day when it was Zacharias's turn to burn incense. This is significant because, given the number of priests who rendered service in the temple, a priest was privileged to burn incense only once in a lifetime. Consequently, this was a special day for Zacharias. In addition, it was a unique moment for God to speak to Zacharias from "the right side of the altar of incense" (see v. 11 and read the commentary regarding the same under MORE LIGHT ON THE TEXT).

It is also interesting to note that God not only chose to speak to Zacharias on this high day in his life; He also chose a day to speak when "the whole multitude of the people were praying without at the time of incense" (v. 1:10). God tends always to speak when the whole church prays.

3. Zacharias and Elisabeth Are Promised a Son (vv. 12-14)

Zacharias's natural response immediately upon seeing the angel was one of uneasiness mixed with fear. The angel's appearance was so sudden and unexpected. Zacharias was not prepared to see what he saw, nor to hear what he heard. After all, he was deeply involved in representing the people to God and praying for Israel's redemption. But God is always gracious and quick to reassure those who walk before Him in righteousness.

The angel speaks comfortingly to Zacharias. The angel's words of comfort confirmed that Zacharias's long-standing prayer had been heard. In the same breath, the angel announced that Zacharias and his wife Elisabeth would be blessed with a son whose future would be linked with the messianic redemption of Israel. The birth of such a son, the angel concluded, would be cause for joy and great celebration.

4. Elisabeth Visits Mary (v. 41a)

During the time of her pregnancy, Elisabeth received a visit from Mary, who was also overwhelmed by an unusual pregnancy of her own. Upon Elisabeth's hearing Mary's greeting, the child within her "leaped" and moved with joy in her womb, causing her to surrender her thought and speech for use by the Holy Spirit.

5. Elisabeth Blesses Mary (vv. 41b-45)

Filled with the Holy Spirit, Elisabeth blessed Mary and the child Mary was carrying. Expressing the generosity of her spirit, Elisabeth is quick and grateful to acknowledge Mary as the mother of the promised Messiah, whom she recognizes in verse 43 as "my Lord." Finally, in verse 45 (NIV), Elisabeth blesses and commends Mary for believing that what the Lord has said to her will be accomplished.

6. A Time to Rejoice (vv. 57-58)

The dramatic months of suspense and holy drama passed, and Elisabeth gave birth to a son. God's promises had been fulfilled, and Elisabeth's "neighbors and cousins heard how the Lord had shown great mercy upon her; and they rejoiced with her."

Whenever God's activity and will are manifested, it is a time for rejoicing; how much more so when God's activity and will are symbolized in the birth of a child. The birth of a child is refreshing and renewing to people in almost any family or group. It is a time to rejoice—and especially so when a child is born to parents who, like Zacharias and Elisabeth, are "both righteous before God" (v. 6).

SEARCH THE SCRIPTURES

1. Zacharias's wife Elisabeth was of the daughters of _____ (Luke 1:5).

2. Zacharias was a priest of the course of _____ (v. 5).

3. Mary went into the _____ with haste, into a city of _____ (v. 39).

4. _____ was the name given to Elisabeth's son, and _____ gave him that name (v. 13).

5. When Elisabeth heard the salutation of Mary, the babe_____ (v. 41).

DISCUSS THE MEANING

1. How are we to understand the phrase, "the babe leaped in her womb"?

2. What is the significance of the right side of the altar of incense?

3. What is meant by the "course of Abia"?

4. What is the meaning of the name Zacharias? The name Elisabeth?

LESSON IN SOCIETY

Quite often, couples wanting children of their own grow bitter and distance themselves from God upon learning that they cannot have children. Rearing children in one's old age is also a challenge. Zacharias and Elisabeth, however, remind us that barrenness need not be the occasion for forfeiting one's faith in God. Barrenness may well be a time for drawing near to God in hope and in the confidence that our times are in God's hands.

Moreover, the increasing number of grandparents who today are challenged to rear their grandchildren will find the story of Zacharias and Elisabeth to be a refreshing source of encouragement.

May those couples who are having difficulty conceiving children ponder Zacharias's and Elisabeth's story. May they take courage and wait patiently for God to work things out for their good.

MAKE IT HAPPEN

This week identify one or two grandparents who are raising their grandchildren. Take time to call and/or visit them in the interest of offering some service or sharing a word of encouragement. Likewise, identify one or two couples who may be discouraged because their efforts to have children have met with difficulties. Call and/or visit them also with some words of encouragement. In any event, give meaningful time this week to praying for all such people.

Your study and review of Zacharias and Elisabeth's story will help you to be sensitive to some of the needs and concerns of grandparents and of couples who may have difficulty conceiving children.

FOLLOW THE SPIRIT

What God wants me to do:

_____

_____

REMEMBER YOUR THOUGHTS

Special insights you have learned:

_____

_____

MORE LIGHT ON THE TEXT
Luke 1:5-14, 39-45, 57-58

Unlike Matthew, who begins his Gospel with the genealogy of Jesus Christ, and unlike Mark, who begins his Gospel with John's baptism of Jesus, Luke begins his Gospel with the birth of Jesus' forerunner, John the Baptist. Luke's narrative style and attention to historical details in these opening verses suggest that an extraordinary story chronicling extraordinary events is about to unfold.

5 There was in the days of Herod, the king of Judaea, a certain priest named Zacharias, of the course of Abia: and his wife was of the daughters of Aaron, and her name was Elisabeth.

"There was in the days of . . . ." Variations of this literary form are used frequently by Luke as a means of putting events about which he is writing in their historical context. Literally translated, it reads "And it came to pass in the days of . . . ." (See Luke 2:1; 6:12; Compare also Luke 8:22; 9:37; 17:26; 20:1. Note also Luke's frequent use of the phrase "in the/those days of" in 1:39; 4:25; 5:35; 9:36.) Using this literary phrase, Luke ties the births of John the Baptist and Jesus to the long reign of Herod the Great, from around 37 B.C. to 4 B.C.

Most historians depict Herod as a bloodthirsty villain who had little, if any, concern for or commitment to the Jewish Law and way of life. However ruthless Herod's reign, he was the "king of Judaea." Luke uses the term "Judaea" in at least two ways. Here, as in Luke 6:17; 7:17; 23:5, it is used to refer to the land of the Jews. Elsewhere, as in Luke 1:65; 2:4; 3:1; 5:17; 21:21, it is used to refer to the Roman province of Judaea in the south (as opposed to Galilee in the north).

Luke proceeds, in verse 5, to introduce Zacharias and his wife Elisabeth. It is obvious that Luke wants his readers to know of the Jewishness and priestly lineage of both Zacharias and Elisabeth; i.e., Zacharias was a "priest . . . of the

Luke, like all the Gospel authors, was a gifted writer. He used words in ways that challenged the hypocrisy and shattered the myths of his day while conveying multiple truths.

For example, Luke's use of the phrase "righteous before God" suggests that the righteousness of Zacharias and Elisabeth was radically and observably different than the righteousness of the Pharisees who sought man's approval (see Matthew 5:20). Unlike the scribes and the Pharisees, Zacharias and Elisabeth walked "in all the commandments and ordinances of the Lord blameless." They guided their lives and ordered their behavior according to God's will and instruction as laid out in the Torah (the first five books of Moses). Zacharias and Elisabeth were "blameless," not in terms of the decision of a human court, but in terms of God's judgment and assessment of their moral conduct and ethical character. This is not to suggest, however, that Zacharias and Elisabeth had achieved sinless perfection. They had not. Like all of us, they had their moments of doubt and lack of faith as revealed in Luke 1:18-20. Rather, Luke's reference in this verse to Zacharias and Elisabeth's "righteous" and "blameless" lifestyle is intended to show that—contrary to the popular thought of their day (see Leviticus 20:20ff and 2 Samuel 6:20-23)—their childlessness was not the result of sin.

Again, Luke demonstrates his gift as a writer and thus sets the stage for how his readers are to approach and understand what is said in the next verse.

course of Abia," and his wife Elisabeth also descended from a priestly line—she was "of the daughters of Aaron." In summary, this is Luke's way of telling his readers that the forerunner of Jesus, John the Baptist, was born of priestly stock.

According to 1 Chronicles 24:1-19 and 2 Chronicles 8:14, the Jewish priesthood was divided into 24 "courses," or groups of four to nine families. Zacharias was "of the course of Abia" (or Abijah, pronounced **uh BEYE juh**). Each of these classes, or divisions, was responsible to service the needs of the temple for two separate weekly courses, from Sabbath to Sabbath, twice a year. All of the divisions, however, were expected to serve during the religious festivals, such as Passover, Pentecost, and the Feast of Tabernacles. Of these 24 divisions, the division of "Abia" was eighth on the list, as noted in 1 Chronicles 24:10. (Those wishing a fuller description of the details of this priestly function are encouraged to read Chapter 8, Section D: "The Ordinary Priest" in Joachim Jeremias's book *Jerusalem in the Time of Jesus*.)

6 And they were both righteous before God, walking in all the commandments and ordinances of the Lord blameless.

7 And they had no child, because that Elisabeth was barren, and they both were now well stricken in years.

Luke seems to assume that his readers are familiar with the Old Testament book of Genesis and therefore know about Sarah (Genesis 11:30;

17:16-17; 18:10-14; 21:1-6), Rebekah (25:21), Rachel (29:31), and Samson's mother (Judges 13:2-24), as well as Hannah, the wife of Elkanah (1 Samuel 1:1-20). Therefore, Luke's calling attention to Elisabeth's barrenness and to the couple's being past childbearing age is a literary device aimed to alert the reader and to heighten the sense of excitement about the miraculous intervention of God in the verses that are to follow.

8 And it came to pass, that while he executed the priest's office before God in the order of his course, 9 According to the custom of the priest's office, his lot was to burn incense when he went into the temple of the Lord. 10 And the whole multitude of the people were praying without at the time of incense.

With all the introductions now completed, Luke turns in verses 8 through 10 to describe the setting within which the event of verses 11 through 14 happened: "And it came to pass, that while . . . ." more literally, "Now it happened when . . . " In other words, the angel's appearance, Zacharias's response to the angel's appearance, and the angel's message all happened when/while "the course of Abia" (the division in which Zacharias served) was engaged in its scheduled turn of temple service.

Fortunately for Zacharias, it fell to his lot to perform the particular service of burning incense. Given the number of priests that served in each of the twenty-four divisions, and given the fact that only one priest was required to offer incense at the daily sacrifices, this was a once-in-a-lifetime privilege for Zacharias. Moreover, it afforded Zacharias the opportunity to go into "the temple sanctuary" (*ton naon*, pronounced **tahn-nah-AHN**), which comprised the holy place and the holy of holies, as opposed to the entire temple complex (*to hieron*, pronounced **taw-hee-eh-RAHN**), as in Luke 2:27, 37, and 46. Few priests were ever afforded this privilege of getting so close to the holy of holies. Because of the large number of priests, no ordinary priest was allowed to burn incense more than once in a lifetime. Consequently, this was the high point of Zacharias's priestly career.

It is clear from verse 10 that while Zacharias

was inside the temple sanctuary burning incense before God, a crowd of worshipers were outside of the temple sanctuary praying. They were not curious onlookers. They were probably pious, devout Jews who, no doubt, had seen the smoke of the burning incense and, like the Psalmist, were moved to pray and to lift up their "hands as the evening sacrifice" (Psalm 141:2).

Luke seems to be saying in verses 8-10 that Zacharias's encounter with the angel in verses 11-14 took place within the context of the worshiping community. God always speaks to His people when they gather for worship. In this instance, God speaks to Zacharias through an angel.

11 And there appeared unto him an angel of the Lord standing on the right side of the altar of incense.

The phrase "an angel of the Lord" is used here in its Old Testament context and is therefore not to be understood merely as referring to some lower angelic being. Rather, it may be a descriptive phrase used here to refer to the visible presence of God.

Luke goes on to say that the angel was "standing on the right side of the altar of incense." To stand at the right of, or to be placed on the right side of someone or something, suggests being favored. In other words, the right side is the favored side—the side of joy and happiness and salvation.

For example, in Matthew 25:31ff, the day of judgment is envisioned, and Jesus describes how the nations will be separated one from another. Jesus comments, "As a shepherd divideth his sheep from the goats. . . he shall set the sheep [which are the ones blessed of the Father] on his right hand, but the goats [which are the ones cursed] on the left." The right side is the favored side. Therefore, in Luke 1:11, when the angel of the Lord appeared "on the right side of the altar of incense," he was positioned to announce a blessing and to bestow a favor upon the one who witnessed his appearance.

12 And when Zacharias saw him, he was troubled, and fear fell upon him.

When Zacharias saw the angel of the Lord, "he

was troubled." Luke uses the Greek word *etarachthe* (pronounced **eh-tah-ROCK-thay**) from the word *tarasso*, which—when used with reference to people—expresses uneasiness mixed with fear. Thus, Luke adds, "and fear fell on him." The New International Version translates this passage as, "he was startled and was gripped with fear." It should be noted, however, that this is the normal reaction of those who experience the supernatural presence of God.

13 But the angel said unto him, Fear not, Zacharias: for thy prayer is heard; and thy wife Elisabeth shall bear thee a son, and thou shalt call his name John.

Throughout the Bible, "fear not" (*me-phobou*, pronounced **may-fah-BOO,** meaning literally "do not fear") is a common statement of reassurance upon witnessing or experiencing the supernatural activity and presence of God (see Genesis 15:1; 26:24; Judges 6:23; Isaiah 41:10, 13-14; Daniel 10:12, 19; Matthew 1:20; 17:7; 28:5, 10; Mark 5:36; 6:50; Luke 1:30; 2:10; 8:50; Acts 18:9; Revelation 1:17).

The basis for the angel's words of reassurance is the good news that Zacharias's prayer has been heard. Exactly what Zacharias had been praying for is not clear. It is reasonable to conclude, however, that Zacharias, like all devout Jews and other priests of his kind, had been praying for the coming of the Messiah and for the salvation and ". . . consolation of Israel" (see Luke 2:25).

If indeed Zacharias had been praying for the salvation of Israel, the angel's declaration and instruction that ". . . Elisabeth shall bear. . . a son, and thou shalt call his name John" was enough to let Zacharias know that his son would, in some way, be involved in Israel's salvation.

In the social culture of Zacharias's day, it was the customary privilege of the father to name his son. In this instance, the name John is divinely provided and therefore has significant meaning; i.e., "the Lord has been gracious." Because of the Lord's graciousness, John's birth will bring heavenly and eternal joy. Thus, the affirmation of the following verse.

14 And thou shalt have joy and gladness; and many shall rejoice at his birth.

This verse points to a special kind of joy that will come to Zacharias and Elisabeth and then spread to many. Luke uses three words in connection with John's birth to describe this special kind of joy: *chara* (pronounced **kah-RAH**), translated "joy"; *agalliasis* (pronounced **ahng-gah-LEE-ah-siss**), translated gladness; and *charesontai* (pronounced **kah-RAY-san-tie**), translated shall or will rejoice. The phrase "many over the birth of him shall rejoice" makes it clear that this joy, gladness, and rejoicing will, in fact, be occasioned by the birth of John and his involvement in bringing about Israel's salvation.

Luke wants his readers to know that God is going to do a special work through Zacharias and Elisabeth's son John that will benefit many in Israel. God is going to involve John in a plan for saving people.

In the following verses, Luke prepares to introduce his readers to what God is going to do through John and through Mary's coming son.

1:39 And Mary arose in those days, and went into the hill country with haste, into a city of Judah; 40 And entered into the house of Zacharias, and saluted Elisabeth.

These two verses set the stage for the miraculous encounter between two yet unborn children: John the Baptist, whose mother lived in a city in the southern part of Judah, and Jesus, whose mother lived in Nazareth in the north.

The trip from Nazareth to the house of Zacharias was an important trip for Mary because of the distance (probably 50 to 70 miles) and because Mary "went . . . with haste" (Greek *meta spoudas*, pronounced **meh-TAH spoo-DACE** and best translated as "with eagerness"). Mary's eagerness to make this trip is explained in part by the angel's message to her in Luke 1:36: "And, behold, thy cousin Elisabeth, she hath also conceived a son in her old age: and this is the sixth month with her, who was called barren." Mary was eager to talk with someone who, like herself, was expecting, and whose pregnancy (also like hers) pointed to the miraculous.

This was also an important trip for Mary because of the blessing she would receive from Elisabeth upon entering the house of Zacharias.

41 And it came to pass, that, when Elisabeth heard the salutation of Mary, the babe leaped in her womb; and Elisabeth was filled with the Holy Ghost: 42 And she spake out with a loud voice, and said, Blessed art thou among women, and blessed is the fruit of thy womb.

Before Elisabeth could respond to Mary's greeting, the babe "leaped" (Greek *eskirtasen*, (pronounced **s-KERR-tay-seh**) from the Greek verb *kirtao*, (pronounced **kerr-TAH-oh**), which denotes joyful movement. Literally, the babe in her womb leaped (jumped and moved) with joy. This meaning is also affirmed later on in verse 44, where the phrase "leaped in joy" *eskirtasen en agalliasei*, (pronounced **s-KERR-tay-sin in ahng-gahl-ee-AH-say**) is more explicit.

Luke wants his readers to know that Elisabeth understood this movement of the child, and therefore adds the phrase, "and Elisabeth was filled with the Holy Ghost . . ." (v. 41). In other words, Elisabeth was inspired to speak. Literally, she called out with a great cry. Filled with the Holy Ghost, Elisabeth was inspired to pronounce the blessing: "Blessed art thou among women, and blessed is the fruit of thy womb."

43 And whence is this to me, that the mother of my Lord should come to me?

Elisabeth is overwhelmed and realizes that she is honored to have the mother of the Messiah visit her.

44 For, lo, as soon as the voice of thy salutation sounded in mine ears, the babe leaped in my womb for joy.

As already noted, this verse helps to affirm the meaning of the action referenced in verse 41. Its being repeated here may suggest that Luke understands the movement of the unborn child, John the Baptist, to be of extreme importance.

45 And blessed is she that believed: for there shall be a performance of those things which were told her from the Lord.

Elisabeth pronounces an additional blessing upon Mary. The first blessing (see v. 42) focused on Mary's being the mother of the Lord. Here, the blessing focuses on Mary's belief that God will

keep and fulfill His Word. In this, Mary is a model for all who may be tempted to question, or even doubt, God's readiness to perform what He has promised.

With these two blessings, Mary is both humbled and elated. She breaks forth in joyous song with the Magnificat (see vv. 46-55). Following Mary's song, Luke has his readers witness the birth of John the Baptist (see vv. 57-58).

1:57 Now Elisabeth's full time came that she should be delivered; and she brought forth a son. 58 And her neighbours and her cousins heard how the Lord had shewed great mercy upon her; and they rejoiced with her.

Here God's mercy is revealed and made known to those who shared village life with Zacharias and Elisabeth. The birth of a child is always an occasion for sharing with others. Moreover, it is a time for sharing joy when there is the safe delivery of a healthy child.

DAILY BIBLE READINGS

M: An Angel Visits Zacharias
Luke 1:5-13

T: Zacharias Questions the Promise
Luke 1:14-20

W: Elisabeth Conceives
Luke 1:21-25

T: His Name Is John
Luke 1:57-66

F: Zacharias Prophesies
Luke 1:67-75

S: John Will Go Before the Lord
Luke 1:76-80

S: Prepare the Way of the Lord
Isaiah 40:3-11

TEACHING TIPS

December 8
Bible Study Guide 2

1. Words You Should Know

A. Virgin (Luke 1:27)—The word refers to a young, unmarried female. As used here, it refers to a young girl who has not had sexual intercourse.

B. Espoused (Luke 1:27)—From the Greek verb *mnasteuo* (pronounced **mnace-TYOO-o**). Here it is used in the passive voice and means to be asked in marriage, to be betrothed, espoused, committed to another for marriage.

C. Son of the Highest (Luke 1:32)—Luke uses this phrase as a means of pointing to the messianic status of the son to be born to Mary. "He shall be great," and His greatness will be derived from his uniquely exalted status and relationship with God.

D. Handmaid of the Lord (Luke 1:38)—The word "handmaid," from the Greek word *doula* (pronounced **DOO-lay**), means female slave or servant. Its use here highlights Mary's trusting submission to God.

2. Teacher Preparation

A. Familiarize yourself with the background Scripture passage by reading Luke 1:26-56 three or four times. If possible, it will help to read the biblical text from at least three different translations: the King James Version, the New International Version, and the Living Bible are suggested.

B. Review the LESSON AIM and read the FOCAL VERSES again.

C. Finally, become conversant with all the other lesson material, including the information in MORE LIGHT ON THE TEXT.

3. Starting the Lesson

A. After a clear and excited vocal reading of the FOCAL VERSES by one of your students, begin your presentation of this lesson by guiding the students in prayer, asking God to help His children to understand more fully what is involved in accepting God's call and claim upon our lives.

B. Review LESSON AIM and share a personal challenge you may have experienced as a result of your study and preparation for this lesson.

4. Getting into the Lesson

A. Review IN FOCUS and ask two or three students to share personal experiences in which they believed God intervened.

B. Discuss how Mary must have felt and what she must have thought when the angel reassured her and announced that she had "found favor with God" and would become the mother of the Messiah.

5. Relating the Lesson to Life

A. Identify and discuss some of the ways in which God reassures us when we are called upon to participate in what seems to be impossible.

B. Identify and discuss some of the ways people react when God uses them to accomplish what seemed to be impossible. In what, or in whom, do they rejoice when God works through them to accomplish a seemingly impossible task?

6. Arousing Action

A. Some of your students may be facing "impossible situations." If they are willing to share and talk about what they are facing, encourage them to do so.

B. Close the session with prayer. Pray especially for those who shared their concerns.

WORSHIP GUIDE

For the Superintendent or Teacher
Theme: When God Calls
Theme Song: "Jesus Calls Us O'er the Tumult"
Scripture: 2 Timothy 1:7-9
Song: "I Have Decided to Follow Jesus"
Meditation: Give us the courage we need, O God, to answer Your call. May we be ready always to answer: "Here am I, send me."

MARY: CHOSEN FOR BLESSING

Bible Background • LUKE 1:26-56
Printed Text • LUKE 1:26-38, 46-49
Devotional Reading • PSALM 146

LESSON AIM

During this lesson, students will identify and explore some of the fears and attitudes that may discourage people from accepting involvement in things that need to be done but that may seem impossible to do.

KEEP IN MIND

"And the angel said unto her, Fear not, Mary: for thou hast found favour with God. And, behold, thou shalt conceive in thy womb, and bring forth a son, and shalt call his name JESUS" (Luke 1:30-31).

FOCAL VERSES

Luke 1:26 And in the sixth month the angel Gabriel was sent from God unto a city of Galilee, named Nazareth,

27 To a virgin espoused to a man whose name was Joseph, of the house of David; and the virgin's name was Mary.

28 And the angel came in unto her, and said, Hail, thou that art highly favoured, the Lord is with thee: blessed art thou among women.

29 And when she saw him, she was troubled at his saying, and cast in her mind what manner of salutation this should be.

30 And the angel said unto her, Fear not, Mary: for thou hast found favour with God.

31 And, behold, thou shalt conceive in thy womb, and bring forth a son, and shalt call his name JESUS.

32 He shall be great, and shall be called the Son of the Highest: and the Lord God shall give unto him the throne of his father David:

33 And he shall reign over the house of Jacob for ever; and of his kingdom there shall be no end.

LESSON OVERVIEW

LESSON AIM
KEEP IN MIND
FOCAL VERSES
IN FOCUS
THE PEOPLE, PLACES, AND TIMES
BACKGROUND
AT-A-GLANCE
IN DEPTH
SEARCH THE SCRIPTURES
DISCUSS THE MEANING
LESSON IN OUR SOCIETY
MAKE IT HAPPEN
FOLLOW THE SPIRIT
REMEMBER YOUR THOUGHTS
MORE LIGHT ON THE TEXT
DAILY BIBLE READINGS

34 Then said Mary unto the angel, How shall this be, seeing I know not a man?

35 And the angel answered and said unto her, The Holy Ghost shall come upon thee, and the power of the Highest shall overshadow thee: therefore also that holy thing which shall be born of thee shall be called the Son of God.

36 And, behold, thy cousin Elisabeth, she hath also conceived a son in her old age: and this is the sixth month with her, who was called barren.

37 For with God nothing shall be impossible.

38 And Mary said, Behold the handmaid of the Lord; be it unto me according to thy word. And the angel departed from her.

1:46 And Mary said, My soul doth magnify the Lord,

47 And my spirit hath rejoiced in God my Saviour.

48 For he hath regarded the low estate of his handmaiden: for, behold, from henceforth all generations shall call me blessed.

49 For he that is mighty hath done to me great things; and holy is his name.

IN FOCUS

In 1961 a close college classmate of mine, who was within a year and a half of graduating, left college to be a part of the youth movement within the Southern Christian Leadership Conference. His decision did not have the support of his parents, nor the support of his college peers. In addition to being a good student, he had a football scholarship and a host of campus friends. Everything seemed to be going his way. However, he felt called to table his college education and join others in a "full-time" fight for civil rights. Questions like: Where will you live? What source of income will you have? What will you do? What about your education? Why forfeit a football scholarship? What about your parents' concerns? etc. were not priorities for him. His mind was made up, and he proceeded to pursue what to many of his peers seemed to be an impossible, if not untimely, dream.

Several years passed, and I had occasion to catch up with my college friend. He had made a significant contribution to the struggle for civil rights and at the time was pursuing a Ph.D. in sociology.

There are many complex, problematic, and seemingly impossible situations in life that beg for solutions that call for our involvement. The question is, Can the seemingly impossible be accomplished through our lives today? The moral behind my friend's story points to an affirming YES! Moreover, those who accept God's call and trustingly submit themselves to Him will, like Mary, come to know the joy of serving One with whom "nothing shall be impossible."

PEOPLE, PLACES, AND TIMES

Although Joseph and Mary's wedding ceremony had not yet taken place, the betrothal ceremony, usually preceded by a period of courtship, had taken place.

While the Bible gives no information about the age at which girls were married, it is believed that people were married at very young ages. The common expectation was that betrothal could take place as early as 12 years old for girls and 18 years old for boys. We do not know, however, how old Mary was when she was betrothed to Joseph. Nor do we know Joseph's age.

According to the customs of that day, the parents, usually the father or guardians involved, assumed responsibility for all decisions when marriages were being arranged. This is not to suggest that the potential bridegroom and bride made no contribution to the marriage arrangements. Nor does it imply a lack of romance between the marriage partners. For example, we know that "Michal was in love with David" (1 Samuel 18:20)

before Saul initiated plans to arrange for their marriage.

Once the proposal of marriage had been made known to the girl's parents, the parents of both families discussed the conditions of the marriage. These discussions focused primarily upon issues related to the loss of the daughter's labor and other financial matters. When an agreement was reached, a marriage contract was drawn up. Although the parties to the marriage were not normally involved in the conversations that ultimately culminated in the marriage contract, the contract was inviolable and had legal consequences. The contract could not be broken except by divorce.

After contractual agreements had been reached and a marriage contract had been drawn up, a betrothal ceremony was conducted. The betrothal ceremony was a time for the groom to give the bride jewelry (e.g., Genesis 24:53) and to make public his commitment to the terms of the marriage contract. It was also during this ceremony that the dowry payments were made. This public betrothal ceremony often involved the services of a priest. In the eyes of the populace, the couple was married although no wedding ceremony had taken place. Moreover, it was expected that the couple would not engage in sexual intercourse until after the wedding celebration, which was usually a year after the betrothal ceremony. It was during the period of betrothal that the angel appeared to Mary.

This helps to explain Mary's puzzlement and inquiry upon the angel's announcement that she, a virgin, would "conceive . . . and bring forth a son" (Luke 1:31), presumably before her wedding celebration and before the consummation of her marriage. The thought was absurd, unbelievable, and preposterous!

BACKGROUND

That God works in mysterious ways is without question. That He works among and with ordinary people is also evident. In last week's lesson, we witnessed God working with the old priest Zacharias as he conducted his temple duties. In this lesson, God calls upon a devout young Jewish girl who, from all indications, hailed from a "no-account" Galilean village called Nazareth. She had no claim to fame and was not yet married. She was, however, betrothed to a poor carpenter named Joseph.

There was nothing about Mary that would cause anyone to think that she would be singled out and called to fulfill a significant and unique role in God's plan of salvation. "God is no respecter of persons" (Acts 10:34), nor is He above bestowing His favors upon those of low estate.

On the day of the angel's announcement of God's intentions for her life, little did Mary know that she was "highly favoured" (Luke 1:28). When the call came petitioning her for special service in the Lord's work, it appears that Mary was making plans for her wedding. Reminiscent of Zacharias's involvement in temple service, Mary was involved in the service of her own routine responsibilities and wedding plans.

God's call was clear and precise. Although she was puzzled at first, and perhaps a bit frightened by the obvious consequences of accepting the call, God reassures Mary, and His reassurance elicits her positive response. Mary accepts the call, submits herself to obedient service, and rejoices in the God of her salvation.

AT-A-GLANCE

1. The Angel Appears to Mary (Luke 1:26-29)
2. The Angel Reassures Mary (vv. 30-33)
3. The Angel Answers Mary's Question (vv. 34-35)
4. The Angel Leads Mary to Accept Her Chosen Role (vv. 36-38)
5. Mary Rejoices and Magnifies God (vv. 46-49)

IN DEPTH

1. The Angel Appears to Mary (Luke 1:26-29)

When the angel Gabriel appeared to Mary and announced her favor with God, she was perplexed and agitated. The Greek wording suggests that Mary was "gripped by fear" (see the commentary on verse 29 under MORE LIGHT ON THE TEXT).

One has to ask: Why is Mary so troubled, agitated, and fearful? Could it be that she does not feel worthy to receive special favor from God? Maybe she

feels that she is not worthy of being greeted by an angel from God. Or maybe Mary was familiar with the popular folk tale told in the apocryphal book of Tobit 3:7-17. According to this apocryphal text, "Sarah, the daughter of Raguel . . . had been married to seven husbands, and the wicked demon Asmodeus had killed each of them before they had been with her as is customary for wives." Maybe the appearance of the angel Gabriel reminded Mary of this folk tale. Perhaps in her fear she mistakenly took the angel Gabriel to be an evil spirit threatening to prevent her marriage or to do some harm to her or Joseph or both of them. After all, the biblical writer Luke does note that Mary "cast in her mind what manner of salutation this should be" (Luke 1:29). In other words, Mary pondered what kind of greeting she had heard.

No matter how one chooses to evaluate Mary's response, one thing is clear: Mary has been put on notice. She cannot escape or disregard the experience that now has her attention. Whenever God wants our attention, He knows how to get it.

2. The Angel Reassures Mary (vv. 30-33)

Recognizing Mary's fear, the angel Gabriel acts quickly to reassure her and to offer a reason why she should not be afraid. The angel reaffirms what he said in verse 28: "Thou hast found favor with God." Mary has no need to think or to feel herself unworthy. Her social status and humble station in life is not an issue with God. Out of all the women in the world, God chose Mary to "bring forth a son" who was to be called Jesus. This Jesus would be the Son of God and rule an endless kingdom. The descriptive and unqualified statement of verses 32 and 33 is the angel's promise and affirmation to Mary that she will bear a son. This son will be the long-awaited Messiah who will "save his people from their sins" (Matthew 1:21).

3. The Angel Answers Mary's Question (vv. 34-35)

The messianic affirmations of verses 30 through 33 leave Mary a bit puzzled and bewildered, not because she has doubts about bearing a son, but because she does not understand how it is to take place. She cannot understand how she can give birth to a son without having had sexual intercourse with a man. Consequently, Mary asks the angel how this could happen.

Mary's question seems to assume that she believed that fulfillment of the angel's promise was to take place before the consummation of her marriage to Joseph. Otherwise, if she had envisioned fulfillment of the angel's promise after consummating her marriage with Joseph, there would have been no need for her question in verse 34.

No one, not even Mary, could have anticipated the angel's answer to her question. The angel explained that the Holy Spirit would come upon her, and through the Spirit's power she would become pregnant. Moreover, because this was to be a work of the Holy Spirit, the child to be born would be holy and would be called the Son of God.

The Apostle Paul's comments in Galatians 4:4-5 help us to understand the mystery of Luke 1:35. According to Paul, it was necessary for Jesus to be born of a woman in order that he might be like those in need of salvation. It was also necessary for Jesus to be holy in order that he might do the work of saving others from their sins.

4. The Angel Leads Mary to Accept Her Chosen Role (vv. 36-38)

When the angel explained to Mary God's infinite power, using Elisabeth's conception as an example, Mary accepted her chosen role. The angel led Mary to reason that if Elisabeth (who had been barren all her life and was now beyond the age of child bearing) could bear a child, then surely what the angel promised Mary would also come to pass. Mary quickly understood what many of us have come to learn: namely, that it is no secret what God can do. What He does for one, he can do for all.

The angel's reference to Elisabeth's blessed situation proved to be a source of encouragement to Mary. Mary's faith is strengthened, and as a result she believed that everything the angel told her was possible. Indeed, "with God nothing shall be impossible." It is important to note that this promise of verse 38 is written in the future tense and therefore speaks to any contemporary situation: "with God nothing **shall be** impossible."

Acting upon such faith, Mary humbly submits herself in trusting reverence to God: "Behold the handmaid of the Lord; be it unto me according to thy word." May it please God that all who hear His call will follow Mary's example and accept the call.

5. Mary Rejoices and Magnifies God (vv. 46-49)

Wrestling with a call from God is encumbered with many fears, sometimes doubts, and questions not easily answered. But thanks to God's reassuring words of comfort and His abiding presence, accepting the call can be an occasion for rejoicing and magnifying God. This was certainly true in Mary's case.

The hymn of praise recorded in Luke 1:46-49 is the expression of a heart set aglow with commitment to God. When one reads this beautiful lyrical poem, popularly known as the "Magnificat," it becomes increasingly obvious that Mary was conversant with many of the scriptural prayers and hymns (spiritual songs) of her people. For example, compare Luke 1:46 with Psalms 34:3 and 69:30; compare Luke 1:47 with Psalms 24:5, 25:5, 27:9, 35:9, and 95:1; compare Luke 1:48 with Psalm 31:7; compare Luke 1:49a with Psalms 71:19; 126:2; and compare Luke 1:49b with Psalms 99:3, 103:1, and 111:9. It is also clear that Mary's hymn of praise owes some of its inspiration to Hannah's song in 1 Samuel 2:1-10.

Luke 1:46-49 clearly indicates that Mary's prayer language and praise vocabulary were both enriched and enhanced by her knowledge of the prayer hymns and scriptural literature of her day.

Believers today would do well to take a cue from Mary and familiarize themselves deeply with the Scriptures. Our increased knowledge of the Scriptures, particularly the Psalms, will add to our capacity to offer a spontaneous and seasonable verbal response to the activity of God in our midst.

SEARCH THE SCRIPTURES

1. In the sixth month the angel Gabriel was sent from _____ (Luke 1:26).

2. Joseph was of the house of _____ (v. 27).

3. And he shall reign over _____ and of his kingdom _____ (v. 33).

4. For with God _____ (v. 37).

5. And Mary said, My son_____ (v. 46).

DISCUSS THE MEANING

1. What does it mean to be the Lord's handmaid?

2. Discuss the reason and motivation for Mary's

question, "How shall this be, seeing I know not a man?"

3. Discuss in what sense Mary was troubled (see Luke 1:29).

4. In what ways can one's knowledge and familiarity with the Scriptures contribute to one's prayer language?

LESSON IN SOCIETY

Prior to the angel Gabriel's announcement, Mary was a little-known young girl of humble origins living in Nazareth and minding her own business. At best she was looking forward to marrying the carpenter Joseph. But God had additional plans for Mary. The angel Gabriel informed her of those plans and announced God's call and claim upon her life. Mary accepted the call, and her life and her life's agenda were changed forever.

It matters not what one's station is in life: accepting the call of God always changes one's life and reorders one's priorities. God can do great things through those who, like Mary, humbly entrust their lives to His use and care. It may be that our greatest service to God is that of simply saying "Yes" to His call. Responding like Mary ("Be it unto me according to thy word") may well be the key to leading a productive and God-fearing life.

God called, and Mary made herself available. God still calls people to serve His purposes. When He calls us, let us make ourselves available in the confidence that He who calls us will also equip us to do the impossible. God has the capacity to turn our limitations into strengths. We need not fear, for with God, nothing shall be impossible.

MAKE IT HAPPEN

If you are not clear about your calling or purpose in life, take some time this week to seek God's will. He has a plan for everyone's life. In prayer, and through conversation with trusted others, ask God to clear your mind and humble your heart to hear His call. When He shows you the path your feet are to take, answer Him quickly, "Be it unto me according to thy word," and your heart will rejoice and magnify the Lord.

FOLLOW THE SPIRIT

What God wants me to do:

_____

_____

REMEMBER YOUR THOUGHTS

Special insights you have learned:

_____

_____

MORE LIGHT ON THE TEXT
Luke 1:26-38; 46-49

The following verses reveal an incredible story filled with drama, suspense, history, theology, the miraculous, and a touch of mystery. In 13 short verses of Scripture, we are told how God became "God with us" in the person of Jesus.

26 And in the sixth month the angel Gabriel was sent from God unto a city of Galilee, named Nazareth.

"In the sixth month" is a reference to the sixth month of Elisabeth's pregnancy and should not be taken to mean the sixth month of the year. Luke's use of this phrase helps connect Mary's story with that of Elisabeth, as is also seen in verse 36. The connection between the two stories is further enhanced by the involvement of "the angel Gabriel," who is God's messenger to both Elisabeth (Luke 1:19) and Mary (Luke 1:26).

Luke's reference to "a city of Galilee, named Nazareth" would have alerted the readers of his day to Mary's humble origins. Nazareth, though referred to here as a city, was an insignificant village located in the hills of the little-respected region of Galilee. Nazareth's claim to fame is best summarized in Nathanael's question to Philip, "Can anything good come out of Nazareth?" (John 1:46, NKJV).

27 To a virgin espoused to a man whose name was Joseph, of the house of David; and the virgin's name was Mary.

A virgin is a young, unmarried female. As used here, the word implies a young girl who has not had sexual intercourse. This understanding of the word is further illustrated by Mary's question in Luke 1:34. The term "espoused" is more accurately translated as "pledged to be married." Again, see WORDS YOU

SHOULD KNOW. Also, review THE PEOPLE, PLACES, AND TIMES.

By using the phrase, "Joseph, of the house of David," Luke prepares his readers for what is to follow in 1:32-33. Luke's aim is to show that Jesus is a descendant of the royal line of David. The significance of the Davidic descent of Jesus is also highlighted in Luke 2:4 and in Luke 3:23-38. It is also interesting to compare Romans 1:3 and 2 Timothy 2:8.

". . . and the virgin's name was Mary" is a thrice-repeated reference to Mary's virginity: twice here in verse 27 and once in verse 34. This repetition underscores the magnitude of Jesus' rare and miraculous conception.

28 And the angel came in unto her, and said, Hail, thou that art highly favoured, the Lord is with thee: blessed art thou among women.

"And the angel came in unto her" in the Greek implies that the angel came into the house where she was. Upon coming into the house, the angel greeted Mary with the common Grecian greeting, "Hail." This word for greeting, from the Greek verb *chairo* (pronounced **KAI-row**), would have been understood by Luke's readers as normal protocol, except that it was immediately followed by an unusual announcement: "thou . . .art highly favoured, the Lord is with thee: blessed art thou among women."

With this normal greeting and unique message, the angel informs Mary that she is the recipient of God's glorious grace—glorious in the sense that she of all women has been singled out for a special encounter with the nearness of the Lord and a once-in-history birthing experience.

29 And when she saw him, she was troubled at his saying, and cast in her mind what manner of salutation this should be.

The entrance of the angel into her house and the content of his message "troubled" Mary. The meaning of the Greek indicates that Mary was perplexed. The Greek word *diatarasso*, pronounced **dee-uh-tah-RAH-so** and translated as "trouble," also means confused or perplexed. It is reasonable to think that Mary's confusion drives her to ask at least two silent questions: *What are you doing in my house? What kind of greeting is this?*

After all, Mary was not accustomed to having angels enter her house, not to mention having an angel speak to her. Luke simply says that she "cast in her mind what manner of salutation this should be."

30 And the angel said unto her, Fear not, Mary: for thou hast found favour with God.

Mary's confusion and inquiries are met with the angel's words of reassurance. The Greek word *charin* (pronounced **KHAR-in**), translated as "favour," literally means grace: "Thou hast found grace with God." The Greek implies an action and choice of God that has nothing to do with Mary's acceptability. Grace is the unearned and unmerited favor of God that, when accepted, causes one to rejoice. Grace expects nothing in return. Its only motivation is the bountiful benevolence of God. It is this grace, says the angel, which God has bestowed upon Mary.

31 And, behold, thou shalt conceive in thy womb and bring forth a son, and shalt call his name JESUS.

The angel proceeds to inform Mary why the bestowal of God's grace is so necessary and significant for her. In short, the angel said, "Mary, you are going to have a baby, a male child, and you will name Him Jesus." Although Luke does not call attention to it, the name Jesus means "Yahweh [or 'the LORD'] saves."

32 He shall be great, and shall be called the Son of the Highest: and the Lord God shall give unto him the throne of his father David:

Here, and spilling over into verse 33, the angel describes the great and royal role that the child to be born to Mary will play. He will be called "the Son of the Highest," which is a reference to the unique relationship that Jesus will have with the God of Israel. This phrase is a Semitic idiom meaning "He will be recognized to be" rather than just being called such. In other words, Jesus will *be* the Son of God.

The phrase, "and the Lord God shall give unto him the throne of his father David" should be taken to mean that Jesus will fulfill the role of Israel's long-awaited Messiah.

33 And he shall reign over the house of Jacob for ever; and of his kingdom there shall be no end.

This verse reaffirms much of what has already been said in verse 32. Like verse 32, this verse describes Jesus as Israel's awaited Messiah. Like His earthly father before Him, Jesus will "reign over the house of Jacob." "The house of Jacob" is an Old Testament idiom used to refer to the nation of Israel (see Exodus 19:3; Isaiah 2:5-6; 8:17; and particularly 48:1).

The messianic nature of Jesus' reign makes His rule and His kingdom eternal: "He shall reign...for ever . . . and of his kingdom there shall

be no end" (see 2 Samuel 7:16; 1 Kings 8:25; Micah 4:7).

34 Then said Mary unto the angel, How shall this be, seeing I know not a man?

It is difficult to ascertain Mary's reasoning and motivation for asking this question. At best we can reason that Mary assumed that what the angel promised was to take place before the consummation of her marriage to Joseph. In view of this assumption and Mary's keen awareness of her virginity, along with her commitment to the custom of celibacy during the period of one's betrothal, the question in verse 34 makes logical sense. For a brief discussion on the logic of Mary's question, see *The Birth of the Messiah* by Raymond Brown, published by Doubleday, 1977, pages 303-309. Also, see *The New International Greek Commentary on Luke* by I. Howard Marshall, published by Eerdmans, 1978, pages 68-70. Also helpful is *The Gospel According to Luke I-IX* by Joseph Fitzmyer, published by Doubleday, 1981, pages 348-350.

35 And the angel answered and said unto her, The Holy Ghost shall come upon thee, and the power of the Highest shall overshadow thee: therefore also that holy thing which shall be born of thee shall be called the Son of God.

Luke, who is fond of talking about the power of the Holy Spirit (see Luke 1:41, 67, 80; 2:25-27), records that the angel answered Mary's question in verse 34 by saying that the Holy Spirit's overshadowing presence would be the causative factor in Mary's impregnation. Because of this connection with the Holy Spirit, the child to be born to Mary would be anointed and set apart for God's service. Indeed, he would be holy and therefore "called the Son of God."

36 And, behold, thy cousin Elisabeth, she hath also conceived a son in her old age: and this is the sixth month with her, who was called barren.

The angel's reference to Elisabeth's old age and barrenness is calculated to enable Mary to believe that God can do the impossible. If God can cause Elisabeth to conceive in her old age after leading a youthful life of barrenness, then surely God can cause Mary to conceive without the involvement of a sexual companion. This reasoning leads to faith's logical conclusion as stated in the next verse.

37 For with God nothing shall be impossible.

When God is at work, nothing is impossible for Him to accomplish. A variant translation is equally accurate: "No word from God will be powerless." In other words, whatever God chooses to make happen will happen, even if it appears to be impossible from our human point of view. Moreover, when His Word goes forth, it never returns to Him void. His Word always accomplishes what He desires, and it achieves the purpose for which He sends it (see Isaiah 55:11).

38 And Mary said, Behold the handmaid of the Lord; be it unto me according to thy word. And the angel departed from her.

Finally, Mary is convinced that God has spoken. She has moved from being confused or perplexed (Luke 1:29) to accepting a call from God. When she realizes that it is God speaking to her, she humbles herself, accepts the call, and becomes submissive to His will. She quickly chooses to become the Lord's "handmaid" and responds in agreement, "Be it unto me according to thy word."

"And the angel departed from her . . ." The concept of departure and return seems to be characteristic of Luke's writings when he wants to bring closure to an event (for examples, see Luke 1:23, 56; 2:20; 5:25; 8:39; 24:12).

46 And Mary said, My soul doth magnify the Lord,

When one struggles with a call from God and lands on the right side of God with a clear awareness of what He wants you to do, coupled with the certain promise that He will be with you (Luke 1:28), songs of praise and adoration flow freely. After her period of struggle with the angel Gabriel and her acceptance of God's claim upon her life, Mary bursts forth in joyful adoration: "My soul doth magnify the Lord." She continues in verse 47.

47 And my spirit hath rejoiced in God my Saviour.

Mary continues to praise God, whom she rec-

ognizes as her Saviour, for what He is about to do and for her privileged part in the unfolding of His purposes.

The repetition in her expressions of praise only helps to highlight the praiseworthiness of God: "My soul magnifies the Lord. My spirit rejoices in God my Saviour." Why? Verses 48 and 49 give the answer.

48 For he hath regarded the low estate of his handmaiden: for, behold, from henceforth all generations shall call me blessed. 49 For he that is mighty hath done to me great things; and holy is his name.

Set forth in lyric prose and poetic imagery, this is the reason behind Mary's hymn of praise! It all has to do with what the Lord has done for Mary and is about to do through her. "For he that is mighty hath done to me great things; and holy is his name." Even Mary's "blessed" status is attributed to what the Lord has done.

Obviously, Mary's experience is unique. But all who accept God's call are also in for a unique experience. Therefore, do not be afraid when you have found favor with God.

DAILY BIBLE READINGS

M: Joseph Believes God
Matthew 1:18-25
T: Visitors from the East
Matthew 2:1-12
W: Joseph Moves the Family to Egypt
Matthew 2:13-18
T: The Family Returns to Galilee
Matthew 2:19-23
F: The Righteous Please God
Proverbs 15:1-9
S: The Lord Watches Over the Righteous
Psalm 1:1-6
S: The Branch of Righteousness
Isaiah 11:1-5

TEACHING TIPS

December 15
Bible Study Guide 3

1. Words You Should Know

A. A just man (Matthew 1:19)—The word "just," from the Greek word *dikaios* (pronounced **DIK-kai-ahss**), is translated elsewhere to mean righteous. It describes those who have conformed their conduct and character to God's standards (see Romans 2:13).

B. Dream (Matthew 1:20; 2:13, 19)—In both the Old and New Testaments, dreams (from the Greek word *onar,* pronounced **OH-nahr,** meaning visions of the night) are viewed as one of the means by which God communicates with certain chosen individuals (see Job 33:14-18; 1 Samuel 28:6).

C. Herod (Matthew 2:13, 15-16, 19, 22)— Herod the Great was made the fiscal administrator of Galilee at the early age of 15. By the time of Jesus' birth, he was the reigning king of Judea, known for his jealousy and cruelty. History records that he killed his wife Marianne and her two sons, Alexander and Aristobulus. He ruled as king of Judea for about 40 years and died in 4 B.C. at the age of 70.

D. Land of Israel (Matthew 2:20-21)—This phrase, found only here in the New Testament, seems to echo Ezekiel 20:36-38 and the story of Moses (see particularly Exodus 2:15ff and 4:19ff). The use of the phrase "land of Israel" shows that Jesus, following the flight into Egypt, returned to the land promised to the people He was sent to save.

2. Teacher Preparation

A. Read the devotional Scripture (Isaiah 11:1-5) and the background Scripture (Matthew 1:18-25; 2:13-23).

B. Put yourself in Joseph's shoes and try to feel and think what he must have felt and thought upon hearing the news of Mary's pregnancy. Then read IN FOCUS and BACKGROUND.

3. Starting the Lesson

A. Open this class session with prayer, asking God to be near those families that are facing difficult situations.

B. After someone has read the FOCAL VERSES to the entire class, divide the class into groups of five. Have students share what they might have felt and thought had they been in Joseph's situation.

4. Getting into the Lesson

A. Bring the small groups together and have someone read the IN FOCUS story aloud. Discuss the various reactions to being in Joseph's situation with the class. Then have the class consider how God would have us to respond to events that seem difficult to understand.

B. Review the questions under DISCUSS THE MEANING and have students volunteer answers.

5. Relating the Lesson to Life

A. Encourage students to share personal experiences in which their faith was shaken and they had many questions to ask God.

B. After several have shared their experiences, ask the students to tell what they have learned about Joseph and how his obedience to God relates to their situations.

6. Arousing Action

A. Encourage students to become more aware of friends who are in situations that may tempt them to make unwise decisions. Explain that by sharing insights with them from Joseph's story, they could help to bring that person closer to faith in God.

B. Remind students to invite their friends to class and to church next Sunday.

WORSHIP GUIDE

For the Superintendent or Teacher
Theme: Joseph: A Righteous Man
Theme Song: "Trust and Obey"
Scripture: Matthew 1:24-25
Song: "Our Best"
Meditation: Give us obedient spirits, O God, that we might always do Your will—even when we do not fully understand Your ways.

JOSEPH: A RIGHTEOUS MAN

Bible Background • MATTHEW 1:18-25; 2:13-23
Printed Text • MATTHEW 1:18-21, 24-25; 2:13-15, 19-21, 23
Devotional Reading • ISAIAH 11:1-5

DEC 15TH

LESSON AIM

During this session, students will be encouraged to recognize that life's difficulties need not destroy our faith nor result in our disobedience and to understand that obedience to God's will does not guarantee comfort.

KEEP IN MIND

"Then Joseph being raised from sleep did as the angel of the Lord had bidden him, And took unto him his wife: and knew her not till she had brought forth her firstborn son: and he called his name JESUS" (Matthew 1:24-25).

FOCAL VERSES

Matthew 1:18 Now the birth of Jesus Christ was on this wise: When as his mother Mary was espoused to Joseph, before they came together, she was found with child of the Holy Ghost.

19 Then Joseph her husband, being a just man, and not willing to make her a public example, was minded to put her away privily.

20 But while he thought on these things, behold, the angel of the Lord appeared unto him in a dream, saying, Joseph, thou son of David, fear not to take unto thee Mary thy wife: for that which is conceived in her is of the Holy Ghost.

21 And she shall bring forth a son, and thou shalt call his name JESUS: for he shall save his people from their sins.

1:24 Then Joseph being raised from sleep did as the angel of the Lord had bidden him, and took unto him his wife:

25 And knew her not till she had brought forth

LESSON OVERVIEW

LESSON AIM
KEEP IN MIND
FOCAL VERSES
IN FOCUS
THE PEOPLE, PLACES, AND TIMES
BACKGROUND
AT-A-GLANCE
IN DEPTH
SEARCH THE SCRIPTURES
DISCUSS THE MEANING
LESSON IN OUR SOCIETY
MAKE IT HAPPEN
FOLLOW THE SPIRIT
REMEMBER YOUR THOUGHTS
MORE LIGHT ON THE TEXT
DAILY BIBLE READINGS

her firstborn son: and he called his name JESUS.

2:13 And when they were departed, behold, the angel of the Lord appeareth to Joseph in a dream, saying, Arise, and take the young child and his mother, and flee into Egypt, and be thou there until I bring thee word: for Herod will seek the young child to destroy him.

14 When he arose, he took the young child and his mother by night, and departed into Egypt:

15 And was there until the death of Herod: that it might be fulfilled which was spoken of the Lord by the prophet, saying, Out of Egypt have I called my son.

2:19 But when Herod was dead, behold, an angel of the Lord appeareth in a dream to Joseph in Egypt,

20 Saying, Arise, and take the young child and his mother, and go into the land of Israel: for they are dead which sought the young child's life.

21 And he arose, and took the young child and his mother, and came into the land of Israel.

2:23 And he came and dwelt in a city called Nazareth: that it might be fulfilled which was spoken by the prophets, He shall be called a Nazarene.

IN FOCUS

To live one's life with a trusting openness toward God is a spiritual discipline worth cultivating. This writer remembers the day he left his grandparent's home intent to pursue a call to prepare academically for full-time service in Christian pastoral ministry. My grandparents raised me and supported me through high school on prayer and a welfare check. Attaining a college and seminary education was a distant dream, but a dream inspired by what was believed to be a call from God to prepare for Christian ministry.

Well do I remember my grandfather's parting words to me on the day I boarded a Greyhound bus intent on going to college: "Son, your grandmother and I have no money to give you, but if you will trust and obey God, He will give you the desires of your heart."

The next eight years were truly a venture of faith. They were years filled with many difficulties and challenges. By working a part-time job during the school years and two full-time jobs during the summer months, plus obtaining several student loans and maintaining a trusting openness toward God, I managed to graduate from college and subsequently from seminary.

This personal story is not shared to brag or boast, but rather to illustrate the results that follow when we live our lives in trusting obedience and openness toward God. Perhaps you have your own story to tell concerning the rewards of trust and obedience.

We may not understand how God's Spirit works in our lives, but like Joseph we can be certain of one thing: God can be trusted!

THE PEOPLE, PLACES, AND TIMES

We know very little about Joseph. We know that he was a righteous man and therefore always tried to do what was right. In the culture of Joseph's day, if a betrothed woman became pregnant by someone other than the man to whom she was betrothed, Jewish law required that her fiancé break off the engagement. Forgiveness was not an alternative prescribed by law. Since Joseph was a righteousness man who always wanted to do what was right, his decision to divorce Mary was the obedient thing to do.

The law also required that the unfaithful woman pay the man for the disgrace she caused him. By law, Joseph could also have had Mary stoned to death, or he could have pursued some other form of public humiliation. Joseph, however, was not that kind of person. He not only wanted to do what was right in the eyes of the law; he also wanted to do what was compassionate in the eyes of God. Consequently, he decided that he would not go public with the divorce, but would end the engagement in the quietest and most private way possible.

BACKGROUND

We meet Joseph after he has decided to divorce his betrothed wife. Upon hearing words of reassurance from the Lord (Matthew 1:20-21), Joseph changes his mind and takes her to be his wife. Rather than pursue a strict adherence to the law, Joseph—prompted by the voice of the living God—sidesteps the letter of the law and acts out of love and concern for the dignity and well-being of another human being. Little did Joseph realize, however, that his reversed decision would cause him to face many more difficulties and dangerous situations.

Joseph's story illustrates what all believers soon come to know: obedience to God does not guarantee comfort. Following God and being involved in His will often takes us along paths of suffering and through many difficulties.

Joseph soon discovers, as this lesson will show, that he must face the difficulty of managing a blended family and living with ridicule and harassment from the community. He must also

AT-A-GLANCE

1. Joseph Resolves to Break the Engagement (Matthew 1:18-19)
2. Joseph is Reassured and Told to Make Mary His Wife (vv. 20, 21)
3. In Obedience Joseph Takes Mary as His Wife (vv. 24-25)
4. In Obedience Joseph Takes His Family to Egypt (vv. 2:13-15)
5. In Obedience Joseph Returns with His Family to Israel (vv. 2:19-21)
6. Joseph Makes His Family's Home in Nazareth (v. 23)

shoulder the responsibility of protecting his family and child from Herod's violence. Even after Herod's death, Joseph is still seen moving his wife and child to a community where he can best provide for their needs (Matthew 2:22-23).

IN DEPTH

1. Joseph Resolves to Break the Engagement (Matthew 1:18-19)

Whereas Luke tells the story of Jesus' birth from the viewpoint of Mary, Matthew tells the story from Joseph's point of view. That Matthew does not tell his readers who Mary and Joseph are suggests that his readers already know. It is also assumed that Matthew's readers know that Mary is a betrothed virgin. Given these assumptions, Matthew then moves quickly to say two things about Mary. First, we are told that Mary's pregnancy is the result of the activity of the Holy Spirit. Second, we are told that her impregnation took place before she and Joseph came together.

When Joseph learns of his betrothed wife's pregnancy, he is embarrassed—indeed, humiliated and disgraced. Since he was committed to obeying the law and did not want to make Mary a public example, Joseph decided to divorce her secretly.

2. Joseph Is Reassured and Told to Make Mary His Wife (vv. 1:20-21)

After Joseph makes up his mind to give Mary a bill of divorce, a messenger from the Lord visits him in a dream. The messenger explains the "how," the "why," and the salvational purpose of Mary's pregnancy. Moreover, Joseph is told to withdraw his plans to give Mary a bill of divorce because God is at work in her pregnancy. Joseph is told not to hesitate, but to proceed with his original plan to take Mary home as his wife.

In addition, the messenger tells Joseph that Mary's child will be a boy and that he is to "call his name Jesus." Under normal conditions, the parents would name the child. This birth, however, was not an ordinary one. This was a special child with a special destiny: "He shall save his people from their sins."

3. In Obedience Joseph Takes Mary as His Wife (vv. 1:24-25)

When Joseph woke up, he obeyed the angel and publicly took Mary as his wife but refrained from marital relations with her until after Jesus was born. Also in obedience to the angel's message, when the child was born, Joseph called his name Jesus.

In addition to assuring readers that Jesus was born of a virgin, these two verses and those that follow show that Matthew is concerned to portray Joseph's obedience. Matthew's constant reference to Joseph's obedience reminds us that the miraculous works of God are usually accomplished through our obedience to His will.

4. In Obedience Joseph Takes His Family to Egypt (Matthew 2:13-15)

These verses continue the theme of Joseph's obedience. Having been warned by an angel that Herod wanted to destroy Jesus, Joseph, again in obedience, takes his family to Egypt. As 1 Kings 11:40, 2 Kings 25:26, Jeremiah 26:21-23, and Zacharias 10:10 will show, Joseph's was not the first Israelite family to leave the homeland and seek refuge in Egypt. Fleeing the famine in Canaan, Jacob and his family also sought refuge in Egypt (see Genesis 46:1ff). Leon Morris has noted that Egypt "was almost a traditional country to which to flee when there was trouble in Palestine" (*The Gospel According to Matthew*, Eerdmans Publishing Company, Grand Rapids, Michigan, 1992, p. 42).

Not only is Joseph instructed to take his family into Egypt; he is told by the angel of the Lord to remain in Egypt "until I bring thee word" to return. Although the angel did not tell Joseph what time of day he should travel, it is interesting to note that Joseph chose to travel "by night." It was about a 75-mile journey to the Egyptian border. Joseph's decision to travel "by night" was wise. It seems that God gives an added measure of "common-sense maturity for making decisions" to those who discipline themselves to obey His Word.

In obedience Joseph and his family remained in Egypt until after Herod's death. Then Matthew

God's faithfulness and ever-present guidance, Joseph's fears were confirmed by God in a dream (Matthew 2:22). As a result, Joseph took his family to the despised region of Galilee, where he made his home in the remote, obscure, and unimportant village town of Nazareth.

6. Joseph Makes His Family's Home in Nazareth (v. 23)

According to Luke 1:26-27 and 2:39, Nazareth was also Joseph and Mary's hometown during the time of their betrothal.

Matthew adds the commentary that Joseph's taking up residence in Nazareth was to fulfill what "was spoken by the prophets": that Jesus was to "be called a Nazarene." Since no such quotation, however, has survived for us in the Old Testament, Matthew's commentary is best understood as a metaphoric reference to the prophecy that the long-awaited Messiah would be "despised and rejected of men" (Isaiah 53:3). This is certainly in keeping with the familiar epitaph, "Can there any good thing come out of Nazareth?" (see John 1:46).

makes a reference to Hosea 11:1 in order to show that the flight into Egypt was to fulfill that "which was spoken of the Lord by the prophet, saying, 'Out of Egypt have I called my son.'"

5. In Obedience Joseph Returns with His Family to Israel (2:19-21)

Joseph's obedience is again exhibited when the angel of the Lord informs him of Herod's death. In response to the angel's message, Joseph arose and took his family and went into the land of Israel. While Herod's death in 4 B.C. may have been a relief to many, Joseph—again exercising his "common-sense maturity for making decisions"—was not unaware of the new danger brewing in Israel. Herod's incompetent and cruel son, Archelaus (pronounced **r-keh-LAY-US**), was bequeathed a portion of his father's kingdom.

Knowing the political chaos that had followed in the wake of Herod's death, Joseph was understandably afraid to take up residence in Archelaus's territory. Moreover, in keeping with

SEARCH THE SCRIPTURES

1. Who sought to destroy Jesus? (Matthew 2:13)

2. After Herod's death, who reigned in Judea? (v. 22)

3. After leaving Egypt, where did Joseph take his family? (vv. 22-23)

4. How were Herod and Archelaus related? (v. 22)

5. What was Joseph's emotional response to the news of Archelaus's reign? (v. 22)

DISCUSS THE MEANING

1. What does it mean to be "a just man"?

2. What did Joseph have in mind when he decided to "put" Mary away "privily"?

3. Why would Herod want to kill Jesus?

4. What lessons can we learn from Joseph's obedience?

LESSON IN OUR SOCIETY

Matthew is very meticulous as he recounts the part that Joseph played in the unfolding story of Jesus' birth. Interestingly enough, however, Matthew never records Joseph's words.

Given all the important things Joseph does, we never hear him speak. When Joseph was disgraced and humiliated by the news of his betrothed wife's pregnancy, we never hear him speak. When Joseph is told to marry the woman with whom by law he should have severed his ties, we never hear him speak. When Joseph learns of Herod's plot to kill Mary's baby, we never hear him speak. When Joseph learns about Herod's death, we never hear him speak a word of joy or sadness. When Joseph's expectations to return to his homeland are frustrated by the news of Archelaus's reign in Judea, we never hear him speak. When Joseph realizes that he must take his young bride and the baby Jesus to live in the despised and unimportant town of Nazareth, we never hear him grumble or complain. Nor do we ever hear Joseph throw up a prayer in opposition to God's commands. Why? *Is he not human like the rest of us?* Surely he must have had strong feelings about the stress and mess of life.

Whatever his feelings may have been, Matthew portrays Joseph as one who guards his tongue. Given all the pressures that obviously caved in upon Joseph, why do we never hear him vent his feelings? Maybe Joseph's silence is attributable to his untiring and tenacious commitment to obey the voice of the living God. Could it be that Joseph's speech was simply that of doing the will of God?

Joseph's aim in life was obedience. The only speaking that Joseph does is through his active response to the Lord's commands. Matthew described Joseph as being "a just man." Simply put, the just man is one who promptly and simply obeys God. Those who desire to learn obedience would do well to emulate Joseph's example.

MAKE IT HAPPEN

This week, reflect upon the question: How committed am I to obeying God's Word? Dare to believe that God is praised when we obey Him. Pray and ask God to help you make decisions and govern your family life and relationships in ways that reflect obedience to His will. Make your speech and actions reflect your dedication to doing the will of God.

FOLLOW THE SPIRIT

What God wants me to do:

_____

_____

REMEMBER YOUR THOUGHTS

Special insights you have learned:

_____

_____

MORE LIGHT ON THE TEXT
MATTHEW 1:18-21, 24-25; 2:13-15, 19-21, 23

1:18 Now the birth of Jesus Christ was on this wise: When as his mother Mary was espoused to Joseph, before they came together, she was found with child of the Holy Ghost.

Matthew begins his story with a clear statement of what he intends to write about: "the birth of Jesus Christ."

Through the work of the Holy Spirit, Jesus' father was God, and His mother was a woman named Mary. Therefore, the church teaches that Jesus is both fully human and fully divine.

The phrase "before they came together" is used to convey the idea that Mary and Joseph did not have sexual intercourse with each other before Mary's pregnancy. Moreover, the phrase "found with child" does not suggest that there was an attempted cover-up of Mary's pregnancy. In our day we would simply say that she was "beginning to show." In other words, her pregnancy had become obvious.

19 Then Joseph her husband, being a just man, and not willing to make her a public example, was minded to put her away privily.

Matthew is quite skilled in helping his readers to sense the tension between Joseph's "being a just man" on the one hand, and on the other hand his not being willing to make Mary "a public example." Matthew's wording makes it obvious that Joseph's commitment to obey the letter of the law is in conflict with his compassionate concern to protect his betrothed wife from suffering the consequences of the law. What a dilemma! Joseph wants to avoid exposing Mary as an adulteress, while also refusing to marry her because her pregnancy has occasioned his humiliation. Joseph does not want to mix his commitment to obedience with what he believes is Mary's sin, nor does he want to see Mary shamed or punished.

This is a great lesson in what it means to be a just or righteous person. Those who are just and righteous do not seek to shame others for their misdeeds.

20 But while he thought on these things, behold, the angel of the Lord appeared unto him in a dream, saying, Joseph, thou son of David, fear not to take unto thee Mary thy wife: for that which is conceived in her is of the Holy Ghost.

After having made his decision to put Mary away "privily," a message from an angel of the Lord causes Joseph to re-frame his response to Mary's pregnancy. First, the angel's greeting, which tells Joseph to "fear not" while addressing him as a "son of David," alerts him to the fact that Mary's baby is of royal linage, and that Joseph as a son of David has a significant role to play. The angel's message helps Joseph realize that his plan to separate himself from Mary and maintain his innocence in the eyes of the law is unnecessary. In short, God is at work fulfilling His plan: "For that which is conceived in her is of the Holy Ghost." Joseph's response shows that he is a compassionate and sensitive man, one with whom God can talk and reason.

21 And she shall bring forth a son, and thou shalt call his name JESUS: for he shall save his people from their sins.

The angel proceeds to fill in the details of God's plan. Joseph is told that Mary's child is to be a son and that Joseph can begin to carry out his part in the plan by naming the child Jesus—meaning "the Lord saves" because "he shall save his people from their sins." This wording makes it clear that this baby's identity and destiny is revealed in His name.

With a new perspective on his perceived dilemma, Joseph is prepared to respond in obedience.

24 Then Joseph being raised from sleep did as the angel of the Lord had bidden him, and took unto him his wife:

In keeping with his commitment to obedience, Joseph did as the angel had commanded. When he awoke from his sleep, he proceeded with the second half of the Jewish marriage ceremony; he took Mary home as his wife. Joseph has now publicly accepted Mary as his wife.

25 And knew her not till she had brought forth her firstborn son: and he called his name JESUS.

Matthew's use of the phrase "knew her not till" makes it clear that Joseph and Mary did not participate in conjugal relations until sometime after Jesus' birth. Then, in keeping with Jewish tradition, Jesus was circumcised eight days after His birth and given the name Jesus. Joseph's naming Jesus signaled the fact that Joseph had legally adopted Jesus.

2:13 And when they were departed, behold, the angel of the Lord appeareth to Joseph in a dream, saying, Arise, and take the young child and his mother, and flee into Egypt, and be thou there until I bring thee word: for Herod will seek the young child to destroy him.

Given Herod's plot to kill Jesus, the angel's message to "flee into Egypt" is imperative. It is commonly believed that Herod's motivation for wanting to kill the baby Jesus was due to his insecurity and fear that the baby might grow up and become a threat to his kingship. It is also worth noting that Matthew does not refer to Jesus as Joseph's child; rather, it is "the young child." This reference serves to remind Matthew's readers that Jesus' conception came about by the Holy Spirit.

14 When he arose, he took the young child and his mother by night, and departed into Egypt:

This verse conveys a certain sense of urgency. That Joseph "arose" and traveled under the cover of night suggests that he acted promptly in the interest of fleeing an immediate danger. Joseph's aim was to take the young child and his mother and leave for Egypt immediately and unobserved.

15 And was there until the death of Herod: that it might be fulfilled which was spoken of the Lord by the prophet, saying, Out of Egypt have I called my son.

This verse speaks of a caring God who goes before and does what is necessary to protect His Son. Egypt is outside the range of Herod's power and is therefore a relatively safe place for Joseph and his family. The phrase "was there until the death of Herod" emphasizes the duration of Joseph's family's stay in Egypt, and should not, therefore, be taken to mean the time of his departure from Egypt.

2:19 But when Herod was dead, behold, an angel of the Lord appeareth in a dream to Joseph in Egypt,

Herod's death removed the threat of danger in Palestine, and the angel is now ready to instruct Joseph to return with his family to Israel.

20 Saying, Arise, and take the young child and his mother, and go into the land of Israel: for they are dead which sought the young child's life.

This verse reminds us of verse 13, and in it the angel seeks to assure Joseph that there is now nothing to fear in returning to Israel. The angel does not indicate, however, where in Israel Joseph is to settle. The only detailed information given is that not only is Herod dead, but presumably those who served at his behest are no longer to be feared.

21 And he arose, and took the young child and his mother, and came into the land of Israel.

Having received the divine instruction, Joseph again responds in obedience and returns with his family to Israel.

2:23 And he came and dwelt in a city called Nazareth: that it might be fulfilled which was spoken by the prophets, He shall be called a Nazarene.

While verse 21 does not tell us where in Israel Joseph and his family went, we are told in verse 23 that it was in Nazareth of Galilee. Notwithstanding the long history of various interpretations of this verse, it is fair to say that Matthew's aim is to associate Jesus with the despised "Servant of the Lord," spoken of in Isaiah 53. Nazareth represented all that was despised. Thus, to call Jesus a Nazarene was to refer to His despised status.

DAILY BIBLE READINGS

M: You Have Found Favor
Luke 1:26-33

T: I Am the Lord's Servant
Luke 1:34-38

W: Elisabeth Greets Mary
Luke 1:39-45

T: Mary's Song of Praise
Luke 1:46-56

F: I Praise God's Mighty Deeds
Psalm 71:15-21

S: Great Are God's Works
Psalm 111:1-6

S: Magnify the Lord with Me
Psalm 34:1-5

TEACHING TIPS

December 22
Bible Study Guide 4

1. Words You Should Know

A. Swaddling clothes (Luke 2:7)—These were strips or swaths of cloth that were wrapped around infants' bodies to help keep them warm and around their legs to help keep the legs straight. Moreover, it is believed that this practice helped to give newborn children a sense of security.

B. Glory of the Lord (Luke 2:9)—This phrase describes the magnificence, grandeur, and brilliance of what is perceived as the presence of God. Fear is the common reaction to the glory of the Lord.

C. Heavenly host (Luke 2:13)—Here the phrase refers to an army or a band of angels.

2. Teacher Preparation

A. Pray for your students. Call them and encourage them to use this Sunday before Christmas as an opportunity to invite some of their unchurched peers to Sunday School. People are often more likely to go to church the Sunday before Christmas than at other times of the year.

B. Review the LESSON AIM and then read the lesson materials. Mentally select one of your students to do a dramatic reading of the FOCAL VERSES.

3. Starting the Lesson

A. After a brief welcoming statement from you and a review of the LESSON AIM, introduce the dramatic reading of the FOCAL VERSES and ask the student to read them aloud.

B. Have two or three students share any childhood memories they may have about this Scripture. Was the passage read in their home, church, or school? If so, what memories can they share?

4. Getting into the Lesson

A. The information in the IN FOCUS section will help frame the concern of the lesson.

B. Ask students to discuss how they might have felt or what they might have considered doing if they had been in Mary and Joseph's situation.

5. Relating the Lesson to Life

A. To the extent that students feel comfortable doing so, ask them to share any situation in which a child was born in difficult circumstances. Ask students to identify the concerns or fears those circumstances may have occasioned. Then discuss how they were dealt with or how they could have been handled.

B. Ask: What can we learn from Mary and Joseph about the wonder and miracle of birth?

6. Arousing Action

A. Ask the students if they know of any parents who do not have the resources or who are not getting the basic services necessary to give adequate care to their young children.

B. If families are identified, discuss what your class might plan and do to help. If not, discuss how your class might help to make a difference for the children in one of your city's child-care agencies.

C. Assignments may need to be made for purpose of follow-up.

D. Close the session with prayer, asking God to help keep us sensitive to the needs of parents with small children.

WORSHIP GUIDE

For the Superintendent or Teacher
Theme: Mary: Mother of the Messiah
Theme Song: "Away in a Manger"
Scripture: Isaiah 9:1-7
Song: "Angels, from the Realms of Glory"
Meditation: We celebrate the miracle of birth, O God, and pray for all those parents who rear children under difficult circumstances. Make us sensitive to their needs and equip us for better and relevant service.

166

MARY: MOTHER OF THE MESSIAH

Bible Background • LUKE 2:1-20
Printed Text • LUKE 2:1, 4-20
Devotional Reading • ISAIAH 9:1-7

LESSON AIM

In this lesson, students will gain an increased awareness of problematic situations that surround the birth and general welfare of many children. Students will also identify and explore ways that they can support and encourage those who are raising children.

KEEP IN MIND

"And she brought forth her firstborn son, and wrapped him in swaddling clothes, and laid him in a manger; because there was no room for them in the inn" (Luke 2:7).

FOCAL VERSES

Luke 2:1 And it came to pass in those days, that there went out a decree from Caesar Augustus that all the world should be taxed.

2:4 And Joseph also went up from Galilee, out of the city of Nazareth, into Judaea, unto the city of David, which is called Bethlehem; (because he was of the house and lineage of David:)

5 To be taxed with Mary his espoused wife, being great with child.

6 And so it was, that, while they were there, the days were accomplished that she should be delivered.

7 And she brought forth her firstborn son, and wrapped him in swaddling clothes, and laid him in a manger; because there was no room for them in the inn.

8 And there were in the same country shepherds abiding in the field, keeping watch over their flock by night.

9 And, lo, the angel of the Lord came upon

LESSON OVERVIEW

LESSON AIM
KEEP IN MIND
FOCAL VERSES
IN FOCUS
THE PEOPLE, PLACES, AND TIMES
BACKGROUND
AT-A-GLANCE
IN DEPTH
SEARCH THE SCRIPTURES
DISCUSS THE MEANING
LESSON IN OUR SOCIETY
MAKE IT HAPPEN
FOLLOW THE SPIRIT
REMEMBER YOUR THOUGHTS
MORE LIGHT ON THE TEXT
DAILY BIBLE READINGS

them, and the glory of the Lord shone round about them: and they were sore afraid.

DEC 22ND

10 And the angel said unto them, Fear not: for, behold, I bring you good tidings of great joy, which shall be to all people.

11 For unto you is born this day in the city of David a Saviour, which is Christ the Lord.

12 And this shall be a sign unto you; Ye shall find the babe wrapped in swaddling clothes, lying in a manger.

13 And suddenly there was with the angel a multitude of the heavenly host praising God, and saying,

14 Glory to God in the highest, and on earth peace, good will toward men. **15** And it came to pass, as the angels were gone away from them into heaven, the shepherds said one to another, Let us now go even unto Bethlehem, and see this thing which is come to pass, which the Lord hath made known unto us.

16 And they came with haste, and found Mary, and Joseph, and the babe lying in a manger.

17 And when they had seen it, they made known abroad the saying which was told them concerning this child.

18 And all they that heard it wondered at those things which were told them by the shepherds.

19 But Mary kept all these things, and pondered them in her heart.

20 And the shepherds returned, glorifying and praising God for all the things that they had heard and seen, as it was told unto them.

IN FOCUS

William Powell Tuck tells about a traveler who, in 1809, met a local resident farmer in Hardin County, Kentucky. "What's new in the world?" asked the farmer.

"Well, they are talking about establishing a national bank," said the traveler, "and we may be having some more trouble with Great Britain. What's new here in Hardin County, Kentucky?"

"Ah, shucks, Mister," the farmer replied, "nothing ever happens here. Nancy and Tom Hanks had a little baby boy last night. But nothing important ever happens here." (Taken from *The Minister's Manual,* James W. Cox, ed., San Francisco: Jossey-Bass Publishers, 1999. p. 340.)

This amusing conversation highlights the lack of significance that is often attributed to the birth and presence of children in our society. Children all over the world seem to be getting the short end of the stick when governmental policy is established, municipal programs are created, and resources are distributed.

It is true that children cannot vote, and rarely, if ever, do they lobby to promote or protest legislation. The grassroots organizations that do lobby for children's rights are often under-funded. As a result, children's needs often do not receive the kind of scrutiny that would advance child-care services.

This sad scenario, however, is not new. One would have thought that someone lodging in the inn at Bethlehem would have given up his or her room for a young pregnant mother in labor. What was the innkeeper thinking about on the day that Mary and Joseph sought lodging for the night? Was the innkeeper unaware of Mary's condition? Or was the innkeeper aware, but unconcerned?

Perhaps it would have made a difference if the innkeeper and his clients had known that they were turning a cold shoulder to a couple who were about to give birth to the Saviour of the world. It was probably Mary and Joseph's appearance of poverty that resulted in the innkeeper's offering them the use of the stable out back.

The impact of poverty often involves some rather difficult societal issues, such as the amount of assistance parents of young children and expectant mothers should depend on. Where children and their parents are concerned, society must decide if the degree of responsibility it currently assumes is adequate. Just as the birth of Christ in a rural Judean village caused an army of angels to break forth in praise, we should rejoice in and care for the children of this century.

THE PEOPLE, PLACES, AND TIMES

It seems strange that the Saviour of the world should be born in such humble surroundings. Jesus' birthplace seems to have been dictated by the government's need to take a census. This census required everyone to go "into his [or her] own city" (Luke 2:3). For Joseph, this meant taking a journey to Bethlehem. Although it is not clear from the text why Joseph took Mary with him, she decided to go. It may be that Joseph took Mary with him to protect her from the potential gossip and slander of people in her own village of Nazareth. Moreover, it is possible that Mary and Joseph were motivated to go to Bethlehem because of their awareness of Scripture. In Micah 5:2, it is prophesied that the Messiah was to be born in Bethlehem. In any event, their traveling together is a tribute to Mary and Joseph's desire to be together during the final days and hours of her pregnancy.

The inn in which Joseph and Mary sought lodging was probably one of two different types of houses. It was either a two-story house with unpartitioned living quarters on the second floor and a first floor that was reserved for animals, or it may have been a one-story house with an adjacent stable. The issue for Mary and Joseph was that of finding privacy for the birth of a child. Their choices were limited. The child could be delivered in the living quarters and therefore in the presence of other tenants, many of whom may have been strangers. Or the birth could have taken place in the animal quarters in the presence of selected individuals. One wonders why the tenants did not vacate their quarters in the interest of Mary's comfort and lodge in the room or stable with the animals.

BACKGROUND

Luke was a doctor, a historian, a theologian,

and an excellent writer. He merged these skills to give us a brief and dramatic version of the birth of Jesus. Luke's account of Jesus' birth is told with passion, simplicity, and restraint.

He divides his record of Jesus' birth into three sections: (1) the social and political setting of Jesus' birth, (2) the announcement of Jesus' birth to the shepherds, and (3) the various reactions to the meaning and significance of Jesus' birth.

Luke ties the social and political setting of Jesus' birth to a census conducted by Rome. While scholarly efforts to reconcile a census associated with Caesar Augustus, Governor Quirinius, and King Herod have not met with complete success, it does not detract from the beauty of the story. Moreover, Luke is not writing a history of the fiscal affairs of imperial Rome. He is merely setting the record straight about the *how* and *why* of Jesus' birth. Therefore, in spite of possibly conflicting historical details about Roman registration for taxation, Luke is clear and accurate about Jesus' divine intervention into human history. Mary and Joseph did, in fact, journey to the "city of David" where the Saviour was to be born in humble surroundings.

Once Jesus is born, Luke draws upon another humble setting—namely, the angelic announcement to shepherds "abiding in the field, keeping watch over their flock by night" (Luke 2:8). Representing plain and common folk, the shepherds responded to the announcement with gratitude, excitement, and a deep desire to "go even

unto Bethlehem, and see this thing . . . which the Lord . . . made known unto" them (v. 15).

Luke approaches the conclusion of the story of Jesus' birth by recounting the shepherds' evangelistic response to what they had experienced and seen: "they made known abroad the saying which was told them concerning this child" (v. 17).

IN DEPTH
1. Joseph and Mary Travel to Bethlehem (Luke 2:1, 4-5)
After Caesar Augustus decreed that all should be registered, Joseph and Mary traveled to Bethlehem, Joseph's ancestral city. Although there is not a consensus as to why Mary went to Bethlehem, it is commonly believed that her pregnant condition encouraged both her and Joseph to remain together. Such were the circumstances that brought Mary and Joseph to the City of David.

During this season of the year, there is devotional value in pondering how we might get to Bethlehem. For the three wise men in Matthew's Gospel, it was their understanding of the science of astrology that brought them to Bethlehem. For the shepherds in Luke's Gospel, it was their response to the invitational announcement of the angel of the Lord that encouraged them to go to Bethlehem. For Mary and Joseph, it was their civic responsibilities that drew them to Bethlehem.

There may be other roads that lead to Bethlehem and many reasons to make the journey. One's hunger to see Jesus is a viable reason that leads people to Bethlehem. Whichever road one chooses, the journey to Bethlehem is a trip worth taking. For it was in this humble place that God was born as a human being.

2. Mary Gives Birth in Bethlehem (vv. 6-7)
Luke's presentation of Jesus' birth is extremely brief. Somewhere in Bethlehem, Mary went into labor and gave birth to a son in the only available place—a place usually reserved for animals. Jesus was then swaddled and placed in a feeding trough, which served as His crib.

Unlike with the birth of children in our day, we cannot be certain of the exact day of Jesus' birth.

AT-A-GLANCE

1. Joseph and Mary Travel to Bethlehem
(Luke 2:1, 4-5)
2. Mary Gives Birth in Bethlehem
(vv. 6-7)
3. Angels Announce the Saviour's Birth
(vv. 8-14)
4. The Shepherds Go to Bethlehem
(vv. 15-18, 20)
5. Mary Meditates on What Happened
(vv. 19)

Nor do we have any biblical data to support December 25 as the day to celebrate Jesus' birthday. According to Norval Geldenhuys (*Commentary on the Gospel of Luke*, Grand Rapids, Michigan: Eerdmans Publishing Company, 1979, p. 102), Christmas was first celebrated in Rome in 354, in Constantinople in 379, and in Antioch in 388. Currently, December 25 is accepted throughout Christendom as the day to celebrate Jesus' birth. It should be remembered, however, that we celebrate an *event*, namely, the *birth* and not the birthday of Jesus.

Although born in humble surroundings, Jesus was not neglected. He received adequate care and attention. We know this because Luke records that Jesus was "wrapped in swaddling cloths" (v. 7). To swaddle a baby was a sign of parental care. Failure to swaddle a baby was tantamount to neglect.

Jesus was then laid in a manger. Whether this was a moveable feeding trough or a cavity in a low rock shelf used as a feeding trough is not clear from Luke's account. Current nativity scenes featuring a cradle-like manger and animals are the result of later interpretations of Luke's story, as well as artistic imagination.

While there may be many questions about the details, circumstances, and resources available to Mary and Joseph, we can be certain that Jesus was born, and the significance of His birth continues to be proclaimed abroad.

3. Angels Announce the Saviour's Birth (vv. 8-14)

Luke turns our attention to an evening pastoral scene: "shepherds keeping watch over their flock." This natural and normal night activity of the shepherds was interrupted by the magnificent, brilliant, and majestic splendor of God's perceptible presence. The response of the shepherds was predictable: "they were sore afraid" (v. 9).

The angel of the Lord acts quickly to allay the shepherds' fears. The shepherds are reassured of God's gracious intentions and invited, even though indirectly, to go to Bethlehem and become eyewitnesses to the Saviour's birth. The message and invitation of the angel was reaffirmed by a band of angels who offered joyful praises unto God: "Glory to God in the highest, and on earth peace, good will toward men" (v. 14).

The angels' praise is not incidental. Men and women of good will still feel a need to praise God when the story and significance of Jesus' birth is told. That God has identified Himself with us through the coming of Jesus merits our gratitude and highest praise. Indeed, Luke wants his readers to identify with the shepherds, to receive the announcement and invitation to go to Bethlehem, and to worship the newborn King.

The shepherds were busy with their flocks when they received the news and the invitation to go to Bethlehem. They were not too busy, however, to make other arrangements for the care of their flock and proceed to Bethlehem. Hopefully, the same can be said of us—that we are not too busy to go to Bethlehem. For there is a child there who deserves our undivided attention and whose calling has implications for our salvation.

4. The Shepherds Go to Bethlehem (vv. 15-18, 20)

The shepherds went "with haste" (v. 16) to Bethlehem and found the Holy Family; then they praised God and told others what they had seen and heard. The shepherds were the church's first evangelists. The "good tidings of great joy" (v. 10) that had been made known to the shepherds and to which they were eyewitnesses, they now desired to make known to others.

This evangelistic spirit of doxology is needed in our day. Those who have truly gone to Bethlehem and are therefore witnesses to the truth that God is with us have a story to tell to the nations. We should tell this story in the confidence that it still has the capacity to amaze and to astonish—ultimately changing the lives of those who hear it.

Luke's story about the birth of Jesus does not end with a scene in Bethlehem. Luke's story of Jesus' birth includes sharing with others the story "concerning this child" (v. 17).

5. Mary Meditates on What Happened (v. 19)

Luke's use of the word "but" contrasts this verse with the preceding verse and suggests that Mary wishes to ponder the meaning and significance of Jesus' birth. While the shepherds reacted with evangelistic zeal, Mary chooses to pursue a more subdued reaction. Luke offers no reason for Mary's desire not to join in the celebration of Jesus' birth. The thrust of the original language suggests that Mary wanted "to get at the right meaning" of Jesus' birth. This is not to suggest that the shepherds did not have the right meaning of Jesus' birth. Certainly, they did. But Mary was the mother of Jesus. Consequently, we should expect Mary's concerns about the past, present, and future to require, if not greater thought, at least a certain depth of contemplation.

SEARCH THE SCRIPTURES

1. What decree did Caesar Augustus issue? (Luke 2:1)

2. Bethlehem is also known as what city? (v. 4)

3. Following His birth, in what was Jesus wrapped? (v. 7)

4. What was the shepherds' first response to the angels' appearance? (v. 9)

5. What did the shepherds do after having seen the baby Jesus? (v. 17)

DISCUSS THE MEANING

1. What is the significance of Jesus' birth?

2. What lessons can we learn from the circumstances surrounding Jesus' birth?

3. What possible dangers do you think were inherent in Mary's traveling with Joseph to Bethlehem? Do you think this was a good decision? Why?

LESSON IN OUR SOCIETY

Luke's story presents us with a new and clear revelation of who God is and what He desires for us. Moreover, we are reminded of the need to be more sensitive to and concerned about God's gift of children to us and to this world.

Like Mary, many women in our day have given birth in difficult situations. Oftentimes, and for a variety of reasons, parents do not get the treatment and services needed to properly care for their children. But God is faithful, and many parents rise above the odds to successfully nurture their children in spite of society's negative influences.

In many ways, Jesus' story is our story. Like Joseph, Mary, and Jesus, we were all born with a special calling and mission to fulfill. While we celebrate Mary and Joseph's obedience and availability to work with God and help fulfill His plan for our salvation, may we consider our own calling and commit to being obedient. May we remember that our status in life need not hinder our capacity to be used of God. Everyone can help contribute to the betterment of the services and social conditions necessary for the safety and healthy growth of children.

MAKE IT HAPPEN

During these few days before Christmas, let's recommit ourselves and our resources to the care of children and families. The birth of a child and its healthy growth ranks high on God's agenda and demonstrates His concern for humanity. We who are disciples of Jesus, and indeed all persons, can take a cue from the story of Jesus' birth and make room in our lives for children and families.

Take time out to celebrate your children and the children of others, and thank God for their presence. Using both your resources and good will, share your commitment with others so that you can work together as much as possible to help make a difference for our children's future.

FOLLOW THE SPIRIT

What God wants me to do:

_____

_____

REMEMBER YOUR THOUGHTS

Special insights you have learned:

_____

_____

MORE LIGHT ON THE TEXT
Luke 2:1, 4-20

2:1 And it came to pass in those days, that there went out a decree from Caesar Augustus that all the world should be taxed.

The phrase, "And it came to pass in those days" is better translated, "At that time." The phrase "all the world" should not be taken to mean the whole inhabited world, but rather the whole land of the Roman Empire.

The story of Jesus' birth begins with Caesar Augustus issuing a decree that resulted in Joseph and Mary's journey to Bethlehem.

4 And Joseph also went up from Galilee, out of the city of Nazareth, into Judaea, unto the city of David, which is called Bethlehem; (because he was of the house and lineage of David).

The terrain of Judea was mountainous. Thus, the phrase "went up from Galilee" is a reference to this mountainous region. The city of Nazareth is where Joseph and Mary lived when Caesar Augustus issued his decree (compare Luke 2:39).

5 To be taxed with Mary his espoused wife, being great with child.

Although theories abound, it is not clear why Mary accompanied Joseph to Bethlehem. Although Mary's journey may appear to have been a risk to our contemporary thinking, it was probably not seen as a problem. Traveling while in an advanced stage of pregnancy may not have been as great an issue in the ancient world as in our world.

6 And so it was, that, while they were there, the days were accomplished that she should be delivered.

At some point during Joseph and Mary's stay in Bethlehem, Mary gave birth. The Greek language used implies that the birth took place while they were in Bethlehem. Nothing more specific is given, nor need it be given. What is important is the event of Jesus' birth and not the date of His birth.

7 And she brought forth her firstborn son, and wrapped him in swaddling clothes, and laid him in a manger; because there was no room for them in the inn.

In verse 7, Luke refers to this child as Mary's "firstborn son." Some scholars would suggest that the term is used here as a literary technique to help introduce the readers to what is to follow in Luke 2:22-24, namely, the dedication of Jesus as the firstborn. The rest of verse 7 describes how Jesus was cared for after His birth. For more information about a child's being "wrapped . . . in swaddling clothes," see WORDS YOU SHOULD KNOW.

The word "manger" has been the source of inspiration for many who have pictured a stable with animals. It is interesting to note, however, that Luke makes no reference to the presence of animals. The contemporary nativity scene is the result of artistic and poetic imagination and is not based upon the description in Scripture. In their desire to have privacy, Joseph and Mary had to be content with space normally reserved for animals because there was no room for privacy in the inn where others were lodging.

8 And there were in the same country shepherds abiding in the field, keeping watch over their flock by night.

This verse demonstrates the motif that runs throughout the Scriptures, that God often works His mysteries and His will through common and lowly people. Leaving the nativity scene, we are taken to a field near Bethlehem where shepherds were keeping night watch over their sheep. The word translated as "watch" is the Greek word *phulaka*, pronounced **foo-lah-KAY,** which translated means to keep watch or guard. Luke uses this word in its plural form. Therefore, the shepherds were keeping watches over their flock. They were "watching the watches of the night." In other words, they were taking turns watching through the night. It was not necessary, therefore, for all the shepherds to be awake at the same time. We can imagine, however, that when the angel spoke amid the glory of the Lord in the following verse, any shepherds who may have been sleeping were surely aroused from their sleep.

9 And, lo, the angel of the Lord came upon them, and the glory of the Lord shone round about them: and they were sore afraid.

While engaged in their natural night activity, the shepherds are startled by the sudden appearance of the "angel of the Lord." The angel's appearance is accompanied by the glory of the Lord (see WORDS YOU SHOULD KNOW), which illumined the area around them. As a result they "were sore afraid." This was, of course, a normal response to the perceptible presence of the Lord.

10 And the angel said unto them, Fear not: for, behold, I bring you good tidings of great joy, which shall be to all people.

Here the angel of the Lord speaks: first, to allay the shepherd's fears, and second, to set the stage for the announcement of the Good News in verse 11. The angel's words of reassurance are linked with the basis for the assurance: "Fear not . . . bring good tidings."

11 For unto you is born this day in the city of David a Saviour, which is Christ the Lord.

The content of the Good News is explained in this verse: that on this day "in the city of David" the long-awaited Messiah has been born.

12 And this shall be a sign unto you; Ye shall find the babe wrapped in swaddling clothes, lying in a manger.

The sign given the shepherds has already been noted in verse 7, i.e., a baby "wrapped in swaddling clothes." Although the angel does not tell the shepherds to go to Bethlehem, the angel seems to assume that they will. Thus, the information is given about where the baby may be found. It is possible that these shepherds were pious men, probably devout Jews. If so, what they needed was not evidence for belief, but instructions as to how they might find and recognize the child. The angelic sign served this purpose.

13 And suddenly there was with the angel a multitude of the heavenly host praising God, and saying, 14 Glory to God in the highest, and on earth peace, good will toward men.

In verses 13 and 14, a band of angels join the angel that appeared in verse 9 to issue a hymn of praise in words that are as clearly understandable as those of the angel in verses 10-12. It should be noted, however, that the KJV rendering of "peace, good will toward men" does not do justice to the meaning of the Greek. A more accurate translation makes those of good will the recipients of peace. Therefore, it is not "peace, good will toward men," but rather "peace to people of good will," or to "people of good pleasure."

It should also be noted that the Greek word for "peace" (*eirana*, pronounced **a-RAY-nay**) is not limited to the cessation or absence of war. The peace referred to by the heavenly host also includes an entire social and political order of prosperity, security, and harmony. In the context of the story of the birth of Jesus, this peace about which the angels sing is to be ushered in by the child born to be the Saviour, which is Christ the Lord.

For a biblical understanding of "peace," see Psalm 29:11; Isaiah 26:3; 32:17; 48:18; Ezekiel 34:25-31.

15 And it came to pass, as the angels were gone away from them into heaven, the shepherds said one to another, Let us now go even unto Bethlehem, and see this thing which is come to pass, which the Lord hath made known unto us.

After delivering God's message, the angels return to God's dwelling place. The shepherds then confer briefly among themselves and decide to go to Bethlehem to see "this thing" about which they have been informed by the Lord's messengers. The thrust of the Greek suggests that they wasted no time in making up their minds. Interestingly enough, Luke says nothing about the provisions the shepherds may have made for the continued care of their flocks.

16 And they came with haste, and found Mary, and Joseph, and the babe lying in a manger.

The phrase "came with haste" confirms the sense of urgency implied in the previous verse. In essence, upon hearing the angel's message, the shepherds hurried off to Bethlehem, where they found Mary and Joseph and the babe, just as the angel had described.

17 And when they had seen it, they made known abroad the saying which was told them concerning this child.

Luke does not specify to whom the shepherds "made known . . . the saying . . . told them concerning this child." Norval Geldenhuys' commentary is the most imaginative in this matter. He contends that since the shepherds lived in the vicinity of Bethlehem, their flock was probably intended for temple offerings. Therefore, the shepherds would have had frequent occasion to go to Jerusalem and to exploit every opportunity to tell the story to all who were living in anticipation of the coming Messiah (*Commentary on the Gospel of Luke,* Grand Rapids, Michigan: Eerdmans Publishing Company, 1979, pp. 113-114).

18 And all they that heard it wondered at those things which were told them by the shepherds.

Those who hear the shepherd's report are filled with wonder, and rightly so, because the news that they have been given is the result of the Lord's initiative.

19 But Mary kept all these things, and pondered them in her heart.

Unlike that of others who received the news of the Saviour's birth, Mary's response is more subdued. She spends her thoughts and emotions on meditating about the meaning of it all. This is a logical response from Mary, primarily because, unlike the others, she has had special experiences that have helped prepare her for this moment.

20 And the shepherds returned, glorifying and praising God for all the things that they had heard and seen, as it was told unto them.

This verse sounds a note of doxology, which recognizes God as the source and initiative for all that the shepherds have heard and seen concerning the Christ child.

DAILY BIBLE READINGS

M: Jesus Is Born
Luke 2:1-7
T: Shepherds Hear the Good News
Luke 2:8-14
W: Mary Ponders the Shepherds' Words
Luke 2:15-20
T: A Sword Will Pierce Your Soul
Luke 2:21-35
F: Anna Sees and Believes
Luke 2:36-40
S: Mary Treasures All These Things
Luke 2:41-51
S: A Child Has Been Born
Isaiah 9:1-7

TEACHING TIPS

December 29
Bible Study Guide 5

1. Words You Should Know

A. Repent (Luke 3:2)–From the Greek word *metanoeo* (pronounced **met-uh-naw-EH-o**), meaning to think differently or, afterwards, to reconsider. It denotes a change of mind or condition. In the context of Luke 3:2, it involves changing one's mind and attitude.

B. Kingdom of heaven (Luke 3:2)—In Jewish thought, this phrase is an indirect way to speak about the "kingdom of God." Both phrases, "kingdom of God" and "kingdom of heaven," are used interchangeably to refer to God's sovereign rule and reign.

C. Pharisees (Luke 3:7)—The Pharisees get their name from a word that means to be separated. Thus, the Pharisees saw themselves as God's special separated ones. They prided themselves on being above other people or better than others, primarily because they gave unprecedented attention to keeping the letter of the law.

D. Sadducees (Luke 3:2)—The Sadducees were members of the high-priestly party. They regarded themselves as descendants of the great priest Zadok. Unlike the Pharisees, who included the general populace, the Sadducees were, for the most part, aristocrats who had the confidence of the wealthy. They were also in cahoots with the Romans and therefore had political clout.

2. Teacher Preparation

A. Read the background Scriptures and the FOCAL VERSES.

B. Then, keeping the LESSON AIM in mind, read all of the lesson material, and read the FOCAL VERSES again.

3. Starting the Lesson

A. Have students share what they know about John the Baptist. You may want to summarize their responses on the chalkboard or on newsprint.

B. Have students read the FOCAL VERSES and list all the things that the text says about John the Baptist.

4. Getting into the Lesson

A. Have students share the new things they learned about John the Baptist. List these things on the chalkboard or on newsprint. Compare the new list with the list of responses from the class discussion in "Starting the Lesson."

B. Ask students to discuss the ways in which John's ministry prepared the way for Jesus' ministry.

5. Relating the Lesson to Life

DEC 29TH

A. We must also ask ourselves: Are we willing to labor and sacrifice to help others realize their ministry and calling?

B. What can we learn from John the Baptist about helping to make a way for others?

6. Arousing Action

A. Ask students to act in ways that support or benefit someone else this coming week.

B. Have students record the feelings or thoughts they have as a result of their actions. Encourage them to use these feelings and thoughts as starting points in offering up prayers of petition and thanksgiving.

WORSHIP GUIDE

For the Superintendent or Teacher
Theme: John the Baptist: Messiah's Forerunner
Theme Song: "Give of Your Best to the Master"
Scripture: Matthew 11:10
Song: "Rise Up, O Men of God"
Meditation: For the opportunity and privilege that is ours, O God, to help advance the good works of others, we give Thee thanks. Give us the courage and generosity of heart to help prepare the way for others.

JOHN THE BAPTIST: MESSIAH'S FORERUNNER

Bible Background • MATTHEW 3; 11:2-19, 14:1-12
Printed Text • MATTHEW 3:1-11; 11:7-10
Devotional Reading • JOHN 1:1-14

LESSON AIM

Using John the Baptist as a model, students will identify and explore ways in which they might fulfill a supportive role in bringing others to faith in Jesus Christ.

KEEP IN MIND

"For this is he, of whom it is written, Behold, I send my messenger before thy face, which shall prepare thy way before thee" (Matthew 11:10).

FOCAL VERSES

Matthew 3:1 In those days came John the Baptist, preaching in the wilderness of Judaea,

2 And saying, Repent ye: for the kingdom of heaven is at hand.

3 For this is he that was spoken of by the prophet Esaias, saying, The voice of one crying in the wilderness, Prepare ye the way of the Lord, make his paths straight.

4 And the same John had his raiment of camel's hair, and a leathern girdle about his loins; and his meat was locusts and wild honey.

5 Then went out to him Jerusalem, and all Judaea, and all the region round about Jordan,

6 And were baptized of him in Jordan, confessing their sins.

7 But when he saw many of the Pharisees and Sadducees come to his baptism, he said unto them, O generation of vipers, who hath warned you to flee from the wrath to come?

LESSON OVERVIEW

LESSON AIM
KEEP IN MIND
FOCAL VERSES
IN FOCUS
THE PEOPLE, PLACES, AND TIMES
BACKGROUND
AT-A-GLANCE
IN DEPTH
SEARCH THE SCRIPTURES
DISCUSS THE MEANING
LESSON IN OUR SOCIETY
MAKE IT HAPPEN
FOLLOW THE SPIRIT
REMEMBER YOUR THOUGHTS
MORE LIGHT ON THE TEXT
DAILY BIBLE READINGS

8 Bring forth therefore fruits meet for repentance:

9 And think not to say within yourselves, We have Abraham to our father: for I say unto you, that God is able of these stones to raise up children unto Abraham.

10 And now also the axe is laid unto the root of the trees: therefore every tree which bringeth not forth good fruit is hewn down, and cast into the fire.

11 I indeed baptize you with water unto repentance: but he that cometh after me is mightier than I, whose shoes I am not worthy to bear: he shall baptize you with the Holy Ghost, and with fire:

11:7 And as they departed, Jesus began to say unto the multitudes concerning John, What went ye out into the wilderness to see? A reed shaken with the wind?

8 But what went ye out for to see? A man clothed in soft raiment? behold, they that wear soft clothing are in kings' houses.

9 But what went ye out for to see? A prophet? yea, I say unto you, and more than a prophet.

10 For this is he, of whom it is written, Behold, I send my messenger before thy face, which shall prepare thy way before thee.

IN FOCUS

The process of moving a large mobile trailer home from one location to another is reminiscent of John's preparing the way for Jesus' ministry. Whenever a mobile trailer home is moved across the city or country, a warning vehicle always precedes its tow truck. The warning vehicle is equipped with the appropriate flashing lights and red flags. Moreover, the warning vehicle carries a highly visible, easy-to-read sign that says, "Caution: Wide Load."

The message of the warning vehicle alerts others that a larger and wider vehicle is coming in its wake. In a very real sense, the warning vehicle clears and prepares the way for the coming of the much larger mobile trailer home. Thus, when other travelers see the warning vehicle, they are alerted to take the appropriate action. The presence of the warning vehicle enables oncoming travelers to better understand what to expect and what is expected of them.

In like manner, in all four Gospels the ministry of John the Baptist precedes Jesus' ministry. John is the "warning vehicle" who goes ahead to prepare the way for the ministry of the Christ. After the long absence of a prophetic voice in Israel, John the Baptist makes his appearance preaching a clear, simple, urgent, and prophetic message: "Repent! Turn your lives around, because the kingdom of heaven is at hand."

THE PEOPLE, PLACES, AND TIMES

Prior to the appearance of John the Baptist, the moral voice of the Hebrew prophets had been silent in Israel for some four hundred years. The people had grown lax in their devotion to God. Every one did that which was right in his own eyes. Even so, because of His love, God had a plan for the salvation of His people. Then "there came a man sent from God, whose name was John" (John 1:6).

With the appearance of John, God's call to moral rectitude and holiness was proclaimed through a new prophet. With great urgency, John called people to "shape up," to get their lives in order and get ready to receive the coming Christ.

John was a sincere and devoted spokesperson for God. He was an outstanding religious leader in his own right. Moreover, John was willing to serve in a supportive role for the benefit of one "whose shoes," said he, "I am not worthy to bear"

(Matthew 3:11). John was keenly aware of both his strengths and his limitations. He knew who he was, and he also knew the scope of his calling. Therefore, he was forthright, courageous, and quick to explain the differences between his mission and that of the one for whom he was preparing the way (see Matthew 3:11). In addition, John was willing to risk ridicule and persecution in order to stir and move people to repentance and to an acceptance of "the kingdom." According to Jesus, "Among them that are born of women there hath not risen a greater than John the Baptist . . ." (Matthew 11:11).

BACKGROUND

There is about a 25- to 30-year lapse of time between the end of Matthew 2 and the beginning of Matthew 3. Near the end of Matthew 2, we leave Jesus as a young child growing up in Nazareth (see Matthew 2:21-23). By the time we reach Matthew 3, John, who was born around the same time as Jesus, is a grown man "preaching in the wilderness of Judaea."

After a long prophetic silence, John bursts on the scene "like the last great prophet of the Hebrew Scriptures and like a walking, breathing law of God, full of doom and holiness and ultimacy" (Frederick Dale Bruner, *The Christbook: A Historical/Theological Commentary,* Waco, Texas: Word Publishers, 1987, p. 70).

John's ministry was a preaching and baptizing ministry that anticipated the ministry of Jesus. While we cannot be certain of the source of John's practice of baptism, we can be certain that his baptism could not grant forgiveness of sins. As Matthew 3:6-12 shows, John's ministry simply called people to a confession of sins, to repentance, and to acknowledgment of the coming one who cleanses us from sins and provides the Spirit who enables right living.

John's ministry was directed to people from all over Judea (v. 5). Because his ministry was in touch with the state of affairs in Israel, and because of his passion for and unselfish interest in the people's social and spiritual welfare, a revival erupted. As a result, people "were baptized of him in Jordan, confessing their sins" (v. 6).

It is obvious from the context and manner of

John's ministry that his baptism was offered as a public sign that those being baptized had received and accepted his message. Forgiveness followed their confession of sin and repentance. John's baptism was a public affirmation that the repentant and now-baptized participants were positioned to receive God's saving grace and presence, thus fulfilling the Scripture: "He that covereth his sins shall not prosper: but whoso confesseth and forsaketh them shall have mercy" (Proverbs 28:13).

AT-A-GLANCE

1. John's Preaching (Matthew 3:1-3)
2. John's Preaching Attracts Many Followers (vv. 4-6)
3. John's Preaching Questions the Integrity of His Contemporaries (vv. 7-10)
4. John's Ministry and the Ministry of Jesus (v. 11)
5. John's Ministry Is Esteemed by Jesus (11:7-10)

IN DEPTH

1. John's Preaching (Matthew 3:1-3)

Matthew introduces John and his preaching and baptizing ministry in terse and quick fashion: "John . . . came, preaching . . . (v. 1), "repent . . . (v. 2), prepare . . . the way of the Lord" (v. 3). These three verses strongly suggest that John was a prominent prophet. He had his own ministry and a significant group of followers. Moreover, John's ministry continued for some time after his baptizing Jesus in the River Jordan (see Matthew 9:14; 11:2-3).

Before describing the content of John's ministry, Matthew takes the time to note the location of John's ministry in "the wilderness of Judaea."

According to verse 2, John's ministry had two emphases. First, his ministry called people to repentance. Second, his ministry announced the nearness of the kingdom of heaven. In view of the nearness of God's kingdom, John urged people to repent, to be sorry for their past behavior, to

change their mind, and to pursue a future behavior that honored God's standard for right and holy living.

John was very assertive in his denunciation of evil. Whether rebuking King Herod because of his unlawful marriage, the Sadducees and Pharisees because of their legalism, or the common folk because of their failure to reverence God, John was intent upon calling people to repent, to turn from their old sinful ways, and to pursue God's kind of righteousness.

Given the ever-present temptation of sin and evil, the church still has need for John's kind of preaching ministry. Moral standards must be set, and people need to be reminded of their potential for growth in the things of God. The message of repentance and forgiveness and the call to right living has the capacity to revitalize and bring spiritual renewal to people.

While Matthew's comment, "for the kingdom of heaven is at hand," gives a reason for John's call to repentance, it also links the story of John's ministry with the story of Jesus' birth and envisioned ministry as told in Matthew 1 and 2. To further explain and affirm the necessary direction of John's ministry, an appeal is made in verse 3 to the prophetic words of Isaiah (see Isaiah 40:3). Matthew, along with all the other Gospel writers, views John's ministry as the direct fulfillment of Isaiah's vision.

2. John's Preaching Attracts Many Followers (vv. 4-6)

Matthew wants his readers to know that there was nothing particularly attractive about John's appearance. His was a very simple lifestyle. His garments were made of camel's hair, and he wore a dried skin belt, reminiscent of Elijah's attire (See 2 Kings 1:8). Moreover, his diet was locusts (see Leviticus 11:22) and honey produced by bees in the wild.

Matthew's description of John's physical appearance begs the question, "What attracted people to him?" People were attracted to John because of the quality and content of his preaching. There is a lesson in this for today's church. While we should seek to have beautiful worship facilities, ultimately it is not our beautiful buildings or fashionable dress that attracts people to Jesus Christ. Real Christian disciples are made as a result of a clear, articulate, and perceptive handling of the Good News concerning life in Jesus Christ. The faithful teaching and preaching "of the gospel of Christ" is still "the power of God unto salvation to every one that believeth" (Romans 1:16).

Verses 5 and 6 report the results of John's ministry. This same result is produced whenever the Good News is preached in ways that meet people's need for God.

3. John's Preaching Questions the Integrity of His Contemporaries (vv. 7-10)

While John's ministry was successful, it did not go unchallenged. John had his audience of critics. Whatever differences the Pharisees and Sadducees may have had between their parties, they were united in their opposition against John's ministry.

It is not clear whether the Pharisees and Sadducees were coming to be baptized or as part of a committee seeking to build a case against John's ministry. John takes the high road and seems to assume that they are coming to be baptized. However, he views their motives with great suspicion and questions the depth of their repentance. This helps to explain the harshness of his statements to them. He calls them "vipers" or snakes and asks them, "Who hath warned you to flee from the wrath to come?" John's question and his demand for evidence of repentance implies that the Pharisees's and Sadducees's motives were questionable. Rather than to demonstrate a commitment to abandon their evil behavior and lead righteous lives, their aim was to escape the certain "wrath to come"—to escape God's punishment for sin.

While the desire to avoid divine retribution may be a motive for right living, it is not the best motive. We should desire to live right because it is the right thing to do in response to God's love for us. It is far better to pour one's energies into bringing forth fruits suitable for repentance in order to glorify God, than to pour one's energies into merely avoiding the wrath to come. Fear of hell need not be an overriding issue for those

who accept God's way. Moreover, God is concerned about right motive as well as right behavior. Repentance that is acceptable to God results in right behavior that is sustained, not by a fear of hell, but by unconditional love for God.

Not only did John the Baptist question the depth of the Pharisees's and Sadducees's repentance, but he proceeds in verses 9 and 10 to question their prideful tendency to desire a relationship with God based upon their religious heritage. A moral God is not interested in the religiosity of one's family tree. Being a child of Abraham secures no brownie points with God. If necessary, God can turn stones into faithful followers of His will. Indeed, according to verse 10, God has already begun to deal with those who think that they can get away with sin: ". . . now also the axe is laid unto the root of the trees . . .which bringeth not forth good fruit . . . ." Fruitless trees will not only be cut down, they will be "cast into the fire," or totally destroyed.

The questions could be asked: Is John too severe? Is he too strict? John is merely fulfilling a supportive role for the Christ who also said, "Every tree that bringeth not forth good fruit is hewn down, and cast into the fire" (Matthew 7:19).

4. John's Ministry and the Ministry of Jesus (v. 11)

John is both clear and emphatic about the relationship of his ministry to that of Jesus. John's purpose was to call people to repentance. Jesus' purpose was to save and empower people for righteous living. Therefore, John's ministry of baptism was essentially preparatory in that it anticipated and prepared the way for the ministry of Jesus.

John is to be commended for his capacity to see the bigger picture and to content himself with playing second fiddle. John was willing to serve in a supportive role for the benefit of one who was superior to him. John's baptism was with water for repentance. Jesus' baptism was with the Holy Spirit for empowerment and with fire for cleansing, purification, and refinement in the things of the Spirit. In other words, John's ministry awakened people's desire for righteousness. Jesus' ministry provides the righteous of God to those who believe and empowers us to live righteously by giving us the Holy Spirit (Acts 1:8; Romans 3:22).

In the plan of God, both ministries were needed to bring us to righteousness. Even today, if the unchurched or the unsaved are to accept Christ and live righteously, they have need for someone to awaken within them the desire for righteousness. This awakening can take place when the Good News about God's saving grace is shared through the testimony of a Christian friend, the sermon of a faithful preacher, or a good deed performed by those of us who claim to be disciples of Jesus.

Like John the Baptist, every believer can fulfill a supportive role by working with God to bring others to faith in Jesus Christ. As born again believers, we can share our faith in the hope and confidence that a desire for righteousness might come alive in those who have not yet accepted Christ as their Lord and Savior.

John's ministry is a model for us all. It is little wonder that Jesus had such high esteem for John and for his ministry.

5. John's Ministry Is Esteemed by Jesus (11:7-10)

In these verses of Scripture, Jesus comments about John and his ministry. Jesus begins by asking a number of rhetorical questions aimed at illustrating the greatness of John's ministry, while leading the people to ask questions about His own ministry.

Jesus' comments are best understood when we remember that the Jews of John and Jesus' day had never seen a prophet. They had heard about the prophets of 400 years ago, but they had never seen one. When they heard that John was doing ministry in the tradition of the prophets, they were eager to go "out into the wilderness to see him," because in the Jewish mind there was no higher human status than that of a prophet. Thus, Jesus' first question was: "When you went out into the wilderness to see the prophet, what did you expect to see?"

Jesus' line of questioning makes the point that the prophet they saw was more than a prophet.

John was the one of whom the prophets prophesied in verse 10: "For this is he, of whom it is written, 'Behold, I send my messenger before thy face, which shall prepare thy way before thee.'" Therefore, if John is greater than the prophets, and if John is simply preparing the way for a greater one to come, then who is this greater one? How great is He?

Matthew wants his readers to know that the greater one, who is Jesus, is also God.

Therefore, they who encounter Jesus encounter God. This truth makes the sharing of our faith critically important. Our supportive role in bringing others to faith in Jesus Christ helps put them in contact with God. For those who have truly met Jesus will have met God. We help advance the kingdom by sharing our faith. May God give us wisdom and courage to fulfill this supportive role of helping to bring others to faith in Jesus Christ.

SEARCH THE SCRIPTURES

1. Where did John the Baptist preach? (Matthew 3:1)

2. What did John wear and eat? (v. 4)

3. What did John call the Sadducees and Pharisees? (v. 7)

4. Every tree which _____ is hewn down. (v. 10)

DISCUSS THE MEANING

1. What does it mean to "bring forth . . . fruits meet for repentance"? (Matthew 3:8-9)

2. What was the relationship between John's ministry and Jesus' ministry? (v. 11)

LESSON IN OUR SOCIETY

Just as the witness of John the Baptist helped to awaken a desire for righteousness in his day, so also can our faithful witness awaken a desire for righteousness in our day. The needed ministry of sharing our testimony and giving witness of Jesus Christ is the call and responsibility of every believer. Like John the Baptist, we too are to go into the "wilderness" of our communities and seek to awaken in people a desire for righteousness. We are to do this in the confidence that when desire is awakened, God will grant salvation through faith in Jesus Christ and convey righteousness by the power of the Holy Spirit to all who will believe.

MAKE IT HAPPEN

Identify five of your close unchurched associates or acquaintances. Write their names, addresses, and phone numbers down. Pray for them daily. Ask God to awaken within them a desire for righteousness. Take the time to talk with them about their desires and their hunger for a more meaningful life. Listen to their concerns and be alert to determine how you might share your faith in response to their expressed desires.

Most people are wooed to faith in Jesus Christ, not by great preaching–though great preaching is needed–but by a friend who dared to share his or her faith about life in Jesus Christ.

FOLLOW THE SPIRIT

What God wants me to do:

_____

_____

REMEMBER YOUR THOUGHTS

Special insights you have learned:

_____

_____

MORE LIGHT ON THE TEXT
Matthew 3:1-11; 11:7-10

3:1 In those days came John the Baptist, preaching in the wilderness of Judaea,

With this verse, Matthew makes a leap of some 25 to 30 years. He leaves the narratives regarding John's and Jesus' birth and begins to talk about John as a grown man involved in a vital preaching ministry. After a 400-year absence of a prophetic voice in Israel, God begins to speak through John.

The phrase, "in those days" refers to the birth of Jesus in Matthew 2 and serves as a reminder that Jesus has also grown older, but is still living with His family in Nazareth.

2 And saying, Repent ye: for the kingdom of heaven is at hand.

John's message of repentance places him within the tradition of the Old Testament prophets. In view of God's anticipated judgment and redemption, responding to the call to turn one's life around and live righteously is the only sane and responsible thing to do.

3 For this is he that was spoken of by the prophet Esaias, saying, The voice of one crying in the wilderness, Prepare ye the way of the Lord, make his paths straight.

This verse describes John's prophesied function as a mouthpiece for God. John's role is referred to in Isaiah 40:3, which Matthew quotes so that the Jews might know that John's preaching and message were predicted and confirmed by the Word of God. The Greek helps to make this emphatically clear by using the phrase *outos gar estin* (pronounced **HOO-tahss gar es-ten**), translated "this is the one." John the Baptist is the one whose ministry is to prepare the way for the long-awaited Messiah.

4 And the same John had his raiment of camel's hair, and a leathern girdle about his loins; and his meat was locusts and wild honey.

While John's raiment was that of the poor, it also helped to link him with the Jewish prophetic tradition. For it is remembered that the Old Testament prophet Elijah dressed in similar fashion (2 Kings 1:8; see also Zacharias 13:4). Moreover, Elijah may have eaten similar food, since locusts were on the Levitical list of approved foods.

5 Then went out to him Jerusalem, and all Judaea, and all the region round about Jordan,

Matthew wants his readers to know the extent of John's influence. Although Matthew does not mention a specific number to indicate how many people were attracted to John's ministry, the implication is that in spite of some opposition there was a great and unusual response. The imperfect tense (i.e., *exeporeueto*) of the Greek verb *ekporeuomai* (pronounced **ek-por-YOO-oh-my**) indicates that they were repeatedly coming out over a period of time to hear John.

6 And were baptized of him in Jordan, confessing their sins.

Not only were the people repeatedly coming out over a period of time to hear John, but a large number were also being baptized by John over a period of time. It should be noted that these baptisms took place in connection with the people's confessions of their sins.

John baptized people in the Jordan River—probably in one of the river's fords since the Jordan was a fast-flowing river.

7 But when he saw many of the Pharisees and Sadducees come to his baptism, he said unto them, O generation of vipers, who hath warned you to flee from the wrath to come?

There has been some debate about how this verse should be interpreted. Were the Pharisees and Sadducees coming to be baptized, or were they merely coming to where John was baptizing? It is quite possible that John had the same or similar questions. In either case, he harshly questioned their motives. In essence, John asked: "Since you show no signs of repentance, why are you coming to this place of baptism?" His statements in verses 8 and 9 provide a logical challenge.

8 Bring forth therefore fruits meet for repentance: 9 And think not to say within yourselves, We have Abraham to our father: for I say unto you, that God is able of these stones to raise up children unto Abraham.

The intent of John's harsh comment is clear. The Pharisees and Sadducees must either repent or prepare to incur the coming judgment of God. Moreover, they cannot escape the judgment of God by hiding behind the religious legacy of their father Abraham. After all, the grace of God extends beyond Jewish borders, and if He chooses to do so, God can "raise up children unto

Abraham" from cobblestones which have absolutely no ethnic origin. It is a humble and contrite heart that draws God's approval (Psalm 34:18; 51:17).

Like everybody else, the Pharisees and Sadducees have a decision to make, and they must make it quickly. For while the kingdom is drawing near, so also is God's judgment. Both the kingdom and God's judgment are imminent. John makes this point in verse 10.

10 And now also the axe is laid unto the root of the trees: therefore every tree which bringeth not forth good fruit is hewn down, and cast into the fire.

John uses the metaphor of an unfruitful tree to talk about the consequences of an unrepentant life. Fruit-bearing trees that bear no fruit are cut down. In like manner, people who were created to live for God but who refuse to do so will ultimately encounter God's retributive justice.

11 I indeed baptize you with water unto repentance: but he that cometh after me is mightier than I, whose shoes I am not worthy to bear: he shall baptize you with the Holy Ghost, and with fire.

It should be noted that the thrust of the Greek does not allow for repentance to be the goal nor the result of baptism. Baptism presupposes that repentance has already taken place. The sequence is repentance, and then baptism. This interpretation guards against any thought that baptism washes away sins. We are not forgiven and made right with God because we are baptized. We are baptized because we have repented and have been forgiven of our sins through faith in Jesus Christ.

There is, however, a greater baptism to follow. It is the baptism of God's conveyance of His righteousness by the Holy Spirit, which enables us to do justice, and to love mercy, and to walk humbly before God. This act of God is concurrent with one's repentance and continues to empower and purify those who live in obedience to God's will.

In Matthew 11:7-10 Jesus talks about the significance of John's ministry and how John's ministry relates to His own. Jesus' comments seem to be directed to a people who, having heard much about John's ministry, did not understand, or at best were confused about the place of John's ministry within the scheme of God's plan for salvation. This is quite understandable, since the people had never experienced the ministry or the message of a true prophet. So when they went to see and hear John, they did not know what to expect. To help the people grasp the significance and meaning of John's ministry, Jesus asked them a series of questions, each of which suggests its own answer.

11:7 And as they departed, Jesus began to say unto the multitudes concerning John, What went ye out into the wilderness to see? A reed shaken with the wind?

Jesus' first question refers to "a reed shaken with the wind." This metaphor suggests weakness and vacillation. In contrast, John's ministry was strong and fixed. There was no vacillation (or wavering) in its orientation or goal.

8 But what went ye out for to see? A man clothed in soft raiment? behold, they that wear soft clothing are in kings' houses.

Jesus' second question refers to "a man clothed in soft raiment." This metaphor suggests a king living in a palace. In contrast, John's attire identified him with the poor, and more specifically with the Old Testament Jewish prophets who were rustic in their demeanor and appearance.

9 But what went ye out for to see? A prophet? yea, I say unto you, and more than a prophet.

Jesus' third question demands an affirmative answer. In other words, if the people went out to see a prophet, they should realize they saw "more than a prophet." The essence of what they saw is amplified in the next verse.

10 For this is he, of whom it is written, Behold, I send my messenger before thy face, which shall prepare thy way before thee.

Jesus wants His audience to know that this one who was "more than a prophet" was also the one promised by the Hebrew Scriptures (Malachi 3:1). Indeed, John was the subject of prophecy. He was the one whose ministry was prophetically destined to "prepare the way" for the coming of the expected Messiah.

DAILY BIBLE READINGS

M: John Proclaims Repentance
Matthew 3:1-10
T: John Baptizes Jesus
Matthew 3:11-17
W: John Testifies to the Light
John 1:1-15
T: I Am Not the Messiah
John 1:19-28
F: No One Greater than John
Matthew 11:2-15
S: John's Death
Matthew 14:1-12
S: John Came in Righteousness
Matthew 21:23-32

TEACHING TIPS

January 5
Bible Study Guide 6

1. Words You Should Know

A. Inherit—To transfer property to; to receive property by the laws of inheritance; to have (certain characteristics) by heredity.

B. Kneel—To bend or rest on one's knee or knees.

C. Grieved—To cause to feel grief; afflict with deep, acute sorrow; make sad; distress.

D. Treasure—Accumulated or stored wealth in the form of money or precious metals; to value greatly; to cherish.

2. Teacher Preparation

A. At the beginning of class, ask the students to list five of their most treasured possessions. You should also make a list of your most treasured possessions and be prepared to share the significance of the items with the class.

B. Study the SEARCH THE SCRIPTURES and DISCUSS THE MEANING questions and prepare your responses.

C. Read and reflect upon the Scriptures for Devotional Reading.

3. Starting the Lesson

A. Open the class with prayer, asking the Lord to order the thoughts of the class members and to help them to establish their priorities. Include in your prayer a request that the Lord would reveal those treasured possessions that have been placed higher than God and His will for your students' lives.

B. Ask students to have their treasured possession lists handy.

C. Review the WORDS YOU SHOULD KNOW with students.

D. Have volunteers read the FOCAL VERSES aloud.

4. Getting into the Lesson

A. Ask a volunteer to read the IN FOCUS story and talk about how it relates to the FOCAL VERSES. Generate a thorough discussion of the Scripture passage.

B. Have various students read the paragraphs in the IN DEPTH section.

C. Have volunteers read and then solicit responses to the SEARCH THE SCRIPTURES questions.

5. Relating the Lesson to Life

A. Divide the class into small groups. Have students share the items on their treasured possession lists with their groups. Ask them to include how they would react if these possessions were stolen or destroyed.

B. Reconvene and discuss various comments from the group sessions.

C. Review and reflect on the questions in LESSON IN OUR SOCIETY. Sum up the comments from the class discussion in light of the principles gleaned from the FOCAL VERSES.

6. Arousing Action

A. Encourage the students to read the DAILY BIBLE READINGS throughout the week.

B. End the class in prayer, thanking God for helping the class members to reorder their priorities and thereby bringing each person even closer to God and His will for their lives.

WORSHIP GUIDE

For the Superintendent or Teacher
Theme: The Rich Man: Wrong Priorities
Theme Song: "Seek Ye First the Kingdom"
Scripture: Matthew 6:25-34
Song: "I Surrender All"
Devotional Thought: My Lord, help me to rid myself of anything that prevents me from following You fully. Amen.

THE RICH MAN: WRONG PRIORITIES

Bible Background • MARK 10:17-27
Printed Text • MARK 10:17-27
Devotional Reading • 1 TIMOTHY 6:6-19

LESSON AIM

By the end of the lesson, students will be able to appreciate the importance and the value of heavenly riches seen through Jesus' encounter with the rich young ruler and will understand why it is wise to choose heavenly treasures above earthly things.

KEEP IN MIND

"Then Jesus beholding him loved him, and said unto him, One thing thou lackest: go thy way, sell whatsoever thou hast, and give to the poor, and thou shalt have treasure in heaven: and come, take up the cross, and follow me" (Mark 10:21).

FOCAL VERSES

Mark 10:17 And when he was gone forth into the way, there came one running, and kneeled to him, and asked him, Good Master, what shall I do that I may inherit eternal life?

18 And Jesus said unto him, Why callest thou me good? there is none good but one, that is, God.

19 Thou knowest the commandments, Do not commit adultery, Do not kill, Do not steal, Do not bear false witness, Defraud not, Honour thy father and mother.

20 And he answered and said unto him, Master, all these have I observed from my youth.

21 Then Jesus beholding him loved him, and said unto him, One thing thou lackest: go thy way, sell whatsoever thou hast, and give to the poor, and thou shalt have treasure in heaven: and come, take up the cross, and follow me.

22 And he was sad at that saying, and went away grieved: for he had great possessions.

LESSON OVERVIEW

LESSON AIM
KEEP IN MIND
FOCAL VERSES
IN FOCUS
THE PEOPLE, PLACES, AND TIMES
BACKGROUND
AT-A-GLANCE
IN DEPTH
SEARCH THE SCRIPTURES
DISCUSS THE MEANING
LESSON IN OUR SOCIETY
MAKE IT HAPPEN
FOLLOW THE SPIRIT
REMEMBER YOUR THOUGHTS
MORE LIGHT ON THE TEXT
DAILY BIBLE READINGS

23 And Jesus looked round about, and saith unto his disciples, How hardly shall they that have riches enter into the kingdom of God!

24 And the disciples were astonished at his words. But Jesus answereth again, and saith unto them, Children, how hard is it for them that trust in riches to enter into the kingdom of God!

JAN 5TH

25 It is easier for a camel to go through the eye of a needle, than for a rich man to enter into the kingdom of God.

26 And they were astonished out of measure, saying among themselves, Who then can be saved?

27 And Jesus looking upon them saith, With men it is impossible, but not with God: for with God all things are possible.

IN FOCUS

There was a man who was the CEO of a large, successful production company. He had worked hard to get the company to its current status. There was nothing he desired materially that he could not have. In essence, money was not an object. If it could be bought, he would buy it. He had put his trust in his wealth. He had stopped attending church to play golf with his peers. His family life suffered because he missed important events, such as anniversaries, birthdays, Little League games, and music recitals. This continued for several years until one day after a routine check-up, he was told that he had cancer. Even though he had the funds to get the best treatment, his money was not enough. He could no longer enjoy his fine cars and beautiful home. Money could not buy what he needed; he needed another form of riches, and that comes only through heavenly treasures.

THE PEOPLE, PLACES, AND TIMES

The kingdom of God. God's rule of grace in the world, a period foretold by the prophets of the Old Testament and identified as beginning with Jesus' public ministry. The kingdom of God is the experience of the blessings of God, like that of Adam and Eve in the Garden of Eden, where evil is fully overcome and those who live in the kingdom know righteousness, peace, and joy. This was the main expectation of the Old Testament prophets about the future.

The expression "kingdom of God" occurs mostly in the Gospels of Matthew, Mark, and Luke. The entire ministry of Jesus is understood in relation to this important declaration of the presence of the kingdom. All that Jesus did is related to the claim that the kingdom of God has dawned through His ministry. His healings were manifestations of the presence of the kingdom. In these deeds, there was a direct confrontation between the power of God and the forces of evil, or Satan and his demons.

Wealth. An abundance of possessions or resources. During the times of the patriarchs, wealth was measured largely in livestock—sheep, goats, cattle, donkeys, and camels. This was true of Abraham (Genesis 13:2), Isaac (Genesis 26:12-14), and Jacob (Genesis 30:43; 32:5). People of the ancient world measured wealth in terms of land, houses, servants, slaves, and precious metals. The prime example is King Solomon, whose great wealth is described in 1 Kings 10:14-29.

Wealth is a major theme in the wisdom literature of the Bible (Proverbs 10:15; 13:11; 19:4). The most important observation of these writings is that wealth comes from God. However, the possession of wealth is not always the sign of God's favor. The question asked by Jeremiah—"Why does the way of the wicked prosper?" (Jeremiah 12:1)—became a familiar theme to the writers of the Old Testament. The popular view that wickedness brings poverty and goodness brings wealth is strongly contradicted by the Book of Job.

In the New Testament, many warnings are given of the dangers of letting money and things possess a person's heart. In the Sermon on the Mount, Jesus spoke of "treasures on earth" and "treasures in heaven," and He called upon His followers to be careful about which treasure they chose.

Many of Jesus' parables, such as those of the rich fool (Luke 12:13-21) and the rich man and Lazarus (Luke 16:19-31), deal with people who made the wrong choice, choosing earthly wealth over heavenly wealth. The only true and lasting wealth is the spiritual riches of God's grace (Matthew 13:44-46).

BACKGROUND

Jesus gave fresh meaning to the theme found in Daniel—the "kingdom of God." The kingdom of God or kingdom of heaven is a place or realm where God is actively reigning. Jesus demonstrated this reign or authority of God by healing numerous people of sickness and demon possession. During Jesus' ministry, He was confronted by people of all backgrounds—rich, poor, educated, uneducated, skeptics, and those who honestly wanted to understand His ministry.

AT-A-GLANCE

1. Material Security or Eternal Security?
(Mark 10:17-20)
2. Choosing Christ Over Earthly
Possessions (vv. 21-22)
3. Difficulties on the Way to Salvation
(vv. 23-27)

IN DEPTH

1. Material Security or Eternal Security ?
(Mark 10:17-20)

As Jesus started on His way to His next destination (He was currently going into the region of Judea and across the Jordan), a young man ran up to Him. Jesus often attracted large crowds that included many types of people from various backgrounds. Perhaps this particular young man was waiting until the crowd dispersed before he made his way to Christ. He wanted a one-on-one session of his own. Upon reaching Jesus, he immediately honored Him by kneeling and calling Him "Good Master." Although the man was a materialist, he knew that you do not get what you need by disrespecting others. Notice that he did not call Jesus "Lord." It was only after kneeling and complimenting Christ that the young ruler asked the question, "What shall I do that I may inherit eternal life?" He had just heard Jesus speak on the topic of a child being able to inherit eternal life, and he wanted to ensure that he, too, would inherit eternal life. Having heard Jesus talk about inheritance, the rich man came kneeling. However, we must not take the fact that he knelt to mean that he considered Jesus to be Lord.

Jesus spoke provocatively by saying, "Why are you calling me good? There is none good but one, that is, God." Jesus was giving proper due to God the Father. At the same time, He was the Son of God. Jesus' provocative response is designed to test his motive. Would he say anything just to participate in the natural aspect of the kingdom? He called Jesus "Good Master." Didn't he know that only God was good? Was he willing to acknowledge Jesus as God standing right there? This leads one to think that he was thinking of "good" in terms of the *goods* of the kingdom. To him, Jesus was good not because of who He is—God with us—but because He held the goods of the kingdom, which this would-be follower might equate with material gain. But he moved beyond seeing Jesus as a "good teacher" to seeing Him as the very good (the true God) for which he searches. But, like many people, he could not move beyond the material to that which is essential.

Jesus responded by referring to the commandments: do not commit adultery, do not kill, do not steal, do not bear false witness, defraud not, and honor thy father and mother. Keeping the commandments God gave to Moses thousands of years earlier was very important. This is perhaps why Jesus first asked the young ruler, "Thou knowest the commandments?" The young master answered by saying he had followed the commandments from his youth. It was perhaps just as important as eating and sleeping. He had mastered the law, but there was one thing he lacked. The real issue Jesus raises with the young man is whether he was willing to let go of his self-righteousness and material security to accept God completely. Having been blessed by God materially, like every good Jew, the man endeavored to live according to the knowledge of the law of God. But even "good Jews" had material goods.

2. Choosing Christ Over Earthly Possessions (vv. 21-22)

Jesus pushes him beyond his material perspective. Because of Christ's love for humankind, He was often moved by compassion. It was love that moved Jesus to tell the rich man that even though he had learned and followed all of the commandments, there was yet one thing he lacked. If Jesus had not loved him, He would not have told him the truth. It's true love that provokes truth in us. Out of love, Jesus told him to sell what he had and give to the poor. Jesus, being God in the flesh, knew the heart of the man. He knew that the man's treasure was in his goods. Jesus told him that once he gave his goods to the poor, he would have treasure in heaven. The ministry of Jesus was to the poor. Perhaps this is why Jesus concluded by saying, "Come, take up the cross, and follow me." In other words, Jesus is saying, "Keeping the commandments is good, but I want your heart."

The rich man was sad and grieved because he had many possessions. His treasure was in his possessions. He was emotionally tied to them, and it provoked sadness and grief to even consider releasing them. He had asked Jesus a very important question— "Good Master, what shall I do that I may inherit eternal life?"—but he was not expecting this answer.

3. Difficulties on the Way to Salvation (vv. 23-27)

Jesus told His disciples that it is hard for those who have riches to enter into the kingdom of God. He repeated that it is hard because they trust in their riches and not in God. This was astonishing to the disciples because they believed that riches were a sign of God's favor. They wondered among themselves, "Who can be saved?" Jesus immediately had to stir up their faith again by saying that humanly these things are impossible, but with God all things are possible. In other words, God is able to change the rich and the poor. He is able to prepare all for the kingdom if they willingly trust Him.

The kingdom of God demands trusting in God completely and totally without distractions. Trust is firm belief or confidence in the honesty, integrity, reliability, justice, etc., of another person or thing. Your faith cannot be properly placed in anything but God.

This rich young man had several difficulties on the way to his salvation. These difficulties were caused by all of his riches. First, he was rich in the knowledge of the law. Second, he was rich in his own righteousness according to the law's external standard. Third, he was rich in physical wealth. From his approach to the Master, we also know that he was rich in his quest for the Word. However, instead of helping him make God his all-in-all, these riches were more important than God. He could not let go of them for the sake of God. He could not reach beyond his material possessions to God. Ironically, there is also another difficulty indicated here.

Though rich in all these ways, the young man was poor regarding compassion for the poor. Suppose Jesus had told him to give his riches directly to God or even to Jesus Himself. He probably would have done it since from His materialistic perspective that would mean that God would owe him—but give to the poor? The poor could not repay him. The final difficulty encountered on the way to his salvation was the needs of the poor, for whom the rich man was unwilling to sacrifice his material comfort. How often do our riches—in gifts, talents, works, even self-righteousness—keep us from taking steps of total submission to God?

SEARCH THE SCRIPTURES

1. What did the rich man ask Jesus? (Mark 10:17)
2. What commandments did Jesus mention? (v. 19)
3. What instructions did Jesus give the rich man? (v. 21)
4. How did he feel when Jesus told him to "sell whatsoever thou hath . . ."? (v. 22)
5. Why does the Scripture say that Jesus was "looking upon them"? (v. 27)

DISCUSS THE MEANING

1. Why do you think Jesus said, "There is none good but one, that is, God"?
2. Why do you think Jesus chose to mention a few of the Ten Commandments? What commandments were missing?
3. Why do you think the rich man was "grieved"?
4. Jesus said that it's hard for those who "trust in riches to enter into the kingdom of God." Explain.
5. What does the verse mean that states, "It is easier for a camel to go through the eye of a needle, than for a rich man to enter into the kingdom of God?"

LESSON IN OUR SOCIETY

It is safe to say that Jesus was not speaking against simply being rich, but rather about how we value our riches. Are our priorities in order? Are the things of God first or secondary? Is the desire to be rich greater than the importance of feeding the poor? If a person is in need, are you willing to share?

MAKE IT HAPPEN

Are your possessions stopping you from worshiping God to the fullest? What's important to you and what is not? Start prioritizing your life today. Get rid of those things that may hinder you from serving God fully. If you lost all possessions today, how would you feel?

FOLLOW THE SPIRIT

What God wants me to do:

_____

_____

REMEMBER YOUR THOUGHTS

Special insights you have learned:

_____

_____

MORE LIGHT ON THE TEXT
Mark 10:17-27

Jesus had just finished dealing with the question about divorce, which the Pharisees posed to test Him (v. 1-10), as well as giving His answer to the disciples on the same topic in verses 11-13. Then, using His disciples' objection about children coming to Him, Jesus taught His audience about the importance of children with regard to entering into the kingdom of God. Entry into the kingdom of God requires a childlike attitude, for He says, "Whosoever shall not receive the kingdom of God as a little child, he shall not enter therein" (v. 10:15). After this, Jesus is confronted with another question about the kingdom: What one can do in order to inherit eternal life (vv. 17-27). This passage can be divided into two main parts: (1) Jesus' encounter with a rich man (vv. 17-22), and (2) Jesus' teaching about how difficult it is for those who are rich to enter the kingdom of God (vv. 23-27).

10:17 And when he was gone forth into the way, there came one running, and kneeled to him, and asked him, Good Master, what shall I do that I may inherit eternal life?

After His encounters with the Pharisees and His disciples and His teaching regarding the kingdom of God, Jesus continues on His journey toward Jerusalem (see v. 17). The phrase, "when he was gone forth into the way" (or, "As Jesus started on His way") suggests that the previous incidents took place at a certain place where Jesus was teaching, and now He continues on His journey. It is unknown whether the "one" was among the audience that Jesus had just addressed, or whether the rich man saw Jesus passing and ran to him and posed his question. If he was among the group Jesus had just finished addressing, he probably wanted to know more about the kingdom of God. Therefore, he ran to meet Jesus. If he was among the crowd, why did he not ask his question when Jesus was teaching? Why did he have to run to meet Jesus on the way? The answer depends on the identity of the person.

Mark does not give us his identity. However, the parallel account in Luke identifies him as a "ruler" (Luke 18:18). He therefore was probably a member of the Jewish ruling council, a Pharisee or a member of the Sanhedrin. Matthew (19:20) calls him a "young man." It is likely that the rich young ruler (as he is generally referred to by scholars) was also a Pharisee. Like Nicodemus who went to Jesus by night (John 3:1ff), this young man probably did not want to ask his question in the presence of the Pharisees. Also like Nicodemus, he seems to be sincere in his inquiry; he wanted to know the truth. This is seen in his approach. First, he ran and knelt down before Jesus, which was a sign of respect and acknowledgment. To "kneel" is the Greek word *gonupeteo*, pronounced **gon-oo-peh-TEH,** and it means to fall on the knees, bow the knee, or prostrate oneself before someone greater. In most ancient cultures, including Jewish culture, it was customary to kneel before one's superiors, kings, or those in authority when speaking to or addressing them. By kneeling down to Jesus, the man showed that he acknowledged Christ's authority and superiority over him. It shows also that he acknowledged Christ's teaching as authoritative, and therefore he wanted to know more.

The second evidence of his sincerity is found in his address to Jesus. He calls Him "Good Master,"

which means good teacher. "Master" is from the Greek noun *didaskalos,* pronounced **dih-DAHSS-kah-lahss,** which means an instructor or teacher. The word "good" used here comes from the Greek adjective *agathos,* pronounced **ah-hag-THASS,** and it is used to describe the Master. The use of the word "good" can be viewed in two ways. First, "good" can here be seen as not referring so much to the moral character of Christ as to the excellent way He taught the people authoritatively (Matthew 7:29; Mark 1:22). Second, "good" here can be viewed with a moral undertone i.e., he is referring to Christ's integrity and moral character. In the light of Christ's reply in the next verse (v. 18), one can strongly assume that it is Christ's moral superiority that is referred to here. The man's question, "What shall I do that I may inherit eternal life?" tends to show that he has Jewish works of righteousness in mind. He wanted to know what he could do to merit everlasting life but seemed to misunderstand Christ's teaching (as implied in v. 15), which indicates that eternal life (the kingdom of God) is a free gift, not a meritorious achievement.

18 And Jesus said unto him, Why callest thou me good? there is none good but one, that is, God. 19 Thou knowest the commandments, Do not commit adultery, Do not kill, Do not steal, Do not bear false witness, Defraud not, Honour thy father and mother.

There seems to be an ambiguity in Christ's reply in verse 18. Jesus asks, "Why do you call me good? No one is good except God alone" (NASB). The question is, what does Christ mean by the statement? A number of suggestions have been made about what Christ had in mind. Probably Christ is saying that the word "good" is not to be used flippantly as praise for anyone because only God has moral goodness. The second probability is that Christ is saying that before he uses such a designation, he should be aware of the implications; he had better mean what he says. He should therefore truly acknowledge Christ as the One who came from the Father. Jesus, therefore, deserves this description because He alone is both fully human and fully divine.

Jesus then gives the man a summary of the contents of the second tablet of the Law (v. 19; cf. Exodus 20:12-17; Deuteronomy 5:16-20). In a similar story in Luke, in which a lawyer asks Jesus the same question, in response Jesus asks him, "What is written in the law?" Then the lawyer quotes the two great commandments regarding loving God and one's neighbor (Luke 10:25-28). Here Jesus reminds the man of the commandments, which assert that one who keeps the law would live (Deuteronomy 30:15-16). Jesus, however, neither affirms nor denies here that the keeping of the law is the only requirement for eternal life. However, keeping the law is the starting point for provoking the man to deeper thought. Jesus starts from the known and reveals the unknown. Keeping the Old Testament law is an important way of acknowledging, submitting to, and loving God. Jesus said later, "If [you] love me, keep my commandments" (John 14:15, 21, 23-24).

The word "defraud," or its Greek equivalent *apostereo*, pronounced **ah-pahss-teh-REH-o,** means to deprive, to rob, destitute, to despoil, to keep back by fraud. It appears only here in the Book of Mark. It probably refers to the commandment against coveting people's things. It should be noted that all six commands mentioned here—do not commit adultery, do not kill, do not steal, do not bear false witness, defraud not, and honor thy father and mother—deal with one's relationship with others (loving our neighbor as ourselves), or the second of the great commandments.

20 And he answered and said unto him, Master, all these have I observed from my youth. 21 Then Jesus beholding him loved him, and said unto him, One thing thou lackest: go thy way, sell whatsoever thou hast, and give to the poor, and thou shalt have treasure in heaven: and come, take up the cross, and follow me. 22 And he was sad at that saying, and went away grieved: for he had great possessions.

The man confidently claims that he has kept all the commandments that Jesus named since his boyhood. The word "youth" (Greek *neotes*, pronounced **neh-AH-tace**) probably refers to the age of 13, when a Jewish boy undergoes *bar mitzvah*. That means he becomes accountable to keep the law (Luke 2:42). To many a Jewish person, obedience to the law may mean only external conformity rather than inner compliance, which is more important. In his pre-Christian knowledge, Paul held to external conformity (Philippians 3:6) as an accepted way of life.

Jesus "beholding him loved him" means that He looks at him admirably. Some would suggest that He placed His hands on him. The main point of interest here is that the man thinks he has lived a decent life,

as evidenced by keeping the law. However, to Jesus, living a decent life according to the law is not good enough for entering eternal life. Jesus therefore prescribes another "recipe" for him: "Go, sell whatsoever thou hast, and give to the poor, and thou shalt have treasure in heaven. . . come and follow me." The statement here means a total surrender to God. Since he claims to "love" his neighbor as evidenced by his keeping the law, the Lord asks him to sell his belongings and give to the poor. What Christ is saying here does not necessarily mean getting rid of all his material wealth and possessions, but all that they represent: security, status, comfort, power, and position. He is to give up his world and accept the kingdom of God like "a little child"(cf. v. 15). Then he will store treasures in heaven—where moths and rust will not destroy nor thieves break in and steal (Matthew 6:19-21).

Christ's prescription seems too hard for the man to swallow, for he "was sad . . . and went away grieved, for he had great possessions." He was prepared to keep the law, but getting rid of worldly possessions for heavenly treasures was another matter entirely. Is there any wonder then that Jesus would say, "No one can serve two masters. Either he will hate the one and love the other, or he will be devoted to the one and despise the other. You cannot serve both God and Money" (Matthew 6:24, NIV).

23 And Jesus looked round about, and saith unto his disciples, How hardly shall they that have riches enter into the kingdom of God! 24 And the disciples were astonished at his words. But Jesus answereth again, and saith unto them, Children, how hard is it for them that trust in riches to enter into the kingdom of God!

The man's reaction prompts one of Christ's most extraordinary declarations. Addressing His disciples, Jesus says, "How hardly shall they that have riches enter into the kingdom of God!" The disciples' amazement reflects their Jewish understanding about riches, which tends to see wealth as a privilege and blessing from God. They see it as approval from God. However, Jesus sees it another way. The word "astonished" is the Greek word *thambeo*, pronounced **tham-BEH'-o,** meaning to stupefy, astound, or amaze. They are shocked at what Jesus says to them. Realizing their amazement, Jesus repeats His declaration but with some explanation. Rather than saying that it is hard for the rich to enter the kingdom, He tells them that it is hard for those "that trust in riches to enter into the kingdom of God." Here He explains to them that the difficulty is not so much having possessions as trusting in and putting confidence in them. In other words, there is nothing wrong with being rich, but it is wrong to trust in riches at the expense of our relationship with God and eternity. Writing to Timothy, Paul reminds him that not money, but "the love of money is the root of all evil" (1 Timothy 6:10). Salvation, therefore, does not depend on what you have or who you are according to the world's standards, but who you are in relation to God and His kingdom. Note how Jesus addresses His disciples here. Jesus calls them "children," or the Greek *teknon,* pronounced **TECK-nahn,** which is an address of endearment, in order to press home His point.

25 It is easier for a camel to go through the eye of a needle, than for a rich man to enter into the kingdom of God.

Jesus further explains His statements in verses 23 and 24 with a proverb to support His point. He tells them how difficult it is for the rich to enter the kingdom of God, which is compared to going through the eye of a needle. To Him "it is easier for a camel to go through the eye of a needle, than for a rich man to enter into the kingdom of God." This is said to be a common proverb in Jewish writings, and conveys the idea of great difficulty or impossibility.

Some modern translators have tried to play down the point and interpretation of this proverb. For example, the "eye of a needle" had been associated with a gate leading into Jerusalem where camels had to kneel before they could get through. However, the existence of such a gate has not been established. Another suggestion is that the word "camel" can mean a "cable rope," which cannot be threaded through the eye of a needle because of its inflexibility. These misinterpretations tend to miss the graphic nature of what Jesus is saying, i.e., it is indeed impossible for the rich person who puts his trust and hope in his earthly possessions to enter the kingdom of God.

26 And they were astonished out of measure, saying among themselves, Who then can be saved? 27 And Jesus looking upon them saith, With men it is impossible, but not with God: for with God all things are possible.

The full meaning of the proverb is not lost on the

disciples. However, they are so perplexed and "astonished out of [beyond] measure" that they ask among themselves, "Who then can be saved?" In verse 24, the disciples are "astonished," but here they are "astonished out of [beyond] measure" (i.e., they are much more surprised and shocked). Why? It is probably because of the universal belief that the rich always get what they want. The disciples cannot comprehend the fact that God's standards of dealing with the rich differ greatly from how humans deal with them. They have yet to understand that God deals with people on an equal basis—whether poor or rich. He is not a respecter of persons (Acts 10:34).

They have yet to learn that both the poor and the rich can be saved, not by what they have done, or what they have or do not have, but by God's grace alone. Realizing their perplexity over His statement and their dilemma in grasping the way God works, Jesus says to them that although "with men it is impossible, [but] not with God: for with God all things are possible." His answer clearly indicates that salvation is possible only through God's grace. Apart from that, it is impossible for anyone, especially the rich, to enter into God's kingdom. Human effort cannot earn God's salvation, but salvation is possible and available for all those who come to Him in faith—both the rich and poor alike. What man cannot do for himself, God through His Son, Jesus, has accomplished on the cross.

DAILY BIBLE READINGS

M: The Rich Man Goes Away Sorry
Mark 10:17-22
T: Hard for the Rich to Enter
Mark 10:23-31
W: Simon Wants to Buy Power
Acts 8:14-24
T: I Will Follow You, But . . .
Luke 9:57-62
F: You Are Lukewarm
Revelation 3:14-20
S: What Tomorrow Will Bring
James 4:13-17
S: Save Your Life and Lose It
Matthew 16:24-28

TEACHING TIPS

January 12
Bible Study Guide 7

1. Words You Should Know

A. Cumbered—To burden in a troublesome way. To perplex or distress.

B. Resurrection—A rising from the dead, or coming back to life. The rising of all the dead at the last judgment.

2. Teacher Preparation

A. Read and meditate on the background Scriptures and the Devotional Reading.

B. Study the FOCAL VERSES.

C. Study and prepare your responses to the SEARCH THE SCRIPTURES and DISCUSS THE MEANING questions.

3. Starting the Lesson

A. Write the LESSON AIM on the board. Explain to the class the importance of staying focused on Jesus and not merely on works that we feel as pleasing to Him.

B. Open in prayer, asking God to reveal His Word today.

4. Getting into the Lesson

A. Review the WORDS YOU SHOULD KNOW terms and briefly discuss.

B. HAVE volunteers read the FOCAL VERSES.

C. After the reading, ask volunteers to answer the questions in the SEARCH THE SCRIPTURES section.

5. Relating the Lesson to Life

A. Divide students into two groups and have them answer the DISCUSS THE MEANING questions.

B. Reconvene the class and discuss each group's answers to the questions.

C. Reflect on the LESSON IN OUR SOCIETY and generate a discussion about the topic.

6. Arousing Action

A. Ask students to reflect on their own ministry to Christ. Are they busy with good works but failing to make time for prayer and meditation before God?

B. Challenge the students to consider the "works" that they do but need to release in order to draw closer to the Savior.

C. Ask them to come back to class next week prepared to share what they have committed to do in response to the challenge.

D. Close the class with prayer.

WORSHIP GUIDE

For the Superintendent or Teacher
Theme: Mary and Martha: Friends of Jesus
Theme Song: "My Faith Looks Up to Thee"
Scripture: James 4
Song: "Great Is Thy Faithfulness"
Devotional Thought: Dear Lord, It is good to know that I have a Saviour who never changes. Thank You for Your strong love in my life.

MARY AND MARTHA: FRIENDS OF JESUS

Bible Background • LUKE 10:38-42; JOHN 11:20-32
Printed Text • LUKE 10:38-42; JOHN 11:20-27, 30-32
Devotional Reading • JOHN 15:12-17

LESSON AIM

By the end of the lesson, students will be able to articulate the importance of our walk with Christ, resolve to avoid being sidetracked with works alone, and focus on an intimate relationship with God through Christ.

KEEP IN MIND

"And Jesus answered and said unto her, Martha, Martha, thou art careful and troubled about many things: But one thing is needful: and Mary hath chosen that good part, which shall not be taken away from her" (Luke 10:41-42).

LESSON OVERVIEW

LESSON AIM
KEEP IN MIND
FOCAL VERSES
IN FOCUS
THE PEOPLE, PLACES, AND TIMES
BACKGROUND
AT-A-GLANCE
IN DEPTH
SEARCH THE SCRIPTURES
DISCUSS THE MEANING
LESSON IN OUR SOCIETY
MAKE IT HAPPEN
FOLLOW THE SPIRIT
REMEMBER YOUR THOUGHTS
MORE LIGHT ON THE TEXT
DAILY BIBLE READINGS

FOCAL VERSES

Luke 10:38 Now it came to pass, as they went, that he entered into a certain village: and a certain woman named Martha received him into her house.

39 And she had a sister called Mary, which also sat at Jesus' feet, and heard his word.

40 But Martha was cumbered about much serving, and came to him, and said, Lord, dost thou not care that my sister hath left me to serve alone? bid her therefore that she help me.

41 And Jesus answered and said unto her, Martha, Martha, thou art careful and troubled about many things:

42 But one thing is needful: and Mary hath chosen that good part, which shall not be taken away from her.

John 11:20 Then Martha, as soon as she heard that Jesus was coming, went and met him: but Mary sat still in the house.

21 Then said Martha unto Jesus, Lord, if thou hadst been here, my brother had not died.

22 But I know, that even now, whatsoever thou wilt ask of God, God will give it thee.

23 Jesus saith unto her, Thy brother shall rise again.

24 Martha saith unto him, I know that he shall rise again in the resurrection at the last day.

25 Jesus said unto her, I am the resurrection, and the life: he that believeth in me, though he were dead, yet shall he live:

26 And whosoever liveth and believeth in me shall never die. Believest thou this?

27 She saith unto him, Yea, Lord: I believe that thou art the Christ, the Son of God, which should come into the world.

11:30 Now Jesus was not yet come into the town, but was in that place where Martha met him.

31 The Jews then which were with her in the house, and comforted her, when they saw Mary, that she rose up hastily and went out, followed her, saying, She goeth unto the grave to weep there.

32 Then when Mary was come where Jesus was, and saw him, she fell down at his feet, saying unto him, Lord, if thou hadst been here, my brother had not died.

JAN
12TH

IN FOCUS

Being a Christian causes us to constantly keep things in perspective. Throughout the teachings of Jesus, He reminds us to "check ourselves" and make sure that we are doing the right thing, not pointing the finger at someone else, but constantly doing a self-evaluation. Let's learn from Mary and Martha today.

THE PEOPLE, PLACES, AND TIMES

Martha and Mary. Two sisters from Bethany (Luke 10:38-41; John 11:1-44; 12:1-3). Their brother's name was Lazarus. All three were sincere followers of Jesus, but Mary and Martha expressed their love for Him in different ways. The account of the two women in the Gospel of Luke reveals a clash of temperaments. Martha "was cumbered about much serving" (Luke 10:40); she was an activist, busy with household chores. Her sister Mary "sat at Jesus' feet, and heard his word" (Luke 10:39); her instinct was to sit still, meditate, and receive spiritual instruction.

On another occasion, Mary anointed Jesus' feet with a "a pound of very costly oil of spikenard" and also wiped his feet with her hair (John 11:2).

Bethany. A village about 1-3/4 miles southeast of Jerusalem on the Mount of Olives and close to Bethphage. It was the home of the sisters Mary and Martha; here Jesus raised their brother Lazarus from the dead. Jesus lodged in Bethany during His last week in Jerusalem, and the palm procession set out from here.

Friend. A person whom one knows, likes, and trusts. One who supports, sympathizes with, or patronizes a group, cause, or movement.

BACKGROUND

Jesus had just taught the disciples the parable of the Good Samaritan. The parable was Jesus' response to a lawyer who asked: "Who is my neighbor?" After using the parable to explain who our true neighbor is, Jesus went to visit His neighbors and friends, Mary and Martha. Martha received Jesus into her home and began to be hospitable, but she was disturbed when her sister Mary chose not to help her. Instead, Mary chose to sit at the feet of Jesus and hear His teachings.

AT-A-GLANCE

1. Jesus Visits Mary and Martha (Luke 10:38-42)
2. Jesus' Friendship with the Bereaved (John 11:20-27)
3. The Impact of Friendship (vv. 30-32)

IN DEPTH

1. Jesus Visits Mary and Martha (Luke 10:38-42)

Once Jesus arrived at Mary and Martha's home, the two women expressed their love for Jesus in different ways. In our walk with Christ, we see various expressions of love for the Lord. Martha chose to busy herself in works. Perhaps she was cooking and cleaning and waiting on Jesus hand and foot as He taught in her home. She was probably sweating, hot, tired, and feeling alone in her works. She was annoyed with her sister, wondering how she could choose to sit down and listen to Christ teaching rather than help her with the household duties. But Mary was intrigued and fascinated by the teachings of Christ (which is not to say that Martha was not). Jesus was in an intimate setting (a home), and she was excited and wanted to grasp all she could, while she could. These Scriptures tell us that there was a multitude that usually followed Christ. On any other occasion, perhaps Mary had to fight the crowd to hear the great teachings of her friend, Jesus. On this occasion, Jesus was close enough for her to sit at His feet.

Martha did not address her sister, but she asked Jesus to address the situation. How many times have we gone to the Lord about other people? "Lord, get them!" Martha felt that she was doing the greater work by doing "much serving." She told the Lord, "Bid her therefore that she help me" (v. 40).

Jesus' response surprised her. He said that

Martha was troubled about "many things." "But one thing is needful: and Mary hath chosen that good part. . ." (v. 42). He was not saying that Martha's works were wrong, but at that particular time, the needful thing was to hear His teachings. Sometimes the people of God can become busy doing a lot of works in the name of the Lord, but Jesus is saying: "Sit down and hear My teachings and then work." Maybe she was trying to do too much at one time; her priorities were out of order. On the other hand, Mary was refilling and feeding her spirit, something that "shall not be taken away from her" (v. 42).

2. Jesus' Friendship with the Bereaved (John 11:20-27)

Lazarus, the brother of Mary and Martha, died of a sickness while Jesus was away teaching. Jesus got word of His friend's death four days prior to His arrival in their hometown of Bethany. When Martha heard that Jesus was coming, she went to meet Him, but Mary stayed at home. Martha told Jesus if He would have been there, "my brother would not have died" (v. 32, NIV). Martha had faith in Jesus, but it was a past-tense faith. To her, the time was past and it was now too late. She knew that Jesus was a miracle worker and capable of healing her brother if He had been in town. Despite her statement, there was still a glimmer of faith. She knew that God would give Him whatever He asked for. Jesus responded to her faith by saying that Lazarus would rise again. This is what happens when you have faith. Isn't it amazing how, though our faith may sometimes be marred by doubt, God reaches that mustard seed and based on it performs miracles on our behalf? Perhaps Martha did not know that before Jesus arrived in Bethany, He said that Lazarus's sickness was "not unto death, but for the glory of God, that the Son of God might be glorified thereby" (John 11:4).

Martha thought that Jesus meant that her brother would rise again during the resurrection on the last day (again we see another human tendency to move faith into the future). Jesus brings her back to the present. Jesus quickly reminded her that He was in fact "the resurrection and the life" and though Lazarus were dead, "yet shall he live." The words of Jesus provoked faith in Martha. She was beginning to see that her beloved Friend was going to raise her brother from the dead, but first she had to believe. Once the Lord got her attention to return to that moment, He proceeded to work. Faith in the presence of God is vital. It settles for us what may or may not have been done in the past, and it corrects our tendency to use the future as an escape from the present.

3. The Impact of Friendship (John 11:30-32)

Before this, Mary was home mourning the death of her brother along with some other Jewish mourners. Jesus had not yet arrived in Bethany, but when she heard that He was coming, she repeated the words of her sister: "Lord, if you had been here, my brother would not have died" (v. 30, NIV). She too had great faith in Jesus' healing power, but forgot that the same power could raise Lazarus from the dead.

Even though Mary was in mourning, she came out to see Jesus. She knew that His presence would bring comfort. Yet He came with comfort, not of words, but of resurrection. The friendship of these three persons with the Lord led to their comfort. Similarly, the experience of a resurrecting friendship with the Master can transform our circumstances, even if it be death.

SEARCH THE SCRIPTURES

1. Whose house did Jesus visit? (Luke 10:38)
2. How did Mary worship Jesus? (v. 39)
3. How did Martha worship Jesus? (v. 40)
4. Why was Martha upset with her sister Mary? (v. 40)
5. Who died? (John 11:21)

DISCUSS THE MEANING

1. Why do you believe Jesus said that Mary's form of worship was the "good part, which shall not be taken away from her"? Do you think Martha was wrong? Explain.
2. What did Jesus mean when He said, "I am the resurrection and the life"? Explain.

LESSON IN OUR SOCIETY

In today's society, friendships are important.

Good friends are by your side throughout life's many phases, whether joyous or painful. You want your friends with you, no matter what. Sometimes, we try hard to please our friends by doing "things." Most of the time, all a true friend wants is your fellowship, a listening ear, and a warm heart of understanding. Are you a true friend? Are your ears and heart open to the voice of your Friend, Jesus?

MAKE IT HAPPEN

Bring your friendships to a new level. Write down the names of all your close friends and schedule a time that is good for both of you just to sit and talk with each other.

FOLLOW THE SPIRIT

What God wants me to do:

_____

_____

REMEMBER YOUR THOUGHTS

Special insights you have learned:

_____

_____

MORE LIGHT ON THE TEXT
Luke 10:38-42; John 11:20-27, 30-32

Jesus and His disciples are on their way to Jerusalem (Luke 9:51-56); Jesus is confronted by a lawyer who desires to know what he has to do to inherit eternal life. This leads us to the famous parable of the Good Samaritan (10:25-37). It seems that Jesus and His followers have stopped at a certain place (see Mark 10:17ff), where these events take place. Like Mark, Luke tells us that Jesus continues on His journey toward Jerusalem.

Luke 10:38-42
38 Now it came to pass, as they went, that he entered into a certain village: and a certain woman named Martha received him into her house.

As they continue on their journey toward Jerusalem, they come to a certain village, most probably Bethany (see John 12:1), where Martha and Mary lived. Bethany is about two miles from Jerusalem on the way to the Jordan River, on the

east slope of the Mount of Olives (Luke 19:29). Bethany must have been a stopping spot for Jesus as He frequently traveled between Galilee and Jerusalem. During His frequent journeys through Bethany, Jesus must have established a close friendly relationship with Martha and her family (cp. John 11:3). We would be correct in assuming that Martha and her siblings were also Christ's disciples. Their home therefore must have been a rendezvous spot for Jesus. Martha seems to have been the older sister. She took the responsibility for the household. The phrase "received him into her house" from the Greek *hupodechomai* (pronounced **hoop-o-DECK-o-my**) simply means that Martha welcomed Him to their home with the idea of entertaining Him.

39 And she had a sister called Mary, which also sat at Jesus' feet, and heard his word.

Verse 39 introduces to us another member of the family—Mary, Martha's sister. According to John, she is the same one who "anointed the Lord [Jesus] with ointment, and wiped his feet with her hair" (John 11:2; cf. 12:3; Matthew 26:6-13). Martha welcomes Jesus to the home and goes to prepare for the Lord's entertainment, but Mary sits down and listens to Jesus' teaching. The Greek word *ekoue* (pronounced **A-koo-eh**) is the third-person singular of the word *akouo* (pronounced **ah-koo-o**), which means to hear or to listen. The tense used here suggests that she is continually listening to His "word." Probably she is in the habit of sitting at the Master's feet and listening to His teaching. It was customary for disciples to sit at their Master's feet to be instructed (cf. 8:35; Acts 22:3).

40 But Martha was cumbered about much serving, and came to him, and said, Lord, dost thou not care that my sister hath left me to serve alone? bid her therefore that she help me.

While Mary sits at Jesus' feet listening to His teaching, Martha is in the kitchen preparing a meal for Jesus. The idea of showing hospitality, which Martha tends to do here, is not bad in itself. But as the phrase "cumbered about much serving" suggests, Martha is distracted and over-burdened with much preparation. The word "cumbered" is a translation of the Greek word *perispao* (pronounced **per-ee-SPAH-o**). It means to be pulled away or to drag around; here it is used figuratively and means to distract (with care). Martha seems to allow her work of hospitality to overcome her. Instead of being a service, it tends to become a burden for her. Overburdened with "much serving" and concerned that she is left alone to serve, she asks Jesus to intervene—to ask Mary to help her. Martha phrases her request in such a way that she expects a positive reply—"Lord, don't you care that my sister has left me to do the work by myself? Tell her to help me!" (NIV)

41 And Jesus answered and said unto her, Martha, Martha, thou art careful and troubled about many things: 42 But one thing is needful: and Mary hath chosen that good part, which shall not be taken away from her.

Instead of getting the reply she expects, Martha would learn the importance of setting her priorities right; she learns that certain things are more important in life than others. Notice the double address "Martha, Martha," which indicates a tender and caring attitude. As on other occasions in Luke, Jesus repeats a name when he wants to make some important and unusually impressive statement or when He wants to press home an important point (see Luke 6:46; 8:24; 13:34; 22:31; cf. Acts 9:4.). He says to Martha that she is "careful and troubled about many things." The word translated as "careful" is the Greek word *merimnao* (pronounced **mer-m-NAH-o**) which means to be worried or to be anxious about something or to "take thought" (Matthew 6:26). The word "troubled" is the Greek word *thorubazo* (pronounced **tho-roo-BAHD`-zo**), which means to be disturbed, upset, or agitated.

Therefore, Jesus tells her that she is easily distracted and worried about many things—things that are less important. "But one thing is needful," i.e., one thing is more important, "and Mary hath chosen that good part." The word "good" (Greek *agathos,* pronounced **ah-gah-THAHSS**) can be translated as "the better or best portion." The phrase, "which shall not be taken away from her" simply means that what she has chosen,

namely, the Word of God and its benefits, cannot be taken away from her. Here Jesus says that we ought to set our priorities straight, that listening to and obeying the Word of God is more important than doing things to impress Him. Implicitly Jesus confirms to Martha the words He spoke to the devil during His temptation: "Man shall not live by bread alone, but by every word that proceedeth out of the mouth of God" (Matthew 4:4).

John introduces us to another member of Martha's family: Lazarus, who is sick and eventually dies before Jesus reaches their home. Jesus is informed about Lazarus's sickness, but He delays and assures His disciples that the sickness would not lead to death. Aware that Lazarus is dead, Jesus decides to go to Bethany (Martha, Mary, and Lazarus's hometown) to "wake Lazarus up" (11:1-19).

John 11:20-27, 30-32
20 Then Martha, as soon as she heard that Jesus was coming, went and met him: but Mary sat still in the house.

Martha and Mary and their friends mourn the death of Lazarus. Then Martha hears that Jesus is on His way into town, so she goes to meet Him. However, Mary stays behind ("Mary sat still in the house") which among Jews (and indeed almost every culture) is a custom of posture in time of grief (Ezra 9:3-4; Nehemiah 1:4). In his description of Israel's agony in captivity in Babylon, the psalmist sings, "By the rivers of Babylon, there we sat down, yea, we wept, when we remembered Zion (Psalm 137:1; cf. Matthew 27:61).

21 Then said Martha unto Jesus, Lord, if thou hadst been here, my brother had not died. 22 But I know, that even now, whatsoever thou wilt ask of God, God will give it thee. 23 Jesus saith unto her, Thy brother shall rise again.

As she approaches the Lord, Martha tells Him that if He had been there on time, her brother would not have died; but she follows that statement with a positive affirmation of faith in the efficacy and power of Christ's prayer. Here, on the one hand she is complaining about Jesus' delay in coming to heal her brother; on the other hand, she is expressing her confidence in the power of Christ to heal. However, she tends to limit Christ's power over death.

The phrase "but I know" is more than head knowledge or an awareness of something; instead, it gives the idea of certainty, as the Greek word *oida* (pronounced **OY-duh**) used here conveys. Martha seems to say, "I am sure that even now, whatever you ask of God, He will definitely grant it to you." What is the basis of this kind of faith? As a friend (see vv. 5, 11) and a disciple of Christ, she must have witnessed several times when Jesus demonstrated His success in getting answers to prayer. Therefore, her faith is based on historical proof. Jesus promises all believers without exception the same: that whatever we ask in prayer in His name, it will be granted.

Such promises are common in the Gospels (Matthew 7:7-11; 17:20; 21:22; Mark 9:23; 11:22-24; Luke 11:1-13; 18:1-14; John 14:1-15; 15:7, 16; 16:23-26). This fact is also demonstrated in Christ's statement in verses 11-16 when He tells His disciples that He is going to raise Lazarus. In His reply to Martha's statement, Jesus assures her that her brother will be raised. The phrase "shall rise again" is from the Greek word *anistemi* (pronounced **ahn-ISS-tay-mee**), which means to stand up, lift up, or be raised up. The noun form of this Greek word is *anastasis* (pronounced **ah-WAHSS-tak-siss**), which means resurrection, standing up, or rising from the dead.

24 Martha saith unto him, I know that he shall rise again in the resurrection at the last day. 25 Jesus said unto her, I am the resurrection, and the life: he that believeth in me, though he were dead, yet shall he live: 26 And whosoever liveth and believeth in me shall never die. Believest thou this?

Martha again asserts her faith in the future hope of resurrection but misses the reality of the present. While Jesus assures her that her brother is about to be physically raised from the dead and her request granted, Martha (probably confused or occupied with grief) is unable to fully understand Christ's intent here. Hence, she focuses her attention on the future resurrection of the believers (1 Thessalonians 4:14-17). One can almost hear her tone of voice, which seems to lack zeal

and is full of despondence. "I know that he shall rise again in the resurrection at the last day," with emphasis on "at the last day." Notice that Jesus does not give the timeframe in His reply (v. 23), but Martha supplies "at the last day" (6:39, 40, 44, 54; 12:48). Jesus then corrects her by drawing her attention to His lordship over life and death—that He is the "resurrection, and the life." That is, in Him is life and death.

Using the present circumstance, Jesus teaches about the future reality, which goes beyond the death and resurrection of Lazarus to all those who will believe in Him. What does Christ mean in the statement (v. 25)? Here, Jesus makes two very significant statements. First, "he that believes in" Him may experience physical death, just as Lazarus has. However, through the power of Christ he will live again, i.e., the believer will be raised from the dead. Second, those who believe will inherit eternal life through faith in Christ. Believers who die in this life will live forever, that is, they will live with Christ in eternity and will never be separated. In fact, whoever believes in Christ in this life will live eternally (v. 26). Then Jesus throws a challenge to Martha: "Do you believe this?" (NIV).

27 She saith unto him, Yea, Lord: I believe that thou art the Christ, the Son of God, which should come into the world.

Her answer confirms her faith in Christ as the expected Messiah and the Son of God. She changes from "I know" (v. 22) to "I believe" (v. 27). The Greek word used here is *pepisteuka* from the root *pisteuo* (pronounced **piss-TYOO'-o**) which means to have faith (in, upon, or with respect to a person or thing), to believe, to commit to, or to trust. However, this particular Greek form is emphatic and means "I firmly or have definitely believed." Although she firmly believes that Christ is the Messiah, there is still the sense that she does not fully comprehend what Christ is about to do or what He means by, "Thy brother shall rise again" in verse 23. She seems to have been caught up with who Christ is, but not with what He is able to do, i.e., to raise Lazarus physically from the dead (see v. 39-40).

It is amazing how many times we (believers)

are just like Martha. We can easily believe in Christ and confess His Lordship, and indeed wait for His coming to raise us from the dead at the last day, but to trust Him to meet our immediate needs (e.g., healing ordinary headaches or supplying our daily needs) is often difficult for us. Jesus is not only Lord of the future; He is also Lord of the present—indeed, the Lord of all times and all circumstances. We need to trust in Him at all times and in His ability to do all things for us.

At the end of this dialogue with Martha, Jesus must have asked her to call Mary her sister. Martha runs home and secretly tells Mary that Jesus is around and is asking for her. As soon as she hears this, Mary goes to meet Jesus (v. 28-29).

11:30 Now Jesus was not yet come into the town, but was in that place where Martha met him. 31 The Jews then which were with her in the house, and comforted her, when they saw Mary, that she rose up hastily and went out, followed her, saying, She goeth unto the grave to weep there.

Verse 30 informs us that Jesus is still at the place where Martha met him, probably at the outskirts of Bethany. According to Jewish custom, burial places were usually outside of the town and villages (Luke 7:12), and Jesus is probably near the place where Lazarus is buried. At the invitation of Christ, and leaving her comforters in the house without a word, Mary goes to meet Jesus. As she sets out, her comforters, thinking that she is going to the grave to weep, follow her. It was customary for bereaved families and friends to go to grave sites to weep for three days (called the days of mourning; Genesis 27:41), when it was believed that the spirit wandered about the sepulcher seeking an opportunity to return to the body.

On the fourth day, decomposition set in and the spirit supposedly left the grave, and the people beat their breasts in loud lamentation for four days (cf. v. 17). This makes a total of seven days of mourning. It is no wonder, then, that Martha finds it difficult to understand Christ's assurance to her that Lazarus will rise again (cf. v. 23, 39-40).

32 Then when Mary was come where Jesus was, and saw him, she fell down at his feet, saying unto him, Lord, if thou hadst been here, my brother had not died.

On meeting Jesus, Mary falls on her knees in honor, and with the same words used by Martha (v. 21), she expresses her disappointment and faith in what would have happened if Jesus had been there earlier before her brother died. However, she does not follow up her statement of faith with a request for resurrection.

The rest of the story in this chapter shows that Christ has power over death, even when the body decomposes; it also demonstrates Christ's relationship with and caring concern for His friends (vv. 33ff). He is always there, both in times of joy (as we see in the Luken passage) and in times of tragedy and need.

DAILY BIBLE READINGS

M: Jesus Visits Mary and Martha
Luke 10:38-42
T: The Sisters Send Jesus A Message
John 11:1-6
W: Lazarus Dies
John 11:7-16
T: Lord, If You Had Been Here
John 11:17-27
F: Jesus Weeps
John 11:28-37
S: Lazarus, Come Out
John 11:38-44
S: Mary Anoints Jesus
John 12:1-8

TEACHING TIPS

1. Words You Should Know

A. Truth—Reality, actual existence, an established or verified fact, sincerity or genuineness.

B. Crucifixion—The method of torture and execution used by the Romans to put Christ to death. At a crucifixion, the victim usually was nailed or tied to a wooden stake and left to die. Because crucifixion was the Romans' most severe form of execution, it was reserved for slaves and criminals.

2. Teacher Preparation

A. Study the FOCAL VERSES intensely. You want to feel as if you were right there with Jesus and Pilate in the judgment hall. You want to fully understand what was going on between the two of them during that time.

B. Answer the SEARCH THE SCRIPTURES and DISCUSS THE MEANING questions. This will help you prepare for the class discussion.

3. Starting the Lesson

A. Before the students arrive, write the LESSON AIM on the board. Later, ask the students if it was accomplished.

B. Have one student lead the class in prayer. Ask him or her to pray that God would bless the class time.

C. Read the IN FOCUS story and ask students if they know of any incidents related to the text.

4. Getting into the Lesson

A. Ask for volunteers to read the BACKGROUND section and THE PEOPLE, PLACES, AND TIMES section.

B. Review the SEARCH THE SCRIPTURES questions together.

C. Discuss the WORDS YOU SHOULD KNOW with the class.

5. Relating the Lesson to Life

A. Have the students read LESSON IN OUR SOCIETY and lead a brief class discussion.

B. Choose volunteers to answer the DISCUSS THE MEANING questions.

6. Arousing Action

A. Have the students individually complete the SEARCH THE SCRIPTURES questions for homework.

B. Encourage the students to complete the DAILY BIBLE READINGS and to be prepared to share their experiences during the next class.

C. Ask a student to end the class in prayer. Also, assign students to pray for one another this week.

WORSHIP GUIDE

For the Superintendent or Teacher
Theme: Pilate: Judge on Trial
Theme Song: "Open My Eyes Lord"
Scripture: James 1:12-18
Song: "Yield Not to Temptation"
Devotional Thought: Father, thank You that truth is available to us in Your Word. Help us not to be deceived by our own thinking or the false words of men, but help us to grow by truth. Amen.

PILATE: JUDGE ON TRIAL

Bible Background • JOHN 18:31-38; 19:12-16a
Printed Text • JOHN 18:31-38; 19:12-16a
Devotional Reading • 1 TIMOTHY 2:1-6

LESSON AIM

By the end of this lesson, students will learn to follow their conscience as informed by the Lord and bear witness to what God has called them to do.

KEEP IN MIND

". . . Thou sayest that I am a king. To this end was I born, and for this cause came I into the world that I should bear witness unto the truth. Every one that is of the truth heareth my voice. Pilate saith unto him, What is truth? . . ." (John 18:37-38).

FOCAL VERSES

John 18:31 Then said Pilate unto them, Take ye him, and judge him according to your law. The Jews therefore said unto him, It is not lawful for us to put any man to death:

32 That the saying of Jesus might be fulfilled, which he spake, signifying what death he should die.

33 Then Pilate entered into the judgment hall again, and called Jesus, and said unto him, Art thou the King of the Jews?

34 Jesus answered him, Sayest thou this thing of thyself, or did others tell it thee of me?

35 Pilate answered, Am I a Jew? Thine own nation and the chief priests have delivered thee unto me: what hast thou done?

36 Jesus answered, My kingdom is not of this world: if my kingdom were of this world, then would my servants fight, that I should not be delivered to the Jews: but now is my kingdom not from hence.

37 Pilate therefore said unto him, Art thou a king then? Jesus answered, Thou sayest that I am a king.

LESSON OVERVIEW

LESSON AIM
KEEP IN MIND
FOCAL VERSES
IN FOCUS
THE PEOPLE, PLACES, AND TIMES
BACKGROUND
AT-A-GLANCE
IN DEPTH
SEARCH THE SCRIPTURES
DISCUSS THE MEANING
LESSON IN OUR SOCIETY
MAKE IT HAPPEN
FOLLOW THE SPIRIT
REMEMBER YOUR THOUGHTS
MORE LIGHT ON THE TEXT
DAILY BIBLE READINGS

To this end was I born, and for this cause came I into the world, that I should bear witness unto the truth. Every one that is of the truth heareth my voice.

38 Pilate saith unto him, What is truth? And when he had said this, he went out again unto the Jews, and saith unto them, I find in him no fault at all.

John 19:12 And from thenceforth Pilate sought to release him: but the Jews cried out, saying, If thou let this man go, thou art not Caesar's friend: whosoever maketh himself a king speaketh against Caesar.

13 When Pilate therefore heard that saying, he brought Jesus forth, and sat down in the judgment seat in a place that is called the Pavement, but in the Hebrew, Gabbatha.

14 And it was the preparation of the passover, and about the sixth hour: and he saith unto the Jews, Behold your King!

15 But they cried out, Away with him, away with him, crucify him. Pilate saith unto them, Shall I crucify your King? The chief priests answered, We have no king but Caesar.

16 Then delivered he him therefore unto them to be crucified.

IN FOCUS

The new cashier at the grocery store where Theresa, a saved sister, worked was accused of taking money, but Theresa knew the real culprit was Lewis. Lew was popular on the job; everyone liked him. He would bring special treats to work to share with fellow employees. He knew how to flatter everyone. "Theresa, that is a nice dress you have on today," he would say. Even though he was nice, Lewis had a problem: he was a thief. Theresa saw him several times stealing cologne, food, small appliances, and anything else he could get away with. In contrast, the new cashier was a teenager who desperately needed the job to help support her mother and two brothers. She came to work on time and never missed a day. She was the model employee. Theresa saw Lewis go into the cash register the night before. Lewis saw Theresa as well. When the supervisor asked Theresa if she saw anything unusual the night before, Theresa initially kept her lips sealed. Then she put herself in the new cashier's shoes. "What is the right thing to do?" she prayed. "What would Jesus want me to do?" Theresa told the truth.

THE PEOPLE, PLACES, AND TIMES

Pilate. The fifth Roman procurator of Judea (ruled 26-36 A.D.), who issued the official order sentencing Jesus to death by crucifixion.

Judge. One who governs and dispenses justice, judgment, and protection. The first judge mentioned in the Old Testament is God Himself (Genesis 18:25). In the New Testament, the high court of Israel was the Sanhedrin, although there were also judges in every town. None of the New Testament judges "protected" the people by leading them into battle (like those in the Old Testament book of Judges did).

BACKGROUND

A band of men and officers from the chief priests and Pharisees led by Judas had just taken Jesus captive. Jesus was bound and taken to the palace of the high priest to be interrogated. Peter

AT-A-GLANCE

1. Pilate: The Reluctant Judge
(John 18:31-35)
2. Jesus Beyond Pilate's Jurisdiction
(vv. 36-38)
3. Powerless Pilate (19:12-16)

followed them but denied that he knew Jesus. From the palace, Jesus is taken to Pilate in the judgment hall. Pilate wants to know why they had brought Jesus to him.

IN DEPTH

1. Pilate: The Reluctant Judge (John 18:31-35)

Pilate was bewildered. He wanted to know why the Jewish leaders had brought Jesus to him. He told them to judge Him according to their own laws. He did not want any part of judging Jesus. Perhaps Pilate had seen and heard of the miracles done by Jesus. He may have heard of the blind gaining sight, the lame learning to walk, and the sick being healed.

One may think that Pilate was being a coward, but that is not really the case. Had they brought an accusation based on Roman law, Pilate would not have asked them to judge Jesus. The statement, "you take him and judge him according to your law" points to Pilate's admission that he was not competent in matters of Hebrew law. Here we see the tangled legal, political, and religious web to which the Romans subjected the Jews. They lived under two laws. According to some interpretations of Mosaic Law, Jesus should die. But according to Roman law, no one should be put to death except by Roman authority. So we find the religious leaders of Judah at that time saying, "It is not lawful for us to put anyone to death." This statement is true regarding Jewish law, but it also goes deeper because it was the Passover season. During the period of preparation for the Passover, it was not lawful for these religious men to put anyone to death. Such action would have made them unworthy to celebrate the Passover. Therefore, it was unlawful on two accounts, but the actions of these leaders were meant to confirm the prophetic statements of the Master about His death (Matthew 20:17-19; John 3:14). It was foretold that the Gentiles (Romans) would kill Him, but also that Israel would deliver Him up.

Pilate continued to try to get Jesus out of his court and back into the hands of the religious leaders. Perhaps he had heard that Jesus called Himself a king. By asking the question, "Are you the king of the Jews?" Pilate would have removed any legal reluctance that he had and would later free his hand to punish Jesus. In Roman law, anyone who claimed monarchy opposed Caesar and had to die. In response, Jesus asked Pilate, "Is this your confession or did you hear someone else say this?" Jesus' tone was accusatory; it is as if He asks, "Are you going by hearsay, Pilate, or is this your conviction?" As a judge, Pilate should know before he speaks. Pilate knew the implication of Jesus' response; it spoke to his tendency to be swayed by opinion rather than facts. If it was discovered that Pilate judged based on opinion and not fact, his career was finished. That is why Pilate got upset and replied, "Am I a Jew?" Pilate was desperately trying to put Jesus back into the hands of the chief priests to be judged by them. The chief priests' role at that time was to administer justice according to Jewish law and to perform sacred service at the temple. However, the chief priests were threatened by Jesus' activities and wanted Him executed.

2. Jesus: Beyond Pilate's Jurisdiction (vv. 36-38)

In verses 36-38, Jesus finally says something that might help to free Him from Pilate. Jesus is indirectly saying, "Yes, I am King of the Jews, but you won't understand the way My kingdom operates. It is not a worldly system." He says, "If My kingdom were of this world, I would call My servants to fight for Me." No, Pilate, Jesus is not interested in your earthly power, neither is He interested in Caesar's kingdom. By placing Himself in another kingdom outside Roman jurisdiction, Jesus removes Himself from Roman authority. In this conversation, it is clear that Pilate did not go out seeking for Jesus. It was Jesus' own Jewish people and priests who delivered Him up. Pilate's next question betrays his feelings. "What have you done?" he asks. The question in the Greek is simple, but quite profound: *ti epoiesus*. The implication is, "What have you done that is so terrible? You must have done something terrible that no one is out there protesting this. Surely Pilate wondered, "How could Jesus' own people turn on Him with such finality?" The answer to that question cannot be a list of evil acts, because the only thing Jesus had done was to go about doing good.

The reason that there were no groups carrying signs to protest this religious lynching is also evident in Jesus' answer. Jesus says, "My kingdom is not of this world." By using the word "world," Jesus is deliberately telling Pilate that the worldly kingdom is fashioned and ordered by human intellect, and in contrast, Jesus' kingdom has heavenly principles and values—it is not of this world. Jesus found no reason to defend Himself. Since He was the Son of God, He already knew His fate. But He confirms that Pilate is correct in saying that He is King. This is why He came into the world, to testify of truth.

Pilate had asked, "What is truth?" After listening to Jesus and knowing deep in his heart there was no reason for this interrogation, Pilate declares that he finds no fault in Him. Jesus is truthful and just. Pilate finds no reason to persecute this man. There is no valid or concrete evidence on which to proceed.

3. Powerless Pilate (John 19:12-16)

The powerlessness of Pilate is revealed in a last desperate attempt to release Jesus, which is again stifled. The religious leaders tell Pilate that he is not a friend of Caesar if he releases Jesus. Truth was being put to the test. The possibility of destroying a relationship and position of power was at stake. Pilate was acting from his own selfish motives. "What if?" He asks himself. "Is this man worth my position? Is He worth me destroying a relationship with the powerful Caesar?" The question was posed in terms of friendship with Caesar.

Pilate chose friendship with Caesar over justice. He chose acceptance of the rich over defense of the poor. It is clear that Pilate had no power to release Jesus because of God's purpose and plan. However, Pilate could have saved himself by deciding in favor of justice. How often our friendship with the world keeps us from standing up for the truth. How often justice suffers in the face of cowardice. By wanting to maintain his hold on power, Pilate lost both friendship with Caesar and the allegiance of the ones he sought to please. Pilate is powerless both to save Jesus and to save himself. His salvation was right in front of him, but he lacked the courage to take it.

What a tragedy! To this day Pilate is known for giving the local leaders authority to execute Jesus He is not known for his allegiance to Caesar. In fact, he is only remembered for his cowardly failure to release Jesus, which led to His crucifixion. The other tragedy is that Pilate knew without question that Jesus was innocent.

SEARCH THE SCRIPTURES

1. What did Pilate tell the Jews to do? (John 18:31)
2. What did Pilate ask Jesus while in the judgment hall? (v. 33)
3. Who delivered Jesus to Pilate? (v. 35)
4. What did the Jewish leaders cry out to Pilate when he wanted to release Jesus? (19:12)
5. What did the Jews want to do with Jesus? (v. 15)

DISCUSS THE MEANING

1. Why didn't Pilate want to crucify Jesus?
2. Why do you think Pilate continued to ask Jesus if he was the King of the Jews?
3. Why did Pilate hand Jesus over to the Jewish leaders?

LESSON IN OUR SOCIETY

In today's society, many people have sacrificed innocent lives for a position or popularity. What about the police officer that knows his fellow officer shot someone in cold blood, but decides to keep silent? Or the nurse who knows that the wrong medication was issued to a patient who later died at the hands of a fellow nurse? Is this what Christ wants us to do?

MAKE IT HAPPEN

Oftentimes we have the power to change a situation, but we won't because it's an unpopular decision. Later we regret that we did not open our mouths. Be aware from this week forward of those opportunities that you have to make a major difference in someone's life—even if it's the most unpopular decision you have ever made. Do it!

FOLLOW THE SPIRIT

What God wants me to do:

_____

_____

REMEMBER YOUR THOUGHTS

Special insights you have learned:

_____

_____

MORE LIGHT ON THE TEXT
John 18:31-38; 19:12-16

Jesus has been transferred from Annas to Caiaphas (the chief priest). From there He is sent to Pilate to face judgment (John 18:24-28). It was during the feast of Passover. Jesus and His disciples have already eaten the Passover (Matthew 26:18-20; Mark 14:12-16; Luke 22:7-15), but the Jewish authorities could not enter the judgment hall lest they be defiled and unable to partake of the feast. Therefore, Pilate goes to meet them outside the judgment hall and questions them concerning their charge against the Lord (John 18:29).

18:31 Then said Pilate unto them, Take ye him, and judge him according to your law. The Jews therefore said unto him, It is not lawful for us to put any man to death: 32 That the saying of Jesus might be fulfilled, which he spake, signifying what death he should die.

Finding no reason for judgment, Pilate offers them the right to judge Jesus according to their law. Why would a Roman official condescend to offer the Jews the right to judge according to their law? Why would he not set Him free since he could not find any reason to condemn Him? Note that Pilate has authority to do whatever he wants without apologies to the Jewish authorities. Indeed, he informs Jesus of his authority to condemn Him or to release Him (19:10). Yet he offers the Jewish leaders the right to judge Jesus according to their law. The word "judge" is the Greek word *krino* (pronounced **KRIH-no**), which means to try, condemn, or punish, with the implication of passing judgment on or condemning someone for committing a crime.

The Jewish officials decline Pilate's offer with the excuse, "It is not lawful for us to put any man to death." Jews had the authority, according to Jewish law, to stone anyone who broke the law (cf. 8:1-11, 59; 10:31; Acts 7:59). Why then would they reject the offer to put Jesus to death? The answer is threefold. The first is that they are lying. By saying to Pilate, "We have a law, and by our law he ought to die, because he made himself the Son of God" (19:7), they are contradicting themselves. The second reason is probably because they are afraid of the people. Therefore, they throw the responsibility of the Lord's death upon Pilate. However, the third and most important reason is so Jesus would die as prophesied—by crucifixion (v. 32; Matthew 20:19; 26:2; John 3:14; 8:28; 12:32-33). Death by crucifixion was not a Jewish method of capital punishment; it was solely the Romans' prerogative. Hence, the Jews reject the offer and intimidate Pilate with the accusation that he is not being Caesar's friend if he sets Christ free (19:12).

33 Then Pilate entered into the judgment hall again, and called Jesus, and said unto him, Art thou the King of the Jews? 34 Jesus answered him, Sayest thou this thing of thyself, or did others tell it thee of me?

After talking with the Jews, Pilate returns to the "judgment hall," or the Greek *praetorion* (pronounced **pry-tow-ree-ahn**), which is also known as the governor's courtroom or a common hall in the governor's palace. Pilate then asks Christ, "Art thou the King of the Jews?" This question suggests that the Jews had accused Him of claiming to be king, which means that He would be guilty of treason against the Roman authority by challenging Caesar's kingship. Rather than giving a straightforward answer, Jesus turns the tables and engages Pilate in dialog. Christ asks him, "Are you saying this on your own initiative, or did others tell you about Me?" (NASB). Here, Jesus seems to put Pilate on trial. Jesus wants to know from him whether His enemies (the religious leaders) have said that of Him or whether this is Pilate's own suspicion.

35 Pilate answered, Am I a Jew? Thine own nation and the chief priests have delivered thee unto me: what hast thou done?

Pilate follows with a rhetorical question ("Am I Jew?"), which of course has a negative answer. In a bid to exonerate himself before Christ and to free himself of any accusation of injustice, Pilate hints to Jesus that he has nothing to do with His being judged. He lays the blame on the Jewish authorities by saying, "Thine own nation and the chief priests have delivered thee unto me," signifying a unanimous participation. With the next question ("What hast thou done?"), Pilate implies, "If you don't claim to be the King of the Jews, what wrong have you done that would cause them to want to kill you?"

36 Jesus answered, My kingdom is not of this

world: if my kingdom were of this world, then would my servants fight, that I should not be delivered to the Jews: but now is my kingdom not from hence.

In His answer, Jesus informs Pilate about His kind of kingdom; His kingdom "is not of this world" i.e., it does not belong to this world. In other words, Christ's kingdom is not an earthly kingdom. It is not of human origin or of a secular nature; therefore, it must be divine or spiritual. Jesus then points out that if His kingdom were of this world, then His servants would have fought for Him and would have prevented Him from being handed over to the religious authorities. Earlier in John, Jesus says to His enemies, "You are from below, I am from above; you are of this world, I am not of this world" (8:23). The word translated "servants" here is the Greek word *huperetes* (pronounced **hoo-peh-REH-tace**) rather than the usual *douloi* (pronounced **DO-lay**), which generally means servants or slaves. *Huperetes* has the idea of assistant, minister, or subordinates. Therefore, the word "servants" refers to His disciples or followers. The word "fight" is the Greek word *agonizomai* (pronounced **ah-go-NIHD'-zo-my**), which means to struggle. Literally it means to compete for a prize; but figuratively it means to contend with an adversary. It has the idea of striving fervently or fighting for something. Here Jesus says that if His kingdom were of this world, His servants would fight for Him like other earthly servants would do for their king.

It is customary for kings to stay home while their subjects fight in wars or guards fight in order to protect their king. "But now," Jesus says, "is my kingdom not from hence." The use of both prepositions "but now" (Greek *nun de,* pronounced **noon-deh**) signifies emphasis, which can be interpreted as "but as it is" or "but, as a matter of fact, my kingdom is not from here." Christ's kingdom does not belong to this world. He does not deny His kingship but affirms it.

37 Pilate therefore said unto him, Art thou a king then? Jesus answered, Thou sayest that I am a king. To this end was I born, and for this cause came I into the world, that I should bear witness unto the truth. Every one that is of the truth heareth my voice.

Of course, Pilate understands Christ's statement. He follows it with a direct question: "Are you then a king?" Jesus answers using a common expression: "Thou sayest that I am a king" (or: "It is you who say that I am a king"), meaning, "Yes, it is so." He then explains that it was for that purpose that He was born and came into the world: so that He might bear witness to the truth. Furthermore, Jesus tells Pilate that everyone who is of the truth listens to and obeys Him. The word "truth" is used over 27 times in John's Gospel (52 times in the NIV), and Jesus repeatedly says that He is the "truth" personified (14:6). According to the New International Version, He uses the phrase "I tell you truth" over 27 times. Therefore, Jesus' testimony is not about truth abstractly, but about the Truth (i.e., Himself). Anyone who finds Jesus and obeys Him belongs to Him (8:32-36; 14:6). Jesus says that He knows His own, His own hear His voice, and He gives them eternal life (8:47; 10:3-4, 16, 27).

38 Pilate saith unto him, What is truth? And when he had said this, he went out again unto the Jews, and saith unto them, I find in him no fault at all.

Continuing the dialogue, Pilate asks Jesus, "What is the truth?" Perhaps confused and unable to comprehend all the religious and philosophical jargon, Pilate could not wait for an answer to the question. He goes out again to his audience and confesses to them, "I find in Him no fault at all," thereby declaring Christ innocent of any treason or criminal act.

John 19:12 And from thenceforth Pilate sought to release him: but the Jews cried out, saying, If thou let this man go, thou art not Caesar's friend: whosoever maketh himself a king speaketh against Caesar.

Finding no reason to condemn Jesus, Pilate seeks ways of releasing Him. Between John 18:39 and 19:11, there are a number of dialogues between Pilate and the Jews and Jesus in which Pilate attempts to set Christ free. Verse 19:12a shows that there are several more attempts to release Christ, but the religious leaders insist that He be put to death. They intimidate Pilate with a threat of reporting Him to Caesar. The phrase, "and from thenceforth" refers particularly to the events of 19:7-11, where the Jews accuse Christ of claiming to be "the Son of God."

We are told in verse 8 that "when Pilate heard

this, he was more afraid." Pilate questions Jesus about His origin. Receiving no answer from Christ, and being driven by fear of this strange person before him and the conviction that Jesus has done nothing worthy of death, Pilate tries all the more to release Him. Probably sensing Pilate's resolve to release Jesus, "the Jews cried [shouted in unison] out" against Pilate's plan and accused him of "high treason" against Caesar. To them, releasing Jesus, who claims to be "king of the Jews" (18:33, 37), is tantamount to challenging the authority and leadership of the ruling emperor. It will mean that Pilate prefers another king to the reigning emperor. They know that if such an accusation came to the emperor (the reigning emperor at this time was Tiberius)—also referred as Caesar—to whom Pilate was responsible, it would be viewed as high treason. Such treason carried a very severe consequence—probably the death penalty.

13 When Pilate therefore heard that saying, he brought Jesus forth, and sat down in the judgment seat in a place that is called the Pavement, but in the Hebrew, Gabbatha.

Pilate knows the magnitude of such an accusation and its consequence, so he is gripped with fear, not only for his political position as governor, but also for his very life. Pilate brings Jesus out to the outer court and sits at the "judgment seat." We learned earlier that Jesus is brought to the judgment hall or Praetorium (where the Jews would not enter lest they be defiled because of the Passover). There, Pilate interrogates Jesus and investigates the people's accusation against Him. The "judgment seat" (Greek *bema*, pronounced **BAY-muh**) or tribunal, also known as the "Pavement" (Greek *lithostrotos*, pronounced **lith-AW-strow-tahss**)—or in the Hebrew "Gabbatha"—was a stone-paved platform in front of the Praetorium, a place for final sentencing, probably where people were declared guilty and condemned to death (Matthew 27:19; Acts 12:21).

14 And it was the preparation of the passover, and about the sixth hour: and he saith unto the Jews, Behold your King!

John gives us the period and precise time of

day when Pilate succumbed to the pressure and intimidation that the Jewish leaders brought and handed Jesus over to them. The day of preparation is the day before the Sabbath, probably equivalent to our own Friday, when the Lamb for sacrifice for the Passover is being prepared. The time is around "the sixth hour" (possibly 12:00 noon). It is not coincidental that at the very time the lamb for the Passover is being prepared for sacrifice, the ultimate and eternal Lamb of God is condemned to death as the ultimate "Sacrifice" for mankind. Pilate, handing Jesus over for crucifixion, says to the Jews, "Behold your King!" Earlier (v. 5) Jesus was robed in purple and crowned with thorns, and here Pilate presents Him to the Jews as their "king." This is probably in mockery, but providentially it is used here to draw from His accusers' lips a complete rejection of God's sovereignty over them and a renunciation of their Messianic promise.

15 But they cried out, Away with him, away with him, crucify him. Pilate saith unto them, Shall I crucify your King? The chief priests answered, We have no king but Caesar.

Pilate's pronouncement ("Behold your King!") aggravates the people all the more into a vehement outburst: "Away with him, away with him, crucify him," signifying a total rejection of the Messiah. The word "away" used here is from the Greek verb *airo* (pronounced **I-row**), which means to lift up, or to take up or away. It is the same word translated "take up" (of serpents) in Mark 16:17-18. Here (v. 15), *airo* is used to express "kill Him" (see also Acts 21:36; 22:22). To them, Jesus was leading people to worship a "strange god," and He needed to be killed according to the law of the land (Deuteronomy 13:12-18). Hence, they burst into outcry: "take Him away, take Him away, crucify Him." Pilate probably mockingly asks them, "Shall I crucify your King?" Degenerating deeper into sin and rejection of God and preferring an enemy over an everlasting Friend, the chief priests (probably including Caiaphas on behalf of the people) shout out, "We have no king but Caesar."

16 Then delivered he him therefore unto them to be crucified.

Finally, Pilate surrenders to the pressure and the threat of facing Tiberius for failure to yield to the Jews' demand to crucify their king. He delivers Jesus to their will to be crucified (Luke 23:25). Speaking later on the day of Pentecost, Peter accuses his audience of crucifying the Messiah. The Romans merely carried out the wish of the people. Pilate did not pronounce sentence but washed His hands of the whole affair (Matthew 27:24). Does that free Pilate from being responsible for Jesus' death? Or does it put Him on trial? Did he not have the authority to condemn or release Christ? (John 19:10). Indeed, Jesus' statement to Pilate—"he that delivered me unto thee hath the greater sin" (v.11)—does not exonerate him in any way. He is therefore also tried and found guilty, just as are those who crucified Christ.

DAILY BIBLE READINGS

M: Jesus Brought before Pilate
John 18:28-32
T: Pilate Questions Jesus
John 18:33-37
W: Pilate's Wife Dreams
Matthew 27:15-19
T: Here Is the Man
John 18:38 19:5
F: Pilate Tries to Release Jesus
John 19:6-12
S: Pilate Washes His Hands
Matthew 27:21-26
S: Jesus Handed Over to Be Crucified
John 19:13-22

TEACHING TIPS

January 26
Bible Study Guide 9

1. Words You Should Know

A. Deny—To refuse to recognize; disown; repudiate.

B. Bitterly—Causing or showing sorrow, discomfort, or pain; acidly; sourly.

2. Teacher Preparation

A. Study the FOCAL VERSES during your quiet time. Reread them throughout the week before class.

B. Read and study the IN DEPTH material and prepare to present it to the class.

B. Write down the answers to the SEARCH THE SCRIPTURES and DISCUSS THE MEANING questions.

C. Pray for your students during your prayer time and ask for God's blessings.

3. Starting the Lesson

A. Write the LESSON AIM on the board and emphasize how studying God's Word helps us to understand how to live according to His Word.

B. Go over the AT-A-GLANCE outline and give a brief overview of each topic.

C. Have students read IN FOCUS quietly together. Begin a brief discussion.

4. Getting into the Lesson

A. Break the class into groups to answer the DISCUSS THE MEANING and SEARCH THE SCRIPTURES questions.

B. Reconvene and discuss the answers together.

C. Share the definitions from WORDS YOU SHOULD KNOW.

5. Relating the Lesson to Life

A. Ask a student to read THE PEOPLE, PLACES, AND TIMES aloud. Have a brief discussion.

B. Ask students to silently read and meditate on the LESSON IN OUR SOCIETY article.

C. Challenge the class to give serious thought and examine themselves in regard to this truth.

6. Arousing Action

A. Have two students share what they learned from today's lesson and tell how they think it's going to make them better Christians.

B. Have the students pair off so that they can pray for each other before the class ends.

C. Challenge the students to read the DAILY BIBLE READINGS throughout the week.

WORSHIP GUIDE

For the Superintendent or Teacher
Theme: Peter: Restored Leader
Theme Song: "Go Tell the Untold Millions"
Scripture: Matthew 28:18-20
Song: "We've a Story to Tell"
Devotional Thought: Dear Lord, as believers we are under the authority of Christ. He has promised to be with us wherever we go as we spread the word of salvation, and for that we thank You. Amen.

208

PETER: RESTORED LEADER

Bible Background • LUKE 22:31-34, 54-62; JOHN 21:1-22
Printed Text • LUKE 22:31-34, 54-62; JOHN 21:17
Devotional Reading • ACTS 4:1-13

LESSON AIM

By the conclusion of the lesson, the students will know that despite Peter's mistakes, he became a great apostle of Jesus Christ. The students will also know that mistakes are not fatal, but a way to draw us closer to our Saviour, who already knows everything there is to know about us.

KEEP IN MIND

"Jesus saith to Simon Peter, Simon, son of Jonas, lovest thou me more than these? He saith unto him, Yea, Lord; thou knowest that I love thee. He saith unto him, Feed my lambs" (John 21:15).

FOCAL VERSES

Luke 22:31 And the Lord said, Simon, Simon, behold, Satan hath desired to have you, that he may sift you as wheat:

32 But I have prayed for thee, that thy faith fail not: and when thou art converted, strengthen thy brethren.

33 And he said unto him, Lord, I am ready to go with thee, both into prison, and to death.

34 And he said, I tell thee, Peter, the cock shall not crow this day, before that thou shalt thrice deny that thou knowest me.

22:54 Then took they him, and led him, and brought him into the high priest's house. And Peter followed afar off.

55 And when they had kindled a fire in the midst of the hall, and were set down together, Peter sat down among them.

56 But a certain maid beheld him as he sat by the fire, and earnestly looked upon him, and said, This

LESSON OVERVIEW

LESSON AIM
KEEP IN MIND
FOCAL VERSES
IN FOCUS
THE PEOPLE, PLACES,
AND TIMES
BACKGROUND
AT-A-GLANCE
IN DEPTH
SEARCH THE SCRIPTURES
DISCUSS THE MEANING
LESSON IN OUR SOCIETY
MAKE IT HAPPEN
FOLLOW THE SPIRIT
REMEMBER YOUR THOUGHTS
MORE LIGHT ON THE TEXT
DAILY BIBLE READINGS

man was also with him.

57 And he denied him, saying Woman, I know him not.

58 And after a little while another saw him, and said, Thou art also of them. And Peter said, Man, I am not.

59 And about the space of one hour after another confidently affirmed, saying, Of a truth this fellow also was with him: for he is a Galilaean.

60 And Peter said, Man, I know not what thou sayest. And immediately, while he yet spake, the cock crew.

61 And the Lord turned, and looked upon Peter. And Peter remembered the word of the Lord, how he had said unto him, Before the cock crow, thou shalt deny me thrice.

62 And Peter went out, and wept bitterly.

John 21:17 He saith unto him the third time, Simon, son of Jonas, lovest thou me? Peter was grieved because he said unto him the third time, Lovest thou me? And he said unto him, Lord, thou knowest all things; thou knowest that I love thee. Jesus saith unto him, Feed my sheep.

JAN 26TH

IN FOCUS

Let's learn from our mistakes and not continue to make the same ones. Instead, repent and start again. Today we will see how Peter was restored as a leader, despite his shortcomings.

THE PEOPLE, PLACES, AND TIMES

Peter (also called Simon). One of the original twelve apostles and their leader following Jesus' ascension. He was originally from the village of

Bethsaida on the northern shore of the Sea of Galilee (John 1:44). Peter was married (Mark 1:30; 1 Corinthians 9:5) and a fisherman by trade together with his brother Andrew. When Jesus called him, he was given the added name Cephas meaning "stone" (Greek: *Petros,* pronounced **PET-trahss,** hence Peter). From the beginning, Peter was a dominant personality among Jesus' disciples who developed a close relationship with his Master. When Jesus chose twelve to form an inner circle, Peter was first among them. Peter regularly acted as their spokesman but often spoke impetuously, not fully understanding what he was saying.

The Gospel of John reports that Andrew and Peter were disciples of John the Baptist before they joined Jesus. Peter is always the first to be named when the apostles are listed (Mark 3:14-16).

Apostle. Means "one who is sent." Conventional Christian language tends to identify the term "apostle" with the twelve closest companions of Jesus during His public ministry. They were chosen by Jesus to preach the Gospel of the kingdom and demonstrate its presence by performing signs and wonders.

Intercession. The act of petitioning God or praying on behalf of another person or group. The sinful nature of this world separates human beings from God. It has always been necessary, therefore, for righteous individuals to go before God to seek reconciliation between Him and His fallen creation. Christ is, of course, the greatest intercessor. He prayed on behalf of Peter and His disciples. Then, in the most selfless intercession of all, He petitioned God on behalf of those who crucified Him. But Christ's intercessory work did not cease when He returned to heaven. In heaven He intercedes for His church.

BACKGROUND

In today's lesson, we see how carefully Jesus chose His disciples. He knew their backgrounds and their characters. He even knew them better than they knew themselves. In this lesson, Jesus tells Peter things that Peter would never have thought about himself, even in his wildest dreams. Jesus also tells Peter that He has prayed for him. This is an example of how Jesus cared for them.

Jesus had performed innumerable miracles. Jesus had walked on the water. Peter had seen the transfiguration. The disciples had seen many people healed, delivered, and set free. The disciples had also seen many who did not receive Jesus and His ministry. After the multitude dispersed, Jesus often gathered His twelve disciples to teach them in a small group. The inner circle received intimate teachings and revelations. In this lesson, Jesus had entered the final phase of His ministry. He was nearing the hour of crucifixion. He wanted to share with the ones closest to Him the things He thought were important—things about themselves that would help them to carry on His ministry. They were the ones who would turn the world upside down forever.

AT-A-GLANCE

1. Peter's Problem (Luke 22:31-34)
2. Peter's Denial of Jesus (vv. 54-60)
3. Jesus' Restoration of Peter (Luke 22:61-62; John 21:17)

IN DEPTH

1. Peter's Problem (Luke 22:31-32)

Jesus ministered to the multitude as well as to His twelve disciples. He knew what they were and were not capable of doing. He was not so preoccupied with the crowd that He lost focus on the intimate group that walked closely with Him. As you see in this verse, Jesus prayed for Simon Peter because He knew the plans that the enemy had for Him.

Peter had vehemently insisted that he would never deny Jesus, but Jesus knew better. Could it be that Peter's arrogant boasting is what made the devil desire to go at him? Jesus says, "Simon, behold, Satan hath desired to have you, that he may sift you as wheat." One can almost see the Master as he shakes his head at the hardheaded disciple who thinks that he can take on the world by himself. Peter could not see that he had, by his presumptuous speech, set himself up for an encounter with the devil.

Jesus reveals a secret here: note that the devil is asking God for permission to go after Peter. The idea here is that Satan needs the permission of God to engage a disciple of Christ in battle. Satan is still under subjection to God even when we deserve a lesson. Why would the devil request to have him? Maybe to show Peter that in his own strength he is no match for the one who holds the mystery of iniquity. There was chaff within Peter that needed blowing away so that the valuable seeds might be revealed. Could it be that Peter still had something in his life that belonged to the devil? How does wheat get sifted from chaff? Is it done by "thrashing," which in life means difficulty or trial?

Peter's weakness was going to be exposed by trial. It is a powerful thing to know that although the Lord knows that Peter will go through this intense trial, He has also made provision for Peter's victory. Jesus said, "I have prayed for thee." This is one of those places where Jesus directly intercedes for one of His disciples.

Our great intercessor, Jesus, is praying for us right now. He told Peter that He prayed that he would have faith and that he would be a source of strength for his brethren. The idea here is not that Peter will not fail, but that even though he fails, his faith will not fail. He would not give up on what he believed. This is true today; Peter is a source of inspiration for us in the 21st century. It is good to know that God knows us and we don't have to pretend with Him. Jesus knew Peter's ways.

In verse 33, Peter wants to assure Jesus that he will follow Him wherever He goes. Peter boldly proclaims he will follow Jesus even to prison and death. It sounds as if Peter was being a bit cocky, because Jesus had revealed some things about him that were not so positive. But God knows us. In verse 34, Jesus knew that it was not going to be very long before Peter would deny Him. As a matter of fact, it was only hours later that Peter denied Him—not once, not twice, but three times!

2. Peter's Denial of Jesus (vv. 54-60)

Jesus' enemies had come and captured Him and taken Him into the high priest's house. Peter said he would go with Jesus wherever he went, but notice that he followed from a distance (v. 54). Peter was lingering behind everyone. If you want be a part of something, you will keep up with the crowd. When you distance yourself, you are trying to disassociate yourself from the subject. Peter did not realize that

this was actually the beginning of the denial process. He distanced himself from Jesus without opening his mouth. When they kindled a fire (v. 55), Peter joined them. The Scripture says he sat down "among" them. It was not long before somebody recognized him. Always beware: someone is always watching you, whether you realize it or not. Peter probably had never noticed the maid who recognized him; otherwise he would not have sat among them. Peter quickly said, "Woman, I know him not." This was the first denial.

It was a little while later when someone recognized him again. Peter was probably saying within himself, "I had no idea this many people knew me." And once again Peter denied knowing Jesus. Peter had forgotten that multitudes followed Jesus, and Peter's face had been seen by many. Jesus was a famous man—the Scripture says His fame went out across the country.

In the next hour, another person "confidently affirmed" that Peter was a follower of Jesus (v. 59). Immediately after Peter denied Jesus for the third time, just as Jesus said, the "cock crew" (v. 60).

3. Jesus' Restoration of Peter (Luke 22:61-62; John 21:17)

Jesus did not give up on Peter even though Peter denied Him. In fact, Jesus did not have to say a word; Peter convicted himself. All Jesus did was look at Peter, and Peter remembered what He had said. But Jesus knew that Peter loved Him, and He knew that Peter would feed His "sheep."

SEARCH THE SCRIPTURES

1. What did Jesus say that Satan wanted to do to Peter? (Luke 22:31)
2. What did Jesus pray? (v. 32)
3. Where did they lead Jesus? (v. 54)
4. What did Jesus say Peter would do? (v. 61)

DISCUSS THE MEANING

1. Why do you think Peter denied Jesus?
2. Why did Peter follow the band of men that took Jesus?
3. Why do you think Jesus asked Peter three times if he loved Him?
4. What does Jesus mean when He says, "Feed my sheep"?

LESSON IN OUR SOCIETY

Many of us are no different than Peter. We might say, "How could Peter deny Jesus after walking so closely with Him and seeing all of the miracles?" But the truth of the matter is this: we deny Jesus every time we don't stand up for righteousness. Do you think Jesus is pleased? He says, "If you love me, feed my sheep."

MAKE IT HAPPEN

Every single day there is an opportunity to witness to someone about Jesus. Every single day there is an opportunity to declare our allegiance to holiness and righteousness. This week, make an extra effort to let someone know that you love Jesus and that you are one of His faithful followers.

FOLLOW THE SPIRIT

What God wants me to do:

_____

_____

REMEMBER YOUR THOUGHTS

Special insights you have learned:

_____

_____

MORE LIGHT ON THE TEXT
Luke 22:31-34, 54-62; John 21:17

Luke 22 contains the events leading to the final stage of Christ's life here on earth. These events include the Last Supper (vv. 7-38), during which Jesus predicts His betrayal and death (vv. 21-23) and teaches His disciples about serving and their future place in His kingdom (vv. 24-30). The next segment deals with Christ's prediction of Peter's denial and restoration (vv. 31-34).

31 And the Lord said, Simon, Simon, behold, Satan hath desired to have you, that he may sift you as wheat: 32 But I have prayed for thee, that thy faith fail not: and when thou art converted, strengthen thy brethren.

The background to Christ's statement to Simon (Peter)—omitted here by Luke—is based on Jesus' prediction of His disciples' failing Him in time of need and their being scattered (see Matthew 26:30-32; Mark 14:26-28). Peter's answer, "Though all men

shall be offended because of thee, yet will I never be offended" (Matthew 26:33) prompts Christ's address to Peter here. The Lord's reaction to Peter's claim of remaining faithful during Christ's trial comes with a strong warning as well as a radiant hope that the Lord Himself is in control. He will uphold Peter so that he will not totally fall away. Note how He addresses Peter by using his Hebrew name, Simon (rather than his Greek name, Peter or *Petros*, pronounced **PET-trahss**; see John 1:42; cp. Matthew 16:18).

Notice the double repetition of the name "Simon," which adds weight and seriousness to the warning. As we learned in our previous study (Luke 10:41), Jesus repeats a name when He wants to make some important and unusually impressive statement or when He wants to press home an important point (Luke 6:46; 8:24; 13:34; 22:31; cf. Acts 9:4). Here Jesus uses Peter's cultural name, probably only used by his family or close friends, to call his attention to the importance of His statement and to the certainty of the event that is about to unfold. Christ uses an agronomic metaphor—"Satan hath desired to have you, that he may sift you as wheat"—to bring the warning. What does Christ mean by this statement?

To understand the statement, we should note that it is not addressed to Peter alone, even though his name is mentioned, but to all the disciples. The pronoun "you," or the Greek *humas* (pronounced **hoo-MAHSS**) of verse 31, is in the plural. It contrasts with the singular pronoun "you," or *sou* (v. 32), where Peter is addressed. The word "desired" is translated from the Greek verb *exaiteomai* (pronounced **ex-i-TEH'-o-my**), which also means to request or demand (for trial). Here we can only speculate that perhaps Satan, as in the case of Job in the Old Testament (Job 1:6; 2:1), has accused the disciples to God of faithlessness and falling away in time of temptation. God probably confirms their steadfastness, and Satan asks for permission to try them by sifting them like a farmer sifts his wheat in order to separate the wheat from the chaff.

As we have already noted in verse 32, "But I have prayed for thee" is addressed to Peter. Knowing the severity of the testing that is coming, Jesus assures Peter of His prayer for him and His confidence that he will overcome the testing. From other passages in the Gospels, it is obvious that Peter is always the spokesman and indeed the leader of the disciples, and Christ is aware that Peter will face Satan's strongest onslaught. Therefore, Christ encourages him and assures him of His prayer so that his "faith may not fail" (NIV). The phrase "may not fail," or *me ekleipe* (pronounced **eh-KLAY-p**), means that his faith will not give way or disappear as the sun disappears during a total eclipse. To assure Peter of the certainty of His prayer and presence with him, Christ gives him the responsibility of strengthening "thy brethren" when he is "converted." This means that when he is restored after Satan's sifting, he should encourage and strengthen his colleagues.

33 And he said unto him, Lord, I am ready to go with thee, both into prison, and to death. 34 And he said, I tell thee, Peter, the cock shall not crow this day, before that thou shalt thrice deny that thou knowest me.

Peter's answer is rash, boastful, and overconfident. He seems to rely on himself instead of trusting in the Lord. This kind of pride usually leads to failure and downfall as Proverbs 16:18 asserts. Paul warns that if you think you are standing firm, be careful you don't fall (1 Corinthians 10:12). Peter boastfully says to Jesus that he is ready to go to prison with Him and even to death, not realizing the magnitude of his utterance and the smallness of his faith in the face of temptation. Peter at this point does not have in mind to deny Jesus, but is ready to make good his promise.

However, Jesus knows how weak Peter's faith is. Then he warns him that the cock shall not crow before Peter denies that he ever knew Him. Jesus knows the future and our hearts and is able to look beyond the physical into the spiritual being of man. Thus, He is able to predict the future and discern what we are able and unable to do. Without Him we can do nothing. As humanistic philosophy teaches, Peter relies on his ego, thinking that he will be able to withstand the impending persecution Jesus is about to face.

What is the significance of the phrase, "the cock shall not crow this day"? One can argue that the crow of the cock is meant to remind Peter of Christ's saying. However, beyond that, the crowing of the cock signifies how soon this denial will take place—that very night, before the cock crows. In ancient times,

before the invention of clocks or watches, people used the crowing of the rooster to tell time. In some parts of the world, especially Africa (particularly some remote villages in Nigeria), people still rely on the rooster as a means of telling time. The cock crows a number of times at early hours of the morning. For example, the first cockcrow is usually 4:00 or 5:00 a.m., when people who plan to rise early get up for their day's work. With this in mind, it is obvious that Jesus' use of the cock's crowing means that before daybreak, in the early hours of the morning (John 18:28), Peter would deny Jesus three times. The prediction is of course fulfilled in the following section (v. 54ff).

54 Then took they him, and led him, and brought him into the high priest's house. And Peter followed afar off.

Jesus is arrested as He comes out with His disciples from the Mount of Olives following His prayers there. He is led to the house of the high priest, but Peter follows afar off. The words "afar off" are translated from the Greek word *makrothen* (pronounced **mah-KRAH'-thin**), which means from a distance. This shows that Peter sneaked along behind out of fear and probably so that he wouldn't be identified as part of the group. Luke does not mention who the high priest is, but from other Gospel accounts, it is probably Annas, the father-in-law of Caiaphas (John 18:13) and the current high priest. This trial is probably before the Sanhedrin (see Matthew 26:59; Mark 14:55). Although Peter follows from a distance, he is the only follower of Christ we know of (according to Luke's account) who follows Christ at all.

55 And when they had kindled a fire in the midst of the hall, and were set down together, Peter sat down among them.

The kindling of fire in the midst of the altar's courtyard signifies the season and time of day that Christ's trial takes place at the house of the high priest. It is most probably at night in the springtime, when it is usually cool in Jerusalem. It is commonplace at such times for people to start fires outside to warm themselves, especially during family gatherings for storytelling in Africa. As the people gather to warm themselves, Peter sits among them to warm himself, probably unnoticed until three people identify and confront him.

56 But a certain maid beheld him as he sat by the fire, and earnestly looked upon him, and said, This man was also with him. 57 And he denied him, saying, Woman, I know him not.

The first to identify Peter is a servant girl— a "certain maid"—who looks earnestly at him and says, "This man was also with him." The phrase "earnestly looked" is the Greek word *atenizo* (pronounced **ah-ten-IHD-zoh**), which means to gaze or look steadfastly, to set one's eyes on something or someone. She is quite certain, but she wants to make sure. Peter is probably trying to hide his face, so she looks at him steadfastly.

The Gospels identify the first speaker as a maid or servant girl of the high priest (Matthew 26:69; Mark 14:66; John 18:25). As she confronts Peter and announces his identity, Peter denies it. The word "denied" is the Greek verb *arneomai* (pronounced **ar-NEH'-oh-my**), which means to disavow, reject, or refuse. It is the opposite of "confess" (Greek *homologeo*, pronounced **hah-mah-lah'-GEH-o**), which means to acknowledge. Both words appear in Matthew 10:32-33, where Jesus cautions His disciples, "Whoever confesses Me before men, him I will also confess before My Father who is in heaven. But whoever denies Me before men, him I will also deny before My Father who is in heaven" (cf. Luke 12:8-9 NKJV). Here Peter denies the Lord, and he says to the girl, "Woman, I know him not."

58 And after a little while another saw him, and said, Thou art also of them. And Peter said, Man, I am not.

After a short time, another person, unidentified by Luke, accuses Peter, "Thou art also of them." Again, Peter denies having any association with Jesus. Although throughout the three denials Jesus' name is never mentioned because the events surrounding Him are well known in the courtyard. Luke also does not reveal the full identity of the second and third speakers. However, Peter's response to one is, "Man, I am not," which sounds emphatic and decisive.

59 And about the space of one hour after another confidently affirmed, saying, Of a truth this fellow also was with him: for he is a Galilaean. 60 And Peter said, Man, I know not what thou sayest. And immediately, while he yet spake, the cock crew.

While Luke does not specify how much time elapsed between the first and second accusations, in verse 59 he specifies the time as "about the space of one hour." We can assume that the time between the second and third accusations is longer than the time between the first and second. This probably would give Peter enough time to consider his answers and remember Christ's prediction regarding his denials.

The third person speaks with confidence and affirms Peter's identity saying, "Of a truth this fellow also was with him: for he is a Galilaean," or "Certainly this fellow was with him, for he is a Galilean" (v. 59, NIV). The words "confidently affirmed" are from the Greek word *diischurizomai* (pronounced **dee-iss-khoo-RID'-zo-my**), which can also be translated as to insist or maintain firmly. There is no doubt at all in his mind that Peter is one of them. The accuser supports his affirmation by identifying his home territory: "for he is a Galilean (too)."

Notice Peter's response: "Man, I know not what thou sayest." He seems so desperate that he pleads ignorance of what the man is saying, which amounts to outright denial of knowing Christ or of having been associated with Him. Peter's desperation is made more evident in Matthew and Mark's accounts, where he accompanies his denials with oaths, cursing, and swearing (Matthew 26:72,74; Mark 14:71). While he is still speaking (i.e., he has not even finished speaking), the cock crows as a fulfillment of Christ's words (v. 34).

61 And the Lord turned, and looked upon Peter. And Peter remembered the word of the Lord, how he had said unto him, Before the cock crow, thou shalt deny me thrice. 62 And Peter went out, and wept bitterly.

As the cock crows, the Lord turns and looks at Peter. The word "looked" is the Greek word *emblepo* (pronounced **em-BLEP'-o**), which means to gaze, look hard, or look straight at someone. It is a type of look that can be either of concern, rebuke, or love. It is probably a look of "I told you, didn't I?" At that moment, the words of the Lord to him ("Before the cock crow, thou shalt deny me thrice") re-echo in Peter's mind. He leaves the fireside, goes out, and weeps bitterly. The events of verses 60-62 seem to happen simultaneously. Verse 62 indicates that Peter's repentance was genuine. Therefore, he is restored (as we shall discover in the following section).

John 21:17 He saith unto him the third time, Simon, son of Jonas, lovest thou me? Peter was grieved because he said unto him the third time, Lovest thou me? And he said unto him, Lord, thou knowest all things; thou knowest that I love thee. Jesus saith unto him, Feed my sheep.

After His resurrection, Jesus catches up with His disciples on a fishing trip and dines with them on the seashore. After breakfast, Jesus questions Peter three times concerning his commitment to Him (John 21:15-17). It is generally assumed by commentators that Christ's threefold interrogation of Peter's commitment corresponds to the threefold interrogation of Peter and his denial in the courtyard. Peter had denied Christ three times before the cock crew, so now the Lord has him make a triple confession and commitment. This triple confession symbolizes not only a commitment, but also a total restoration of Peter to his role as leader. Verse 17 records the third time Jesus questions Peter, using the same formula and his Hebrew name, "Simon, son of Jonas, lovest thou me?"

After being asked the same question three times, Peter is grieved. The word "grieved" is the Greek verb *lupeo* (pronounced **loo-PEH'-o**), which means to make sorrowful, cause grief, or to make uneasy and to sadden. Why is Peter saddened? It is because the Lord asks him the question three times, "Do you love Me?" What is going through Peter's mind at this time? Someone has suggested that Peter probably becomes uneasy and irritated because he is unsure why Christ has to repeat the question three times. Does Jesus know something about Peter that he himself is not aware of and that might lead to another fall? Is Jesus about to tell him of it? Peter's response,

"Lord, thou knowest all things; thou knowest that I love thee," demonstrates his sense of humility. In Luke, Peter thinks that he knows more about himself than Jesus does, but now he humbles himself and confesses his limitations and Christ's omniscient ability (to know all things).

This is also the type of confession Christ expects from him, and indeed from all who will confess Him as Lord. After Peter's confession, Jesus gives him the final charge to "feed my sheep." The word "feed" is the Greek verb *bosko* (pronounced **BAHSS-ko**), which may be interpreted in a number of ways, including to tend to a flock, provide pasture for, take care of, guide, lead, defend or govern, and shepherd. "Sheep," or the Greek equivalent *probaton* (pronounced **PRAH'-bah-ton**), is a figurative term that Jesus uses often to refer to His followers or believers (cf. 10:11ff). Jesus says that He is the Shepherd, and now He hands over that responsibility to Peter the restored leader.

DAILY BIBLE READINGS

M: When You Have Turned Back
Luke 22:24-34

T: Peter Denies Jesus
Luke 22:54-62

W: Peter Goes Fishing
John 21:1-6

T: It Is the Lord
John 21:7-14

F: Simon, Do You Love Me?
John 21:15-19

S: Repent and Be Baptized
Acts 2:37-42

S: In Jesus' Name, Walk
Acts 3:1-7

TEACHING TIPS

February 2
Bible Study Guide 10

1. Words You Should Know

A. Encouragement (Acts 36)—The act of exhortation, encouragement, and comfort. Barnabas is called the "son of encouragement," referring to his gift of helping and motivating others.

B. Grace (Acts 11:23)—In regard to salvation, grace is a state of affairs in which the favor of God is bestowed on people based solely on the work of Christ.

2. Teacher Preparation

A. Read through all four lessons of this last unit and be prepared to introduce the unit and the last four lessons to the class.

B. Try to recall a time when you needed and received encouragement or comfort from someone. Be prepared to share your testimony with the class.

3. Starting the Lesson

A. Have students silently read the FOCAL VERSES. Then ask: "What are some of the key points in the verses? How can we relate those points to where we are today? Is there anything we can see in Barnabas's character that can help us?"

B. Have a student lead the class in prayer, focusing on the LESSON AIM, and thanking God for the opportunity of studying His Word this week.

4. Getting into the Lesson

A. Read the AT-A-GLANCE outline to the class and assign different students to focus on specific aspects of the outline, and assign the corresponding SEARCH THE SCRIPTURES questions to go along with their part of the discussion.

B. It is important for students to understand that Barnabas was a man who was called the "son of encouragement or consolation" because he was able to help and encourage many people. Ask students: What kind of spiritual gift did Barnabas have? How effective was he in using his gift?

C. Discuss THE PEOPLE, PLACES, AND TIMES

background information to help the students understand the importance of Antioch and why it was a region where the disciples were first called Christians.

5. Relating the Lesson to Life

A. Share your testimony of a time you needed and received encouragement or comfort from someone.

B. Have students think back to a time when they were discouraged and consider what happened when someone encouraged them. How can they use those examples to prompt them to do the same with others who may feel hopeless and discouraged?

C. Discuss the LESSON IN OUR SOCIETY article to help students see how the lesson from Scripture parallels with many present-day situations. Ask students what they plan to do in order to find people who are discouraged with life and encourage them.

6. Arousing Action

The MAKE IT HAPPEN section contains a suggestion of how to apply the principles learned. Discuss it with the class and encourage them to implement this suggestion during the coming week.

WORSHIP GUIDE

For the Superintendent or Teacher
Theme: Barnabas: Encourager and Enabler
Theme Song: "I'm Encouraged to Serve The Lord"
Scripture: Deuteronomy 3:27-28
Song: "Thank You, Lord"
Confession of Faith: Lord, I thank You for encouraging me even though I often fail in encouraging others. Help me to be an encourager to everyone I meet. In Jesus' name. Amen.

BARNABAS: ENCOURAGER AND ENABLER

Bible Background • ACTS 4:36-37; 9:26-27; 11:19-30; 15:36-40
Printed Text • ACTS 4:36-37; 9:26-27; 11:22-26; 15:36-41
Devotional Reading • HEBREWS 10:19-25

LESSON AIM

At the conclusion of today's lesson, students will understand the value of people who bring comfort and encouragement to others, be able to explain the impact Barnabas had on the early church, and determine to follow Barnabas's example by looking for opportunities to encourage and comfort others.

KEEP IN MIND

"Who, when he came, and had seen the grace of God, was glad, and exhorted them all, that with purpose of heart they would cleave unto the Lord. For he was a good man, and full of the Holy Ghost and of faith: and much people was added unto the Lord" (Acts 11:23-24).

LESSON OVERVIEW

LESSON AIM
KEEP IN MIND
FOCAL VERSES
IN FOCUS
THE PEOPLE, PLACES,
AND TIMES
BACKGROUND
AT-A-GLANCE
IN DEPTH
SEARCH THE SCRIPTURES
DISCUSS THE MEANING
LESSON IN OUR SOCIETY
MAKE IT HAPPEN
FOLLOW THE SPIRIT
REMEMBER YOUR THOUGHTS
MORE LIGHT ON THE TEXT
DAILY BIBLE READINGS

FOCAL VERSES

Acts 4:36 And Joses, who by the apostles was surnamed Barnabas, (which is, being interpreted, The son of consolation,) a Levite, and of the country of Cyprus,

37 Having land, sold it, and brought the money, and laid it at the apostles' feet.

9:26 And when Saul was come to Jerusalem, he assayed to join himself to the disciples: but they were all afraid of him, and believed not that he was a disciple.

27 But Barnabas took him, and brought him to the apostles, and declared unto them how he had seen the Lord in the way, and that he had spoken to him, and how he had preached boldly at Damascus in the name of Jesus.

11:22 Then tidings of these things came unto the ears of the church which was in Jerusalem: and they sent forth Barnabas, that he should go as far as Antioch.

23 Who, when he came, and had seen the grace of God, was glad, and exhorted them all, that with purpose of heart they would cleave unto the Lord.

24 For he was a good man, and full of the Holy Ghost and of faith: and much people was added unto the Lord.

25 Then departed Barnabas to Tarsus, for to seek Saul:

26 And when he had found him, he brought him unto Antioch. And it came to pass, that a whole year they assembled themselves with the church, and taught much people. And the disciples were called Christians first in Antioch.

15:36 And some days after Paul said unto Barnabas, Let us go again and visit our brethren in every city where we have preached the word of the Lord, and see how they do.

37 And Barnabas determined to take with them John, whose surname was Mark.

38 But Paul thought not good to take him with them, who departed from them from Pamphylia, and went not with them to the work.

39 And the contention was so sharp between them, that they departed asunder one from the

FEB
2ND

other: and so Barnabas took Mark, and sailed unto Cyprus;

40 And Paul chose Silas, and departed, being recommended by the brethren unto the grace of God.

IN FOCUS

Here are some good beauty tips for all believers.

For attractive lips, speak words of kindness.

For beautiful eyes, look for the good in other people.

To lose weight, let go of stress, hatred, anger, discontentment, and the need to control others.

To improve your ears, listen to the Word of God. Rather than focus on the thorns of life, smell the roses, and count your blessings, giving thanks for each one of them.

For poise, walk with knowledge and self-esteem.

To strengthen your arms, hug at least three people a day. Touch someone with your love.

To strengthen your heart, forgive yourself and others. Don't worry and hurry so much.

Rather than walk this earth lightly, walk firmly with determination and leave your mark.

For the ultimate in business, casual, or evening attire, put on the robe of Christ; it fits like a glove but allows room for growth. Best of all, it never goes out of style and is appropriate for any occasion.

Doing these things on a daily basis will certainly make you a much more beautiful person.

Our study today centers on Barnabas, a man who displayed many of the qualities listed above and who left his mark on the Christian church.

THE PEOPLE, PLACES AND TIMES

Antioch. There were at least 16 cities called Antioch in the ancient world, but the capital of Syria was the greatest. The city, located about 300 miles north of Jerusalem, had a population of about half a million, making it the third largest city in the Roman empire.

As a busy port city, Antioch attracted all kinds of people from all over the Roman world. With its large cosmopolitan population and great commercial and political power, Antioch presented the church with an opportunity to evangelize various cultures. Other than Jerusalem, no city is more intimately identified with early Christianity.

Not only was the first Gentile church established in Antioch, but the Antioch church commissioned Paul and Barnabas to begin the first of the missionary journeys that would eventually bring the Gentile world to Christ.

BACKGROUND

Barnabas is probably the best-known missionary of biblical times. Nothing is known of Barnabas's life before his initial appearance in the Book of Acts. However, once he comes on the scene, he becomes a prominent character in the founding of the early church and the spread of the Gospel.

Paul accompanied Barnabas on the very first missionary journey to take the Gospel to the Gentile world. This journey resulted in a chain of predominantly Gentile churches reaching far into Asia Minor. Ultimately, Barnabas became a leader in the church and a missionary to the Gentiles. He may also have been influential in the Christian activities in Syria since it is there that Saul became a Christian. The great missionary played an instrumental role in the development of Paul's early ministry.

Luke describes Barnabas as a man of triple grace—a good man, full of the Holy Ghost and of faith. His ministry was one of inspiration and encouragement.

AT-A-GLANCE

1. A Generous Beginning (Acts 4:36-37)
2. An Act of Consolation (9:26-27)
3. An Act of Exhortation (11:22-26)
4. A Sad Ending (15:36-40)

IN DEPTH

1. A Generous Beginning (Acts 4:36-37)

After the outpouring of the Holy Spirit on the Day of Pentecost, the Church grew rapidly (Acts 2:46-47). These early Christians were united in spirit; they were of "one heart and one soul" (v. 32). A church that is of one heart and one mind can effectively fight the forces of darkness in a community. That is why Scriptures teach us that we must endeavor to keep the unity of the Spirit in the bond of peace (Ephesians 4:3).

The people also realized that all their possessions were blessings from God, so they shared their possessions with the other saints in the church. Christians who understand and live by the principles of stewardship are eager to share with others.

One of the people who was a part of the Jerusalem church was a man name Joses, a Levite from Cyprus. Barnabas' given name was Joses (Acts 4:36). The name Barnabas comes from the Greek phrase *huios parakles* (pronounced **hwee-AHSS pah-rah-KLAY-seh-ose**), which literally means "son of consolation." The reason the apostles changed Joses's name to Barnabas was probably because he comforted other believers who may have been discouraged and wanted to return to Judaism. Barnabas was the one who admonished, encouraged, and strengthened believers to hold on to their faith.

It is vitally important that we have men and women in our churches whose job is to admonish, strengthen, and encourage people who may be going through trials and tribulations in their lives. What better place to get encouragement than from other believers who may have had similar problems in their lives but are now experiencing victory?

2. An Act of Consolation (9:26-27)

The next time that we see Barnabas is shortly after Paul's conversion experience. After his conversion, Paul immediately began preaching the Gospel in Damascus. The Jews in the city were completely dumbfounded at his change and new message. After preaching in the city for nearly three years, the Jews decided that the only way to stop their former ally was to kill him. When word of the Jewish plot reached the disciples, they helped Paul escape the city, and he went up to Jerusalem (see Acts 9:20-25).

When Paul arrived in Jerusalem, his situation was difficult. The Jews there had originally commissioned Paul (Saul) to apprehend Christ's followers in Damascus and bring them back to Jerusalem. At his conversion, Paul not only turned against his Jewish leaders, but he joined the oppo-

sition. These Jews would be less than pleased at his return to the city.

On the other hand, the disciples remembered how viciously Paul had pursued and persecuted believers. They may have felt he was a spy, and his three-year disappearance may also have caused some concern (Galatians 1:17-18). There were many unanswered questions that helped to create an air of suspicion. Paul had been run out of Damascus, he was hated by the Jews in Jerusalem, and he was not trusted by the disciples there.

This was a low point in Paul's life and ministry. If anyone ever needed the comfort of a friend, it was Paul. He found this friend in Barnabas, the "son of comfort." Though the other disciples refused to believe that Paul had changed, Barnabas stepped in to help. Perhaps Barnabas could see the call of the Lord on Paul's life, or maybe he felt bad about the way the other believers treated him. Whatever the reason, the "son of consolation" took Paul directly to the apostles and introduced him to them.

Barnabas was excited about what he had seen and heard of Paul's conversion experience and the way he preached boldly in the Damascus synagogue. As a result, Barnabas vouched for Paul's integrity and character. Paul had enemies among the religious leaders and skeptics among the other disciples, but he had a true friend in Barnabas.

Barnabas' stature with the apostles and members of the Jewish community in Jerusalem was so high that he was able to vouch for Paul's integrity and guarantee his conversion. After listening to Barnabas speak on Paul's behalf, the disciples of Jerusalem were reassured and welcomed Paul into their midst.

3. An Act of Exhortation (11:22-26)

After the stoning of Stephen, the Jews persecuted the church, and many believers fled Jerusalem and scattered to other parts of Palestine, including Phoenicia, Cyprus, and Antioch. In spite of severe persecution, the disciples persisted in preaching the Word to Jews and Gentiles in every city and village they came to. Many people throughout Palestine accepted Jesus Christ as their Saviour.

News of the conversion rapidly spread throughout the region and soon reached the apostles in

Jerusalem. The apostles were anxious to find out what was going on. So they sent Barnabas—the "son of consolation"—to Antioch to get a firsthand report of events.

When Barnabas arrived in Antioch, he was over-joyed at what he saw. The grace of God was evident among the people, and Barnabas, true to his name, "encouraged them all to remain true to the Lord with all their hearts" (v. 23, NIV). The origi-nal disciples did not assume that new converts would always remain true to the Lord. They knew that the world, the flesh, and the devil would tempt new believers to turn away from their newfound faith. Barnabas provides an excellent example of how new believers should be treated and encour-aged.

The Greek word for "exhort," *parakaleo* (pro-nounced **pah-rah-kah-LEH-oh**), means to comfort, encourage, and to come alongside to console oth-ers. Jesus uses the same word to describe the Holy Spirit, who is called to our side as our encourager and comforter (John 14:16). These verses affirm Luke's description of Barnabas as "a good man, full of the Holy Spirit and faith" (v. 24, NIV).

Barnabas was so excited about the events in Antioch that he left the city to go to Tarsus to search for Paul. Paul had been sent to Tarsus by the apostles after certain Jewish leaders had plot-ted to kill him (Acts 9:2-30). Once Barnabas found Paul, he explained to him what was happening in Antioch and convinced him to come to Antioch to assist him in the church's growth.

Barnabas and Paul spent a year in Antioch, teaching the people and establishing authority, order, and government in the church. In fact, Barnabas and Paul had such an impact on the city that the disciples were first called "Christians" in Antioch (v. 26). This name was given to followers of Jesus Christ by non-believers, and it was not commonly used by Christians themselves at first. The name "Christian" is found only two other times in Scripture: Acts 26:28 and 1 Peter 4:16.

4. A Sad Ending (15:36-40)

It is somewhat tragic that our last encounter with Barnabas is spoiled by an argument between the great missionary and his dear friend, Paul. However, Scripture does not give us pictures of perfect people, but of ordinary people with faults as well as strengths.

A little while after the Jerusalem Council, where the matter of Gentile circumcision was resolved, Paul suggested to Barnabas that they revisit the towns where they had planted churches. Barnabas was naturally excited about the idea and suggested that they take his cousin John Mark along with them (see Colossians 4:10). John Mark had accom-panied the pair on their first missionary journey but had left them in Galatia and returned to Jerusalem.

Paul disagreed with Barnabas's suggestion because John Mark had deserted them, and Paul thought he should not be given a second chance. The disagreement between the two men was so sharp that they parted company. "Barnabas took Mark and sailed for Cyprus" (Acts 15:39, NIV).

There will be times when disagreements will occur between even the most loving believers. When these disagreements cannot be resolved, it is sometimes best to separate and continue the work of the Lord separately. The key is to never allow disagreements over God's work to sink to the level of hostility and bitterness.

Whenever we encounter Barnabas in Scripture, he is consoling, exhorting, or encouraging others to be their best for Jesus. Not all believers are going to impact the kingdom publicly like Peter, nor are we all going to plant churches like Paul, but we can all be like Barnabas and give God and His people our very best.

SEARCH THE SCRIPTURES

1. What does the name Barnabas mean in Aramaic? (Acts 4:36)

2. What act did Barnabas perform that demon-strated his generosity? (v. 37)

3. Who helped Saul after the disciples in Jerusalem rejected him? (Acts 9:26-27)

4. How did Paul become involved with the church in Antioch? (Acts 11:25-26)

DISCUSS THE MEANING

1. What are some ways that Christians can allow the indwelling Holy Spirit to manifest Himself through their character?

2. The disciples were called Christians for the

first time at Antioch. What characteristics do you think they possessed that prompted the people to call them Christians?

LESSON IN OUR SOCIETY

There was a movie a couple of years ago in which a young boy attempted to change the world through acts of kindness. Each action included the stipulation that the person who received the kindness perform an act of kindness for someone else and ask them to do the same.

What do you think would happen if believers performed acts of kindness, comfort, or encouragement for strangers with the only stipulation being that they do the same for someone else? Do you think it's possible to encourage enough people to become involved to change a community, a city, or maybe a nation?

What specific "Barnabas-like" steps can you take to start the process? Write out a plan that can be shared with the other members of your Sunday School so that you can make a difference in your community.

MAKE IT HAPPEN

There are many people in your circle of friends, relatives, and church members who could use some encouragement or comfort. Make it a point this week to encourage or comfort at least one person each day. Be prepared to share your experiences with the class next week.

FOLLOW THE SPIRIT

What God wants me to do:

_____

_____

REMEMBER YOUR THOUGHTS

Special insights you have learned:

_____

_____

MORE LIGHT ON THE TEXT
Acts 4:36-37; 9:26-27; 11:22-26; 15:36-41

4:36 And Joses, who by the apostles was surnamed Barnabas, (which is, being interpreted, The son of consolation,) a Levite, and of the country of Cyprus, 37 Having land, sold it, and brought the

money, and laid it at the apostles' feet.

Barnabas' given name was Joses or Joseph. The apostles who spoke Aramaic nicknamed Joses "Barnabas," meaning "son of prophecy," from the Hebrew *bar* meaning "son of" and *nebu a* meaning prophecy. Some have given the nickname a slightly different meaning, translating it as "son of refreshment." Based on his intimate knowledge of the man, Luke translated the Aramaic into the Greek as *huios parakleseos,* which is translated variously as "son of consolation, exhortation, or encouragement."

Parakleseos comes from the same root as the word Jesus used in His promise to send the Holy Spirit: "And I will pray to the Father and He will give you another Comforter [*parakletos*], that He may abide with you forever" (John 14:16). Luke uses these exact words to indicate that the Holy Spirit had distinguished Himself in Barnabas. Whenever we see Barnabas in the pages of the New Testament, he is consoling, exhorting, or encouraging others to be their best for Jesus.

Although Barnabas is probably the best known non-apostolic missionary of biblical times, nothing is known of his life before he makes his initial appearance in Acts. The great missionary came from a Jewish-Cypriot family, but he had family in Jerusalem including the Apostle John Mark (Colossians 4:10).

In our Scriptural introduction to Barnabas, he has sold some property and given all the proceeds to the apostles to distribute to the church as they saw fit. Barnabas was a descendent of the tribe of Levi. The Levites came into prominence in connection with Moses and Aaron. After Aaron led the Israelites into apostasy with the golden calf, the children of Levi avenged the Lord's honor by punishing the wrongdoers (Exodus 32:25-28).

The Levites served as priests in the sanctuary and distributed the tithes to the needy. They also taught and interpreted the law (Deuteronomy 10:8-9, 17:9-11; Numbers 3:5-9). As a Levite, Barnabas was not allowed to own any land in Israel (Numbers 18:20; Deuteronomy 10:9), so the property he sold was either land in his hometown of Cyprus or was his burial plot.

Barnabas' act of generosity is contrasted with the self-serving lie of Ananias, who sold his property and kept back part of the proceeds for himself (see Acts 5:1-11). Barnabas's gift may even have caused Ananias to lie, thinking he would be elevated in the esteem of the apostles like Barnabas.

9:26 And when Saul was come to Jerusalem, he assayed to join himself to the disciples: but they were all afraid of him, and believed not that he was a disciple. 27 But Barnabas took him, and brought him to the apostles, and declared unto them how he had seen the Lord in the way, and that he had spoken to him, and how he had preached boldly at Damascus in the name of Jesus.

To understand the chronology of the events in this passage of Scripture, we must look to Paul's account in Galatians. "But when God, who set me apart from birth [or from my mother's womb] and called me by his grace, was pleased to reveal his Son in me so that I might preach him among the Gentiles, I did not consult any man, nor did I go up to Jerusalem to see those who were apostles before I was, but I went immediately into Arabia and later returned to Damascus. Then after three years, I went up to Jerusalem to get acquainted with Peter [Greek, *Cephas*] and stayed with him fifteen days" (Galatians 1:15-18, NIV).

After Paul's conversion, he immediately began to preach the Gospel in Damascus, and the Jews in the city were completely dumbfounded at his change and new message. After he had preached in the city for nearly 3 years, the Jews there were fed up with Paul and conspired to kill him. When word of the plot reached the disciples, they helped Paul escape from the city, and from there he went up to Jerusalem (see Acts 9:20-25). Paul's conversion has been dated to 33 A.D. and his return to Jerusalem around 35 A.D.

When Paul went back to Jerusalem, he found himself in a tenuous position. His previous associates were well aware of his defection and hated him for it. The disciples, on the other hand, remembered how viciously Paul had persecuted believers in Jerusalem and pursued them when they fled to other cities.

Paul had been run out of Damascus, and he was hated by the Jews in Jerusalem and not trusted by the disciples there. This was a low point in Paul's life and ministry. If anyone ever needed the comfort of a friend, it was Paul. He found this friend in Barnabas, the "son of comfort." In the Greek, the phrase, "But Barnabas took him, and brought him" implies that Barnabas literally took Paul by the hand and led him before the apostles to confirm his belief that Paul was a changed man.

It appears that Barnabas was already acquainted with Paul and knew his conversion was genuine. Barnabas's stature with the apostles and members of the Jewish community in Jerusalem was so high that he was able to vouch for Paul's integrity and guarantee his conversion. After listening to Barnabas speak on Paul's behalf, the disciples of Jerusalem were reassured and welcomed Paul into their midst.

11:22 Then tidings of these things came unto the ears of the church which was in Jerusalem: and they sent forth Barnabas, that he should go as far as Antioch. 23 Who, when he came, and had seen the grace of God, was glad, and exhorted them all, that with purpose of heart they would cleave unto the Lord. 24 For he was a good man, and full of the Holy Ghost and of faith: and much people was added unto the Lord.

Up to this point, the Christians who had fled from the persecution in Jerusalem had restricted their evangelizing to the Jewish communities in the cities to which they fled. All this changed in Antioch.

There were at least 16 cities called Antioch in the ancient world, but the capital of Syria was the greatest. The city, located about 300 miles north of Jerusalem, had a population of about one-half million, making it the third largest city in the Roman empire. Antioch was a busy port city that attracted all kinds of people from all over the Roman world. The city's large cosmopolitan population and great commercial and political power presented the church with an opportunity to evangelize various cultures. Other than Jerusalem, no city is more intimately identified with early Christianity than Antioch. Antioch would eventually replace even Jerusalem as the center of the Christian movement.

The evangelism of Antioch began when certain Christians from Cyprus and Cyrene began sharing the Gospel message with Gentiles. The

Gentiles in the city took to the Christian message, and a large number of them became believers.

When word of the Gentile converts reached the leaders of the church in Jerusalem, they sent Barnabas to Antioch to investigate the situation.

Verse 24 gives us a splendid spiritual profile of Barnabas, who possessed a triple grace: "He was a good man." *Agathos* is the Greek adjective that Luke uses to describe Barnabas' innate goodness. He was morally honorable, pleasing to God and therefore beneficial to others. Barnabas was "full of the Spirit" or God-possessed, and he was full of "faith," which demonstrated the way in which he encouraged others.

When Barnabas arrived in the city, he found the grace of God blessing both Jew and Gentile alike. Barnabas's generous heart was filled with joy at what he found. True to his name, the great missionary encouraged the believers to persevere in their devotion to the Lord.

Barnabas stayed in Antioch and led the church there. The church grew even more as a result of his ministry.

25 Then departed Barnabas to Tarsus, for to seek Saul: 26 And when he had found him, he brought him unto Antioch. And it came to pass, that a whole year they assembled themselves with the church, and taught much people. And the disciples were called Christians first in Antioch.

Soon the church grew to such a point that Barnabas could no longer oversee it alone. He needed help, and Barnabas knew just the man— if only he could find him.

Barnabas set out for Tarsus "to seek for Saul." Finding Paul appears to have been a difficult task. The Greek verb *anaseteo,* translated "to seek for," is used especially to denote searching for human beings with some difficulty. Close to nine years had passed since Paul had left Jerusalem and sailed home to his native land of Tarsus (Acts 9:29-30). The search would have been especially difficult if in fact Paul had been disinherited because of his Christian beliefs, as Paul implies in his letter to the church in Philippi. "I consider everything a loss compared to the surpassing greatness of knowing Christ Jesus my Lord, for

whose sake I have lost all things" (Philippians 3:8). In spite of the apparent difficulty, Barnabas found Paul and took him back to Antioch. For the next year, the two worked in tandem and many more converts were added to the church.

It was in Antioch that the disciples "were called Christians" (Greek *chrematisai Christianous*). The Greek word *Chrematsai* primarily meant "to have business dealings with." Because the main activity of Antioch's believers was spreading the Gospel of Christ, they were publically called Christians. The word "Christian" has lost a lot of its significance since the time of the early church, when it referred to one who turned away from sin and received salvation through faith in Christ.

The word "Christian" occurs only three times in the New Testament: here in Acts 11:26, Acts 26:28, and 1 Peter 4:16. The passive verb *chrematizo,* translated "were called," literally means to be called or named. This implies that the early Christians did not assume the name themselves.

The Jews of Antioch would not have given them the name because the Hebrew/Aramaic word is "Messiah." Furthermore, the Jews referred to believers as "Nazarenes" (Acts 24:5), a derisive term that alluded to the proverb, "nothing good came out of Nazareth" (John 1:47). The name was probably given to believers by the Gentiles in the city. These Gentiles did not understand that "Christ" was a title referring to the Anointed. They thought it was a personal name, which they converted to a party name. The suffix *ian* is a Latin word and means "belonging to the party of."

15:36 And some days after Paul said unto Barnabas, Let us go again and visit our brethren in every city where we have preached the word of the Lord, and see how they do. 37 And Barnabas determined to take with them John, whose surname was Mark.

Shortly after the Jerusalem council where the issue of Gentile circumcision was decided (15:1-35), Paul proposed to Barnabas that they revisit the churches they had planted on their first missionary journey to Cyprus and Asia Minor (13:1—14:28). "In every city" comes from the Greek phrase *kata pasan polin* and literally means "city by city." Barnabas quickly agreed and suggested that they take John Mark with them.

38 But Paul thought not good to take him with them, who departed from them from Pamphylia, and went not with them to the work.

Paul immediately disagreed with this suggestion. He felt that John Mark had deserted them in Perga during their last journey. The apostle may have felt that John Mark's desertion indicated some character flaw that made him unfit for missionary work. On the other hand, Barnabas, who was John Mark's cousin (Colossians 4:10), probably saw the promising potential of the young apostle that could be developed under his care.

39 And the contention was so sharp between them, that they departed asunder one from the other: and so Barnabas took Mark, and sailed unto Cyprus;

Some believe that an earlier incident contributed to the falling out of the two friends. Peter had come to Antioch and often ate with Gentile converts. But when a delegation arrived from Jerusalem, Peter drew back and refused to eat with the uncircumcised Gentiles. Barnabas joined with Peter in this hypocrisy (Galatians 2:12-13). Whether or not this was a contributing factor, Paul's point-blank refusal to take John Mark along started a heated argument between the two men. "The contention was so sharp" (Greek *egeneto paraxumos*) is more correctly rendered "there arose a sharp contention." The Greek noun *paraxumos* (from which we get our English word "paroxysm") means to provoke or arouse anger, indignation, and resentment.

This disagreement was so heated that the only thing the two men could agree on was to disagree and go their separate ways. Barnabas took John Mark and sailed for his homeland of Cyprus. This is the last mention of Barnabas in the Book of Acts.

The partnership between the two great men of faith may have been broken, but not their friendship. We know that Barnabas, John Mark, and Paul were later reconciled. Paul would later write of John Mark, "Get Mark and bring him to me

because he is helpful to me in my ministry (2 Timothy 4:11).

40 And Paul chose Silas, and departed, being recommended by the brethren unto the grace of God.

Paul chose Silas as his new traveling companion. Silas was a distinguished member of the apostolic church in Jerusalem. He accompanied Paul and Barnabas back to Antioch after the council's decision on circumcision (Acts 15:22). His double qualification as a leading Jewish Christian and a Roman citizen (16:37) made him eminently qualified to replace Barnabas on Paul's next missionary journey. Paul and Silas were "recommended by the brethren," which was not the case with Barnabas and John Mark. They visited the churches in Syro-Cilicia, encouraging them and handing down to them the commands of the elders (Acts 15:41; 16:4).

> ### DAILY BIBLE READINGS
>
> **M: Barnabas, Son of Encouragement**
> Acts 4:32-37
> **T: Barnabas Speaks Up for Saul**
> Acts 9:23-30
> **W: Barnabas Exhorts Antioch Believers**
> Acts 11:19-24
> **T: Barnabas Brings Saul to Antioch**
> Acts 11:25-30
> **F: Barnabas and Saul Are Set Apart**
> Acts 13:1-5
> **S: They Relate All God Has Done**
> Acts 14:21-28
> **S: Barnabas Chooses Mark**
> Acts 15:36-41

TEACHING TIPS

February 9
Bible Study Guide 11

1. Words You Should Know

A. Persecutest (Acts 26:14)—From the Greek verb *dioko* (pronounced **dee-OH-keh**), meaning to pursue and prosecute with repeated acts of hatred.

B. Minister (v. 16)—In the Greek, literally means "underrower." The word refers to a lowly servant on a galley ship.

2. Teacher Preparation

A. Read the Scriptures for the Devotional Reading and Bible Background.

B. Write out or type your testimony, and be prepared to share it with the class.

3. Starting the Lesson

A. Review last week's lesson and challenge students to share testimonies of how they applied the lesson to their lives during the week. Remind students that they are called to be encouragers to others.

B. Read the SEARCH THE SCRIPTURES questions aloud to allow students the opportunity to consider them while the FOCAL VERSES are being read.

C. Have a student pray for the class to achieve the LESSON AIM.

4. Getting into the Lesson

A. Now have the class participate in an open discussion, using the FOCAL VERSES as the foundation of the discussion. Keep the discussion as focused as possible on Stephen and his connection with the Lord.

B. Have a student read aloud the information in the BACKGROUND section.

C. Ask students to discuss the SEARCH THE SCRIPTURES questions in groups. Allow time to find the answers and for responses.

D. Discuss THE PEOPLE, PLACES, AND TIMES background information to help students understand the setting for today's text.

5. Relating the Lesson to Life

A. Have students answer the DISCUSS THE MEANING questions. Open the discussion so the students can ask whatever questions they may have concerning the Scriptures.

B. Select three students and have them share the most significant points they have learned from this lesson regarding Paul's testimony. Ask: "What is the most important principle we can take with us today that can help another believer this week?"

C. Use the LESSON IN OUR SOCIETY exercise to help students connect the biblical significance of this lesson with their social context.

D. Ask students what they have learned from the lesson and if the class achieved the LESSON AIM.

6. Arousing Action

A. The MAKE IT HAPPEN section suggests that the students write or type their testimonies, and share them with someone else this week. Encourage them to carry out this suggestion and be prepared to share their experiences and their testimonies next week.

B. Challenge students to develop good study habits by reading God's Word and applying it to their lives daily.

PAUL: OBEDIENT MESSENGER

Bible Background • ACTS 25:23—26:32
Printed Text • ACTS 26:12-23, 27-29
Devotional Reading • EPHESIANS 3:1-13

LESSON AIM

At the conclusion of today's lesson, students will be able to tell the story of Paul's conversion, commission, and commitment to preach the gospel; realize the importance of their personal testimony; and determine to share their testimony with at least one person this week.

KEEP IN MIND

"Whereupon, O king Agrippa, I was not disobedient unto the heavenly vision" (Acts 26:19).

FOCAL VERSES

Acts 26:12 Whereupon as I went to Damascus with authority and commission from the chief priests,

13 At midday, O king, I saw in the way a light from heaven, above the brightness of the sun, shining round about me and them which journeyed with me.

14 And when we were all fallen to the earth, I heard a voice speaking unto me, and saying in the Hebrew tongue, Saul, Saul, why persecutest thou me? it is hard for thee to kick against the pricks.

15 And I said, Who art thou, Lord? And he said, I am Jesus whom thou persecutest.

16 But rise, and stand upon thy feet: for I have appeared unto thee for this purpose, to make thee a minister and a witness both of these things which thou hast seen, and of those things in the which I will appear unto thee;

17 Delivering thee from the people, and from the Gentiles, unto whom now I send thee,

18 To open their eyes, and to turn them from darkness to light, and from the power of Satan unto God, that they may receive forgiveness of sins, and

LESSON OVERVIEW

LESSON AIM

KEEP IN MIND

FOCAL VERSES

IN FOCUS

THE PEOPLE, PLACES, AND TIMES

BACKGROUND

AT-A-GLANCE

IN DEPTH

SEARCH THE SCRIPTURES

DISCUSS THE MEANING

LESSON IN OUR SOCIETY

MAKE IT HAPPEN

FOLLOW THE SPIRIT

REMEMBER YOUR THOUGHTS

MORE LIGHT ON THE TEXT

DAILY BIBLE READINGS

inheritance among them which are sanctified by faith that is in me.

19 Whereupon, O king Agrippa, I was not disobedient unto the heavenly vision:

20 But shewed first unto them of Damascus, and at Jerusalem, and throughout all the coasts of Judaea, and then to the Gentiles, that they should repent and turn to God, and do works meet for repentance.

21 For these causes the Jews caught me in the temple, and went about to kill me.

22 Having therefore obtained help of God, I continue unto this day, witnessing both to small and great, saying none other things than those which the prophets and Moses did say should come:

23 That Christ should suffer, and that he should be the first that should rise from the dead, and should shew light unto the people, and to the Gentiles.

26:27 King Agrippa, believest thou the prophets? I know that thou believest.

28 Then Agrippa said unto Paul, Almost thou persuadest me to be a Christian.

29 And Paul said, I would to God, that not only thou, but also all that hear me this day, were both almost, and altogether such as I am, except these bonds.

IN FOCUS

There was a schoolteacher who asked her class of first-graders to draw a picture of something they were thankful for since Thanksgiving Day was approaching. As they began to draw, she thought of how little these poor Black children from poverty-stricken neighborhoods actually had to be thankful for. She imagined that most of them would probably draw things that they hoped for—like cars, toys, or maybe tables of food for Thanksgiving Day. The teacher was completely surprised by the picture little Douglas handed in—a simple, childishly drawn hand.

"But whose hand?" she wondered. The class was also captivated by the abstract image.

"I think it must be the hand of God that brings us food," said one child.

"It's the president's hand," said another, "because he gives us food stamps."

Finally, when the others were at work, she bent over Douglas's desk and asked whose hand it was. "It's your hand, Teacher," he shyly mumbled.

She was moved to tears. She recalled that frequently at recess she had taken Douglas, a scrubby forlorn child, by the hand as she walked and talked with him. She often did that with the children to give them personal attention. But it meant so much more to Douglas, who was from a broken, troubled family. This small act of kindness made a world of difference to a little boy who otherwise may not have known compassion.

When we take the time to give of ourselves to others, we become an expression of God's love. In today's lesson, we will examine the testimony of Paul, a man who gave his all to others for the cause of Christ.

THE PEOPLE, PLACES, AND TIMES

Festus. Nothing is known of the life of Porcius Festus before he succeeded Felix as governor of Judea around 59 A.D. Festus died in office two years after his appointment.

Although Felix was convinced of Paul's innocence (Acts 26:31), he was prepared to sacrifice the apostle to the Jews to maintain good relations. He suggested to Paul that he go to Jerusalem to stand trial before the Sanhedrin, and Paul refused. Felix was so baffled by Paul that he brought his case before Herod Agrippa II and his sister Bernice. Paul is shown to be clearly innocent but is still sent to Rome for trial because of his appeal to Caesar.

BACKGROUND

On Paul's journey back to Jerusalem, he was twice warned not to go there. At a stopover in Tyre of Syria, the disciples urged "through the Spirit" that Paul should not go up to Jerusalem (Acts 21:4). Later in the journey, Paul stopped in Caesarea to spend some time with deacon Philip. While there, a believer named Agabus arrived from Jerusalem. Paul and Agabus had previously worked together in a famine relief program for Judea (11:27-30). When Agabus visited Paul and Philip, he took Paul's belt from around his waist and tied it around his own hands and feet. He then prophesied, "The Holy Spirit says, 'In this way the Jews of Jerusalem will bind the owner of this belt and hand him over to the Gentiles'" (21:11).

When Paul arrived in Jerusalem, he joined with four other believers in the city in a Nazarite vow and purified himself for seven days. At the end of the seven days, he went to the temple to offer a sacrifice to God. It so happens that some of Paul's enemies from Asia were in the city and spotted him. These men lied and stirred up the people against Paul. A riot ensued, and Paul had to be rescued by Roman soldiers.

Later, the captain of the guard found out that some Jews were plotting to assassinate Paul. He hurriedly moved the apostle to Caesarea to be tried by Felix, the governor of Judea. When Felix questioned Paul, he found no cause to hold him. But since Paul would not offer him a bribe, he allowed Paul to remain in prison for two years until Felix was replaced as governor by Festus (21:17—24:27).

When Festus took office, Jewish leaders urgently requested that Paul be turned over to them for trial so they could kill him. Instead of turning Paul over to them, in an attempt to appease the Jews, Festus asked Paul if he would be willing to go to Jerusalem to stand trial. Paul immediately appealed to be tried by Caesar. Because this was a right afforded to all Roman citizens, Festus had to agree.

This seemed to satisfy the Jews, but Festus still had a problem. He had to send Paul to Caesar for trial, but he did not know what crime to charge Paul with. Festus discussed the situation with Herod Agrippa II, who agreed to hear the case and help Festus out (25:1-27). When Paul was brought before King Agrippa, the king's sister Bernice, and Festus, he saw it as an opportunity to share his testimony with unbelievers and took full advantage of it.

1. Paul's Conversion (Acts 26:12-15)
2. Paul's Commission (vv. 16-18)
3. Paul's Commitment (vv. 19-23, 26-27)

IN DEPTH

1. Paul's Conversion (Acts 26:12-15)

Paul begins his testimony before Festus, King Agrippa, and Bernice by recapping his life as a devout Pharisee who zealously persecuted and imprisoned Christian believers in Jerusalem. When believers were sentenced to death, Paul gave His "voice against them" (Acts 26:10). This phrase actually means he cast his vote against them, which implies that Paul may have been a member of the Sanhedrin. Paul's persecution of the believers caused many to flee Jerusalem (8:4).

Not content with his harassment of the believers in Jerusalem, Paul asked for and was given permission to pursue believers in distant cities. It was his ardent zeal to persecute believers that brought the conflicted Saul to his fateful encounter on the Damascus road.

This is the third account of Paul's conversion, the first being in Chapter 9 and the second in 22:2-16. Paul adds a few new details to the story here, such as the time of day. As Paul was traveling on the road to Damascus, his mind was made up, but his heart may have been troubled. He had witnessed the heroic death of Stephen and was probably amazed at how the tortured believers had tenaciously clung to their faith in Jesus.

"At midday" (v. 13), or at high noon, a light flashed around Paul and his escort. This light, which was brighter than even the noonday sun, was the overpowering glory of the Lord. Paul and his escort fell to the ground. The men who were with Paul got to their feet and stood speechless (9:7) while Paul lay blinded on the ground. Jesus Christ called out to Paul in the familiar Hebrew language of his birth, and He addressed Paul by his Hebrew name: "Saul, Saul, why persecutest thou me?" (v. 15). Paul thought that he had been defending his faith from

heretics, when in truth he had been persecuting the Lord he thought to serve. As he lay on the ground, the stricken Pharisee called out, "Who art thou, Lord?" (15a). This is the most important question any human can ever ask. The answer to this question determines the eternal destiny of us all. The risen Lord answered, "I am Jesus whom thou persecutest" (15b).

That day on the Damascus road, Saul of Tarsus made several life-altering discoveries. First, he discovered that Jesus Christ was alive. This meant that Paul had to change his mind about who Jesus was. Paul also discovered that he was a lost sinner in danger of judgment. He thought he was doing good but discovered he was "persecuting" the one he thought to serve. This meant that he had to turn away from the life he had led and submit himself to his Lord, Jesus Christ. There are many good people who believe they are earning their way into heaven by their works. Like Paul, these good people need a face-to-face confrontation with the risen Lord. Isn't it wonderful that God has chosen believers to serve as the modern-day "Damascus road" to lead other people to Him?

2. Paul's Commission (vv. 16-18)

Although Paul does not mention it in his testimony to Festus, Agrippa, and Bernice, his next question was, "Lord, what wilt Thou have me to do?" (Acts 9:6) Jesus replies by telling Paul to get to his feet. He then explains that He has appeared to Paul to call him into service and to give him his commission. From this moment on, Paul will serve as Christ's minister and witness to the Gentiles.

Paul's mission was twofold. First, he was sent to "open their eyes" (v. 18a). Lost people are blinded by the darkness of their existence. They cannot see the reality of their situation and so fail to realize that they are "strangers from the covenants of promise, having no hope, and without God in the world" (Ephesians 2:12). They are not aware that "the hour is coming, in the which all that are in the graves shall hear his voice, And shall come forth; they that have done good, unto the resurrection of life; and they that have done evil, unto the resurrection of damnation" (John 5:28-29). Paul was to bring the light of Christ into their lives by preaching the Gospel in the power of the Holy Spirit.

Second, Paul's mission was to turn them "from the power of Satan unto God" (v. 18b). Satan is the ruler of this world (John 12:31; 14:30), and all the unsaved serve his evil purposes and are enslaved by his power. Sharing our testimonies in the power of the Holy Spirit will rescue people from the dominion of darkness and bring them into the kingdom of Christ (Colossians 1:13).

The believer's benefit package includes "forgiveness of sins" (v. 18c). This forgiveness comes through faith in Christ and is based on His sacrificial death on the cross. It also includes an "inheritance among them which are sanctified by faith that is in me" (v. 18d). Not only are believers delivered from the power of darkness and forgiven for our sins; we are indwelt by Holy Spirit. The Holy Spirit within us sets us apart from the world, and we live in sweet communion with God and His people. What a marvel this salvation is. How could any believer neglect to share the wonders of our deliverance with anyone who will listen?

3. Paul's Commitment (vv. 19-23, 26-27)

Paul affirms that he was "not disobedient unto the heavenly vision" (v. 19). In Acts 9:6, when Paul asked Christ, "Lord, what wilt thou have me to do?" he was serious. When Jesus explained His mission, Paul got it immediately. From the instant he recognized Christ as Lord and Savior, Paul dedicated his life to serving Him.

He began his ministry right there in Damascus. In the same city he had come to terrorize, he became a force for the kingdom. His preaching was so powerful that the Jews in that city soon began plotting to kill him (Acts 9:20-25). Later, when he preached in Jerusalem, the Jews there also attempted to kill him. But Paul would not be deterred—he continued to preach the Gospel "throughout all the coasts of Judaea, and then to the Gentiles." He never wavered from the message Christ gave him that people "should repent and turn to God, and do works meet for repentance" (Acts 26:20).

Paul explains that it was because of his testimony of the living Christ and because of his ministry to the Gentiles that he had been attacked and almost killed in the temple. For that reason, he stood before the governor and the king on this occasion.

Paul's statement, "I continue unto this day, witnessing both to small and great" (v. 22), may have been a veiled reference to the proceedings that were taking place. One thing is sure: Paul never missed an opportunity to share his faith. Talking to Agrippa, he affirms that his witness is based on the teachings of Moses and the prophets. Then he goes on to summarize the Gospel message as proclaimed by the prophets: "That Christ should suffer, and that he should be the first that should rise from the dead, and should shew light unto the people, and to the Gentiles" (v. 23; see Isaiah 52:12-15; 53:12; Psalm 16:8-11).

At the end of his presentation, Paul spoke directly to the king. "King Agrippa, believest thou the prophets?" With this question, Paul was forcing Agrippa to take a stand. As king of Israel, Agrippa could not disclaim what every Jew believed. Agrippa knew that if he affirmed his belief in the writings of the prophets, the next question would be whether he believed that Jesus was the One of whom the prophets wrote. Agrippa managed to sidestep the question by sarcastically remarking, "Paul, almost thou persuadest me to be a Christian" (Acts 26:28). This was actually asking Paul: "Are you trying to make a Christian of me?" Paul could only answer in the affirmative. His prayer was that not only Agrippa, but all those listening to him that day would be saved.

Even with his life on the line, Paul was reaching out to others with his testimony and the Good News of Christ. He was God's obedient messenger regardless of the circumstances. His is an example that should be followed by all believers.

SEARCH THE SCRIPTURES

1. What time of day was it when Paul had his encounter with the risen Lord? (Acts 26:13)

2. Who answered Paul when he asked the name of the person speaking to him from heaven? (v. 15)

3. In what city did Paul first proclaim the Good News of Christ after his conversion? (v. 20)

4. Who asked Paul if he was trying to convert him to Christianity? (v. 28)

DISCUSS THE MEANING

1. In view of the two prophecies through the Holy Spirit, do you think Paul should not have gone to Jerusalem? If it was God's will for Paul to preach the

Gospel in Rome (Acts 23:11), why was he twice warned not to go to Jerusalem?

2. Do you think that all believers have an obligation to share their testimony or the good news of Christ with others? Does this include strangers as well as friends and loved ones?

LESSON IN OUR SOCIETY

Many people in our society have given up hope of ever having any joy or peace in their lives. Some of these people are the elderly in nursing homes, and some are children who have no one to love and care for them. Becoming foster parents or regularly visiting nursing homes are a couple of ways believers can live out their testimony. What other ways can you think of to show the love of Christ to others?

MAKE IT HAPPEN

Everyone's story of how he or she came to know Christ as Lord and Saviour is eternally valuable. The testimony of those who have practically always lived Christian lives is just as valuable as that of people who were dramatically saved from completely immoral lives. Take some time this week to write down your personal testimony of salvation. Then rehearse sharing it with someone. Finally, share your testimony with at least one person this week and affirm that what God has done for you, He can do for them.

FOLLOW THE SPIRIT

What God wants me to do:

_____

_____

REMEMBER YOUR THOUGHTS

Special insights you have learned:

_____

_____

MORE LIGHT ON THE TEXT
Acts 26:12-23, 27-29

12 Whereupon as I went to Damascus with authority and commission from the chief priests, 13 At midday, O king, I saw in the way a light from heaven, above the brightness of the sun, shining round about me and them which journeyed with me.

After his third missionary journey, Paul returned to Jerusalem. While purifying himself in the temple,

he was assaulted by a Jewish mob and rescued by a contingent of Roman soldiers. The Jewish mob accused Paul of desecrating the temple, and Paul was arrested.

The Jews then hatched a plot to kill Paul, but the Roman centurion found out about the plot and had Paul taken to Caesarea to stand trial before Felix, the Roman procurator of Judea (52 A.D. to around 58 A.D.). The Jews could not prove any of their charges against Paul, but Felix held Paul under loose confinement for two years until Porcius Festus replaced Felix as procurator of the province. At his trial before Festus, Paul appealed his case to Caesar. As a Roman citizen, Paul had a right to have his case heard by the emperor himself.

Festus had no choice but to grant Paul's appeal, but this presented a difficulty. Festus had to send to Rome a report of the case as he understood it. The problem was he did not understand it. Listening to the arguments of Paul and his accusers had only confused him more. Fortunately, a way out of the difficulty soon appeared. Herod Agrippa II, ruler of the petty kingdom of Chalcis, came to pay his respects to the new representative of Rome (Acts 21:1—25:12).

King Agrippa was the son of Herod Agrippa I, king of Judea from 41 to 44 A.D. When his father died, Agrippa II was only 17 years old. The Roman emperor thought of appointing the young Agrippa to the throne but was persuaded that he was too young. Judea reverted to a procuratorial administration. Soon after the death of the king of Chalcis in 48 A.D., the young Agrippa was appointed king.

Agrippa was considered an authority on the Jewish religion, and Festus decided that he was the man who could help him frame the report he had to send to Rome. Paul was brought before Festus and Agrippa and presented his case. The apostle began his defense by explaining his Jewish heritage (26:2-8), then tells of his zeal in persecuting Christians. Then his story takes an abrupt turn, and Paul begins to explain his conversion and his teachings.

Paul was not content with just driving the Christian believers from Jerusalem; he pursued them wherever they fled. Armed with authority from the chief priest, he went from house to house and from synagogue to synagogue in city after city to punish believers. The obsessed Pharisee's intent was to turn the believers into apostates by making them blaspheme the name of Christ (v. 11). When he failed to get the believers to blaspheme, the believers were put on trial, and Paul cast his vote for their condemnation, demanding the death sentence.

When the believers fled to cities outside of Israel, Paul pursued them into those cities where the writ of the Sanhedrin was accepted. The high priest, as head of the Sanhedrin, was head of the Jewish state. Under Roman law, the decrees of the Sanhedrin were binding, not only for Jews, but also in many communities outside of Israel. Armed with the high priest's commission, Paul set out for Damascus.

Damascus, the capital of Syria, had a large Jewish population. It is believed that the city had 30 to 40 synagogues in it. The fact that there were already believers in the city is an indication of how effective believers had been in spreading the Gospel.

This is the third account of Paul's conversion, the first being in Acts 9 and the second in Acts 22:2-16. There are a few new details given here. The first is the time of day. At "midday," or around high noon, a light flashed around Paul and his escort. This light was the overpowering glory of the Lord, and it was far brighter than the high noon sun.

14 And when we were all fallen to the earth, I heard a voice speaking unto me, and saying in the Hebrew tongue, Saul, Saul, why persecutest thou me? it is hard for thee to kick against the pricks. 15 And I said, Who art thou, Lord? And he said, I am Jesus whom thou persecutest.

In Acts 9 and 22, Paul speaks of only himself as being knocked to the ground. In this verse (26:24), he informs us that his traveling companions were knocked over as well. We are told that the voice Paul heard spoke in the Hebrew language (he was now speaking to King Agrippa and Festus in Greek). Although the men traveling with Paul saw the great light and were knocked to the ground, the message was for Paul alone, and Jesus addressed him by his given name.

Jesus makes Paul aware that not only was He alive, but that He knew Paul personally, and spoke to him intimately in the language of his birth.

The question, "Why persecutest thou me?" stimulates Paul's thinking. The word "persecutest," from the Greek verb *dialo*, means to pursue and prosecute with repeated acts of hatred. Jesus identifies with

believers to the point that He actually experiences our trials and persecutions. The statement, "It is hard for thee to kick against the pricks" is an ancient agricultural proverb. The saying referred to a long-handled pointed instrument called a "prick" or "goad." The instrument was used to urge oxen along when plowing. The farmer would stick the animals with the prick, and the oxen would kick at the offending instrument.

This metaphor leads us to believe that the Holy Spirit was pricking Paul's conscience. Perhaps Stephen's argument and death had made a deep impression on Paul. Paul's hatred and persecution of believers could have been his attempt to kick against the pricks of the Holy Spirit. In answer to Paul's question, "Who art thou, Lord?" Jesus replies, "I am Jesus whom thou persecutest." At that moment, Paul identifies Jesus with the Lord Jehovah, whom he had tried so zealously to serve. From that moment on, Paul would serve the Lord Jesus with all his heart.

16 But rise, and stand upon thy feet: for I have appeared unto thee for this purpose, to make thee a minister and a witness both of these things which thou hast seen, and of those things in the which I will appear unto thee; 17 Delivering thee from the people, and from the Gentiles, unto whom now I send thee, 18 To open their eyes, and to turn them from darkness to light, and from the power of Satan unto God, that they may receive forgiveness of sins, and inheritance among them which are sanctified by faith that is in me.

In Paul's second recitation of his conversion, the apostle does not find it necessary to relate how he was blinded by the light and sent to Straight Street to await Ananias, who would baptize him. Instead, Paul gives us additional details of his commissioning by Christ.

Christ begins His commissioning of Paul by telling him to "rise." The word "rise" is a translation of the Greek verb *anistemi*, which literally means to stand again. This verb is the same one used to describe Christ's resurrection from the dead (Acts 2:32) and of the resurrection of believers (John 6:39-40, 44; Acts 13:33-34; 17:31). Paul was dead in sin, and Christ calls him to rise up to his new life.

Christ reveals the reason for his appearance to Paul and commissions him as a minister and witness to the Gentiles. The word "minister," from the Greek word *huperetes*, is a nautical term literally translated as "underrower." The term came to refer to a subordinate servant who waits to accomplish the commands of his master. "Witness" is from the Greek word *martura*, meaning one who bears testimony.

Paul would testify of the things he had seen, that is, the risen Lord. It was necessary that the apostle of the Gentiles should see Christ. He must be a witness that the Lord had risen. As Christ's servant, Paul was to open the eyes of the blind and turn their spiritual darkness into light. Paul would later restate this commission as the blessing of all believers: "Giving thanks to the Father, who has qualified you to share in the inheritance of the saints in the kingdom of light. For he has rescued us from the dominion of darkness and brought us into the kingdom of the son he loves" (Colossians 1:12-13, NIV).

The apostle would also testify of "those things in the which I will appear unto thee," or literally, "of those things I will show you." The word "appear" is from the Greek word *optomai* and in this case means to experience a revelation. The word is found in most dictionaries as *horao*, meaning to see.

Jesus gives Paul a threefold mission to the Gentiles: to open their eyes, to turn them from darkness to light, and to turn them from the power of Satan to God.

The word "open" in the command "open their eyes" is from the Greek *anoigo* and generally refers to that which is closed by a cover or door. Used metaphorically, it means to open the eyes of understanding of the mind or to cause one to perceive or understand.

The second part of Paul's mission is "to turn them from darkness to light." The word "turn" (Greek *epistrepho*) means to convert to something and embrace it. What Christ wants us to turn away from is darkness. This is a translation of the Greek word *skotos*, which refers to moral and spiritual wickedness caused by ignorance or error and leading to misery and damnation. Turning away from something also means to turn to something, and the something believers turn to is light (Greek *phos*). In the figurative sense, *phos* refers to moral and spiritual goodness. The word implies knowledge that enlightens the mind, soul, and conscience and includes the idea of moral goodness, purity, and holiness and the

consequent reward of happiness and eternal life.

The final part of Paul's commission is to turn them "from the power of Satan unto God." The Greek word for "power," *exousia*, refers to the permission, authority, right, or liberty to do something while denying the presence of a hindrance. It means to operate under the power of Satan completely, to give in to the lusts of the flesh while denying God's absolute authority to challenge or hold one accountable for one's actions.

Christ's ultimate purpose in commissioning Paul was to bestow on the Gentiles a double blessing: "That they may receive forgiveness of sins." The word "forgiveness" (Greek *aphieme*) literally means to send away. The verb signifies the elimination of punishment due to sinful conduct. The elimination is based on the vicarious and propitiatory sacrifice of Christ.

The second blessing is a heavenly "inheritance" (Greek *kleronomos*). This word is derived from *kleros*, meaning a lot. As God's heir (Hebrews 1:2), Christ enters into possession of all things because of His relationship to the Father. Believers in a sense share the divine sonship by reason of adoption and therefore share in the divine inheritance (Romans 8:17). We follow in the footsteps of Abraham as heirs to the promise. Our inheritance is something that is given by God's grace because of our status in His sight and is in no way earned.

Finally, Christ tells Paul who will receive this double blessing: "them which are sanctified (*hoi hagiasmenoi*, literally "those who are sanctified"), which refers to Christians in general. Metaphorically, "sanctified" means rendered morally clean and holy.

19 Whereupon, O king Agrippa, I was not disobedient unto the heavenly vision: 20 But shewed first unto them of Damascus, and at Jerusalem, and throughout all the coasts of Judea, and then to the Gentiles, that they should repent and turn to God, and do works meet for repentance.

Paul states, "I was not disobedient unto the heavenly vision." Even after this miraculous encounter, Paul could have disobeyed. His will was free, but he could act in good conscience only by obeying Christ. Paul immediately began to carry out his mission, preaching repentance first in Damascus, then in Jerusalem and Judea and throughout the Gentile nations, by preaching the message "that they should repent." Paul preached more than theory or religion; he preached a whole new life.

21 For these causes the Jews caught me in the temple, and went about to kill me.

The only reason the Jews attacked and tried to kill Paul was because he obeyed and preached Christ. Festus had found it difficult to understand why Paul had been arrested in the first place, but it was important that he find out to conclude his report to Rome. Agrippa's understanding of the Jews provided him with special insight into why they would have such animosity toward a former rabbi who offered an equal footing to the Gentile believers.

22 Having therefore obtained help of God, I continue unto this day, witnessing both to small and great, saying none other things than those which the prophets and Moses did say should come: 23 That Christ should suffer, and that he should be the first that should rise from the dead, and should shew light unto the people, and to the Gentiles.

Because of divine help that had protected him and because he was doing God's work, Paul was enabled to witness "unto this day" to all ranks of people, "both great and small." What he proclaimed was only what Moses and the prophets had said should come: "That Christ should suffer, rise, shew light to the people, and to the Gentiles." In these things, he had the support of Moses and the prophets, and for these things he was accused. He was not in disagreement with the Law of Moses but preached its true meaning.

27 King Agrippa, believest thou the prophets? I know that thou believest. 28 Then Agrippa said unto Paul, Almost thou persuadest me to be a Christian. 29 And Paul said, I would to God, that not only thou, but also all that hear me this day, were both almost, and altogether such as I am, except these bonds.

King Agrippa professed to believe in the prophets. Yet those very prophets, as Paul had shown, testified to all the facts of the career of Jesus of Nazareth and His claims to Messiahship. This personal appeal deeply moved the king, as

his reply shows: "Almost thou persuadest me to be a Christian." The king, like Felix (24:35), was deeply moved; the fact that he and Festus decided that Paul was not a transgressor (v. 32) shows that they were favorably impressed; it was no occasion for an ironical answer, and Paul took the remark as in earnest and added still another appeal.

Paul's reply to Agrippa is courteous but of intense earnestness, a last effort to save souls that were deeply stirred. He would that the king and governor, and indeed all Jews and Gentiles, share his hope of a glorious inheritance and were, like himself, at peace with God—such as he, "except these bonds." It is probable that his chains were then hanging upon his arms and that he indicated them by a gesture.

DAILY BIBLE READINGS

M: Paul Stands before Festus
Acts 25:1-12
T: Festus Explains Paul's Case
Acts 25:13-22
W: Paul Comes before Agrippa
Acts 25:23-27
T: Paul Begins His Defense
Acts 26:1-8
F: Paul Tells of His Conversion
Acts 26:9-18
S: I Was Not Disobedient
Acts 26:19-23
S: Paul's Appeal to Agrippa
Acts 26:24-32

TEACHING TIPS

February 16
Bible Study Guide 12

1. Words You Should Know

A. Well reported (Acts 16:2)—From the Greek word *martureo,* pronounced **marr-toor-REH-oh**, meaning to be a witness. In this case, it implies commendation of one's character.

B. Proof (Philippians 2:22)—Convincing evidence that satisfies a test or examination and demonstrates approved character.

C. Apostle (1 Timothy 1:1)—From the Greek word *apostololos,* which literally means one sent forth.

2. Teacher Preparation

Begin prepararation by reading all the FOCAL VERSES for the lesson. Then read through the entire Bible Study Guide, making note of specific highlights you will want to emphasize.

3. Starting the Lesson

A. Have a student lead the class in prayer, using the LESSON AIM.

B. Ask the students to share their experiences from last week's MAKE IT HAPPEN assignment and what they learned from their DAILY BIBLE READINGS during the week.

C. Assign one student to read today's IN FOCUS story. Ask students to explain why family is so important to the social and spiritual growth of both the young and the old.

D. Assign four students to read the FOCAL VERSES according to the AT-A-GLANCE outline.

4. Getting into the Lesson

A. The BACKGROUND section will help set the stage for today's lesson. Have students silently read the section and write down their thoughts in the REMEMBER YOUR THOUGHTS section.

B. Refer to the SEARCH THE SCRIPTURES questions as you begin the discussion of the lesson.

C. Discuss the background information in THE PEOPLE, PLACES, AND TIMES section to help students understand the impact of Timothy's mother on his personal and spiritual growth.

5. Relating the Lesson to Life

A. Use the DISCUSS THE MEANING questions to help students observe some relationships between the lesson and their personal situations that can help students put the "meat on the bones."

B. The LESSON IN OUR SOCIETY section should also be used to help students see how the lesson parallels their present-day situation. Ask students what can happen to the youths in their communities who are successfully mentored by those in the church.

C. Share your personal experiences with students. Sometimes students have difficulty believing that teachers may have some questions about spiritual mentoring. If you share your experience with students, they may find it easier to open up and share with you and the other members of the class.

6. Arousing Action

A. Sum up the lesson with the KEEP IN MIND verse. Have students read it in unison while contemplating how they can apply the verse to their everyday lives.

B. Challenge students to follow through on the MAKE IT HAPPEN assignment.

C. Close the class with prayer.

WORSHIP GUIDE

For the Superintendent or Teacher
Theme: Timothy: Valued Helper
Theme Song: "God Has His Hands on Me"
Scripture: 2 Timothy 4:16-18
Song: "My Faith Looks Up to Thee"
Meditation: Thank You, Lord, for Your faithfulness and commitment to my life. Help me to be faithful to You in all that I do this week. In Jesus' name. Amen.

TIMOTHY: VALUED HELPER

Bible Background • ACTS 16:1-5; PHILIPPIANS 2:19-24;
1 TIMOTHY 1:1-3; 2 TIMOTHY 1:1-5
Printed Text • ACTS 16:1-5; PHILIPPIANS 2:19-24;
1 TIMOTHY 1:1-3; 2 TIMOTHY 1:3-5
Devotional Reading • 2 TIMOTHY 2:1-7

LESSON AIM

After today's lesson, students will be able to relate the circumstances of Paul and Timothy's first meeting and ongoing relationship, understand the importance of mentoring younger Christians, and determine to take someone under their wing and contribute to their spiritual growth.

KEEP IN MIND

"But ye know the proof of him, that, as a son with the father, he hath served with me in the gospel" (Philippians 2:22).

FOCAL VERSES

Acts 16:1 Then came he to Derbe and Lystra: and, behold, a certain disciple was there, named Timotheus, the son of a certain woman, which was a Jewess, and believed; but his father was a Greek:

2 Which was well reported of by the brethren that were at Lystra and Iconium.

3 Him would Paul have to go forth with him; and took and circumcised him because of the Jews which were in those quarters: for they knew all that his father was a Greek.

4 And as they went through the cities, they delivered them the decrees for to keep, that were ordained of the apostles and elders which were at Jerusalem.

5 And so were the churches established in the faith, and increased in number daily.

Philippians 2:19 But I trust in the Lord Jesus to send Timotheus shortly unto you, that I also may be

LESSON OVERVIEW

LESSON AIM
KEEP IN MIND
FOCAL VERSES
IN FOCUS
THE PEOPLE, PLACES, AND TIMES
BACKGROUND
AT-A-GLANCE
IN DEPTH
SEARCH THE SCRIPTURES
DISCUSS THE MEANING
LESSON IN OUR SOCIETY
MAKE IT HAPPEN
FOLLOW THE SPIRIT
REMEMBER YOUR THOUGHTS
MORE LIGHT ON THE TEXT
DAILY BIBLE READINGS

of good comfort, when I know your state.

20 For I have no man likeminded, who will naturally care for your state.

21 For all seek their own, not the things which are Jesus Christ's.

22 But ye know the proof of him, that, as a son with the father, he hath served with me in the gospel.

23 Him therefore I hope to send presently, so I shall see how it will go with me.

24 But I trust in the Lord that I also myself shall come shortly.

1 Timothy 1:1 Paul, an apostle of Jesus Christ by the commandment of God our Saviour, and Lord Jesus Christ, which is our hope;

2 Unto Timothy, my own son in the faith: Grace, mercy, and peace, from God our Father and Jesus Christ our Lord.

3 As I besought thee to abide still at Ephesus, when I went into Macedonia, that thou mightest charge some that they teach no other doctrine,

2 Timothy 1:3 I thank God, whom I serve from my forefathers with pure conscience, that without ceasing I have remembrance of thee in my prayers night and day;

4 Greatly desiring to see thee, being mindful of thy tears, that I may be filled with joy;

5 When I call to remembrance the unfeigned faith that is in thee, which dwelt first in thy grandmother Lois, and thy mother Eunice; and I am persuaded that in thee also.

FEB
16TH

IN FOCUS

There is a story of a frail old man who went to live with his son, daughter-in-law, and four-year-old grandson. The old man's hand trembled, his eyesight was blurred, and his step faltered.

The family ate together at the table, but the elderly grandfather's hands and failing eyesight made this difficult. Peas rolled off his spoon onto the floor. When he lifted his glass, milk spilled on the tablecloth. The son and daughter-in-law soon became irritated with the old man's mess. So the son and his wife set a small table in the corner. There Grandfather ate alone while the rest of the family ate at the table. Because the old man had broken a couple of dishes, his food was served to him in a wooden bowl. At mealtime when the family sometimes glanced over in Grandpa's direction, there was an occasional tear in the old man's eye. The four-year old watched all this in silence.

One day the father noticed his son playing with wood scraps on the floor. "What are you making, son?" he asked. The little boy innocently looked up at his dad and replied, "I'm making a little bowl for you and Mama to eat from when I grow up."

That evening, the father took his father's hand and led him back to the family table. For the remainder of his days he ate his meals with the family and no one ever complained when he dropped his fork or spilled his milk.

Family relationships and experiences are where our earliest values are developed. Today's lesson explores the ministry of Timothy, whose character and love for God were developed under the loving guidance of his mother and grandmother.

THE PEOPLE, PLACES, AND TIMES

Eunice. Timothy's mother, who was born Jewish but became a Christian, the wife of a Gentile (Acts 16:1). Influenced by her mother, Lois, Eunice gave Timothy religious instruction (2 Timothy 1:5; 3:14-15), but he was not circumcised until he joined Paul's mission (Acts 16:3; 2 Timothy 3:10-11).

BACKGROUND

On their second missionary journey, Paul and Barnabas got into a heated argument over whether or not to take John Mark with them on the trip. Paul did not want John Mark to accompany them because the young man had deserted them in the middle of their first journey (see Acts 13:13). Paul was not prepared to give John Mark another chance, while Barnabas wanted to give his young cousin another opportunity to prove himself.

The debate became so significant that Paul and Barnabas decided to separate from each other. Barnabas and John Mark sailed for Cyprus, while Paul took Silas with him to Syria and Cilicia (see Acts 15:36-41).

Feelings of remorse about the separation from Barnabas over John Mark may have been what first attracted Paul to Timothy, or it may have simply been that Paul recognized the young man's potential. Whatever the reason, Timothy, whose name means "honored of God," would become a constant companion and beloved friend of the great apostle.

It is appropriate that the last recorded words of Paul are in a letter he wrote to Timothy from his prison cell in Rome. Later, Timothy would also be imprisoned (Hebrews 13:23), but no other details are given and nothing is known of his fate.

AT-A-GLANCE

1. Paul Selects Timothy (Acts 16:1-5)
2. Paul Sends Timothy
(Philippians 2:19-24)
3. Paul Sponsors Timothy
(1 Timothy 1:1-3)
4. Paul Supports Timothy
(2 Timothy 1:3-5)

IN DEPTH

1. Paul Selects Timothy (Acts 16:1-5)

Paul and Silas's first stops were in Derbe and then Lystra. Both cities were in the region of Lycaonia in central Asia Minor and Galatia and within miles of each other. While there, Paul received favorable reports about Timothy from many of the people in the region. Timothy's mother, Eunice, was a Jew and had become a Christian (Acts 16:1). Both she and Lois, Timothy's grandmother, had instructed the young man in the Scriptures (see 2 Timothy 1:5).

As a result, Timothy's exuberance and Christian influence were felt in the community.

Paul wanted Timothy to replace John Mark and join him and Silas on their missionary journey. However, there was one problem that still had to be addressed. Because Timothy's mother was Jewish and his father was a Greek (v. 3), Timothy had not been circumcised. Even though the Jerusalem Council had declared circumcision unnecessary for Gentile believers, Paul had Timothy circumcised. The great apostle felt that, because Timothy was half-Jewish, his not being circumcised could cause other Jews to focus more on the circumcision issue than the Gospel message. With that issue taken care of, Timothy would be able to witness to both Jew and Gentile.

Once Timothy was circumcised, he joined Paul and Silas on their travels through the region of Galatia, proclaiming the Gospel to the Gentiles and reminding them of the ordinances and doctrinal statements that were written by the Jerusalem Council. Those ordinances were concerned with: abstaining from things polluted by idols, sexual immorality, eating things that were strangled, and blood (Acts 15:29).

Paul had his reasons for circumcising Timothy, but Timothy had to volunteer for the procedure. Timothy was willing to undergo this ritual to remove any barriers to his witness for Christ. Sometimes we must be willing to sacrifice our rights to effectively communicate the Gospel message.

2. Paul Sends Timothy (Philippians 2:19-24)

Paul wrote the letter to the Philippians while in prison, either awaiting trial or a verdict, for preaching the Gospel of Christ. The church, which Paul founded on his second missionary journey, was the first church established in Europe. Paul's love for the people of Philippi is evident throughout this epistle, which is one of the most personal letters the apostle wrote.

Even though the apostle was languishing in prison, he wrote this letter to encourage the Philippian believers to keep their eyes on Jesus Christ in the midst of a crooked and perverse generation of people (see vv. 13-15).

Paul realized that he could not personally be with the people to encourage them to hold on their faith,

so he decided to send Timothy. Timothy was with Paul in Rome when the apostle wrote this letter. He traveled with Paul on his second missionary journey when the church in Philippi was established (Acts 16:4-5, 11-40). The young missionary had proven himself to the apostle with the people of Philippi, so he wasn't the least bit hesitant to ask his protege to check on the people.

One reason why Paul wasn't hesitant to send Timothy was that he trusted the church to the Lord Jesus Christ (v. 19). We don't always know people's motives, but if we trust them—and our lives—to the Lord Jesus, we will never go wrong.

The second reason why Paul would send Timothy is because Timothy and he were "likeminded." The Greek word used is *isopsuchos* (pronounced **iss-SAW-soo-kahss**), which comes from two words: *isos*, which means equal, and *psuche* (pronounced **soo-KAY**), which means soul or mind. Paul is saying that he and Timothy were both motivated by their love for Jesus and their desire to give their best to the building of His kingdom.

Paul knew that a lot of believers were too preoccupied with their own needs to spend quality time working for Christ. Paul knew that Timothy was not out for fame and glory for himself. Instead, his motives were his desire to lift up Jesus Christ as well as his concern was for his spiritual father and the churches that he oversaw. Paul was confident that whatever he gave Timothy to give to the people, it would get there.

The apostle was preparing his young apprentice to carry on the ministry in his absence. All believers who work in the church should be mentoring someone to stand in for them when necessary and eventually to replace them.

3. Paul Sponsors Timothy (1 Timothy 1:1-3)

Paul wrote 1 Timothy after the events recorded in Acts 28. The apostle's first Roman imprisonment had apparently ended with his release (2 Timothy 4:16-17). Paul had appointed Timothy as his apostolic representative in Ephesus, and at the time of this writing, Paul was probably in Macedonia (1 Timothy 1:3).

In the letter, Paul calls himself an apostle "by the will of God" (1 Timothy 1:1). This statement refers back to Acts 13:2, where the Holy Spirit commanded, "Separate me Barnabas and Saul for the work whereunto I have called them." He refers to Timothy as "my own son in the faith" (1 Timothy 1:2). Many believe that this phrase refers to the men's spiritual relationship. While in Iconium, Paul may have visited Timothy's home and led the young man to the Lord. In his second letter to Timothy, Paul expresses the depth of their personal relationship by addressing Timothy as "my dearly beloved son" (2 Timothy 1:2). He repeats this phrase in his letter to the Corinthian church, adding, "He is faithful in the Lord" (1 Corinthians 4:17).

The purpose of Paul's first letter to Timothy was to defend the purity of the Gospel from the corruption of false teachers. Many years before, Paul had warned the Ephesian church that false teachers would try to distort the Gospel, and now it was happening. Paul urges Timothy to confront the erroneous teachers and "to command certain men not to teach false doctrines any longer" (1 Timothy 1:3, NIV).

Today, just as in the days of Paul and Timothy, false teachers are distorting the purity of the Gospel. All believers have the responsibility to seek the truth of God for themselves under the guidance of the Holy Spirit and the direction of godly teachers. When we challenge certain interpretations of Scripture, we both grow in our knowledge of Scripture and defend the Gospel message.

4. Paul Supports Timothy (2 Timothy 1:3-7)

Paul's second letter to Timothy was written from a prison cell in Rome toward the end of the great apostle's life around 66 A.D. Paul sensed that his death was near and wrote his spiritual son to encourage him to continue the work of ministry despite the predicament that the apostle was in.

Paul opened his heart to his young apprentice and told him how thankful he was for Timothy's service and friendship and that he prayed constantly for him. The best way any believer can express appreciation for others is to remember them in prayer.

We do not know when Paul and Timothy parted for the last time, but it may have been when Paul was arrested and taken to Rome for his second imprisonment. The tears that Timothy shed at their parting obviously touched the old apostle's heart.

Here Paul expresses to Timothy his desire see

him, and that he remembers the tears the young man shed while in the service of the Lord. It is very probable that Paul had warned Timothy that ministry was not easy and that he would cry many nights. Paul wanted to be with Timothy to hear him share about those times when ministry made him cry. Timothy's personal experiences would have brought the apostle so much joy.

Timothy was experiencing opposition both to his message and to himself as a leader. Paul warned Timothy that he would face persecution, false teachers, confusion, and turmoil in the congregations he would lead. Therefore, it was important that the apostle remind Timothy of some things he had learned but may have forgotten over the course of the years that they had worked together.

Paul knew that no matter what happened, Timothy would never lose hope because he knew that Timothy sincerely trusted in God. The young man's faith had been passed on to him by his mother Eunice and his grandmother Lois. Paul had probably led these women to Christ, and their teachings had produced a harvest of blessing in the young man's life. Paul knew that Timothy's faith would be tested in the days to come, and he wanted Timothy to exhibit the three main characteristics of Christian leadership: power, love, and self-discipline. Paul knew Timothy possessed these qualities because of the Holy Spirit who lived within him.

Like most people of Scripture, Timothy's strengths and weaknesses are evident. He was affectionate (1 Timothy 1:4), loyal (1 Corinthians 16:10; Philippians 2:19ff), and a student of the Word (2 Timothy 3:15). On the other hand, Timothy was fearful (2 Timothy 1:4) and maybe sometimes ashamed of the Gospel.

Most believers are like Timothy. We have areas in which we excel and other areas in which we are lacking. Unfortunately, some people are written off as being ineffective because of their weaknesses. We would all do well to remember that it is the Holy Spirit who empowers all of us to succeed.

SEARCH THE SCRIPTURES

1. When Paul and Silas came to Derbe and Lystra, who did they meet? (Acts 16:1-2)

2. Why did Paul have Timothy circumcised? (vv. 3-4)

3. Why did Paul write to the Corinthian believers? (1 Corinthians 4:14-15)

4. Who was Paul going to send to Corinth to see about the church? (v. 17)

5. Why wasn't Paul afraid to send Timothy to see the Philippian believers? (Philippians 2:19-21)

DISCUSS THE MEANING

1. How important is it for young people to have mentors in the body of Christ? Explain.

2. Why was Timothy's reputation so important to the churches of Corinth and Philippi, where Paul sent him on his behalf? Discuss.

LESSON IN OUR SOCIETY

So often we condemn the youths in our communities because of their actions. How important is it to mentor a young person so that he/she may reach their fullest potential and become what God desires them to be? What specific steps can we take to ensure the mentoring process takes place? Discuss.

MAKE IT HAPPEN

This week, identify a young person or a person new to the faith in your family or church who needs your help. Ask the Lord for specific directions on how you might reach out to this person and positively impact his or her life. Be prepared to share your experiences with the class next week.

FOLLOW THE SPIRIT

What God wants me to do:

_____

_____

REMEMBER YOUR THOUGHTS

Special insights you have learned:

_____

_____

MORE LIGHT ON THE TEXT

Acts 16:1-5; Philippians 2:19-24; 1 Timothy 1:1-3; 2 Timothy 1:3-5

Acts 16:1 Then came he to Derbe and Lystra: and, behold, a certain disciple was there, named Timotheus, the son of a certain woman, which was a Jewess, and believed; but his father was a Greek: 2 Which was well reported of by the brethren that were at Lystra and Iconium.

On their second missionary journey, Paul and Silas traveled north around the tip of the Mediterranean and then westward toward the cities of Derbe and Lystra. On this second journey, the order of the cities listed in the Galatian territory are reversed from the first journey. On their first visit to the Galatian territory, Paul and Barnabas traveled from the west rather than the east.

On this second journey, Paul revisits the cities that had been evangelized during his first journey two or three years earlier. When Paul and Barnabas began their ministry in Lystra, the people had proclaimed them Greek gods. Their short ministry in the Galatian cities ended with Paul's being stoned and left for dead outside the walls of Lystra.

However, one of the fruits of that short, violent time was a young man and his mother. The young man's name was Timothy. Timothy and his mother may have been among the group of disciples that surrounded the apparently lifeless body of the apostle outside the walls of Lystra after Jews from the cities of Iconium and Antioch had stoned Paul (vv. 19-20). The young man certainly would have been among those souls Paul confirmed on his second visit to the city, exhorting them "to continue in the faith" (v. 22).

Timothy's mother was a Jewish Christian. The fact that she had married a Greek and not had her son circumcised leads one to question whether or not she was a practicing Jew before her conversion. Such mixed marriages, though practiced little and disliked by the stricter Jews in Palestine, probably occurred frequently among the Jews of the dispersion, especially in remote districts.

Even at a young age, Timothy was well reported of by the brethren that were at Lystra and Iconium. The phrase "well reported of" is a translation of the Greek verb *martureo,* which in the passive voice means to have a good reputation or good character.

3 Him would Paul have to go forth with him; and took and circumcised him because of the Jews which were in those quarters: for they knew all that his father was a Greek.

During the years Paul was away, Timothy had grown in faith, and Paul decided to take the young man under his wing. He asked Timothy to join him and Silas on their journey. Timothy was the first Gentile who became a missionary after his conversion. Later, Titus would join Paul, but he would not be circumcised because he was a true Gentile (Galatians 2:3).

Mosaic Law commanded that on the eighth day of life, all Hebrew boys were to have the fold of skin covering the end of the penis cut off. This rite was called circumcision. After God reconfirmed His promise to Abraham for the third and last time, the Lord said of Abraham's descendants, "Any uncircumcised male, who has not been circumcised in the flesh, will be cut off from his people; he has broken my covenant" (Genesis 17:14). This meant the uncircumcised Israelite male was not covered by the covenant promise given to Abraham.

The rite of circumcision symbolized submission to God and faith in His promise. However, God also required a "circumcision of the heart" (Deuteronomy 10:16; 30:6; Jeremiah 4:40), which is explained as having a faith-rooted heart and soul and a love for God that is evidenced through obedience to His commands.

Paul would later argue that Abraham was justified by faith even while he was uncircumcised, years before the rite was given. Circumcision was a sign, a seal of the righteousness Abraham had by faith while he was still uncircumcised (Romans 4:11; cf Genesis 15:6-7; 17:10-27).

The act of circumcision was not carried over into the church. However, many Jewish Christians tried to impose circumcision and the Mosaic Law on new Gentile believers (Acts 15:1). But the Jerusalem Council rejected the requirement of circumcision (15:1-29). Paul explained his take on the subject in the letter he later wrote to the Corinthians: "Was a man already circumcised when he was called? He should not become uncircumcised. Was a man uncircumcised when he was called? Circumcision is nothing and uncircumcision is nothing. Keeping God's commands is what matters" (1 Corinthians 7:18-19, paraphrased).

The point of Paul's argument is that God has never been concerned about the symbol of the thing itself. God cares about the reality. It is our heart's response to Him that counts. As Paul would later write, "For we are the circumcision, we who worship by the Spirit of God, who rejoice in Christ Jesus, and who put no confidence in the flesh" (Philippians 3:3, NIV).

In mixed marriages, Jewish mothers were not permitted to circumcise their sons against the Gentile father's wishes. This explains why all the religious heritage of Timothy is traced to the female side of the family (2 Timothy 1:5).

Paul had Timothy circumcised because of his parentage. In the eyes of the Jews, Timothy was a Gentile because his father was a Greek. However, in the eyes of Gentiles, Timothy was a Jew, having been raised in his mother's religion. Paul's methodology was to preach the Gospel to the Jew first and then to the Gentile. But such a course would have been impossible had not Timothy been circumcised. He would have been rejected by the people who later attempted to murder Paul because they imagined he had taken a Greek into the temple (Acts 21:19).

4 And as they went through the cities, they delivered them the decrees for to keep, that were ordained of the apostles and elders which were at Jerusalem. 5 And so were the churches established in the faith, and increased in number daily.

The new threesome continued their ministry in Derbe, Lystra, Iconium, and other cities in Lycaonia, and in Phrygia and Galatia. They advised the churches in these cities and taught rules of Christian conduct to be observed and followed by them, such as those concerning the abstinence of the Gentiles from things offered to idols, from blood, from things strangled, and from fornication (Acts 15:20-29). As a result of these apostolic visits, the churches were strengthened and the number of believers multiplied daily.

Philippians 2:19 But I trust in the Lord Jesus to send Timotheus shortly unto you, that I also may be of good comfort, when I know your state. 20 For I have no man likeminded, who will naturally care for your state.

The letter to the church in Philippi differs from most of Paul's letters. It contains less logic and more of the apostle's heart. The letter is distinguished by the absence of didactical teaching and the presence of a tender affection that is more apparent than in other of Paul's letters.

The church in Philippi was founded in 50 or 51

A.D., and the account of its establishment is given in Acts 16. Paul's letter to the church was written from Rome during Paul's first imprisonment, sometime around 63 A.D. The mention of his bonds, of the palace or praetorian camp (1:12), and of Caësar's household (4:22) as well as other references (1:25; 2:24) all show that Paul was in the Roman capital at the time of writing.

In Philippians 2:19, Paul turns to personal matters concerning the church. He planned to send Timothy and Epaphroditus (v. 25) to minister and report back to him on the church's progress. He looked forward to receiving encouraging news from the Philippian church. The Greek verb *eupsycheo,* translated here as "be of good comfort," is probably better translated, "so I may be encouraged when I learn of your condition."

The old apostle describes Timothy, his young apprentice, as being "likeminded." This is a translation of the Greek adjective *isppychos.* This word combines *iso,* meaning equal, and *phyche,* meaning mind or soul, and thus can be translated as "equal-minded." The word means to be inspired by the same motives or to share like character.

21 For all seek their own, not the things which are Jesus Christ's.

The expression "all" (Greek *pantes)* is limited and does not include "most of the brothers in the Lord," who have been encouraged to speak the Word of God more courageously and fearlessly (1:14). The people Paul refers to here were more concerned with popular applause and the honor and glory of men. One such person was Demas, who, "loving this present world" (2 Timothy 4:10), deserted the imprisoned apostle in his time of need.

22 But ye know the proof of him, that, as a son with the father, he hath served with me in the gospel.

Timothy had traveled with Paul for several years and had proved himself a trustworthy minister of the Gospel. The word "proof" is from the Greek word *dokimos,* meaning tried as metals are by fire and thus purified; hence, to be approved as acceptable in the furnace of adversity.

23 Him therefore I hope to send presently, so I shall see how it will go with me. 24 But I trust in the Lord that I also myself shall come shortly.

The phrase, "shall see how it will go with me" expresses the apostle's confusion regarding his ultimate fate. Whether he would be set free or called to suffer martyrdom for Christ's sake was a matter that he expected to be determined in a very short time. Whatever the outcome, he fully expected Timothy to be spared. Paul maintained a secret hope that he would be delivered from imprisonment; if that hope was realized, his intention was to visit the church himself.

1 Timothy 1:1 Paul, an apostle of Jesus Christ by the commandment of God our Saviour, and Lord Jesus Christ, which is our hope; 2 Unto Timothy, my own son in the faith: Grace, mercy, and peace, from God our Father and Jesus Christ our Lord.

When Paul wrote the first letter to Timothy from Macedonia (1:3), he was on his way to Nicopolis (see Titus 3:12). Paul had left the young Timothy in charge of the work at Ephesus. The apostle greatly desired to visit Timothy (3:14; 4:13), but in the meantime this letter would serve to guide Timothy in his personal conduct and pastoral responsibilities.

One of the objectives of Paul's first letter to Timothy was to strengthen Timothy's authority, so Paul writes as an apostle. His apostolic office gave him authority over overseers and deacons of the various churches. The word "apostle," from the Greek word *apostololos,* literally means one sent forth. Paul did not meet the qualifications of apostleship as described by Peter: "men which have companied with us all the time that the Lord Jesus went in and out among us, Beginning from the baptism of John, unto that same day that he was taken up from us" (Acts 1:21-22). However, Paul had been commissioned directly by the Lord Jesus Himself after His ascension to carry the Gospel to the Gentiles.

Certain Judaizing believers claimed that Paul was inferior to Peter and the other apostles. Paul uses the phrase, "by the commandment of God" to emphasize that his appointment did not come from the apostles and that he was independent of them. The Lord sent him to the Gentiles, as the other apostles were sent to the Jews (Acts 9:15).

Although the phrase "God our Saviour" (Greek *Theou soteros hemon*) is frequently employed in the Old Testament, it is unique in the New Testament and is used only in the pastoral Epistles (See also 2:3; 4:10; Titus 1:3; 2:10; 3:4). One of the most interesting Old Testament uses of this title occurs in Isaiah: "I, even I, am the LORD; and beside me there is no saviour" (Isaiah 43:11). Since God proclaims that beside Him there is no saviour, how is it that Paul refers to Jesus as Lord and Saviour (Philippians 3:20; Titus 1:4)? The answer is that the two are one. Referring to Jesus as Lord and Saviour is a confirmation of His deity and an affirmation of Trinitarian doctrine.

The apostle refers to Timothy as "my own son in the faith" because the young man was converted to Christianity as a result of Paul's ministry. "My own" is a translation of the Greek word *gnesios,* which properly means lawfully begotten, true, or genuine.

3 As I besought thee to abide still at Ephesus, when I went into Macedonia, that thou mightest charge some that they teach no other doctrine,

On his previous visit to Ephesus, Paul thought it necessary to leave a trusted minister in the city to counteract the errors that were arising there. The apostle urged Timothy to stay behind as his representative. One of Timothy's responsibilities was to ensure "that they teach no other doctrine" other than the Gospel that they had been taught. This phrase is all one word in the Greek, *heterodidaskalein.* It is a compound of *heteros,* meaning different, and *didaskaleo,* meaning to teach. The other doctrine referred to here is described as "fables and endless genealogies" (v. 4). These fables and genealogies were mythical legends added to Old Testament history.

2 Timothy 1:3 I thank God, whom I serve from my forefathers with pure conscience, that without ceasing I have remembrance of thee in my prayers night and day;

When Paul wrote his second letter to Timothy, he was imprisoned in Rome as a result of the Christian persecution under Rome (see vv. 8, 16). He realized that the time of his death was drawing near (4:6-8) and penned this intensely personal letter to his young son in the faith.

The phrase, "whom I serve from my forefathers" explains how Paul, like Timothy (v. 5), had been taught by his parents to fear and serve the Lord. Even before he became a Christian, Paul tried his best to serve God (see Acts 23:1, 24:14; Romans 11:23-24, 28). The word "forefathers," from the Greek word *progonos,* is an adjective meaning born before. It generally refers to living parents or grandparents but can also mean ancestor.

4 Greatly desiring to see thee, being mindful of thy tears, that I may be filled with joy; 5 When I call to remembrance the unfeigned faith that is in thee, which dwelt first in thy grandmother Lois, and thy mother Eunice; and I am persuaded that in thee also.

There is something pitiable in the language Paul uses here. "Greatly desiring to see thee" expresses how much the imprisoned apostle misses his young protege. The lonely prisoner recalls Timothy's tears at their last parting and feels a yearning desire to see and counsel him face to face once more. When Paul thought back to Timothy's youth, he recalled the faith instilled in Timothy at an early age by his mother and grandmother and he spoke with confidence concerning Timothy's continuation in the faith.

DAILY BIBLE READINGS

M: Paul Takes Timothy with Him
Acts 16:1-5
T: I Have No One Like Him
Philippians 2:19-24
W: A Loyal Child in the Faith
1 Timothy 1:1-5
T: A Man of Sincere Faith
2 Timothy 1:1-7
F: Timothy and Silas Stay in Berea
Acts 17:10-15
S: Paul Sends Timothy to Encourage
1 Thessalonians 3:1-6
S: Come to Me Soon
2 Timothy 4:9-15

TEACHING TIPS

February 23
Bible Study Guide 13

1. Words You Should Know

A. Persuaded (Acts 18:4)—To move or influence by kind words or motives.

B. Mighty (v. 24)—From a Greek word (*dunatos*, pronounced **doo-nuh-TAHSS**) meaning powerful or able. Also refers to someone who is capable.

2. Teacher Preparation

Plan to arrive in class about 30 minutes early. Spend some time in prayer for your students and today's lesson. Make sure your classroom is set up the way you like it. When your students arrive, greet them individually at the door and tell them how much you enjoyed studying this quarter's lessons with them.

3. Starting the Lesson

A. Open the class in prayer, focusing on the LESSON AIM and thanking God for the opportunity to study His Word.

B. Ask the students to share their favorite New Testament personality and why. Ask the students to identify some of the similarities of the characters and some of their main differences. How did these similarities and differences affect the growth of the church?

4. Getting into the Lesson

A. Have students silently read the FOCAL VERSES. Then review the SEARCH THE SCRIPTURES questions.

B. Ask students to discuss why it was necessary for Paul, Aquila and Priscilla to meet. How much of their lives influenced Paul's ministry and helped him focus on the wider picture of ministry? Discuss.

5. Relating the Lesson to Life

A. Divide the students into three groups and assign each group a section of the IN DEPTH commentary. Allow five minutes for students to discuss their sections and prepare a summary of the key points. Bring the class back together and assign one person from each group to present their findings.

B. The LESSON IN OUR SOCIETY article will also help students to understand the specific points in the lesson and how they can apply to us today. Ask students to talk about the communities in which they live and whether or not there is a need for more Aquilas and Priscillas in society.

C. Read THE PEOPLE, PLACES, AND TIMES to give students the opportunity to note some of the similarities in their own communities with that of Paul's.

6. Arousing Action

A. Sum up the lesson with the KEEP IN MIND verse. Have students read it in union. Challenge the class to commit the verse to memory to remind themselves of the importance of influencing others in ministry.

B. Challenge students to make use of the MAKE IT HAPPEN assignment. It is important that they apply the truths they've learned today to their individual lives.

WORSHIP GUIDE

For the Superintendent or Teacher
Theme: Priscilla and Aquila: Partners in the Gospel
Theme Song: "I'm a Soldier in the Army of the Lord"
Scripture: Luke 24:28-32
Song: "Use Me to Be a Blessing, Lord"
Confession of Faith: Lord, we thank You for the opportunities You give us to work as a team to accomplish Your will. Help us to be faithful and committed to the call that You have upon our lives for accomplishing Your will. In Jesus' name. Amen.

FEB 23RD

PRISCILLA AND AQUILA: PARTNERS IN THE GOSPEL

Bible Background • ACTS 18:1-4, 24-26; ROMANS 16:3-4;
1 CORINTHIANS 16:19; 2 TIMOTHY 4:19
Printed Text • ACTS 18:1-4, 24-26; ROMANS 16:3-4;
1 CORINTHIANS 16:19; 2 TIMOTHY 4:19
Devotional Reading: EPHESIANS 4:1-13

LESSON AIM

After studying today's lesson, students should be able to relate the story of Paul's meeting and ongoing relationship with Aquila and Priscilla; understand how working together in ministry or a profession can contribute to marital relationships; and determine to find an area of ministry, work, or recreation they can share with their spouse.

KEEP IN MIND

"Greet Priscilla and Aquila my helpers in Christ Jesus: Who have for my life laid down their own necks: unto whom not only I give thanks, but also all the churches of the Gentiles" (Romans 16:3-4).

FOCAL VERSES

Acts 18:1 After these things Paul departed from Athens, and came to Corinth:

2 And found a certain Jew named Aquila, born in Pontus, lately come from Italy, with his wife Priscilla; (because that Claudius had commanded all Jews to depart from Rome:) and came unto them.

3 And because he was of the same craft, he abode with them, and wrought: for by their occupation they were tentmakers.

4 And he reasoned in the synagogue every sabbath, and persuaded the Jews and the Greeks.

LESSON OVERVIEW

LESSON AIM
KEEP IN MIND
FOCAL VERSES
IN FOCUS
THE PEOPLE, PLACES,
AND TIMES
BACKGROUND
AT-A-GLANCE
IN DEPTH
SEARCH THE SCRIPTURES
DISCUSS THE MEANING
LESSON IN OUR SOCIETY
MAKE IT HAPPEN
FOLLOW THE SPIRIT
REMEMBER YOUR THOUGHTS
MORE LIGHT ON THE TEXT
DAILY BIBLE READINGS

18:24 And a certain Jew named Apollos, born at Alexandria, an eloquent man, and mighty in the scriptures, came to Ephesus.

25 This man was instructed in the way of the Lord; and being fervent in the spirit, he spake and taught diligently the things of the Lord, knowing only the baptism of John.

26 And he began to speak boldly in the synagogue: whom when Aquila and Priscilla had heard, they took him unto them, and expounded unto him the way of God more perfectly.

Romans 16:3 Greet Priscilla and Aquila my helpers in Christ Jesus:

4 Who have for my life laid down their own necks: unto whom not only I give thanks, but also all the churches of the Gentiles.

1 Corinthians 16:19 The churches of Asia salute you. Aquila and Priscilla salute you much in the Lord, with the church that is in their house.

2 Timothy 4:19 Salute Priscilla and Aquila, and the household of Onesiphorus.

IN FOCUS

A young man noticed an elderly couple sit down to lunch at a restaurant. He saw that they only ordered one meal and an extra drinking cup. As he watched, the elderly gentleman carefully divided the hamburger in half, then counted out the fries, one for him, one for her, until each had half of them.

Then he poured half of the soft drink into the extra cup and set that in front of his wife. Then the old man began to eat, and his wife sat watching, with her hands folded in her lap. The young man decided to ask if they would allow him to purchase another meal for them so that they didn't have to split theirs. The old gentleman said, "Oh, no. We've been married 50 years, and everything has always been and will always be shared, 50/50."

The young man then asked the wife if she was going to eat, and she replied, "Not yet. It's his turn with the teeth."

This cute little story illustrates the commitment that goes into making a marriage partnership successful. In today's lesson, we will look at the marriage partnership of Aquila and Priscilla, a godly couple who dedicated themselves to the ministry of the Gospel.

THE PEOPLE, PLACES, AND TIMES

Claudius. The fourth Roman emperor, who assumed power after Gaius Caligula's assassination (41 A.D.). His weak constitution and ill health contributed to the emergence of rich and powerful freedmen. Though generally conciliatory toward the Jews, he expelled some from Rome because of rioting (see Acts 18:2).

Corinth. As a major city of antiquity, located on the isthmus between mainland Greece and the Peloponnesus, it was founded by Greeks in the tenth century B.C. However, in 44 B.C. Julius Caesar undertook refining the city, naming it Colonia Laus Julia Corinthiensis and populating it with Italian freedmen. Latin seems to dominate the public inscriptions of the city well into the second century A.D., although most of the people probably spoke Greek by the time Paul arrived around 50 A.D.

In 27 A.D., Corinth was named capital of the senatorial province of Achaia and seat of the ruling proconsul. Corinth was an important commercial center, and Jewish communities were well established in the city. The Apostle Paul arrived in the city on his first visit, met Aquila and Priscilla, and preached in the synagogue despite a suit brought against him by some Jews before Gallio, the proconsul. Apollos also visited Corinth (Acts 18:27—19:1; 1 Corinthians 1:12; 3:3-9; 4:6), which may have contributed to the factionalism and difficulties that Paul addressed in his letters to Corinth. Also, Paul may have written his letter to the Romans while living in Corinth. (*Harper's Bible Dictionary*, 1985, pp. 173, 182-3.)

BACKGROUND

Luke, the author of the Acts of the Apostles, portrays the husband and wife team of Aquila and Priscilla as an ideal model of Christianity. They are friendly, hospitable, and generous. Aquila was a tentmaker who traveled extensively throughout the New Testament world with his wife Priscilla (see Acts 18:2-28: 1 Corinthians 16:19). It is also suggested that Priscilla may have been a woman who had inherited wealth and held tremendous influence in her community. This may be one reason why she is often mentioned before her husband in Scripture.

The Bible does not say how Paul met this couple, but it is clear that the apostle formed a friendship with Aquila and Priscilla. Through their influence and friendship, Paul was able to continue his missionary journey while leaving a faithful ministry team in Ephesus to preach the Gospel on his—and Jesus'—behalf.

AT-A-GLANCE

1. Paul Meets Aquila and Priscilla
(Acts 18:1-4)
2. Apollos Meets Aquila and Priscilla
(vv. 24-26)
3. Paul Salutes Aquila and Priscilla
(Romans 16:3-4; 1 Corinthians 16:19; 2 Timothy 4:19)

IN DEPTH

1. Paul Meets Aquila and Priscilla (Acts 18:1-4)

Paul ministered in Athens, sharing the Good News with the people. Some believed, while others were still unsure of the power of the Gospel.

But Paul didn't let that deter him from his missionary journey. His next stop was Corinth, approximately 50 miles west of Athens. While there, Paul met a Jewish-Christian couple named Aquila and Priscilla.

Along with his wife Priscilla, Aquila had lived in Italy for a while. Aquila was born in Pontus, a province of Asia Minor that stretches along the southern shore of the Black Sea from Bithynia to Armenia. Many Jews lived throughout Pontus, and by 100 A.D., Christianity had caused so much unrest in the province that the Jews became a permanent minority in the area.

Aquila and Priscilla were Hebrew Christians who had to leave the Roman province because Claudius, the fourth Roman emperor, wrote an edict that commanded that all Jews be expelled. It is not clear how Paul met this couple, but we know that God had a divine purpose for their paths crossing.

Although Paul was a scholar, like every Jewish male child he was taught the trade of tentmaking to earn a living. The Scriptures affirm that Aquila and Priscilla were also tentmakers, so it is quite probable that Paul felt a kindred spirit with this couple. The three of them worked at their tentmaking trade during the week, while Paul engaged in ministry on the Sabbath, preaching to both Jews and Gentiles in the synagogue.

Tents were portable shelters made of cloth or animal skins. They were often used by soldiers as living quarters. Some tents were made by weaving goat hairs together, while others were made of piecemeal materials like leather.

Most would agree that Paul was a great apostle and evangelist, but dedicated friends helped Paul achieve many of his accomplishments. Christian friends, like Aquila and Priscilla, are vitally important to ministry and evangelism. It was through people like this godly couple that Paul learned firsthand what it means to "bear ye one another's burdens and so fulfill the law of Christ" (Galatians 6:2). God's church is not made of brick and mortar; it is made of people who are co-dependent on one another and Christ. It is possible that God will place people of "like precious faith" (2 Peter 1:1) together to do a specific work

in a particular region at a particular time. Our responsibility is to make ourselves available to God's call and God's people.

2. Apollos Meets Aquila and Priscilla (vv. 24-26)

Paul remained in Corinth more than 18 months, teaching the Word of God and making tents to support himself. Paul made quite a few friends and enemies in the city, and he and Aquila and Priscilla became very close.

However, Paul was on a divine timetable, and there were other cities that needed his ministry. So Paul left Corinth and traveled southeast to Syria along with Priscilla and Aquila. Before leaving for Syria, Paul shaved his head because he had taken the Nazarite vow at Cenchrea, a harbor city approximately seven miles east of Corinth.

The word "Nazarite" means one who is separated unto the Lord. By the terms of the vow, a person would voluntarily separate himself for a specific period of time. Once the days of the separation were fulfilled, the Nazarite would offer a sacrifice unto the Lord and shave his head as a sign of his purification and sacrifice (see Numbers 6:13-21). Paul may have felt the need to take the vow since he was going further into Gentile territory to win many people to Christ.

When Paul, Aquila, and Priscilla arrived in Ephesus, they parted company. Paul went immediately into the synagogue to preach to the Jews before continuing his missionary journey. Aquila and Priscilla remained in the city to do ministry.

The Bible doesn't give specific information, but it is possible that Aquila and Priscilla had a hand in the development of the church in Ephesus, nurturing and overseeing the people. Sometime later, Apollos, a Jew who was born in Alexandria, came to Ephesus. Apollos must have been a man excited about the Word of God and the Lord Jesus Christ, because Luke describes him as "an eloquent man, [and] mighty in the Scriptures" (v. 24).

Apollos possessed great biblical skills, having the ability to teach the Word diligently, even though he only knew about the baptism of John. However, Apollos' ministry caught the attention of Aquila and Priscilla. They were impressed with his teaching and his boldness as he spoke in the synagogue, but they realized that Apollos lacked a fuller understanding of Jesus.

Aquila and Priscilla took to Apollos and became his mentor in the things of the Spirit. We all need spiritual "mentors" who can help us expound the Word of God in a more complete way. We should not be afraid to ask others who may be more spiritually mature to help us get a better understanding of the Scriptures.

3. Paul Salutes Aquila and Priscilla (Romans 16:3-4; 1 Corinthians 16:19; 2 Timothy 4:19)

At the close of his letter to the Romans, the Apostle Paul greets 26 people by name. At the top of this list is the ministry team of Priscilla and Aquila. He refers to the couple as "my helpers in Christ Jesus." The word "helper" is probably better translated as "companion in labor" or "fellow worker." The couple did much more than assist Paul with his ministry. They were actively involved in their own ministry. In describing them as "my helpers," Paul is probably looking back to their love and aid to him when he arrived in Corinth. When Paul left Corinth for Ephesus, this godly couple packed up their belongings and their tent-making business and moved with him. Then they helped him to establish a new church, and eventually they stayed behind to care for the Ephesian church when Paul returned to Antioch. In Paul's first letter to the Corinthian church, he again mentions a church in their home and sends the couple's greetings to the church there.

The apostle says that the couple "laid down their own necks," or risked their lives in his behalf. Scripture does not record the incident where this took place, but at some point the couple was willing to sacrifice their own lives for the Gospel. At the time of the writings the couple was back in Rome conducting church services in their home. It was common for early churches to meet in the homes of believers. The fact that Aquila and Priscilla opened the door of their home to the Roman congregation is another indication of a willingness to give their all to the Lord.

In Paul's last letter to Timothy before his death, the apostle writes, "Salute Priscilla and Aquila" (2 Timothy 4:19). Timothy was the leader at the church in Ephesus, and Aquila and Priscilla had stayed on to help him. The couple were dedicated to God's ministry, not God's ministers. They worked just as hard under the leadership of Timothy as they had under the leadership of Paul.

It is the faithfulness of people like Aquila and Priscilla that makes ministry a joy for others. The effectiveness of their ministry says a lot about their personal relationship with each other and with God. Their hospitality became the doorway of salvation for many.

Christian homes and solid Christian marriages remain two of the best tools for spreading the Gospel. Husband-and-wife teams can be tremendous blessings for the body of Christ.

SEARCH THE SCRIPTURES

1. Why had Aquilla and Priscilla left their home in Rome and relocated to Corinth? (Acts 18:2)

2. Paul and Aquila were both trained craftsmen. What craft did they practice to earn their living? (v. 3)

3. Who is the young man that Aquila and Priscilla took under their wing to mentor after hearing him preach in the synagogue at Ephesus? (vv. 24-26)

4. What phrase did Paul use to describe Aquila and Priscilla's ministry with him? (Romans 16:3)

5. Where did members of the church in Ephesus conduct their services? (1 Corinthians 16:9)

DISCUSS THE MEANING

1. Many people believe that working with one's spouse professionally or in ministry can cause problems in the home because work problems or ministry disagreements follow the couple home and cause friction. Do you believe this? If so, why? If not, why not?

2. What are some of the reasons that people do not take on the responsibility of mentoring younger people? How should these issues be resolved?

LESSON IN OUR SOCIETY

More than half the marriages in the United

States end in divorce. List some of the positive features and negative hindrances that can affect husband-and-wife businesses/partnerships (and marriages). Report on your list next week.

MAKE IT HAPPEN

In today's lesson, Aquila and Priscilla took young Apollos under their wing and mentored him in the Gospel. Examine your life to see who you are influencing in the body of Christ. If you can't think of anyone, ask God to help you make a specific contribution in someone's life this week. Perhaps making a phone call or writing a letter to lift someone's spirit is a good place to start. Before the class is over today, make a commitment to find someone this week.

FOLLOW THE SPIRIT

What God wants me to do:

_____

_____

REMEMBER YOUR THOUGHTS

Special insights you have learned:

_____

_____

MORE LIGHT ON THE TEXT
Acts 18:1-4, 24-26; Romans 16:3-4; 1
Corinthians 16:19; 2 Timothy 4:19

Acts 18:1 After these things Paul departed from Athens, and came to Corinth:

After the apostle's debate with the philosophers and his sermon in the Areopagus (Acts 17:16), "Paul departed from Athens, and came to Corinth." Corinth, located about seven miles from the Aegean seashore, abounded in riches and luxury and was well known for its debauchery. The city was originally called Ephyra, and many believe the city received its new name because of multitudes of prostitutes there. The Greek phrase *corai entha* means "here are girls, or whores." The centerpiece of the city was the temple of Venus/Aphrodite, the goddess of love and beauty, where no less than a thousand prostitutes provided services.

2 And found a certain Jew named Aquila, born in Pontus, lately come from Italy, with his wife Priscilla; (because that Claudius had commanded all Jews to depart from Rome:) and came unto them.

Jewish guilds always kept together, whether in the street or in the synagogue, so Paul would have little trouble finding a place to ply his trade in the city and to meet others who were similarly employed. He was in such a guild when he first met the husband-and-wife team, Aquila and Priscilla. The couple would prove to be valuable assets to the apostle's ministry.

"Aquila" seems to have been his Roman name, which he had taken or was given him while he was at Rome. His Jewish name may have been "Nesher," which signifies an eagle, as does "Aquila." Aquila was born in Pontus, a country in Asia where many Jews lived. Though he was born in a heathen country, his parents were Jews. The name "Priscilla" literally means primitive; thus, "worthy of veneration and honor" as belonging to the good old days.

The couple had recently arrived in Corinth from Italy because Claudius, the Roman emperor, "had commanded all Jews to depart from Rome." This Claudius was the fourth emperor of Rome, and this decree was passed sometime between the ninth and eleventh year of his reign, about the year 51 or 54 A.D. It is believed that Claudius issued his edict because the Jews in Rome were continually at odds with the Christians about Jesus being the Messiah. Claudius, who was a timid person, was afraid that the conflict would lead to unrest, so he banished all the Jews from Rome. At that time, heathens saw no difference between Christians and Jews, so they were all ordered to leave. As a result, Aquila and Priscilla were obliged to leave Rome and come to Corinth. When Paul found out about the couple, he came and visited them and stayed in their home.

3 And because he was of the same craft, he abode with them, and wrought: for by their occupation they were tentmakers.

What attracted Paul to the couple was a shared skill. In Greek, the phrase "same craft" is one word, *homotechnos*. The word is composed of the prefix *homo,* meaning same, and the suffix *technos,* meaning trade. Like Paul, Aquila and Priscilla were tentmakers who "wrought," or worked with their own hands to support themselves. Paul was a stranger in Corinth, and as yet there was no church to support him. However, when he was there he would take nothing from the converts because he knew that false teachers might rise up among them and accuse him of greed.

Tentmaking was a prosperous trade. The tents were either for the soldiers or the general public. The soldier's tents were made of sackcloths of hair, of leather, or of the skins of various animals sewed together. Other tents were canopies made of linen or other materials and were erected in the summer to shade and screen people from the heat of the sun.

4 And he reasoned in the synagogue every sabbath, and persuaded the Jews and the Greeks.

There was a synagogue in Corinth where the Jews of the city met together for worship on the seventh day of the week, which was their "sabbath." Each Friday Paul went to the synagogue and "reasoned" with the Jews out of the Scriptures concerning the person and offices, incarnation, obedience, sufferings, and death of Christ, and the redemption and salvation that came through Him. The word "reasoned" is from the Greek *dialegomai.* The word combines the prefix *dia,* meaning from or separation, with the word *lego,* meaning to speak. The literal translation is "to speak back and forth" or "to intelligently dispute."

The effect of Paul's reasoning was that many Jewish and Gentile proselytes who attended synagogue worship were convinced by his arguments, were convinced of the truth of the Gospel and embraced it. The word "persuaded" from the Greek *peitho* means to convince or affect by kind words or motives. The word here is in the imperfect tense of continuous (not completed) action. A better interpretation is "trying to persuade," especially since we know that Paul did not succeed in persuading everyone.

Acts 18:24 And a certain Jew named Apollos, born at Alexandria, an eloquent man, and mighty in the scriptures, came to Ephesus.

After Paul's departure from Ephesus while Aquila and Priscilla were there, one of John's disciples named Apollos arrived in the city and began preaching the Word. Apollos was a cultured, educated Jew from Alexandria, a thriving Egyptian metropolis that was home to a great number of Jews. "Apollos" is a Greek name that means a destroyer or a youthful god of music.

Luke describes the young man as being "eloquent." The Greek word for eloquence is *logio*, which means skilled in speech as well as wise and learned. Apollos was also "mighty in the Scriptures." In this case, the Greek adjective *dunatos* means capable rather than strong. The word "Scriptures" refers to the Old Testament, particularly the prophecies concerning the Messiah. Apollos had thoroughly read them, carefully examined them, could readily cite them, had great knowledge of them, and was capable of explaining them; he was "skillful in the Scriptures."

25 This man was instructed in the way of the Lord; and being fervent in the spirit, he spake and taught diligently the things of the Lord, knowing only the baptism of John.

The word "instruction" suggests that Apollo's parents, who may have been disciples of John, trained him in the Scriptures. Apollo had only been taught the rudiments of the Christian faith, here called the "things of the Lord." Apollos knew of Christ, but he did not know Christ as Lord and Saviour. In spite of his incomplete training, Apollo was "fervent (Greek *zeo*) in the spirit." In other words, Apollos was boiling with enthusiasm to preach the Good News. The word "spirit" in this case refers to Apollos' own spirit; in other words, his soul burned with zeal for the glory of God, and he diligently proclaimed the Word according to the measure of grace and knowledge he had received. Apollo taught the people all he knew of the person, work, and office of the Lord Jesus.

The phrase "knowing only the baptism of John" must be understood as the entire ministry of John, including John's doctrine of repentance and remission of sins, which looked forward to the Christ who was to come as well as to His baptism. Scholars are not in agreement, but whatever Apollos was lacking he received from Aquila and Priscilla.

26 And he began to speak boldly in the synagogue: whom when Aquila and Priscilla had heard, they took him unto them, and expounded unto him the way of God more perfectly.

Apollo spoke out boldly in the synagogue without fear of the Jews. While attending a synagogue meeting, Aquila and Priscilla heard Apollo preach and observed that there was some deficiency in his message. Being concerned for the young minister's message, they "took him unto them" or "they took him aside" when he came out of the synagogue and privately conversed with him. Over time they "expounded [or explained] unto him the way of God more perfectly." The word "perfectly" is a translation of the Greek word *akribos* and means accurately. In other words, Aquila and Priscilla supplied the knowledge that Apollos was lacking.

Aquila and Priscilla had received a considerable measure of evangelical revelation and knowledge from the Apostle Paul during their time together, and they imparted their knowledge to Apollos. Later, Apollos would became one of Paul's trusted friends and companions (1 Corinthians 16:12; Titus 3:13). He was such an effective preacher that some of the Corinthians put him before Paul and Peter (1 Corinthians 1:12; 3:4-6). There are many who credit Apollos with writing the epistle to the Hebrews.

Romans 16:3 Greet Priscilla and Aquila my helpers in Christ Jesus:

When Priscilla's name is mentioned before her husband's, it is without design, for sometimes he is put before her, as in Acts 18:2, 26 and 1 Corinthians 16:19. Because it is a rule with the Jews that there is "neither first nor last" in the Scriptures, strict order is not always observed. Therefore, the suggestion by some that she was first converted or was the leader of the church in their home is uncertain.

The date that the couple left Ephesus and returned to Rome is unknown, but at that time either Claudius had died or his edict that ordered the Jews to depart from Rome had been revoked. The couple returned again to Rome, and they were there when the apostle wrote this epistle to the church in Rome. Paul salutes them and refers to them as "my helpers in Christ Jesus." The couple assisted Paul in spreading the Gospel and promoting the kingdom and Lordship of Christ. They were helpful in encouraging young converts and comforting them with their own experiences and therefore they were greatly appreciated by the apostle in the work of the Lord Jesus.

4 Who have for my life laid down their own necks: unto whom not only I give thanks, but also all the churches of the Gentiles.

When Paul says that Aquila and Priscilla have "for my life laid down their necks," he is intimating that the couple exposed themselves to great danger to save his life. The allusion is to the ancient practice of beheading, and to some one laying down his head and offering his neck to the executioner in place of another. We should not suppose that Aquila and Priscilla literally did this, but the intent of the expression is that in some way they risked their own lives for Paul's. We are given no further details of this courageous act, but there are a couple of plausible possibilities. The incident may have occurred at the insurrection in Corinth, when the Jews dragged Paul to the judgment seat of Galileo and beat Sosthenes, the ruler of the synagogue before him (Acts 18:17).

Or it might have been in Ephesus, where Demetrius and the craftsmen incited a riot against Paul and his companions (Acts 19:24). Aquila and Priscilla were present at both events and were no doubt actively protecting the apostle. Whatever the case, Paul was very grateful for their heroic assistance.

1 Corinthians 16:19 The churches of Asia salute you. Aquila and Priscilla salute you much in the Lord, with the church that is in their house.

The phrase, "the churches of Asia salute you" indicates that the letter was written from Ephesus during Paul's three-year ministry there with Aquila and Priscilla on his third missionary journey (Acts 20:31). The couple had helped Paul establish the church in Corinth during his 18-month stay there on his second missionary journey (Acts 18:1-17). The church in Ephesus was meeting in the home of Aquila and Priscilla at the time.

2 Timothy 4:19 Salute Priscilla and Aquila, and the household of Onesiphorus.

Paul wrote his first letter to Timothy after the events recorded at the end of Acts. His first Roman imprisonment (Acts 28) apparently ended with the apostle being set free (2 Timothy 4:16-17). Based on the information in the "pastoral letters," Paul eventually returned to Greece and Macedonia. During this time (64-65 A.D.), Paul commissioned Timothy to pastor the church in Ephesus.

The letter of 2 Timothy was the last letter Paul wrote before his death. At the time of its writing, the Roman emperor Nero was attempting to wipe out Christianity in Rome by severely persecuting Christians, and Paul had again been taken prisoner. In the final benediction of Paul's last letter, the apostle salutes Priscilla and Aquila, who were now assisting Timothy in his pastoral ministry.

DAILY BIBLE READINGS

M: They Were Tentmakers
Acts 18:1-10
T: Aquila and Priscilla Teach Apollos
Acts 18:24-28
W: They Risked Their Necks
Romans 16:1-5
T: The Church in Their Home
1 Corinthians 16:13-24
F: Greet Priscilla and Aquila
2 Timothy 4:16-22
S: Maintain the Unity of the Spirit
Ephesians 4:1-8
S: Gifts for Equipping the Saints
Ephesians 4:9-16

NOTES

INTRODUCTION TO MARCH 2003 QUARTER

The Quarter at-a-Glance

JESUS: GOD'S POWER IN ACTION

This quarter's lessons are taken from the Gospel of Mark, a Gospel that emphasizes Jesus' acts. It contains teachings of Jesus, but it is a Gospel of rapid-fire action. Mark presents God's power at work in Jesus to change people's lives. The narrative of the Gospel of Mark moves quickly from one act to another in lightning fashion in a way depicting the swiftness of the power of God and God's ability to respond to those who are need. This is a Gospel of power encounter. In fact, only one discursive teaching is recorded. It portrays Jesus as the doer or the worker of great works. The Book of Mark can be divided into three movements: The first unit focuses on Jesus' early ministry. The second unit examines Jesus' death and resurrection. The third unit presents Jesus' responses to the faith of various persons.

UNIT 1. JESUS' EARLY MINISTRY

Unit 1 is composed of five lessons that explore the beginning of Jesus' ministry and the conflict that He encountered almost immediately. The first lesson examines Jesus' baptism, temptation, and beginning ministry. The second lesson presents the beginning of conflict. The third lesson focuses on Jesus' authority. The fourth lesson explores Jesus' rejection at Nazareth. The fifth lesson is a study of Jesus' teaching about what actually defiles a person.

LESSON 1: March 2
The Beginning of the Gospel
Mark 1:9-26

The biblical content emphases for this lesson deals with the commencement of the of Jesus' ministry. In this Scripture we see that Jesus was baptized by John, affirmed as God's Son (Mark 1:9-11), and tempted by Satan in the wilderness (vv. 12-13). Jesus began His Galilean ministry by proclaiming the coming of the kingdom of God (vv. 14-15). He then called fisher-men to be His first disciples (vv. 16-20), and healed a man with an unclean spirit while in the synagogue on the Sabbath day (vv. 21-26).

How did the Gospel begin? What are the things which happened at its onset? What are the significance of the events in this beginning? The topic of this lesson "The Beginning of the Gospel" shows us certain things about Jesus. We learn that this Son of the Most High went to John to be baptized. We are reminded of the need for affirmation from others who have been in the kingdom as we set out on our own journey. We also see that Jesus, upon His open revelation of how He was going to serve the Lord God, experienced temptation. Many of us have experienced temptation following our declaration of commitment to the course of the Lord. We will be tempted to turn our gifts to bad use. We will be tempted to go against the will of God. We will be tempted to impose our power upon others. But in this lesson we learn that we can choose to follow in the pathway of the Lord. As we follow this lifestyle at a cost to ourselves, the victory and healing of Jesus is always available. When we struggle with the pressures of temptation, we can remember that the Lord has been through similar experiences and will strengthen us.

LESSON 2: March 9
The Beginning of Conflict
Mark 2:3-12, 14-17

In this text, the scribes thought it was blasphemy when Jesus forgave the sins of a paralyzed man who had been lowered through the roof (Mark 2:3-7). Knowing the scribes' thoughts, Jesus confronted them and then, to the amazement of all, He healed the paralyzed man and told him to go home (vv. 8-12). After Jesus called Levi, the tax collector, as His disciple, He went to Levi's house and ate with tax collectors and sinners (vv. 14-15). When the scribes and Pharisees discovered Jesus dining with "sinners," they voiced their objections to Jesus' disciples (v. 16). Jesus responded to their objection by telling them He came to heal the sick (v. 17).

In this lesson we see how "Jesus Calls Sinners." Sin

is a serious concern in this life. That there is one who by His call can bring us out is important. There is forgiveness to those who respond. In this call is the core belief that forgiveness is crucial to leading healthy lives. The call is to sinners. This is not about our occupations or our perceived significance or comparative worth to others. Rather, the lesson is about breaking down barriers that exclude others being part of the kingdom of God. This lesson calls us to reach out and invite others to the community of faith and participate in the important task of extending the reign of God. This lesson calls, not just sinners to repentance, but all who need freedom of spirit and deliverance for their soul. There is a sense in which this lesson calls us to develop empathy for others who are suffering or are in need of the Saviour. If we have grown in our capacity to understand and accept God's forgiveness, then we ought to offer that same forgiveness to others.

LESSON 3: March 16
Jesus' Authority
Mark 4:36-41; 5:2-13

In the midst of a threatening storm at sea, Jesus responded to the cries of the terrified disciples and stilled the storm (Mark 4:36-39). Because the disciples were unable to grasp the significance of Jesus' words and deeds and did not understand who Jesus really was, Jesus chided them for their fear and lack of faith (vv. 40-41). As Jesus and the disciples came ashore, they were met by a man possessed by demons who could not be restrained (5:2-5). The demon-possessed man immediately recognized Jesus as the Son of the Most High God and invoked God's name to get Jesus to leave him alone (vv. 6-7). Jesus called out an unclean spirit from the man (v. 8). The spirits, called Legion because there were many of them, begged Jesus to let them enter some swine, rather than to send them out of the country; and Jesus gave them permission (vv. 9-13).

In this lesson we see the display of "The Power of Jesus." The need for the manifestation of the power of God has not abated since Jesus went into heaven. We need the power of God in our lives. In this day when many show a lack of trust in God's power working through Jesus, this lesson calls us to see and acknowledge His power today. God's saving presence and power is with us even our crises.

In this lesson we are called to hold on to this power and not panic in times of crisis. May the Lord help us.

Those who know this power will not be so fearful and repelled by people who are violent, on drugs, or display other kinds of out-of-control behaviors. In this lesson we see the display of such awesome power that we are led to the assurance that we are not victims but victorious with Jesus on our side. We must believe that God's power in us can enable us to overcome the worst evils in human experience. Divine power can conquer any situation. The display of power in this text leaves no doubt that "all things are possible." When you sometimes find yourself in frightening situations, lean on His power. When your resources recede, trust that you will overcome in the power of His might. Do not be impressed by the power and authority of the world; rely on the power of Jesus. When you may wonder why God allows storms and other natural phenomena to occur, wonder even more about the awesome power of the Lord.

LESSON 4: March 23
Rejection and Mission
Mark 6:1-13

The biblical context and content of this lesson looks at Jesus' visit to Nazareth. We read that as Jesus taught in the synagogue in His hometown, the people refused to acknowledge His authority and they took offense at Jesus (Mark 6:1-3). Jesus acknowledged their disbelief by quoting a common proverb (v. 4). He was able to do only a few miraculous works because of the people's disbelief (vv. 5-6). Jesus sent the disciples out two-by-two to preach and heal (vv. 7-11). The disciples preached repentance, cast out demons, and healed the sick (vv. 12-13).

"Mission Accomplished" is the topic for this day's lesson. What does it take to accomplish the mission on which the Lord sent us? What tools do we need? In this lesson we learn how the Lord sent His disciples out equipped to accomplish the task before them. We learn in this lesson that the Lord is able to help us solve problems which we are unable to solve on our own. We are obligated to continue Jesus' work through our individual lives and the ministry of the church. But this must be done in the power of Jesus. We are the disciples of Christ and have been sent to manifest his power in all that happens in all the corners of the world. This lesson raises the need for believers to answer the call to a deeper commitment of God. It also calls us to develop a divine concern for those who do not know God.

LESSON 5: March 30
What Really Defiles
Mark 7:1-15

The Pharisees and scribes, who observed extremely strict rules about washing hands and utensils, asked Jesus why His disciples did not adhere to the same rules (Mark 7:1-5). Jesus challenged the religious leaders with a quotation from Isaiah that castigated the people because they substituted human teaching for true devotion to God (vv. 6-8). Jesus explained how they replaced God's laws with human traditions by citing an example based on the commandment to honor one's own parents (vv. 9-13). Jesus asserted that nothing one eats or drinks can defile a person, but impurity comes from within (vv. 14-15).

UNIT 2. JESUS' CRUCIFIXION AND RESURRECTION

This unit looks at Jesus' final week on earth. The first session focuses on Jesus' entrance into Jerusalem and his cleansing of the Temple. The second session examines Jesus' instituting the Lord's Supper. The third session explores Jesus' death and resurrection.

LESSON 6: April 6
Entering Jerusalem and Cleansing the Temple
Mark 11:1-9, 15-18

The biblical content of this lesson contains the following: Jesus sent two of his disciples to the village to bring a colt that had never been ridden (Mark 11:1-2) The two disciples went away and found a colt (v. 4). The people questioned the disciples' actions and the disciples responded as Jesus told them (vv. 5-6). Jesus rode the colt into Jerusalem while many people welcomed Him and spread their cloaks and branches on the road with shouts of praise (vv. 7-9). When Jesus and His disciples came to Jerusalem, Jesus entered and cleansed the temple (vv. 15-17). People from the religious establishment kept looking for a way to kill Jesus because the crowd was captivated by His teaching (v. 18).

LESSON 7: April 13
A New Meaning for Passover
Mark 14:12-25

As the Jewish Passover approached, Jesus' disciples asked how they should prepare for this observance (Mark 14:12). Jesus instructed the two disciples to follow a man carrying a jar of water and to make preparations for the Passover in a home where Jesus had

arranged for using a large room upstairs (vv. 13-16). During the Passover meal, Jesus announced that one of the twelve would later betray Him (vv. 17-18). As each distressed disciple openly questioned himself, Jesus described and pronounced judgment on the one who would betray Him (vv. 19-21). Jesus blessed and broke a loaf of bread, giving it to the disciples as a symbol of His body (v. 22). Jesus gave thanks for the cup, passing it to all of the disciples and describing it as a covenant in His blood (vv. 23-25).

The meeting at the upper room was about the preparation for the death of the Lord, but it also served as re-interpretive context. Here the Lord gave new meaning for old traditions. In the context of the celebration of life and death Jesus raised for us the issue of having good plans, anticipating future needs, and addressing them successfully. It also raises for us the need to find occasions to be together with family and friends especially when darkness seems near. Here again we see the mystery of the service of Jesus to humanity who, though He had been unheralded for the great service He provided to the poor and marginalized, continued to the end. Here also we see that just because we do the work of God this does not keep us from betrayal. This lesson from Jesus shows us that we must not hold back completely from intimate and personal relationships because someone has betrayed us.

LESSON 8: April 20
The Cross and the Empty Tomb
Mark 15:21-24, 34-37; 16:1-8

The biblical content emphasis includes passages which tell us that Simon of Cyrene was ordered to carry Jesus' cross to Golgotha, the place of the crucifixion (Mark 15:21-22). The soldiers offered Jesus wine mixed with myrrh, but He did not take it (v. 23). The soldiers crucified Jesus, drew lots, and divided His clothes among themselves (v. 24). At three o'clock Jesus cried out with a loud voice, "My God, my God, why have you forsaken me?" (v. 34). The bystanders thought Jesus was calling for Elijah and waited to see if Elijah would come (vv. 35-37). On the first day of the week, the three Marys found Jesus' tomb empty; and a young man told them that Jesus had been raised and to tell the disciples to meet Him in Galilee (16:1-8).

Christianity is triumphant. Jesus is a triumphant Saviour. Our God is triumphant. In the resurrection of Jesus we see triumph over adversity. Life presents us with many adversities, the deepest of which is death. This lesson does not deny that we experience hardships; instead rather by looking at the suffering of Jesus, it encourages us to believe that our sufferings for the cause of God do benefit others. There are all kinds of adversities in the world today. We are judged by our association with others, often causing us emotional pain. Some of us have even experienced punishment more severely than others for the same or lesser crimes. Like the Lord on the cross, we sometimes wonder why our experiences are so severe and if anyone really cares. Through it is difficult to accept the inexplicable nature of painful events even when they bring fulfillment to others, we must encourage ourselves with the triumph of Jesus. Because He overcame, we can overcome also. Because He triumphed, we are also triumphant. Jesus' victory over death is our assurance that trouble doesn't last always. Though death is a part of life, it is not the last word.

UNIT 3. JESUS' RESPONSES TO FAITH

The first lesson emphasizes the importance Jesus placed on the people's faithful response to Him. The second session examines the bold faith of a woman and of the persons who brought a man to Jesus. The third session focuses on Peter's confession that Jesus was the Messiah and God's affirmation of that truth in the transfiguration. The fourth session presents the honest faith of a father who was concerned deeply for his son. The fifth session contrasts the disciples' lack of faith with the blind man's exercising faith in Jesus and receiving his sight.

LESSON 9: April 27
The Importance of Belief
Mark 5:22-36, 41-42

A crowd followed Jesus as He went with a ruler of the synagogue to visit the ruler's dying daughter (Mark 5:21-24). A woman was in the crowd who had suffered from hemorrhages for twelve years, had spent all of her resources, but grew worse (vv. 25-26). Hearing about Jesus' power to heal, the woman reached through the crowd to touch the cloak of Jesus and was immediately healed of her disease (vv. 27-29). When Jesus asked, "Who touched my clothes?" the woman confessed; and Jesus told her, "Your faith has healed you" (vv. 30-34). Some men

from the ruler's house brought news of his daughter's death; but Jesus told the ruler, "Do not fear, only believe" (vv. 35-36). Three of Jesus' disciples accompanied Him to the ruler's house, where the girl who was reported to be dead rose from her bed at Jesus' command and walked (vv. 37-42).

In this lesson, we learn that faith conquers fear. Oftentimes fear keeps us from entering into relationships with others. As a result, many people are not willing to go out of their way to help others; but for those of us who have experienced faith in Jesus there arises a willingness to help others, and an acceptance of the requirements, responsibilities, and standards necessary to begin a new life. Fear says that we are afraid of being disappointed by others, but faith goes out with joy, is led by peace, and openly inspires others. Fear is a normal response when human beings are faced with death. But faith helps us deal with the fear of death.

LESSON 10: May 4
Bold Faith
Mark 7:24-37

This lesson continues the call to act boldly in faith. In this lesson, a Gentile woman asked Jesus to cast the demon out of her little daughter (Mark 7:24-26). When Jesus put her off with an enigmatic statement, she persisted; and Jesus honored her request and healed her daughter (vv. 27-30). Friends brought to Jesus a man who was deaf and spoke with an impediment and asked that He heal the man (vv. 31-32). Jesus took the man aside in private and healed him (vv. 33-35). Jesus ordered the people to tell no one about this healing, but the amazed crowd could not keep this news quiet (vv. 36-37).

The key to building extraordinary faith in life is to act boldly on that faith. The call to act boldly in faith is answered by striving daily to overcome barriers designed to keep us from accomplishing God's purpose in life. Bold faith compels us to accept responsibility and to confront any form of discrimination in a spirit of humility and love. Bold faith takes initiative to do things for those who cannot act for themselves. Bold faith requires praise, which in turn makes it difficult to keep silent about the goodness of Jesus toward us.

LESSON 11: May 11
Confession of Faith and Affirmation
Mark 8:27-35; 9:2-7

This biblical passage turns on the question of the identity of the Messiah. In this text we come upon the time when Jesus asked His disciples, "Who do people say that I am?" The disciples indicated that many people said Jesus was a prophet (Mark 8:27-28). Peter, however, declared that Jesus was the Messiah and Jesus ordered the disciples not to tell anyone (vv. 29-30). Jesus openly told the disciples of His approaching death and rebuked Peter for interfering with the plan of God (vv. 31-33). Jesus defined discipleship in terms of taking up a cross and laying down one's life for the sake of the Gospel (vv. 34-35). Jesus was transfigured before His closest disciples, and they were frightened and awed by their experience (9:2-6). A voice from an overshadowing cloud instructed the disciples to listen to Jesus, God's beloved Son (v. 7).

The lesson for today leads us to the need for confession and affirmation of faith in the Lord Jesus. We must follow in faith. Popular opinion often affects the decisions we make as they relate to our faith in Jesus. True confession of faith in Jesus calls us to focus, not on our well-being, but inculcate self-denial as a way to greater fulfillment. Confession of faith may mean that we become willing to deny ourselves for the greater good of others. Here in this lesson, we see one who affirmed and confessed his faith, but still was unwilling to follow Jesus to the place of sacrifice. We must understand what it means to live with the consequences of faith decisions, be they pleasant or otherwise. Our recognition of Jesus and the confession of His uniqueness places an obligation on us to share in His calling even when that calling leads to pain.

LESSON 12: May 18
Honest Faith
Mark 9:14-29

The biblical content of this lesson begins with an argument between Jesus' disciples and the scribes which drew a large crowd and prompted Jesus to inquire about the cause of the dispute (Mark 9:14-16). A man indicated that the disciples had been unable to heal his son, who was afflicted by an unclean spirit (vv. 17-18). Jesus addressed the crowd and admonished them for their lack of faith (v. 19). The man brought his son to Jesus and asked if Jesus could help him (vv. 20-22). Jesus affirmed that all things can be done for anyone who believes, and the man confessed his belief and asked for help with his unbelief (vv. 23-24). Jesus healed the boy and later explained to the disciples why they had not been able to heal the boy (vv. 25-29).

Unbelief is the bread of the modern age. We tend to doubt everything. Yet many of us will not face the fact that we have unbelief. The first step to developing faith is acknowledge that we have unbelief and to ask God to help us. "Facing Our Unbelief" is the topic here as we meet with the father who faced his unbelief when confronted by Jesus. Jesus causes us to come face to face with our lack of faith in the power and possibility which God has made available to us.

LESSON 13: May 25
Faith and Sight
Mark 10:37-52

When James and John, the sons of Zebedee, asked Jesus to grant them special places in the kingdom of God, Jesus asked the disciples if they were prepared to assume such great responsibilities (Mark 10:37-38). When James and John asked Jesus to let them sit at His right and left in glory, Jesus said their request was not for Him to grant (vv. 39-40). The other disciples became angry at James and John because of their boldness, but Jesus taught them about rendering service to others (vv. 41-45). As they left Jericho, a blind beggar called out to Jesus, asking for His mercy (vv. 46-47). Many persons rebuked the beggar, but Jesus told them to bring the beggar to him (vv. 48-49). When the beggar asked Jesus to give him his sight, Jesus healed him and told him his faith had made him well (vv. 50-52).

"How Bold Is Your Faith?" is the topic for this lesson. Faith is not abstract but involves life's everyday concerns. A bold faith demands that we press on to follow Jesus until we get what He has for us. Bold faith, as in the case of this blind beggar, has the capacity to amaze even those who feel that they know us. Bold faith has learned to believe that God will act even when such belief is unexplainable. Bold faith holds on to God's promise even when our circumstances and the opinions of friends and strangers suggest that we stop believing.

Spiritual Keys to Transformative Leadership: Becoming the Leader Who Changes Lives

Jeanne Porter and Samira E. Robinson

Author Fred Smith says in his book *Learning to Lead*[1], "The right concept of leadership is vital. And without a solid concept of leadership, you have a faulty leadership." As leaders in the service of the Lord, we must have the right concept of what it is we are called to do, and why. We must ask ourselves pertinent questions such as: What is a leader? What are the assumptions we make about leadership, and the places in which we lead? Transformative leadership provides us with a model of leadership that is necessary for the twenty-first century.

Many of us grow up believing that leadership is merely about a position–the Sunday School superintendent, the pastor, the usher board president. Transformative leaders realize that spiritual leadership is a process; it's doing God-ordained things to effectuate change in the lives of people. It is a process whereby leaders motivate others to be and do their best, accomplish goals, and realize their divine destiny. For instance, a significant leader in the church is the Sunday School teacher. The Sunday School teacher who sees herself as a transformative leader realizes that her aim and purpose are to shape, mold, and stimulate thoughts, beliefs, and attitudes about the Lord. She is to bring forth truth and thus lead her students out of the darkness of misinformation. The lessons taught, while universal, hold a unique meaning in each Sunday School class. The teacher sets the tone for the class, and based on the level of study, spirituality, and biblical knowledge of her students, she influences and impacts youth and adults in positive or not-so-positive ways.

Transformative leaders realize that spiritual leadership is a process; it's doing God-ordained things

There are old models of leadership styles, secular in nature, that we have followed that have undoubtedly run their course. Often these models reflect a worldly agenda instead of God's purpose. A review of the traditional versus the transformative leadership model allows us to compare the thrust, and resulting outcomes, of each model. Traditional leadership has a history of viewing the leadership role as a call to dominate or control, and a number of overt and covert methods are used to get what we want. Transformative leadership realizes that leadership is a call to service, first to God and then to the people. Secular leadership often focuses on certain techniques and tactics to get a job done. Transformative leadership relies on God's prompting and leading. The secular leadership model emphasizes taking charge, and often the leader takes pride in his or her abilities. The transformative leadership model is activated by one's faith in one's position in Christ and the call of God in one's life. The secular leadership model is often defined by what the world system says is important. The transformative leadership model comes from God's Word and is defined by God.

Based on the transformative leadership model, church leaders must adapt an approach to leadership that reflects their faith in God and desire to please Him. Church leaders who desire to be transformative leaders will have to acclimate themselves to utilizing biblical principles with a revelatory understanding of the needs of today's Sunday School student. The goal must not be to simply get our message to them, but to learn what their message is. What is troubling them? What are their goals? What do they want to be when they grow up? What gifts has God given them, and what skills do they have? Transformative leaders must work at knowing the answers to these questions. That is not to say that one has to know the personal history and be personally involved with each student. But one should be concerned enough to go beyond the surface, to the depths of caring about each person. It is then that our message will be heard loud and clear. Today's generation encompasses those often referred to as the "unchurched" and those who were raised in church but have not applied the Word to their lives. The transformative leader is in tune with the heart of God, and the heart of the student.

There are nine spiritual keys to transformative leadership that, when grasped, will take you to the next level in your spiritual growth and fulfillment of your purpose as a leader. These principles help you function more effectively in your calling to help others. The principles are as follows:

1. Understand who you are as a person. The transformative leader must understand who he or she is as a person—who God has created him or her to be versus who society has constructed him or her to be. Leadership is personal. It is about the individual—the unique person whom God has created, not the generic label that society has attempted to construct. The leader is a person first, not a role model. Remember that God blesses people with gifts, not roles or positions. The transformative leader will carry his or her God-given special mark.

2. Discover and tap into your purpose. God designed each person with a specific purpose in mind. We are His workmanship (Ephesians 2:10) or His special creation. Every new product comes from the manufacturer or maker with instructions. Each person should imagine that he or she is a new product. How would the instructions describing your purpose and function read? What have you been created to do? You are a distinct creation and a model of excellence. What are the unique features, gifts, talents, and abilities with which you have been equipped? Until you can get in touch with this purpose, you will flounder or be less than effective as a leader.

3. Determine the proper place for your leadership. Placement is very important to God. Like Esther, Joseph, Paul, and Daniel, God strategically situates His leaders in places to fulfill His purposes in the lives of people. He assigns us to work in churches, businesses, service agencies, professional service agencies, and the community. Too often people get frustrated with where they are, and fail to see the working of God—that He has strategically placed him or her. As you pray about placement, ask God where He wants you to offer your gifts and where you can be of the best service for kingdom building.

4. Accept God's preparations for you. Even as Jesus went through extensive preparation for His public ministry, so will every leader go through a preparation phase. Before every harvest, there is a season of sowing. For every walk, there is a toddle. In Jesus' preparation we see isolation and testing—out of which came a clarified purpose. A transformative leader must accept God's mode of preparation for them. God prepares leaders in His time frame. The leader's preparation includes formal and informal lessons that come from living. Every experience, trial, and triumph is part of the preparation process.

5. Develop the process that is in line with who you are and where God has placed you. Transformative leaders must develop the process that is in line with who they are and where God has placed them. The process refers to the way in

which the leader accomplishes his or her goals, tasks, and objectives. The process depends upon the people with whom you are in a leadership relationship, the tasks or things that need to be accomplished, and the steps you take to do it based on your leadership style.

6. Utilize the power that you have been given. Transformative leaders must practice using the power that God has given them. Traditionally leaders have relied upon power that comes from holding a formal position or title. These leaders operated under the theory, "I get you to do what I want because I'm the boss and I can reward or punish you." Other traditional leaders persuade people using charisma, charm, or personality. God is calling for leaders to rely on the dynamic power of the Holy Spirit to guide the leader, grant the leader wisdom to envision possibilities for their organization or department, and to enable leaders to work with people to get results.

7. Follow the plan that God has laid out for you. Transformative leaders follow the plan the Lord has laid out for them. In Jeremiah 29:11, God told the nation of Israel, "I know the plans I have for you... They are plans for good and not for disaster, to give you a future and a hope" (New Living Translation,(NLT)). His plan was to give Israel a future and a hope. God has laid out plans for nations as well as for individuals. He has the master plan and the task of the transformative leader is to tap into the Master's plan for their lives and for their organization or group. They do not introduce their own agendas but go where God says to go and do what He says to do.

8. Love the people God has given you. Transformative leaders love and accept the people God has given them. They do not seek out others with whom they would rather work. The transformative leader resists treating students like needy people and interacts with them as treasures of God entrusted to the leader. The transformative leader learns wisely to utilize the gifts of the people who have been assigned to him or her. Too often traditional leaders blame their staffs for the leader's own inadequacies. Worse yet, these traditional leaders perpetually look for people who can produce for them, instead of learning how to cultivate the resources they already have to get a maximum yield.

9. Develop proficiencies that facilitate spiritual transformation. Transformative leaders develop proficiencies or skills that facilitate spiritual transformation. They realize that God works on the inside and that divine purpose starts in the heart of every believer and works its way out. They practice integrity and work on self-improvement, building on their skills and talents.

This transformative leadership model embodies the concept of collaborative leadership, which in actuality many organizations and corporations are beginning to use because they now realize that the traditional model has lost its effectiveness. They adopt the new model because they feel the winds of change in society and do not want to be left behind. Corporations and businesses fully intend to be successful in this new millennium. The church, the Body of Christ on earth, must not fall behind but rather set the standard for others to follow, especially when the foundational paradigm supporting collaborative leadership is spiritual and relational.

People need transformative leadership. In this fast-paced and morally-impoverished society, our church and community members need leaders to be dynamic individuals who are willing to accept change and use new ways to reach and teach them. They hunger and thirst for church leaders who are grounded in the Word of God and His divine purpose. It is our challenge, our call, and our responsibility to become the leaders whom God has ordained—transformative leaders or leaders who change lives for the kingdom of God.

[1] Fred Smith, "Learning to Lead," Christianity Today, Inc./Word, Inc., 1986. Distributed by Word Books; p. 24.

Dr. Jeanne L. Porter is an Associate Minister at the Apostolic Church of God. She is founder of TransPorter Communications and has contributed to two recently published books. Dr. Porter holds Bachelors and Masters of Science degrees from Ohio State University in Columbus, Ohio as well as a Ph.D. in Communications from Ohio University in Athens, Ohio.
Samira E. Robinson is a member of the Apostolic Church of God in Chicago. She has a Masters of Arts degree.

SPIRITUALS AS INSTRUMENTS OF SURVIVAL FOR AFRICAN AMERICANS

Jennifer D. King

More than 200 years after their creation, African American religious folks songs, or spirituals as they came to be known, remain with us and are still routinely performed in the smallest of churches as well as large concert settings. In the traditional African American church settings, these songs continue to be a regular part of the musical repertoire. The impact of these lyrics on individuals varies widely. Many people find the jubilant and rejoicing spirit of many of the spirituals uplifting. "Every time I feel the spirit moving in my heart, I will pray!"[1] Still others, like Frederick Douglass, who was himself a slave, found listening to spirituals too agonizing to bear. He wrote that these songs "breathed the prayer and complaint of souls boiling over with the bitterest anguish. Every tone was a testimony against slavery, and a prayer to God for deliverance from chains."[2] Indeed, it is only the most bitter of anguish that inspires lyrics such as "Lord, how come me here?/I wish I never was born."[3]

Perhaps the answer to why the spirituals are received so differently lies in the paradox of their content. The spirituals are not "simple" religious songs. Attempts to read them as such lead to misinterpretations of the invaluable way they assisted in the psychological survival of the enslaved Blacks who created them. Through the spirituals, the slaves created for themselves an expression of their religious and cultural beliefs that commented not only on their particular circumstance, but on their worldview. Specifically, the spirituals not only pay homage to a God who acknowledges their humanity and suffering but reaffirmed the sense of humanity, identity, and community that the institution of slavery labored to destroy.

The savagery of that "peculiar institution" that separated both close family members and kinsmen created a tremendous loss within the slave community. The slaves lost their homeland, their families, their language, and their culture. This overwhelming loss gave way to intense desperation that was alleviated through the musical interpretation of certain biblical texts. In the only arena that was relatively free of White control—the performance of song—the enslaved Blacks created in the spirituals an expression for their religious and cultural beliefs that commented on their particular worldview.

These religious folk songs were most "likely fashioned by combining verses from the Bible and hymns with portions of sermons and prayers given during the worship."[4] The spirituals certainly had as their topics God, heaven, Jesus, and salvation. We must remember, however, that the God of the slaves was a divine champion of the victims of injustice. This God of their fashioning allowed them, at least in song, to transcend the narrow limits of slavery.

While the dancing and drumming they had brought with them from African was often forbidden, the White owners generally encouraged singing. The Whites did not foresee that when the slaves began adopting specific biblical narratives as lyrics for their songs, the slaves would use them as vehicles to unify themselves by addressing one another in song, using lyrics that countered the racist assertions of their subhumanness.

The transmission of biblical information from the Whites to the slaves was a slow process. First, there was the problem of legal prohibitions against teaching slaves to read. The second problem was that the slave owners were divided on the question of religious training for their slaves. On one hand, their thought was that perhaps christianizing the slaves would make them more obedient. After all, many of the Old Testament

Scriptures proved that slavery was a recognized institution, and some of New Testament Scriptures taught that slaves ought to "obey" their masters.

On the other hand, there was the growing concern that many of the biblical accounts could actually encourage rebellion and insurrection. This debate was ended largely through the evangelizing efforts of the Baptist, Methodist, and Presbyterian denominations throughout the South. Able at last to attend gatherings to listen to Scripture readings, preaching, and singing alleviated the isolation from one another that typified slavery. The religious gatherings provided a relief from the strict monitoring of movement from plantation to plantation and the monitoring of what slaves said to one another. The slave owners did not forsee that a people who had been so isolated from one another would seize the opportunity to use music as a medium for communicating between themselves.

The narrative accounts from the Old Testament, with their vast selection of heroes and adventures, and the easily identifiable themes of loss and displacement, suffering, and redemption, were especially appealing to the slaves. In these Scriptures, the slaves encountered a spiritual force with a proven track record of defending and liberating the underdog.

The attributes of this new God of the Bible were similar in nature and power to the African high gods worshiped by the slaves in their homeland. Because the slaves were already familiar with the concept of deity, their transfer of allegiance to the Christian God should not be surprising.

In addition to imbuing God with extraordinary presence, the slaves often indicated that their relationship with the Creator is less that of magnanimous guardian and benefactor that many Whites perceived Him to be, and more of friend and confidante. The lyrics of one spiritual declares, "When I get to heaven, gonna be at ease/Me and my God gonna do as we please . . . Gonna chatter with the Father, argue with the Son/Tell 'em 'bout the world I just come from."[5] This familiarity and intimacy with God allowed the slaves to view themselves very differently than their owners did. The singers' insistence that they were close enough to God to address Him so informally is an implicit argument that the singers were claiming for themselves a far more personal and privileged role with God than that held by the Whites. Such songs also argued that the Blacks were not simply disposable property. Rather, such lyrics allowed them to view and identify themselves as God's "chosen."

As the elect of the Most High God, the songs of the slaves insisted that God could be counted on to fight on their behalf and execute judgment upon those who merited destruction. Old Testament texts offered the slaves a continual affirmation that God is on the side of the oppressed. It is not surprising then that the African slaves identified so strongly with the oppression of the Children of Israel—the ultimate victims of loss. In the face of the harshness of chattel slavery endured by the Blacks, it stood to reason that the all-powerful God, who had so deftly delivered Israel out of bondage, could be counted on to deliver them from their captivity. A large body of the spirituals reflects this affinity with the historical burdens suffered by the Israelites and other Old Testament heroes. The comparison between themselves and Old Testament narratives and heroes is constant in the spirituals: "Didn't my Lord deliver Daniel, and why not every man?"[6]

These songs not only offered a hope of eventual salvation, they presented varying possibilities about the role of the vanquished sufferer while he waited for his deliverance. The Old Testament presented some enslaved people of God who took a proactive role in their deliverance, as in the case of Moses' demand that "Ol' Pharaoh let my people go." Still other songs insisted on patience and declared that salvation lay in resisting the temptation to fight and waiting for God to act on one's behalf. These songs urged a more passive approach to freedom. They called on the believer to be "laying down" one's burdens and "studying war no more."

The portrayals of Jesus in spirituals offered many of these same unique Black perspectives of God. The closeness and familiarity the spirituals claimed with God is also shared with His Son. In the lyrics "Nobody knows da trouble I sees, Nobody knows but Jesus," there was an insistence that only a people of true value and worth could be worthy of such special kinship with Jesus. Similarly, singing "Talk about a child that do love Jesus, here is one"[7] was further evidence of heightened self-esteem.

Often in the songs, Jesus was presented as a New Testament Moses, a deliverer to whom the slaves could cry out for physical and spiritual deliverance (see Matthew 10:34). "King Jesus is my Captain/He is my all in all/He gives me grace to conquer/And take me home to rest."[8] The repetition of the pronoun "my" intensifies the personalization of the relationship between the singer and Jesus.

It is not at all surprising that the slaves could so easily wholly identify with Jesus. The biblical account of His life closely mirrored the life of the enslaved Black. Jesus was innocent of any crimes, yet He was hated and persecuted by the authorities (who bore a curious resemblance to the slaveholders in their religious hypocrisy).

The slaves sang of Jesus, not only because He could save their souls, but because He could reward and deliver them. The spirituals are replete with references to rewards for the long-suffering faithfulness of the believers. These rewards ran the gamut from the simple—long white robes, wings, harps, and golden slippers to trod upon streets of gold—to spectacular, low-swinging chariots accompanied by bands of angels, drinking from wells that never run dry and perpetual rest in a kingdom that offered "no sorrow there."

The "heaven" of the spirituals expressed the slave's vision of a new home where simple pleasures would abound, relief from their suffering would be enjoyed, and where they would be recognized as worthy and welcome residents.

In addition to the rewards He offered, the Jesus contained in the lyrics of the spirituals held the key to their removal from the harsh conditions of slavery.

The creation and singing of spirituals allowed the slaves to recreate for themselves a new home. The creators of this music—those enslaved Blacks

working in the cotton, rice, and tobacco fields of Georgia, the Carolinas, and Louisiana—had no way of knowing how to get back home, yet they knew the place and condition in which they found themselves was not home. The spirituals filled in the gaps of the tremendous losses these people suffered as slaves. In the spirituals, the African slaves literally sang their humanity into being. Through the spirituals they created for themselves a God who loved, valued, and privileged them in a place that held them in such low esteem. The spirituals provided a mechanism by which the slaves, borrowing from the Bible, recreated a history for themselves that cast them as chosen sufferers, rather than captured chattel.

Just like the pattern of their singing, the spirituals contained a call and response. The enslaved Africans made a call for an understanding or an explanation of their horrific and seemingly hopeless situation: "Lord, How Come Me Here?" It was through their construction of this musical art form that they created for themselves a self-defining response which countermanded the master's insistence on their inferiority. In the skillfully poetic hands of the slaves, biblical texts took on a life of their own. The themes of loss, displacement, divine intervention, and deliverance were reinterpreted to allow for a universal adoption, better suited for the condition in which the slaves found themselves. These songs remain with us as proof of the slave's ability to react creatively, constructively, and responsively to the brutal realities of their new life.

---

[1] Traditional African-American Spiritual, "Every Time I Feel the Spirit."

[2] Douglass, Frederick. Narrative of the Life of Frederick Douglass. The Classic Slave Narratives. New York: Penguin 1987.

[3] Traditional African-American Spiritual, "Lord, How Come Me Here?"

[4] Nelson, Angela. "The Spiritual." Christian History (10), 1991. p. 30.

[5] Traditional African-American Spiritual, "Hold the Wind."

[6] Traditional African-American Spiritual, "Didn't My Lord Deliver Daniel?"

[7] Traditional African-American Spiritual, "Talk About a Child that Do Love Jesus."

[8] Traditional African-American Spiritual, "I'm Walking With Jesus."

Jennifer D. King is Superintendent of Sunday School for Bay Area Christian Connection. She holds a B.A. with honors in English and is currently working toward a Masters of Arts degree.

THEMATIC ESSAY

GOD'S POWER IN ACTION

Overseer Terry Goodlow

Several years ago a tornado came through Omaha, Nebraska and devastated an area of the city. The tornado completely uprooted several homes from their foundations. Structures that had taken several years to erect were suddenly destroyed in a matter of seconds. That tornado reminded me of the magnitude of God's power.

Power is the ability or strength to perform an activity or deed. Power is sometimes used with the word authority. If power suggests physical strength, authority suggests a moral right or privilege. One can have power to perform a task but not authority to do it. Thus, the power of God must be understood as God's authority and ability to do anything He desires to fulfill His purpose. God is said to be omnipotent. The noun "omnipotence" is not found in the English Bible, nor any noun exactly corresponding to it in the original Hebrew or Greek. However, the adjective "omnipotent" occurs in Revelation 19:6 (KJV); the Greek for this is *pantokrator.* It is also found frequently in the Septuagint, especially in the rendering of the divine names *Yahweh tsebha'oth* and *'El Shadday.* Although the concept of omnipotence as it is worked out in theology does not occur in the Old Testament, the substance of the idea is conveyed in various ways. The notion of "strength" is inherent in the Old Testament conception of God from the beginning, being already represented in one of the two divine names inherited by Israel from ancient Semitic religion, the name *'El.* According to one etymology it is also inherent in the other, the name *'Elohim,* and in this case the plural form, by bringing out the fullness of power in God, would mark an approach to the idea of omnipotence (from *International Standard Bible Encyclopedia*).

Beginning in Genesis with the creation to the culmination of all things in Revelation, the power of God is demonstrated. In the Old Testament, God demonstrated His power in creation: "In the beginning God created the heaven and the earth" (Genesis 1:1). As He spoke, things began to happen by the power of His word. God was able to bring things into existence by His Word. Once God created man He breathed into His nostrils and man became a living soul by the power of the living God. The same God took the man He had created and made a woman from him. Only a God of unlimited power could do this.

> *Power is the ability or strength to perform an activity or deed.*

He also demonstrated His power in terms of His "strength" to Israel. The language of God's "strength" is highly metaphorical. God's right hand gloriously manifests His "power" in Exodus 15:6. His voice is loud: "The voice of the Lord is powerful; the voice of the Lord is full of majesty" (Psalm 29:4). In His "power" He delivered Israel from Egypt (Exodus 32:11) and brought them through the Red Sea (Exodus 15:6). Even as He advances the rights of the poor and needy (Isaiah 50:2), He brought the Israelites as a needy people into the Promised Land with His "power": "He hath shewed his people the power of his works, that he may give them the heritage of the heathen" (Psalm 111:6). God delights in helping His people. However, the Lord does not tolerate self-sufficiency on the part of human beings. Isaiah rebuked the king of Assyria for his arrogance in claiming to have been successful in his conquests (Isaiah 10:12-14). Likewise God had warned His people against pride in taking the land of Canaan: "And thou say in thine heart, My power [*koach*, pronounced **KOW-ahk**] and the might of mine hand hath gotten me this wealth. But thou shalt remember the Lord thy God: for it is he that giveth thee power [*koach*] to get wealth, that he may establish his covenant which he swore unto thy fathers, as it is this day" (Deuteronomy 8:17-18). Every believer must learn to depend upon God and trust in Him: "This is the word of the Lord unto Zerubbabel, saying, Not by might, nor by power, but by my spirit, saith the Lord of hosts" (Zechariah 4:6).

The principal words for "power" in the New Testament are *dunamis* (pronounced **DOO-nuh-miss**) and *exousia* (pronounced **x-oo-SEE-uh**). In the latter case the Revised Version (British and American) frequently changes it to "authority" (Mark 3:15; 6:7; Ephesians 1:21, etc.) or "right" (Romans 9:21; 1 Corinthians 9:6; 2 Thessalonians 3:9, etc.). The supreme manifestation of the power, as of the wisdom and love of God, is found in redemption (1 Corinthians 1:18, 24). None but the living God could manifest Himself in the world by His only begotten Son. John records: "And the Word was made flesh, and dwelt among us (and we beheld his glory, the glory as of the only begotten of the Father), full of grace and truth" (John 1:14, KJV). God demonstrated His great power by providing Himself the lamb that would be offered, the high priest that would offer the sacrifice, and the God to whom the sacrifice would be made. Jesus came with both power and authority over disease, demons, nature, and death. Miracles, as "mighty works," are denoted by the term "powers" (see Matthew 11:21, 23, Revised Standard Version, RSV). Jesus taught as one who had authority and not as the religious leaders of His day: "And they were astonished at his doctrine: for he taught them as one that had authority, and not as the scribes" (Mark 1:22). He had power to lay His life down and take it up again (John 10:18). What great power God the Father has shown by causing the shed blood of His only Son to produce salva-

tion for all who will receive it. After His resurrection, Jesus testified that all power in heaven and earth had been given to Him: "And Jesus came and spake unto them, saying, All power is given unto me in heaven and in earth" (Matthew 28:18).

In the Scripture we notice how God's power was put into action through the lives of various people. This is only possible by the indwelling of the Holy Spirit. Jesus even tells us that we shall do greater works than He did. As He was preparing to return to glory, He instructed the disciples to wait until they were empowered by the Holy Spirit. What this means is that God gives you the authority and strength through His Son to live and speak for Him. He also supplies everything you need to fulfill His purpose in you. After receiving the Holy Spirit, the

Power is sometimes used with the word authority.

disciples were able to perform great work for Jesus. This became evident on the day of Pentecost. God poured out His Spirit on all of the disciples, and they began to speak in languages previously unkown to them as the Spirit gave them utterance. We find Peter, who had denied knowing Jesus, now standing in the midst of his fellow Jews preaching Christ and Him crucified. When the Spirit of God moves into the heart of an individual, His wonderful power enables that person to do and say what he or she otherwise could not do or say.

Moses delivered the Children of Israel by the power of God from Egypt. Moses turned aside to see the burning bush on Mount Horeb. Never before had he witnessed so great a power as God was displaying to him in the burning bush. At that moment Moses became a vessel whom God would use to show His power in fulfilling His divine will of delivering the Children of Israel from Egypt. Moses knew that he did not have the power to do this, so he became totally dependent on God for His authority and strength to stand before Pharaoh and lead Israel out of Egypt.

David gives us an example of depending on the

power of God when he faced the Philistine giant, Goliath. As he was preparing to fight Goliath, he remembered that his source of strength was not in himself, but in the Almighty God. He had learned this as a young lad while he was tending his father's sheep. God gave him the victory over a lion and a bear. He knew that the battle belonged to God, not man, and with God all things are possible.

The Prophet Elijah trusted in the power and might of God when he to challenged the 450 prophets of Baal. He knew that the Lord God not only had the power to answer his prayer, but that He would answer. Elijah believed in the power of God so much that he had the sacrifice drenched with water and a trench around the sacrifice filled with water. God answered by fire, lapping up the sacrifice and the water (1 Kings 18:24-39). God overcomes all obstacles, for He is all-powerful.

If power suggests physical strength, authority suggests a moral right or privilege.

Just as God's power worked in the lives of Moses, David, Elijah, Jesus, and the disciples, He wants to manifest His power through you. The challenge is not whether God has wonder-working power, but the challenge is for the people of God to make themselves available for the power of God to work in them. It is God's desire to deliver all from the bondage of sin, and it is wonderful to think that He will use us to spread His message of salvation to the lost. Although the Gospel has saving power within itself, God uses weak men and women like you and me to declare His Word to the world. God will empower us by imparting His Spirit in us. It is amazing to think that our heavenly Father would choose us to fulfill His desire to save the world. Think about it, God can take a sinner like you and turn you into a powerful influence in the world. Perhaps the Apostle Paul says it best: "Not that we are competent in ourselves to claim anything for ourselves, but our competence comes from God. He has made us competent as ministers of a new covenant—not of the letter but of the Spirit; for the letter kills, but the Spirit gives life" (2 Corinthians 3:5-6, NIV). Paul said that he was not ashamed of the Gospel of Christ, for it is the power of God for the salvation of all humankind.

Many people believe in the power of God as it relates to the Bible, but few ever experience His magnificent power in their lives. Many Christians believe that God can do anything for and through others but not through them. They often have ability but not availability. Have you experienced His power in your life? Can you recall a time when the power of God acted on your behalf? Has the Almighty chosen you to manifest His power in the earth? God wants to unleash His power in our lives to perform His divine will. However, He can only manifest His power when we make ourselves available to Him and put all of our trust and confidence in Him.

To those who will open their lives to the Almighty God, He will also provide eternal blessings. He has promised eternal life and rewards to the faithful servants. Will you become a faithful servant and allow the power of God to work through you?

Overseer Terry Goodlow is Pastor of the Church of the Living God Temple Number 41 in Beaumont, Texas. Overseer Goodlow holds an A. S. in Psychology and is also Superintendent of the National Sunday School Department of the Church of the Living God.

PERPETUA

Perpetua was a great African Christian woman who died at the hands of the Roman government because she would not offer sacrifice to the emperor as god. This was both a religious and political statement to many Africans of this time. Perpetua was a highly educated African woman, and a daughter of one of the town chiefs. She was still in the new believers' class, and had an infant child when she was arrested and put into a dungeon with other Christians. People pleaded with her to deny Jesus Christ as her Saviour, but she held fast to her faith. Consequently, she was condemned to die in the coliseum as a public spectacle. It is said that she had so much spiritual power that when they threw her to the mad cow, she still survived. After all of her suffering, she continued to praise God. Though she did not recover from this experience, her bravery inspired many people to believe in the Messiah. Perpetua was a woman filled with the Holy Spirit and gifted with vision. She was also a great theological thinker in a time when many women were not allowed to theologize.

FELICITAS

Felicitas, Perpetua's midwife, was also arrested while in church. At the time of her arrest, she was eight months pregnant. This strong African woman did not want pity because she was pregnant. Her condition did not keep them from arresting Felicitas and placing her in a cold, damp, and dark dungeon. She went into labor while in prison because of her suffering. In fact, she was in such great difficultly that nonbelievers looked on and mocked her. She delivered a baby girl who was then taken by the Christian community to be brought up in the faith. Meanwhile, the Romans beat Felicitas with scourges and forced her to fight wild beasts in the amphitheater. Then she was thrown to a bull in the arena and returned to the dungeon. Later on she was brought out and killed with the sword.

TEACHING TIPS

March 2
Bible Study Guide 1

1. Words You Should Know

A. Gospel (Mark 1:1); Greek *euangelion* (pronounced **u-ahng-GHEL-lee-ahn**)—"Good message," also a word of Anglo-Saxon origin meaning "God's spell" (good news).

B. Baptize (v. 9); Greek *baptidzo* (pronounced **bahp-TIDZ-oh**)—To symbolically cleanse or make clean by submerging in water; to overwhelm.

C. Tempted (v. 13); Greek *peiradzo* (pronounced **pehr-AHD-zuh**)—To test; to make a trail of.

2. Teacher Preparation

A. Pray for the students in your class, asking God to open their hearts to today's lesson.

B. Read and study the FOCAL VERSES, paying attention to how Jesus began His ministry.

C. Carefully review Bible Study Guide 1, making any notes for clarification.

D. Be prepared to tell the class about a new beginning you experienced (moving to a new city, starting a new job, and so forth).

E. Materials needed: a chalkboard and chalk, Bible, and a small spiral notebook or journal.

3. Starting the Lesson

A. Before the students arrive, write the word "Beginnings" on the board.

B. After the students arrive and are settled, lead the class in prayer, specifically asking for godly insights on the lesson and blessings on the lives of the students.

C. Point to the word "Beginnings" and talk about how exciting a new start can be. Now tell the class about a new experience you have had, and invite students to tell their stories as well. Talk about the joys, fears, and conflict that involve new beginnings.

4. Getting into the Lesson

A. Ask a volunteer to read IN FOCUS and then spend time in a class discussion.

B. Ask volunteers to read THE PEOPLE, PLACES, AND TIMES and BACKGROUND.

C. Ask a student to read the FOCAL VERSES and then the corresponding IN DEPTH section. For example, a student will read Mark 1:9-11, followed by "Jesus is Baptized by John." Continue in this manner until the class has completed all the Scripture verses and the IN DEPTH section. Allow time for discussion between each section.

5. Relating the Lesson to Life

A. Spend time answering the questions in DISCUSS THE MEANING.

B. Ask the class if anyone has insights to express regarding today's lesson.

6. Arousing Action

A. Read LESSON IN OUR SOCIETY to the class. Tell the class that during the month of March they will keep a journal called "My New Beginning." Direct the students to MAKE IT HAPPEN and discuss it with the class.

B. As a review, tell the students to complete SEARCH THE SCRIPTURES during the week.

C. End the session with prayer.

WORSHIP GUIDE

For the Superintendent or Teacher
Theme: The Beginning of the Gospel
Theme Song: "Come to Jesus"
Scripture: Mark 1:1-8
Song: "I Surrender All"
Devotional Thought: Father, thank You for sending Your Son, Jesus, to preach the Good News. Help me to be a disciple of Jesus, one in whom You are well pleased.

THE BEGINNING OF THE GOSPEL

Bible Background • MARK 1:1-45
Printed Text • MARK 1:9-26
Devotional Reading • LUKE 4:14-21

LESSON AIM

By the end of the lesson, students will know that beginning a work for God requires total obedience and will involve temptation and conflicts. They will become convinced that victory is possible through the power of God.

KEEP IN MIND

"And there came a voice from heaven, saying, Thou art my beloved Son, in whom I am well pleased" (Mark 1:11).

FOCAL VERSES

Mark 1:9 And it came to pass in those days, that Jesus came from Nazareth of Galilee, and was baptized of John in Jordan.

10 And straightway coming up out of the water, he saw the heavens opened, and the Spirit like a dove descending upon him:

11 And there came a voice from heaven, saying, Thou art my beloved Son, in whom I am well pleased.

12 And immediately the spirit driveth him into the wilderness.

13 And he was there in the wilderness forty days, tempted of Satan; and was with the wild beasts; and the angels ministered unto him.

14 Now after that John was put in prison, Jesus came into Galilee, preaching the gospel of the kingdom of God,

15 And saying, The time is fulfilled, and the kingdom of God is at hand: repent ye, and believe the gospel.

16 Now as he walked by the sea of Galilee, he saw Simon and Andrew his brother casting a net into the

LESSON OVERVIEW

LESSON AIM
KEEP IN MIND
FOCAL VERSES
IN FOCUS
THE PEOPLE, PLACES, AND TIMES
BACKGROUND
AT-A-GLANCE
IN DEPTH
SEARCH THE SCRIPTURES
DISCUSS THE MEANING
LESSON IN OUR SOCIETY
MAKE IT HAPPEN
FOLLOW THE SPIRIT
REMEMBER YOUR THOUGHTS
MORE LIGHT ON THE TEXT
DAILY BIBLE READINGS

sea: for they were fishers.

17 And Jesus said unto them, Come ye after me, and I will make you to become fishers of men.

18 And straightway they forsook their nets, and followed him.

19 And when he had gone a little farther thence, he saw James the son of Zebedee, and John his brother, who also were in the ship mending their nets.

20 And straightway he called them: and they left their father Zebedee in the ship with the hired servants, and went after him.

21 And they went into Capernaum; and straightway on the sabbath day he entered into the synagogue, and taught.

22 And they were astonished at his doctrine: for he taught them as one that had authority, and not as the scribes.

23 And there was in their synagogue a man with an unclean spirit; and he cried out,

24 Saying, Let us alone; what have we to do with thee, thou Jesus of Nazareth? art thou come to destroy us? I know thee who thou art, the Holy One of God.

25 And Jesus rebuked him, saying, Hold thy peace, and come out of him.

26 And when the unclean spirit had torn him, and cried with a loud voice, he came out of him.

IN FOCUS

Beginning a new venture can be difficult and requires motivation, faith, and discipline. Wilma

Rudolph (1940-1994), the first American woman to win three gold medals in the Olympics in 1960, exhibited such stamina. This great African-American athlete faced major challenges, including racism and a severe case of childhood polio.

Yet she overcame and made this statement in *I Dream a World* by Brian Lanker: "It took sheer determination to be able to run a hundred yards and remember all of the mechanics that go along with it. . . . From the moment you walk into the stadium, you block out everything and everybody, until you get the command to start."

In today's lesson we will learn about the beginning of the Gospel and the temptation Jesus faced.

THE PEOPLE, PLACES, AND TIMES

John the Baptizer. The son of Zacharias and Elizabeth, little is known about his early years. The prophets declared that he would precede the Messiah and that his purpose was to reform the Jews and prepare them to receive the Messiah (Isaiah 40:1-8; Malachi 4:5-6).

Unclean Spirits. Unclean spirits were demons. Both Jews and Greeks believed these spirits possessed living persons and controlled them.

Galilee. One of three provinces in Palestine, along with Judea and Samaria. The place where Jesus preached His first sermon, this northern province becomes the focal point of His ministry.

BACKGROUND

John Mark wrote the Gospel of Mark in Rome sometime after Peter was martyred about A.D. 64. The Gospel writer's name is both Jewish (John) and Roman (Mark or Marcus). It is the only book among the four Gospels that uses the term the "Gospel of Jesus Christ," and most scholars believe it is the oldest Gospel. Also, the Book of Mark, unlike Matthew and Luke which begin with the stories of Jesus' birth, focuses on the mission and miracles of Christ.

Although it is the shortest Gospel, Mark is filled with great detail about Jesus' miracles and does not include long discourses on His teachings. Scholars consider this Gospel as one filled with action and have called it the "Gospel of Power."

The title "Gospel of Power" is certainly appropriate as the Book of Mark begins with Jesus' baptism, temptation, and then proceeds to His authoritative

presence in Galilee as teacher, preacher, and healer. His public entrance into ministry is set in motion by His forerunner, John the Baptist. John the Baptist, son of priest Zacharias and Elizabeth, who preaches in the wilderness of Judea and in the Jordan valley, is to prepare the people for the Messiah. Although John preaches repentance and tells people of the arrival of one greater than he who will baptize with the Holy Spirit (Matthew 3:1-12), Jesus' ministry still meets opposition and rejection. Today's study and succeeding lessons show how Jesus experiences conflict, not only with Satan in the wilderness, but also among the religious leaders and His own townsfolk.

AT-A-GLANCE

1. Jesus Is Baptized by John (Mark 1:9-11)
2. Jesus Faces Temptation (vv. 12-13)
3. Jesus Preaches and Calls Disciples (vv. 14-20)
4. Jesus Teaches and Heals in the Synagogue (vv. 21-26)

IN DEPTH

1. Jesus Is Baptized by John (Mark 1:9-11)

John baptizes Jesus in the Jordan River, the main north-south river of Palestine. This baptism represents Jesus' initial outward preparation for His entrance into public ministry. As evidence of this confirmation Jesus saw and heard signs from heaven. He saw the heavens open and the Spirit descend on Him like a dove. Some scholars believe that the people saw and heard these signs, while others declare that Jesus alone witnessed the events.

God's voice was an affirmation of Jesus's identity: "Thou art my beloved Son," as well as an endorsement of what Jesus would do: "in whom I am well pleased." Although Jesus had just begun His public ministry, God was already pleased.

Jesus' baptism represented full and complete obedience to God. In Matthew 3:15 Jesus tells John that baptism fulfills all righteousness: "Let it be so now; it is proper for us to do this to fulfill all righteousness" (NIV). The very act of baptism was one of humility and total obedience on behalf of Jesus because He was already totally committed to doing the Father's will.

2. Jesus Faces Temptation (vv. 12-13)

After His confirmation at baptism, Jesus undergoes a wilderness experience. Mark uses the expression "the spirit driveth him forth," which means that Jesus submitted to the will of God. The Scripture is clear about the purpose of the wilderness—Satan there tempted Him. Anytime God sets His seal of approval upon us for ministry, temptation or conflict will often follow.

What type of place was the wilderness? Located beyond Jericho and extending along the western shore of the Dead Sea, the wilderness was a place of isolation, barrenness, and peril. Verse 13 tells us that wild animals freely roamed this desolate place, so Jesus' life was in jeopardy. In addition to being physically weak, having fasted for 40 days, Satan presented Jesus with three temptations (Matthew 4:1-10). Satan not only presented the temptations, but also questioned the essence of who Jesus proclaimed to be by stating, "If you are . . ." (NIV). Nevertheless, Jesus knew He was the Son of God.

Do you know who you are in Christ? When the enemy questions your identity, are you able to say, "I am a child of the Father?"

3. Jesus Preaches and Calls Disciples (vv. 14-20)

Jesus came on the scene preaching after John was placed in prison. His message was clear: "repent and believe the good news" (NIV). Christians and religious leaders have often made salvation difficult to understand and complex to fulfill. But Jesus' call is simply "repent and believe the good news."

Jesus knew that He would need to employ others to assist Him in His work. He did not look among kings, princes, or royalty, but He called ordinary people like fishermen. Note that Jesus' call was for His followers to "come after me." These four fishermen— Simon, Andrew, James, and John—responded to Jesus immediately. No doubt they had heard and seen Jesus on other occasions, but this time was different. "They forsook their nets, and followed him." Two key words here are *forsook* and *followed*, which could be viewed as outward expressions of

repent and *believe*. They forsook or left their old way of life, and even more their livelihood. So for these rugged fishermen to *follow* Jesus required faith— faith that Jesus had something better to offer.

4. Jesus Teaches and Heals in the Synagogue (vv. 21-26)

Capernaum, a town on the northwest shore of the Sea of Galilee, was the place Jesus began His ministry. His going to the synagogue was customary (Luke 4:16), but on this day He taught. And His teachings were unlike the scribes, who taught out of tradition, perhaps in rote, ritualistic manner. In *The Layman's Bible Commentary*, Paul S. Minear makes this statement about the scribes: "The other scribes relied upon the authority of the Scriptures and of their tradition; [Jesus] spoke as a prophet, relaying a message straight from heaven and acting as if he had been assigned to speak in God's own name."

Although Mark's Gospel does not state what Jesus said in the synagogue, the power in which He spoke amazed the audience. Instead of speaking on the authority of Moses or the elders as the scrbes did, Jesus spoke on His own authority. Throughout Matthew (5:18, 20, 22) we hear Jesus saying, "I say unto you."

Jesus' authoritative teaching was demonstrated with power when He encountered the man with an unclean spirit. The unclean spirit had ruled the man for a period of time, we do not know how long, but assuredly it did not want to relinquish control and submit to Jesus. In fact, the demon's response, "What have we to do with thee?" means "leave me to act as I please."

Jesus' purpose was to destroy the works of the devil, so He would not permit the demon to control. Jesus responded with a rebuke, and in only eight words, He commanded the unclean spirit to come out.

Jesus set free the man who was once dominated by a demonic spirit. He was not only set free physically, but mentally, emotionally, and spiritually.

SEARCH THE SCRIPTURES

1. What was the Father's response to Jesus' baptism? (Mark 1:11)

2. In which province of Palestine did Jesus begin His ministry? (v. 14)

3. How did the people respond to Jesus' teachings? (v. 22)

4. What did Jesus say to the man with an unclean spirit? (v. 25)

DISCUSS THE MEANING

1. As children of God we are always faced with various forms of temptation. What actions can we take to keep us from yielding to temptation?

2. Simon, Andrew, James, and John forsook their way of life and followed Jesus. What things, people, or places might Jesus be calling us to forsake today in order to follow Him?

3. The people were amazed because Jesus taught with authority. What is the difference between hearing a scholarly preacher or teacher versus one who is both knowledgeable and speaks with God's anointing?

4. Share with the group a time when Jesus healed you. It does not have to be a physical healing but might include an emotional or spiritual healing.

LESSON IN OUR SOCEITY

If there ever was a time in which the world needed to hear the simple message "repent . . . and believe the gospel," it is now. Murders are taking place in the schools, among family members, at the workplace, and even in churches. New Age beliefs and cults have drawn people away from the church. Unfortunately many churches are places of schisms and strife.

Today Jesus is still saying there is hope; just come follow Me. As He brought complete healing to the man with the unclean spirit, Jesus wants to do the same for us. Jesus is always beckoning us to come.

Jesus sees us, with our broken hearts, our weary spirits, and our fractured souls, and He bids come to Him—to come just as we are.

MAKE IT HAPPEN

During the month of March why not start a journal called "My New Beginning?" If you are new to journaling, a journal is a place to record prayers, concerns, and any spiritual insights regarding your daily experiences. It is not a diary, so you do not have to record routine events that happen during the day. Also, your journal does not have to be elaborate; a small spiral notebook will work fine.

What will you write in your journal? First, ask God to show you one area in your life where you need to start anew. Perhaps you need to begin eating a balanced diet opposed to unhealthy foods. Have you been holding a grudge against someone and need to release it? Is it an unhealthy relationship in which you need to let go? Do you struggle with pride? Be honest with God so that you can receive the healing and deliverance that you need.

In your journal write, "I will begin anew by _____ (write your area of concern). After you have written down your struggle, find a Scripture that you can meditate on to encourage your victory over this problem or sin. Write that Scripture, or other passages if you found more than one, in your journal.

Then prayerfully ask God to show you things you need to do, or stop doing, to gain victory. Remember, temptation will come, but be determined to follow God. Last, let your spouse, a close friend, or prayer partner know what you are doing and ask that person to keep you in prayer.

FOLLOW THE SPIRIT

What God wants me to do:

_____

_____

REMEMBER YOUR THOUGHTS

Special insights you have learned:

_____

_____

MORE LIGHT ON THE TEXT
Mark 1:9-26

The Gospel of Mark begins with the beginning of Christ's earthly ministry but leaves out His nativity narrative and biography as in Matthew and Luke. We can only speculate about the reason for the absence of these elements in Mark's Gospel. Either Mark lacks knowledge concerning the birth and early childhood of Christ, or they are of no use in his purpose for the book. Therefore, we are immediately confronted with the announcement of the preparation of "the beginning of the gospel of Jesus Christ" (v. 1); it leads us to Christ's public ministry, which begins around A.D. 27 when He was about 30 years old. His ministry is preceded by two major events—

His baptism by John the Baptist and His temptation by the devil.

9 And it came to pass in those days, that Jesus came from Nazareth of Galilee, and was baptized of John in Jordan.

Mark begins his story about Jesus with a formula that is common in the Gospels. "And it came to pass," or the Greek *ginomai* (pronounced **ghin-oh-my**) is often translated as "it happened" or "came about," a formula often used to connect stories. The phrase "in those days" *en ekeinais tais hemerais,* (pronounced **in eh-kay-nice tice heh-merr-ice**) can also be rendered "at that time" and links us to the preceding story (vv. 1-8). As John is baptizing in the Jordan River, Jesus comes from Nazareth of Galilee, His boyhood hometown, and is baptized by John. Mark omits some of the details of Christ's baptism contained in Matthew 3:14-15.

10 And straightway coming up out of the water, he saw the heavens opened, and the Spirit like a dove descending upon him:

Mark uses the adverb "straightway," or Greek *euthys* (pronounced **you-thoose**), which he uses as many times as all the other New Testament writers combined. It can also be translated as immediately, forthwith or as soon as, to describe the immediacy of the occurrence of the event that follows the baptism of Christ. The frequency of the adverb in Mark gives the Book a certain degree "of breathlessness," as one writer puts it. The use of *euthys* here seems to suggest that as soon as Jesus leaves the water, "the heaven opened and the Spirit" descends upon Him, almost simultaneously. According to Mark's account, it seems that only Jesus witnessed the strange phenomenon. The word translated "opened" here (KJV) is dramatically rendered in the Greek with the verb *schizo* (pronounced **skih-zuh**) which is better translated split, rend, or sever. Matthew 3:16 and Luke 3:21 use a different Greek verb *anoigo* (pronounced **ah-noy-go**), ordinarily used for "open." The only other place the word *schizo* appears in the Gospel is in 15:38 when Mark reports that at Jesus' death the curtain in the temple split from top to bottom. A number of other scriptural passages refer to human experiences of heaven opening. In the Acts of the Apostles, when he is being stoned to death,

Stephen declares, "I see the heavens opened, and the Son of man standing on the right hand of God" (Acts 7:56).

As the heaven splits, the "Spirit like a dove" descends upon Jesus. The descent of the Spirit on Jesus here indicates His anointing and equipping for His earthly ministry. He promises the same anointing to His disciples prior to His ascension into heaven (Acts 1:8). Earlier, speaking in the synagogue at Nazareth, Jesus declares, "The Spirit of the Lord is upon me" (Luke 4:18).

11 And there came a voice from heaven, saying, Thou art my beloved Son, in whom I am well pleased.

The descent of the Spirit in the form of a dove is followed with a "voice from heaven" which affirms the messianic status of Jesus by God. Here the voice addresses Jesus directly: "You are My beloved Son, in You I am well-pleased" (NASB), but at the Transfiguration the voice confirms Jesus' status to the disciples (Peter, James, and John) using the third person: "This is my beloved Son: hear him" (Mark 9:7). This echoes the prophetic song of Psalm 2:7 that refers to the Lord's anointed as God's beloved Son. At the beginning of the Book of Mark (1:1), Mark confesses Jesus as the Son of God, and here God Himself testifies that Jesus is His Son. The word "beloved" comes from the Greek *agapeto,* (pronounced **ah-gah-pay-tahass**), a noun derivation of the verb *agapao* (pronounced **ah-gah-pah-oh**), meaning to love. The word *agapetos* therefore means loved one or one who is dearly loved. The phrase "I am well pleased" (Greek *eudokesa,* pronounced **you-dough-keh-sa**) comes from the verb *eudokeo* (pronounced **you-dough-keh-oh**). It means to think well of (i.e., approve), to have or take pleasure in. Here God not only confirms Christ as His Son He also declares His confidence and the pleasure He has in Him. This indicates God's approval of Christ's ministry.

12 And immediately the spirit driveth him into the wilderness. 13 And he was there in the wilderness forty days, tempted of Satan; and was with the wild beasts; and the angels ministered unto him.

Using his characteristic word *euthys,* Mark emphasizes the urgency and immediacy of the temptation of Christ following His baptism. *Euthys* will be correctly translated "at once." That means immediately following this announcement (v. 11), the Spirit (the same Spirit who descended on Him) drives Jesus into the desert. The word "drive" is the Greek *ekballo* (pronounced **eck-bah-low**) and can be rendered send away or thrust with the idea of being compelled, though without the notion of resistance. He spends 40 days in the desert being tempted of the devil or Satan. Mark's account of the temptation is brief compared with Matthew and Luke's account (see Matthew 4:1-11; Luke 4:1-13). While in Matthew and Luke's account we read that Jesus spends 40 days in the wilderness without food, which prompts the first of the threefold temptations, Mark makes no mention of His fasting. Mark gives no specific temptation but mentions that "the angels ministered to Him." What is the significance in being in the wilderness 40 days? It has been suggested that the 40 days is reminiscent of Moses' 40 days and 40 nights on Mount Sinai (Exodus 24:18), Israel's 40 years of wandering in the wilderness (Numbers 14:33), or Elijah's experience in the desert (1 Kings 19:8, 15). Mark does not develop these themes. Rather he mentions that Jesus "was with the wild beasts," which suggests a continuous conflict and temptation with Satan for the period of 40 days. Forty days, as someone has suggested, perhaps is symbolic of an extended period of time. The word "ministered" Mark uses here is the Greek verb *diakoneo* (pronounced **dee-ah-kow-neh-oh**) and suggests that Jesus is continuously attended to or served throughout the 40 days by angels. Contrary to some suggestions, service here does not imply that the angels were feeding Him. Rather it could mean that they ministered to Him by encouraging and strengthening Him (Matthew 4:11; Luke 22:43).

14 Now after that John was put in prison, Jesus came into Galilee, preaching the gospel of the kingdom of God, 15 And saying, The time is fulfilled, and the kingdom of God is at hand: repent ye, and believe the gospel.

Verse 14 serves as transition to the narrative of the

beginning of Christ's ministry. It states the time frame when Christ begins to preach following His temptation by the devil. Again, without the details concerning John's imprisonment and death as in Matthew (11:2; 14:1-12), Mark tells us where Jesus begins His ministry in the regions of Galilee. He begins ministry in His own region (v. 9) "preaching the gospel of the kingdom of God." Mark summaries the theme of Christ's ministry in verse 15: "The time is fulfilled, and the kingdom of God is at hand: repent ye, and believe the gospel." This echoes the message of John the Baptist (Matthew 3:2), the same message the disciples are charged to preach (Matthew 10:7-10; Mark 6:7-13). Indeed, this is the gist of the whole Gospel message for believers of all times. Matthew's account of Christ's ministry in the region of Galilee includes preaching, teaching, and healing (4:23).

The mention of John's imprisonment seems to suggest that Jesus' public ministry began only after John is imprisoned (i.e., after John as the forerunner has completed his own task). The content of Christ's preaching is about "gospel of the kingdom of God." The "gospel," or the Greek *euaggelion* (pronounced **you-ahng-ghel-ee-ahn**), is generally translated as good news or good message. The "good news of the kingdom of God" is both about God as the object and from God as the subject. Here Jesus announces that "the time is fulfilled and the kingdom of God is at hand." The phrase "time (*kairos*) is fulfilled" means the season or a previously promised period of time (i.e., the consummation of God's plan for Israel, Galatians 4:4). "The kingdom of God" refers to the sovereign rule of God. The divine rule Jesus says is "at hand" or, more appropriately, has drawn near. The kingdom of God referred to here is not the world-sphere but the rule of God within the human heart. Thus, the condition for the reality of this kingdom is through repentance from sin and believing the Gospel. By doing this, we allow God's sovereign rule in our hearts.

16 Now as he walked by the sea of Galilee, he saw Simon and Andrew his brother casting a net into the sea: for they were fishers. 17 And Jesus said unto them, Come ye after me, and I will make you to become fishers of men. 18 And straightway they forsook their nets, and followed him.

The next four verses give details of the call of Christ's first disciples. As He passes along the shores of the Sea of Galilee, He sees two brothers, Simon and Andrew, fishing. Mark does not tell us whether these brothers had any encounter with Jesus prior to this time (see John 1:35-42); he does not tell us how big their fishing business was. The only information that Mark considers necessary is that, seeing these brothers casting their net, Jesus invites them to follow Him. Fishing was common in the region because the sea abounded with fish. Without hesitation, Simon and his brother abandon their nets and follow Him. In His invitation, Jesus tells them that they will be fishing for people, rather than catching fish. Mark uses the adverb "straightway" again here (see v. 10) to describe how quickly the two brothers accepted the invitation to follow Jesus. That means when Jesus asks them to follow Him, they at once, or instantly, left their nets and followed Jesus. The word "follow" is the Greek word *akoloutheo* (pronounced **ah-kaw-loo-theh-oh**) which means to accompany, specifically as a disciple.

19 And when he had gone a little farther thence, he saw James the son of Zebedee, and John his brother, who also were in the ship mending their nets. 20 And straightway he called them: and they left their father Zebedee in the ship with the hired servants, and went after him.

As He walks a little farther, Jesus sees two brothers named James and John with their father and their servants fishing. Jesus extends the same invitation to them to follow Him. Likewise, James and John respond immediately, leaving their father and their servants and follow Jesus. The mention of the "hired servants" seems to suggest that Zebedee's fishing business is a big one, but how big is not indicated. It also tends to indicate that by leaving their father, the two brothers are not leaving their father alone to run their business all by himself. However, the main point here is the immediate response they gave to Jesus' call just as in the case of Simon and Andrew. This call also demonstrates the cost of discipleship, which includes not only abandoning everything to follow Jesus, but also breaking the family ties.

21 And they went into Capernaum; and straightway on the sabbath day he entered into the synagogue, and taught.

With His newly acquired disciples, Jesus goes to Capernaum. The phrase "and straightway on the Sabbath day" seems to suggest that as soon as Jesus and the four arrive in the city of Capernaum on the Sabbath, He goes into the synagogue and begins to teach the people. Alternatively, they have been in the city and then on the Sabbath day they go into the synagogue where He teaches the people.

Capernaum was a city in the north of Galilee. It was the home of the Apostle Peter and became the headquarters of Jesus' ministry (2:1-6; 9:33; cf. Matthew 4:13; 17:24-27; Luke 4:31; 7:1-10; 10:15; John 4:46-53; 6:17-25, 59). The word "synagogue" is an English transliteration of the Greek *sunagoge* (pronounced **SOON-ah-go-GAY**) which refers both to a local assembly and the place where the congregation meets. Synagogues originated during the Babylonian exile and were erected in numerous cities for worship and instruction. Synagogues served other purposes, such as a place for a court of justice where both religious and civil cases were tried (Luke 12:11; Acts 9:2; see also Matthew 10:17; 23:34; John 9:22, 34; 12:42; 16:2; Acts 22:19; 26:11; etc.). Jesus frequently made use of the synagogue for His teaching. He made use of the freedom of the Jewish custom whereby teachers were invited to teach in the synagogues (Luke 4:14-22; cf. Matthew 4:23; 13:54; Mark 6:2), reading the Scriptures and expanding on the Law. The apostles also often made use of synagogues (Acts 13:5, 15; 14:1; 17:10-17; 18:19).

22 And they were astonished at his doctrine: for he taught them as one that had authority, and not as the scribes.

As Jesus enters the synagogue in Capernaum, He begins to teach the congregation. His teaching is described as being with authority "and not as the scribes." The word "authority" comes from the Greek *exousia* (pronounced **ex-oo-SEE-ah**) which can also mean power, with the idea of being in control and confident. Although we are not told what He taught them in this instance, His teachings have such authority and power that the people are astonished. The word translated "astonished" here is the Greek word *exeplessonto*, which is a compound word from *plesso* (pronounced **PLAY-so**). It means to strike with panic, astound, to be struck with amazement, to be overwhelmed. To them this is a new way of teaching, which differs from how the scribes or the teachers of the law taught. The "scribes," or its Greek equivalent *grammateus* (**grah-mah-TOOSE**) were professional writers or secretaries, custodians of the law, professionally trained and charged with interpretation and application of the Jewish law (Ezra 7:6-21; Nehemiah 8:1-13; Matthew 23:2-34; Luke 5:17; etc.). What is the difference between Jesus' teaching and that of scribes? The difference is that while the scribes quote from other sources, Jesus speaks independently without referring to or relying on external sources. He speaks directly from God. No wonder He astounds them. This authority is not only demonstrated abstractly through the preaching and teaching of the Word, but in the demonstration and power over sickness and unclean spirits as we can see in the next few verses.

23 And there was in their synagogue a man with an unclean spirit; and he cried out, 24 Saying, Let us alone; what have we to do with thee, thou Jesus of Nazareth? art thou come to destroy us? I know thee who thou art, the Holy One of God.

In the synagogue among the congregation is a man possessed with an unclean or evil spirit, sometimes called a demon. As Jesus is teaching, the possessed man disrupts the service as he shouts with a loud voice, asking Jesus to let them alone. The use of the plural pronouns indicates that the "unclean spirit" works in a group of other spirits. The phrase "what have we to do with thee" is from the Greek *ti hemçn kai soi*, (pronounced **tih-hey-min-KAI-soy**). It literally means "what is [there] to us and to you," i.e., "what do we have in common?" In other words "what do you want from us?" The unclean spirit identifies both the earthly and heavenly natures of Jesus. In the earthly realm He is "Jesus of (from) Nazareth," and in the heavenly realm He is "the Holy One of (from) God." Not only do demons know Jesus, they also recognize His authority (Acts 19:15) and ability to overcome them. Hence they ask, "Art thou come to destroy us?" The devil's purpose here is not to confess Jesus, but to deceive people and discredit Jesus.

Belief in the work and activities of demons has between minimized in our modern society, especially among churches in the so-called developed or civilized nations. Such beliefs have often been dismissed as superstition or attributed to a "third world" phenomenon or something that happens in the most remote sections of the world. Many fail to recognize their existence and therefore they remain unprepared, unequipped, and unable to fight them. However, this attitude is changing. Many churches are now coming to grips with the existence of the devil and his work and are now getting spiritually equipped to face and fight him.

25 And Jesus rebuked him, saying, Hold thy peace, and come out of him. 26 And when the unclean spirit had torn him, and cried with a loud voice, he came out of him.

Jesus recognizes the demon's craftiness, and He commands him to "hold thy peace," i.e., to be quiet and to "come out of" the man. Jesus used no magical formula only His authority based on the Word of God. After ordering the demon to come out, He speaks the word. The spirit, crying with a loud voice, convulses the man and comes out of him. The people are astonished more at this miracle, and His fame spread in all the region of Galilee.

DAILY BIBLE READINGS

M: Jesus Is Baptized, Tempted
Mark 1:1-13

T: Jesus Calls Four Fishermen
Mark 1:14-20

W: Follow Me
John 1:43-51

T: You Will Catch People
Luke 5:1-11

F: Jesus Casts Out an Unclean Spirit
Mark 1:21-28

S: Jesus Heals Many Sick Persons
Mark 1:29-38

S: Jesus Preaches Throughout Galilee
Mark 1:39-45

TEACHING TIPS

March 9
Bible Study Guide 2

1. Words You Should Know

A. Sick of the Palsy (Mark 2:4); Greek *paralutikos* (pronounced **Pah-rah-lit-ih-kahass**)—Disabled due to the lack of functioning of certain nerves (paralysis).

B. Speak Blasphemy (v. 7); Greek *blasphemeo* (pronounced **Blahs-feh-meh-oh**)—To speak evil against God. According to *The American Heritage Dictionary* it is "the act of claiming for oneself the attributes and rights of God."

2. Teacher Preparation

A. Study the Devotional Reading, and pray for your students asking God to strengthen and provide wisdom as they start their new beginning journal.

B. Study the BACKGROUND section.

C. Be prepared to ask students to imagine that they are the following characters in the Scripture passage "The Faith of Friends" (Mark 2:3-12). You will serve as the narrator.

D. Materials needed: Bible, chalkboard and chalk, an illustration of a New Testament house, and a *New International Version* Bible.

3. Starting the Lesson

A. Before the students arrive, write "The Faith of Friends" on the board and underneath this title write the following words: the four friends, the paralytic man, the scribes (teachers of the law), and Jesus.

B. After the students arrive have prayer. Then read and discuss IN FOCUS.

4. Getting into the Lesson

A. Have a volunteer read THE PEOPLE, PLACES, AND TIMES and clarify any questions students might have. Make sure students understand who the Pharisees were since some students will role-play this group later in the lesson.

B. Explain to the students the definitions of to "speak blasphemy" and "sick of the palsy."

C. Let students know that they will become biblical characters in today's lesson. Ask for volunteers to represent each person making sure each character is rep-

resented. Tell students to close their eyes and imagine that they are the characters they choose. Read with clarity and expression (Mark 2:3-12, NIV). After you read the passage, allow them to talk about how they felt being their character, why they thought or acted the way they did, and so forth.

D. Read the remaining FOCAL VERSES and discuss them.

5. Relating the Lesson to Life

A. Direct the students to read DISCUSS THE MEANING and allow time for them to express their answers to questions 1 and 3. Then spend time discussing question 3, and ask students if they encountered any opposition this week as they began their new start.

B. Read and discuss LESSON IN OUR SOCIETY.

6. Arousing Action

A. Direct the students' attention to the MAKE IT HAPPEN suggestion and encourage them to practice it this week.

B. Encourage and remind students to write in their journal this week, specifically noting any conflicts they have encountered in their new beginning.

C. Tell the students to review today's lesson this week by completing SEARCH THE SCRIPTURES.

D. Close the session with prayer.

WORSHIP GUIDE

For the Superintendent or Teacher
Theme: The Beginning of Conflict
Theme Song: "He Looked Beyond My Fault"
Scripture: Psalm 63:1-8
Song: "I Know the Lord Laid His Hands on Me"
Devotional Thought: Father, thank You for Your unconditional love and Your power to heal the body, mind, and spirit.

THE BEGINNING OF CONFLICT

Bible Background • MARK 2:1—3:6
Printed Text • MARK 2:3-12, 14-17
Devotional Reading • LUKE 15:1-7

LESSON AIM

By the end of the lesson, students will understand that Jesus has the power to heal and forgive sins, and that His main purpose was to make sinners whole. Students will be motivated to reach out and help a needy person during the week.

KEEP IN MIND

"When Jesus heard it, he saith unto them, They that are whole have no need of the physician, but they that are sick: I came not to call the righteous, but sinners to repentance'" (Mark 2:17).

FOCAL VERSES

Mark 2:3 And they come unto him, bringing one sick of the palsy, which was borne of four.

4 And when they could not come nigh unto him for the press, they uncovered the roof where he was: and when they had broken it up, they let down the bed wherein the sick of the palsy lay.

5 When Jesus saw their faith, he said unto the sick of the palsy, Son, thy sins be forgiven thee.

6 But there were certain of the scribes sitting there, and reasoning in their hearts,

7 Why doth this man thus speak blasphemies? who can forgive sins but God only?

8 And immediately when Jesus perceived in his spirit that they so reasoned within themselves, he said unto them, Why reason ye these things in your hearts?

9 Whether is it easier to say to the sick of the palsy, Thy sins be forgiven thee; or to say, Arise, and take up thy bed, and walk?

LESSON OVERVIEW

LESSON AIM
KEEP IN MIND
FOCAL VERSES
IN FOCUS
THE PEOPLE, PLACES,
AND TIMES
BACKGROUND
AT-A-GLANCE
IN DEPTH
SEARCH THE SCRIPTURES
DISCUSS THE MEANING
LESSON IN OUR SOCIETY
MAKE IT HAPPEN
FOLLOW THE SPIRIT
REMEMBER YOUR THOUGHTS
MORE LIGHT ON THE TEXT
DAILY BIBLE READINGS

10 But that ye may know that the Son of man hath power on earth to forgive sins, (he saith to the sick of the palsy,)

11 I say unto thee, Arise, and take up thy bed, and go thy way into thine house.

12 And immediately he arose, took up the bed, and went forth before them all; insomuch that they were all amazed, and glorified God, saying, We never saw it on this fashion.

2:14 And as he passed by, he saw Levi the son of Alphaeus sitting at the receipt of custom, and said unto him, Follow me. And he arose and followed him.

15 And it came to pass, that, as Jesus sat at meat in his house, many publicans and sinners sat also together with Jesus and his disciples: for there were many, and they followed him.

16 And when the scribes and Pharisees saw him eat with publicans and sinners, they said unto his disciples, How is it that he eateth and drinketh with publicans and sinners?

17 When Jesus heard it, he saith unto them, They that are whole have no need of the physician, but they that are sick: I came not to call the righteous, but sinners to repentance.

IN FOCUS

He was beaten by a mob, jailed over twenty times, bombed at home and church, and sued for three and a half-million dollars. This man is the Reverend Fred Shuttlesworth, a gallant leader of the Civil Rights Movement in the 1950's and 60's. He worked with Dr.

Martin Luther King, Jr. in Birmingham, Alabama, and for forty years fought for desegregation and equality. Despite the opposition Shuttlesworth faced, he did not retreat from the battle to see justice prevail and stood steadfast on his faith in God. During a sermon at John Wesley United Methodist Church in Ohio he made this statement: "I've faced death eight times (during the civil rights movement), but God has never let me die" (*The Cincinnati Enquirer,* October 1999).

In today's lesson we will discover the conflict that Jesus encountered with the scribes and Pharisees because of His stand for righteousness. Jesus confronted these religious accusers by clearly articulating His mission and purpose: "I came not to call the righteous, but sinners to repentance" (Mark 2:17). What is your response when others question your work for God? Do you know your mission and purpose as a child of God?

THE PEOPLE, PLACES, AND TIMES

Religious Sects. The following religious sects existed in Palestine during Jesus' time:

Pharisees. This sect, which means "the separated ones," numbered around 6,000. They were the most influential and pledged themselves to obey every aspect of tradition and often added rules to assure not breaking the Law in any minute fashion. Thus the Pharisees added rules and regulations which became a burden to the Jews, and Jesus often rebuked them for their self-righteousness and hypocrisy (Matthew 15:1-9). Not all Pharisees were hypocrites, however; some were sincere in their reverence for God and the Law.

Sadducees. Not as large as the Pharisees, some scholars believe this group (also called Zadokites) originated from the sons of Zadok. Zadok was a priest during the reign of King David (1 Kings 1:32-33). Unlike the Pharisees, they did not believe in the resurrection of the body after death. Although the Sadducees also exhibited a self-righteous demeanor, they were not quite sticklers for the law as the Pharisees were, and they also strongly opposed Jesus.

The Essenes. With only a few thousand in this sect, they opposed the Greek influence on the Jewish religion. They believed in self-denial, temperance, and strict adherence, in some ways more so than the Pharisees, to the law. They had their own purification rites and did not worship in the temple. The group is not mentioned in the New Testament.

The Zealots. This sect solidly opposed Rome, even resorting to violence. They were against paying taxes and the Roman pagan beliefs. Simon, one of the disciples, was a Zealot (Luke 6:15).

Scribes. Often called lawyers and doctors of the law (Matthew 22:35), they were not considered a sect or a party, nor were they priests. Their expertise in the law was their occupation, so they received payment for their teachings. The scribes, who often served as judges, strongly opposed Jesus and His teachings.

BACKGROUND

The news of Jesus, the worker of miracles, spread throughout Capernaum. This was an exciting time, for the community had never experienced a healer and teacher like Jesus. No wonder Mark 1:32-33 speaks of the townspeople bringing all the sick and demon-possessed to Jesus. And in Jesus' great compassion He healed every one of them, but He too needed a time of restful healing. So the next morning He departed to be alone with the Father.

The Scriptures do not tell the length of Jesus' solitude, but His time was shortened by the disciples' appearance. Jesus did not appear to be irritated by the disciples presence, but informed them that He must preach in other places: "Let us go on to the neighboring towns, so that I may proclaim the message there also; for that is what I came out to do" (Mark 1:38, New Revised Standard Version NRSV). Of a certainty there were more people in need of healing in Capernaum, but Jesus knew His mission was to spread the Gospel to everyone, so He traveled to other towns.

AT-A-GLANCE

1. The Faith of Friends (Mark 2:3-5)
2. The Threatening Thoughts (vv. 6-12)
3. The Call to a Collector (v. 14)
4. The Supper with Sinners (vv. 15-17)

IN DEPTH

1. The Faith of Friends (Mark 2:3-5)

Luke does not provide any great detail about the four friends who brought their paralyzed man to Jesus, but we can sum up their character in two words: persistent and resourceful. In fact, their ingenuity was a by-product of their persistence. They observed the crowd gathered and saw no way of getting near the door to see Jesus.

The oriental house structures in those days were one or two stories, built in the form of a rectangle or square. They had one door that opened into an open space called the porch. Often the porch contained a stairway that led to the roof. So these friends saw the roof as a means to reach Jesus.

The four friends tore up the roof of this house, which apparently belonged to Simon Peter. What were these men thinking? They were destroying another man's property. What did others think of this act? Alexander Maclaren in his *Expositions of Holy Scripture* states it eloquently:

"No doubt, their act was inconvenient; for, however light the roofing, some of the rubbish must have come down on the heads of some of the notabilities below. . . But here was a sick man, and there was his Healer; and it was their business to get the two together somehow. It was worth risking a good deal to accomplish. The rabbis sitting there might frown at the rude intrusiveness; Peter might object to the damage to his roof; some of the listeners might dislike the interruption to His teaching; but Jesus read the action of the bearers and the consent of the motionless figure on the couch as the indication of their faith, and His love and power responded to the call."

The four friends help us realize that we cannot be too concerned about what others think when we bring someone to Christ. Jesus was impressed with their faith, and that's all that really matters. The Master saw the man's physical need but looked beyond that to bring spiritual healing: "Son, thy sins be forgiven thee."

2. The Threatening Thoughts (vv. 6-12)

The teachers of the law said nothing but were outraged as they pondered Jesus forgiving the sins of another. That was God's right and authority, they

reasoned. "How dare he talk against God like this?" (v. 7, Today's English, TEV)). Responding to the scribes' thoughts, Jesus declares His authority as One who is able not only to heal but also to forgive sins. The Savior's desire is for us to be whole in body, soul, and spirit. The man, once a paralytic, now had his physical strength and activity restored as well as the weight of sin lifted off him.

3. The Call to a Collector (v. 14)

The Jews despised the publicans (tax collectors) who were charged with the task of collecting revenue for the Roman government, for they were extortioners and used any opportunity they could to overcharge the Jews. Publicans were considered the basest of people and considered defiled because of their conformity to Roman heathenism. What made matters worse was that many of the Jews were themselves collectors. Such was the case for Levi (Matthew), who sat at the tollgate and collected for Herod Antipas. As he sat, no doubt many passed by and looked at him with disgust, but Mark says that Jesus *saw* Levi, not like the other villagers. Jesus saw who Levi could become, and the Master acted upon this perception by inviting Levi to follow Him.

Levi's whole life changed as a result of accepting Jesus' call. He changed from sitting in the seat of sinners (the tax collector's booth) to walking in God's will and worshiping the Saviour. He changed from fraudulently taking from society to freely giving to others the message of deliverance.

4. The Supper with Sinners (vv. 15-17)

Jesus not only called Levi, He went to his home for dinner. Joining someone for a meal during Jesus' time was in some respects different from the way we gather for meals today. We may nonchalantly dine with people we do not like for our own selfish gain, or we speak disparagingly about our hosts when the meal is over. Conversely, a meal with someone in biblical times usually meant that the two parties were bound by mutual covenant. Thus, the meal at Levi's house meant that he and Jesus were in covenant. Since word about Jesus had spread throughout Galilee, other tax collectors and sinners were there, too, out of curiosity. They wanted to get a glimpse of Jesus and hear His teachings firsthand.

The sight of Jesus, a "religious man," eating with

outcasts and transgressors appalled the Pharisees and scribes. Jesus again makes clear His mission and purpose to these self-righteous leaders. "I have not come to call the respectable people, but the outcasts" (v. 17, TEV). This statement provides the clarion call that Jesus' ministry is to the lowly and the lost.

SEARCH THE SCRIPTURES

1. Why did the scribes accuse Jesus of blasphemy? (Mark 2:7)

2. What was Levi's occupation? (v. 14)

3. What was the purpose of Jesus' ministry? (v. 17)

DISCUSS THE MEANING

1. Is there a connection between sickness and unforgiveness? Can unforgiveness lead to sickness?

2. How can conflict weaken or strengthen our faith?

3. What might cause a person to feel unwelcome in church? What might Christian leaders do to welcome people in the church?

LESSON IN OUR SOCEITY

In today's lesson we see Jesus healing and forgiving sins, calling tax collectors to join Him in ministry, and eating with sinners. These actions bothered the religious leaders, but we again see our purposed-minded Healer. He was equipped during the biblical days, and He is equipping today. Likewise, whatever God has called you to do, He has already readied you for the job. "You are equipped with everything you need to fulfil your purpose," states Miles Munroe (*In Pursuit of Purpose*). He has called us as Christians to minister to the outcasts and people whom others do not want to touch. Despite the conflicts that you might encounter, even among other Christians and religious leaders, keep your faith in Jesus and be persistent like the four friends in today's lesson.

MAKE IT HAPPEN

This week ask God for a discerning spirit that you might reach out and touch someone that you normally overlook. God might lead you to buy lunch for a homeless person, speak words of encouragement to a store clerk, or pray with someone who is dis-

couraged. Don't look for something elaborate to do; simply follow the Spirit's leading as you meet people in your routine, daily activities. You will be blessed, and so will the other person.

FOLLOW THE SPIRIT
What God wants me to do:

_____

_____

REMEMBER YOUR THOUGHTS
Special insights you have learned:

_____

_____

MORE LIGHT ON THE TEXT
Mark 2:3-12, 14-17

The first chapter of the Gospel according to St. Mark records the beginning of Jesus' ministry, a ministry characterized by teaching, healing, and miracles. With these remarkable happenings and miracles, Jesus' fame spread all over the region. As a result, people from all walks of life came to Jesus bringing the sick, both to hear Him and to be healed. Among them were four people who brought a man sick of palsy to Jesus when He returned to Capernaum. Verse 2 states that Jesus "was in the house," probably Peter's house, which became His headquarters (Matthew 4:13; 9:1; Mark 1:21, 29).

3 And they come unto him, bringing one sick of the palsy, which was borne of four. 4 And when they could not come nigh unto him for the press, they uncovered the roof where he was: and when they had broken it up, they let down the bed wherein the sick of the palsy lay.

Jesus is apparently in Simon Peter's house in Capernaum preaching and teaching. The people, hearing that He is around, gather to hear Him. The crowd is so great that there is not room enough to contain them (vv. 1-2). To understand the full impact of this story, one needs to have knowledge of the layout of Palestinian houses at this time. It is believed that houses were flat-roofed with railings so that people would not fall off (Deuteronomy 22:8; Judges 16:27; 2 Samuel 11:2). On the top of some houses there was access via outside stairs. These types of houses are still common in the northern part of the African continent, especially in northern Nigeria. Houses there are built flat-roofed with mud and wooden beams and thatch covered over them.

As Jesus teaches in the small one-room house, four people bring a man "sick of the palsy" to be healed. As they arrive, they discover that there is no room or access through the doorway by which they can get to the Lord. They therefore carry the sick man up the outside stairs to the roof of the house. They lower the man down to Jesus. They evidently dig through the roof tiles (Luke 5:19) and lower the man in front of Jesus. There the sick man lay at Jesus' feet. The word "palsy" is the Greek word *paralutikos* (pronounced **pah-rah-loo-tih-KAHSS**) from which we derive the English paralytic or paralysis. The man is paralyzed, hence, he is unable to walk by himself to meet Jesus. Four of his friends or relatives carry him in a "bed" (stretcher or pallet) and place him before Jesus.

5 When Jesus saw their faith, he said unto the sick of the palsy, Son, thy sins be forgiven thee.

As he lay before Him, "Jesus saw their faith." Whose faith is referred here? Apparently, it is the faith of both the paralytic and the faith of his four friends or relatives. Their faith is demonstrated in their action carrying the man to the house and the creativity and perseverance in getting him to Jesus in spite of the obstacles. Prayers are often granted when faith is demonstrated (Matthew 21:22; Mark 9:23; 11:22-24; Hebrews 11:6; James 1:5-8). Here Jesus acknowledges their faith and says to the sick man, "Son, thy sins be forgiven thee." Of course this is not what the man or his friends are looking for. It does not mean that the man is particularly sinful, but he comes under the universal disunion between man and his Creator caused by man's sinful nature from the Garden of Eden. The pronouncement of forgiveness here also illustrates the common belief in the Old Testament that every suffering is embedded in man's alienation from God. To Jesus the man's deepest need is the healing of the soul (conversion and the forgiveness of sins), then the physical; it also illustrates Jesus' fundamental purpose established at the beginning of His ministry (1:15). Jesus, therefore, calls the people's attention to this need by proclaiming forgiveness to the man. This single act provokes controversy and conflict among the scribes and Jewish authorities against Jesus. It is also, according to Mark's records, the beginning of conflict in Christ's ministry on earth.

6 But there were certain of the scribes sitting there, and reasoning in their hearts, 7 Why doth this man thus speak blasphemies? who can forgive sins but God only?

Among the crowd gathered in the house to hear Jesus are some scribes—"teachers of the law" (see 1:22). According to Luke (5:17) these doctors of the law included the Pharisees who come from "every town of Galilee, and Judaea, and Jerusalem" to hear Him. Their purpose in coming is not made known. However, they must have come out of curiosity upon hearing the news of the nature of His teaching as compared with their own (1:22) and the numerous miracles He had already performed. It will also not be out of place to suggest that they come in order to ensnare Him on theological issues. This opportunity comes as Jesus proclaims forgiveness to the sick man.

These learned lawyers, on hearing this, begin to question within their individual hearts Christ's authority to forgive sins. The word "reasoning" is the Greek equivalent of *dialogizomai* (pronounced **dee-ah-log-IDZ-oh-my**) from which we have the English word "dialogue." It means to cast in mind, consider, dispute, or muse. To these learned scribes, Christ's pronouncement constitutes "blasphemy" (*blasphemia*, **blahs-fy-ME-uh**), i.e., speaking against God or speaking irreverently). Therefore, each of them, and probably the Pharisees also, debates within their mind why Jesus is blaspheming, since to them no one "can forgive sins but God only."

8 And immediately when Jesus perceived in his spirit that they so reasoned within themselves, he said unto them, Why reason ye these things in your hearts? 9 Whether is it easier to say to the sick of the palsy, Thy sins be forgiven thee; or to say, Arise, and take up thy bed, and walk?

As they contemplate this in their heart, Jesus through the Holy Spirit perceives their thoughts. Mark uses the adverb "immediately," *euthus* (**YOO-thoos**) a word he uses frequently in his Gospel which can be translated "forthwith" or "straightway."

It signifies immediacy or how close the two actions take place. The word "perceived" is from the Greek verb *epiginosko* (pronounced **epp-ihg-NOHS-koh**) meaning to know or recognize or acknowledge. It has the idea of being fully acquainted with or having knowledge of. Here Jesus through the Spirit discerns their thoughts right away. Both actions (vv. 7-8) are simultaneous. Knowing their thoughts, Jesus confronts them with the following questions. First, "Why reason ye these things in your hearts?" Although they have not expressed their thought openly, through His question Jesus implicitly makes them know who He is because only God can know and discern the inner thoughts of man. Following that Jesus poses another more revealing question to them, "Which is easier: to say to the paralytic, 'Your sins are forgiven,' or to say, 'Get up, take your mat and walk'?" (NIV). Humanly speaking, and to the scribes, both seem impossible. Although speaking forgiveness could be termed easier since its fulfillment is not verifiable. However, asking a paralyzed man to get up and walk is subject to verification. Therefore, to them it is impossible for an ordinary human being to do. But Jesus is not an ordinary human. He is the Son of God, which is not accepted by the teachers.

10 But that ye may know that the Son of man hath power on earth to forgive sins, (he saith to the sick of the palsy,) 11 I say unto thee, Arise, and take up thy bed, and go thy way into thine house.

Without waiting for an answer from the lawyers, Jesus reveals His true identity. He addresses the Jewish authorities first, and then he probably turns and addresses the paralytic. He identifies Himself as the "Son of man" to the scribes. To show them that He has authority on earth to forgive sins—contrary to their belief— He heals the paralytic. He does this in an unconventional way. He says to the sick man, "Arise . . . take up thy bed and go thy way into thine house." This physical and outward healing corroborates His claim of authority to forgive sins. It makes the crowd realize that since He is able to do the miracle of healing, which they can see, He can also do the other miracle, which they cannot see. Indeed, the invisible miracle (forgiveness) has already been realized.

12 And immediately he arose, took up the bed, and went forth before them all; insomuch that they were all amazed, and glorified God, saying, We never saw it on this fashion.

The sick man's response is instant and his healing instant. He picks up his bed, according to Jesus command, and walks away to the amazement of all in the crowd, including the teachers of the law who have challenged His authority to forgive sins. The word "amazed" comes from the Greek verb *existemi* (pronounced **ex-ISS-tay-mee**) which literally means to put (stand) out of [wits], be beside oneself, to be astounded, or astonished, or to become astounded, or insane. The reaction of the crowd moves from being "amazed" and bewildered to praising God. The word "glorify" is the Greek verb *doxazo* (pronounced **dox-AHD-zoh**), which means to render (or esteem) glorious, to honor and magnify. They praise God because never before have they seen anything like that. The main thrust of this story, is not rooted in terms of Jesus' pity on and healing of the helpless paralytic, but on His ability to forgive sins. Sin is the sick man's (indeed, all humanity's) major problem, to which Jesus first declares forgiven and thereby proclaims the presence of the kingdom of God to mankind—the thrust of His earthly mission.

2:14 And as he passed by, he saw Levi the son of Alphaeus sitting at the receipt of custom, and said unto him, Follow me. And he arose and followed him.

Verse 13 serves as a transition. It tells us about Jesus' destination. It tells us that Jesus passes along the seashore with a large crowd following Him. He comes across a man called Levi (also named Matthew; cf. Matthew 9:9), a tax collector and the son of Alphaeus, sitting in his office. Jesus calls on him to follow Him. Just as in the case of Simon and his brother Andrew, and James and his brother John (1:16-20), Levi leaves everything (Luke 5:27-28) and follows Jesus.

15 And it came to pass, that, as Jesus sat at meat in his house, many publicans and sinners sat also together with Jesus and his disciples: for there were many, and they followed him. 16 And when the scribes and Pharisees saw him eat with publicans and sinners, they said unto his disciples, How is it

that he eateth and drinketh with publicans and sinners?

Levi (Matthew) prepares a great dinner and invites Jesus to his house (Luke 5:29). Among the guests are other publicans and sinners, and Jesus' disciples also. It seems the scribes and the Pharisees are among the crowd as well. Whether they are the at table with Him or they stay outside the house (which is most probable since they regard the publicans or tax collectors as sinful), Mark is silent. However, he does tell us about their reaction. As Jesus sits eating and drinking at Levi's house, the Pharisees and scribes see Him with the tax collectors, so they complain to Jesus' disciples. Levi must have arranged the dinner as a farewell party to his friends, and perhaps as a means of inviting his friends to meet Jesus. At any rate, Jesus dines with those regarded by the Jewish authorities as sinful—the "publicans [tax collectors] and sinners" those that need to be isolated from the religious or "the righteous."

The "publicans" *telones,* (pronounced **tell-OH-nace**) are collectors of public revenue for the Roman authorities and are regarded by the Jews as traitors and sinners. The publicans are notorious for their corrupt and fraudulent methods of carrying out their duties. Pharisees are a Jewish sect known for the rigorous way they follow the oral and written law and the strict way they maintain ceremonial purity. Anyone who does not adhere to the strictness of following the commandments is regarded as a sinner. "Sinners" is from the Greek noun *hamartolos* (singular, pronounced **ham-ar-to-los'**) derived from the verb *hamartano* (**ham-ar-tan'-o**) which literally means to miss the mark, to err, (especially morally), to offend or trespass. To the Pharisees, these are people who do not follow the precepts of the law. Accordingly, the publicans, because of the nature of their work, "miss the mark"—they do not measure up. Therefore, they are grouped together as sinners. Thus when the Pharisees see Jesus banqueting with the publicans, they complain to Jesus' disciples (according to Luke's record, they murmur against Jesus). They question the disciples about why Jesus, who is "supposedly" religious and an observer of the Jewish law, eats and drinks with publicans and sinners.

17 When Jesus heard it, he saith unto them, They that are whole have no need of the physician, but they that are sick: I came not to call the righteous, but sinners to repentance.

In answer to their query (murmuring), using a metaphor Jesus makes one of the most profound statements in the whole of the Gospels. Here He declares the essence of His ministry on earth and the foundational basis of Christianity. It is common sense that doctors do not minister to the healthy but to the sick. Therefore, it is the sick who go to the doctor to be healed. Likewise, it is only sinners who see the need for their salvation and come to Jesus. Jesus therefore "came not to call the righteous [the self-righteous], but sinners" (i.e., those who have missed the mark and are unable to reach God's standards of righteousness or those who have been alienated from society and from God) to salvation. The Good News of the Gospel is that the *"Son of man is come to seek and to save that which was lost"* (Luke 19:10). This means "all" *"For all have sinned, and come short of the glory of God"* (Romans 3:23).

DAILY BIBLE READINGS

M: Your Sins Are Forgiven
Mark 2:1-12

T: Jesus Eats with Tax Collectors
Mark 2:13-17

W: Joy Over a Sinner Who Repents
Luke 15:1-7

T: New Wine in Old Wineskins
Mark 2:18-22

F: Sabbath Was Made for Humankind
Mark 2:23-28

S: Jesus Heals on the Sabbath
Mark 3:1-6

S: You Are the Son of God!
Mark 3:7-12

TEACHING TIPS

March 16
Bible Study Guide 3

1. Words You Should Know

A. Authority Greek *exousia* (pronounced **x-oo-SEE-uh**)—The ability or strength that one possesses or exercises; power of influence and privilege.

B. Faith (v. 40); Greek *pistis* (pronounced **PISS-tiss**)—Conviction of the truth; "belief with the predominate idea of trust (or confidence) whether in God or in Christ, springing from faith in the same" (*Strong's Concordance*).

2. Teacher Preparation

A. Study the Devotional Reading and pray for your students.

B. Read Bible Study Guide 3 at least twice, and make notes on any insights you want to share with the class.

C. Study IN DEPTH ("Where Is Jesus in Your Storm?").

3. Starting the Lesson

A. Before the students arrive, write AT-A-GLANCE questions on the board.

B. After the students arrive ask a volunteer to pray. Then read and discuss the IN FOCUS section.

4. Getting into the Lesson

A. Ask volunteers to read THE PEOPLE, PLACES, AND TIMES and BACKGROUND.

B. Direct the class to IN DEPTH question, "Where Is Jesus in Your Storm?" Now read FOCAL VERSES Mark 4:36-41.

C. Ask a volunteer to read the remaining FOCAL VERSES, and allow time for discussion pointing out any insights from IN DEPTH question 2, "Who's Really in Control?"

5. Relating the Lesson to Life

A. Read and discuss LESSON IN OUR SOCIETY.

B. Invite students to talk about insights they have learned while keeping their "My New Beginning Journal" or any other experiences related to the journal. Let them know that they do not have to share if they feel uncomfortable discussing their journal entries.

6. Arousing Action

A. Direct the students to the MAKE IT HAPPEN section and encourage them to practice it this week.

B. Tell the students to review today's lesson this week by completing SEARCH THE SCRIPTURES.

C. Ask if there are any prayer concerns and then end the session with prayer.

WORSHIP GUIDE

For the Superintendent or Teacher
Theme: Jesus' Authority
Theme Song: "I Will Trust in the Lord"
Scripture: Hebrews 11:1-6
Song: "The Storm Is Passing Over"
Devotional Thought: Lord, Your power and knowledge are beyond my comprehension. Help me to trust You with all my heart.

JESUS' AUTHORITY

Bible Background • MARK 4:35—5:20
Printed Text • MARK 4:36-41; 5:2-13a
Devotional Reading • JOHN 5:2-17

LESSON AIM

By the end of the lesson, students will understand that Jesus has all authority they will reaffirm their intent to put complete faith in Him.

KEEP IN MIND

"What manner of man is this, that even the wind and the sea obey him?" (Mark 4:41).

FOCAL VERSES

Mark 4:36 And when they had sent away the multitude, they took him even as he was in the ship. And there were also with him other little ships.

37 And there arose a great storm of wind, and the waves beat into the ship, so that it was now full.

38 And he was in the hinder part of the ship, asleep on a pillow: and they awake him, and say unto him, Master, carest thou not that we perish?

39 And he arose, and rebuked the wind, and said unto the sea, Peace, be still. And the wind ceased, and there was a great calm.

40 And he said unto them, Why are ye so fearful? how is it that ye have no faith?

41 And they feared exceedingly, and said one to another, What manner of man is this, that even the wind and the sea obey him?

5:2 And when he was come out of the ship, immediately there met him out of the tombs a man with an unclean spirit,

3 Who had his dwelling among the tombs; and no man could bind him, no, not with chains:

4 Because that he had been often bound with fetters and chains, and the chains had been

LESSON OVERVIEW

LESSON AIM
KEEP IN MIND
FOCAL VERSES
IN FOCUS
THE PEOPLE, PLACES,
AND TIMES
BACKGROUND
AT-A-GLANCE
IN DEPTH
SEARCH THE SCRIPTURES
DISCUSS THE MEANING
LESSON IN OUR SOCIETY
MAKE IT HAPPEN
FOLLOW THE SPIRIT
REMEMBER YOUR THOUGHTS
MORE LIGHT ON THE TEXT
DAILY BIBLE READINGS

plucked asunder by him, and the fetters broken in pieces: neither could any man tame him.

5 And always, night and day, he was in the mountains, and in the tombs, crying, and cutting himself with stones.

6 But when he saw Jesus afar off, he ran and worshipped him,

7 And cried with a loud voice, and said, What have I to do with thee, Jesus, thou Son of the most high God? I adjure thee by God, that thou torment me not.

8 For he said unto him, Come out of the man, thou unclean spirit.

9 And he asked him, What is thy name? And he answered, saying, My name is Legion: for we are many.

10 And he besought him much that he would not send them away out of the country.

11 Now there was there nigh unto the mountains a great herd of swine feeding.

12 And all the devils besought him, saying, Send us into the swine, that we may enter into them.

13 And forthwith Jesus gave them leave.

IN FOCUS

Little Cory was afraid of the dark. One night his mother told him to go out to the back porch and bring her the broom. The child turned to his mother and said, "Mama, I don't want to go out there. It's dark."

The mother smiled reassuringly at her son. "You don't have to be afraid of the dark," she explained. "Jesus is out there. He'll look after you and protect you."

The little boy looked at his mother real hard and asked, "Are you sure He's out there?"

"Yes, I'm sure. He is everywhere, and He is always ready to help out when you need Him," she said.

Cory thought about that for a minute and then went to the back door and cracked it open a tiny bit. Peering into the darkness, he called, "Jesus? If You're out there, would You please hand me the broom?"

THE PEOPLE, PLACES, AND TIMES

The Times. Word of Jesus' name and teachings had spread throughout Galilee and large crowds followed Him (Mark 3:7). The Pharisees and scribes, who were among the crowd, watched Jesus's every move to see how they might trap and accuse Him (Mark 3:23). They had built such a case against Jesus that they not only accused Him of being possessed by Satan but also wanted to kill Him.

Gadarenes. (Gerasenes and Gergasenes in some manuscripts) This refers to the city of Gadara, which was a large city situated on the summit of a mountain approximately six miles southeast of the Sea of Galilee. Although Garasenesare is mentioned in the passage (Mark 5:1-13), scholars are not sure if the miracle of Jesus healing the demon-possessed man (vv. 2-13) actually took place in Gadara or in another place with overlapping names.

BACKGROUND

Mark 4 opens with a litany of parables that Jesus tells to a large crowd gathered by the Sea of Galilee. He sits in a boat and teaches so that everyone can see and hear Him. Although Jesus may have taught using parables before, this is the first recorded case of a series of these stories.

What is a parable? The Greek term *parabole* (pronounced **pah-rah-BO-lay**) means "placing side by side for the purpose of comparison." In other words the parable uses the familiar to clarify the unfamiliar. Thus Jesus speaks of the sower, the lamp, and mustard seed—all items with which His listeners are familiar. In the Parable of the Sower Jesus provides a detailed explanation of its meaning to the disciples. After teaching, Jesus and

the disciples leave that evening by boat.

AT-A-GLANCE

1. Where Is Jesus in Your Storm? (Mark 4:36-41)
2. Who's Really in Control? (5:2-13)

IN DEPTH

1. Where Is Jesus in Your Storm? (Mark 4:36-41)

After teaching the multitudes in a ship by the sea of Galilee, Jesus instructs the disciples to go to other side of the shore. Weary from his daylong delivering of sermons, Jesus falls asleep in the stern (lower or back part of the ship). Then a fierce storm arises. The disciples fear for their lives and see the imminent danger as water fills the ship. The next action that the disciples take is one we should study closely, for it reveals our own reactions to difficulties. Frantically, they wake up Jesus and say, "Teacher, don't you care that we are about to die?" (Mark 4:38, TEV). Isn't this the same question we as Christians often ask the Saviour when we encounter the storms and problems of life: "Jesus, don't you see what I'm going through? Can't you do something about it?"

Jesus did do something about the storm on the Sea of Galilee by simply speaking to it "Peace, be still" and of a certainty He wants to protect us when we experience life's turbulence. Jesus requires that we have faith in Him, and even reprimands the disciples for their lack of trust (Mark 4:40). Although the disciples are aware that Jesus is with them, the storm appears to be greater than their faith in the Saviour. One ancient writer, Saint Ephrem the Syrian, sums up this passage in Mark powerfully: "The ship carried His [Jesus'] humanity, but the power of His Godhead carried the ship and all that was in it" (*Ancient Christian Commentary on Scripture* edited by Thomas C. Oden and Christopher A. Hall).

As you face life's storm, remember that God is carrying the ship. He has total control over the tempest that you face. Where is Jesus in your storm? He is right there with you saying, "Peace, be still."

2. Who's Really in Control? (5:2-13)

In this passage we see another instance of Jesus confronting a demoniac. Although any person controlled by an evil spirit is in bondage, the man in the tombs is a severe case, for he had been possessed for a long time. During Jesus' time people believed that evil spirits dwelt among the tombs. Since the demon-possessed man was uncontrollable, he was a menace to society. Even worse, he was a danger to himself for he mutilated his own body with stones. This man had thousands of demons as his name, "Legion" (v. 9), so indicates. (A legion was a division of the Roman army containing four to six thousand men.)

Yet the unclean spirit that totally dominated the man had to submit to Jesus (v. 6). This act demonstrates Jesus' superior power and authority. Not wanting to relinquish control of the man, the unclean spirit gives the same response recorded in Mark 1:24: "What do you want with me?" or "Leave us alone." Jesus exercised total control and commanded the demon to come out of the man. The passage concludes with Jesus permitting the demons' request to be cast into a herd of swine. Being possessed by so many demons, the swine ran down a steep cliff and drowned in the sea.

SEARCH THE SCRIPTURES

1. How did the disciples react when faced with the storm? (Mark 4:38)

2. What was the condition of the demoniac? (5:3-5)

3. What did Jesus do to show His authority over the demons? (v. 8)

DISCUSS THE MEANING

1. Allow the students to spend time discussing the question, "Where Is Jesus in Your Storm?" Why is it often difficult to have faith in a crisis?

2. Jesus shows His power and authority during the storm and when He heals the demoniac. As Christians, has Jesus also given us authority over unclean spirits and illnesses? Why or why not?

LESSON IN OUR SOCIETY

In today's lesson we discovered that Jesus is in control at all times. What He asks of us is to have complete faith and confidence in Him. Often it is difficult for us to have faith because we feel the need to be in control and resort to trusting our own reasoning. But there are some things that only God knows, and He will not reveal them to us because He wants us to trust Him. We must let God be our confidence in the midst of a storm, for He has ALL power and authority.

MAKE IT HAPPEN

Read the following Scriptures on faith, select one of the passages, and share it with someone this week: Matthew 17:20; Romans 10:17; and Hebrews 11:1. You will strengthen your faith by meditating on the Word as well as by sharing the Scriptures with others.

FOLLOW THE SPIRIT

What God wants me to do:

_____

_____

REMEMBER YOUR THOUGHTS

Special insights you have learned:

_____

_____

MORE LIGHT ON THE TEXT
Mark 4:36-41; 5:2-13a

The first part of this chapter introduces us to the teachings of Jesus by the Sea of Galilee. Jesus had gone to the seaside and a great number of people had gathered to hear Him teach them. The crowd grew so large that Jesus entered into a ship, while the crowd stood by the seashore, and from there He taught them using many parables (vv. 1-34). Mark does not inform us in this passage when Jesus began His teaching that day. However verse 35, which serves as a transition, reveals to us that He taught the multitude until the evening, probably till sunset. This suggests that it was a whole day. He requests His disciples to sail across the sea to the other sea shore. Mark does not tell us why Jesus decided to go to the other side of the lake. He probably wanted to change venue or to go away from the crowd to recuperate after a long day's work.

36 And when they had sent away the multitude, they took him even as he was in the ship. And there were also with him other little ships.

After dismissing the multitude, Jesus and His disciples begin sailing in the same ship (or boat) from which He taught (v. 1). "They took Him even as He was in the ship" seems to suggest that they begin sailing without going to shore. Other suggestions as to the meaning of this statement include that He sailed without a change of clothes, or that they took Him directly without waiting to make accommodations for the passage. Who does the pronoun "they" refer to? Some might say that Mark does not tell us to whom the boat belongs. "They" probably refers to the owners of the boat who might not be Jesus' disciples or who may not have come in contact with Him before this time. If that is correct, then the statement would then mean "they took Him as an ordinary person, thinking nothing special about Him." They looked at Him as an ordinary passenger. Hence their reaction and question of verse 41. However, Matthew 8:23-25 and Luke 8:22 indicates that Jesus' disciples were involved.

The mention of "other little ships" does not seem to have any significance to the story other than giving a detailed account of an eyewitness. Mark does not tell us what happened to them whether they perished in the storm, were driven back to shore, or that they were also rescued when Jesus calmed the storm. Any suggestions here are purely speculative.

37 And there arose a great storm of wind, and the waves beat into the ship, so that it was now full.

As they sail across the lake, they encounter a "great storm," with "the waves" beating the ship, and filling the ship with water. The Sea of Galilee is well-known for its sudden violent storms. The sea is situated in a valley surrounded by a range of mountains and is usually calm at night and early morning. However, "when storms come at those times, they are all the more treacherous."

(Walter W. Wessel, Mark: The Expositor's Bible Commentary with the NIV, vol. 8, Frank E. Gaebelein, general editor. Grand Rapids: Zondervan Publishing House, 1984, p. 655).

Here is one writer's eyewitness account of the storm that usually occurs at the Sea of Galilee:

The position of the lake makes it liable to sudden storms, the cool air from the uplands rushing down the gorges with great violence and tossing the waters in tumultuous billows. Such storms are fairly frequent, and as they are attended with danger to small craft, the boatmen are constantly on the alert. Safe in very settled conditions, they will not venture far from the shore. Occasionally, however, tempests break over the lake, in which a boat could hardly live . . . Only twice in over five years the present writer witnessed such a hurricane. Once it burst from the south. In a few moments the air was thick with mist, through which one could hear the roar of the tortured waters. In about ten minutes the wind fell as suddenly as it had risen. The air cleared, and the wide welter of foam-crested waves attested the fury of the blast. On the second occasion the wind blew from the East, and the phenomena described above were practically repeated.

(from International Standard Bible Encyclopaedia, Electronic Database. Copyright ©1996 by Biblesoft).

38 And he was in the hinder part of the ship, asleep on a pillow: and they awake him, and say unto him, Master, carest thou not that we perish?

Being tired after the long day's teaching, Jesus goes into "the hinder part of the ship" and there He falls asleep "on a pillow." The phrase "hinder part of the ship" or the Greek equivalent *prumna* (pronounced **PRUHM-nah**) means the rear of a ship. The word "pillow" or the Greek *proskephalaion* (pronounced **prahs-teeff-AH-lie-ahn**) can also be translated as cushion, i.e., something for the head. He must have been very tired because He sleeps through a violent tempest to the amazement of the other people in the boat. While every other person is worried and anxious, probably doing everything they can to survive the storm, Jesus is in the back of the ship fast asleep. This becomes troubling to His disciples who wake Him up and say to Him, "Master, carest thou not that we perish?" The word "care" or *melo* (pronounced **MEH-low**) means being concerned. The question can be rendered, "Master, don't you care" or "Are you not concerned that we about to perish?" The word "perish" is the Greek *apollumetha* from the verb *apollumi* (pronounced **ah-PAW-loo-mee**), which also means to die, to lose, or destroy. In this contest, it will also mean going down. This story is reminiscent of the story of Jonah's encounter with the storm (Jonah 1:4-6).

39 And he arose, and rebuked the wind, and said unto the sea, Peace, be still. And the wind ceased, and there was a great calm. 40 And he said unto them, Why are ye so fearful? how is it that ye have no faith?

The difference between this story and that of Jonah is that while Jonah had not control of the storm and asks the sailors to throw him overboard (Jonah 1:7ff), Jesus demonstrates His authority and control over the cosmic order. Jesus wakes up from sleep, and He "rebukes" the storm. The word "rebuke" is the Greek verb, *epitimao* (pronounced **epp-ih-tih-MAH-oh**), which means to charge, admonish, command, or forbid. Here Jesus first addresses the stormy wind to cease its operation. To the sea He says, "Peace, be still." The phrase "Peace, be still" just means: be calm. Both the wind and the waves obey Him. The storm ceases and the waves die off and there is calm in the sea. There is the implicit notion that the ceasing of the storm and calming of the waves was instant.

Jesus then turns to His disciples and rebukes them for their being fearful and their lack of faith. Here fear is the opposite of faith; indeed, the presence of fear means the lack or absence of faith. Why would Jesus rebuke them as He does in other instances (cf. 7:18; 8:17-18, 21, 9:19) of being faithless? Elsewhere the disciples have witnessed all kinds of miracles which Jesus performed that should have caused them to put their faith in God and trust Him. Still, they are afraid. So Jesus rebukes them for their lack of faith in God and His providence.

41 And they feared exceedingly, and said one to another, What manner of man is this, that even the wind and the sea obey him?

The miracle of the storm and waves brings greater fear to them. The word "fearful" Jesus uses to describe the disciples' disposition in verse 40 is

the Greek *deilos* (pronounced **day-LASHSS**); it has the idea of timidity, cowardice and, by implication, faithlessness. The "fear" expressed by the phrase "feared exceedingly" (v. 41) is from the verb *phobeo* (pronounced **faw-BEH-oh**) and has the idea of being astounded with wonder and awe coupled with a sense of reverence. The Greek expression translated here as "they feared exceedingly," *ephobeethesan phobos megan* (pronounced **eh-fob-BAY-thay-sahn-FAH-bahss-MEG-gahn**) literally means that they "feared a great fear." They are gripped with such awe and wonder that they question among themselves, "What manner of man is this?" or "Who is this? Even the storm and waves obey Him!" The disciples are startled even though they have seen Him heal the sick and cast out evil spirits, but to order a boisterous wind and waves to cease is another "ball game." They have never seen such a mighty act before. Here Jesus reveals that He is the Creator of the cosmos and that He has authority over all its affairs.

5:2 And when he was come out of the ship, immediately there met him out of the tombs a man with an unclean spirit,

After calming the sea, Jesus and His disciples then continue their journey eastwards to the region of the Gerasenes (5:1). Verse 2 seems to suggest that as soon as Jesus steps out the ship, the possessed man immediately confronts Him. However, verse 6 indicates that the man sees Jesus from afar and runs towards the Lord. Verse 2 therefore is a leading sentence, introducing us to the main character of the next event that takes place—the man possessed by demons. The next few verses give a detailed description of this man.

3 Who had his dwelling among the tombs; and no man could bind him, no, not with chains: 4 Because that he had been often bound with fetters and chains, and the chains had been plucked asunder by him, and the fetters broken in pieces: neither could any man tame him.

Mark probably thinks it important to give us vivid, detailed information regarding this man. Why such detail? The detail here is probably intended to give us a graphic picture and show the severity of this man's case. It is also intended to reveal how strong demons can operate in humans, how they can operate supernaturally, but how their power is limited compared with the limitless power of the supreme God.

First, Mark tells us that the man lived among the tombs. From there he runs out to meet Jesus. In the Ancient Near East people were either buried in tombs carved out of rocks or in natural caves. It was customary for each family to have their family tombs, and each tomb contained many niches in each of which they put their dead. The entrances to the tombs were sealed with big circular rocks. Most tombs were hewed on the hillside away from the city. As such, the tombs were isolated from the people and lonely. So the man must have been driven away from the city to live among the tombs by the unclean spirits.

The second information about this man is that he is so strong that no one could restrain him. He has often been "bound with fetters and chains," but he breaks the chain and fetters in pieces. The phrase "had been plucked asunder" is the Greek verb *diaspao* (pronounced **dee-ahs-PAH-oh**) which means to draw apart, to sever, to dismember, or to pull in pieces. The word "fetters" is the Greek word *pede* (pronounced **PED'-aa**) i.e., shackles for the feet. Shackles are usually made of iron. So the man was bound hand and feet with chains and shackles, but he dismantled and breaks them into pieces. No one was able to subdue him.

5 And always, night and day, he was in the mountains, and in the tombs, crying, and cutting himself with stones.

The next information we have regarding this man is his erratic behavior. He is always in the mountains and in the tombs crying day and night, mutilating himself with stones. It is said that the rocks and cliffs of the country of the Gadarenes (v. 1) were filled with tombs cut out of the limestone, which served not only for burial, but are dwelling places for the poor and insane (Isaiah 65:4) and hiding places for criminals. From these places men continuously cried day and night. These were usually the signs of lunatics or people possessed by demons. Modern scholars label this type of behavior psychosis or psychological disorder and thereby undermine the power of Satan. Instead of dealing with the problem spiritually and supernaturally by the power of the Holy Spirit (through prayer), they rationalize it and treat it intellectually usually resulting in failure.

6 But when he saw Jesus afar off, he ran and worshipped him,

Having seen Jesus from a distance, probably from the mountain ranges as Jesus is passing along the shores of the lake, the possessed man runs to Him and falls on his knees before Him. The word translated "worshipped" (KJV) is the Greek verb *prosekuneesen* (third person singular) from *proskuneo* (pronounced **prahs-kooh-NEH-oh**) from which the English word "to prostrate" is derived. It means to fall on one's knees as a gesture of respect before a superior. The unclean spirit acting through this man falls before Christ in recognition of Christ's superiority and authority over him, but not as in worship. Therefore, the New Intertational Version translation of the word *prosekuneesen* tends to be the preferred rendering rather than the King James Version.

In many cultures a common practice to pay homage to elders, kings, or people of authority is shown by falling on the knees. Some kiss the king's or elders' feet as an expression of respect or to make supplication. In Africa (Nigeria in particular), people of the Yoruba tribe fall upon their knees and touch the ground with their forehead as an expression of reverence before their Oba (kings) or their elders.

7 And cried with a loud voice, and said, What have I to do with thee, Jesus, thou Son of the most high God? I adjure thee by God, that thou torment me not. 8 For he said unto him, Come out of the man, thou unclean spirit.

As he falls on his knees in front of Jesus, the demon speaking through the man recognizes the person of Jesus as the "Son of the most high God" and cries loudly, "What have I to do with thee?" The Greek phrase *tí émoí jaí soí* (pronounced **tih-eh-MOY-kai-soy**) is a way of saying, "What do you want with me?" or "What do we have in common?" Note that the demon uses Christ's personal name "Jesus" and His title "Son of the most high God" in recognition of Christ's divinity. His recognition of the person and deity of Christ here, as in the earlier encounter with Jesus (1:24), does not imply a belief that leads to "worship of Christ," but a means of trying to gain control over Him (cf. Matthew 4:3, 6; Luke 4:3, 9).

The demon recognizes also the power and authority Christ has over him, so he pleads for leniency. He says to Jesus, "I adjure thee by God, that thou torment me not." The word "adjure" *horkizo* (pronounced **hor-KID-zoh**) means to put under oath, i.e., make to swear; or to solemnly implore, to charge. He pleads with Christ to swear to God that He would not torture *basanizo* (pronounced **bah-sahn-NID-zoh)** him.

It seems that as soon as the man approached Jesus and fell at His feet, Jesus ordered the demon to come out of the man. Verse 8 is therefore Mark's explanation of what took place and why the demon reacted the way they did.

9 And he asked him, What is thy name? And he answered, saying, My name is Legion: for we are many. 10 And he besought him much that he would not send them away out of the country.

Jesus asks the man to identify himself. Again the demon through the man replies "My name is Legion: for we are many." Some say that casting out demons involves discovering their names. The word "legion" is of Latin origin and refers to a body of soldiers numbering over 6,000. Note the use of both the singular and plural third person pronouns: "And he besought . . . not (to) send them away out of the country." This shows that the demons were using the lips of the demoniac. The phrase "he besought him much" from the Greek *parekálei auton pollá* (pronounced **parr-eh-KAH-lay-OW-TAHN-pah-LAH)** has a sense of urgency and insistence. This means that the demons plead urgently that they not be sent "out of the country [or region]." In a parallel passage in Luke (8:31) the request is that they not be sent into the abyss Greek *abussos,* (pronounced **AH-boo-sahn**) or bottomless pit, where Satan and his angels will be confined for a 1000 years (Revelation 20:1-3).

11 Now there was there nigh unto the mountains a great herd of swine feeding. 12 And all the devils besought him, saying, Send us into the swine, that we may enter into them. 13 And forthwith Jesus gave them leave.

Rather than being sent out of the area, the demons prefer being sent into a "a great herd of swine feeding" near the mountainside. Jesus grants them their request. The presence of pigs in this area seems to suggest that the eastern region was largely Gentile. However, we are not specifically told that the man was a Gentile. The significance of sending the demon into the pigs is not clear. Any suggestions will be only speculative at best. However, the aim of the narrative the calming of the sea (4:36-41), the casting away of the demons (5:1-13), and the healing of Jairus (vv. 21ff)—demonstrate the power and authority of Christ over nature, Satan and his angels, and over sickness. It signifies the presence of the kingdom of God (1:15).

DAILY BIBLE READINGS

M: Peace! Be Still!
Mark 4:35-41

T: Jesus Walks on Water
Mark 6:45-51

W: Jesus Confronts the Demoniac
Mark 5:1-10

T: Everyone Is Amazed
Mark 5:11-20

F: Jesus Turns Water into Wine
John 2:1-11

S: The Son Gives Life
John 5:19-24

S: He Taught as One with Authority
Matthew 7:24-29

TEACHING TIPS

March 23
Bible Study Guide 4

1. Words You Should Know

A. Prophet (Mark 6:4)—One who speaks on God's behalf; the Hebrew word *nabi* means one who announces declarations of God.

B. Commission Greek—*epitrope* (pronounced **epp-ih-troh-PAY**)—To grant permission and power. Jesus commissions the disciples by authorizing them to preach and heal the sick on His behalf.

C. Mission—A calling or vocation.

2. Teacher Preparation

A. Study the Devotional Reading and pray for your students.

B. Read Bible Study Guide 4 at least twice and make notes on any insights you plan to share with the class.

C. Write or type (double-spaced) your class roll on a sheet of paper, and make enough copies to distribute to each student.

D. Materials needed: Bible, chalkboard, chalk, and copies of your class roll.

3. Starting the Lesson

A. Before the students arrive, write AT-A-GLANCE on the board.

B. After the students arrive, ask if they have prayer concerns, specifically relating to their new beginning. After the students have expressed their concerns, ask the group to form a circle and join hands. Tell them, "We are going to pray for one another." You will begin the prayer by praying for the person to your right and the group will continue in that manner.

C. Spend a brief time reviewing Lesson 3 by letting the class answer questions in SEARCH THE SCRIPTURES in that lesson.

D. Read and discuss IN FOCUS.

4. Getting into the Lesson

A. Read and discuss THE PEOPLE, PLACES, AND TIMES and BACKGROUND sections.

B. Ask volunteers to read the FOCAL VERSES and the corresponding IN DEPTH section. Continue in this manner until the class has completed all the verses and IN DEPTH. Allow time for discussion between each section. In the discussion point out how the people of Nazareth's rejection of Jesus prevented them from receiving the blessings, the miracles, and teachings of Jesus.

MAR 23RD

5. Relating the Lesson to Life

A. Spend time answering the questions in DISCUSS THE MEANING.

B. Ask the class if anyone has insights to express regarding today's lesson.

6. Arousing Action

A. Direct the students to DISCUSS THE MEANING and let them express answers to the questions. Then discuss LESSON IN OUR SOCIETY.

B. Give students a copy of the class roll, and tell them that they are going to pray for one another this week. Ask students if they have special requests, and if they do, direct the class to write the special request beside the person's name on the roll sheet. Now point the class to MAKE IT HAPPEN and read the section. Clarify any questions students might have.

WORSHIP GUIDE

For the Superintendent or Teacher
Theme: Rejection and Mission
Theme Song: "I Shall Not Be Moved"
Scripture: John 12:44-50
Song: "Where He Leads Me"
Devotional Thought: Lord, help me to stay focused on You when others reject the work You have called me to do. Thank You for providing the strength and wisdom I need in the midst of opposition.

REJECTION AND MISSION

Bible Background • MARK 6:1-13
Printed Text • MARK 6:1-13
Devotional Reading • JOHN 12:44-50

LESSON AIM

By the end of the lesson, students will understand that the people of Nazareth rejected Jesus' ministry and that He commissioned the disciples and gave them authority and power to fulfill His work.

KEEP IN MIND

"But Jesus said unto them, A prophet is not without honour, but in his own country, and among his own kin, and in his own house" (Mark 6:4).

FOCAL VERSES

Mark 6:1 And he went out from thence, and came into his own country; and his disciples follow him.

2 And when the sabbath day was come, he began to teach in the synagogue: and many hearing him were astonished, saying, From whence hath this man these things? and what wisdom is this which is given unto him, that even such mighty works are wrought by his hands?

3 Is not this the carpenter, the son of Mary, the brother of James, and Joses, and of Judah, and Simon? and are not his sisters here with us? And they were offended at him.

4 But Jesus said unto them, A prophet is not without honour, but in his own country, and among his own kin, and in his own house.

5 And he could there do no mighty work, save that he laid his hands upon a few sick folk, and healed them.

6 And he marvelled because of their unbelief. And he went round about the villages, teaching.

7 And he called unto him the twelve, and began to

send them forth by two and two; and gave them power over unclean spirits;

8 And commanded them that they should take nothing for their journey, save a staff only; no scrip, no bread, no money in their purse:

9 But be shod with sandals; and not put on two coats.

10 And he said unto them, In what place soever ye enter into an house, there abide till ye depart from that place.

11 And whosoever shall not receive you, nor hear you, when ye depart thence, shake off the dust under your feet for a testimony against them. Verily I say unto you, It shall be more tolerable for Sodom and Gomorrha in the day of judgment, than for that city.

12 And they went out, and preached that men should repent.

13 And they cast out many devils, and anointed with oil many that were sick, and healed them.

IN FOCUS

Marian Anderson (1897-1993) was the first African-American singer to perform at the Metropolitan Opera House in New York City. Anderson, like all other Black artists during her time, faced blatant racism. In 1939 the Daughters of the American Revolution, who owned Constitution Hall in Washington, prohibited her from performing there solely because she was Black. While her talents were not appreciated in her own country initially, she went to Europe and gained wide recognition.

Like Anderson, the people did not accept Jesus in His hometown. In their eyes He had no status, and they saw Him only as a carpenter's son. Today we will discover the responses Jesus received from the people in Nazarath and how He responded to their rejection.

THE PEOPLE, PLACES, AND TIMES

Nazareth. This hometown of Jesus, located in the lower part of Galilee in the north, belonged to the tribe of Zebulun. Approximately 15-20,000 inhabitants lived in the land, located about 14 miles from the Sea of Galilee. The name, meaning separated and sanctified, is quite appropriate for the Messiah. Yet ironically, the town was viewed with contempt by Judeans. Some scholars believe this to be so because the Galileans were less cultivated and had more contact with the heathen. This contempt caused Nathanael to ask, "Nazareth! Can anything good come from there?" (John 1:46, NIV).

The Twelve. This was the name given the disciples listed as follows: Simon Peter; brothers James (the son of Zebedee) and John, also called Boanerges ("The sons of thunder"); Andrew; Philip; Bartholomew; Matthew; Thomas; James the son of Alpheus; Thaddaeus; Simon the Canaanite; and Judas Iscariot (the one who betrayed Jesus).

BACKGROUND

Mark 5:22-43 recounts two notable miracles of Jesus: the woman with the issue of blood and Jarius's daughter. The first report that Jesus hears is that Jairus's daughter is sick, and later messengers tell Him that the little girl is dead. Jesus' response to the second report is a significant one because He ignores the fatal message and speaks words of faith to Jairus: "Be not afraid, only believe" (v. 36). When Jesus reaches the house to heal the girl, the people laugh Him to scorn because He states that she is asleep, rather than dead as they believed (vv. 39-40). So Jesus puts the mockers out of the room and performs the miraculous healing of Jairus's daughter.

We do well to learn from Jesus' actions. First, we must learn to ignore folk who deliver negative reports regarding our work and mission for God. That is, we mush not allow negative words to gain power over our lives. Second, in some cases we have to go even further and "put [some folk] out"—out of our lives, because all they are doing is hindering what Jesus wants to do through us.

Next, when Jesus healed the woman with the issue of blood, the Scriptures state that Jesus asked, "Who touched my clothes?" (v. 30) Although the woman touched Him physically, she also touched His divinity with her faith, and faith moves Jesus.

AT-A-GLANCE

1. Disrespect and Disbelief (Mark 6:1-6)
2. Commission and Repentance (vv. 7-13)

IN DEPTH

1. Disrespect and Disbelief (Mark 6:1-6)

Jesus astonished the listeners in the synagogue on this Sabbath day, but their amazement was changed to contempt. They could not accept this messenger or His message because they knew Him too well. He was their neighbor, their brother, their relative, the boy down the street. He was the son of peasants, a carpenter's son. So the town of Nazareth rejected Jesus, and in response to their offense Jesus quotes a proverb that the prophet is without honor in his native land.

As the Nazareth community marveled with suspicion at Jesus, He was likewise shocked at their lack of faith. Thus, their lack of faith hindered their own spiritual gain, for Jesus could not work many miracles there.

2. Commission and Repentance (vv. 7-13)

Despite the opposition to Jesus in Nazareth, He stayed centered. He was not distracted by these homefolk, and He left there and continued preaching (v. 6). He not only taught, but also commissioned the Twelve and gave them power over demonic influences. Jesus heavily equipped the disciples spiritually but instructed them to be featherweights in the physical realm—taking nothing for their journey. Though Jesus' instruction may appear strange, He knew that the preoccupation with "things" and belongings would weigh them down and offset their focus and mission. Jesus even provided details as to where they were to stay: "Wherever you are welcomed, stay in the same house until you leave that town" (Mark

6:10, TEV). During biblical times hospitality and welcoming strangers were the responsibility of the village.

On the other hand, if the hearers (the village) did not receive the disciples, Jesus simply told them to move on. According to *The Interpreter's Bible* the phrase "shake the dust" was "a symbolic act disclaiming responsibility if the townspeople persistently refused to hear." Last, the disciples' message was simple and was the same as John the Baptist's—they preached repentance.

SEARCH THE SCRIPTURES

1. Why was it difficult for Jesus to preach in His hometown? (Mark 6:2-3)

2. What did Jesus instruct the disciples to take with them when He sent them out? (vv. 8-9)

3. What were the results of the Twelve's obedience? (vv. 12-13)

DISCUSS THE MEANING

1. Why is it often difficult to receive the message and wisdom of people we know well?

2. What is the best way to handle rejection or opposition when you are doing a work ordained of God?

3. Can a lack of faith in God hinder your blessings? If so, how?

LESSON IN OUR SOCIETY

In his poem "Death of the Hired Man" Robert Frost wrote, "Home is the place where, when you have to go there, they have to take you in." This quotation did not hold true in Jesus' case. He met disrespect and disbelief during His hometown visit to Nazareth. The community, including His relatives and friends, summed up their rejection with one phrase: "Who in the world does Jesus think he is?" Yet, Jesus knew who He was—the Son of God in whom His Father was well pleased. Likewise, we must know who we are during times of rejection and challenge. With our faith focused on and rooted in our identity with Jesus, we are unstoppable.

MAKE IT HAPPEN

During the last three lessons the class has been writing in "My New Beginning Journal." Since we need the prayers and support of others, spend time this week praying for your classmates on the class roll. Pray specifically for any prayer concerns listed.

FOLLOW THE SPIRIT

What God wants me to do:

_____

_____

REMEMBER YOUR THOUGHTS

Special insights you have learned:

_____

_____

MORE LIGHT ON THE TEXT
Mark 6:1-13

Jesus has returned to Capernaum on the west side of the Sea of Galilee (5:21) after His teaching and miraculous works on the east side (4:35ff), including the region of Gadarenes (5:1ff). In His return to Capernaum, a great multitude gathers at the seashore to hear Him teach. He heals a woman who has been sick for twelve years and raises a girl from death (5:21ff).

6:1 And he went out from thence, and came into his own country; and his disciples follow him.

Having had a successful ministry in Capernaum and other regions, Jesus returns to His hometown of Nazareth with His disciples. This seems to be His second trip back home and His second mission in the synagogue (Luke 4:16; cf. Matthew 13:53ff). "Country" here is the Greek *patris* (pronounced **pah-TREECE**), which means a fatherland, native town, or city. Although Jesus was born in Bethlehem (Matthew 2:1), he grew up in Nazareth (Matthew 2:23) from which Joseph and Mary went to Bethlehem to register (Luke 2:4ff).

2 And when the sabbath day was come, he began to teach in the synagogue: and many hearing him were astonished, saying, From whence hath this man these things? and what wisdom is this which is given unto him, that even such mighty works are wrought by his hands?

On the Sabbath day, He goes into the synagogue, a habit He has formed from childhood (cf. Luke 2:41-50). Since He grew up in the town, He was therefore a familiar face to the worshipers and rulers of the synagogue. He was also familiar with the worship rituals and was no stranger.

According to Jewish customs in synagogue service, which include Scripture reading (cf. Luke 4:17), Jesus read from the Scriptures and then begins to expound the Word of God. The nature of His teaching is so profound that His audience and worshipers in the synagogue are amazed and dumbfounded at the wisdom with which He is teaching. They begin to question among themselves, "From whence hath this man these things?" Probably many of the people have not heard Him speak before and so this is their first experience. They are amazed. However, there is an undercurrent of skepticism among some of them as to the source of His authority and power as implied in the questions: "Where did this man get these things?" and "What's this wisdom that has been given him, that he even does miracles!" (NIV). In other words, "Where does this man get all this?" "What sort of wisdom does He possess that all these miracles are wrought through Him?" By implication, it is either from God or from Satan. To skeptics, it must have come from Satan, since no one (including rabbis and scribes) has ever taught and done miracles as He does. Although there is no record of Jesus performing any miracles in Nazareth before, His fame has spread all over the place because of the miracles and the authority with which He taught (1:21-28; 3:32ff; Luke 4:14-15).

3 Is not this the carpenter, the son of Mary, the brother of James, and Joses, and of Juda, and Simon? and are not his sisters here with us? And they were offended at him.

The people's hostile and negative attitudes toward Jesus become more apparent in the following rhetorical and derogatory questions. "Is not this the carpenter?" In Matthew He is referred to as the carpenter's son; Joseph was a carpenter by trade. Growing up Jesus must have learned carpentry from His adoptive father, Joseph. Before going into His public ministry at age 30, Jesus must have worked in that trade. Carpenters were regarded as common peasants, unlearned, at least not to the degree of the rabbis and scribes. Therefore Jesus, to them, is just an ordinary man who worked

with His hands as other common people did.

The next question is both derogatory and demeaning: "Isn't this the son of Mary?" In the Jewish culture, and indeed in almost all cultures of the world, both ancient and modern, men are not usually described or identified as sons of their mother, even if their fathers were no more. Describing Jesus as the "son of Mary" here is probably intended as a put-down, and perpetuates the rumor being circulated at that time that He was an illegitimate child because of the nature of His birth (John 9:29, 34). It is clear from the Scripture that Jesus was the son of Mary and was not the actual son of Joseph (Matthew 1:18-25; Luke 1:30-35; John 1:14, 18; 3:14-20; Hebrews 1:1-2). However, the people's intent here is still disdainful.

Equally contemptuous are the next questions: "Is not this . . . the brother of James, and Joses, and of Juda, and Simon?" And "Are not his sisters here with us?" All this implies that He is an ordinary person that they know very well and probably grew up with Him. Why does He parade Himself as a rabbi and miracle-worker? With such a knowledge and familiarity of His background, the people became "offended at Him." "Offended" is the Greek verb *skandalizo* (pronounced **skan-dah-LID-zoh**) from which the English "scandalize" is derived. It literally means "trip up," i.e., stumble or to cause displeasure. It is to be offended at someone, that is, to see in another what I disapprove of and what hinders me from acknowledging his authority; it is to cause a person to begin to distrust and desert one whom he ought to trust and obey.

The mention of Jesus' siblings substantiates the fact that subsequent to the birth of Jesus other biological children were born to Mary and Joseph. James is the one at the council at the Jerusalem church (Acts 12:17; 15:13; 21:18; 1 Corinthians 15:7; Galatians 1:19; 2:9, 12) and the author of the Epistle of James (James 1:1). Juda (Jude) is the author of the Book of Jude, but little is known about the rest of His brothers and sisters.

The people therefore upbraid him with the meanness of His relations and upbringing. Although astonished at His doctrine (v. 2), they are offended at His person (v. 3). Prejudiced against Him, they look at Him with contempt and for that reason reject His teaching. Even the testimony of the blind (John 9:27ff) would not induce the people to believe in the Lord Jesus. What disbelief!

4 But Jesus said unto them, A prophet is not without honour, but in his own country, and among his own kin, and in his own house. 5 And he could there do no mighty work, save that he laid his hands upon a few sick folk, and healed them. 6 And he marvelled because of their unbelief. And he went round about the villages, teaching.

Jesus acknowledges their unbelief and reproves them with a supposedly common proverbial saying: that a prophet is not recognized in his own country, among his people, and in his own family. Unlike other places and regions where we see Jesus perform miracles of stilling the storm (4:35ff), casting out demons (5:1ff) and healing the sick (5:21ff), He could not do such miracles in His own homeland because of their obstinate unbelief. However, He is able to lay hands on a few sick people and they are healed. "Unbelief" is from the Greek *apaistia* (pronounced **ah-piss-TEE-ah**). It means faithlessness, i.e. disbelief, unfaithfulness, or disobedience.

Their unbelief cost them the privilege of experiencing miracles and healing as other regions had. What does this mean? Does it mean that their unbelief or their faithlessness limited Christ's ability to heal? The answer is no. We read nowhere in the Scriptures that Jesus failed to heal anyone or any case that is brought to Him, nor did unbelief of anyone present prevent Him from healing anyone who came to Him. Indeed, we read repeatedly in the Bible phrases stating that He "healed them all" or "every one" (1:32-35, 3:10; 6:5, cf. Matthew 4:23-24; 8:14-17; 9:35; 11:5; 12:15; 14:14; 19:2; Luke 4:40; 5:15, 17; 6:10; 7:21-23; Acts 10:38; etc.). Rather, their unbelief and their contempt of His person kept them from bringing their sick to Christ to be healed. Surprised at their unbelief, Jesus goes "round about the villages, teaching." The word "teaching" is the translation of the Greek *didasko* (pronounced **dih-DAHS-koh**), i.e., to instruct or to hold discourse with others in order to instruct them.

7 And he called unto him the twelve, and began to send them forth by two and two; and gave them power over unclean spirits;

Not only does He go about the villages instructing the people, but Jesus also sends out the Twelve (cf. 3:14-19) in pairs with special authority and direction. We remember that Jesus has earlier promised them He would make you "fishers of men" (1:17) when He called them. This, therefore, is the beginning of the fulfillment of that promise. In preparation for their mission the Twelve have learned first-hand from Jesus, their Master, by being with Him everywhere He went, observing all the miracles and healing, and listening to His teachings. He now sends them out with this purpose *"to preach, and to have power to heal sicknesses, and to cast out devils,"* (3:14-15).

The word "send" is the Greek verb *apostellein* a third person singular from *apostello* (pronounced **ap-pahs-TELL-oh**), which means to send forth, or to order one to go to an appointed place. It has the idea of delegation with liberty as a representative to work or do something on behalf of another. From this word we have the word "apostles" by which the Twelve are commonly known. As an authorized group, they are to represent Christ. Therefore, He commissions them by sending them in pairs for the mission and gives them authority to perform miracles, including casting out "unclean spirits." The purpose of sending them in pairs probably originates from Jewish custom (11:1; 14:13; Acts 13:2, 4; 16:40) so that their testimony could be established on the account of *"two or three witnesses"* (Deuteronomy 17:6).

8 And commanded them that they should take nothing for their journey, save a staff only; no scrip, no bread, no money in their purse: 9 But be shod with sandals; and not put on two coats.

In His commission of the Twelve, He implicitly instructs them to rely totally on God's providence to supply all their material needs during their journey. Therefore, they are to carry no provision with them, "no scrip, bread i.e., food of any kind, no money in their purse"—except "a staff," "sandals," and one coat. That means no formal preparation. They are to go with just what they have, which not only emphasizes their absolute trust in God to supply their daily physical needs but signifies the extreme urgency of their mission. Knowing that their mission will involve a lot of hard walks, including the rocky hills of Palestine, Jesus allows them to go with their sandals for protection. The prohibition of other materials seems to apply only to the mission Christ sent them at that time (Matthew 10:10; Luke 9:3). That prohibition is later removed and the disciples are instructed (Luke 22:35-36) to be prepared, probably because Jesus will longer be with them and because proclaiming the Gospel will mean persecution, so much that hospitality will be limited.

10 And he said unto them, In what place soever ye enter into an house, there abide till ye depart from that place. 11 And whosoever shall not receive you, nor hear you, when ye depart thence, shake off the dust under your feet for a testimony against them. Verily I say unto you, It shall be more tolerable for Sodom and Gomorrah in the day of judgment, than for that city.

Missions demand dignity, integrity, and good reputation. Perhaps in order to protect these virtues, Jesus instructs the Twelve to remain in the same house where they have been accepted until they leave that town. They should not leave their first lodging even if they are offered a better, more attractive, or more comfortable accommodation.

With His personal experience, Jesus knows the difficulty the Twelve are about to face—rejection. He therefore reminds them that their mission will not always be accepted; He instructs them on how to react in the face of such rejection. They are to "shake off the dust under your feet for a testimony against" the town or place where they are not accepted. The act of shaking dust off of one's feet originates from the Jewish custom in which they considered the dust of heathen lands as defiling in contrast to the holy land (Ezekiel 45:1; Amos 7:17). To shake the dust of any land off their feet declares that city heathenish that rejects God (Matthew 10:14; Luke 9:5; Acts 13:51). Note Christ's instruction to the Twelve in Matthew: *"Do not go among the Gentiles or enter any town of the Samaritans. Go rather to the lost sheep of Israel,"* (10:5-6, NIV). The phrase "for a testimony against them" suggests that the act will be a means of judgment against them on the day of judgment. Compared to the judgment the people will face in the end time, Jesus says that the punishment of Sodom and Gomorrah would be "child's play."

12 And they went out, and preached that men should repent. 13 And they cast out many devils, and anointed with oil many that were sick, and healed them.

Verses 12 and 13 describe the actual mission of the Twelve. Their mission is threefold: preaching the Gospel of repentance and salvation, casting away evil spirits from those possessed, and healing the sick. These are patterned after Christ's own ministry. They also formed the model of the ministry of the apostles and the early Church's ministry and mission after Christ's death and resurrection. This model remains the same today even though there is debate and disagreement in many churches and denominations whether the three mandates apply, especially the miraculous aspects of the Gospel—the casting out of demons and the healing of the sick.

DAILY BIBLE READINGS

M: A Prophet Without Honor
Mark 6:1-6
T: People Question Jesus as Messiah
John 7:37-44
W: No Prophet Comes from Galilee
John 7:45-52
T: The Kingdom of Heaven Is Near
Matthew 10:5-15
F: Be Wise Serpents, Innocent Doves
Matthew 10:16-26
S: Whoever Welcomes You
Matthew 10:37-42
S: Jesus Sends Out the Twelve
Mark 6:7-13

TEACHING TIPS

March 30
Bible Study Guide 5

1. Words You Should Know

A. Tradition (Mark 7:3); Greek *paradosis* (pronounced **pah-RAH-doh-siss**)—Giving over by word of mouth or in writing.

B. Hypocrite (v. 6); Greek *hupokrites* (pronounced **HOO-pock-KRIH-tace**)—An actor, a pretender.

C. Defile (v. 15); Greek *koinoo* (pronounced **koy-NAH-oh**)—To make unclean.

2. Teacher Preparation

A. Study the Devotional Reading and pray for your students.

B. Read Bible Study Guide 5 at least twice, and make notes on any insights you want to share with the class.

C. Materials needed: Bible, chalkboard, and chalk.

3. Starting the Lesson

A. Before the students arrive, write AT-A-GLANCE on the board.

B. After the students arrive, ask if they have prayer concerns and then lead the group in prayer.

C. Read and discuss IN FOCUS.

4. Getting into the Lesson

A. Read and discuss THE PEOPLE, PLACES, AND TIMES and BACKGROUND.

B. Ask volunteers to read the FOCAL VERSES and the corresponding IN DEPTH section. Continue in this manner until the class has completed all the verses and IN DEPTH. Allow time for discussion between each session.

5. Relating the Lesson to Life

A. Spend time answering the questions in DISCUSS THE MEANING.

B. Ask the class if anyone has insights to express regarding today's lesson. Also, tell them to think about the study for the last four Sundays and provide any comments and insights on this study as a whole.

6. Arousing Action

A. Direct the students to MAKE IT HAPPEN.

B. Remind the students that their journaling does not have to end because the unit study for March has concluded. Encourage them to continue writing in their journals and feel free to share testimonies of their spiritual success in the future.

C. Ask the group to stand, form a circle, join hands, and then close the session with prayer.

WORSHIP GUIDE

For the Superintendent or Teacher
Theme: What Really Defiles
Theme Song: "My Faith Looks Up to Thee"
Scripture: Philippians 4:8
Song: "Nothing Between"
Devotional Thought: Lord, thank You for the wonderful example of holiness represented in Your Son. Help me to purify my mind and thoughts daily.

WHAT REALLY DEFILES

Bible Background • MARK 7:1-23
Printed Text • MARK 7:1-15
Devotional Reading • PSALM 51:10-17

LESSON AIM

By the end of the lesson, students will realize how the Pharisees' traditions, as well as some church traditions today, hinder true worship of God. Students will determine to avoid empty ritual in private and public worship.

KEEP IN MIND

"For from within, out of the heart of men, proceed evil thoughts, adulteries, fornications, murders" (Mark 7:21).

FOCAL VERSES

Mark 7:1 Then came together unto him the Pharisees, and certain of the scribes, which came from Jerusalem.

2 And when they saw some of his disciples eat bread with defiled, that is to say, with unwashen, hands, they found fault.

3 For the Pharisees, and all the Jews, except they wash their hands oft, eat not, holding the tradition of the elders.

4 And when they come from the market, except they wash, they eat not. And many other things there be, which they have received to hold, as the washing of cups, and pots, brasen vessels, and of tables.

5 Then the Pharisees and scribes asked him, Why walk not thy disciples according to the tradition of the elders, but eat bread with unwashen hands?

6 He answered and said unto them, Well hath

LESSON OVERVIEW

LESSON AIM
KEEP IN MIND
FOCAL VERSES
IN FOCUS
THE PEOPLE, PLACES, AND TIMES
BACKGROUND
AT-A-GLANCE
IN DEPTH
SEARCH THE SCRIPTURES
DISCUSS THE MEANING
LESSON IN OUR SOCIETY
MAKE IT HAPPEN
FOLLOW THE SPIRIT
REMEMBER YOUR THOUGHTS
MORE LIGHT ON THE TEXT
DAILY BIBLE READINGS

Esaias prophesied of you hypocrites, as it is written, This people honoureth me with their lips, but their heart is far from me.

MAR 30TH

7 Howbeit in vain do they worship me, teaching for doctrines the commandments of men.

8 For laying aside the commandment of God, ye hold the tradition of men, as the washing of pots and cups: and many other such like things ye do.

9 And he said unto them, Full well ye reject the commandment of God, that ye may keep your own tradition.

10 For Moses said, Honour thy father and thy mother; and, Whoso curseth father or mother, let him die the death:

11 But ye say, If a man shall say to his father or mother, It is Corban, that is to say, a gift, by whatsoever thou mightest be profited by me; he shall be free.

12 And ye suffer him no more to do ought for his father or his mother;

13 Making the word of God of none effect through your tradition, which ye have delivered: and many such like things do ye.

14 And when he had called all the people unto him, he said unto them, Hearken unto me every one of you, and understand:

15 There is nothing from without a man, that

entering into him can defile him: but the things which come out of him, those are they that defile the man.

IN FOCUS

Larry Crabb and Dan Allender in their book *Encouragement* tell the story of a young male foreigner who visits the United States for a long period of time. While in the United States, he attends a church and during an evening fellowship service, someone introduces him to the congregation. After the service, several people welcome the man and tell him they would love to have him over for dinner soon. Soon never comes nor does an invitation to dinner. Later the foreigner explains to someone that he had to adjust to the American culture and learn that many words are spoken without meaning.

In addition to words spoken without meaning, our actions are often pointless as well. Such was the case of the Pharisees in today's lesson. In this lesson we will learn how the church can become entangled in traditions that are devoid of God's love and contrary to His commandments.

THE PEOPLE, PLACES, AND TIMES

Tradition of the Elders. The Pharisees believed that Moses received additional commandments that he communicated orally to the elders. These elders in turn handed down these extra commands through the generations. They regarded these traditions as equal in authority with the written word, the Law. For example, the Mosaic Law did specify different kinds of uncleanness, but the Pharisees took it further by adding their own. They stated that a person who went to the marketplace and touched an unclean person would himself become unclean. They even stated that certain cups and pots were unclean unless they were washed, when this was not in Moses' Law at all. So they were extremists in keeping their self-made laws and expected everyone else to keep them as well.

BACKGROUND

Several major events and miracles take place in Mark 6 leading up to today's lesson: John the Baptizer is beheaded upon the request of Herodias's daughter during Herod's birthday party; Jesus feeds a crowd of over 5,000; and the disciples see Jesus walk on water. Jesus' ministry is reciprocal. As the Great Physician, He touched and healed all that were sick, and in turn all who were sick sought to touch Him. Verse 56 indicates that the people begged just to touch the edge of His cloak so that all who touched Him were healed. While the infirmed touched Jesus and received healing, the scribes and Pharisees continued to remain detached and suspicious of Jesus.

AT-A-GLANCE

1. Empty Tradition (Mark 7:1-13)
2. Inner Corruption (vv. 14-15)

IN DEPTH

1. Empty Tradition (Mark 7:1-13)

The scribes and Pharisees held Jesus under close scrutiny constantly. They followed Jesus only to seek ways to destroy Him and His message. In so doing, they were always asking Jesus why He and the disciples exercised certain practices. In this case it was these religious leaders' concern for eating with unwashed hands. What did it mean in biblical times to eat with unwashed hands? First, the washing of hands was not for personal hygiene but for ceremonial cleanness. It indeed was a ceremony because the hands had to be washed in a certain way. According to William Barclay (in his commentary entitled *The Gospel of Mark*) some rules for this hand washing ritual of the Pharisees consisted of the following:

1. The hands had to be free of sand, gravel, or any other substance.

2. The water for washing had to be kept in large stone jars.

3. The hands must be washed with the fingertips pointing upwards, and water was poured over them.

4. The fist of one hand was rubbed in the palm of the other.

So if a person failed to follow this ritual, the Pharisees considered the person unclean in the sight of God. Not only did the Pharisees and many Jews wash their hands, but they also added to the law by washing pots and pans, tables, and other utensils.

How did Jesus view the Pharisees' hand washing ceremony? He described their actions as only lip service and vain worship, for their hearts were impure. The word "vain" here means fruitless. Thus the Pharisee's piety, or worship, was futile and rendered no honor to God. Worst still, they had "rejected" God's law and were following their own rules. What a dangerous path upon which to travel, but many Christians today, like the Pharisees, are trekking on the tradition trails. Many a churchgoer's response is, "We cannot do it a different way. We've always done it this way." Unfortunately, they do not stop to ask themselves, "Is **this way** God's way?"

Jesus pointed to a specific example of the Pharisees' vain traditions and laws when He spoke of honoring father and mother. The Old Testament clearly stated that children should respect their parents (Exodus 20:12; Leviticus 20:9), but the Pharisees' law asserted a different obligation. In *The Laymen's Bible Commentary*, Paul S. Minear explained the text: "If a son had made a vow to offer to God, or to the Temple, property which was later needed to support his parents, he should give this vow priority over his family obligation." Thus, by changing the law to their own profit, Jesus declared that the Pharisees made the Word ineffective.

2. Inner Corruption (vv. 14-15)

The Pharisees were concerned about washing their hands, cups, and utensils outer purity. But Jesus confronted them with a deeper issue the issue of the heart and taught on inner corruption in Mark 7:18-23. These corrupt things that come from the heart include fornication, evil thoughts, adultery, murder, and foolishness. In conclusion, when we stand before God in judgment, He will not look to see if we washed our hands and cups, but rather if our souls have been washed in the blood of the Lamb.

SEARCH THE SCRIPTURES

1. Name two traditions of the Pharisees. (Mark 7:3-4)

2. What did Jesus have to say about the Pharisees' tradition? (vv. 6-8).

3. What defiles a person? (vv. 14-15)

DISCUSS THE MEANING

1. In what ways can church/religious traditions do more harm than good?

2. Jesus accused the Pharisees of placing a heavy burden on the people with all of their legalistic laws and replacing God's commandments with their own. Do we have Pharisees in the church today? If so, how are they placing burdens on the body of Christ?

LESSON IN OUR SOCIETY

In today's lesson we learned about the useless traditions that the Pharisees followed. Reading about this religious group provides an example of what is still happening in the church more than 2000 years later. Many churches are holding on to rituals, but are not experiencing the presence and power of God. Some Christian leaders have made the Word of God of no effect by using Scriptures to justify sins such as homosexuality and fornication. While other Christians feel they are righteous solely because they go to church, pay large sums of money, or work on church committees. All worship that is rendered out of an impure heart is in vain. Jesus' desire for the church today is to be renewed in mind, heart, and spirit so that we worship Him in spirit and in truth.

MAKE IT HAPPEN

The key verse today teaches that it is from within, from the human heart, that evil intentions come. This week read the FOCAL VERSES again and answer the questions in SEARCH THE SCRIPTURES. After you have answered the questions, write in your journal any insights that you learned from your reading as well as from today's class. Pray with your prayer partner this week, telling him or her about any struggles you are having with your new beginning. If you do not have a partner, join with someone that you feel comfortable with in your class and the two of you should plan to pray together this week.

events must have spread all over the region so that a delegation of Jewish authorities was sent from Jerusalem to meet Him, probably to investigate Him.

7:1 Then came together unto him the Pharisees, and certain of the scribes, which came from Jerusalem. 2 And when they saw some of his disciples eat bread with defiled, that is to say, with unwashen, hands, they found fault.

We have learned earlier (3:22) that scribes and Pharisees have come down from Jerusalem to investigate Christ's activities at Galilee. This time they have probably come to Gennesaret where Jesus has performed many miraculous healings (6:53-56). On their arrival they find out that Jesus' disciples are breaking the Jewish laws and traditions by eating with their hands unwashed. They are offended and complain about it. Their complaint is that the disciples eat with defiled hands. The disciples are not necessarily unhygienic by their failure to wash their hands before the meal, but rather they break the ceremonial ritual of purification—a tradition of the elders.

3 For the Pharisees, and all the Jews, except they wash their hands oft, eat not, holding the tradition of the elders. 4 And when they come from the market, except they wash, they eat not. And many other things there be, which they have received to hold, as the washing of cups, and pots, brasen vessels, and of tables.

Verses 3 and 4 try to explain the meaning of this tradition. According to the elders' tradition, "the Pharisees and all the Jews" are expected to wash their hands often or they are not allowed to eat. It is believed that Mark's Gospel is aimed at a Gentile audience. Therefore, the explanation here is to benefit his Gentile readers. The word

FOLLOW THE SPIRIT
What God wants me to do:

_____

_____

REMEMBER YOUR THOUGHTS
Special insights you have learned:

_____

_____

MORE LIGHT ON THE TEXT
Mark 7:1-15
The latter verses of chapter 6 in Mark's Gospel report a number of outstanding miracles of Christ during His ministry. These include feeding of over 5,000 (vv. 32-44), walking on the sea, calming of the storm (vv. 45-52), and healing of the sick (vv. 53-56). The news of these extraordinary

"wash" is the Greek verb *nipto* (pronounced **NIP-toe**), which means to cleanse the hands or the feet or the face, or to perform ablution—a sort of ritualistic ceremony.

In verse 4 Mark gives His readers examples of such rituals. For example, when one returns from the market, one ought to wash oneself or he or she would not eat. Note the Greek used here for "wash" is *baptizo* (pronounced **bap-TID-zoh**), which means to immerse, submerge; to make overwhelmed (i.e., fully wet). This is the original of the English word "baptize" from which the ordinance of Christian baptism is derived. The idea here is not only washing of the hands but having a bath—immersing oneself in water (cp. v. 3; cf. Hebrews 9:10). The object of this observance is believed to be cleansing oneself after mingling with Gentiles or non-conformists of the traditions of elders. Mark explains further that the Pharisees observe many rituals and tradition such as "washing of cups, and pots, brasen vessels, and of tables."

5 Then the Pharisees and scribes asked him, Why walk not thy disciples according to the tradition of the elders, but eat bread with unwashen hands? 6 He answered and said unto them, Well hath Esaias prophesied of you hypocrites, as it is written, This people honoureth me with their lips, but their heart is far from me.

In their complaint, the Pharisees and scribes ask Jesus why His disciples are not keeping the tradition of their elders by eating with their hands unwashed. "Tradition" is the translation of the Greek *paradosis* (pronounced **pah-RAH-doh-siss**). It means a precept or ordinance, the Jewish traditional law. These traditions were mainly oral and created by the rabbis and teachers of the law to supplement the law, especially on issues where the commandment or the law is not explicit. These traditions were passed from generation to generation until they become binding. The traditions were so numerous in the Jewish religion that it was impossible to keep them all. Jesus came into the world not only to do away with the burdens of the Old Testament Law but also to liberate the people from the numerous enslaving traditions.

In answer to their inquiry, Jesus quotes from

the Prophet Isaiah and comments that "Isaiah was right when he prophesied about you hypocrites," (29:13, NIV). According to Him, Isaiah quotes God as saying that "this people honoureth me with their lips, but their heart is far from me." The English word "hypocrite," a transliteration of the Greek *hupokrites* (pronounced **hoo-POCK-krih-tace**) meaning an actor under an assumed character (a stage player), a dissembler or a pretender. Here Jesus accuses the Pharisees and scribes as people who falsely assume what they are not. While they pretend to be holy and show outward piety, their lives reflect the contrary. Their hearts are far away from worshiping the true God.

7 Howbeit in vain do they worship me, teaching for doctrines the commandments of men. 8 For laying aside the commandment of God, ye hold the tradition of men, as the washing of pots and cups: and many other such like things ye do. 9 And he said unto them, Full well ye reject the commandment of God, that ye may keep your own tradition.

Like the people of the Old Testament the people substitute the commandment of God for man-made commandments. They replace God's commandment with man-made traditions which include the ceremonial "washing of pots and cups: and many other such like things." Jesus accuses them of nullifying and rejecting God's law and holding to their own teaching which contradicts the commandment of God. They set aside God's law in order promulgate their own tradition.

10 For Moses said, Honour thy father and thy mother; and, Whoso curseth father or mother, let him die the death: 11 But ye say, If a man shall say to his father or mother, It is Corban, that is to say, a gift, by whatsoever thou mightest be profited by me; he shall be free.

Quoting the Old Testament, Jesus gives an example of how they set aside the commandment in order advance their own tradition. The first quote comes from Exodus 20:12, the fifth commandment, which deals with a person's responsibility toward one's parents: "Honour thy mother and thy father." He combines it with the second quote from Exodus 21:17, which stipulates the penalty for failure to obey the fifth commandment, i.e., death for anyone who curses his father or mother.

In order to circumvent this law and avoid caring for one's parents, one would declare a gift as "corban." "Corban" is from the Hebrew *korban* or may be of Aramaic origin *korbanas* (pronounced **kohr-hah-NAHS**). That means a gift or a consecrated present dedicated to God for the temple fund. Rather than taking care of one's parent, one would give an excuse that sounds like "all that I can spare of material things have been dedicated to God, and I cannot now help my parents." It was a common practice for children who did not want to support their parents to enter into an agreement with a corrupt priest for a small percent to dedicate things to God, thus excluding their parents from benefitting from such a gift. Thus, they would be free of their obligation to their parents.

12 And ye suffer him no more to do ought for his father or his mother; 13 Making the word of God of none effect through your tradition, which ye have delivered: and many such like things do ye.

The Pharisees and scribes condone this action, Jesus says, and He condemns them. By encouraging this type of attitude, Jesus accuses the Pharisees and scribes of nullifying the Word and commandments of God and promoting their own traditions. Jesus accuses them of many other things, especially hypocrisy.

14 And when he had called all the people unto him, he said unto them, Hearken unto me every one of you, and understand: 15 There is nothing from without a man, that entering into him can defile him: but the things which come out of him, those are they that defile the man.

Before this Jesus has been addressing the religious authorities in reply to their accusation against the disciples (v. 5). He condemns them for their hypocrisy and religiosity. He now calls for the attention of the crowd together around Him (v. 14). He invites them to pay close attention to what He is about to teach in answer to the Pharisees' accusation. The word "hearken" is from the Greek verb *akouo* (pronounced **ah-KOO-oh**) which means to hear or to listen with the purpose of understanding what is being said. He solicits their undivided attention to His teaching. Jesus informs them what does and does not defile or make one unclean. He states clearly that what enters into a person—i.e., what one eats for sustenance, such as food—does not defile one, even if it is eaten with unwashed hands. (Such things do not, however, include intoxicated drinks, narcotics, poisons, tobaccos and other things that bind and destroy the mind and body.) Rather, what defiles a person, Jesus says, is what comes from within—a person's motives, thoughts, and what the person says, desires and does—these are what make a person unclean.

DAILY BIBLE READINGS

M: Holding to Human Tradition
Mark 7:1-8

T: What Comes Out Defiles
Mark 7:9-15

W: Evil Things Come from Within
Mark 7:17-23

T: God Knows the Heart
Luke 16:10-15

F: Do Not Follow Human Tradition
Colossians 2:6-10

S: Create in Me a Clean Heart
Psalm 51:10-17

S: Take the Log from Your Eye
Luke 6:37-42

TEACHING TIPS

April 6
Bible Study Guide 6

1. Words You Should Know

A. Colt (Mark 11:2)—A young donkey which had never been ridden.

B. The house of prayer (v. 17)—Greek *oikos proseuches* (pronounced **OY-kahss prahs-you-KACE**) God's temple. In the New Testament each individual believer is God's temple.

2. Teacher Preparation

A. Familiarize yourself with all the 13 lessons of the quarter. The QUARTER-AT-A-GLANCE will help you with this.

B. Begin your study for this week's lesson by reading the entire Book of Mark.

C. The key words for this week's passage are defined in the WORDS YOU SHOULD KNOW section. Be sure to review them.

D. Review the KEEP IN MIND verse and reflect on how it applies to you personally. You may want to share the application with the class.

3. Starting the Lesson

A. Open the session with prayer. Thank God for all that He taught you in the last lesson and ask that the Holy Spirit open your hearts and minds to the eternal truths of the new lesson.

B. Welcome the students to the new lesson, and ask someone to read the UNIT 2 INTRODUCTION in the QUARTER-AT-A-GLANCE section. Invite another student to read the lesson overview for today's lesson.

4. Getting into the Lesson

A. Have the students read the LESSON AIM in unison, then silently read the IN FOCUS story.

B. Assign one of the students to read aloud the BACKGROUND information, then ask for three volunteers to read the FOCAL VERSES according to the AT-A-GLANCE outline.

5. Relating the Lesson to Life

A. Lead the students in answering the SEARCH THE SCRIPTURES questions. Then focus on THE PEOPLE, PLACES, AND TIMES section.

B. Allow ten minutes or so for the students to silently read the IN DEPTH commentary, then go over the highlights with them.

C. Now call the students attention to the DISCUSS THE MEANING questions and the LESSON IN OUR SOCIETY section. This will help them to see how the lesson applies to our modern day experiences.

D. Have the students share the most significant point they have learned from today's lesson and how they plan to use it during the week.

6. Arousing Action

APRIL 6TH

A. Call the students attention to the MAKE IT HAPPEN suggestion, and encourage them to practice it this week.

B. Remind students to use the DAILY BIBLE READINGS, REMEMBER YOUR THOUGHTS, and FOLLOW THE SPIRIT sections. This will help build their faith and plant the seeds of God's Word in their hearts.

C. Close the class with prayer, thanking God for our redemption and restoration.

WORSHIP GUIDE

For the Superintendent or Teacher
Theme: Entering Jerusalem and
Cleansing the Temple
Theme Song: "Oh, Worship the King"
Scripture: Mark 11:1-9, 15-18
Song: "I Will Call upon the Lord"
Devotional Thought: Lord, cleanse our
hearts, our words, our thoughts, and
especially our bodies today, that we might
offer up worship which is worthy of You.
Amen.

ENTERING JERUSALEM AND CLEANSING THE TEMPLE

Bible Background • MARK 11:1–12:12
Printed Text • MARK 11:1-9, 15-18
Devotional Reading • LUKE 19:28-40

LESSON AIM

By the end of the lesson, students will be able to explain the meaning of Jesus' triumphant entry into Jerusalem and His cleansing of the temple. They will commit themselves to the cleansing of God's temple, their bodies. They will follow through on the MAKE IT HAPPEN challenge.

KEEP IN MIND

"And they come to Jerusalem: and Jesus went into the temple, and began to cast out them that sold and bought in the temple, and overthrew the tables of the moneychangers, and the seats of them that sold doves" (Mark 11:15).

FOCAL VERSES

Mark 11:1 And when they came nigh to Jerusalem, unto Bethphage and Bethany, at the Mount of Olives, he sendeth forth two of his disciples,

2 And saith unto them, Go your way into the village over against you: and as soon as ye be entered into it, ye shall find a colt tied, whereon never man sat; loose him, and bring him.

3 And if any man say unto you, Why do ye this? say ye that the Lord hath need of him; and straightway he will send him hither.

4 And they went their way, and found the colt tied by the door without in a place where two ways met; and they loose him.

5 And certain of them that stood there said unto them, What do ye, loosing the colt?

LESSON OVERVIEW

LESSON AIM
KEEP IN MIND
FOCAL VERSES
IN FOCUS
THE PEOPLE, PLACES,
AND TIMES
BACKGROUND
AT-A-GLANCE
IN DEPTH
SEARCH THE SCRIPTURES
DISCUSS THE MEANING
LESSON IN OUR SOCIETY
MAKE IT HAPPEN
FOLLOW THE SPIRIT
REMEMBER YOUR THOUGHTS
MORE LIGHT ON THE TEXT
DAILY BIBLE READINGS

---

6 And they said unto them even as Jesus had commanded: and they let them go.

7 And they brought the colt to Jesus, and cast their garments on him; and he sat upon him.

8 And many spread their garments in the way: and others cut down branches off the trees, and strawed them in the way.

9 And they that went before, and they that followed, cried, saying, Hosanna; blessed is he that cometh in the name of the Lord:

11:15 And they come to Jerusalem: and Jesus went into the temple, and began to cast out them that sold and bought in the temple, and overthrew the tables of the moneychangers, and the seats of them that sold doves;

16 And would not suffer that any man should carry any vessel through the temple.

17 And he taught, saying unto them, Is it not written, My house shall be called of all nations the house of prayer? But ye have made it a den of thieves.

18 And the scribes and chief priests heard it, and sought how they might destroy him: for they feared him, because all the people was astonished at his doctrine.

IN FOCUS

Shannon and David were married less than one year, and soon David's parents were coming to visit them. Since Shannon's in-laws lived out of state, they had never come to their little apartment before. Shannon was wildly cleaning everything in sight—every closet, every drawer, ever corner of every room. She called her mama to find out the most perfect things she could cook. Still she was very nervous. She knew that David's mother was a perfect housewife and wonderful cook.

What do you think were some of Shannon's motivations in the hospitality extended to her in-laws? Sometimes our welcome has many layers of meaning—some explicit, some that we may be hiding even from ourselves. Why do you think the people welcomed Jesus on that first Palm Sunday? How did they view Jesus? What were they expecting of Him? Can our own worship be motivated by conflicting emotions?

THE PEOPLE, PLACES, AND TIMES

Jerusalem. The capital and holy city of Israel since the time of King David (about 1000 B.C.).

Bethphage. A suburb of Jerusalem, on the southeastern slope of the Mount Olives. It was near Bethany.

Bethany. A suburb of Jerusalem (about 2 miles), on the eastern slopes of the Mount of Olives.

Mount of Olives. A mountain east of Jerusalem, 2660 feet above sea level, known for its many olive trees.

The Temple. The first temple was built by King Solomon (about 957 B.C.). It was destroyed by the Babylonians in 587/6 B.C. Zerubbabel built the second temple after the exile (about 515 B.C.). Antiochus Epiphanes (pronounced **ann-TIE-uh-kuss ee-PIFF-uh-neez**) despoiled it and desecrated it. The third temple was built by Herod the Great (37 A.D.–4 B.C.). It is the one referred to in Mark. Although Herod's temple was actually the third temple, scholars have traditionally referred to it as the second temple, because it surpassed the actual second temple in importance.

BACKGROUND

Mark 11:1-9, 15-18 is part of a section (chapters 11 and 12) concluding Jesus' earthly ministry. Jesus is in His last week. The events and teachings are set in and around Jerusalem. In this section there is a recurring pattern of entrance into the city during the day and withdrawal to Bethany in the evening (11:11, 19).

The section consists of symbolic actions, such as Jesus' entry into Jerusalem (11:1-11), the cleansing of the temple (11:15-18), the cursing of the fig tree (11:12-14, 19-26), and the parable of the vineyard (12:1-11). It also describes the conflict with the Jewish authorities (11:27-33; 12:12-44) thus preparing the way for Jesus arrest, trial, and crucifixion (chapters 14 and 15).

The section is in contrast to Jesus' early ministry. In His early ministry Jesus used to withdraw Himself from public notice, often passing His time in the remote part of Galilee (see Isaiah 42:2). But here, by His own choice, He deliberately made a public entry into Jerusalem surrounded by a crowd crying "Hosanna," like King David returning to his palace in triumph (2 Samuel 19). The cleansing of the temple also brought upon Him more public notice.

AT-A-GLANCE

1. Jesus Enters Jerusalem as a King
(Mark 11:1-9)
2. Jesus Cleanses the Temple
(vv. 15-18)

IN DEPTH

1. Jesus Enters Jerusalem as a King (11:1-9)

On Sunday Jesus was on His way to Jerusalem. His road led Him through Bethany and Bethphage. He sent two of His disciples. They were to go into the village ahead. They would find a colt. The description of the colt as one which had never been ridden is significant in the light of the Old Testament provision that an animal devoted to a sacred purpose must be one that had not been put to ordinary use (Numbers 19:2; Deuteronomy 21:3; 1 Samuel 6:7).

The two disciples were to untie the colt and bring it back. If anyone asked questions, they were to say, "The Lord hath need of him." He promised to return it!

The execution of the command is recorded in terms identical with Jesus' instruction. Things happened just as Jesus had said.

The disciples put their outer garments on the animal in place of a saddle, and Jesus began His ride to the gates of Jerusalem. The disciples and the crowd threw clothing and branches for Jesus to ride over, expressing a spontaneous expression of homage to Jesus. They began singing the great psalms of ascent to Jerusalem (Psalms 113–118). They were crying out "Hosanna" which strictly means "Please save" but through liturgical use came to have the sense of "Hallelujah" or "Praise God." They shouted out their conviction that Jesus was coming in the name of God, that He was bringing God's kingdom, and that He was the promised Son of David.

Jesus came to die in Jerusalem, and He desired all the people to be witness of His death. Thus He purposely made public His entry into the city.

2. Jesus Cleanses the Temple (vv. 15-18)

Jesus now had some support after His triumphant entry into Jerusalem. He had been treated as Israel's Messiah and, for the moment, He could do anything He wanted in the temple.

On Monday, He forcefully ejected the small-time businessmen who had been using the temple as their marketplace. The scene was the outermost court of the temple, the court of the Gentiles. It was a wide enclosure, which provided access to the interior parts of the temple precincts from which it was separated by a high partition wall. By the colonnades around it, the scribes were teaching their pupils. On the pavement, the traders conducted their business of selling wine, salt, oil, and sacrificial animals. In a country where the circulating currency consisted primarily of Roman money, provision had to be made for the people to pay the annual temple tax of one half shekel (Exodus 30:13-16). Thus, at certain seasons, the moneychangers exchanged the Greek or Roman money of the pilgrims into Jewish or Tyrian currency required for the payment of the temple tax. Regulations prohibited the use the courtyard as a thoroughfare. A temple that is not a house of prayer anymore is not a temple, but a cavern of thieves (v. 17). What was Jesus' intention in driving out the merchants and overthrowing the moneychangers' tables?

A. Jesus was horrified at the disregard for the sanctity of an area consecrated for the use of Gentiles who had not yet become full proselytes to Judaism. His act was an evidence of respect for the sacredness of the temple precincts.

B. His gesture against the merchants was a

prophetic, symbolic act accompanied by a warning about God's impending judgment on the temple and Israel.

C. Jesus' action was an extraordinary display of zeal for God. The weapons Jesus carried on the eve of His passion are certainly not those of the armed revolutionary but those of an authoritative teacher whose prophetic word terrified the religious authority of Israel. By cleansing the temple courtyard, Jesus bore witness to the conditions of "that day" when God would gather the nations to His temple to worship Him (Zechariah 14:16).

The scriptural basis for Jesus' "violent" action is from Isaiah 56:7. The clause "all nations" indicates that Jesus expelled the merchants from the temple courtyard in order to safeguard rights and privileges authorized by God. The use of the courtyard as an open market prevented the temple from being a place of prayer.

One might imagine that the religious authorities would be happy to have a clean temple (v. 18). The cleansing of the temple was actually one more incident that made them increase their efforts to arrest Jesus. They did not arrest Him immediately because of Jesus' popularity with the people. In contrast to the hostile response of the chief priests and the scribes, the people were fascinated at Jesus' remarkable display of authority.

The temple cleansed by Jesus was destroyed by the Romans in A.D. 70. The Bible describes Christians as the new temple of God (1 Corinthians 3:16-17; 6:19-20; 2 Corinthians 6:16; Ephesians 2:19-22; 1 Peter 2:5).

SEARCH THE SCRIPTURES

1. What did Jesus do when he came near Jerusalem? (Mark 11:1-3)

2. What did the crowd say as they followed Jesus? (v. 9)

3. What did Jesus call the temple? (v. 17)

DISCUSS THE MEANING

1. Jesus accepted worship from the people and He authoritatively judged sin. Both of these actions imply His deity. Why are these things that only God can do?

2. Why did Jesus cleanse the temple? Is there a temple that we are called to clean? First

Corinthians 3:16 tells us that our physical bodies are the Lord's temple. When we abuse our bodies in any fashion, we are abusing the temple of the Lord. What are some common ways that people abuse their bodies today?

LESSON IN OUR SOCIETY

Our secular society sees and understands only the physical and earthly. That anything could be considered holy is thought to be an antiquated idea. Lack of respect for people, places, and things is a key component of our society. Consider how people used to show respect for preachers, churches, and Bibles. How can we show respect for the house of the Lord, for Christian leaders, and the Bible in the context of our society? Are traditions of past generations of African American believers relevant for today? Which of the former customs should we follow today? Which need to be discarded? How can we modify some of the former manners to be in line with God's command for holiness, along with His hatred of customs that merely cause a pharisaical self-righteousness?

MAKE IT HAPPEN

Jesus cleansed the temple so that it can be used for its rightful purpose. The Bible says that we are the temple of God (1 Corinthians 3:16-17; 6:19-20; 2 Corinthians 6:16; Ephesians 2:19-22; 1 Peter 2:5). It is our responsibility to respond enthusiastically to the message of God and with His help cleanse our bodies, His temple.

FOLLOW THE SPIRIT

What God wants me to do:

_____

_____

REMEMBER YOUR THOUGHTS

Special insights you have learned:

_____

_____

MORE LIGHT ON THE TEXT
Mark 11:1-9, 15-18

11:1 And when they came nigh to Jerusalem,

unto Bethphage and Bethany, at the Mount of Olives, he sendeth forth two of his disciples,

The Greek word *apostellei* (pronounced **ah-pah-STELL-aa**) or "he sendeth forth" denotes the sending of a messenger with a special task, a commission and with full authority. The emphasis is on the one who sends, not on the one who is sent. The disciples were sent as ambassadors with a precise message and speaking in the name of their Master. Their mandate is described in the next verse. By sending two of His disciples, Jesus was accomplishing a prophecy from Zechariah, thus giving the event a messianic meaning.

2 and saith unto them, Go your way into the village over against you: and as soon as ye be entered into it, ye shall find a colt tied, whereon never man sat; loose him, and bring him.

The Greek word *Polon* (pronounced **POH-lahn**) means literally a young colt. The description of the young animal as one which had never been ridden is significant in the light of many Old Testament passages. Such an animal was consecrated to a unique and holy use (Numbers 19:2; Deuteronomy 21:3; 1 Samuel 6:7). The messianic meaning of Jesus's action is pointed out in His instruction about the young colt (Zechariah 9:9).

3 And if any man say unto you, Why do ye this? say ye that the Lord hath need of him; and straightway he will send him hither.

The Greek word *Ho kurios* (pronounced **haw KOOR-ee-ahss**) meaning Lord is less likely to refer to the owner of the colt; it refers to Jesus Himself, showing His supreme authority over all things. It is possible that Jesus' relationship with the owner of the young animal was well known in the village. In any case Jesus armed his two emissaries against possible difficulties, by furnishing them with the word to speak. He promised to return the young animal promptly (*eutheos*) after He has used it.

4 And they went their way, and found the colt tied by the door without in a place where two ways met; and they loose him.

Jesus' ambassadors found the young animal

exactly as He had said. It was outside the house and fastened by the door.

5 And certain of them that stood there said unto them, What do ye, loosing the colt?

Precisely what Jesus said would happen did happen.

6 And they said unto them even as Jesus had commanded: and they let them go.

The fact that the people standing by were satisfied with the answer given by the disciples is explained by the consideration that Jesus was well-known in the neighborhood. He was well-known for His miraculous deeds and for the fact that He taught with authority (see John 7:46; Mark 11:18). They knew that this Master could be trusted. They probably were proud of the fact that the young colt would be used by the Master.

7 And they brought the colt to Jesus, and cast their garments on him; and he sat upon him.

The disciples placed their outer garments on the colt in place of a saddle. Jesus sat and began His ride to the gates of Jerusalem.

8 And many spread their garments in the way: and others cut down branches off the trees, and strawed them in the way.

He was met by a spontaneous expression of homage. The crowd provided "a red carpet" for Him, the King. They threw into the road their garments. The Greek word *eis* (pronounced **ace**) meaning "into" denotes that the crowd threw their garments into the way and spread them there for Jesus to ride over.

The carpeted way was not made of garments only. The crowd also cut down branches off the trees and strewed them into the road. The Greek word *stoibadas* (pronounced **stoy-BAH-dahss**) speaks of a mass of straw, rushes, or leaves beaten together or strewed loosely so as to form a carpet.

9 And they that went before, and they that followed, cried, saying, Hosanna; Blessed is he that cometh in the name of the Lord

The Greek word *Hosanna* comes from the

Hebrew word *Hosiana* (pronounced **ho-she-ah-nah**). Its original meaning is a cry for help: "O save" or "Help, I pray" as in Psalm 118:25-26. Coupled with the blessing that follows, as in Mark, it denotes an expression of praise, rejoicing, or greeting. The Greek word *eulogemenos* (pronounced **you-log-a-MEN-ahss**) or "blessed" means to speak well of or to praise. The blessing is from God who is the source of all blessings. He who comes is blessed by the Lord God to whom He belongs. Jesus was eulogized by the crowd which subjected itself to Him and recognized Him as the Messiah (see Psalm 118:26).

11:15 And they come to Jerusalem: and Jesus went into the temple, and began to cast out them that sold and bought in the temple, and overthrew the tables of the moneychangers, and the seats of them that sold doves;

Jesus began His day by throwing out the money-makers from the temple. They were using the court of the Gentiles as a market. Jesus made no distinction between sellers and buyers.

16 And would not suffer that any man should carry any vessel through the temple.

Jesus prohibited anyone from carrying a vessel through the temple, using it as a shortcut when going between the city and the Mount of Olives.

17 And he taught, saying unto them, Is it not written, My house shall be called of all nations the house of prayer? but ye have made it a den of thieves.

The Greek word *edidasken* (pronounced **eh-DIH-dass-KEN**) translated "he taught" has a meaning of an act done continuously. It denotes that Jesus was teaching continually. Thus Jesus' cleansing of the temple is brought under the cover of His teaching activity. He started to teach them about the purpose of the temple of God. He quoted from the Prophet Isaiah (56:7) to explain His action. The perfect tense in the statement "ye have made it a den of thieves" emphasizes the incurable character of the action of the people and points forward to the severe warning in Mark 13:2. They are insensitive to the holiness of the area where they practiced their trade. Jesus'

action freed the place and made possible the worship of the Gentiles at the Passover feast, which commemorated God's redemption of His people. The phrase "for all the nations" stresses the fact that the day of exclusion is now over. In Christ all nations can have access to God.

18 And the scribes and chief priests heard it, and sought how they might destroy him: for they feared him, because all the people was astonished at his doctrine.

The Greek word *exeplesseto* (pronounced **x-eh-PLAY-seh-taw**) or "astonished" literally means to strike out of one's senses. Jesus' teachings were in such contrast to that of the scribes that the people saw the difference at once, and they were struck out of their senses because of it. The people were used to receiving formal, dry, stereotyped, without power, and over-their-heads type of teachings. But now they are receiving a simple, powerful, and challenging teaching from Jesus (see 1:22, 27; 6:2; 7:37).

DAILY BIBLE READINGS

M: Jesus Rides into Jerusalem
Mark 11:1-11
T: The King Comes Riding a Donkey
Zechariah 9:9-12
W: The Stones Would Shout
Luke 19:28-40
T: Jesus Cleanses the Temple
Mark 11:12-19
F: Have Faith in God
Mark 11:20-25
S: By What Authority?
Mark 11:27-33
S: The Story of Wicked Tenants
Mark 12:1-12

TEACHING TIPS

April 13
Bible Study Guide 7

1. Words You Should Know

A. The Son of Man (Mark 14:21)—A title of Jesus pointing to His incarnation.

B. The Kingdom of God (v. 25)—Refers to God's possession and the exercise of His power.

2. Teacher Preparation

A. Familiarize yourself with the all 13 lessons of the quarter. The QUARTER-AT-A-GLANCE will help you with this.

B. Read the UNIT 2 INTRODUCTION and subsequent lesson overviews.

C. Begin your study for this week's lesson by reading the entire Book of Mark.

C. The key words for this week's passage are defined in the WORDS YOU SHOULD KNOW section. Be sure to review them.

D. Review the KEEP IN MIND verse and find ways in which it applies to you personally. You may want to share the application with the class.

3. Starting the Lesson

A. Open the session with prayer. Thank God for all that He taught you over the last lesson, and ask that the Holy Spirit open your hearts and minds to the eternal truths of the new lesson.

B. Welcome the students and ask someone to read the UNIT 2 INTRODUCTION in the QUARTER-AT-A-GLANCE section. Invite another student to read the lesson overview for today's lesson.

4. Getting into the Lesson

A. Have the students read the LESSON AIM in unison, then silently read the IN FOCUS story.

B. Assign one of the students to read aloud the BACKGROUND information, then ask for three volunteers to read the FOCAL VERSES according to the AT-A-GLANCE outline.

5. Relating the Lesson to Life

A. Lead the students in answering the SEARCH THE SCRIPTURES questions. Then focus on THE PEOPLE, PLACES, AND TIMES.

B. Allow ten minutes or so for the students to silently read the IN DEPTH commentary, then go over the highlights with them.

C. Now call the students attention to the DISCUSS THE MEANING questions and the LESSON IN OUR SOCIETY section. This will help them to see how the lesson applies to our modern-day experiences.

D. Have the students share the most significant point they have learned from today's lesson and how they plan to use it during the week.

6. Arousing Action

A. Call the students attention to the MAKE IT HAPPEN suggestion, and encourage them to practice it this week.

B. Remind students to use the DAILY BIBLE READINGS, REMEMBER YOUR THOUGHTS, and FOLLOW THE SPIRIT sections. This will help build their faith and plant the seeds of God's Word in their hearts.

C. Close the class with prayer, thanking God for our redemption and restoration.

WORSHIP GUIDE

For the Superintendent or Teacher
Theme: A New Meaning for Passover
Theme Song: "His Blood Will Never Lose Its Power"
Scripture: Hebrews 9:11-14
Song: "Amazing Grace"
Devotional Thought: Lord God Almighty, we thank You for the blood of Jesus, for through His blood we are made righteous. Amen.

A NEW MEANING FOR PASSOVER

Bible Background • MARK 14:1-25
Printed Text • MARK 14:12-25
Devotional Reading • MATTHEW 26:17-30

LESSON AIM

By the end of the lesson, students will be able to explain the new meaning for Passover given by Jesus, relate to Jesus as He is betrayed by someone close, and re-dedicate themselves to the One who shed His blood for them to enter the new testament of God. They will follow through on the MAKE IT HAPPEN challenge.

KEEP IN MIND

"And he said unto them, This is my blood of the new testament, which is shed for many" (Mark 14:24).

FOCAL VERSES

Mark 14:12 And the first day of unleavened bread, when they killed the passover, his disciples said unto him, Where wilt thou that we go and prepare that thou mayest eat the passover?

13 And he sendeth forth two of his disciples, and saith unto them, Go ye into the city, and there shall meet you a man bearing a pitcher of water: follow him.

14 And wheresoever he shall go in, say ye to the goodman of the house, The Master saith, Where is the guestchamber, where I shall eat the passover with my disciples?

15 And he will shew you a large upper room furnished and prepared: there make ready for us.

16 And his disciples went forth, and came into the city, and found as he had said unto them: and they made ready the passover.

17 And in the evening he cometh with the twelve.

18 And as they sat and did eat, Jesus said, Verily I say unto you, One of you, which eateth with me shall betray me.

19 And they began to be sorrowful, and to say unto him one by one, Is it I? And another said, Is it I?

20 And he answered and said unto them, It is one of the twelve, that dippeth with me in the dish.

21 The Son of man indeed goeth, as it is written of him: but woe to that man by whom the Son of Man is betrayed! good were it for that man if he had never been born.

22 And as they did eat, Jesus took bread, and blessed, and brake it, and gave to them, and said, Take, eat: this is my body.

23 And he took the cup, and when he had given thanks, he gave it to them: and they all drank of it.

24 And he said unto them, This is my blood of the new testament, which is shed for many.

25 Verily I say unto you, I will drink no more of the fruit of the vine, until that day that I drink it new in the kingdom of God.

IN FOCUS

Rachel inherited her father's old Oldsmobile when he died. It was not the sort of car she would have chosen for herself. It was beige and she preferred silver. She wanted a jeep, but this looked like the grandfatherly car it was. She even left the plate on the front with her parents' names. Why did she continue driving this car? It was the memories. Driving this car

---

APRIL 13TH

made her think of her father and the many family trips of her youth she had made with her father always at the wheel of a car. Somehow she felt closer to him and protected still by him.

As human beings we need memorials to help us remember the good things in our lives. Communion, or the Lord's Supper, is a memorial to what our Lord has done for us. Although memorials only make us feel closer to events and people of the past, Communion has a genuine spiritual power, because it causes us to think on what the Lord has done for us. And to partake of Communion is the Lord's command.

THE PEOPLE, PLACES, AND TIMES

The Passover. A feast commemorating God's deliverance of the Israelites from slavery (Exodus 12). It was also called the feast of unleavened bread.

The Son of Man. A title of Christ pointing to His incarnation.

The Kingdom of God. A phrase used to refer to God's possession and exercise of His power. It describes God's rule. It has both a present and future aspect.

BACKGROUND

Jesus is constantly portrayed in the company of His disciples from chapter 1 to chapter 13. But as His death approached, He is *estranged* and goes alone to His death (Chapters 14—15). He is abandoned by those close to Him.

The section (14:1-25) points out the plot of the religious authorities, Judas's plan to betray Jesus, and the Last Supper. It is divided as follows: the plot (vv. 1-2), the anointing at Bethany (vv. 3-9), Judas's plan to betray Jesus (vv. 10-11), the preparations for the

Passover (vv. 12-16), the prophecy of the betrayal (vv. 17-21), and the Last Supper (vv. 22-25).

IN DEPTH

1. Preparation for the Last Supper (Mark 14:12-16)

Jesus' disciples took the initiative to ask Him where they should prepare the Passover meal. He commissioned two of them to get the provisions. They will meet a man who will guide them through the streets of Jerusalem to a house whose owner will provide the accommodations they need. It works out as Jesus says.

A man has been led by God to provide what is needed. Jesus was led by the Holy Spirit to know what to do.

2. Jesus Announced His Betrayal (vv. 17-21)

At evening they gathered to eat the Passover meal. Jesus warns the disciples of betrayal. This is in effect giving a warning to Judas, yet it is also giving him time to change his ways. By not mentioning his name, Jesus avoids publicly disgracing Judas. No one yet knew that Judas was different from the others. No one thought of saying, "Is it Judas?" They all said, "Is it I?" It also seems that Judas was present during the Lord's Supper. Jesus was showing Judas an amazing love. Jesus' words emphasize the seriousness of his sin (v. 20), the impossibility of defeating God's plan, and the terrible destiny awaiting the betrayer (v. 21).

3. The Institution of the Lord's Supper (vv. 22-26)

Jesus began by giving thanks. Then He took the symbols of His coming death. The bread stands for Jesus' dying in His body and carrying our sins (1 Peter 2:24). The breaking of the bread stands for Jesus' suffering. Jesus' death involved great suffering. He was broken in His sufferings. Although not a bone of His body was broken, He was broken within by the sufferings He endured. There was disgrace, ridicule, loneliness, shame, pain, and worst of all the feeling of abandonment by the Father.

The wine stands for blood atonement, which began a new testament. A testament had to be initiated with a sacrifice. It was a relationship in which an oath is given. God's oath is unconditional. He promises to receive and save all who come to Him based on the merit of His Son who has paid the

---

AT-A-GLANCE

1. Preparation for the Last Supper (Mark 14:12-16)
2. Jesus Announced His Betrayal (vv. 17-21)
3. The Institution of the Lord's Supper (vv. 22-26)

penalty for our sin (Jeremiah 31:33-34). Our being in covenant with Jesus means that there is a fixed relationship between Him and us. He is asking us to live a life of persistent faith in Him. As we do so, He promises to bless us. It all takes place by the blood of Jesus.

It is by the blood of Jesus that we get daily cleansing (1 John 1:9). It is by persistent faith in the blood of Jesus that we live constantly for God. The eating and drinking stand for the persistent faith in the atoning blood of Jesus. We get life and energy by feeding on Jesus and what He did for us on the cross. We are to eat Jesus and drink His blood. This means that we are to persistently get liveliness and confidence by a never-ending trust in the blood of Jesus. When we pray, when we sin, when we are weary, when we are suffering, in every situation, we turn in faith to the Jesus who is in covenant with His Father and us by means of the atoning blood.

The blood is poured out for many. Jesus' death benefits the entire human race. It has taken place for everyone. Everyone is invited to respond to Jesus in faith that He has died for him or her.

Jesus tells the disciples how they and their successors must live until He returns. They will be living by faith in a crucified Saviour. Not until His return in glory will they eat again with Him in precisely this way, with Him literally and physically present.

SEARCH THE SCRIPTURES

1. What did the disciples ask Jesus? (Mark 14:12)
2. What sad news did Jesus tell His disciples while they where reclining at the table? (vv. 18-21)
3. What did Jesus do while they were eating? (vv. 22-25)

DISCUSS THE MEANING

1. Note how Jesus treats Judas, even though He knew from the beginning the sort of person that he was. What does this tell us about the way Jesus treats all people, even those who do not believe in Him or follow Him? How should the example of Jesus in His treatment of Judas affect the way we treat others?

2. Why do you believe Jesus told His disciples about His betrayal and death? Again and again Jesus prophesied His death on the cross to His dis-

ciples, sometimes implicitly, other times explicitly. In what phrases in today's Scripture passage does Jesus imply that He is going to die? (See verses 18, 21, 22, 24, and 25.) Although Jesus did not speak of His crucifixion directly this time as He did at others, He is very explicit as to the meaning of His coming death. What does verse 24 tell us about why Jesus was going to die? Why do you think it was important at this time for Jesus to explain His crucifixion to His disciples? Why is it important for us to understand the reason? How should an understanding of our Lord's Last Supper make a difference in our lives?

LESSON IN OUR SOCIETY

In recent decades, people have discovered that having great financial resources is not enough, especially if it means neglecting the spiritual side of life. Christians are also finding that even though we may have beautiful churches with very busy programs, there is a need to slow down, meditate on what our Lord has done for us, and worship Him. Communion, as many call this special ordinance, is meant to draw us close to Christ, so close that we are in communion with Him and with His people as we remember what He has done for us. Communion is God's design for our hearts' deep need.

MAKE IT HAPPEN

Jesus involved His disciples in the Passover preparation, even though He knew where to find the location and the other things needed. In the same way, He involves us in preparation for special worship times. In what ways can we be involved in our church's preparation for worship, especially for Communion? Perhaps your class or your church may plan a special celebration of the Lord's Last Supper with His disciples. As you celebrate Communion together, think of the meaning that Jesus gave to this ordinance of His church. Prepare your hearts for worship as you prepare for the physical implements of Communion.

FOLLOW THE SPIRIT

What God wants me to do:

_____

_____

317

REMEMBER YOUR THOUGHTS
Special insights you have learned:

_____

_____

MORE LIGHT ON THE TEXT
Mark 14:12:25

14:12 And the first day of unleavened bread, when they killed the passover, his disciples said unto him, Where wilt thou that we go and prepare that thou mayest eat the passover?

The story begins with "and" as do many New Testament stories. The subject, "Jesus," is not indicated. The chronological indications refer to the day before Passover, starting Thursday at sundown. The disciples took the initiative and asked Jesus where they should prepare the meal. Their question indicates that they were not aware of any practical arrangements in advance by Jesus.

13 And he sendeth forth two of his disciples, and saith unto them, Go ye into the city, and there shall meet you a man bearing a pitcher of water: follow him.

The episode of the preparation of the passover meal has some analogy with the one in 11:1-7. They are parallel in structure. The precise knowledge of what they will encounter and the exact response to be given to the responsible party characterized both stories. The commissioning of the disciples shows that Jesus often sent out His disciples. In this case, two among them would be enough for this particular mission. The carrying of water was usually a woman's job. But here they will meet a man carrying a pitcher. He is merely a guide and may or may not have been unconscious of his role. The disciples are to follow him to the house where he will enter and give Jesus' message to the *oikodespotes* (pronounced **oy-koh-dess-POT-tace**) or the "goodman of the house."

14 And wheresoever he shall go in, say ye to the goodman of the house, The Master saith, where is the guest chambers, where I shall eat the passover with my disciples?

The Greek *kataluma* (pronounced **kah-TAH-loo-mah**) translated "chamber" can also mean guest room or dining room. It is modified by the pronoun

mou (pronounced **moo**) or "my" (first person in the genitive case) literally meaning "my room" or "my dining room." Such a construction seems to suggest something agreed upon before.

15 And he will shew you a large upper room furnished and prepared: there make ready for us.

The owner of the house himself would show them a large upstairs room. The upstairs rooms were usually furnished with carpets and couches for the guests to recline on as they ate the meal.

16 And his disciples went forth, and came into the city, and found as he had said unto them: and they made ready the passover.

The disciples entered the city. They found that Jesus' instructions were precise, so they prepared the meal.

17 And in the evening he cometh with the twelve.

In the evening (Thursday after sunset), Jesus came to Jerusalem with His disciples fully aware that He was to accomplish the Passover in His own person.

18 And as they sat and did eat, Jesus said, Verily I say unto you, One of you which eateth with me shall betray me.

Jesus warned the disciples of the betrayal. He announced that one them would betray Him (see Psalm 41:10; 49:9). The betrayal described in the Scriptures was clearly foreseen by Jesus.

19 And they began to be sorrowful, and to say unto him one by one, Is it I? And another said, Is it I?

The betrayal was a surprise to the disciples. The word "sorrow" in Greek is *lupeo* (pronounced **loo-PEH-oh**) meaning "to be grieved" or "distress." This word points out the strong reaction of the disciples. The question they ask "one by one" shows that they did not understand that it was too late.

20 And he answered and said unto them, It is one of the twelve, that dippeth with me in the dish.

In His answer Jesus removed all ambiguity and said that it was one of the twelve "that dippeth with me in the dish." The Greek word *embaptomenos* (pronounced **m-bah-TAH-men-ahss**) literally means to plunge or soak his hand with me in the dish. Thus, the betrayal is revealed as all the more horrible because of the betrayer's intimate fellowship with Jesus.

21 The Son of man indeed goeth, as it is written of him: but woe to that man by whom the Son of Man is betrayed! good were it for that man if he had never been born.

The expression "as it is written" refers to the Scriptures in general and not a particular passage. The death of the Son of Man is in harmony with the Scriptures. Judas's betrayal is within the context of God's plan and purpose. The word "woe" expresses compassion, sorrow rather than intimidation. Judas was responsible for his act. Here it is his existence that was being deplored and the terrible destiny awaiting him.

22 And as they did eat, Jesus took bread, and blessed, and brake it, and gave to them, and said, Take, eat: this is my body.

The word "bread" (Greek *artos*, pronounced **R-tahss**) usually denotes a flat cake of leavened bread. He took the symbols of His coming death. Here He "blesses" the bread, in Greek *Eulogesas* (pronounced **you-lahg-GAY-sahss**) means to bless or speak well of, and He gave it to them. The bread stands for His dying in His body. The breaking of the bread stands for Jesus' suffering. It is a means of participating in the presence of Jesus. The Greek expression *to soma mou* (pronounced **taw SO-mah**) translated "my body" can mean the whole being.

23 And he took the cup, and when he had given thanks, he gave it to them: and they all drank of it.

He took the cup and after giving thanks (or in Greek *Eucharistesas* (pronounced **you-kar-iss-TAY-sahss**), He gave it to them. The cup stands for blood atonement, which inaugurates a new covenant. His blood is poured out for many.

24 And he said unto them, This is my blood of the new testament, which is shed for many.

"Many" is a Hebrew way of saying "everyone."

"Shed for many" is probably both a reference to Exodus 24:8 and to the work of the Servant in Isaiah. The making of a new covenant is part of the mission of the Servant (Isaiah 42:6; 49:8; Luke 22:20; 1 Corinthians 11:25). "Shed for many" is a participle involving a near future; "for many" probably refers to Isaiah 53 and shows the great number of the beneficiaries of the sacrifice.

25 Verily I say unto you, I will drink no more of the fruit of the vine, until that day that I drink it new in the kingdom of God.

Jesus was referring to the messianic banquet at His advent (Isaiah 25:6). Jesus' death is placed in the light of the coming kingdom of God.

DAILY BIBLE READINGS

M: A Woman Anoints Jesus
Mark 14:1-9
T: Plans Made for Passover
Mark 14:10-16
W: The Cup and the Bread
Mark 14:17-25
T: Jesus Washes the Disciples' Feet
John 13:1-5
F: I Have Set You an Example
John 13:12-20
S: Where I Go, You Cannot Come
John 13:31-35
S: In Remembrance of Me
1 Corinthians 11:23-28

TEACHING TIPS

April 20
Bible Study Guide 8

1. Words You Should Know

A. Crucified (Mark 15:24)—A form of execution for a criminal. Only the lowest and worst offenders were crucified, because it was such a terrible way to die. Large nails were driven through the wrists and heel bones of the victim to hang him to a cross. If the victim allowed his weight to fall, he suffocated; so against the pain of the nails in the feet, he would brace himself up as much and as long as possible. If the victim lingered too long, his legs were broken to hasten the death.

B. Casting lots (v. 24)—A form of gambling similar to tossing coins to determine who won. Those executing a criminal were given the right to divide up the few possessions He had. In the case of Jesus, He probably had an under and an over-garment, a belt, sandals, and possibly a head covering.

2. Teacher Preparation

A. Review the key words for this week's passage as defined in the WORDS YOU SHOULD KNOW.

B. Review the KEEP IN MIND verse and find ways in which the verse applies personally to you. You may want to share the application with the class.

3. Starting the Lesson

Open the session with prayer. Thank God for His many blessings and ask that the Holy Spirit open your hearts and minds to the eternal truths contained in the lesson.

4. Getting into the Lesson

A. Have the students read the LESSON AIM in unison, then silently read the IN FOCUS story.

B. Assign one of the students to read aloud the BACKGROUND information,

C. Ask for three volunteers to read the FOCAL VERSES according to the AT-A-GLANCE outline.

5. Relating the Lesson to Life

A. Lead the students in answering the SEARCH THE SCRIPTURES questions. Then focus on THE PEOPLE, PLACES, AND TIMES. Allow ten minutes or so for the students to silently read the IN DEPTH commentary, then go over the highlights with them.

B. Now call the students' attention to the DISCUSS THE MEANING questions and the LESSON IN OUR SOCIETY section. This will help them to see how the lesson applies to our modern-day experiences.

C. Have the students share the most significant point they have learned from today's lesson and how they plan to use it during the week.

6. Arousing Action

A. Call the students attention to the MAKE IT HAPPEN suggestion, and encourage them to practice it this week.

B. Remind students to use the DAILY BIBLE READINGS, REMEMBER YOUR THOUGHTS and FOLLOW THE SPIRIT sections. This will help build their faith and plant the seeds of God's Word in their hearts.

C. Close the class with prayer, thanking God for our redemption and restoration.

WORSHIP GUIDE

For the Superintendent or Teacher
Theme: The Cross and the Empty Tomb
Theme Song: "Were You There When They Crucified My Lord?"
Scripture: Romans 5:6-8
Song: "Christ Arose"
Devotional Thought: Lord, thank You for dying on the cross for our sins. Give us strength to bear our crosses daily. Amen.

THE CROSS AND THE EMPTY TOMB

Bible Background • MARK 15:21-16:8
Printed Text • MARK 15:21-24, 34–37; 16:1-8
Devotional Reading • JOHN 20:11-18

LESSON AIM

By the end of the lesson, students will be able to identify the steps leading to Jesus' crucifixion and resurrection, commit themselves to serving others, and follow through on the MAKE IT HAPPEN challenge.

KEEP IN MIND

"And he saith unto them, Be not affrighted: Ye seek Jesus of Nazareth, which was crucified: he is risen; he is not here: behold the place where they laid him" (Mark 16:6).

FOCAL VERSES

Mark 15:21 And they compel one Simon a Cyrenian, who passed by, coming out of the country, the father of Alexander and Rufus, to bear his cross.

22 And they bring him unto the place Golgotha, which is, being interpreted, The place of a skull.

23 And they gave him to drink wine mingled with myrrh: but he received it not.

24 And when they had crucified him, they parted his garments, casting lots upon them, what every man should take.

15:34 And at the ninth hour Jesus cried with a loud voice, saying, Eloi, Eloi, lama sabachthani? Which is, being interpreted, My God, my God, why hast thou forsaken me?

35 And some of them that stood by, when they heard it, said, Behold, he calleth Elias.

36 And one ran and filled a spunge full of vinegar, and put it on a reed, and gave him to drink, saying, Let alone; let us see whether Elias will come to take him down.

37 And Jesus cried with a loud voice, and gave up

the ghost.

Mark 16:1 And when the sabbath was past, Mary Magdalene, and Mary the mother of James, and Salome, had bought sweet spices, that they might come and anoint him.

2 And very early in the morning the first day of the week, they came unto the sepulchre at the rising of the sun.

3 And they said among themselves, Who shall roll us away the stone from the door of the sepulchre?

4 And when they looked, they saw that the stone was rolled away: for it was very great.

5 And entering into the sepulchre, they saw a young man sitting on the right side, clothed in a long white garment; and they were affrighted.

6 And he saith unto them, Be not affrighted: Ye seek Jesus of Nazareth, which was crucified: he is risen; he is not here: behold the place where they laid him.

7 But go your way, tell his disciples and Peter that he goeth before you into Galilee: there shall ye see him, as he said unto you.

8 And they went out quickly, and fled from the sepulchre; for they trembled and were amazed: neither said they any thing to any man; for they were afraid.

IN FOCUS

Once there was a young man who served several Supreme Court justices. One justice was liberal in his politics but never acknowledged the Black man who

APRIL 20TH

321

brought him his food and even helped him dress for court. Another justice supported laws that hindered the success of African Americans, while treating him as a friend, as well as an assistant. This judge even celebrated their mutual birthdays together. Yet in both circumstances this man performed his tasks with integrity and dignity. Today his children are successful in a variety of fields, including one who is the president of an African American Christian publishing company.

We think of the Roman soldier who grabbed Simon of Cyrene to carry the cross for Jesus. Was racial prejudice operating even then? Whatever the soldier's motivation, Simon's deed is memorialized in our Bibles and he went on to serve the church as an elder and to raise sons who were respected Christian leaders. What crosses do we bear and how do we carry them?

THE PEOPLE, PLACES, AND TIMES

Simon a Cyrenian, the Father of Alexander and Rufus. A man from Cyrene in North Africa.

Golgotha. *Golgotha* in Aramaic or *Calvary* in Latin means the place of a skull. It was the place where Jesus was brought to be crucified.

Ninth Hour. Time of day corresponding approximately to 3 p.m.

Elias. A prophet (1 Kings 17-19, 21; 2 Kings 1-2) named Elijah in the Old Testament. He was considered one of Israel's greatest prophets.

Sabbath. A holy day and the seventh day of the week on which no work was permitted.

Mary Magdalene, Mary the Mother of James and Salome. They were among the followers of Jesus during His earthly ministry (Mark 15:40-47; Luke 8:2; John 20:1-18).

Jesus of Nazareth. A title of Jesus linking Him to the place where He was from and where He grew up.

Peter. A disciple of Jesus also called Simon. He was the leader of the disciples.

Galilee. The northern region of Palestine which was the scene of Jesus' boyhood and early ministry.

BACKGROUND

An African adage says, "In suffering you know your true friends." Mark 15:21-24, 34-37; 16:1-8 is part of the passion story. The section describes the suffering Jesus went through from His arrest and His sentencing to His crucifixion and death. He was unjustly condemned and abandoned by all. But He won the victory over death. He rose from the dead.

Although the scriptural reference to Simon of Cyrene is very brief, we see a tantalizing hint of the composition of the band of followers of Christ. Obviously the disciples knew Simon, for they mention the names of his two sons, Rufus and Alexander. Early church history refers to Alexander, the bishop in Africa, and it is thought that he was the son of Simon. In Acts 13:1, the cross-cultural group of elders of the church at Antioch are listed, including Simon called Niger (black). This probably was the same Simon who carried the cross of Jesus. Then in Romans 16:13, Paul sends his greetings to Rufus and his mother. Scholars believe that this Rufus was the son of Simon of Cyrene. Paul also mentioned that Rufus's mother ministered to him as a mother. (Does not this remind us of the African American church mothers involved in prison ministry today?) Prisoners in the days of Paul were often dependent upon others or upon their own means for provision of food. What tasty treats can you imagine this African mother brought to Paul?

AT-A-GLANCE

1. The Crucifixion (Mark 15:21-24, 34-37)
2. The Resurrection (Mark 16:1-8)

IN DEPTH

1. The Crucifixion (Mark 15:21-24, 34-37)

As Jesus is led out of Pilate's court, the Roman officials force a man passing by, Simon of Cyrene, to help Jesus carry His cross. Jesus at this point was evidently so physically weak that someone else was forced to do the work. It was a Roman habit to get the man to be crucified to carry his own cross.

Simon was coming in from the country when suddenly the Romans grabbed him and demanded he carry Jesus' cross. His cross-bearing brought him honor and fame worldwide. It also brought him the high privilege of relieving Jesus of some suffering at the time of His crucifixion. Jesus had said that the way to follow Him is to carry a cross, to willingly accept the painful chastening that God lays upon us. The event here is quite literal, but it illustrates Jesus' point.

Jesus was taken to Golgotha outside the city to be crucified. He was offered wine mixed with myrrh to dull His senses, but He refused to drink. He evidently preferred to be wide-awake on the cross, since He did not want to bear the sins of the world while being asleep or drugged.

The soldiers took away His clothes and gambled over who should have them. This was a great shame and embarrassment for Jesus.

On the cross for three hours, His suffering was intense. He asked a question in Aramaic, *"Eloi, Eloi, lama sabachthani?"* meaning "My God, my God, why hast thou forsaken me?" At this point some were still wondering whether there would be a last minute miracle. But Jesus surrendered His life to the Father.

2. The Resurrection (Mark 16:1-8)

Late on Saturday night at about 6 p.m. after the Sabbath had past, three women went to buy spices to anoint the body of Jesus. One of the women was Mary Magdalene. Another was Mary the mother of James. The other woman was Salome. They agreed to anoint Jesus' body early the following morning.

The next day early in the morning, the three women, wondering how to get the stone rolled away from the tomb entrance, went to the tomb of Jesus. The stone was already rolled away when they got there. A young man was there dressed in a way that indicated that he was an angel. He told the women of the resurrection of Jesus. They were invited to see the place where Jesus had been. Then the angel gave them a commission. They were to tell Peter and the disciples to go to Galilee where Jesus would appear to them. Shocked and fearful they hurried away, saying nothing to anyone.

The Resurrection of Jesus was a historical event. His body was raised. An angel appeared to explain what had happened. It was not any kind of hallucination. The women were not expecting to find Jesus raised from the dead. On the contrary, they had bought special anointing oil to use on His dead body. The Resurrection took them by surprise and made them hurry with fear, and saying nothing to anyone.

SEARCH THE SCRIPTURES

1. What led to Simon relieving Jesus from bearing the cross? (Mark 15:21)

2. What question did Jesus ask at the ninth hour? (v. 34)

3. What did Jesus do as He breathed His last breath? (v. 37)

4. What had the women intended to do when they reached the tomb? (Mark 16:1)

5. What did the angel tell the women? (vv. 6-7)

DISCUSS THE MEANING

1. Matthew 16:24 tells us to take up our cross and follow Jesus. What can we learn from the way Jesus bore His cross concerning how we are to bear our crosses today? Jesus was not always quiet and passive. In what instances did He speak up? When was He silent? What sort of cross might a Christian bear today?

2. Resurrection Day is the Good News of the empty tomb. What is the meaning of the empty tomb for our salvation? What does the Resurrection prove? In spite of the witness of Old Testament prophecy and the witness of Jesus Himself, the women had not expected to find Him risen. How does this further prove the reality of His resurrection?

LESSON IN OUR SOCIETY

Christianity is often presented today as a magical charm. Trust Jesus and you will be rich, healthy, and famous. Yet Jesus Himself suffered the indignity and agony of the cross. Standing up for Jesus in our society has little cost, comparatively speaking. But we should not expect that everything will go well just because we have faith in our Lord. We should not make our decisions on how to follow Jesus based on what we think will be the consequences for our own reputations and comfort.

MAKE IT HAPPEN

When have you suffered for Jesus? What was your response? Did you observe anything positive coming from your suffering? Most of the time we do not see anything good happen, but occasionally God blesses us with a glimpse of the things He is accomplishing through our pain. Pray for God's help in whatever trouble you may experience for His sake.

FOLLOW THE SPIRIT
What God wants me to do:

_____

_____

REMEMBER YOUR THOUGHTS
Special insights you have learned:

_____

_____

MORE LIGHT ON THE TEXT
Mark 15:21-24, 34-37; 16:1-8
15:21 And they compel one Simon a Cyrenian, who passed by, coming out of the country, the father of Alexander and Rufus, to bear his cross.

As Jesus was led out of Pilate's court, the soldiers compelled Greek *aggareuousin* (pronounced **ah-gah-RYOU-oo-sin**) or "requisitioned" Simon of Cyrene to help Jesus carry His cross. It happened very suddenly to him. He was coming in from the country when they grabbed him and demanded he carry Jesus' cross. He was a sojourner from outside Jerusalem, a pilgrim from Africa who probably came to observe the Passover, but happened upon the scene.

22 And they bring him unto the place Golgotha, which is, being interpreted, The place of a skull.

Jesus was taken to a place outside Jerusalem called *Golgotha* in Aramaic or *Calvary* in Latin meaning "the place of a skull."

23 And they gave him to drink wine mingled with myrrh: but he received it not.

The Greek word *edidoun* (pronounced **eh-DID-doon**) literally means "to give to" or "offered." They offered Him wine mixed with myrrh, a sedative or analgesic potion with the goal of reducing His suffering. But Jesus was willing to drink His cup (the cup of suffering) to the dregs (see 10:38; 14:36).

24 And when they had crucified him, they parted his garments, casting lots upon them, what every man should take.

"Casting lots" is a clear reference to Psalm 22:18-19. The custom was that the soldiers in the death squad could keep the personal belongings of the person they executed. In the case of Jesus, the four men of the death squad cast lots to divide His garments (see John 19:23).

15:34 And at the ninth hour Jesus cried with a loud voice, saying, Eloi, Eloi, lama sabachthani? Which is, being interpreted, My God, my God, why hast thou forsaken me?

After three hours, the suffering was intense. Jesus cried in Aramaic, *"Eloi, Eloi, lama sabachthani,"* or "My God, my God, why hast thou forsaken me?" The Greek words translated mean "why," "for what reason?" Here is a reference to Psalm 22:1. Jesus probably had in mind the whole psalm, a prayer of a righteous sufferer. This cry expressed Jesus' unshaken faith in God at this horrible hour. He had faith in God's continual protection and final vindication. The scene is to be understood in the perspective of the holy wrath of God and the character of sin, which cuts the sinner off from God (see Isaiah 59:2). Jesus identified Himself completely with sinners and bore on the cross the judgment of God upon human rebellion (see 10:45; Romans 5:8; Galatians 3:13; 2 Corinthians 5:21).

35 And some of them that stood by, when they heard it, said, Behold, he calleth Elias.

Some spectators, who probably misunderstood Jesus or were mocking Him, said "Behold, he calleth Elias." They believed that He was calling Elijah to rescue Him (Malachi 3:1; 4:5).

36 And one ran and filled a spunge full of vinegar, and put it on a reed, and gave him to drink, saying, Let alone; let us see whether Elias will come to take him down.

A soldier soaked a sponge in vinegar and reached it up to Jesus' mouth on the end of a reed. It was intended to keep Him conscious for as long as possible. But some were still wondering whether there would be a last minute miracle. They said, "Let us see whether Elias will come to take him down." According to popular Jewish beliefs, Elias (Elijah) would come to the help of the just in their time of distress.

37 And Jesus cried with a loud voice, and gave up the ghost.

The loud cry of Jesus before He expired indicates that His death was different from others who died on a cross. He died suddenly (see vv. 39, 44). He died for us (8:31; 10:45; 14:24). His death was voluntary. His life was not taken, for He "gave up the ghost" (His spirit).

16:1 And when the sabbath was past, Mary Magdalene, and Mary the mother of James, and Salome, had bought sweet spices, that they might come and anoint him.

Saturday after the sun went down, three women went to buy spices to anoint the body of Jesus. They agreed to anoint Jesus' body early the next day. The women are the same as those mentioned in Mark 15:40. Their act shows their love for Jesus. It also indicates that they had no expectation of an immediate resurrection of Jesus.

2 And very early in the morning the first day of the week, they came unto the sepulchre at the rising of the sun.

Apparently the women started the journey while it was still dark (John 20:1), but by the time they had arrived at the tomb, it was daylight.

3 And they said among themselves, Who shall roll us away the stone from the door of the sepulchre?

The Greek verb *elegon* (pronounced 'EH-leh-gahn) means "they kept on saying among themselves." The women were wondering how to get the stone rolled away from the tomb entrance.

4 And when they looked, they saw that the stone was rolled away: for it was very great.

When they were near the tomb, they looked up and noticed immediately that the stone was already rolled away. The stone was big enough for them to see it easily.

5 And entering into the sepulchre, they saw a young man sitting on the right side, clothed in a long white garment; and they were affrighted.

They probably entered the external chamber of the sepulchre and saw a young man dressed in white sitting on the right side, probably facing the chamber. The dress of the young man suggests an angelic being, thus a divine messenger. The women were terrified.

6 And he saith unto them, Be not affrighted: Ye seek Jesus of Nazareth, which was crucified: he is risen; he is not here: behold the place where they laid him.

The angel told them of the Resurrection and invited them to see the place where Jesus had been. Jesus is called the Nazarene and the Crucified.

7 But go your way, tell his disciples and Peter that he goeth before you into Galilee: there shall ye see him, as he said unto you.

The women were sent to tell the disciples to go to Galilee (over 70 miles north) where Jesus would appear.

8 And they went out quickly, and fled from the sepulchre; for they trembled and were amazed: neither said they any thing to any man; for they were afraid.

Shocked and fearful, the women hurried away, saying nothing to anyone. The phrase "for they were afraid" refers not to a religious fear, but it shows that the women were deeply troubled. The Resurrection took the women by surprise and made them hurry away with fear, saying nothing to anyone. They did not expect Jesus to be raised from the dead.

DAILY BIBLE READINGS

M: The Place of the Skull
Mark 15:21-32
T: Why Have You Forsaken Me?
Mark 15:33-41
W: Joseph Asks for Jesus' Body
Mark 15:42-47
T: He Is Not Here
Mark 16:1-8
F: Jesus Joins Two on the Road
Luke 24:13-27
S: The Lord Has Risen Indeed!
Luke 24:28-35
S: Touch Me and See
Luke 24:36-49

TEACHING TIPS

April 27
Bible Study Guide 9

1. Words You Should Know

A. Issue of blood (Mark 5:25)—Thought to be a chronic menstrual disorder or a uterine hemorrhage.

B. Damsel (v. 41)—A young, unmarried woman of noble birth.

2. Teacher Preparation

A. First, familiarize yourself with all thirteen lessons of the quarter. The QUARTER-AT-A-GLANCE will help you with this.

B. Read the UNIT 3 INTRODUCTION. Begin your study for this week's lesson by reading the entire Book of Mark.

C. The key words for this week's passage are defined in the WORDS YOU SHOULD KNOW section. Be sure to review them.

D. Review the KEEP IN MIND verse and see how it applies to you personally. You may want to share the application with the class.

3. Starting the Lesson

Open the session with prayer. Thank God for all that He taught you over the last lesson and ask that the Holy Spirit open your hearts and minds to the eternal truths of the new lesson.

4. Getting into the Lesson

A. Have the students read the LESSON AIM in unison, then silently read the IN FOCUS story.

B. Assign one of the students to read aloud the BACKGROUND information, then ask for three volunteers to read the FOCAL VERSES according to the AT-A-GLANCE outline.

5. Relating the Lesson to Life

A. Lead the students in answering the SEARCH THE SCRIPTURES questions.

B. Focus on THE PEOPLE, PLACES, AND TIMES character. Allow ten minutes or so for the students to silently read the IN DEPTH commentary, then go over the highlights with them.

C. Call the students attention to the DISCUSS THE MEANING questions and the LESSON IN OUR SOCIETY section. This will help them to see how the lesson applies to our modern day experiences.

D. Have the students share the most significant point they have learned from today's lesson and how they plan to use it during the week.

6. Arousing Action

A. Call the students' attention to the MAKE IT HAPPEN suggestion and encourage them to practice it this week.

B. Remind students to use the DAILY BIBLE READINGS, REMEMBER YOUR THOUGHTS, and FOLLOW THE SPIRIT sections. This will help build their faith and plant the seeds of God's Word in their hearts.

C. Close the class with prayer, thanking God for our redemption and restoration.

WORSHIP GUIDE

For the Superintendent or Teacher
Theme: The Importance of Belief
Theme Song: "Trust and Obey"
Scripture: Mark 5:22-36, 41-42
Song: "Trusting Jesus"
Devotional Thought: Dear gracious heavenly Father, thank You for Your help when we are in desperate situations. Give us patience to keep on trusting You. For we pray in Jesus' name. Amen.

THE IMPORTANCE OF BELIEF

Bible Background • MARK 5:21-43
Printed Text • MARK 5:22-36, 41-42
Devotional Reading • HEBREWS 11:1-6

LESSON AIM

By the end of the lesson, students will be able to describe the faith of Jairus and the woman with an issue of blood, relate to their suffering, commit themselves to becoming women and men of faith, and follow through on the MAKE IT HAPPEN challenge.

KEEP IN MIND

"As soon as Jesus heard the word that was spoken, he saith unto the ruler of the synagogue, Be not afraid, only believe" (Mark 5:36).

FOCAL VERSES

Mark 5:22 And, behold, there cometh one of the rulers of the synagogue, Jairus by name; and when he saw him, he fell at his feet,

23 And besought him greatly, saying, My little daughter lieth at the point of death: I pray thee, come and lay thy hands on her, that she may be healed; and she shall live.

24 And Jesus went with him; and much people followed him, and thronged him.

25 And a certain woman, which had an issue of blood twelve years,

26 And had suffered many things of many physicians, and had spent all that she had, and was nothing bettered, but rather grew worse,

27 When she had heard of Jesus, came in the press behind, and touched his garment.

28 For she said, If I may touch but his clothes, I shall be whole.

29 And straightway the fountain of her blood was dried up; and she felt in her body that she was

healed of that plague.

30 And Jesus, immediately knowing in himself that virtue had gone out of him, turned him about in the press, and said, Who touched my clothes?

31 And his disciples said unto him, Thou seest the multitude thronging thee, and sayest thou, Who touched me?

32 And he looked round about to see her that had done this thing.

33 But the woman fearing and trembling, knowing what was done in her, came and fell down before him, and told him all the truth.

34 And he said unto her, Daughter, thy faith hath made thee whole; go in peace, and be whole of thy plague.

35 While he yet spake, there came from the ruler of the synagogue's house certain which said, Thy daughter is dead: why troublest thou the Master any further?

36 As soon as Jesus heard the word that was spoken, he saith unto the ruler of the synagogue, Be not afraid, only believe.

5:41 And he took the damsel by the hand, and said unto her, Talitha cumi; which is, being interpreted, Damsel, I say unto thee, arise.

42 And straightway the damsel arose, and walked; for she was of the age of twelve years. And they were astonished with a great astonishment.

IN FOCUS

The newly married couple was anxious to begin a family. After several years, they sought out a doc-

APRIL 27TH

tor. They prayed and prayed. When the young wife would see other women with babies, she felt so desirous of having one of her own that she felt a lump in her throat and tears in her eyes. She had surgery. He had surgery. And she had surgery again. Still no children. Then they decided to adopt a child. They were only able to adopt one child, but this child is now a grown woman, very much involved in Christian ministry. The situation that seemed to grow more hopeless by the month had bcome a great blessing as the years go by. What desperate situations have you encountered? How long did you wait for an answer? How did God answer your prayers? What difficult situation are you in today? Don't give up hope!

THE PEOPLE, PLACES, AND TIMES

Jairus. A ruler of the synagogue whose daughter was restored to life by Jesus. The ruler of a synagogue was a lay person with administrative responsibilities, such as looking after the worship and supervising any work on the facilities. Usually a synagogue had just one ruler. Jairus may have been the ruler of the syagogue in Capernaum where a home across from the synagogue from Jesus' time has been excavated. Jairus may have lived in this home.

Synagogue. After the Jews returned from exile, they built local synagogues for public worship. They only went to the big temple in Jerusalem for the three big religious holidays. Since the rule was that ten males were required to form a group large enough for corporate worship, large towns had several synagogues and even most small towns had one. The synagogues were important buildings. Jesus always went to the synagogue in whatever town He was in for worship on the Sabbath.

BACKGROUND

People are willing to spend a lot money and do anything possible to see their favorite movie or sports star. They want to get his/her autograph. Here, in these two intertwined stories, two people wanted to see the "Master"—Jesus. They had faith that Jesus could help them through their trials. They were willing to do anything it took to bring to Him their concerns. What would be the reac-

tion of the "Master" to these two people?

AT-A-GLANCE

1. Jesus, Lord of Disease (Mark 5:25-34)
2. Jesus, Lord of Death (vv. 35-36, 41-42)

IN DEPTH

1. Jesus, Lord of Disease (Mark 5:25-34)

The story of a woman with an issue of blood for 12 years is told within another story, the sickness and death of Jairus's daughter. Jairus, a synagogue official, had come to ask Jesus to heal his daughter. As He was going along with His disciples and the crowd, a woman suffering from a constant hemorrhage followed closely after Jesus. Jairus's daughter was 12 years old, and the woman had been suffering for 12 years. Many physicians had been unable to help her (v. 26).

Let us take notice of the following: One does not back off from spending a lot of money and doing anything possible to keep or recover one's health. But how many are willing to do the same for their souls? (see Proverbs 17:22)

The woman believed that one tiny bit of faith in Jesus would bring her healing. As soon as she touched Jesus, she was healed (v. 29). The contact with Jesus is a blessing only for the ones who come to Him in faith, recognizing their helplessness (Hebrews 4:2). Jesus was conscious that something had happened and soon found out about the woman. She fell down at His feet and told Him "all the truth" (v. 33). At the feet of the "Master" is a good place to tell all the truth. He reassured her and told her that her faith had brought her healing.

2. Jesus, Lord of Death (vv. 35-36, 41-42)

Jairus, a synagogue official, came to Jesus, asking for his dying daughter to be healed. Jesus went with him, followed by a great crowd who was eager to see another miracle.

Halfway there, news came that Jairus's daughter had died. But Jesus insisted on continuing the journey to Jairus's home. He told Jairus, "Be not afraid, only believe." When they reached Jairus's home, Jesus took Jairus's daughter by the hand and she was raised from the dead.

Two Intertwined Stories

The intention of the two stories is to point us to the very great power of Jesus over the worst kind of human distress. Jairus and the woman have problems which are overwhelmingly painful. Jairus has seen his daughter steadily deteriorate; she is at the point of death when he turns to Jesus (v. 23). The woman has been suffering for 12 years and had received many disappointments in her attempts to get help from physicians (vv. 25-26). She has used all her financial resources in her attempts to get assistance. In both cases, they had faced great disappointments, and it seemed almost impossible that anyone would be able to help.

Sometimes God allows some problem to continue in our lives for a long time. He also lets some problems run to an extreme point, where it seems that a change in the situation is impossible. Both the woman and Jairus had great faith in Jesus, despite the severity of their predicaments. Jairus believed that one touch from Jesus would bring restoration to his child (v. 23). The woman believed that such power radiated out from Jesus, that even the slightest touch of His clothes would bring her healing (v. 28). Both Jairus and the woman found that at the very point where they were about to get an answer, great challenges.

The woman was hoping to get a secret healing. One can understand why she felt this way. She was ceremonially unclean. According to Mosaic Law, a woman was considered unclean during her menstrual period. Anyone touching her or even sitting on anything she sat upon would have to wash his clothes and bathe with water (Leviticus 15:20-33). The same rules applied to any woman with any bleeding from the genital area. The woman being in a crowd and being touched by many people would make them angry if they discovered she was ceremonially unclean. At the point where she seems to have received a miracle without anyone knowing it, she is suddenly exposed. Jesus demands to know who touched Him. Full of fear and trembling, she comes forward. Is she going to get into trouble? Will her

healing be canceled since she took it without permission? At the very point where she seems to be getting rescued from her 12 years of suffering, there comes a challenge to her hopes.

Jairus has something similar happen to him. He is finding all his hopes are blasted just at the point when he was about to get something wonderful from Jesus. Jesus gives both Jairus and the woman strong encouragement in a gentle and compassionate way (vv. 34, 41). They both experience Jesus' mighty power.

SEARCH THE SCRIPTURES

1. What did the woman say would happen if she may touch Jesus' clothes? (Mark 5:28)
2. What did Jesus say to her after she told Him the truth? (v. 34)
3. What did Jesus tell Jairus after he had received news about his daughter's death? (v. 36)

DISCUSS THE MEANING

1. Discuss the manner in which Jesus' healing of the woman with the issue of blood differed from the way His healing of Jairus's daughter came about. Think of various healings in the Bible and discuss the differences in Jesus' methods. Why do you think the method of healing differed from case to case? Can you think of people you know who have been healed in various ways? Why do you think their healings came about in different ways?

2. Some Christians think that God will instantly heal any disease as soon they have enough faith and go to the right person for a gift of healing. Name some cases, both from the Bible and from your own experience, in which a follower of the Lord had to wait a long time for healing. Name some cases in which there was no healing. Why do you think some people have to wait a long time for deliverance from a physical illness or disability? Why do you think some people are never healed? Support your answers with Scripture.

LESSON IN OUR SOCIETY

During the days when Jesus ministered here on earth, people avoided those who were ritually unclean. What sort of people do we avoid today? What reasons or excuses do we give? Jesus touched the lepers and others who had unclean diseases. What was His attitude toward those with disgusting physical conditions? What illnesses do people avoid today? What would be some Christ-like responses to those with these health problems?

MAKE IT HAPPEN

What troubling things are going on in your life right now? Which of those things have been going on for a long time and with seemingly no answer in sight? Think back on other situations which involved a great period of waiting. How did God bring about a resolution? What things did you learn about God's faithfulness to us in desperate situations? What can you do to be patient in today's problems?

FOLLOW THE SPIRIT

What God wants me to do:

_____
_____

REMEMBER YOUR THOUGHTS

Special insights you have learned:
_____
_____

MORE LIGHT ON THE TEXT
Mark 5:22-36, 41-42

5:22 And, behold, there cometh one of the rulers of the synagogue, Jairus by name; and when he saw him, he fell at his feet,

The phrase "one of the rulers of the synagogue" is a title pointing out Jairus's position of authority and influence within his society. He was head or president of the synagogue. He was a man of high standing in the Jewish community. It must have been a difficult decision for him to come and fall at Jesus' feet and then beg (Greek *parakalei*, pronounced **pah-rah-KAH-lay**) Him to

come and heal his daughter since Jesus was not recognized and accepted by the Jewish leaders.

23 And besought him greatly, saying, My little daughter lieth at the point of death: I pray thee, come and lay thy hands on her, that she may be healed; and she shall live.

The Greek word *Thugatrion* (pronounced **thoo-GAH-tree-ahn**) literally means little daughter, little girl (cf. *Korasion*, pronounced **koh-RAH-see-ahn**) in v. 41 from *kore* (pronounced **Koh-Ray**) a virgin or young girl). My little girl is (Greek *Eschatos echei*, pronounced **s-KAH-tose ECK-aa**) "at the point of death," literally "is at the end." He begged Jesus to come and lay hands of healing upon his daughter. He was confident that if Jesus would come, his daughter's life would be saved.

The Greek word *Sodzo* (pronounced **SOHD-zoh**) translated by "heal," literally means "save." "To heal by laying hands on" reflects a common practice of the day (see 6:5; 7:32; 8:23, 25). The laying on of hands was much more familiar in the

Jewish context in connection with sacrifice, blessing, and ordination than with healing.

24 And Jesus went with him; and much people followed him, and thronged him.

Jesus went with him followed by a great crowd, which was pressing on Him from all sides, eager to see another miracle.

25 And a certain woman, which had an issue of blood twelve years,

As Jesus was on His way to Jairus's house with the crowd pressing from all sides, a woman suffering from a constant hemorrhage follows closely after Jesus. Just as Jairus's daughter was 12 years old, so also the woman had been suffering for 12 years.

26 And had suffered many things of many physicians, and had spent all that she had, and was nothing bettered, but rather grew worse,

The woman had suffered under, or at the hands of, many physicians who were unable to help her. In fact, her condition "was nothing bettered, but rather grew worse." The statement prepares the way for divine intervention. Thus human skill had not healed her of her chronic ailment. She was in a constant state of uncleanness and contact with her would make others unclean (Leviticus 15:25-33).

27 When she had heard of Jesus, came in the press behind, and touched his garment.

The Greek expression *Ta peri tou Iesou* (pronounced **tah puh-REE too ee-AA-soo**) can be understood as "things (said) about Jesus" or "the deeds concerning Jesus." The name Jesus has here a definite article before it, marking Him out as a particular Jesus, not any Jesus. He was "The Jesus," distinguishing Him from any other Jesus, since the name Jesus or Jehoshua was very common. She came from behind, since her sickness made her ritually unclean, and reached out to Jesus' garment. It is possible that her attitude came from a bad conscience or the fear of being reprimanded (see v. 33).

28 For she said, If I may touch but his clothes,

I shall be whole.

The Greek *Elegen* (pronounced **EH-leh-ghen**) in this context means "saying (to herself)" or "thinking that" (see 3:10). Just like Jairus, she believed that one tiny bit of faith in Jesus would bring her healing.

29 And straightway the fountain of her blood was dried up; and she felt in her body that she was healed of that plague.

The phrase "fountain of blood" (Greek *He pege tou haimatos* (pronounced **hey pay-GAH too HI-mah-tahss**) literally means "the spring of blood (see Leviticus 12:7) dried up." She knew from experience or "she felt" (Greek *egno*, pronounced **EGG-no**) from *ginosko* (pronounced **gih-NO-skoh**) meaning to know that she was healed.

30 And Jesus, immediately knowing in himself that virtue had gone out of him, turned him about in the press, and said, Who touched my clothes?

The word "virtue" translated in the Greek is *dunamis* (pronounced **DOO-nah-miss**) which is generally translated "power." In other words, Jesus knew that power had gone out from Him and healed this sick woman. The interesting thing here is that out of all the people who touched Jesus, only one woman was healed.

31 And his disciples said unto him, Thou seest the multitude thronging thee, and sayest thou, Who touched me?

The disciples did not understand what had taken place. They said that the crowd was pressing hard around Jesus, and He said, "Who touched me?"

32 And he looked round about to see her that had done this thing.

Jesus kept on looking around to see who "had done this thing." The feminine participle is used here, probably implying that Jesus knew that it was a woman who touched Him.

33 But the woman fearing and trembling, knowing what was done in her, came and fell down before him, and told him all the truth.

The woman acknowledged with fear and trembling what had been done to her. She knew that she had experienced healing; she declared the truth to Jesus. She may have also been afraid because she feared the consequences of defiling a holy man by touching Him.

34 And he said unto her, Daughter, thy faith hath made thee whole; go in peace, and be whole of thy plague.

Jesus reassured her. He told her that her faith had brought her healing. The Greek word *Thugater* (pronounced **THOO-gah-tare**) or "daughter" expresses a relation of father to child. It is an expression of sympathy. The woman is brought into close relationship with Jesus. The Greek word for "whole," *sesokeh* (pronounced **SEH-so-keh**) means to save or rescue. It can be used both for the healing of the body as well as of the soul. Jesus was reassuring her that now her healing was permanent; she had nothing to fear. The phrase "go into peace" is a customary Hebrew farewell. The corresponding Hebrew word is *shalom* (pronounced **shah-LOAM**) which speaks of the health of the body and the soul. The woman's faith in Jesus had made it possible for her to experience wholeness, completeness of life.

35 While he yet spake, there came from the ruler of the synagogue's house certain which said, Thy daughter is dead: why troublest thou the Master any further?

The phrase "while he was still speaking" shows the simultaneity of two actions. As Jesus was speaking to the woman, the news came that Jairus's daughter had died. In the expression "why trouble (or weary) the teacher" the Greek verb means to annoy, even if ever so slightly. The remark here shows the hopelessness of the situation on the human level—"thy daughter is dead." It prepares the way for divine intervention.

36 As soon as Jesus heard the word that was spoken, he saith unto the ruler of the synagogue, Be not afraid, only believe.

Jesus overheard the conversation. Without noticing what was said, He insisted on continuing the journey to Jairus's house. He said to Jairus,

"Be not afraid, only believe." Jesus called Jairus to an intense faith. The father had already shown faith by coming to Jesus. He had witnessed the healing of the woman. Now, in the presence of death, he must keep on believing.

5:41 And he took the damsel by the hand, and said unto her, *Talitha cumi*; which is, being interpreted, Damsel, I say unto thee, arise.

Jesus took the girl by the hand and spoke in Aramaic. The phrase "I say unto thee" (Greek *soi lego,* pronounced **soy LEG-oh**) stresses the authority of Jesus over death.

42 And straightway the damsel arose, and walked; for she was of the age of twelve years. And they were astonished with a great astonishment.

The Greek word *euthus* (pronounced **you-THOOSE**) or "straightway" stresses the immediacy of the action. The girl got up and walked to the great amazement of the people standing by. The Greek phrase for "were astonished" literally means "to stand outside oneself" with a big bewilderment.

TEACHING TIPS

May 4
Bible Study Guide 10

1. Words You Should Know

A. Unclean Spirit (v. 25)—A demon representing defilement and was grounds for prohibiting a person from participating in the worship of God.

B. Gentile—One who is not of the Jewish faith. Also known as a pagan or heathen.

2. Teacher Preparation

A. Begin preparing for the lesson by reading Matthew's account of the story (Matthew 15:21-28) and then Mark's account (Mark 7:24-30).

B. Locate two historical and two current event stories which clearly highlight a woman or a racial group who experienced prejudice or rejection. Bring the clippings or video for use in the class.

C. Prepare discussion questions that connect what the class sees on the video or reads from the news clippings to the lesson.

3. Starting the Lesson

A. Arrive about 30 minutes early and label the seats with the names of the students. Put all of the females in one section or all on the back rows. If your class has all females or mostly females, label the seats with signs about who can speak and who should be silent.

B. After about 20 minutes into the lesson, discuss feelings of rejection and prejudice experienced by the students who were either relegated to the back rows of the classroom or those who were not allowed to speak.

C. Write their reactions on the board so that all the students can see them.

D. Ask the class to compare them to the feelings that the Syrophenician woman may have been experiencing because of her race, religion, and her gender.

4. Getting into the Lesson

A. Read the LESSON AIM as a group.

B. Have a student read the FOCAL VERSES aloud.

C. Divide the class into groups of two and have them read and discuss selections from the IN DEPTH section and present a two-sentence summary to the class. This exercise should take no more than 15 minutes.

5. Relating the Lesson to Life

A. Ask the students to discuss any special insights they received from today's lesson.

B. Ask students if they have had similar experiences which resemble those of the Syrophenician woman.

C. Compare how her faith and the student's faith was strengthened or weakened through these experiences.

6. Arousing Action

A. Assign the FOLLOW THE SPIRIT section for homework and ask the students to be prepared to discuss the results at the beginning of the next class session.

B. Discuss the MAKE IT HAPPEN section and ask each student to select an action project for the coming week.

WORSHIP GUIDE

MAY 4TH

For the Superintendent or Teacher
Theme: Exercising Faith Boldly
Theme Song: "Have Faith in God"
Scripture: Hebrews 4:16
Song: "All the Way My Savior Leads Me"
Devotional Thought: Thank You, dear
Lord, for inviting us to exercise our faith
by coming boldly to You for our needs
and the needs of those to whom and with
whom we minister.

333

BOLD FAITH

Bible Background • MARK 7:24-37
Printed Text • MARK 7:24-37
Devotional Reading • LUKE 7:1-10

LESSON AIM

By the end of the lesson, students should understand how Jesus transcends racial boundaries they will commit themselves to helping and sharing Christ with those who are of a different race or religious faith.

KEEP IN MIND

"And were beyond measure astonished, saying, He hath done all things well: he maketh both the deaf to hear, and the dumb to speak (Mark 7:37).

FOCAL VERSES

Mark 7:24 And from thence he arose, and went into the borders of Tyre and Sidon, and entered into an house and would have no man know it: but he could not be hid.

25 For a certain woman whose young daughter had an unclean spirit, heard of him, and came and fell at His feet:

26 The woman was a Greek, a Syrophenician by nation; and she besought him that he would cast forth the devil out of her daughter.

27 But Jesus said to her, "Let the children first be filled: for it is not meet to take the children's bread and cast it unto the dogs."

28 And she answered and said to him, "Yes, Lord: yet the dogs under the table eat of the children's crumbs."

29 And he said unto her, "For this saying go thy way; the devil is gone out of thy daughter."

LESSON OVERVIEW

LESSON AIM
KEEP IN MIND
FOCAL VERSES
IN FOCUS
THE PEOPLE, PLACES, AND TIMES
BACKGROUND
AT-A-GLANCE
IN DEPTH
SEARCH THE SCRIPTURES
DISCUSS THE MEANING
LESSON IN OUR SOCIETY
MAKE IT HAPPEN
FOLLOW THE SPIRIT
REMEMBER YOUR THOUGHTS
MORE LIGHT ON THE TEXT
DAILY BIBLE READINGS

30 And when she was come to her house, she found the devil gone out, and her daughter laid upon the bed.

31 And again, departing from the coasts of Tyre and Sidon, he came unto the sea of Galilee, through the midst of the coasts of Decapolis.

32 And they bring unto him one that was deaf, and had an impediment in his speech; and they beseech him to put his hand upon him.

33 And he took him aside from the multitude, and put his fingers into his ears, and he spit, and touched his tongue;

34 And looking up to heaven, he sighed, and saith unto him, Ephphatha, that is, Be opened.

35 And straightway his ears were opened, and the string of his tongue was loosed, and he spake plain.

36 And he charged them that they should tell no man: but the more he charged them, so much the more a great deal they published it;

37 And were beyond measure astonished, saying, "He hath done all things well: he maketh both the deaf to hear and the dumb to speak."

IN FOCUS

Discrimination is the practice of unfairly targeting an individual or group on the basis of difference. Because of the severity of discrimination experienced by some groups, the United States

House of Representatives directed a panel to look into the charges of discrimination by the United States Customs Department. The testimonies of the people they interviewed were alarming. In testimony before the panel, witnesses told of being detained, forced to drink laxatives, and then strip-searched. All were people of color and suspected of drug smuggling. Representative John Lewis, the Democratic representative for Georgia, said, "There are figures showing that 43 percent of the people that are detained—that are searched—happen to be Black and Hispanic."

THE PEOPLE, PLACES, AND TIMES

Times. Jesus was in search of a place away from the crowd of Jews in order to rest and prepare Himself and His disciples for the end of His ministry on earth.

Gentile. (*ethnos,* pronounced **ETH-nahss**) or "Heathen," the name or term given to all non-Jewish people.

Canaanites. Descendants of Canaan (Numbers 13:29; Deuteronomy 7:1) and traders. They were ancestral enemies of the Jews (Genesis 15:18-20).

Tyre and Sidon. Cities of Phoenicia which were a part of Syria. Syria stretched north from Carmel, along the coastal plain. It lay between Galilee and the seacoast. Tyre lay 40 miles northwest of Capernaum. It means "the Rock" because it was located between two great rocks joined by a three thousand foot-long ridge. This made the city a great natural harbor and naturally fortified.

Sidon was 26 miles northeast of Tyre and 60 miles north of Capernaum. Like Tyre, Sidon also had a natural breakwater and its origin as a harbor and a city was so ancient that no one knew who founded it. Although Phoenician cities were part of Syria, they were independent and rivals. They had their own kings, gods, and coinage.

BACKGROUND

Jesus was at a point in His ministry/journey when He needed rest. In this passage He is seen deliberately withdrawing into the borders of Gentile country. It was only in this northern area that Jesus felt He could find freedom from the crowds and His opponents.

The Syrophenician (or Canaanite) woman was a Greek-speaking, non-Jew and therefore a Gentile. She was from one of the seven nations to be driven out of the land of Canaan in the Old Testament. These seven nations were all descended from Ham, whose name means "black." Though the Israelites broke their power, they did not eliminate them from the land. Phoenicians were noted for their invention of the alphabet, commerce, and their sea-faring abilities.

The Canannite woman came with an urgent request. Jesus, aware of the enmity between His people and hers, allowed her to come, although He appeared to be troubled by the interruption. Believing Jesus was the only source of help for her child, the mother endured Jesus' rekindling of their ethnic boundaries. She heard that Jesus was the one with the power to help her. Before help is offered, however, she is faced with embarrassment and degradation. In spite of this, she refused to let Him go until He granted her request.

There are only two individuals whose faith Jesus pronounced to be "great." The Canaanite woman in our story (Matthew 15:28) and the centurion (Matthew 8:10). They both were Gentiles.

AT-A-GLANCE

1. Jesus' Search for Rest (Mark 7:24)
2. A Woman's Search for Help (vv. 25-26)
3. A Woman's Faith Is Challenged (vv. 27-28)
4. A Woman's Faith Is Rewarded (vv. 29-30)

IN DEPTH

1. Jesus' Search for Rest (Mark 7:24)

This is the only recorded time that Jesus left Jewish territory. Ideally Tyre and Sidon were part of the realm of Israel. Under Joshua the tribe of Asher was allocated the land from Sidon to the city of Tyre (Joshua 19:28-29). Because they were not able to conquer the inhabitants of the land, they were not able to take possession of it. It is into this land that Jesus went to find rest.

2. A Woman's Search for Help (vv. 25-26)

A mother was in search of someone who could help her daughter who was possessed by a demon. Her search ended when she heard that Jesus was on the outskirts of the town where she lived. Apparently she had heard that Jesus was a miracle worker and was able to heal people from terrible diseases. Immediately she sought Him out, and when she found Him she would not let Him go on His way until He healed her daughter.

3. A Woman's Faith Is Challenged (vv. 27-28)

Jesus, in previous verses, had just chided the Jewish leadership for voiding the law of Moses with their tradition. He speaks concerning what is clean and what is unclean concerning the ritual of washing the vessel of food. Jesus tells the disciples that it is not what goes into a person that makes them unclean, but what comes out. The encounter with the Syrophenician woman is another opportunity for Jesus to teach on what is clean or unclean.

Based on Jewish tradition Gentiles are unclean. The woman approaches Jesus on behalf of her daughter who is unclean because of a demon. Jesus made several attempts to reject the Syrophenician woman. His first attempt was to ignore her (Matthew 15:23) she would not be ignored. Then Jesus rebukes her and says that the "children" must have their fill first before any is given to the "dogs." In other words, His mission was not to the Gentiles, but to the Children of Israel. Still the woman would not be deterred. She continues the metaphor and says that even the "dogs" get the crumbs that fall from the table. Because she is a Gentile and thought of as unclean does not mean that she should wait until Israel has had its fill. All she was asking for was the droppings or crumbs from the Master's table. She refused to allow such a characterization of her ethnicity to deter her from receiving her request.

Was Jesus rejecting this woman of color, or was He testing and challenging her faith? Was Jesus demonstrating to His disciples that persons outside Judaism could have more faith than Jews?

4. A Woman's Faith is Rewarded (vv. 29-30)

Jesus takes this opportunity to show the disci-
ples that faith transcends racial and ethnic barriers. He recognizes her faith galling it "great" and then heals her daughter. She refused to allow such a characterization of her race to deter her from receiving her request. Her daughter needed help and that was all that mattered. As a result the Syrophenician woman and her daughter became clean or acceptable members of the faith community. Her humility, tenacity, and steadfast faith, gained Jesus' attention and He granted her request.

SEARCH THE SCRIPTURES

1. Where was Jesus headed on His visit to Tyre and Sidon? (Mark 7:24)

2. What was wrong with the woman's daughter? (v. 25)

3. What did the woman request of Jesus? (v. 26)

4. What was Jesus' initial response to the woman's request? (v. 27)

5. What did the woman find when she returned home? (v. 30)

DISCUSS THE MEANING

1. Why was Jesus seeking rest in Tyre and Sidon?

2. Explain the Syrophenician woman's response to Jesus: "Yes, Lord, yet the dogs under the table eat of the children's crumbs."

3. What does the phrase "let the children be filled first" mean?

4. Compare your definition of faith with that expressed by the Syrophenician woman.

5. What can we learn from the Syrophenician woman's persistence?

LESSON IN OUR SOCIETY

Many people have refused to be molded by the pressures and expectations of what the media, society, and history deem proper. Facing the biases of society, many of us have had to exhibit an attitude and persona of strength and wisdom. Like the Syrophenician woman, we must forge ahead in the midst of controversy and succeed against the odds. How would you persevere in the face of gender, racial, and religious prejudice and rejection?

MAKE IT HAPPEN

When was the last time you made a difference in someone's life by breaking the cycle of prejudice and rejection? The cycle can be broken beginning with you. You can become a mentor to young women women who face prejudice and rejection because of being a single parent. You can volunteer at a homeless shelter once a month. You can volunteer at a domestic violence shelter or at your church to be a host-site for monthly Alcoholics Anonymous (AA) meetings.

FOLLOW THE SPIRIT

What God wants me to do:

_____

_____

REMEMBER YOUR THOUGHTS

Special insights you have learned:

_____

_____

MORE LIGHT ON THE TEXT
Mark 7:24-37

7:24 And from thence he arose, and went into the borders of Tyre and Sidon, and entered into a house and would have no man know it, but he could not be hid.

In Mark the story of the Syrophenician woman is presented as a key transcending of boundaries which Jesus and His disciples experienced beginning in Mark 6:45—8:21. The detour through Gentile country began after Jesus' disciples failed to go ahead of Him to Bethesda on the other side of the Sea of Galilee.

This coastal area seemed to have been the only place He could find rest from the crowds and His opponents. Jews were not likely to enter Gentile territory, so Jesus probably felt assured that He could remain anonymous and receive some much needed rest. Jesus was not entering into alien territory because the land was actually given to His ancestors by God. Coming to this area suggests that Jesus was known to the Jews who had settled in the area, so it must have been in the home of Jews that Jesus retreated.

25 For a certain woman, whose young daughter had an unclean spirit, heard of him, and came and fell at his feet.

Because of her gender, the Syrophenician woman experienced the usual rejection and limitations imposed on females of her day. The very action of approaching Jesus, a male and a stranger, on behalf of her family was unconventional and deemed unacceptable based on Jesus and His disciples' initial response to her (see Matthew 15:23). The care and protection of an honorable family was the responsibility of the father or other senior male relatives (Mark 1:29-34; 5:21-24a, 33-34). The request, coming from a "woman," was considered shameful.

There is no mention of a father, husband, or any other male relative in this passage. The father may have been unwilling or unable to seek help for his family. This mother may have been a widow or unwed. Her daughter may have been her only family. As a woman, her status was already lower than her male counterparts. If she was a widow, her status was even lower, and it was lower still if she was unwed. Women could not own property, be the legitimate heads of families, or be the direct recipients of their family inheritance. If that were not enough, she had a daughter who was gravely ill, and the only person she was able to find to assist her was a historical enemy, a Jew.

26 The woman was a Greek, a Syrophenician by nation; and she besought him that he would cast forth the devil out of her daughter.

Because of her lineage, and based on the customs of the day, this woman had a double strike against her. Not only was she female, she was also Syrian, a descendant of the early inhabitants of the coastland of Phoenicia. Matthew's account says that she was a "woman of Canaan" (15:22). The term Canaanite indicates an inhabitant of Canaan, meaning a non-Jewish inhabitant of Palestine. The Canaanites founded Sidon (Genesis 10:19) and the Phoenicians were their descendants. All the people of this region were African/Asiatic, including the Jews. Therefore, the distinction is not one of color but of culture and ethnicity. The term "Syrophenician" was an even narrower description of this woman's ethnicity. It was used to describe a Syrian who lived in Phoenicia, and as such it distinguished the Phoenicians from the other Syrians. Phoenicia was a narrow strip near the northeast corner of the Mediterranean Sea. It was about 28 miles long and about one mile wide.

Mark's goal in his Gospel is to present Jesus as God's Servant. This is different from Matthew's goal, which is to present Jesus as King of the Jews. Therefore, Mark leaves out this mother's cry of pleading for Jesus' help by referring to Him as "Son of David" and "Lord." Mark merely writes that she asks Jesus for help. This mother's desperate pleas for help is diminished to a mere, almost quiet, "cry" for assistance, as opposed to a dramatic never-ceasing pleading of her case for her spirit-possessed child.

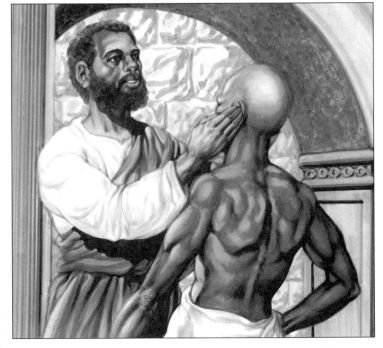

In Matthew we can almost hear the mother pleading with Jesus as she describes her daughter's condition: "My daughter is grievously vexed with a devil" (15:22c). Being possessed by an unclean spirit is not presented as a mild experience (Mark 5:1-15; Matthew 17:14-21). Although it appears to be unintentional, Mark pushes this woman even further to the fringes of society by quieting her yearnings for help for her tormented child by merely stating (in Greek), "She kept asking . . . ."

This mother seemed to know that Jesus had the power to help her daughter. Without question she speaks with Jesus as if she knows He has the ability to heal her daughter. She speaks with power and unwavering faith and trust: "She besought Him to cast forth the devil out of her daughter." Whether she heard of Jesus' fame or was just aware of His power to heal people is uncertain. What is certain is that she believed that Jesus could, and she fully expected Him to heal her daughter.

27 But Jesus said unto her, Let the children first be filled: for it is not meet to take the children's bread, and cast it unto the dogs.

When compared to Matthew's account, the disciples also appealed to Jesus to grant this woman's request (15:23). Their concern was not for her child, but that she was making too much noise. They were concerned that her cries would draw attention to Jesus, which would probably alert the sick, lame, diseased, blind, mute, deaf, and even Jesus' enemies to their retreat location. Sadly, the disciples were not interested in this mother's daughter being healed but in rest and safety for themselves. Louis Barbiri in the *Bible Knowledge Commentary* believes the disciples are in fact implying, "Lord, why don't you go ahead and help this woman? She isn't going to give up until you do something for her."

When Jesus did speak, His response appeared to be demeaning, with ethnic overtones, and not in keeping with the "Jesus" from whom we have come to expect fairness, equality, mercy, grace and healing. When Mark wrote, "But Jesus said unto her," some scholars suggest that Jesus was addressing the statement to the disciples and not directly to this mother, and that the disciples' request for Jesus to help her was their way of silencing her. Regardless of whether this statement was directed to the disciples or to her, it is clear that Jesus said it and it had the *appearance* of ethnic overtones.

"Let the children first be filled: for it is not meet to take the children's bread and cast it unto the dogs." Some scholars suggest that when making this statement Jesus was only quoting a popular proverb. Earlier Jesus had expressly directed the disciples not to go into the way of the Gentiles but to go only in the way of the Jews (Matthew 10:5-6). For consistency's sake, here He observed His own admonition. It would seem impossible to evangelize the Gentiles without setting aside the Jewish customs, the Law of Moses, and confronting the bitterness and prejudices of the Jews. The evangelizing of the Gentiles would have to wait until the Jews completely rejected Jesus and ordered His execution. Once crucified, the risen Lord's Gospel would be available to all who would believe on His name (Matthew 28:18-20; Acts 1:8).

"Let the children first be filled" expressly implies that Jesus' ministry was to the Jews first and that they were God's chosen people and must be reached first. Some suggest that this statement was one of fact, not of rejection. In making this statement to the woman, it is also suggested that she needed to be taught at least two lessons. The first lesson was persistence, humility, and trust; and the second lesson was that there was only one true religion and one true Messiah.

"For it is not meet to take the children's bread and cast it unto the dogs." Jesus' use of the word "dogs," which was occasionally used for Gentiles, did not mean He recognized this description as being an accurate way of addressing a person, regardless of his or her ethnicity. It is suggested that these words, although harsh in nature, were not meant to be harsh because Jesus never spoke harshly or rejected anyone who came to Him, especially those with a desperate need. It would appear that Jesus spoke these words to lead her to persist and believe.

The term "dog" has at least two connotations. First, it was used to refer to wild street dogs.

Second, it could refer to a house puppy or lap dog. Was the use of either reference a clear implication of someone who is considered not human but animalistic in nature? Was the use of the term "dog" an ethnic slur by Jesus to degrade this woman? Hardly. Rather, it was to illustrate that the Gospel of the kingdom was to Jews first, and then Gentiles.

28 And she answered and said unto him, Yes, Lord: yet the dogs under the table eat of the children's crumbs.

"Yet the dogs under the table eat of the children's crumbs" seems to be an acknowledgment that she and her daughter are undeserving and without legal covenant rights to the children's bread. She then uses the Greek word for "dog," *kunarion* (pronounced **koo-nar-ee-on**), meaning "puppies." In humility she was requesting the crumbs that fall to the floor when the children are eating. She was claiming the "puppies" scraps for her and her daughter which would have been thrown away.

Through all her endeavors she finally sees an opening where she is hopeful that her daughter's chance for healing will come. Her faith had been challenged, and she met the rejection and racial comments with grace and tenacity. Now she waited for Jesus' response.

29 And he said unto her, For this saying go thy way; the devil is gone out of thy daughter.

"For this saying go thy way." Matthew's presentation of her reward for her persistence and unwavering faith gives us a more acceptable rendition of events. "Then Jesus . . . said unto her, 'O woman, great is thy faith!'" (Matthew 15:28). In this account Jesus actually compliments this mother on her commitment and trust in Him to fulfill her heart's desire. It is noted that here, Jesus Himself congratulates her, a Gentile woman, on her faith. Jesus immortalizes her in history as one of only two persons whom He congratulated on having "great" faith (Matthew 8:10-13; 15:28).

This mother is a model of faith in the Lord's mercy, even when rejection and prejudice comes from the most unlikely persons. Her greatness of faith was manifested in that she came to Jesus despite the differences of religious beliefs and culture. She persevered when it seemed that her prayer would be denied. She continued her quest in spite of the obstacles, and she waited until Jesus extended mercy to her. This kind of faith prevails in the most difficult circumstances and Matthew vividly describes what resulted from this woman's faith: "and her daughter was made whole from that very hour" (15:28b).

30 And when she was come to her house, she found the devil gone out, and her daughter laid upon the bed.

When arriving home, this mother found her daughter, no longer raving or in convulsions, but lying quiet on the bed. This posture of her daughter indicated the physical exhaustion that would naturally follow the intense nervous strain of demon possession, especially the last attack produced by the departing demon. Finally, she had been healed as a result of her mother's faith and prayers.

31 And again departing from the coasts of Tyre and Sidon, He came to the sea of Galilee, through the midst of the coasts of Decapolis.

Jesus continued His travels through Sidon and along the coast of the Decapolis. Decapolis was a confederacy of ten Roman-controlled cities, mostly east of the Jordan River and settled by the Greeks. It was formed after 63 B.C. and dominated by Damascus. This also was a largely Gentile area with large Jewish colonies, the region where the demoniac was healed (Mark 5:20).

Some scholars suggest that Jesus was going from Tyre in the north, to Galilee in the south. This route would have eventually taken Jesus south by heading north first, if he started by going to Sidon. It is because of this geographical meandering that scholars believe Jesus was in search of quietness and rest for Himself and His disciples, as well as preparation and training of the disciples before facing opposition in Galilee. This portion of Jesus' journey, which ended in Galilee, took around eight months. It is at the completion of this journey that Jesus is now in the

regions of Galilee and comes into the district of the Decapolis.

32 And they bring unto him one that was deaf and had an impediment in his speech; and they beseech Him to put his hand upon him.

Mark alone records the specific healing of this deaf man. Matthew's version of this same time includes a mass of people being healed by Jesus as He sits on a mountain and people are brought to Him (Matthew 15:29-30). Mark's Gospel pulls this deaf man apart from the crowd to highlight Jesus' ministry to an individual, which emphasizes Jesus' servanthood.

The phrase "impediment in his speech" occurs only this once in the New Testament. It is found in the Old Testament only in Isaiah (35:6). The use of this Greek word implies that the man could scarcely speak. This condition is the result of a long-term deafness, which can be inferred by the fact that his hearing had been totally lost.

33 And he took him aside from the multitude, and put his fingers into his ears, and he spit, and touched his tongue.

Taking the man aside from the multitude indicates two things. First, the man went where Jesus led him, which was an exercise in faith, expecting Jesus to fully heal him. Second, there must have been a crowd there as indicated by Matthew's account (15:30). It seems that Mark tries to avoid mentioning the crowd in order to highlight this man's story, but he cannot avoid mentioning the crowd. Therefore, he includes "and he took him aside from the multitude."

Three points may be suggested as to why Jesus removed the man from the crowd: 1) Jesus could have been trying to keep the man from experiencing additional embarrassment because of his disability; 2) He did not want the Gentiles present to assume that He was practicing some sort of magic; and 3) He wanted to avoid publicity and undue attention from those whom He was trying to elude.

"And put his fingers into his ears, and he spit, and touched his tongue." These were symbolic acts which were common among Greek and Jewish healers. These acts suggested to the sufferers that they might be healed. This could also have been Jesus' attempt to communicate with the man because of his inability to hear language. Jesus touched the parts affected to apprise the man of His intention to reach the seat of the infirmities and remove the maladies.

34 And looking up to heaven he sighed, and saith unto him, Ephphatha, that is, be opened.

The motion of "looking up" was a continuation of the signs Jesus used to communicate with the man. In looking "up to heaven" Jesus was communicating to him that the power which He received to heal him came from the God of heaven, the God above all and not one of the many gods the Gentiles worshiped. Jesus' sigh was also a part of the process of communicating with this man, but it also symbolized the heartfelt compassion that Jesus felt for the man's condition.

"And saith unto him, Ephphatha." It cannot be assumed that this man was a Gentile. He could have been a Jew, since Jesus spoke to him in Aramaic. After using the signs of touch, taste, and sight, at this point Jesus decided to use speech and announced "Ephphatha," meaning "be opened," to the man's condition.

35 And straightway his ears were opened, and the string of his tongue was loosed, and he spake plain.

As soon as the word was pronounced, immediately the man's hearing came to him. The difficulty of speech seems to have arisen from the man's deafness. Once he was able to hear, he immediately was able to speak plainly. "His ears were opened" implied that, like most of us, his hearing resulted from the channels through which sounds are transmitted to the inner ear. Once healed he was now able to speak clearly.

36 And he charged them that they should tell no man: but the more he charged them, so much the more a great deal they published it.

Jesus insisted that the man who was healed, the people who brought him to Jesus, and those who witnessed the healing should all keep quiet about the miracle they witnessed. "That they should tell no man" was Jesus' attempt at anonymity. He also

was trying to keep the news from the scribes and Pharisees. "But the more he charged them, so much the more a great deal they published it." This is an indication of Jesus' attempt to keep the knowledge of His presence and fame at a minimum. It is to be noted that after several miracles Jesus cautioned the people to keep quiet (Matthew 8:4; Luke 5:14; 8:56; 9:21). It can be gathered from Jesus' admonitions of silence that He did not want to be publicly recognized as the Messiah by the fickle and easily excitable multitudes.

37 And were beyond measure astonished, saying, he hath done all things well: he maketh both the deaf to hear, and the dumb to speak.

All those around were amazed at the miracle Jesus did that day. This verse is reflective of Matthew 15:30-31. This crowd, the majority of which were probably Gentile, came to the conclusion that Jesus did all things well. This may have been primarily based on the miracles that were performed during that time. But these words are also reflective of the words spoken by God in Genesis 1:31a: "And God saw everything that he had made, and, behold, it was very good."

DAILY BIBLE READINGS

M: A Gentile Woman Seeks Out Jesus
Mark 7:24-30

T: He Has Done Everything Well
Mark 7:31-37

W: Do You Not Understand?
Mark 8:11-21

T: A Centurion's Faith
Luke 7:1-10

F: Peter and John Show Boldness
Acts 4:5-14

S: We Cannot Keep from Speaking
Acts 4:15-22

S: Prayer for Boldness
Acts 4:23-31

TEACHING TIPS

May 11
Bible Study Guide 11

1. Words You Should Know

A. Messiah (Mark 8:29)—The anointed one. "Messiah" in Hebrew; "Christ" in Greek.

B. Elders (v. 31)—Older Jewish men chosen from among the people to represent them on the Sanhedrin.

C. Sanhedrin—The 71 member Jewish governing council and supreme court presided over by the High Priest and made up of elders, scribes, Pharisees, and Sadducees. Jesus referred to this group in Mark 8:31.

D. Chief Priests (v. 31) Jewish men who were in charge of worship in the Temple.

2. Teacher Preparation

A. Read the Bible BACKGROUND in various translations and in the other Gospel accounts.

B. Read Bible Study Guide 11 in its entirety and complete the SEARCH THE SCRIPTURES and the DISCUSS THE MEANING questions.

C. Call students and give them the assignments that they will need to participate in class.

3. Starting the Lesson

A. Before students arrive, write the lesson title, AT-A-GLANCE outline, and sub-headings from the IN DEPTH section on the board.

B. As the students arrive for class, have them complete the SEARCH THE SCRIPTURES section.

C. When the rest of the students are present and seated, begin the class by asking for reports of praise and requests for prayer.

D. After prayer ask a preassigned student to read and explain the LESSON AIM.

4. Getting into the Lesson

A. Begin the lesson with a review of the WORDS YOU SHOULD KNOW.

B. Generate a discussion on to the lesson's central question: Who is Jesus?

C. Have three students make preassigned presentations from the perspectives of a Moslem, a Jew, and a Christian.

D. Now, using the outline on the board and the information from the IN DEPTH section, take students through the lesson focusing on the question: Who is Jesus?

5. Relating the Lesson to Life

A. Now pose the question: If one of your non-Christian friends asked you who Jesus is, what would you say?

B. Give the students two minutes to think and one minute each to answer.

6. Arousing Action

A. Ask students to turn to the MAKE IT HAPPEN section and encourage them to put the suggestion into practice this week.

B. Remind them to read the DAILY BIBLE READINGS for the week.

C. Close the class by singing one verse and chorus of "Tell Me the Story of Jesus."

WORSHIP GUIDE

For the Superintendent or Teacher
Theme: God's Son, Our Saviour, Lord, and Example
Theme Song: "Everybody Ought to Know Who Jesus Is"
Scripture: 2 Peter 1:16-18
Song: "Fairest Lord Jesus"
Meditation: Dear Lord, we thank You for Jesus and all that He means to us and has done for us. Help us to accept Him as our Saviour and Lord and to follow Him as our example.

CONFESSION OF FAITH AND AFFIRMATION

Bible Background • MARK 8:27; 9:8
Printed Text • MARK 8:27-35; 9:2-7
Devotional Reading • PHILIPPIANS 2:5-11

LESSON AIM

By the lesson's end, students can clearly state their understanding of Jesus as the Messiah and God's Son, will appreciate some of the complexities of these relationships, and will determine to share their commitment with someone during the coming week.

KEEP IN MIND

"And he saith unto them, But whom say ye that I am? And Peter answereth and saith unto him, Thou art the Christ" (Mark 8:29).

FOCAL VERSES

Mark 8:27 And Jesus went out, and his disciples, into the towns of Caesarea Philippi: and by the way he asked his disciples, saying unto them, Whom do men say that I am?

28 And they answered, John the Baptist: but some say, Elias; and others, One of the prophets.

29 And he saith unto them, But whom say ye that I am? And Peter answereth and saith unto him, Thou art the Christ.

30 And he charged them that they should tell no man of him.

31 And he began to teach them, that the Son of man must suffer many things, and be rejected of the elders, and of the chief priests, and scribes, and be killed, and after three days rise again.

32 And he spake that saying openly. And Peter took him, and began to rebuke him.

33 But when he had turned about and looked

LESSON OVERVIEW

LESSON AIM
KEEP IN MIND
FOCAL VERSES
IN FOCUS
THE PEOPLE, PLACES,
AND TIMES
BACKGROUND
AT-A-GLANCE
IN DEPTH
SEARCH THE SCRIPTURES
DISCUSS THE MEANING
LESSON IN OUR SOCIETY
MAKE IT HAPPEN
FOLLOW THE SPIRIT
REMEMBER YOUR THOUGHTS
MORE LIGHT ON THE TEXT
DAILY BIBLE READINGS

on his disciples, he rebuked Peter, saying, Get thee behind me, Satan; for thou savourest not the things that be of God, but the things that be of men.

34 And when he had called the people unto him with his disciples also, he said unto them, Whosoever will come after me, let him deny himself, and take up his cross, and follow me.

35 For whosoever will save his life shall lose it; but whosoever shall lose his life for my sake and the gospel's, the same shall save it.

36 For what shall it profit a man, if he shall gain the whole world, and lose his own soul?

37 Or what shall a man give in exchange for his soul?

9:2 And after six days Jesus taketh with him Peter, and James and John, and leadeth them up into an high mountain apart by themselves: and he was transfigured before them.

3 And his raiment became shining, exceeding white as snow; so as no fuller on earth can white them.

4 And there appeared unto them Elias with Moses: and they were talking with Jesus.

5 And Peter answered and said to Jesus, Master, It is good for us to be here: and let us make three tabernacles; one for thee, and one for Moses, and one for Elias.

6 For he wist not what to say; for they were sore afraid.

7 And there was a cloud that overshadowed

MAY 11TH

them: and a voice came out of the cloud, saying, This is my beloved Son: hear him.

IN FOCUS

"Whodunits" are my favorite television programs. Even a fictional program like *Law and Order* can hold my attention for an hour or for several episodes. But the true "whodunits," like *America's Most Wanted*, are the most intriguing and educational to me. Very seldom can I predict who the bad guy is or how he will be caught. The criminal is usually the person who is the least suspicious, either to the victim or the viewer. On the other hand, the criminal is usually someone whom the victim knows or thinks he/she knows, somebody who is a relative, co-worker, or close friend. In one true story the wife of the criminal knew him as a loving husband, a U.S. Air Force reserve pilot, and a father to her five children. She had no idea that over the past few years he had murdered fourteen young women and buried one of them in her backyard.

Who do you know or think you know? One of the lessons of these "whodunit" episodes is that we really don't know anyone for certain. If we're honest and have lived a while, we'll confess that we really don't know ourselves. Just when we think we've "found ourselves" and have ourselves all figured out, we'll do something or say something that will surprise us.

So perhaps we shouldn't be too hard on the disciples in today's lesson because they really didn't know Jesus. The focus of our lesson today is the question: Who is Jesus? To get the fullest impact of today's lesson, be sure to read Matthew's report (Matthew 16:13-20). When we put together Matthew, Mark, and Luke's reports, we come away with the impression that only God really knows who Jesus is (and who we are). So when we talk about our knowledge of Jesus (or ourselves), we must do so with humility and reliance on the Scriptures.

THE PEOPLE, PLACES, AND TIMES

Casearea Philippi. Built by Philip, the son of Herod the Great, and located in the vicinity of Sidon, Tyre, and Damascus. The beautiful marble shrine to Caesar, the head of the Roman empire, is near the source of the Jordan River. The shrine's location and some of the surrounding towns are named for Caesar and Philip.

Satan. In the Bible, Satan is an actual spiritual being who is the personification of everything evil. When Jesus called Peter Satan, he was not saying that Peter was equated with this being, but that he was being used as Satan's instrument.

For further information on Satan, see Halley's Handbook (Grand Rapids: Zondervan Publishing House).

BACKGROUND

As presented by Mark, since the beginning of His ministry, Jesus has spent most of His time in Galilee (Mark 1:9—7:23). He had made a visit to the Tyre and Sidon region and has stopped in Dalmanutha (8:10-12).

In our lesson today He has gone to the Caesarea Philippi (pronounced **sess-uh-REE-uh FILL-ih-pie**) area, which is north of Galilee. He is bringing His Galilean ministry to a close and getting ready to go to Jerusalem where He will end His earthly ministry. He is seeking the peace and quiet of out-of-the-way places where He can give His disciples their preparation to carry on His ministry after His ascension. He is trying to teach them two lessons: 1) who He is and is not and 2) that He, and all who follow Him, are going to have to suffer.

AT-A-GLANCE

1. Jesus Is the Messiah (Mark 8:27-30)
2. Jesus Is a Suffering Messiah (vv. 31-37)
3. Jesus Is the Son of God (9:2-7)

IN DEPTH

1. Jesus Is the Messiah (Mark 8:27-30)

In the first story of today's lesson, Jesus gave His disciples a two-question quiz. The first question they passed with flying colors, but even though they had been with Jesus for at least two years, they failed the second question embarrassingly. The drama probably went something like this:

Jesus: What are people saying about me? Who do they think I am?

First Disciple: Some say you remind them of John the Baptist.

Jesus: Why?

Second Disciple: Well, he came right before you. He introduced you and your ministry and at first, your message of repentance sounded the same as his (Mark 1:4-10, 15).

Jesus: Well, that makes sense.

Third Disciple: Other people say you remind them of Elijah.

Jesus: Elijah?

Third Disciple: Yes, like Elijah, you speak out against the corrupt religious leaders (1 Kings 18:16-19; Mark 7:5-13).

Fourth Disciple: You also control nature like Elijah did, and you work miracles of healing (1 Kings 17:1, 17-24; Mark 3:1-6; 6:45-52).

Narrator: Other disciples chimed in with other names such as Jeremiah and some of the other Jewish prophets (Matthew 16:14; Luke 9:18-19). Jesus waited until they quieted down and spoke quietly.

Jesus: How about you? You're my disciples, my followers, and my students. Who do you say I am? (Mark 8:29, TEV)

Narrator: A hush fell over the disciples. They were on the spot. They all focused on the ground as if a revelation was going to rise from the earth. Finally Peter broke the silence. His mouth was moving and he spoke in his usual bold manner. But the words seem to be coming through him rather than from him.

Peter: You are the Christ (8:29, NIV).

Narrator: All the disciples were tense. Peter often gave the wrong answer. They didn't know if Peter had again spoken out of turn. Matthew tells us that Jesus approved of Peter's answer by telling him it was a divine revelation (Matthew 16:17). Then, just as everybody was relaxing and thanking the Lord for saving them from a truly embarrassing situation, Jesus spoke again.

Jesus: Don't tell anyone about me (8:30, TEV).

Disciples: No one?

Jesus: No one!

Why do you think Jesus didn't want the disciples spreading the word that he was the Messiah?

Jesus was not a conquering Messiah. Through most of their history—after Joseph and before Moses in Egypt, and after their golden age under David—the Jews had suffered oppression. They had been oppressed either by some of their own kings or under the foreign governments of Assyria, Babylon, Persia, Egypt (again), and now Rome.

For many years, in many ways, the Jews had been "trampled under the iron feet of oppression" (Dr. King's phrase). During their time of oppression they developed a belief that God would send two champions to deliver them from their suffering. The first person would be as Elijah (Mark 9:11-13) who would bring order to the nation's internal chaos. As he settled internal disputes and strife, he would also rigorously announce the coming of the Messiah. The second person would be a conqueror, a leader like David, who would bring freedom, peace, and prosperity.

In Jesus' day, the Jews longed for a Messiah who would conquer the Romans, give the Jews their independence, and restore Jerusalem to its former glory. When Peter announced that Jesus was the Messiah, that's the kind of person he and the disciples had in mind. That's why Jesus said, "Don't tell anyone that I'm that person!"

2. Jesus Is a Suffering Messiah (vv. 31-37)

After Jesus said, "Don't tell . . ." Mark said Jesus began to teach the disciples that He was a "suffering Messiah." Jesus was convinced that the way to initiate change was to change people—their hearts, minds, and spirits—and therefore their behavior. He believed that the major human problem is not environmental but personal. He believed that the central source of evil is not external but internal. In Mark 7:20-23 Jesus says that "from within, out of the heart [of people] proceed evil thoughts, adultery, fornication, murder, theft, covetousness, wickedness, deceit . . . all these things, come from within; and defile."

So Jesus said in effect, "Peter, I'm not trying to get the Romans off of you. I'm trying to get the Romans out of you. In order to do that I'm going to have to 'suffer many things' including rejection and death. But this death is not permanent. After three days I'll rise again" (8:31).

Peter was so upset that he grabbed Jesus "by the arm" (8:32, pharaphrased) and screamed, "No! No! No! Jesus, not more suffering! Haven't we suffered enough? Haven't we already been enslaved? Beaten down? Oppressed? Taken advantage of? Demeaned? Haven't we suffered enough?" (8:32)

Jesus turned around in silence and looked at the disciples—probably with tears in His eyes because He knew, humanly speaking, that Peter was right and was expressing their feelings and the feelings of most of the poor, marginalized, and dispossessed of the earth. But to make a very important and crucial point, He said, "Peter, while you are right—historically, economically, and politically—morally and spiritually you are thinking like the devil. That is the way Satan wants us to think. In order to carry out my divine mission, I've had to put that kind of thinking behind me. I challenge you, Peter, not to think mere human thoughts but God's thoughts" (8:31).

Then He turned to the crowd that had gathered during the conversation and challenged them, "If there is anyone here who wants to join me in my mission, let him put away his self-centered thinking, pick up an instrument of suffering, and join me in my crusade to bring love, peace, and justice to this world. For anybody who commits his or her life to avoiding physical pain will surely suffer spiritual pain. But whoever commits himself or herself to suffering on behalf of others will experience a life beyond pain. How much profit will a person have left who is materially full, but spiritually empty?"

What is the quality of a person's life who lives in external wealth and internal poverty? If you had all of the material wealth, comfort, and luxury you desired, how much of it would you be willing to exchange for love, peace, and joy? Some of it? All of it? None of it?

3. Jesus Is the Son of God (9:2-7)

The theme regarding Jesus' identity continues in the second dramatic episode. There Jesus experiences a radical change in His appearance. We call it the Transfiguration. In this section Mark tells us that Jesus took three special disciples on a mountain retreat probably to Mt. Hermon which is 9,200 feet high and located not too far from Caesarea Philippi. This event happened about a week (Mark says six days, while Luke says eight) after the previous episode so the matter of Jesus' identity was still fresh in their memory.

While Jesus was in prayer (Luke 9:28), He suddenly began to glow. Even His clothes began to shine like snow in the sun and became whiter "than anyone in the world could bleach them" (Mark 9:3, NEB). As Jesus prayed and the disciples slept, the Lord sent Moses and Elijah to talk to Jesus about His suffering and death in Jerusalem (Luke 9:30-31). As these three of the Lord's most outstanding servants conversed, the disciples woke up and were absolutely flabbergasted at what was taking place. As Moses and Elijah were saying their goodbyes, Peter blurted out, "Master, it's a good thing that we're here [meaning the three disciples]. We can put up some tents, so that Moses and Elijah can stay on longer." Mark tries to help Peter's image by saying he didn't know what to say because he, James, and John were "so frightened" (Mark 9:6, TEV). (No apology needed for us. We know Peter had problems coordinating his mouth and his brain!)

Just as Peter closed his mouth, a cloud appeared and blocked out the sun. Out of the cloud came the voice of God, saying: "This is my Son. I love Him. Listen to Him" (9:7).

Now what is this dramatic experience all about? It is about prayer. Jesus is about to go through the most challenging experience of His life. It is an experience that He believes has been ordained by God, so as is His habit, He takes time to talk to the One who gave Him the assignment.

It is about assurance. Moses and Elijah were sent by God to assure Jesus that He was in God's will. As a divine being He needed no assurance, but as a human creature who was undertaking a unique assignment God knew He needed someone to say, "Yes, Jesus, you're doing the right thing" and perhaps to share their experiences with Him. Moses, the founder of Judaism, had experienced being asked by God to do what no one before him had been asked to do. He had really put his life on the line to get the children of Israel out of Egypt, through the Red Sea, and across the wilderness. He had presented them with the Ten Commandments, built their Tabernacle, and taught them how to worship and how to live together as an emerging nation. And then, because of his zeal and frustration with them, he was not able to go into the Promised Land.

Elijah's assignment was to help bring a wayward nation back to God in the midst of material prosperity and spiritual bankruptcy. He also, literally, put his life on the line to carry out God's assignment for him.

Now Jesus, who had given His life in ministry to the poor, the brokenhearted, the blind, the lame, and the demon-possessed, was on His way to Jerusalem to suffer and give His life a ransom for many (10:45). As a divine being, He understood precisely the what and why of this God-ordained assignment. But, as a human, the Son of man needed some assurance from persons who had already gone through the life-sacrificing process. Moses and Elijah were two such persons.

It was about confirmation. Moses and Elijah were helpful, but after they left, there were lingering doubts. Jesus' circumstances were different from theirs. After all of their efforts and all of the years in between, was another human sacrifice necessary? Was He the chosen one? Was He as special as He believed Himself to be? Was John right in identifying Him as God and as God's lamb? (John 1:1-5, 29) He needs a direct word, an unmistakable word from God.

As He pondered these questions, a cloud came over and blocked out the sun. Out of the cloud, a voice spoke. He had heard this voice before when John baptized Him. Now here on the mountain as He faced the most difficult assignment of His life, the voice spoke again: "This is my Son. I love Him." And then a special word to the disciples: "Listen to Him" (v. 7).

With that word of confirmation, Jesus took His disciples down the mountain to minister to a demon-possessed boy.

What does Jesus' experience mean for us? 1) It means that at some point in our Christian lives we can expect the Lord to give us a special assignment. 2) We can expect that as a result of the assignment we will have human experiences of doubt and uncertainty. 3) We can expect that the Lord will send a person or persons with similar experiences to assure us that our assignment is genuinely God-given and that God will supply what we need to carry it out. 4) We can expect that the Lord will give us direct confirmation through His Word and in the way that we can best hear Him.

SEARCH THE SCRIPTURES
Match the names and places below with the appropriate Scripture references.

1. _____ Mark 8:27   A. My beloved Son
2. _____ Mark 9:4-5   B. Christ
3. _____ Mark 8:33   C. Caesarea Philippi
4. _____ Mark 9:7   D. John the Baptist
5. _____ Mark 8:31   E. Elijah and Moses
6. _____ Mark 8:29   F. Elders, chief priests, and scribes

7. _____ Mark 8:28   G. Satan

DISCUSS THE MEANING
1. Why do Moslems, Jews, and Christians perceive Jesus differently?
2. What differences do history, geography, and culture make?

LESSON IN OUR SOCIETY
Should Christians insist on prayer in the public schools if Christian prayers offend Moslems, Jews, and Buddhists? If so, why? If not, why not?

In a pluralistic society, is it proper to insist on our beliefs and religious expressions as the only legitimate beliefs and expressions?

MAKE IT HAPPEN
This week briefly discuss with two or three non-Christians the question, "Who is Jesus?" See how long you can listen without interrupting to insist on your interpretation. Plan to be friendly and to smile and give each person a small gift of love—perhaps a book, picture, or other token.

FOLLOW THE SPIRIT
What God wants me to do:

_____

_____

REMEMBER YOUR THOUGHTS
Special insights you have learned:

_____

_____

MORE LIGHT ON THE TEXT
Mark 8:27-33; 9:2-7

8:27 And Jesus went out, and his disciples, into the towns of Caesarea Philippi: and by the way he asked his disciples, saying unto them, Whom do men say that I am?

The TEV says, "Then Jesus and his disciples went . . . ." The word "then" connects the present events to the past episode of the healing of "Mr. Trees" in 8:22-26. After Jesus left Bethsaida, He headed in the direction of Caesarea Philippi. This town was previously called Balinas, once an important center of Baal worship. It is still in existence but is now called "Banias," a form of "Panias." It got the name of Panias because on a nearby hillside is a cavern where Pan, the Greek god of nature was supposed to have been born. It is also from a cave in the hillside that the waters of the Jordan River are supposed to have originated. Near the top of the hill, Philip built a beautiful white marble temple in honor of Caesar, the Roman emperor, then ruler of the world.

Some people worshiped Caesar as a god. All of this beauty and the legends surrounding it attracted people, so those villages of various sizes developed around this shrine. It was to this area that Jesus brought His disciples to get away from the crowds of Galilee. He wanted to spend some quality time to prepare them for the terrible experiences of Jerusalem.

The KJV says that they went "into the towns," while the NIV, NEB, and TEV say "on the way to the towns" which suggests that they were in the vicinity but not necessarily in the towns. Being in the towns would have probably defeated Jesus' intention of time alone in peace and quiet.

He didn't want to repeat His episode with "Sister Crumbs" in 7:24-30, so while they were out-side of the towns He asked the disciples about His identity.

28 And they answered, John the Baptist: but some say, Elias; and others, One of the prophets.

The KJV reads, "Whom do men say that I am?" The NEB reads, "Who do men say I am?" The NIV reads, "Who do people say I am?" and the TEV reads, "Tell me, who do people say that I am?" The question is the same in all four translations. The NIV and TEV use inclusive language—"people" instead of "men." But what Jesus is leading up to is the crucial question. He uses the first question to move the disciples' minds into an identity thought-pattern: Who is Jesus? He could have used a more direct approach and simply told them who He was.

There's a lesson here for all who want to be effective teachers. A good question by the teacher is better than a good answer. We also see a principle of readiness at work here. Jesus used the first question to get their minds ready for the answer to the second. Of course, they were still taken by surprise, as shown by Peter's reaction to Jesus' disclosure of the kind of Messiah He was. The disciples were not ready to know who Jesus really was. Without the first question they would have been caught totally off guard.

29 And he saith unto them, But whom say ye that I am? And Peter answereth and saith unto him, Thou art the Christ.

Peter's words have become known as the Great Confession: "You are the Messiah" or as Matthew recorded it: "Thou art the Christ, the Son of the living God" (Matthew 16:16, KJV). "Messiah" is Hebrew; "Christ" is Greek. Both words mean "anointed one."

30 Then charged he his disciples that they should tell no man that he was Jesus the Christ.

After Peter's confession Jesus immediately says, "Do not tell anyone about me," (8:30, TEV). This statement is part of what Markan scholars call "the Messianic Secret." Over and over Mark records Jesus saying, "Don't tell anybody" (3:12; 5:43; 7:36). There is much discussion about this phrase among scholars. Several reasons emerge. The most radical

man must suffer many things, and be rejected of the elders, and of the chief priests, and scribes, and be killed, and after three days rise again. 32 And he spake that saying openly. And Peter took him, and began to rebuke him. 33 But when he had turned about and looked on his disciples, he rebuked Peter, saying, Get thee behind me, Satan: for thou savourest not the things that be of God, but the things that be of men.

The "Who is Jesus?" question to the disciples also remained unanswered. It seems quite obvious in Matthew, Mark, and Luke that the disciples didn't fully understand what Jesus came to do. Even after Peter received the revelation from God, Jesus said, "Flesh and blood hath not revealed it unto thee but my Father which is in heaven" (Matthew 16:17). It is obvious that the answer came *through* Peter, not *from* him, because shortly afterward he began to rebuke Jesus. Now if Peter didn't understand his own words, we certainly can't ask the other disciples to be more perceptive, can we?

Notice Jesus never asks them that question again. He knew it was useless. The concept of being a suffering Messiah was just too much for them. And we should not be too disappointed with the disciples. They were small businessmen, fishermen, and the like—not Bible scholars, theologians, or Christian philosophers. Even after 2000 years of church history and Christian experience, how many people do you know who can explain who Jesus is? A Christian is not a person who can fully explain Jesus but a person who believes and accepts Him by faith and commits to following Him by faith.

Paul reminds us that we are saved by grace through faith; it is the gift of God (Ephesians 2:8-9). Study is important. Research is important. Thinking is important. But when it comes to our relationship with God through Jesus Christ, it is by God's grace through faith. We'll never be smart enough to understand Jesus.

is that Jesus said "don't tell" because He was not the Messiah and in Mark's account never claimed to be. This view is not acceptable.

A second reason Jesus said "don't tell" was that He was not the kind of Messiah the people of His day were expecting. He was a suffering Messiah rather than a conquering Messiah.

A third reason given for his "don't tell" policy was that if He traveled around making Messianic claims, He would be assassinated by the authorities "before his time."

A fourth reason given was that a Messianic claim would attract too much attention and not allow Him to prepare His disciples to carry on after His resurrection and ascension.

A final reason was that He didn't want to attract the wrong kinds of people as followers, namely anarchists, insurrectionists, and political revolutionaries.

After much discussion in lectures, debates, books, and journals, the answer remains a mystery. Perhaps even Mark didn't know. If he did, he didn't disclose it in his book.

31 And he began to teach them, that the Son of

9:2 And after six days Jesus taketh with him Peter, and James, and John, and leadth them up into a high mountain apart by themselves: and he was transfigured before them. 3 and his raiment became shining, exceeding white as snow; so as no fuller on earth can white them.

Just as we'll never be smart enough to understand Jesus, neither will we be able to understand the transfiguration. Does anybody know how it happened? Mark tells us when it happened—six days later. Luke said it was eight days later (9:28). We would say it was about a week—six to eight days. But neither Matthew (17:1-13), Mark (9:2-10), nor Luke (9:28-36) tell us exactly why it happened.

4 And there appeared unto them Elias with Moses: and they were talking with Jesus.

We have some ideas (see IN DEPTH) about why Moses and Elijah appeared. Luke tells us what they talked about (9:30-31).

5 And Peter answered and said to Jesus, Master, it is good for us to be here: and let us make three tabernacles; one for thee, and one for Moses, and one for Elias. 6 For he wist not what to say, for they were sore afraid.

Peter acted the way we have come to expect, running his mouth before putting his brain in gear. But we cannot be too hard on Peter because we find "Peters" all around us—in church, business, the arts, and sports. In our quietest, most honest moments, we recognize some of Peter qualities within ourselves. Two of the Lord's most valuable gifts to us are lips that close!

7 And there was a cloud that overshadowed them: and a voice came out of the cloud, saying, This is my beloved Son: hear him.

There is nothing so wonderful as a word of confirmation from the Lord. How could Jesus go through the passion experience? After having done so much good He had to face denial, betrayal, and abandonment by His disciples; be denounced and delivered by the religious leaders of His people; be spat upon, cruelly beaten, and crucified by the enemies of His people, the Romans, who didn't even know Him. How could

Jesus endure it? He had heard the voice saying, "This is my Son whom I love" (9:7, NIV). The assurance of the message took Him through all of the horror. Have you heard the voice? Don't attempt to go to Jerusalem until you hear the voice!

Fear not, I am with thee; O be not dismayed,
For I am thy God, and will still give thee aid;
I'll strengthen thee, help thee, and cause thee to stand
Upheld by my gracious, omnipotent hand.
When through the deep waters thy pathway shall lie,
My grace, all sufficient, shall be thy supply:
The flame shall not hurt thee; I only design
Thy dross to consume, and thy gold to refine.
That soul that on Jesus hath leaned for repose
I will not, I will not desert to his foes;
That soul, though all hell should endeavor to shake,
I'll never, no never, no never forsake.
(From How Firm A Foundation, author unknown).

DAILY BIBLE READINGS

M: Who Do You Say I Am?
Mark 8:27-33
T: Take Up Your Cross
Mark 8:34—9:1
W: This Is My Son
Mark 9:2-8
T: You Have the Words of Life
John 6:60-69
F: Zacchaeus Sees Jesus
Luke 19:1-10
S. Every Tongue Shall Confess
Philippians 2:5-11
S: Confess That Jesus Is Lord
Romans 10:5-13

TEACHING TIPS

May 18
Bible Study Guide 12

1. Words You Should Know

A. Scribes (Mark 9:14)—Among the Jews, a scribe (Hebrew *sopher*, pronounced **so-FAYER**) originally was a copyist of the Law or a secretary, but eventually he became a literary man, learned in Scripture, preoccupied with the letter of the Law.

B. Fasting (v. 29)—Has been practiced for centuries in connection with religious ceremonies. Fasts are observed among Christians, Jews, Muslims, Confucianists, Hindus, Taoists, and adherents of other religious faiths. Among the Jews and some early Christians, fasting was a form of penitence and purification.

2. Teacher Preparation

A. Read the story in all of the Gospel accounts.

B. Write out the answers to the SEARCH THE SCRIPTURES and DISCUSS THE MEANING questions.

C. If you have activities that require prior planning or research by the students, call and remind them of their assignments.

3. Starting the Lesson

A. Before the students arrive, write the lesson title and AT-A-GLANCE outline on the board.

B. As the students enter class, ask them to complete the SEARCH THE SCRIPTURES questions.

C. When the class has assembled, briefly review these questions with the class, after opening the class with prayer.

4. Getting into the Lesson

A. Ask a pre-assigned student to summarize the lesson BACKGROUND, and another student to present THE PEOPLE, PLACES, AND TIMES information.

B. Let students take turns reading the FOCAL VERSES.

C. Using the AT-A-GLANCE outline, lead the class though the lesson, keeping in mind the LESSON AIM.

5. Relating the Lesson to Life

A. Divide the class into two groups. Have group 1 review and discuss the DISCUSS THE MEANING section and group 2 review and discuss the LESSON IN OUR SOCIETY section.

B. Reassemble the class and have reports from a representative of each group.

6. Arousing Action

A. Direct the students' attention to the MAKE IT HAPPEN section and ask how they intend to carry out this part of the lesson.

B. Remind students to read the DAILY BIBLE READINGS.

C. Close the class session with an appropriate poem or song and prayer.

WORSHIP GUIDE

For the Superintendent or Teacher
Theme: Rebuilding Faith
Theme Song: "Tis So Sweet to Trust in Jesus"
Scripture: Luke 7:1-10
Song: "My Faith Looks Up to Thee"
Meditation: Thank You, Lord, for the gift of speech. Help us to use our words to heal, not wound; to understand, not criticize, to cooperate, not compete. Help us to love and encourage the members of our Christian family— whatever their denomination may be.

MAY 18TH

351

HONEST FAITH

Bible Background • MARK 9:14-37
Printed Text • MARK 9:14-29
Devotional Reading • JOHN 16:25-33

LESSON AIM

By the end of the lesson, students will be able to recall the story, to appreciate God through honest faith, and commit to assist in rebuilding the faith of others.

KEEP IN MIND

"And straightway the father of the child cried out, and said with tears, Lord, I believe; help thou mine unbelief" (Mark 9:24).

FOCAL VERSES

Mark 9:14 And when he came to his disciples, he saw a great multitude about them, and the scribes questioning with them.

15 And straightway all the people, when they beheld him, were greatly amazed, and running to him saluted him.

16 And he asked the scribes, "What question ye with them?"

17 And one of the multitude answered and said, Master, I have brought unto thee my son, which hath a dumb spirit.

18 And wheresoever he taketh him: he teareth him; and he foameth, and gnasheth with his teeth, and pineth away: and I spake to thy disciples that they should cast him out; and they could not.

19 He answereth him, and saith, O faithless generation, how long shall I be with you? how long shall I suffer you? bring him unto me."

20 And they brought him unto him: and when he saw him, straightway the spirit tare him; and he fell on the ground, and wallowed foaming.

21 And he asked his father, How long is it ago

LESSON OVERVIEW

LESSON AIM
KEEP IN MIND
FOCAL VERSES
IN FOCUS
THE PEOPLE, PLACES,
AND TIMES
BACKGROUND
AT-A-GLANCE
IN DEPTH
SEARCH THE SCRIPTURES
DISCUSS THE MEANING
LESSON IN OUR SOCIETY
MAKE IT HAPPEN
FOLLOW THE SPIRIT
REMEMBER YOUR THOUGHTS
MORE LIGHT ON THE TEXT
DAILY BIBLE READINGS

since this came unto him? And he said, Of a child.

22 And ofttimes it hath cast him into the fire, and into the waters, to destroy him: but if thou canst do any thing, have compassion on us, and help us.

23 Jesus said unto him, If thou canst believe, all things are possible to him that believeth.

24 And straightway the father of the child cried out and said with tears, Lord, I believe; help thou mine unbelief!

25 When Jesus saw that the people came running together, he rebuked the foul spirit, saying unto him, Thou dumb and deaf spirit, I charge thee, come out of him, and enter no more into him!

26 And then the spirit cried, and rent him sore, and came out of him: and he was as one dead; insomuch that many said, He is dead.

27 But Jesus took him by the hand, and lifted him up; and he arose.

28 And when he was come into the house, his disciples asked him privately, Why could not we cast him out?

29 And he said unto them, This kind can come forth by nothing, but by prayer and fasting.

IN FOCUS

Spiritual immaturity, a propensity for the fantastic, persons with charm and charisma coupled with persons desperate for signs from God, or those in need of physical or emotional healings—these are the ingredients which can create an atmosphere of spiritual deception for those in desperate need of a miracle.

While watching an investigative type TV program, the host caught my undivided attention when he announced that the featured story would be about "faith healers." The story was about television evangelists who sensationalize their "healing ministry" with demonstrations of choreographed spiritual slaying and supernatural healing.

In one case they presented a particular "faith healer" after 25 years of ministry, and through overly dramatized theatrics and emotional crusades, he was only able to *take pain away* which led his admirers to believe that they had been truly healed.

These healings included conditions of asthma, arthritis, multiple sclerosis, fibromyalgia, blood and heart conditions. The difficulty was that the healing almost never included the type of physical healing as those described in the Bible. The program's host commented that these television evangelists do not call paraplegics, those who suffer from terrible burns, those who are crippled or stroke victims on stage or in front of the auditorium to either testify of their healing, nor are there genuine demonstrations of these healings taking place.

A family brought their son to be prayed for after having been in a serious car accident resulting in paralysis and a diminished mental capacity. The "faith healer" proclaimed that their son was healed and that the parent's faith, coupled with a generous donation, would result in their son experiencing a full and miraculous recovery over time. Their son died shortly thereafter. When interviewed they had convinced themselves that their son's untimely death and non-recovery was because of some insufficiency in their faith and not the inability of the "faith healer" to produce what was promised.

Surrounded by an audience hungry for signs and wonders, an ability to mesmerize with music, lighting, and oration, a need for the fantastic, and an ego thirsty for praise can lead the most seasoned "faith healer" down the road of spiritual immaturity. With the focus taken off God and placed on one's self, some well-meaning genuine "faith healers" have left the carcasses of innocent miracle seekers in their path as they seek glory, wealth, and fame.

THE PEOPLE, PLACES AND TIMES

The Times. Jesus had returned from the mountain where God had affirmed Him. At the bottom of the mountain He encountered a crowd. It seems that some scribes and the rest of His disciples had been engaged in a frantic verbal confrontation.

Scribes. Men who acted not only as copyists but also as editors, interpreters, and expert scholars of the Law.

Fasting. Abstention from food and often also from drink for a longer than usual period.

BACKGROUND

Jesus had been on a mountain that biblical scholars call the Mountain of Transfiguration with three of His disciples—Peter, James, and John. On this mountain it had been confirmed by the voice of God the Father that Jesus was God's beloved Son and that the disciples should listen to Him. It was also on this mountain that Elijah and Moses ministered to Jesus. Later, Jesus traveled down from the mountain of praise and preparation to the valley of pessimism and problems. At the center of the controversy were the other nine disciples.

AT-A-GLANCE

1. Spiritual Immaturity Shames
(Mark 9:14-18)
2. Spiritual Immaturity Grieves Jesus
(vv. 19-27)
3. Spiritual Immaturity Must Be
Dealt With (v. 28)
4. Spiritual Immaturity Can Be
Transformed (v. 29)

IN DEPTH

1. Spiritual Immaturity Shames (Mark 9:14-18)
Jesus came down from a mountain peak expe-

rience of illumination and spiritual saturation to a valley of confusion and confrontation. He noticed that a crowd had gathered around the nine disciples left at the foot of the mountain. To His dismay there were some scribes in the crowd. From that moment, Jesus seemed to have known that the disciples were in a bad situation. It seemed that the scribes had succeeded in shaming the disciples in front of a large crowd of people. The humiliation stemmed from a religious confrontation between these two groups. The disciples' inability to heal a boy with a lunatic spirit seemed to have exacerbated the situation. The disciples probably felt that healing the man's son was a winnable challenge. After all, they had cast out demons before.

Not only were they losing the debate, but to add insult to injury, the man's son began to act out. The scribes probably used this man's situation and the disciples' failed attempt at healing the boy as an opportunity to entice the crowd and build opposition against Jesus. Using their failure as ammunition against Jesus made the situation for the disciples even more embarrassing. More humiliation ensued when the excited crowd joined the ridiculing of their failed efforts.

2. Spiritual Immaturity Grieves Jesus (9:19-27)

The faithlessness of the people gathered there seemed to have upset Jesus. He had performed many miracles in that region and yet their faith seemed to be non-existent. To make matters worse, it seemed that the disciples' lack of faith was somehow intertwined with the people's lack of faith. In the last few months the disciples had personally witnessed Jesus feeding over four thousand people with only a few small fish and seven loaves of bread (8:1-9). They witnessed the healing of a deaf and dumb man (7:31-37) and the healing of a blind man (8:22-26). Jesus seemed to have become exhausted with the shakiness of their sometimes up, sometimes down, sometimes level-with-the-ground faith.

In the midst of all the confusion, a father's pleas for his demonized son were ignored. The scribes' taunting of the disciples, the disciples' inconsistent spiritual life, and the crowd's fickle reasoning set Jesus' temper ablaze. He repri-

manded the entire generation for their unbelief. This reprimand is comparable to His reprimand of another religious situation in which those who sought refuge in the practice of the Law degraded the plight of the needy (12:38-40).

3. Spiritual Immaturity Must Be Dealt With (v. 28)

The father acknowledged his immature faith right away (9:24). The disciples, on the other hand, must be dealt with in private. They had suffered enough humiliation and embarrassment already. The scribes never acknowledged their part in the faithless generation. As at other times when Jesus began to reprimand them, their silence was astoundingly deafening (Matthew 23:13-33; Mark 12:34).

When the disciples were alone with Jesus, they wanted to know what happened. Why were they not able to heal the man's son? Jesus had given them power to heal, cast out demons, and basically do what they had seen Him do (3:14-15; Luke 9:1; 10:17). Their religious confrontation had put them in a precarious situation and seems to have made them lose their focus, their concentration, and for the moment, cost them their religious authority.

4. Spiritual Immaturity Can Be Transformed (v. 29)

Jesus needed His disciples to understand how to develop and maintain spiritual maturity. They needed to learn how to be consistent in exercising their faith. The extreme fluctuation in their faith was creating costly and unnecessary failure at the expense of the needy. They had to learn how to sustain their faith, especially when the arrest, trial, and crucifixion of Jesus loomed just over the horizon.

Immaturity can be overcome by first seeking spiritual power. The disciples needed to understand why they had failed, and they sought spiritual direction from Jesus. Second, it can be overcome by prayer and fasting. The statement by Jesus—"This kind can come forth by nothing, but by prayer and fasting"—highlights the fact that the disciples were not living close enough to God. They were not praying and fasting enough nor taking the time needed to prepare for the ministry needs they would encounter. They needed to follow Jesus' teachings concerning prayer (Matthew 5:44; 6:6, 9; 21:22; 26:41; Luke 18:1) and Jesus' example as a man of prayer. We read that on many occasions Jesus went off alone to pray (Luke 3:21; 5:16; 6:12; 9:18, 28; 11:1 and 22:41-44). Following Jesus' example and teachings would have given them the kind of spiritual stamina enjoyed by Christians who are mature in their faith.

SEARCH THE SCRIPTURES

1. What was happening at the foot of the mountain? (v. 14)

2. What was the father's problem? (v. 17)

3. What was the boy's problem? (v. 18)

4. What did Jesus do about the boy's problem? (v. 25)

5. What did the disciples ask Jesus privately? (v. 28)

DISCUSS THE MEANING

At the center of the religious confrontation between the disciples and the scribes is a father whose son is extremely ill. The situation is so out of control that a young man's illness is ignored because of the exaggeration of tempers and religious posturing.

Jesus appears and is confounded to see the men He has been mentoring in such a quandary. Not only did a crowd immediately swarm to Jesus, but He is unable to receive a private briefing by His mentees. Put on the spot, coupled with the blatant cries of a desperate father, Jesus decides to heal the terminally ill young man.

In addition, Jesus encourages the father, who is desperate and honest enough to confess his lack of faith. Jesus simultaneously chastises the scribes for their taunting of what appeared to be the crippled faith and inability of the disciples to perform a healing on demand. Jesus then privately reprimands and explains to His disciples what they lacked in order to perform this type of healing.

1. What was the father's situation in the story?

2. Which disciples were a part of the failed healing?

3. What was the crowd's faith issue?

4. With whom was Jesus upset and why?

5. How would fasting and prayer have helped the disciples in building their faith?

LESSON IN OUR SOCIETY

When persons who have been blessed with "spiritual gifts," which manifest themselves in dramatic ways, lose sight of the Giver of the gift, the one to whom the gift has been bestowed can cause the gift to become ineffective. To maintain the power which comes with the gift, the possessor of the gift must stay in constant communication and alignment with the Giver of the gift.

Imagine that you are selected to be on the board of the World Council of Churches. You and the other members have been given the task of regulating the operating procedures for television evangelists who have been labeled "faith healers." You have been asked to bring two or three recommendations with you to the next committee meeting. What would be your recommendations?

MAKE IT HAPPEN

It's a Saturday afternoon. There is a knock on your front door. You answer it and to your delight, or dismay, it's your neighbors. They have heard rumors that you belong to a church whose pastor has a reputation for being able to heal people. They have received a message from their doctor that medical science has run its course. Your neighbors believe that their only hope is a miracle.

In the coming week seek out a person who has lost his or her faith in churches or religious persons. Listen closely as they explain what happened to make them lose faith. Discuss with them what they need in order for their faith to be restored and how you can assist in that process. Remember to pray for God's guidance as you assist them in a more informed and closer walk with the Lord.

FOLLOW THE SPIRIT

What God wants me to do:

_____

_____

REMEMBER YOUR THOUGHTS

Special insights you have learned:

MORE LIGHT ON THE TEXT
Mark 9:14-29

9:14 And when he had come to his disciples, He saw a great multitude about them, and the scribes questioning with them.

The Transfiguration appears to have taken place at night, and so it was the next day when they came down from the mountain. When Jesus, along with Peter, James, and John returned to the other disciples, there were a lot of people, some of whom were scribes. The nine disciples and the scribes seemed to have been in an intense debate. It could have been over the disciples' inability to perform a healing upon demand.

The scribes (Latin *scribere*, "to write"), *grammateus* from the word *gramma* means writing, or a man of letters, or a teacher of the law. The scribes are often mentioned in the Matthew, Mark, and Luke's Gospels along with the Pharisees (Luke 5:21). Scribes were also mentioned along with the chief priests (Mark 8:31; 10:33; 11:18, 27). They were considered qualified to teach in the synagogues, and they expected honor from their pupils and others, because of their knowledge and ability to interpret of the Law of Moses.

15 And straightway all the people, when they beheld him, were greatly amazed, and running to him saluted him. 16 And he asked the scribes, What question ye with them?

Jesus' return was unexpected and therefore the disciples and the crowd were amazed. This phrase "were greatly amazed" is sometimes compared to that used of Moses as he descended from Mount Sinai (Exodus 34:29-33). This question is addressed to the scribes. Because of the verbal confrontation, it seems that the crowd's greeting toward Jesus went unnoticed. The presence of the scribes may indicate that they were sent out by the Sanhedrin in Jerusalem to gather evidence which could be used against Jesus. This would explain why the scribes were questioning the disciples, especially in Jesus' absence. This may also explain why Jesus' abrupt questioning seemed directed to everybody and particularly to the scribes.

To Jesus' question there is a noticeable absence of a reply from both the scribes and the disciples. Neither was in a position to take a stance and explain to Jesus what the debate was about. The disciples were probably too embarrassed to publicly confess their inadequacies. The scribes were probably waiting to see if the "all-knowing Jesus," as on other occasions, would tell them the issue and then offer an explanation. Or they could have been taken by surprise by Jesus' unexpected return, thus putting a halt to their tyrannical treatment of the disciples.

17 And one of the multitude answered and said, Master, I have brought unto thee my son, which hath a dumb spirit; 18 and wheresoever he taketh him, he teareth him: and he foameth, and gnasheth with his teeth, and pineth away: and I spake to thy disciples that they should cast him out; and they could not.

A person in the crowd finally speaks up and confesses that he has brought his demon-possessed son in hopes of getting help from Jesus. Instead he finds nine of Jesus' disciples whom he expected to be able to do what Jesus would have done. But they were unable to carry out his agonizing request. As Jesus' disciples, their preparation for ministry included some "on-the-job" training. Part of their preparation was Jesus' empowering them to cast out demons. They were then sent out to practice what they had seen Jesus do (Mark 3:14-15; Luke 9:1; 10:17).

Matthew adds that the boy also had a lunatic spirit (Matthew 17:15). The lunatic spirit is said to have done ten things to this boy: caused dumbness, deafness, foaming at the mouth, fits, gnashing of teeth, pining away (lifelessness, complete exhaustion), prostrations, suicidal tendencies, screaming, and lunacy or insanity. It is suggested that these symptoms indicate a major form of epilepsy. The description of the destructive energy released at unexpected intervals by the demonic spirit indicates the seriousness of the boy's condition and the desperateness of the father's search for help. "I spoke to thy disciples that they should cast him out and they could not" implies that the disciples had tried various ways of casting out the demon but were unsuccessful.

19 He answereth him, and saith, O faithless generation, how long shall I be with you? how long shall I suffer you? bring him unto me.

The statement "O faithless generation, how long shall I be with you? how long shall I suffer you?" seems also to embody not only Jesus' frustration with the people, but with the nine disciples and the scribes as well. Jesus addresses His responses to the entire generation, but His rebuke seems to be personalized and directed to the disciples. It is the disciples who had been with Him and who had many times witnessed His power.

On many occasions they had heard Jesus announce that it was the person's faith, or the faith of others, that directly contributed to the healing (Mark 2:5; 5:34; 5:36; 7:29 and Matthew 15:28). Some say that the scribes were included in Jesus' rebuke and that Jesus was frustrated at their willingness to ignore the boy's illness, the father's cry for help, and to celebrate in the impotence of the nine disciples. "Bring [the boy] to me" could have been, in part, Jesus' attempt to salvage the situation, the reputation of the disciples, and to diminish the scribes' agenda. Jesus' focus immediately turned to the father and his epileptic son's condition.

20 And they brought him unto him: and when he saw him, straightway the spirit tare him; and he fell on the ground, and wallowed foaming.

"And they brought him unto him" implies that the boy's condition was so acute that it required several persons to assist in getting him to Jesus. Upon seeing Jesus, the spirit in the boy began showing the amount of control it had over the boy. "Straightway the spirit tare him; and he fell on the ground, and wallowed foaming" signals that the boy had an epileptic attack. Epilepsy, also called seizure disorder, is a chronic brain disorder that briefly interrupts the normal electrical activity of the brain and causes seizures. It is characterized by a variety of symptoms, including uncontrolled movements of the body, disorientation or confusion, sudden fear, or loss of consciousness.

21 And he asked his father, How long is it ago since this came unto him? And he said, "Of a child." 22 And ofttimes it hath cast him into the fire, and into the waters, to destroy him: but if thou canst do any thing, have compassion on us, and help us.

In asking the father this question, Jesus is allowing the father to express some of the distress he has had to endure for the past years. Jesus does this in other instances where there had been a prolonged illness (John 5:5-9). Allowing the father to share his story also helps him articulate for the crowd the boy's full condition and the enormous request he is making of Jesus.

"And ofttimes it has cast him into the fire, and into the waters, to destroy him." This type of epilepsy can be characterized as generalized seizure, tonic clonic, grand mal, or convulsion. The whole brain is involved. It is often signaled by an involuntary scream caused by a contraction of the muscles that control breathing. As loss of consciousness sets in, the entire body is gripped by a jerking muscular contraction. The face reddens, breathing stops, and the back arches. Subsequently, alternate contractions and relaxation of the muscles throw the body into sometimes violent agitation, and the person may be subject to serious injury. After the convulsion subsides, the person is exhausted and may sleep heavily. Confusion, nausea, and sore muscles are often experienced upon awakening, and the individual may have no memory of the seizure. These attacks can be fatal.

"But if thou canst do any thing, have compassion on us, and help us." This father had a tremendous setback in his faith, having first brought his son to the disciples, who had failed to do anything for him or his son. They not only failed to heal his son, but they also were caught up in religious posturing with the scribes which further marginalized the man's desperate situation. His plea for Jesus' help also implies that he was not sure of the extent of Jesus' power to heal his son. Maybe he assumed that Jesus' power was limited as well. This could explain the father's timid request: If you can do anything, have compassion and help us. This seems to be the father's expression of his desperate need for help, not only for his son, but also for himself and his entire family.

23 Jesus said unto him, If thou canst believe, all thing are possible to him that believeth. 24 And straightway the father of the child cried out, and said with tears, Lord, I believe; help thou mine unbelief.

"If thou canst believe, all thing are possible to him that believeth." This may have been the only glimmer of hope the man had encountered for years. Jesus seems at this point attempting to build on the spark of faith the father had left, encouraging him to dig deep and find just a little more faith. Some scholars suggest that this statement in some ancient text reads, "If you can." Thus it really means that Jesus' reply to the father's statement was: The question is not whether "I" am able, but whether "you" believe.

"And straightway the father of the child cried out, and said with tears, Lord, I believe; help thou mine unbelief." This shows the depth of despair to which this father had sunk. His crying out at the slightest glimmer of hope is extremely moving for any parent who senses hope and seeks healing for a terminally ill child. "I believe; help thou mine unbelief" is the mustard seed type of

faith that Jesus requires of all who seek healing and help from Him (Matthew 17:20; Luke 17:6).

The father confesses his part as one of the persons in the unbelieving generation. He also confesses his need for help in making his faith stronger. It is important to note here that Jesus has not made necessary the faith of the son as he is incapable of making rational decisions in his present state. Therefore, Jesus relies on the faith of the person making the petition on his behalf, his father.

25 When Jesus saw that the people came running together, he rebuked the foul spirit, saying unto him, Thou dumb and deaf spirit, I charge thee, come out of him, and enter no more into him.

Here again it appears that Jesus, the father, and the boy were at a distance from the crowd, which seems to have scattered. Jesus now fulfills the promise implied when He first asked that the boy be brought to Him. "He rebuked the foul spirit."

A rebuke of the opposition is seen throughout Mark's Gospel (4:39; 8:32; 10:13). These possessing spirits are often called "unclean" in the Gospels. "Thou dumb and deaf spirit" indicates the double symptom effect of the unclean spirit. This may have been prompted by the unclean spirit's display of contempt for Jesus which exhibited itself in the severe convulsions seen in verse 20. "I charge thee, come out of him, and enter no more into him" is clearly Jesus' expression of His authority over unclean spirits.

His explicit command to "enter him no more" assures the father that his son is delivered now and will continue to be delivered. Epileptics may seem all right at times and then, without warning, can have another attack. The force of Jesus' command is that the unclean spirit is to leave once and for all.

26 And the spirit cried, and rent him sore, and came out of him: and he was as one dead; insomuch that many said, He is dead. 27 But Jesus took him by the hand, and lifted him up; and he arose.

The unclean spirit makes a last ditch effort to

retain control over the boy by throwing him into convulsions. The force of the exiting demon is so great that it tears at the very life of the boy, giving him the appearance of being dead. By now the crowd appeared. Their abrupt presence seems to be an implication that Jesus' attempt at healing the boy had failed as had that of His disciples.

Jesus completes the miracle by grasping the boy's hand and helping him to his feet. Mark emphasizes "and he arose," indicating the boy's strength had been renewed. This was uncommon after a violent epileptic attack. (See full commentary of epilepsy under vv. 21-22. After the convulsion subsides, the person is exhausted and may sleep heavily. Confusion, nausea, and sore muscles are often experienced upon awakening.)

Matthew adds that the boy was healed from that very hour, indicating the immediacy of the healing (Matthew 17:18). Luke reports the amazing effect this healing had on the crowd that was gathered (Luke 9:43). Undoubtedly the scribes were among the crowd and was also amazed at the power of Jesus. They would undoubtedly have to confess, "Jesus not only controls but He is also able to cast out unclean spirits."

28 And when he was come into the house, his disciples asked him privately, Why could not we cast him out? 29 And he said unto them, This kind can come forth by nothing, but by prayer and fasting.

Matthew and Mark provide us with a glimpse of the disciples questioning of Jesus about their lack of power. Earlier Jesus had given them power to do what He had just done (6:7, 13; Matthew 10:1). They had practiced the casting out of demons and reported their successes to Jesus (Mark 6:30). "Why could not we cast him out?" The nine disciples wanted to know why they had failed, especially since they seemed to be included in Jesus' reprimand of the "faithless generation." Somehow they seemed to have ignored that "their faith" was at issue.

Since they assumed it was not their faith that made them incapable of healing the boy, it must have been something else. "This kind can come forth by nothing, but by prayer and fasting." This response of Jesus seemed to be yet another of

Jesus' explanations that went right over the disciple's head. Fasting and prayer empowers faith to do the kind of work Jesus was expecting of them. Even the Pharisees accused Jesus' disciples of not fasting (Mark 2:18, 20). They could not have mistaken their need for prayer because Jesus was their example. It seems that before performing miracles Jesus had just either returned from praying (Mark 1:35-39; 6:45-46; Luke 9:28-36) or prayed out loud in the midst of performing some miracles (Mark 6:41; 7:34).

The disciples' emphases had been on the confrontation with the scribes. This religious confrontation between these two groups, both of whom professed to be God's representatives, had neglected the needs of the father and his son. Their focus on each other is a clear example of how religions groups can be misguided and spend precious time fighting each other while losing sight of the needs of the world.

DAILY BIBLE READINGS

M: They Could Not Cast It Out
Mark 9:14-18

T: Help My Unbelief
Mark 9:19-27

W: This Kind Comes Out through Prayer
Mark 9:28-32

T: Do You Now Believe?
John 16:25-33

F: Jesus Prays for Future Believers
John 17:20-24

S: One Healed Leper Returns
Luke 17:11-19

S: Whoever Believes Has Eternal Life
John 6:43-48

TEACHING TIPS

May 25
Bible Study Guide 13

1. Words You Should Know

A. In thy glory (Mark 10:37)—This phrase refers to the kingdom of God. Today's English Version translates the phrase "your throne in the glorious kingdom."

B. Cup and Baptism (vv. 38-39)—The "cup" is a symbol of Jesus' suffering; the "baptism" is a symbol of Jesus' death and resurrection.

C. Gentiles (v. 42)—Persons who are not Jews by birth or religion.

D. Minister (vv. 43-45)—Servant or slave.

E. Ransom for many (v. 45)—Some see this phrase as the basis for Paul's doctrine of the atonement. Others see it as expressed in the *Interpreter's Bible*, (vol. 7, 1967, p. 818): ". . . To Jesus His death was not an accident, not a tragedy, but an offering from which [people] would receive great blessings."

2. Teacher Preparation

A. Read Mark chapter 10 in a modern translation (NIV, TEV, NKJV).

B. Read *William Barclay's Commentary* on Mark 10:32-52 in his *Daily Study Bible* (Philadelphia: Westminster Press).

C. Also read Matthew and Luke's account of the FOCAL VERSES.

D. Be sure to write out your answers to the SEARCH THE SCRIPTURES and DISCUSS THE MEANING questions.

3. Starting the Lesson

A. Before the students arrive, write the title of the lesson and the AT-A-GLANCE outline on the board.

B. As the on-time students are arriving, ask them to answer the SEARCH THE SCRIPTURES questions.

C. After most of the students have finished the questions, ask for praise reports and prayer requests.

D. Read the LESSON AIM in unison and ask one or several of the students to lead the class in prayer. The LESSON AIM should be included in the prayer time.

4. Getting into the Lesson

A. Divide the students into groups. Ask one group to think of definitions for the WORDS YOU SHOULD KNOW, a second group to read THE PEOPLE, PLACES AND TIMES, and a third group to read the lesson BACKGROUND.

B. After a few minutes, ask each group to report to the whole group.

C. Now using the AT-A-GLANCE outline on the board, lead the students through the two stories in today's lesson.

5. Relating the Lesson to Life

A. Direct the students' attention to the LESSON IN OUR SOCIETY section and encourage discussion.

B. Review and discuss the DISCUSS THE MEANING questions. Help the students to see how the lesson applies to their own life.

6. Arousing Action

A. Direct the students to the MAKE IT HAPPEN section and challenge them to put the suggestion into practice during this week.

B. Encourage them to read the DAILY BIBLE READINGS.

C. Close the class session with prayer.

WORSHIP GUIDE

For the Superintendent or Teacher
Theme: Exercising Our Faith
Theme Song: "Have Faith in God"
Scripture: Hebrews 11:1-6
Song: "My Faith Looks Up to Thee"
Meditation: Thank You, dear Lord, for the gift of faith. Help us to exercise our faith in You for the things we need and want and in our ministry to others.

FAITH AND SIGHT

Bible Background • MARK 10:32-52
Printed Text: • MARK 10:37-52
Devotional Reading: • JOHN 20:24-31

LESSON AIM

By the end of this lesson, students will be able to retell the stories of James and John's request for special places in Jesus' kingdom and the healing of blind Bartimaeus. They will appreciate Jesus' emphasis on humble service and faith and desire to practice service and faith in their daily lives.

KEEP IN MIND

"Jesus said unto him, Go thy way; thy faith hath made thee whole. And immediately he received his sight, and followed Jesus in the way" (Mark 10:52).

FOCAL VERSES

Mark 10:37 They said unto him, Grant unto us that we may sit, one on thy right hand, and the other on thy left hand, in thy glory.

38 But Jesus said unto them, Ye know not what ye ask: can ye drink of the cup that I drink of? and be baptized with the baptism that I am baptized with?

39 And they said unto him, We can. And Jesus said unto them, Ye shall indeed drink of the cup that I drink of; and with the baptism that I am baptized withal ye shall be baptized:

40 But to sit on my right hand and on my left hand is not mine to give; but it shall be given to them for whom it is prepared.

41 And when the ten heard it, they began to be much displeased with James and John.

42 But Jesus called them to him, and saith unto them, Ye know that they which are accounted to rule over the Gentiles exercise lordship over them;

LESSON OVERVIEW

LESSON AIM
KEEP IN MIND
FOCAL VERSES
IN FOCUS
THE PEOPLE, PLACES, AND TIMES
BACKGROUND
AT-A-GLANCE
IN DEPTH
SEARCH THE SCRIPTURES
DISCUSS THE MEANING
LESSON IN OUR SOCIETY
MAKE IT HAPPEN
FOLLOW THE SPIRIT
REMEMBER YOUR THOUGHTS
MORE LIGHT ON THE TEXT
DAILY BIBLE READINGS

and their great ones exercise authority upon them.

43 But so shall it not be among you: but whosoever will be great among you, shall be your minister:

44 And whosoever of you will be the chiefest, shall be servant of all.

45 For even the Son of man came not to be ministered unto, but to minister, and to give his life a ransom for many.

46 And they came to Jericho: and as he went out of Jericho with his disciples and a great number of people, blind Bartimaeus, the son of Timaeus, sat by the highway side begging.

47 And when he heard that it was Jesus of Nazareth, he began to cry out, and say, Jesus, thou son of David, have mercy on me.

48 And many charged him that he should hold his peace. but he cried the more a great deal, Thou son of David, have mercy on me.

49 And Jesus stood still, and commanded him to be called. And they call the blind man, saying unto him, Be of good comfort, rise; he calleth thee.

50 And he, casting away his garment, rose, and came to Jesus.

51 And Jesus answered and said unto him, What wilt thou that I should do unto thee? The blind man said unto him, Lord, that I might receive my sight.

52 And Jesus said unto him, Go thy way; thy faith hath made thee whole. And immediately he received his sight, and followed Jesus in the way.

MAY
25TH

IN FOCUS

Mother Teresa, Albert Schweitzer, Jimmy Carter, Mary McLeod Bethune, George Washington Carver, and Martin Luther King, Jr. What do these people have in common? They're *not* all Black or White, dead or alive, Americans or foreigners, but they are all persons of faith who can accurately be described as humble servants. They have enhanced people's quality of life. Isn't that what Jesus taught and did in our stories for today?

In almost every page of Mark's Gospel account, Jesus is preaching the Good News, healing somebody, casting out demons, teaching somebody, or suffering and dying to save somebody. His whole life was spent going "about doing good" (Acts 10:38).

The focus of the two stories in today's lesson is on Jesus' teaching His disciples and healing a blind man who exercised persistent faith. These two stories are important to us because these are two lessons that we can absorb and put into practice.

THE PEOPLE, PLACES, AND TIMES

Jesus. He is called five different names. The disciples called Him "Master" (v. 35), meaning Rabbi or teacher. The crowd called Him "Jesus of Nazareth" (v. 47), recognizing His humanity and the city of His birth. Bartimaeus called Him "Son of David" (vv. 47-48), recognizing His Jewish heritage and perhaps His royal lineage. Mark, as narrator, refers to Him simply as "Jesus" (vv. 38, 42, 49, 51-52).

Jesus refers to Himself as the Son of Man (v. 45), which emphasizes His role as our representative, redeemer, servant, and example.

James and John. Both are sons of Zebedee, perhaps co-owners with their father of a fishing business that was prosperous enough to have hired servants (1:19-20). Jesus called them "Sons of thunder" probably because of their stormy tempers (Luke 9:49-56). Along with Peter, they were Jesus' inner-circle of three.

Bartimaeus. His "real" name is not known. Mark (10:46) refers him to as the son of Timaeus, his father. He is outstanding because of his persistent faith and because in Mark he is the last person Jesus healed.

Jericho. A city about fifteen miles from Jerusalem. It was the home of 20,000 priests who served the temple in Jerusalem (William Barclay, *The Gospel of Mark*, Daily Bible Study Series, Philadelphia: Westminster, p. 260). It is perhaps most famous as the city where Joshua fought his battle and "the walls came tumbling down" (Joshua 6:20).

BACKGROUND

In our lesson Jesus is closing the second phase of His ministry. He is on His way to Jerusalem where, as He has prophesied, He will be condemned by His own people and then handed over to the Roman authorities who will treat Him cruelly and crucify Him. However, Jesus assured His disciples that His death was not His final destiny and that on the third day He would be resurrected (Mark 10:33-34).

How does it feel to have done so much good, to help so many people, and then to face such a cruel death and such a glorious resurrection? Only Jesus knows.

AT-A-GLANCE

1. Jesus Teaches about Ministry (Mark 10:37-45)
2. Bartimaus Teaches about Faith (vv. 46-52)

IN DEPTH

Just as Socrates and Plato, Booker T. Washington and W.E.B. Dubois, Maria Montessori, and Mary McLeod Bethune were teachers, there are two teachers in our lesson today. Jesus is an intentional teacher who used the questions raised by His disciples to teach them some lessons that they didn't especially want to learn. The other teacher is Bartimaeus, an unintentional teacher who taught those around him some lessons they did not expect to learn—especially from a blind beggar. If we read carefully, it would be surprising if we couldn't learn something of tremendous value from both of these teachers.

1. Jesus Teaches about Ministry
(Mark 10:37-45)

James and John must have been surprised and chagrined at the way things turned out. It seems they came to Jesus trying to play a little patronage game. They got Jesus off by Himself and said in effect, "Jesus, you the man. We know you just finished talking about suffering and dying, but we believe you're really a king, and one day you're going to be crowned as king. When you do, we want to be your Vice President and Secretary of State" (10:37).

The Challenge of Ministry—Jesus looked them straight in their faces and said, "You brothers don't know what you're asking for. Can you drink the cup of suffering? Can you go through the deep, icy waters of the baptism of death?"

They looked right back at Jesus and said, "We can" (10:38-39). Wow, the confident ignorance of youth.

Jesus didn't blink but stayed in their faces and said prophetically, "You shall." Luke tells us in the Book of Acts (12:2) that James fulfilled Jesus' prophecy, and church tradition tells us that John lived a long time but might have also suffered martyrdom.

Jesus went on to say, "But to sit at my right or left is not for me to grant. These places belong to those for whom they have been prepared" (10:40, NIV). These were not the words James and John wanted to hear. But had they reflected a bit, they might have concluded that if God had prepared places for others, God had also prepared places for them. Jesus could have made those additional facts clear to them, but He wanted to give them the challenge of ministry, which is "no cross, no crown."

The Contrast of Ministry—The conversation did not end with Jesus' prophecy because by this time the word was out that James and John were trying to pull a fast one. The other disciples were HOT. So Jesus called a special meeting of all the disciples. He gave them a brief lecture on the contrast between Christian leadership and secular leadership. He reminded the disciples that in the political arena, leaders used the authority of their office to make their subordinates serve them and their purposes. But as Christian lead-

ers, He said, "You are to use your authority to serve those who can benefit from your gifts, talents, resources, and positions of power" (paraphrased) "If one of you wants to be great, he must be the servant of the rest; and if one of you wants to be first, he must be the slave of all" (10:43-44, TEV).

The disciples were probably not happy, but they shouldn't have been surprised. Jesus was always doing that, wasn't He—making the last first, the strong serve the weak, and the rich serve the poor? Jesus insisted on teaching by contrast.

The Example of Ministry—Jesus closed His lesson on ministry by referring to His own ministry of commitment. He said even the Son of Man did not come to this planet to be waited on hand and foot, to be catered to, and carried from place to place. "For even the Son of Man did not come to be served, but to serve, and to give his life as a ransom to many" (Mark 10:45, NIV).

2. Bartimaeus Teaches About Faith (vv. 46-52)

We don't know whether or not Brother Bart was expecting Jesus, or whether he just happened to be in the right place at the right time to exercise his faith. It seems almost obvious that he knew who Jesus was and had probably heard about His healing powers. Had the news of Jesus' encounter with Zaccheus reached his ears (Luke 19:1-10), or had the news of the healing of the daughter of Sister Crumbs drifted down from Tyre (Mark 7:24-30), or perhaps the healing of the deaf and dumb man from Ten Towns? (7:31-37) How could he not hear about the unusual healing of the blind man of Bethsaida? (8:22-26)

Faith Uses Available Resources—In any case, when Brother Bart heard that it was Jesus of Nazareth who was passing by, he used his available resources to get his healing. He couldn't see, but he could hear. So he used his ears. He couldn't see, but he could think. So he used his brain to recall Jesus' reputation. He couldn't see, but he could use his voice. So he hollered, screaming, "Jesus, Son of David, have mercy on me" (10:47).

Faith Ignores Objections—Some people in the crowd started saying, "Shhh—be quiet, be cool." But Brother Bart wouldn't be quiet, primarily because he knew that the people who were shushing him could afford to be quiet because they could see! So he turned up the volume and kept turning it up until Jesus heard him and called him.

Faith Makes Specific Requests—Notice Jesus asked Brother Bart the same question that He asked the Zebedee Brothers, "What do you want me to do for you?" (vv. 36, 51) Brother Bart didn't hem and haw; he said immediately, "I want to see again." Actually this was Bart's second request. His first request was for mercy (v. 48). Now that his cry for mercy had caught Jesus' attention, he proceeded to ask for healing. Is there a lesson here? Do you want to get Jesus' attention? Don't scream about your virtues, your talents, your resources and assets. Ask Him for mercy. If He gives you mercy, as He certainly will, He will surely give you everything that goes along with it.

Faith Follows Jesus—The little phrase that Mark put at the end of the story is so precious: "[Bartimaeus] followed Jesus on the road" (v. 52, TEV). An unknown poet has written: "Many there be who worship at [Jesus'] shrine, but few there be who follow in His steps."

Oh, I wish we knew more about Brother Bart. Did he follow Jesus the 15 miles into Jerusalem? Was he one of those shouting, "Hosanna in the highest" during the triumphal entry? (11:10) Was he at the cross? Was he in the Upper Room when the Spirit "fell?" We don't know. All Mark tells us is that "he followed." Are you willing to follow Jesus? How far?

SEARCH THE SCRIPTURES

1. What was Jesus' destination in today's lesson? (Mark 10:32-33)

2. What was the request of James and John? (v. 37)

3. What did Jesus say His two purposes were in coming to this planet? (v. 45)

4. What were Bartimaeus' two requests? (vv. 47-48, 51)

5. What was Bartimaeus' response when he received his sight? (v. 52)

DISCUSS THE MEANING

1. The disciples had been with Jesus about three years. Should they have been able to under-

stand His purpose in going to Jerusalem? (10:33-34)

2. If you were elected to a high office in your church, list three or four things you would do to show your commitment to Jesus' leadership style as expressed in Mark 10:42-45.

LESSON IN OUR SOCIETY

Imagine that you have been elected president of a large company like Ebony Magazine or Motown Records, or a government agency like the FBI or the IRS, or Bishop of the African Methodist Episcopal Church (AME) or the Church of God in Christ (COGIC). List two or three problems you would have in practicing Jesus' leadership style as outlined in Mark 10:42-45. Would Jesus' leadership style work? If not, why not? If so, how?

MAKE IT HAPPEN

You either are or will be a Christian leader. As a preparation project this week, go to the library or Christian bookstore and select and read a good book on servant leadership.

FOLLOW THE SPIRIT

What God wants me to do:

_____

_____

REMEMBER YOUR THOUGHTS

Special insights you have learned:

_____

_____

MORE LIGHT ON THE TEXT
Mark 10:32-52

The two stories in our text are a part of Jesus' journey from Galilee where, according to Mark He spent most of His ministerial life, to Jerusalem where His earthly ministry and life ended.

32 And they were in the way going up to Jerusalem; and Jesus went before them: and they were amazed; and as they followed, they were afraid. And he took again the twelve, and began to tell them what things should happen unto him, 33 Saying, Behold, we go up to Jerusalem; and the

look." They wanted to catch up to Him and say something encouraging or ask what's wrong? But "those who followed were afraid: (10:32, NIV).

When Jesus sensed their terror, He slowed His pace, let them catch up with Him, and "took again twelve" or called a conference to explain His strange actions. He had done this before (8:31; 9:31), but now He had to do it again. He got right to the point, "Look," He said, "we are on our way to Jerusalem. There the religious leaders—the chief priests and the scribes—are going to

Son of man shall be delivered unto the chief priests, and unto the scribes; and they shall condemn him to death, and shall deliver him to the Gentiles: 34 And they shall mock him, and shall scourge him, and shall spit upon him, and shall kill him: and the third day he shall rise again.

In the verses above, we have moved the text back to verse 32. There Mark writes that they were in the "way going up to Jerusalem." In other words, Jesus and His disciples were on the main road that went through Jericho and on to Jerusalem. The word "up" describes the fact that when David chose a spot on which to establish his capital city, He chose a high spot. Jerusalem was sometimes, especially in the Old Testament, referred to as Mount Zion (2 Samuel 5:7), and some of the Psalms (120—134) were sung by pilgrims as they ascended the long steep road that led up to their holy city.

As they were walking along the road, it seems that Jesus stepped up His pace and strode ahead of the Twelve. His look of determination, deep sorrow, and loneliness frightened the disciples. We might say that Jesus had on His face a "death

condemn me as a criminal and turn me over to the Roman authorities (the Gentiles). The Roman soldiers are going to make fun of me, beat me (tear my flesh with leather straps inserted with bits of bone or metal), spit on me, and hang me on a cross until I'm dead. And on the third day I will rise again."

Before, Jesus had told them of His rejection by the Jewish leaders, His death, and resurrection (8:31; 9:31). This time He added the details of His suffering, that He would be made fun of, beaten, and spat on. Mark just lets Jesus' words stand there in all their stark nakedness, without further comment. Luke provides a transition by telling His readers that "the disciples did not understand any of this. Its meaning was hidden from them, and they did not know what he was talking about" (Luke 18:34, NIV).

10:35 And James and John, the sons of Zeedee, come unto him, saying, Master, we would that thou shouldest do for us whatsoever we shall desire. 36 And he said unto them, What would ye that I should do for you? 37 They said unto him.

Grant unto us that we may sit, one on thy right hand, and the other on thy left hand, in thy glory.

We do not find the disciples' lack of understanding hard to believe in light of the next actions of James and John. In Mark's account, it seems that the request for a favor from Jesus immediately follows Jesus' statement about His suffering, death, and resurrection. Can this be so? Is it inconceivable that even the sons of thunder could be that insensitive? Maybe Jesus closed the conference with prayer and sent the disciples off to think about what He had said. Then while everybody else was off in little groups and Jesus was by Himself, the Zebedee Brothers came to Jesus and made their requests.

They said, "When you sit on your throne in the glorious kingdom, we want you to let us sit with you, one at your right and one at your left" (v. 37, TEV). James and John have often been accused of wanting positions of power. We really don't know why they wanted to be so close to Jesus. Did they want positions of privilege and power, or just positions of identification with Jesus? Or did they simply want to be constantly in Jesus' presence?

10:38 But Jesus said unto them, Ye know not what ye ask: can ye drink of the cup that I drink of? and be baptized of with the baptism that I am baptized with? 39 And they said unto him, We can. And Jesus said unto them, Ye shall indeed drink of the cup that I drink of; and with the baptism that I am baptized withal shall ye be baptized:

Whatever their motive, Jesus introduced the matter of price. Jesus asked in effect, "Do you know how much it costs to be that close to me? Are you willing to pay the same price that I have to pay to sit in the center seat? Can you drink from the cup of suffering and go through the baptism of death?"

"We can" (v. 39). Didn't they answer too soon? They didn't ask, "What is the cup or the baptism?" In their youthful enthusiasm, confidence, and ignorance, they said, "Whatever it is, we can do it." Jesus should have slapped them with words of reality, "Look, don't make any such commitments. You don't know what the future holds. Slow down, find a quiet place and do some serious thinking and come back when you grow up

and learn some sense!" No, Jesus just looked at them and affirmed, "You will drink the cup and experience the baptism. You will share my suffering and death experiences."

40 But to sit on my right hand and on my left hand is not mine to give; but it shall be given to them for whom it is prepared.

Jesus said in effect: "Yes, I will occupy the center seat because it is my seat. But I cannot determine who will sit in the seat to my right and left. The One who planned that I sit in the center seat (Philippians 2:9-11) has also determined who will sit in the other seats."

41 And when the ten heard of it, they began to be much displeased with James and John.

The ten were mad, upset, angry when they heard that the Zebedee brothers were trying to pull a fast one on the rest of the group. They were so filled with resentment that Jesus had to call another quick conference to avoid an emotional explosion and maybe a fistfight. Remember that Peter was one of the ten. Peter was considered a rebel and later cut off a man's ear (John 18:10).

42 But Jesus called them to him, and saith unto them, Ye know that they which are accounted to rule over the Gentiles exercise lordship over them; and their great ones exercise authority upon them.

Jesus said, "Look, brothers, you are not Gentiles, so don't act like it." Gentile leaders "have power over the people." The test of non-Christian leadership is how much control they have over how many people. How many people serve them and obey them. How many people are at their beck and call. How many jump when they say jump and ask how high on the way up? How many people can they hire and fire. How many resources do they control? Jesus tried to impress on the disciples that non-kingdom leadership has to do with power, authority, and control.

43 But so shall it not be among you: but whosoever will be great among you, shall be your minister. 44 And whosoever of you will be the chiefest, shall be servant of all.

"Leadership in my kingdom," Jesus said, "operates on another principle, the opposite principle of the Gentiles. It's not how many people you can control, but how much service you can give." President John F. Kennedy stated this principle and challenged his generation: "Ask not what your country can do for you, but what you can do for your country."

That is the attitude of Christian heroes and she-roes like Dr. Martin Luther King, Jr. and Mother Teresa and millions of pastors, Sunday School teachers, deacons, youth leaders, stewards, missionaries, and other church and community leaders. Without these persons and others who serve humanity, many churches, hospitals, schools, libraries and community volunteer organizations would cease to exist; much of the world, as we know it, would grind to a halt. Jesus emphasized that in the Christian community of faith and love, greatness is determined by service and the person whose ambition it is to be greater than everybody else must serve everybody else.

In a sermon called "the Drum-Major Instinct" Dr. King said that Jesus did not condemn James and John for wanting to be great. In fact, Dr. King said, "The desire for greatness is a part of the normal human instinct—the desire to be out front, to be first, to be a drum major." Jesus encouraged greatness based not on power but service. King said that in this way Jesus put greatness within everybody's reach because everybody can serve.

45 For even the Son of man came not to be ministered unto but to minister and to give his life a ransom for many.

Jesus closed His conference with the disciples by using Himself as an example of humble service. In Mark, Jesus usually referred to Himself as the "Son of man." Scholars have not been able to agree on the exact meaning of this title, but it certainly emphasizes Jesus' humanity and presents him as a representative of humanity. And when we look at the title as used by Daniel and Ezekiel, it does not help us to be definitive in a dogmatic sense. But we do know that Jesus is saying in simple but profound terms that I, as humanity's chief representative, did not come to have people serve me but to be a servant to people. The inference is

that Jesus is the Christian disciple's example.

46 And they came to Jericho; and as he went out of Jericho with his disciples and a great number of people, blind Bartimaeus, the son of Timaeus, sat by the highway side begging.

Between verses 45 and 46, there is a shift of scenes. A new story begins. It centers around an exciting incident near Jericho. To discover what was so exciting, you need to read Luke's story of Zacchaeus (19:1-10). There you'll find that a despised little tax collector's life was radically changed by the power of Jesus' love. That was *inside* of Jericho. Mark tells us what happened on Jesus' *way out* of Jericho. Another man's life was radically changed. Jesus is still in the business of changing people's lives radically. If yours has not been changed, right now can be your Jericho.

47 And when he heard that it was Jesus of Nazareth, he began to cry out, and say, thou son of David have mercy on me.

In a sense Bartimaeus' blindness is a metaphor that can be applied to all of Chapter 10. In the discussion of divorce in 10:1-12, the Pharisees and the disciples were blind to God's view of the importance of the family. In 10:13-16, the disciples were blind to the significance of children; in 10:17-31, Richard, the man we call the rich, young ruler and the disciples were blind to the importance of the kingdom; and in 10:32-34 the disciples were blind to the meaning of Jesus' suffering, death, and resurrection (see Luke 18:34). Immediately before Brother Bartimaeus's story, the disciples again display their blindness in their desire for supremacy in the kingdom of God (Mark 10:35-45). So the story of Bartimaeus's blindness is a fitting close to this whole chapter on blindness.

48 And many charged him that he should hold his peace: but he cried the more a great deal; thou Son of David have mercy on me.

The crowd is also a part of the metaphor, isn't it? By their questions (vv. 10, 26, 35) and actions (vv. 13, 32), weren't the disciples, like Bartimaeus, crying out for the light of understanding? And wasn't Jesus by His answers trying to cure their blindness? From this chapter, it would seem that spiritual blindness is more difficult to cure than physical blindness. In spite of the opposition of the crowd, Bartimaeus refused to stay blind.

49 And Jesus stood still, and commanded him to be called. And they call the blind man, saying unto him, Be of good comfort, rise; he calleth thee.

Bible students do not have to read the rest of the story to know what happened. Whenever anybody calls on the Lord for mercy, we know how the story will end. If we come to the Lord in jest or in boast, the answer to our request is very uncertain, but when we come confessing and sincerely asking for mercy, we are certain that our prayers will be answered (1 John 1:9). We know that the Lord will have mercy and will abundantly pardon (Isaiah 55:7).

In a sense, we might say that one measure of a person is what it takes to call him or her to attention. What does it take to stop you? What does it take to stop your schedule? Your routine? The pursuit of your legitimate goals and priorities? Who can call you to attention? Your wife? Your children? Your banker? Your boss? The IRS? How about a bunch of little children? (Mark 10:13) Or a confused young person? (vv. 17-22) A street beggar? (v. 47) A hungry person? A homeless person? A sick person or a prisoner? (Matthew 25:34, 44-45)

Notice also how quickly the crowd changed its tune when Jesus showed Bart some attention. All of a sudden they soften their tone from "Shut up!" to "Be encouraged!" (Mark 10:49)

50 And he, casting away his garment, rose, and came to Jesus.

Why did he cast away or throw off his garment? There's been much speculation, but the scholars seem not to know. They don't even know why Mark included that phrase in his account. But the important action here is that Bart not only knew whom to call on but he also knew who to go to. He went straight to Jesus.

51 And Jesus answered and said unto him, What wilt thou that I should do unto thee? The blind man said unto him, Lord, that I might receive my sight.

Jesus is such a gentlemen, isn't He? "Now that you're here brother, what do you want?" Bart not only knew the right person, he knew the right answer. "Lord, I want to see."

52 And Jesus said unto him, Go thy way; thy faith hath made thee whole. And immediately he received his sight, and followed Jesus in the way.

Bartimaeus not only knew the right person, and the right answer, but he also made the right response—he received, he followed. And Luke said that he gave thanks and inspired the previously hostile crowd to praise God also (see Luke 18:43).

Have you asked and received? Then give thanks and follow.

DAILY BIBLE READINGS

M: Can You Drink the Cup?
Mark 10:32-40

T: The Great Must Become Servants
Mark 10:41-45

W: Jesus Gives Bartimaeus Sight
Mark 10:46-52

T: Believing Without Seeing
John 20:24-31

F: Abraham's Faith Did Not Weaken
Romans 4:16-22

S. Promises Seen from a Distance
Hebrews 11:8-16

S: Looking Ahead to the Reward
Hebrews 11:23-28

NOTES

NOTES

INTRODUCTION TO JUNE 2003 QUARTER

The Quarter at-a-Glance

GOD RESTORES A REMNANT

This quarter deals with the period after the return of the exiles as the different institutions of the life of the nation were renewed or reestablished in the land. During the quarter the students will study the books of Ezra, Nehemiah, Daniel, Joel, Obadiah, Haggai, Zechariah, and Malachi. Some scholars include these prophets in what is usually called the Minor Prophets. All of them had something to do with exile or the post-exilic community of Israel. Of course, Ezra and Nehemiah chronicle the leadership that came with the first group of returning exiles. Daniel deals with the life of the exiles within the land and customs of their captors. In all of the works here, except for Ezra and Nehemiah, there is a forward look to the future peace and deliverance of Israel.

Unit 1: BEGINNING THE RETURN

Unit 1 deals with the leadership of Jeshua and Zerubbabel as exiles began to return to the land. In this unit the study relates to the struggles and hopes of the newcomers, the resistance from enemies around them, and the victories of the exiles as they hear the voice of the prophets Haggai and Zechariah.

LESSON 1: June 1
Return of the Exiles
Ezra 1

The biblical content deals with the fact that the Lord stirred up the spirit of King Cyrus of Persia to have the temple at Jerusalem in Judah rebuilt (vv. 1-2). The king invited any of God's people in exile to join him in this divine endeavor; he invited them to return to Jerusalem to rebuild the temple (v. 3). God also moved the king to help the returning people by contributing material resources of

silver, gold, animals, and other goods (v. 4). Cyrus also gave the returning exiles the temple vessels that Nebuchadnezzar had taken away from Jerusalem when he captured the city (vv. 5-11).

Our theme for this lesson is Facing God-Given Opportunity. The life-concerns in this lesson deal with how we address pressure and stress. For those of us who have suffered loss of possessions, this lesson shows us that there is still the possibility of restoration in God. Though we may have been devastated by disappointment, there is still a God who keeps His appointments. This lesson calls us to stop longing for the past, but rather to face the future with God. This lesson is not meant to keep us from cherishing our family, cultural, and religious history, but to see God at work in all of these. In this lesson we learn that though some of us have been cast aside by society, God still reaches out to us. Those of us who know what it is like to live in a strange, unfamiliar place far from our original home can take heart from this lesson.

LESSON 2: June 8
Beginning to Rebuild
Ezra 3:1-3, 6-7, 10-13

This biblical passage tells us what happened when the exiles had returned to Judah. They built an altar and offered burnt offerings when they gathered in Jerusalem (vv. 1-3). The people also pulled their financial resources together to provide supplies for the building of the temple (vv. 6-7). Once the foundation of the temple was laid, the priests and Levites led the people in a celebration of praise (vv. 10-11). The celebrations caused some of the older priests, Levites, elders, and others who had seen the previous temple to weep (vv. 12-13).

The adult topic for this lesson is "Laying Foundations." One of the concerns that arises from this lesson as it relates to life is the desire to continue traditional forms of worship while reaching out to a new generation. Also arising from this lesson is the need to seek God's help to protect us

371

from physical and spiritual dangers. In this lesson we see that we all need help and sometimes we need to seek help from others even as it relates to forms of spirituality which we have developed. The lesson also calls us to remember to praise the Lord when we have achieved success and when we are frustrated in our plans.

LESSON 3: June 15
God's Message to the Exiles
Haggai 1:2-14

Our biblical content emphasizes that God sent the prophet Haggai with a message to Zerubbabel and the people. Haggai scolded the people for not finishing the work of rebuilding the temple (v. 2). This lesson shows how Haggai challenged the people to examine their lives and their motives for not completing the rebuilding project (vv. 3-6). Haggai told the people that the Lord was commanding them to continue the work (vv. 7-8). In his prophetic soundings Haggai showed the people that they were to blame for not finishing the temple (vv. 9-11). The text tells us that the people obeyed the words of the Lord spoken through Haggai (v. 12). Their obedience led Haggai to assure the people of God's presence. This assurance was the catalyst the people needed to rebuild the house (vv. 13-14).

"Getting Back on Track" is the topic of this lesson. After we have strayed from the command given to us by the Lord, how can we get back on track? The lesson raises several life-concerns appropriate to context in which we, as people of African descent, may find ourselves. In today's world, people of African descent, like other people, are looking to spiritual mentors, preachers, and all kinds of religious leaders for guidance.

So many are still more concerned about material possessions than the things of God. Many times our misprioritization leads us to seek happiness in the wrong places. The key for these times, as in any times of spiritual hunger, is to obey God's word. Even though our times are times of spiritual searching, such spiritual searches are accompanied by uncertainties that can only be assuaged by the assurance of the presence of the Lord. It is God's word and God's presence that can lead us back on track, assure us that things can be better, and encourage us to keep on the track of doing God's work. The lesson also shows how one person committed to God can encourage others to return to their appointed task.

LESSON 4: June 22
Hope for a New Era
Zechariah 8:1-13

The biblical content of this lesson is taken from the Scripture through the prophet Zechariah. God promised His people that He would again dwell in the land of Zion and in the city of Jerusalem (v. 3). In this promise God said that people of all ages would again enjoy life in Jerusalem (vv. 4-5). Zechariah said the impossible would be made possible through the Lord, who saves the people in faithfulness and righteousness, by gathering them to Jerusalem (vv. 6-8). Zechariah told the people to be strong and God would make them productive and blessed (vv. 9-12). God would also make them a blessing, not a curse, among the nations (v. 13).

The topic of this lesson is "Hope for the Future." The concern raised within this lesson is for needed reassurance. Many of us want to be productive but sometimes run into walls and need some encouragement. In our day, when many people do not know what family is anymore, there is a desire to be restored to family. This lesson addresses that issue of restoration. If you have experienced a sense of hopelessness, this lesson is meant to instill a sense of hope again into your context. This sense of hope is directed to having you recall or even re-experience the faithfulness of God. It is in this context of experiencing the faithfulness of God that we rekindle our own faithfulness. If you have been unfaithful, God gives you another opportunity to be faithful.

LESSON 5: June 29
Dedication of the Temple
Ezra 6:13-22

The key verse is Ezra 6:16. When the temple was finished, the people of Israel celebrated the dedication of the house of God with joy. The biblical content of this lesson emphasizes how the people rejoiced when they finished building the Lord's house (vv. 13-16). At the dedication of the temple, the people of Judah offered sacrifices, and the priests and Levites performed services according to the law of Moses (vv. 17-18). After the dedication of the temple, the people celebrated the Passover at the appropriate time (vv. 19-20). The returned exiles, and others who had joined them, all ate the Passover lamb and celebrated joyously the festival of unleavened bread for seven days (vv. 21-22).

The lesson topic is "Celebrating Victories." How important it is to celebrate the victories that the Lord provides for us on our way. This lesson points out the importance of such celebrations. This lesson taps into the feeling of satisfaction which accompanies feelings of accomplishment. Though many of us feel more comfortable worshiping in familiar surroundings, many of our victories come when we follow God to new territories. This lesson calls us to be aware of the meaning and symbolism of special observances and religious holidays. Are you conscious of the fact that all your accomplishments are due to God working in and through you? If so, then celebrate in thanksgiving.

UNIT 2: THE RENEWAL OF THE NATION

The theme for Unit 2 is "The Renewal of the Nation." This unit offers students the opportunity to study Ezra's and Nehemiah's effort to share a new vision with the exiles. Using the passages from the books of Ezra and Nehemiah, the lessons in this unit deal with some of the troubles and changes necessary to recreate and restore the nation.

LESSON 6: July 6
Nehemiah's Work Begins
Nehemiah 1:1-4; 2:4-5, 13, 16-18

A key verse of this lesson reads: "They replied, 'Let us start building.'" So they committed themselves to the good work (2:18, NIV). This verse introduces the biblical content that this lesson emphasizes. According to the text, Nehemiah asked about Jerusalem and its survivors. The men told Nehemiah that the people were ashamed because the wall of Jerusalem was broken down and the gates burned (1:1-3). This news prompted Nehemiah to mourn; he then prayed and fasted for days before God (v. 4). Nehemiah asked King Artaxerxes to grant him permission to return to Judah to rebuild Jerusalem (2:4-5). Nehemiah inspected the walls at night, and he did not disclose his plans to anyone (vv. 13, 16). He reported to the people what he had seen, how God had been with him, and what the king had permitted (vv. 17-18). Upon hearing Nehemiah's report, the people were ready to build and committed themselves to the task (v. 18).

Challenges confront us for the work of God today including challenges to rebuild community,

to raise up families that honor God, and to live godly lives in a world filled with ungodliness. The topic for today's lesson is "Accepting a Challenging Task." God is calling us to commit ourselves to particular tasks that can help bring divine transformation in the world. Are we up to the challenge? It is one thing to respond emotionally to bad news, but it is another to rise to the challenge with the good news of the power of God. You and I may not know where to start, but we must seek help to accomplish plans from the One with the master plan, God himself. This lesson calls us to make commitments and stop waiting for others to do it or tell us to do it. It is enough that God has given us the Word.

LESSON 7: July 13
The Wall Completed
Nehemiah 6:1-9, 15-16

"When all our enemies heard of it, all the nations around us were afraid and fell greatly in their own esteem; for they perceived that this work had been accomplished with the help of our God" (6:16). This is the focal verse on which this lesson turns. It is that heart of the biblical content which emphasizes the interaction between the people of Judah who were building the wall and those who sought to stop the wall. The text tells us that the enemies of the Jews found out that the wall of the city was built (v. 1). As a result of the enemies receiving this information, Sanballat and Geshem tried to get Nehemiah to leave the work to meet with them. Nehemiah discerned that they were trying harm him, and he would not leave (vv. 2-4). Sanballat sent a letter to Nehemiah, and he threatened to tell the king that the Jews were rebuilding the wall so they could rebel (vv. 5-7). Nehemiah recognized this as a ploy to frighten the people and make them stop work on the wall (vv. 8-9). When the wall was finished, it was a sign of God's power that made the enemy nations afraid (vv. 15-16).

We are called in this lesson to persevere in the face of persecution and ridicule when we strike out to do the will of God. The topic for today is "Persevering with Faith." This is a very appropriate life-concern for us today. This lesson reminds us that many of us will face opposition as we proceed to do the work of the Lord. Sometimes we may even feel defeated when something goes wrong. In fact, people who claim to be on our side may be our greatest hindrance and try to stop us from the good work to which God has called us. We must persevere in spite of difficulties. We are encouraged to call on God in times of difficulties and to discern the hand of God through the actions of others. Though opposition arises, know that God is present and that divine protection is available. Though the enemy rises like a flood, we must refuse to be intimidated by demonic bullies. Through it all we must persevere; we must stay our course because the Lord God who called us into this work is never going to leave us.

LESSON 8: July 20
Called to Obey the Law
Nehemiah 8:1-3, 5-6, 8-12

Nehemiah 8:8 reads, "So they read in the book, in the law of God distinctly, and gave the sense, and caused them to understand the reading." This passage of Scripture brings clarity to the way God intends for His people to combine head and heart and not separate the two. The passage on which today's lesson is founded deals with the explanation of the law in terms that could be understood by the people. The passage notes that after the returned exiles were settled in their towns, the people met in the square before the Water Gate in Jerusalem and asked Ezra to present the Law of Moses (vv. 1-2). From early morning to midday, Ezra read the Law to men and women and all who could understand it; the people listened attentively (v. 3). The people reverenced the Word of God by standing while Ezra read. When Ezra blessed the Lord, the people bowed to worship God (vv. 5-6). To help the people understand the Law, other priests helped to interpret it (v. 8). When the people heard the words, they wept; however, the leaders instructed them to rejoice because the day was holy to the Lord (vv. 9-11). The people then rejoiced when they understood the words that were declared to them. (v. 12).

The topic for this lesson is "Responding to God's Law." How do we respond to the law of the Lord? How does a people who have been separated from the Law come to respond rightly to the Law of the Lord? In our everyday life we are concerned about how to respond to situations in a godly manner. It is true that many of us take the

Word of God seriously. But that in itself does not mean that we are always clear on how to apply it in the particular contexts of our daily lives. Even the most erudite of us may once in a while need to help others to understand Scripture. Under the New Covenant, the Holy Spirit is that helper, but we still need others whom God has called to interpret the text for our gain. We must take pleasure in hearing God's Word, read and cherish God's Word, and be open conviction by the Word of God. In this way we will be able to obey and apply it in our everyday context. This lesson is meant to help us see how the Word was obeyed by God's people in the past for our own learning.

LESSON 9: July 27
Renewal of the Covenant
Nehemiah 10:28-33, 35-37

The biblical content of this lesson emphasizes that the people renewed their allegiance to God by vowing to follow the commandments of the Lord (vv. 28-29). They pledged not to intermarry and not to buy merchandise on the Sabbath or other holy days (vv. 30-31) They also committed to honor the sabbatical year (v. 31). As part of their renewal, the Jews agreed to pay for the service of the house of God (vv. 32-33). They vowed to bring the first of all they had to the house of God (vv. 35-37).

The topic for this lesson is "Renewing Spiritual Commitments." The lesson focus concerns recommitment as people attempt to follow God's commandments. One of the areas where commitment seems to rise and fall is in financial commitment to the work of God. This lesson calls us to support the work of God with resources and talents and our presence. Our commitment to follow Jesus Christ must reach beyond words to actual sacrifice. We must guard against the idea of just doing enough to get by. We must give our best effort.

UNIT 3: THE MESSAGE OF THE PROPHETS

Unit 3, "The Message of the Prophets," focuses on messages that helped the nation renew itself and that helped the people believe in a new era. The prophets Obadiah, Joel, Malachi, and Daniel reminded the exiles of past difficulties and of God's call for their lives.

LESSON 10: August 3
Edom's Condemnation
Obadiah 1-4, 10-11, 15, 21

"As you have done, it shall be done to you; your deeds shall return on your own head" (v. 15). This serves as the key to the biblical content emphasis of the lesson. In the text God spoke to Obadiah in a vision; He gave Obadiah a message of judgment on Edom (vv. 1-2). Edom's people were very prideful and felt invincible, but God would bring them down (vv. 3-4). Edom would be judged for helping the Babylonians capture Jerusalem (vv. 10-11). Obadiah said that the Lord would do to the Israelites' enemies what those enemies had done to them (v. 15) Obadiah proclaimed that the Lord reigned, and His people would reign over Edom (v. 21).

The topic "Peril of Pride" speaks to a common human life—concern. Pride lies behind many of the injustices in our world. We look at the high and mighty and the evil they inflict upon the poor and wonder whether God is concerned with correcting injustices. In fact, many who are involved in the pain of injustice do not see themselves as accountable to God. They proudly think that they control their own destiny and that neither their victims nor God will call them to account. This lesson should be an encouragement to all those who have suffered injustice. If you have experienced injustice and betrayal at the hands of the powerful, remain hopeful and know that God will call the oppressor to account. In this lesson God is telling Edom, who in pride had persecuted Israel, that she will receive the same kind of treatment she has handed out to others. So we are encouraged not to lose hope. If we remain faithful to the cause of God, there is a reward waiting for us. God will not disappoint. Those oppressors will receive their reward. Edom's problem was pride, which led them to victimize and treat others with injustice and betrayal. In this lesson, God is saying to Israel that she will not be oppressed forever. Thank God who calls oppressors to account even to the end of the ages.

LESSON 11: August 10
Call to Repentance
Joel 2:1-2, 12-14, 28-29

God's call in this lesson is a call to repentance.

As a symbol of pending judgment and darkness, God sent a plague of locusts (2:1-2). Joel told the Children of Israel that judgment could be avoided if they repented (vv. 12-14). God promised the people a day in which God's Spirit would be poured out on the people (vv. 28-29). Repentance is a life-concern to which we can all relate from children to adults. Repentance is that insight and perception of the long-term consequences of our behavior, which causes us to run to God and change our behavior. If we have been wayward, God offers us repentance as a way to make significant changes in our lifestyles. It is our way back from hopelessness, which is the result of our sin. We throw ourselves upon the righteousness of God. This is the doorway to find hope and security in faith. If we have lost our sense of God's presence because of our sins, repentance brings us back to God and opens us to experience the presence of God's Spirit again. This lesson is meant to teach the importance of repentance.

LESSON 12: August 17
A Promise to the Faithful
Malachi 3:1-4, 16-18; 4:1-3, 6

The content of this lesson tells us that God will send a messenger to prepare the way for the Lord's coming, which will be for purifying judgment (3:1-4). The Lord is aware of those who have been faithful (v. 16). The Lord counts those who have been faithful as precious possessions and will deal differently with them than with those who have been wicked (vv. 17-18). On the day of the Lord, the evildoers will be destroyed (4:1). On the day of the Lord, the faithful will be blessed and will stamp on the wicked (vv. 2-3). The Lord promises to send the prophet Elijah before the day of the Lord to restore love in the family so that God will not destroy the land (v. 6).

Today's topic is "Different Destinies." This lesson deals with the people's misconceptions about God's expectations. When we suffer at the hands of wicked people, we sometimes wonder whether God knows or cares. Many of us live in fear of what may come in the future because deep inside we aren't sure that God is in the future. Yes, we do have a "book knowledge" of God's care for the future, but we lose faith when our future seems threatened by evil. Notwithstanding, we need to remain optimistic about the future and believe all will work out in the end. The fate of the wicked may concern us as believers, but we must commit even that into the hands of God. This lesson calls us to be faithful even in the face of what may seem like evil. Those of us who are faithful are assured in God's Word of receiving unique blessings in this life and the life to come.

LESSON 13: August 24
An Eternal Reign
Daniel 2:26, 36-45

The scriptural text on which this lesson is based deals with the great dream of Nebuchadnezzar. The text tells us that after God revealed King Nebuchadnezzar's dream and its meaning to Daniel, he interpreted the dream to the king (vv. 26, 36-38). Daniel reveals that the gold, silver, bronze, and iron-clay parts of the statue in the dream symbolize four kingdoms, Nebuchadnezzar's kingdom and those that would follow (vv. 39-43). The stone that crushed the four parts of the statue in the dream symbolized the kingdom of God that would endure forever (vv. 44-45).

How do we find certainty in this uncertain world? This lesson seeks to direct us in discovering the response to this question. This lesson is therefore entitled "Certainty in an Uncertain World." In today's world many people seem concerned with foretelling the future. Some want to know the future through both scientific analysis and others by superstition. We are also aware of the fact that while some governments are more powerful than others, none are invincible. We are now aware that while some economic systems are better than others, they are flawed because they are based on human sinfulness and desire. We know that they can all fail. This causes many people anxiety. In the midst of such great shifting, which reveals the fluidity of human control, people long for a sense of security. This lesson takes us back to the place of our security, which is found in God. God is the only certainty in the midst of uncertainty. While the interest in dreams and supernatural experiences may seem spiritual, we must not allow such things to replace the Word of God or our faith in God.

LESSON 14: August 31
The End of the Days
Daniel 12:1-9

This lesson is taken from a text of Scripture in which Daniel the prophet peers into the future. It discusses the plight of those who trusted in the word of the Lord and the agony of those who refused to believe and act accordingly. In this text we read that after a time of anguish, those whose names are written in God's book will be delivered (v. 1). The dead will be raised and some will have everlasting life and some will experience everlasting contempt (v. 2). God will honor the wise who have led many to righteousness (v. 3). Before the end of time many people will seek knowledge, but evil will increase (v. 4). However, the duration of the time of anguish will be limited (vv. 5-7). Complete understanding of the end will not be realized until the end (vv. 8-9).

While many seek to understand the reasons for suffering in this world, the truth is that we do not have the answer right now. It may sound like a cliche, but "we will understand it better by and by." There are so many theories about life after death. What we know as believers is that we will be with the Lord after this life. Our task in this life is not to attempt to figure out what eternity is like, but to eagerly share our faith with others so that they will partake of the great revelation of life when we see the Lord of life, Jesus our Savior. While we must place high priority on gaining knowledge, we must remember that the knowledge of God is greater than any knowledge that we seek from this world. One type of knowledge, which according to this lesson is important, is knowing that difficult times will end. This is a knowledge that helps us to endure and remain faithful to the end.

MODES OF LEARNING

Deborah Branker Harrod

Do you remember grade school? I remember. I remember thick oak doors that looked so heavy that they would not budge. Somehow though, polished golden doorknobs made them yield to a small child's hand. I remember rooms that smelled of contraband candies, slightly sour milk and the crisp autumn air that clung to our clothes from the walk to school. I remember desks evenly spaced in neat rows, facing the blackboard as if ready for learning to commence. I remember cavernous windows that made our relatively small, somewhat cramped rooms seem larger. I remember sitting at my desk, usually in the front of the classroom. I remember peering through those windows and finding that the clarity of the sky offered me a clean slate to ponder the ideas that my teachers were introducing. I remember how it felt when a new idea started to make sense to me and become a part of my thinking.

Back then my teachers always seemed to introduce ideas by writing them on the blackboard. As a teacher wrote an idea on the board and discussed it, it was as if she wrote the idea on a slate in my head and as if my brain recorded a summary of what she was saying. I could see the words with my mind's eye and as the idea played across the TV screen of my brain, I could hear my teacher articulate the idea in my head. It was as if my brain were a VCR that had been programmed to record the images and sounds that were the focus of the day's lesson. The new idea caused me to think of other ideas that I had stored in my memory. Staring out into the clean, clear sky helped me to discover how the new idea was connected to my old ones. As my gaze fell upon the nearest window, I could see in my mind's eye both the new and the old ideas. I would enter into a dialogue with myself to determine how the old and the new were linked. I would pose questions to myself that would help me to examine the connection between old and new.

My answers to these questions would often lead to more questions and subsequently more answers until, finally, I understood how the new idea was connected to my old ideas. Pondering the link between the new and the old felt like trying to match the pieces of a puzzle that, when put together, formed a clear picture. When I had pieced together my ideas, it was clear to me that the new idea was no longer something strange and unfamiliar that stood apart from my old ideas. In fact, there ceased to be a new idea and some old ideas. Now there was a seamless body of knowledge that my mind had constructed as a result of seeing and hearing a new idea. As a child, I always absorbed ideas best when I could see and hear them. I still learn best through these modes of learning. I am a visual and an auditory learner.

Modes of learning are the unique ways in which individuals intercept new ideas that they will ponder and blend into their stores of knowledge. Specifically, we use our senses of sight, hearing, touch, smell, and taste to take in new ideas. Each of us uses these senses on a daily basis and, as a result, we learn things. Clearly, our sight allows us to take in new ideas as we glance at billboards while driving along the highway. Our hearing allows us to learn the tune to a song that a passerby hums. Our sense of touch allows us to perceive the heat of a pot that should be handled with an oven mitt. Our sense of smell allows us to detect the aroma of freshly baked cookies. Our taste buds allow us to sample the sweetness of those cookies. Therefore, our senses allow us to absorb new ideas in the world around us all the time, even when we are not actively pursuing knowledge.

When we are trying to pursue knowledge, however, one (or more) of our senses instinctively works to harness the new ideas. For example, when I am attempting to learn a new hobby, I seek to hear and see the concepts that I need to know to master this new interest. While I could probably learn by assimilating ideas through my senses of touch, smell or taste (either singly or in combination), taking in ideas through visual and auditory means is natural to me. It is like breathing. My senses of sight and hearing comprise my dominant modes of learning, and each of us has our own modes of learning, which are our natural ways of taking in ideas. Those of us who are visual learners take in new ideas by reading or writing the ideas or seeing visual representations of them. Ideas can be written or read in the form of poems, songs, fiction, or non-fiction. Film, television, video, museum exhibits, and cultural tours can provide visual representations of ideas. Watching people interact with one another during the course of a day can also furnish visual representations of ideas. Auditory learners take in new ideas by hearing themselves or others discuss the ideas. Ideas can be heard when listening to songs, poetry, debates, sermons, lectures, or casual conversations.

Tactile learners rely on their sense of touch to absorb new ideas. They often need to manipulate physical representations of an idea to take it in. Young tactile learners thrive in "touch and feel" museums, which are usually designed for children between the ages of 3 and 10. They give children a chance to learn about something through a hands-on exploration of it. For example, one museum that I frequent with my daughter has a six-foot replica of the human ear for children to climb on, run through and play in. The children learn about the ear by touching this huge model of it. Those devoted to culinary pursuits, such as chefs, use their sense of taste and smell as receptors of new information. Newborn infants also rely on their sense of smell and taste (and also touch) to take in new information about the world around them because their other senses are not fully developed at birth. Lastly, chemists who design perfumes and florists use their sense of smell to take in new ideas that relate to the world of nature.

Our modes of learning seem to automatically kick in to help us master leisurely pursuits such as a new dance, the lyrics to a popular song, or how to cook a new dish. They should also kick in when we are trying to master the subject matter taught in academic settings. In formal learning situations, teachers can provide students with the opportunity to use their unique ways of learning. They can do so by designing lesson plans that support a variety of learning styles. For example, a church school teacher wants his second grade students to understand some of the lessons in the story of Noah and the ark (Genesis 6:9-

9:17). Some of those lessons are: (1) all living things on earth are supposed to obey God, (2) disobeying God without repenting can result in death, (3) God works to cleanse the earth of evil, and (4) God sticks to His promises.

To help his students understand these abstract concepts, the teacher would have the class examine the setting and important symbols in the story using their senses of sight, touch, hearing, taste, and smell. Given that the ark is central to the story, it would be the symbol that the class studies. To help visual learners understand what an ark is, the teacher would show the class pictures of one. To reinforce the visual learners' understanding of the ark, he would ask each student in the class to draw or paint his/her own ark, and then he would provide the chance for each ark to be viewed by each member of the class. To assist tactile learners in comprehending what an ark is, the teacher would allow the class to touch and study a small-scale model of an ark. To solidify the tactile learners' understanding of an ark's structure, the teacher would allow the members of the class to build their own arks (from ice cream sticks, perhaps) and then ask them to show their creations to one another. The students would be allowed to touch each other's arks. To aid auditory learners in comprehending what an ark is, the teacher would state the components of an ark aloud (maybe in the form of a rap or a poem) and then have the members of the class discuss whether their drawings and models included these components. The students would also discuss why God told Noah to build an ark, and not some other buoyant structure, and what the ark symbolizes in the story.

In order to support the students who learn through the senses of taste and smell, the class would study the setting of the story. To help those students who learn by tasting, the teacher would have the class prepare and taste some of the types of foods consumed by those who perished in the flood, the types of food that may have sustained Noah and the inhabitants of the ark, and the food consumed after the flood. This exercise would give the class insight into the behaviors that prompted the flood, life on the ark, and life after the flood. The members of the class would then prepare a meal in which they would share modern-day foods that represent the prevailing attitudes before the flood, the feeling that reigned in the ark, and the spirit that surfaced after the flood. A class discussion of attitudes before, during, and after the flood would accompany the sharing of food. To help those students with keen senses of smell to learn, the teacher would have the class stand about and smell the air of a humid (early summer) day and describe it. Then he would ask them to smell the air after a long, hard rain and to compare how the air smelled on the two days. Following this activity, he would ask the class to imagine how the air on Earth smelled before Noah entered the ark and after he emerged from it. This exercise can give the class insight into the notion that evil permeated the very air that the people breathed before the flood and that a spirit of renewal flowed through the air after the flood. Class discussion would accompany this exercise.

Clearly, the activities outlined above are designed to help children with all of the different learning styles to understand the importance of the ark and the setting of the story. Activities such as these help the teacher, as well as the students, to learn. By designing and frequently executing lessons such as these, the teacher gets to observe and discover each child's learning style. Those students who seem consistently excited and particularly engaged by the visual representations of an idea might be visual learners. Those who often seem mesmerized by lecture or discussion of an idea are probably auditory learners. Those who seem enthralled by examining physical representations of ideas are usually tactile learners. Those intrigued and riveted by learning through tasting or smelling might learn best through those respective modes of learning.

When teachers know the learning styles of their students, they can make the learning process more engaging, personally relevant, and effective for each individual student. Likewise, students become more enthusiastic and confident learners when their modes of learning inform the design of the curriculum.

Students learn more when they feel respected by their teachers and peers and when they are excited about the course of study. A classroom where learners are engaged and respected is a classroom where ideas flourish. Ideas are exchanged, and the lives of the members of this learning community are enriched as a result. The ideas are like the essence of God Himself inhabiting us and motivating us to act in ways that sustain life and honor Him. The ideas come from our minds, which God formed from the same soil He used to form our hands, our feet, and our hearts. In shaping our minds, God shaped the manner in which we take in new ideas. When breathing the breath of life into us, He molded us into visual learners, auditory learners, or individuals who learn by touching, tasting or smelling. The many different ways in which we take in ideas reflect the complexity of our Maker. God is one entity with infinite dimensions. Likewise, human beings are one people with many unique ways of learning. We are truly made in God's image.

Yet some educators do not see diverse ways of intercepting ideas as a reflection of the complex beauty of God. They fail to celebrate the fact that God has allowed humankind many different ways of perceiving and appreciating His Creation. Instead, these individuals favor a single mode of learning in their classrooms. For example, some of these educators may be visual learners themselves, and they may create classroom environments which encourage only visual learning. Such classrooms have lots of educational materials that can be read or viewed such as posters, books, and videotapes. Yet they do not have a lot of materials to support the learning of students who learn using their other four senses. Continually forcing students to adopt a favored mode of learning is asking them to ignore the beauty of their own God-given brilliance. It is asking them to extinguish what is Godly in them. It is denying the world of the ideas and the goodness that could have come from that God-inspired brilliance.

When we extinguish the lights of others, we become the architects of a world that breeds self-loathing, apathy, and chaos. When we stand idly by and witness others' lights being extinguished, our passiveness fosters the emergence of a world without the beauty and grace of God. So often we comment that we are in search of the Lord to rid the world of its ills. Yet, in our search for a larger-than-life God who will make everything better overnight, we fail to see Him as He presents Himself to us every day. Perhaps if we saw evidence of God's creativity in each other, our world and our lives would make sense again. If we saw the driving design of God that resides in all living things, we would not need to look for the Lord's comfort, guidance, and mercy. They would be with us always. Imagine a world where each little light could shine. Imagine a world where we allow ourselves to be as brilliant as God knows we are.

ON DOING THE RIGHT THING:
A Moral Mandate for Ministry

Leonard Lovett, Ph.D.

The Moral Context of Leadership

Leadership requires and demands much more of us today. This holds true especially within the African American community and particularly the larger society. Those who lead God's people in today's world often find themselves living either in the center or on the edge of the ethical quandary. In a society encumbered by ethical mishaps, a few words of pastoral wisdom forged on the anvil of pastoral experience may be in order. The years of 1987 and 1988 are etched in our moral memory. It was during that time that the religious world was rocked by the exposé of publicly admitted moral improprieties. Such revelations reveal all the more that we have "feet of clay" and survive only by the grace of God.

Leadership requires ethical restraint and moral boundaries. While ethics deals with what ought to be in light of what is, it also deals with the values we embrace. Can you imagine what our cities would be like without stop signs and traffic signals to regulate our high-powered, turbo-charged automobile engines? What would society be like without rules, regulations, and laws? What would civilized societies be like without moral outcries and outrage? Moral relativism is an ethical theory which contends that all the values we embrace are relative and there are no moral absolutes. Moral relativism, reduced to its basic essence, can only lead to a glorified humanism that asserts "self" is the sole determiner of moral behavior and rules for day-to-day choices. In the African American community, we often hear people on the streets make statements such as, "I alone decide what is best for me." It leads us to believe that we alone are the masters of our souls and sole determiners of our fate.

Immorality in the ministry is a rather complex issue that involves a number of factors. Such delicate factors as one's self-image, identity, and lifestyle surface as we come under the mirror of human scrutiny. The sins that plague us in ministry are often more than just a spiritual problem. More often they have a history rooted in our moral behavior. The interpersonal dynamics of moral failure must be critically assessed if we are to mature and learn from the mistakes of others.

Ministers are often like physicians who care deeply for the patients they treat but end up dying from the very diseases they are trained to cure. We listen to the sins and the failures of others in counseling sessions but refuse to disclose our pain or engage in self-disclosure even with those we deem to be close. Because of our ego, it is far too risky. A careful reading of the Old Testament biblical narrative is revelatory of the fact that "giants do fall." The problem becomes involved as you search for someone you can trust and engage in open disclosure without the fear of having to share our pain and those deep-seated fears that also increase our stress levels. Moral leadership is not some separate calling in ministry, it lies at the very core of who we are and what we do in leading God's people. Whenever the "blind leads the blind" both can be victimized by falling into a ditch according to the wisdom of our Lord.

The Minister as a Person

Spirituality. Those who serve in ministry should seek to render their best service by being morally, mentally, physically, and spiritually whole. A minister should daily find a specific time to be in the presence of God. It may be finding a quiet place for meditation on Scripture or prayer. I have discovered that my day does not proceed with a sense of purposeful destiny when I forfeit my "quiet time." The late E. Stanley Jones, a great Methodist missionary to India, described prayer as "entering God's presence for cleansing and decision-making." Prayer is the fuel that supplies us for the long pilgrimage. It enhances what we do or say and influences those we touch.

Communion with God is to those who minister the fountain and source of renewal and replenishment. We are channels for God's grace and power but not the source. Indeed, we are compelled to drink from the "fountains of living water" if we are to lead the people of God. Those who give must be receivers. All rivers originate somewhere. The roaring, mighty Mississippi River with its scores of tributaries and streams originates and ends somewhere. The source of burnout in ministry does not always occur because of the quantity of what one does in ministry. It is more often related to lack of balance in one's disciplined duties that also require nurture and replenishment. Focused spirituality is necessary to give substance to who we really are before God. Encountering God at the deepest level of our being enables us to come to grips with our identity. We must be in touch with our humanity in order to effectively motivate others to maximize their potential, which is the primary task of leadership.

Physical Wholeness. Those who serve in ministry must be physically and mentally sound in order to effectively lead the people of God. One should find time to engage in some form of exercise compatible with your condition of health. Friends who walk five miles a day in Los Angeles told me about a man who had all kinds of health problems with his heart combined with hypertension. This man in his early seventies had been spending a major amount of money on medication monthly. He had never engaged in any kind of physical exercise. Within months after adopting walking as a daily form of exercise, he dropped all medications and has been told that his hypertension and heart condition has receded.

Recently, I have become a frequent walker/jogger after having been an avid racquetball player since 1979. I have observed that whenever I am consistently on task with a balanced exercise program, my energy level is high. Occasional use of a vitamin supplement provides astounding energy for most tasks. Diet, rest, and proper exercise increases blood circulation and impacts my total energy level. Mental alertness is one of the positive consequences of a regular fitness program. Exercise helps to relieve us of stress. Do you receive annual physical exams? If not, why not? Do you drink enough water? A friend of mine recently disclosed that a surgeon told him after his operation for colon cancer that had he drank enough water instead of soda, his surgery would have been unnecessary. We should drink one half of our body weight in ounces of water daily to be physically fit. Water alone has so may functions within the human body.

Social Relationships. Those who are bearers of the Gospel are also social beings. Jesus was a special guest at a wedding in Cana of Galilee. The issue is not whether we are social beings or not but rather what are the limitations and boundaries imposed on our social behavior. Should we be viewed as "ecclesiastical snobs"? Should we be viewed as human beings too "holy" to laugh or play? What are the risks to our ministry when we cross the boundaries of our professional behavior for personal aggrandizement? The ancient words of Scripture are still appropriate in our time, "Can a man take fire in his bosom and his clothes not be burned?" (Proverbs 6:27, KJV) As an ethicist it appears that discernment is the normative key to setting limitations on our social behavior.

Those who minister must be discerning at all times. Most of us are aware of ministers who were excellent communicators and motivators but failed because they crossed the ethical boundaries of professionalism and developed inappropriate relationships with those they sought to help. The ministers' relationship with those of the opposite sex must be free, guarded, and yet responsible. Counseling should take place only in a professional setting. Reputation has to do with who people say we are. Character has to do with who we are. We must be discerning so that we will not do anything that will violate another as we seek to lead the people of God.

I have been in settings where it was social to imbibe in drinking a cocktail. My choice was a soft drink. I did not superimpose my judgement on those who sipped their cocktail. I was comfortable and unembarrassed as I sipped my Coke. Discernment was the key in making such a decision. I had imposed on my lifestyle the co-efficiency of consistency and discipline. It is important that my witness be coherent and clear at all times. Most of us are familiar with ministers who crossed the boundaries of social drinking and ended up strung out on alcohol or drugs. Those of us who bear the witness of the claims of Jesus Christ must never surrender our convictions simply to go along with the crowd. I have friends who have paid the price for the loss of their ministry for failing to be discerning and taking a stand. Lifestyle witnessing continues to be an effective tool for ministry.

GOD RESTORES A REMNANT

> *God does not restore us, or these exiles, to the same old thing which we knew; rather, with restoration God offers the opportunity to ponder, rethink, and give new effort to a new vision.*
>
> **A. O. Ogbonnaya, Ph.D.**

The plight of Israel prior to the Exile and after the return of the exiles is a portrait of the ability of God to salvage and to restore even in the midst of the most problematic of situations. It is an archetypal manifestation of the life cycle of an institution's demise, renewal, disrepair, and reestablishment. It also typifies a pattern of our own life cycle; our ups and our downs, our sickness and our health, our sins and our forgiveness, our death and our resurrection. Scripturally, the evidence for Israel is found in the major prophets as well as the so-called minor prophets, Ezra, Nehemiah, Daniel, Joel, Obadiah, Haggai, Zechariah, and Malachi. Here we see that when we return from our negative situation to a positive one, we may not return with all that we once possessed.

The restoration of the remnant of Israel presents us with several lessons. In order to restore the remnant, God raised up leadership in the persons of Joshua and Zerubbabel. They themselves were exiles who began to return to the land. The word remnant is instructive also because there is an implication for those who are so named in the interweaving of struggles and hopes, the mixture of the old and the new, the commingling of acceptance and resistance, the juxtaposition of new friends and old enemies. We see little setbacks in the broad canvas of divine victories. Also, in restoration we see that the returning exiles were not left without a word from God; the voice of the Lord continued to be heard through the prophets.

The restoration of the remnant also entailed "the renewal of the nation." God does not restore us, or these exiles, to the same old thing which we knew; rather, with restoration God offers the opportunity to ponder, rethink, and give new effort to a new vision. Using our experiences of failure and pain from spiritual entanglement, God deals with some of our troubles and moves us to the changes necessary for re-creation and newness. The message of the restored remnant is that we can be helped, that there is renewal. We must then believe that a new era is possible and that this hope is not just a figment of the imagination. The prophets Obadiah, Joel, Malachi, and Daniel remind us within their texts that in the past God's hand had done great things; therefore, the difficulties we may encounter as we seek renewal can also be overcome.

Restoration calls for courageous action. The statement made by King Cyrus underscores the need for courage by the remnant: "Anyone of his people among you may his God be with him, and let him go up to Jerusalem in Judah and build the temple of the LORD, the God of Israel, the God who is in Jerusalem" (Ezra 1:3, NIV). For the remnant who are weak and overlooked, restoration does not come because they will it to be so, as much as it comes because the Lord stirs up the spirit of His people, charging them to build a highway of the Lord for freedom.

Restoration means that we are faced with a God-given opportunity. We are presented with the divine opportunity to move from captivity, pressure, and the stress of exile to the land of liberated joy. It is a call to place the losses we have suffered because of possessions or honor in the light of God's great power and promise. It is time to reconsider our disappointment in light of divine appointments. It is a move to balance our nostalgia, or even nausea, for the past with a new vision of the future. It contains

Restoration means that we are faced with a God-given opportunity. We are presented with the divine opportunity to move from captivity, pressure, and the stress of exile to the land of liberated joy.

within it a message that says being cast aside by society is not the last word; rather, divine restoration and renewal is the persistent word.

So now, because God has promised restoration, we are in a place to begin to rebuild. What was Israel called to rebuild? Was it not their religious-spiritual foundation? For us to be restored completely, we need to begin with the rebuilding of our personal, family, and communal altar. Could it not be said that like Jerusalem before the restoration, our altars and places of worship lie in waste? As the altar remains desolate, return from exile and our gathering church will be ineffective, and joy will remain half-empty. But the fullness of our joy comes when we rebuild the altar and offer ourselves completely to God. When many people speak of restoration, they seem to think that it means continuing with stale music and unemotional worship. For some it is the continuation of their racist hegemony and ethnocentric control of the welfare of others. But this restoration is the act of the Lord and must place Him at the center. As Haggai 1:2-14 insists, the act of restoration must make God our priority or it is not genuine. One who is truly restored to the Lord will answer the question: "Is it a time for you yourselves to be living in your paneled houses, while this house remains a ruin?" (Haggai 1:4) with an unequivocal, "No."

TERTULLIAN

In addition to writing in Greek, he is also considered the founder of Western theology since most theological concepts in Western thought can be traced to him.

Tertullian was one of the greatest African scholars. Born in Carthage, he was a father of the church. Carthage was in what is known today as Tunisia and what was referred to by the ancients as Libya. He was very proud of his Carthaginian heritage. It is important to know that the Carthaginians, led by Hannibal, were Africans who fought and defeated the Romans. Tertullian was one of the most educated people in the western world in his time. In fact, he traveled to Rome to become a lawyer. Upon his conversion to Christianity in a.d. 195, he returned to Africa to proclaim the Gospel to his own people. In Africa he taught new members and older Christians principles of the Christian faith. Tertullian authored several books and was the first African to write theology in the Latin language. Because his first language may not have been Latin, he was able, like present day Africans and African Americans, to express thoughts in new terms that were unfamiliar to traditional Latin speakers. In addition to writing in Greek, he is also considered the founder of Western theology since most theological concepts in Western thought can be traced to him. The Roman church condemned this great African for heresy. In fact, they condemned him for believing in the power of the Holy Spirit and refusing to accept the power of the bishop of Rome. Tertullian, like all of us, was not perfect and held many views that we may not accept, but he was the church father who determined the direction of the Western church. About forty of his books still remain with us. Later in his life Tertullian began his own group, which scholars call the Tertullianists.

TEACHING TIPS

June 1
Bible Study Guide 1

1. Words You Should Know

A. Mouth–(Ezra 1:1) Hebrew *Peh* The word is used to declare God's divine revelation.

B. Stir–(v. 1:1) The act of God opening up one's eyes; to arouse.

2. Teacher Preparation

A. Read Ezra 1 from several translations. You should also read God's promise to Israel revealed through Jeremiah (pay particular attention to Jeremiah 25:11-12 and 29:10-14). You may want to review the lessons in the September 2002 quarter. Be prepared to refresh your class's memory about God's promise to the exiled Israelites.

B. Read the INTRODUCTION and make appropriate notes to share with the students to help them understand the quarter's theme of restoration.

C. Read the LESSON AIM and focus your teaching on achieving these goals. Answer the SEARCH THE SCRIPTURES and MAKE IT HAPPEN questions so you can be prepared to assist the students.

3. Starting the Lesson

A. As students arrive, ask them to try to remember the lesson from the September 2002 quarter. Ask them why were the Israelites in captivity. Ask them who captured them and what happened to Jerusalem, the holy city. Then ask them to discuss God's promise to the exiles.

B. Discuss how God *always* fulfills promises, regardless of how bleak our current circumstances seem. You may ask students to write down some promises God has made to them. Encourage them to keep those promises in mind as they study this lesson.

C. Lead the class in prayer, using the objectives listed in the LESSON AIM.

4. Getting into the Lesson

A. Ask several students to read the FOCAL VERSES and the KEEP IN MIND verse. Use the IN DEPTH section to discuss the meaning of the verses.

B. Read IN FOCUS section. Ask students to name messengers who have been obedient to God's calling. Ask them to consider how open they are to hearing from God and being obedient to God's calling.

C. Read THE PEOPLE, PLACES, AND TIMES and discuss how Cyrus was obedient to God's stirring.

D. Assign SEARCH THE SCRIPTURES and DISCUSS THE MEANING questions to students. Give them a few moments to find the answers, then discuss them as a class.

5. Relating the Lesson to Life

A. Read and discuss LESSON IN OUR SOCIETY. Remind students that God shows us mercy so we should show others mercy also. Invite students to think of ways they can help others.

B. Encourage students to read the MAKE IT HAPPEN section and develop a plan to help someone this week. Ask them to be prepared to share what happened in next week's class.

6. Arousing Action

A. Ask students to record their reflections on the lesson in the FOLLOW THE SPIRIT and REMEMBER YOUR THOUGHTS sections of the lesson.

B. Encourage them to use today's lesson as evidence of God fulfilling promises. Tell them to also be open to God's stirring.

C. Close the class with prayer.

WORSHIP GUIDE

For the Superintendent or Teacher
Theme: Return of the Exiles
Theme Song: "Great Is Thy Faithfulness"
Scripture: Ezra 1
Song: "Thank You"
Devotional: Lord, thank You for always keeping your promises. Help me to be open to hear from You and willing to obey your commands. In Jesus' name. Amen.

RETURN OF THE EXILES

Bible Background • EZRA 1
Printed Text • EZRA 1
Devotional Reading • ISAIAH 52:7-12

LESSON AIM

By the end of the lesson, students will know that God has true messengers who hear His voice and obey His commands. They will learn to discern and follow true messengers of God.

KEEP IN MIND

"Who is there among you of all people? His God will be with him, and let him go up to Jerusalem, which is in Judah, and build the house of the LORD God of Israel, (he is the God,) which is in Jerusalem" (Ezra 1:3).

FOCAL VERSES

EZRA 1:1 Now in the first year of Cyrus king of Persia, that the word of the LORD by the mouth of Jeremiah might be fulfilled, the LORD stirred up the spirit of Cyrus king of Persia, that he made a proclamation throughout all his kingdom, and put it also in writing, saying

2 Thus saith Cyrus king of Persia, The LORD God of heaven hath given me all the kingdoms of the earth; and he hath charged me to build him an house at Jerusalem, which is in Judah.

3 Who is there among you of all his people? his God be with him, and let him go up to Jerusalem, which is in Judah and build the house of the LORD God of Israel (he is the God,) which is in Jerusalem.

4 And whosoever remaineth in any place where he sojourneth, let the men of his place help him with silver, and with gold, and with goods, and with beasts, beside the freewill offering for the house of God that is in Jerusalem.

LESSON OVERVIEW

LESSON AIM
KEEP IN MIND
FOCAL VERSES
IN FOCUS
THE PEOPLE, PLACES,
AND TIMES
BACKGROUND
AT-A-GLANCE
IN DEPTH
SEARCH THE SCRIPTURES
DISCUSS THE MEANING
LESSON IN OUR SOCIETY
MAKE IT HAPPEN
FOLLOW THE SPIRIT
REMEMBER YOUR THOUGHTS
MORE LIGHT ON THE TEXT
DAILY BIBLE READINGS

5 Then rose up the chief of the fathers of Judah and Benjamin, and the priests, and the Levites, with all them whose spirit God had raised, to go up to build the house of the LORD which is in Jerusalem.

6 And all they that were about them strengthened their hands with vessels of silver, with gold, with goods, and with beasts, and with precious things, beside all that was willingly offered.

7 Also Cyrus the king brought forth the vessels of the house of the LORD, which Nebuchadnezzar had brought forth out of Jerusalem, and had put them in the house of his gods;

8 Even those did Cyrus king of Persia bring forth by the hand of Mithredath the treasurer, and numbered them unto Sheshbazzar the prince of Judah.

9 And this is the number of them: thirty chargers of gold, a thousand chargers of silver, nine and twenty knives,

10 Thirty basins of gold, silver basins of a second sort four hundred and ten, and other vessels a thousand.

11 All the vessels of gold and of silver were five thousand and four hundred. And these did Sheshbazzar bring up with them of the captivity that were brought up from Babylon unto Jerusalem.

IN FOCUS

When Africans were taken from their homeland

and sold into slavery, they were forced to leave behind their wealth, land, prestige, culture, and language. They were forced to adapt to another way of living. Everything was stripped from them and they became slaves. Webster's dictionary defines slave as a human being who is owned by and absolutely subject to another human being, as by capture, purchase, or birth; a bond servant divested of all freedom and personal rights. This is much like what the children of Israel suffered at the hands of the Babylonians. It was a time of prayer to the Lord for deliverance from the oppressor. God was sure to answer and send a messenger, just like He had with the slaves in America. In today's lesson God sends a messenger, a deliverer to lead His people to freedom.

THE PEOPLE, PLACES, AND TIMES

Cyrus, King of Persia from 559 to 530 B.C., captured the city of Babylon, which Nebuchadnezzar had ruled and also where Jews were in captivity. Cyrus had a policy of allowing conquered people to return to their homelands. As a result of the conquest the Jews were set free to return to Jerusalem and rebuild the temple.

Cyrus was deemed a heroic figure and messenger of God to redeem Israel. Persia an ancient world empire that flourished from 539-331 b.c. The Babylonian Empire previously fell to the Persians, setting the stage for the return of the Hebrew people to Jerusalem about 538-445 b.c. following their long period of captivity by the Babylonians. Among the kingdoms of the ancient world, Persia is remembered because it built many important cities.

BACKGROUND

The children of Israel had experienced a period of sheer rebellion against God. Because God is merciful, He sent this prophets to speak to them concerning their ways, but "they mocked the messengers of God, and despised his words, and misused his prophets until the wrath of the LORD arose against his people, till there was no remedy" (v. 16). As a result the young, old, male, female, rich, and poor were led into captivity. Second Chronicles 36:20 reads, "And them that had escaped from the sword carried he away to

Babylon; where they were servants to him and his sons until the reign of the kingdom of Persia."

Ezra 1 begins with God fulfilling His promise to return His people to the land of promise after seventy years of exile. This has been called by some as Israel's "second exodus."

> ### AT-A-GLANCE
>
> **1. The Revelation of a Stirred Heart**
> **(Ezra 1:1-4)**
> **2. The Proclamation of a Stirred Heart**
> **(vv. 1-4)**
> **3. The Response of Stirred Hearts**
> **(vv. 5-11)**

IN DEPTH

1. The Revelation of a Stirred Heart
(Ezra 1:1-4)

King Cyrus was in his first year of leadership over Persia when the LORD "stirred up" his spirit. This "stirring" was a fulfillment of Scripture spoken by the prophets Jeremiah and Isaiah (Isaiah 45:1; Jeremiah 51:11). For many years the children of Israel had been in captivity while their land laid in waste. King after king had made sure that they would never return for fear that they would regain their ancient glory. It is true, of course, that Israel got into this mess because of its rebellion, yet one cannot help but wonder how those who took them captive could have (through all the sixty-nine years of their captivity) never thought about their plight. Rather every ruler sought to use them for his own goal. Some of these leaders must have thought Israel was going to be in bondage forever. But deep in the mind of the Israelites was the promise of God from his prophets, especially Jeremiah. The Scripture in Jeremiah promises that God will deliver His people after a period of bondage. At the appointed time God began to move. No matter how long one may be held in captivity by the devil or by sinister human machination, God has promised deliverance.

In fulfillment of the word, which God had spoken through Jeremiah and through Isaiah, God began to move. When God wants to change a situation, the divine Spirit searches for those whose hearts are malleable to the stirring of God.

According to verse one, God did three things. He stirred Cyrus's spirit. This stirring is represented by the Hebrew word *uwr* (pronounced **oor**), which means that God opened his eyes. Hitherto every ruler had been blind to the plight of God's people. God caused Cyrus to understand the plight of those of lower rank than he was. This implies the idea that he saw beyond their culture. He gained insight into the injustice of their situation. Oh that God would cause us to see the plight of those who are around us.

There is another way to look at it. The LORD God of Israel caused him to wake up figuratively to the group of people in his kingdom who had borne the brunt of all the prejudices in the kingdom. We also need for God to stir our spirit for the plight of others. We must lift up ourselves from the bed of complacency. The great thing about the word "stir" is that it implies that God is saying to Cyrus: get up from your complacency; lift up yourself and do something for me. One cannot help but wonder how many people God had tried to stir but who (because the plight of God's people gave them economic power) would not wake up and do something about it. Many of us wish for the suffering to be helped, but are we willing to put our names on the line, our kingdoms on the line to stand for "the least of these"? We thank God that Cyrus did not just get stirred by the spirit in his house so he jumped up and down and felt good, but he followed through with an obedient spirit and a listening ear to hear "thus saith God."

2. The Proclamation of A Stirred Heart (vv. 1-4)

Cyrus proclaimed (v. 2) that God had given him all the kingdoms of the earth and appointed him to build a temple in Jerusalem. This stirring led him to cross over to God's side. When we are stirred by God, we are called to transition to God's way. Here we see the king being transformed from being antagonistic to Israel to being her friend. Instead of alienating himself from

God, he is now aligning himself with the will and word of God. When divine stirring is in place, we want everyone to know. The king sought to bring others to the place of obedience to God. The idea here is not mere talk. The Hebrew word for proclamation implies carrying over, persuading others to come over by means of the transformation of their conduct. In this context the king did not just talk; his word brought results. People like king Cyrus who hear the word of the Lord and are stirred by it tend to seem as meddlers. They let it be known that God has spoken to them.

The proclamation was also a challenge directed at the people of God. It was a time for rebuilding and refreshing. God wanted His people and temple again, and He was going to use King Cyrus to put things in motion. Cyrus was the king God was waiting for. All the kingdoms of the earth were given to him, and he freely obeyed God. Note the way the proclamation is put.

"Who is there among you of all his people?" (v. 3). The question is not about identity. This "who?" is meant to draw out the willing. Who is he among you who is willing? Why will the people not be willing? Just because people are God's people does not always mean that they will go when God calls. The statement "His God be with him, and let him go up to Jerusalem, which is in Judah, and build the house of the LORD God of Israel (he is the God,) which is in Jerusalem" suggests that there was reason to fear. Cyrus is here calling not just those who claim to belong to God, but those who have faith in God's ability to protect and keep those who step out for God. Cyrus is very clear that he was not speaking about just a god, but of the God who is at Jerusalem.

3. The Response of a Stirred Heart (vv. 5-11)

God works at various levels to release His people. At one level God was working in the life of the king. At another level God was creating a willing heart in His people. At another level God was granting them favor in the sight of the Persians around them. This story reminds one of the Exodus. There God moved Pharaoh and then moved his people and then moved the ordinary Egyptians to supply the freed slaves with material to start a new life.

How awesome God is. At that time God was calling His people from bondage to freedom to work and fulfill this great commission. He was also telling the captors to release His people. As they began to respond to God's stirring, God began to provide them with provision for the work to which they were being called. They needed silver, gold, goods, livestock, and freewill offerings for the house of God. Having been captives for many years in a foreign land, they could not afford these things. But God had already made a way. The temple needed to be rebuilt. Upon its rebuilding, even while it was in the process of being rebuilt, offerings had to be made daily. This was very costly, but God made a way because both the king and God's people were willing to follow the divine stirring. When God stirs the heart of His people for a task, there is always a favor waiting.

What a glorious time this must have been! A form of jubilee. The family heads of Judah and Benjamin with the priests and Levites were preparing to "go up to build the house of the Lord" (v. 5). It was a time of forgetting about the past because God had promised a bright future. God had a remnant of people to fulfill the next phase of Israel's spiritual journey. The leaders were preparing to go forth in the power and might of God's promise to His people. God wanted a house to dwell in, and it was time to do it. They were strengthened to do the work of the Lord. Generations had been in bondage and now there was a releasing!

There was restoration, all because someone was willing to listen to the divine stirrings that awaken one (vv. 7-8). First, there is spiritual restoration, a willing heart to answer the call of God. Second, there is physical restoration of the temple, which was destroyed by Nebuchadnezzar. Third, there is restoration of the people who had been removed from the land where they were meant to worship God. Fourth, there is a restoration of material things, which were not meant just to make them rich but for the purpose of effectively carrying out the glorification of God by His people. All that the officials of Babylon stole, valuable vessels, candlesticks, incense burners, linens were now being returned. The inventory of the vessels listed (vv. 9-11) is not so much about material things as it is about the possibility of again worshiping God as He had commanded them to do, in the place which He had chosen for Himself. It also signifies the power of the God of Israel over the gods and kings who laid claim to what belonged to the people of God. No matter how long it takes, God can bring His people back to the place of true worship and restore all that has been lost. In this sense Cyrus is a type (or picture) of the Messiah who seeks by His Word and work to restore humanity to the place of true worship and celebration. The people of God were getting their freedom and their goods. God will restore.

SEARCH THE SCRIPTURES

1. What did the LORD do to the spirit of Cyrus king of Persia? (Ezra 1:1)

2. What was Cyrus the king charged to do? (v. 2)

3. The men "of his place" were to help with what? (v. 4)

4. Who rose up? (v. 5)

5. What was the number of vessels ? (vv. 9-11)

DISCUSS THE MEANING

1. Why do you think it was important that the Scriptures be fulfilled that were spoken by the prophet Jeremiah?

2. Why did the temple have to be rebuilt?

3. Why do you think God thought it was so important not to send the captives out empty-handed? What does this reveal about our God?

LESSON IN OUR SOCIETY

There are people in our society who have been cast aside due to some unfortunate event in their lives. Not only have they been cast aside, but their possessions may have been taken away from them as well. The individual may have placed himself or herself in a position that caused these misfortunes to occur. But when God shows mercy, we must show mercy and lend a helping hand and strengthen these individuals to stand on their own two feet again.

In this lesson God supplied His people with a portion of gold, silver, and cattle to get them started again. How can we help someone who was once in jail and now has served that sentence?

MAKE IT HAPPEN

This week think of someone who needs your help. What kind of people may have lost their job, house, and possessions due to disobedience to God and His ways? They may be recovering drug addicts, alcoholics, or prisoners. They are trying their best to get back on track. How can you help? Ask God to help, lead, and guide you.

FOLLOW THE SPIRIT

What God wants me to do:

_____

_____

REMEMBER YOUR THOUGHTS

Special insights you have learned:

_____

_____

MORE LIGHT ON THE TEXT
Ezra 1

1:1 Now in the first year of Cyrus king of Persia, that the word of the LORD by the mouth of Jeremiah might be fulfilled, the LORD stirred up the spirit of Cyrus king of Persia, that he made a proclamation throughout all his kingdom, and put it also in writing, saying,

"The first year of Cyrus king of Persia" refers to the first year that Cyrus ruled over Babylon, which would have been 538 B.C Cyrus's reign partly began in 559 B.C. when he succeeded his father as king of Anshan. Cyrus defeated the king of Media and welded the empires into a dual monarchy called Medo-Persia. In 539 B.C. Cyrus's army marched into the city of Babylon, bringing the Babylonian empire to a close. The Persian empire, including Persia, Media, Babylonia, and Chaldea, with many smaller dependencies, was founded by Cyrus (536 B.C.).

"That the word of the LORD might be fulfilled" is a parenthetical statement of the writer and not a part of the Cyrus's proclamation. "Mouth" is a translation of *Peh*. There are fifty occurrences of *peh* which speaks of God's mouth in the sense of divine revelation. When the

prophets spoke, they were only passing on God's message.

Before the fall of Judah, the prophet Jeremiah predicted that Judah would be taken into Babylonian captivity and the land would remain desolate for seventy years. After seventy years God would punish the Babylonians for their cruelty and sinfulness (Jeremiah 25:12). The prophet further predicted that at that time He would cause the Jews to return to Judah (29:10). The seventy-year captivity began with the first of the Jews taken into captivity in 605 B.C. during the reign of Jehoiakim (2 Kings 24:1; Daniel 1:1). The period ended when the captives began their return in 538 B.C., approximately seventy years later.

Ezra tells us that "the LORD stirred up the spirit of Cyrus king of Persia" to issue the proclamation. "Stirred" is from the Hebrew word *uwr* meaning to "arouse." "Spirit" is a translation of the Hebrew *ruah* (pronounced **ROO-AHCK**). In this case the word refers to the seat of human will and intellect and emotion. The phrase may be best rendered "the LORD moved the heart of Cyrus" (NIV). By stirring Cyrus's heart to be kind toward these exiled people, God enabled the word of His promise to Jeremiah to be fulfilled.

2 Thus saith Cyrus king of Persia, The LORD God of heaven hath given me all the kingdoms of the earth; and he hath charged me to build him an house at Jerusalem, which is in Judah.

"The LORD God of heaven hath given me all the kingdoms of the earth" is hyperbole (accepted exaggeration), but it was literally true that the Persian empire was the greatest ruling power in the world at that time. "God" in this case is a translation of the Hebrew "El" meaning "mighty one." In the Ancient Near East "El" was the most widespread word for God. "Heaven" from the Hebrew *shamayim* (pronounced **shah-MY-yim**), refers to the abode of God, a higher realm where celestial beings dwell.

"He hath charged me to build him an house at Jerusalem." The phraseology here offers evidence that Cyrus had seen (probably through means of Daniel) the prophesies of Isaiah which were written two hundred years before he was born: "That saith of Cyrus, He is my shepherd, and shall perform all my pleasure: even saying to Jerusalem, Thou shalt be built; and to the temple, Thy foundation shall be laid" (Isaiah 44:28; see also 45:1-2).

The existence of these remarkable predictions led Cyrus to acknowledge that all his kingdoms were gifts bestowed on him by "the LORD God of heaven" and prompted him to fulfill the duty which had been laid upon him long before his birth. This was the principal reason of the great favor he showed to the Jews. Although Cyrus acknowledged the Lord, Scripture clearly states that he was an unbeliever: "For Jacob my servant's sake, and Israel mine elect, I have even called thee by thy name: I have surnamed thee, *though thou hast not known me*" (v. 4).

3-4 Who is there among you of all his people? his God be with him, and let him go up to Jerusalem, which is in Judah, and build the house of the LORD God of Israel, (he is the God,) which is in Jerusalem. And whosoever remaineth in any place where he sojourneth, let the men of his place help him with silver, and with gold, and with goods, and with beasts, beside the freewill offering for the house of God that is in Jerusalem.

His "people" is from the Hebrew *am* and means "nation, tribe or people." In this case the word signifies a group of people unified by religion and/or ancestral relationships. This is a reference to the Jews throughout the empire. "Whosoever remaineth" speaks to the Jews who chose to remain in Babylon. Although 49,897 Jews chose to return (Ezra 2:64-65), the vast majority chose to remain in Babylon. "The men of this place" are the Gentile neighbors who were asked to help by giving donations. To "go up," from the Hebrew *alah* (pronounced ah-LAH) in this case means to travel from a lower elevation to a higher one. The temple of God was located on a mountain and anyone going there had to "go up."

The purpose of Cyrus's proclamation was to grant full permission to those Jewish exiles, in every part of his kingdom, who chose to return to their own country. Also, this charge recommended to those of their countrymen who chose to remain to aid the returnees on their way and to contribute liberally towards the rebuilding of the temple

5-6 Then rose up the chief of the fathers of Judah and Benjamin, and the priests, and the Levites, with all them whose spirit God had raised, to go up to build the house of the LORD which is in Jerusalem. And all they that were about them strengthened their hands with vessels of silver, with gold, with goods, and with beasts, and with precious things, beside all that was willingly offered.

"The chief of the fathers" is a reference to paternal and ecclesiastical leader chiefs of the captivity. These leaders were primarily elders of the tribes of Judah and Benjamin, but members of the other ten tribes were also represented (1 Chronicles 9:3) who retained the pure worship of God. These elders naturally took the lead in this movement. They were followed by all those Jews whose love for God and patriotism were strong enough to leave the comforts of captivity for the hardships of the repatriation.

Many of the Jews who had been born in Babylonia or had comfortably established themselves decided to stay behind. Although they would remain behind, they generously contributed to the venture. It also appears that some of their international friends and neighbors displayed hearty goodwill and great liberality in aiding and promoting the views of the emigrants. The phrase "willingly offered" is a translation of the Hebrew *nadab*, which means "to give freely. The word denotes the inward attitude of those who spontaneously gave to the construction of the temple.

7 Also Cyrus the king brought forth the vessels of the house of the LORD, which Nebuchadnezzar had brought forth out of Jerusalem, and had put them in the house of his gods;

Nebuchadnezzar had looted the temple of God and taken the vessels of the house of the LORD as prizes and proof of the power of the Babylonian gods. Some of the vessels had been taken in 605 b.c. (Daniel 1:2), others in 597 B.C. (2 Kings 24:13), and the rest in final deportation in 586 B.C. (2 Kings 25:13-15). These items were placed in the temple of the Babylonian gods. Although the writer of Kings says that these were "cut in pieces" (2 Kings 24:13), that would not be done to the large and magnificent vases, and if they had been divided the parts could be reunited. But it may be doubted whether the Hebrew word *qatsats* (pronounced **kaht-SAHTS**), rendered "cut in pieces" can also mean to "cut off;" that is, from further use in the temple.

8 Even those did Cyrus king of Persia bring forth by the hand of Mithredath the treasurer, and numbered them unto Sheshbazzar, the prince of Judah.

"Numbered them unto Sheshbazzar" indicates that the items were inventoried and a written record was given. "Numbered" is from the Hebrew *safar* (pronounced **sah-FAHR**), meaning to enumerate or count, usually through a written record.

Many believe that Sheshbazzar and Zerubbabel are two different people, but it is more likely that they were the same person. "Sheshbazzar" may refer to the protection of the Babylonian moon-god (compare Ezra 3:8 and 5:16). The Babylonian name indicates that Sheshbazzar may have served in the royal court where Babylonian names were given to young men chosen to serve to make them more Babylonian. The most evident case of Babylonian renaming is the case of Daniel, Hananiah, Mishael, and Azariah whose names were changed to Belteshazzar, Shadrach, Meshach, and Abed-nego (Daniel 1:7; also see Esther 2:7).

Sheshbazzar was the son of Shealtiel who was the son of Jeconiah and an ancestor of Christ (Matthew 1:12). Sheshbazzar was born in Babylon, and called by his family "Zerubbabel" meaning "offspring of Babylon" or "begotten in Babylon." Because of his royal bloodline he was recognized among the exiles as a "hereditary prince of Judah." He led the exiles in their return to Judah from their Babylonian captivity (Ezra 2:1-64). In the ruined city of Jerusalem Sheshbazzar and Jeshua, the high priest, led the people in the restoration of the temple (3:1-9).

9-11 And this is the number of them: thirty chargers of gold, a thousand chargers of silver, nine and twenty knives, Thirty basins of gold, silver basins of a second sort four hundred and ten, and other vessels a thousand. All the vessels of gold and of silver were five thousand and four hundred. All these did Sheshbazzar bring up with them of the captivity that were brought up from Babylon unto Jerusalem.

Of the 5,400 total vessels only 2,499 are listed here. It is probable that the larger, most valuable vessels are mentioned, while the inventory of the whole, including great and small, came to the gross sum stated in the text.

All the Jewish exiles did not embrace the privilege which the Persian king granted them. The great proportion, born in Babylon, preferred continuing in their comfortable homes instead of undertaking a distant, expensive, and hazardous journey to a desolate land. Nor did the returning exiles all go at once. The first band went with Zerubbabel, others afterwards with Ezra (7:1-10:44), and a large number with Nehemiah at a still later period (Nehemiah 1:1 2:20).

DAILY BIBLE READINGS

M: Cyrus Is the Lord's Anointed
Isaiah 45:1-5

T: Cyrus Will Build God's City
Isaiah 45:7-13

W: Israel Is Saved by the Lord
Isaiah 45:14-19

T: The Lord Will Go Before You
Isaiah 57:7-12

F: The People Prepare to Return
Ezra 1:1-5

S: Their Neighbors Aid Them
Ezra 1:6 2:2

S: Freewill Offerings for God's House
Ezra 2:64-70

TEACHING TIPS

June 8
Bible Study Guide 2

1. Words You Should Know

A. Altar–(Ezra 3:2) An elevated place or structure before which religious ceremonies may be enacted or upon which sacrifices may be offered.

B. Foundation–(v. 6) The act of founding.

C. Mason–(v. 7) One who builds or works with store or brick.

D. Carpenter–(v.7) A worker who makes, finishes, and repairs wooden structures.

2. Teacher Preparation

A. To prepare for today's lesson, read several translations of Ezra 2-4. Read the BACKGROUND and MORE LIGHT ON THE TEXT sections for insight on the text. Underline or highlight specific points you will want to bring out in class.

B. Read the section on Lesson 2 from the QUARTER AT-A-GLANCE. Reflect on how this lesson applies to the quarter's theme of restoration.

C. Read and reflect upon the devotional reading, Psalm 100. Ask yourself how the devotional reading relates to the lesson.

D. Read the LESSON AIM and focus your teaching on achieving these goals. Answer the SEARCH THE SCRIPTURES and MAKE IT HAPPEN questions so you can be prepared to assist the students. You may also think of additional questions that address your students' specific needs and concerns.

3. Starting the Lesson

A. As students arrive, ask them to think about a project that they would like to do as a group. Ask them to briefly sketch out a plan for the project, including what they would need to develop and implement the project.

B. Open the class with a prayer, using the goals of the LESSON AIM.

C. Discuss the Words You Should Know section with students.

4. Getting into the Lesson

A. Have each student take turns reading the FOCAL VERSES, the KEEP IN MIND verse, and the IN DEPTH section. Discuss the meaning of the verses.

B. Ask a volunteer to read the IN FOCUS section. Ask students to discuss Langston Hughes' quote. How does it relate to the lesson? How does it relate to their lives?

C. As a group discuss the SEARCH THE SCRIPTURES questions.

5. Relating the Lesson to Life

A. Divide the class into small groups. Allow the groups to answer the DISCUSS THE MEANING questions. Reconvene and share what was discussed.

B. As a group reflect on the LESSON IN OUR SOCIETY section.

C. Refer back to the projects students thought about at the beginning of class. Allow them to present their ideas. Then decide which one you'd like to use as a part of the MAKE IT HAPPEN assignment.

6. Arousing Action

A. Encourage the students to read the DAILY BIBLE READINGS throughout the week. Encourage them to write journal entries, reflecting on how the Scriptures apply to them.

B. End the class in prayer.

WORSHIP GUIDE

For the Superintendent or Teacher
Theme: Beginning To Rebuild
Theme Song: "We Are One In The Spirit"
Scripture: Ezra 3:1-3, 6-7, 10-13
Song: "Let Us Break Bread Together"
Devotional: Lord, show us how to be one, even as the Father, Son, and the Holy Spirit are one. When we are one, great accomplishments can be completed and great joy will be our results. In Jesus' name. Amen.

BEGINNING TO REBUILD

Bible Background EZRA 3–4
Printed Text EZRA 3:1-3, 6, 10-13
Devotional Reading PSALM 100

LESSON AIM

By the conclusion of this lesson, students should see the power of unity in Ezra's work and grasp the importance of unity in doing God's work.

KEEP IN MIND

"And all the people shouted with a great shout, when they praised the LORD, because the foundation of the house of the LORD was laid" (Ezra 3:11).

FOCAL VERSES

Ezra 3:1 And when the seventh month was come, and the children of Israel were in the cities, the people gathered themselves together as one man to Jerusalem.

2 Then stood up Jeshua the son of Jozadek, and his brethren the priests, and Zerubbabel the son of Shealtiel, and his brethren, and builded the altar of the God of Israel, to offer burnt offerings thereon, as it is written in the law of Moses the man of God.

3 And they set the altar upon his bases; for fear was upon them because of the people of those countries: and they offered burnt offerings thereon unto the LORD, even burnt offerings morning and evening.

6 . . . the foundation of the temple of the LORD was not yet laid.

7 They gave money also unto the masons, and to the carpenters; and meat, and drink, and oil, unto them of Zidon, and to them of Tyre, to bring cedar trees from Lebanon to the sea of Joppa, according to the grant that they had of Cyrus king of Persia.

10 And when the builders laid the foundation of the temple of the LORD, they set the priests in their apparel with trumpets, and the Levites the sons of

LESSON OVERVIEW

LESSON AIM
KEEP IN MIND
FOCAL VERSES
IN FOCUS
THE PEOPLE, PLACES, AND TIMES
BACKGROUND
AT-A-GLANCE
IN DEPTH
SEARCH THE SCRIPTURES
DISCUSS THE MEANING
LESSON IN OUR SOCIETY
MAKE IT HAPPEN
FOLLOW THE SPIRIT
REMEMBER YOUR THOUGHTS
MORE LIGHT ON THE TEXT
DAILY BIBLE READINGS

Asaph with cymbals, to praise the LORD, after the ordinance of David king of Israel.

11 And they sang together by course in praising and giving thanks unto the LORD; because he is good, for his mercy endureth forever toward Israel. And all the people shouted with a great shout, when they praised the LORD, because the foundation of the house of the LORD was laid.

12 But many of the priests and Levites and chief of the fathers, who were ancient men, that had seen the first house, when the foundation of this house was laid before their eyes, wept with a loud voice; and many shouted aloud for joy:

13 So that the people could not discern the noise of the shout of joy from the noise of the weeping of the people: for the people shouted with a loud shout, and the noise was heard afar off.

IN FOCUS

A local schoolteacher had seven days to organize her students for a science fair. This year the rules for the science fair had changed. There would not be individual science projects but classroom projects. She told the children that Langston Hughes said, "I have discovered in life that there are ways of getting almost anywhere you want to go, if you really want to go."

After absorbing those words daily, the children eventually (after many obstacles) discovered that together they were going to get the job done. They went on to win first place in the local and state science fair.

THE PEOPLE, PLACES, AND TIMES

Burnt Offerings. This kind of offering was described as "that which goes up [to God]." This sacrifice, offered every morning and evening, pointed to Christ's atoning death for sinners (2 Corinthians 5:21) and His total consecration to God (Luke 2:49). The burnt offering spoke of Christ's passive obedience and His submission to the penalty required by man's sinfulness.

Jeshua. A high priest of Judah, Jeshua (also called Joshua) was born during the exile of the Jews in Babylon (587-538 B.C.). Before the exile, high priests had been subordinate to the kings of Judah. But when King Cyrus of Persia permitted the Jews to return to Jerusalem and rebuild their temple, Jeshua assumed a major leadership role along with the Jewish governor, Zerubbabel, who remained subject to the Persian ruler. Together the pair saw to it that an altar was erected and worship restored in Jerusalem.

Levites. Descendants of Levi served as assistants to the priests in the worship system of the nation of Israel. As a Levite, Aaron and his sons and their descendents were charged with the responsibility of the priesthood, offering burnt offerings and leading the people in worship and confession.

BACKGROUND

The children of God were getting organized to rebuild. After so many years of captivity, they had to start over again. A type of census was taken to see how many people there were; how much silver and gold; and the people's occupations. In Ezra 2 we learn that there were 42,360 in the congregation. This did not include the 7,337 menservants and maidservants and 200 men and women singers. They had 736 horses, 245 mules, 435 camels, and 6,720 donkeys. Ezra 2:68-70 reads like this from the NIV:

"When they arrived at the house of the LORD in Jerusalem, some of the heads of the families gave freewill offerings toward the rebuilding of the house of God on its site. According to their ability they gave to the treasury for this work 61,000 drachmas of gold, 5,000 minas of silver and 100 priestly garments. The priests, the Levites, the singers, the gatekeepers and the temple servants settled in their own towns, along with some of the other people, and the rest of the Israelites settled in their towns."

AT-A-GLANCE

1. The Children of Israel Gather to Build and Offer Burnt Offerings (Ezra 3:1-3)
2. The Children of Israel Organize Monies and Skilled Persons Needed to Build the Temple (vv. 6, 7)
3. The Children of Israel Lay the Foundation and It's Time for Rejoicing (vv. 10-13)

IN DEPTH

1. The Children of Israel Gather to Build and Offer Burnt Offerings (Ezra 3:1-3)

It was the seventh month, the number of completion and the children of Israel did an awesome thing. They gathered themselves together with one purpose. They also understood that it would take solid unity to rebuild the temple. They were just freed from captivity and settled in their towns when the assembly was called.

Just as with any task, there must be a leader or leaders. There must be someone to point the way and organize the people. Jeshua and Zerubbabel and assistants rose up first to build an altar and offer burnt offerings to the God of Israel. They were doing things in order. Before they would take on the great task of rebuilding the temple, they would make a sacrifice, according to the law of Moses. The Scripture says that despite their fear of those around them, they built an altar and offered sacrifices day and night.

2. The Children of Israel Organize Monies and Skilled Persons Needed to Build the Temple (vv. 6, 7)

The people were making the daily burnt offerings, but the foundation of the temple was not laid. The command was to build the temple. This reveals to us that sometimes we can get so involved in ceremonial rituals and forget about the more important job at hand. It was wonderful that the offerings were going on, but God gave a commandment to work.

They were freed from captivity; now it was time to take the next step.

In verse 7, they proceeded with the plan of rebuilding the temple. They gave money to the masons and carpenters. The workers were being paid for their work and supplies. The business was being taken care of properly. Food, drink, and oil were given to Sidon and Tyre to bring by sea, the trees from Lebanon. The temple would be restored in style! The best of everything. This is what Cyrus king of Persia granted.

3. The Children of Israel Lay the Foundation and It's Time for Rejoicing (vv. 10-13)

Phase one was completed and the people were rejoicing. The builders laid the foundation. No longer was building the temple a faraway dream; their eyes of faith were seeing the final project. The foundation encouraged them that the end was not far. They started a good work, and God was going to see them through it all. God promised that He would.

SEARCH THE SCRIPTURES

1. The people gathered themselves as _____ _____in Jerusalem. (Ezra 3:1)
2. They offered burnt offerings thereon unto the Lord, even burnt offerings _____and _____ (v. 3).
3. They gave _____also unto the _____, and to the _____; and meat, and drink and oil unto them of Zidon (v. 7).
4. And when the _____ laid the _____ of the temple of the Lord, they set the priests in their _____ with trumpets . . . (v. 10)
5. When the foundation of this house was laid before their eyes, wept with a loud _____; and many shouted aloud for joy.

DISCUSS THE MEANING

1. Explain what it means to be "as one man"?
2. Why did the children of Israel offer burnt offerings to the Lord?
3. Why do you think the foundation was not "yet laid" in verse 6?
4. What does "according to the grant that they had of Cyrus king of Persia" mean?

5. Why do you think the people wept and shouted once the foundation was laid?

LESSON IN OUR SOCIETY

Some wonderful things can be accomplished when people come as "one man" as we see in today's lesson. The power of unity is awesome. It takes unity to build a business, a family, a church, and a country. If Christian people will become like the "one man" Christ, there is nothing we cannot do. Think of some projects you were a part of where wonderful results were accomplished because of unity. Also, think of some projects that have failed because of discord.

MAKE IT HAPPEN

Develop an idea for a project and use the principles of today's lesson to complete that project. Afterwards, discuss how you reached your goal in that project.

FOLLOW THE SPIRIT

What God wants me to do:

_____
_____

REMEMBER YOUR THOUGHTS

Special insights you have learned:

_____
_____

MORE LIGHT ON THE TEXT
Ezra 3:1-3, 6-7, 10-13

3:1 And when the seventh month was come, and the children of Israel were in the cities, the people gathered themselves together as one man to Jerusalem.

The direct route from Babylon to Palestine was about 530 miles; however, traveling by land northward over the fertile crescent extended the journey to about 900 miles and would have taken the exiles several months to reach their destination. Later Ezra would make the same journey, departing Babylon on the "first day of the first month" and arriving in Jerusalem on the "first day of the fifth month" a journey of four months (Ezra 7:8-9).

The exiles left in the spring and arrived in Palestine in the early fall. For some time after their arrival they were occupied in the necessary work of rearing habitations for themselves amid the ruins of Jerusalem and its neighborhood. After the people were settled in their cities and towns, a general assembly was called and all the people gathered in Jerusalem on the "first day of the seventh month."

On the Jewish calendar the seventh month was Tishri (September-October). Tishri is most noted for its three holy feasts: the Feast of Trumpets on the first of the month, the Day of Atonement on the tenth of the month, and the Feast of Booths or Tabernacles that begins on the twentieth of the month (Leviticus 23:1-36). The leaders of the people resolved to celebrate their feasts just as if the temple had been fully restored.

The "Children of Israel" is a translation of the Hebrew *bene Yisrael* (pronounced **beh-NAY-YISS-rah-ale**), which is literally translated "sons of Israel." *Bene* generally means "son" but is often used idiomatically to denote children or descendants. Thus the phrase sons of Israel refers to all the people of Israel and not just the males.

"People" is from the Hebrew *am* and essentially refers to people in general. However, the noun usually signifies a group of people united by sustained relationships, such as by religious (Genesis 17:14) and ancestral (25:8, 17) relationships. The Israelites were called "the people of God" (Exodus 15:13; Deuteronomy 32:36), the "holy people" (Deuteronomy 7:6) and the "people of [His] inheritance" (4:20).

2 Then stood up Jeshua the son of Jozadak, and his brethren the priests, and Zerubbabel the son of Shealtiel, and his brethren, and builded the altar of the God of Israel, to offer burnt offerings thereon, as it is written in the law of Moses the man of God.

Jeshua was the grandson of Seraiah, the high priest whom Nebuchadnezzar put to death at Riblah (2 Kings 25:18-21). His father, Jozadak, had been carried captive to Babylon, and died there. His "brethren" were not his actual brothers, but relatives from the line of Aaron (Numbers 3:10).

In 1 Chronicles, Zerubbabel is designated as the son of both Shealtiel and his brother Pedaiah, which suggests a levirate marriage. Levirate (from the Latin meaning "husband's brother") marriages took place when a married brother died. The surviving brother was obligated to marry his brother's widow.

Zerubbabel's "brethren" are the other princes from the Davidic bloodline. Together these princes and priests encouraged the people to build the altar.

The first priority of the exiles was to build an altar to the Lord. It would take a while to get the temple built, but getting the altar built immediately was an absolute necessity. The altar, also called "the altar of burnt offering" (see Exodus 30:28; Leviticus 4:7), was the center of Jewish worship. The altar was the place where atonement for their sins was made. It was also the place to obtain the divine blessing on their preparations for the temple, as well as stimulate their feelings of piety and patriotism for the completion of this national work.

The "burnt offering" from the Hebrew *olah* (pronounced **oh-LAH**) meaning "to go up or bring up." The *olah*, or burnt offering, was the most frequently recurring offering. Individual offering could be a bull (Leviticus 1:3-5) or a sheep or goat (1:10). The offerer placed his hand on the head of the animal to be sacrificed, symbolizing the transfer of sin to the animal. The priest then killed the animal and took the blood and presented it to the LORD, sprinkling it on the horns of the altar which were projections on the four corners of the altar. Then the sacrifice was divided and the purified parts were carefully placed on the altar and burned (Leviticus 1:6-9, 12-13). The burnt offering typified the Lord Jesus offering Himself as our eternal sacrifice.

The reference to the "Law of Moses" alludes to Deuteronomy 12:5-6: "But unto the place which the LORD your God shall choose out of all your tribes to put his name there, even unto his habitation shall ye seek, and thither thou shalt come: And thither ye shall bring your burnt offerings, and your sacrifices, and your tithes, and heave offerings of your hand, and your vows, and your freewill offerings, and the firstlings of your herds and of your flocks."

3 And they set the altar upon his bases; for fear was upon them because of the people of those countries: and they offered burnt offerings thereon unto the LORD, even burnt offerings morning and evening.

The motivation for the building of the altar was the people's understanding of their role on earth as "a kingdom of priests, and an holy nation" (Exodus 19:6). They could only fulfill their divine calling by becoming what God intended them to be. A second reason for getting the altar built quickly was because of the danger of the "people of those countries" or the nations around them. The people realized that God would protect them from their enemies, but only if they approached Him in faith and obedience (see Exodus19:5; Hebrews 4:16).

Setting "the altar upon his bases" means that the people reared the altar upon its old foundation, so that it occupied as nearly as possible the site on which it had formerly stood. Deeming it their duty to perform the public rites of religion, they did not wait until the temple was rebuilt and dedicated.

6 . . . the foundation of the temple of the LORD was not yet laid.

After erecting the altar the people immediately began sacrificing the burnt offerings. They celebrated the "new moon" offering on the first day of the month, three special feasts that occurred in the seventh month, and they resumed the twice-daily sacrifice prescribed by the law. Every day two male lambs were sacrificed one in the morning and one in the evening according to the command: "The one lamb shalt thou offer in the morning, and the other lamb shalt thou offer at evening" (Numbers 28:4). Even though the work on the temple had not even begun, the people knew it was necessary to revive the daily oblation or sacrifice.

7 They gave money also unto the masons, and to the carpenters; and meat, and drink, and oil, unto them of Zidon, and to them of Tyre, to bring cedar trees from Lebanon to the sea of Joppa, according to the grant that they had of Cyrus king of Persia.

The returned exiles followed the same pattern that King Solomon had used to construct the original temple (1 Kings 5:7-12). The Israelites opened negotiations with the Tyrians for workmen, as well as for timber, on the same terms and with the same views as Solomon had done. In exchange for a certain amount of wheat, timber, wine, and olive oil Tyrians and Sidonians would cut down cedars from Lebanon (north of Israel) and float the logs down by sea to Joppa. The Israelites would pick up the logs at Joppa and transport them to Jerusalem (2 Chronicles 2:15-16).

"Masons" from the Hebrew *chatsab* (pronounced

kaht-SAHV), meaning to cut or carve. The word generally referred to wood and stone cutters. "Carpenters" is a translation of the Hebrew *haras* (pronounced **kah-RAHSH**), meaning craftsmen. The term is used in a variety of contexts and encompasses those who possess a wide variety of skills.

King Cyrus's public proclamation that was read to the people (Ezra 1:2-4) did not contain all the details of the order. Some of these details, including "the grant that they had of Cyrus king of Persia," would be spelled out later. The details included the size of the temple which would be 90 feet high and 90 feet wide. The grant to help pay for goods, services, and labor would be covered by money taken from the royal treasury (6:3-5).

10 And when the builders laid the foundation of the temple of the LORD, they set the priests in their apparel with trumpets, and the Levites the sons of Asaph with cymbals, to praise the LORD, after the ordinance of David king of Israel.

"Foundation" is from the Hebrew *yasad* (pronounced **yah-SAD**), meaning to establish, set, or build up. The word carries the idea of fixing or establishing something firmly. The most famous use of *yasad* occurs in the messianic prophecy of Isaiah: "I lay in Zion for a foundation of stone, a tried stone, a precious corner stone, a sure foundation" (28:16).

When the foundation of the temple was finally laid, the priests were clothed "in their apparel." "Apparel" is a translation of the Hebrew *labash* (pronounced **lah-BASH**), which generally refers to garments or clothing. In the case of the priest, the word alluded to their sacred vestments. These vestments included: (1) a breastplate, which was a square containing 12 precious stones placed in four horizontal rows of three. The name of each of the 12 sons of Israel was engraved on each stone; (2) a robe; (3) a tunic; (4) a turban; (5) a sash; and (6) an ephod, which was a loose-fitting sleeveless garment that extended to the knees. It was worn like an apron over the priest's robe. The temple musicians began to play and the people began to praise the Lord according to the prescribed system by David who had given clear instructions on the use of music in the temple (1 Chronicles 25:1-6).

11 And they sang together by course in praising and giving thanks unto the LORD; because he is good, for his mercy endureth for ever toward Israel. And all the people shouted with a great shout, when they praised the LORD, because the foundation of the house of the LORD was laid.

The work of rebuilding the temple began the year after the Israelite exiles arrived in Jerusalem (Ezra 3:8). It took seven months (from the seventh in year 1 to the second month in year 2) just to prepare to build the temple. The preparation time demonstrates the importance the people attached to the holy project. The "second month" is the month of Iyyar (April-May) 535 B.C. Many people believe the laying of the temple's foundation signified the end of the seventy years of captivity begun when the first Israelites were taken into captivity in 605 B.C. (2 Kings 24:1-2; Daniel 1:1).

The people sang songs of praise to the LORD when they saw the foundation of the temple laid because it represented God's answer to their prayers and His goodness to them. Their song of praise pointed back to David's song of thankfulness after the Ark of the Covenant had been brought into Jerusalem (1 Chronicles 16:1-36, especially v. 34).

Old Testament writers used three different basic words to call people to praise and worship. The first word which is used here for praise is the word *halal*, from which we get the word "hallelujah," meaning praise the LORD. *Halal* basically means to celebrate and glorify the LORD.

12 But many of the priests and Levites and chief of the fathers, who were ancient men, that had seen the first house, when the foundation of this house was laid before their eyes, wept with a loud voice; and many shouted aloud for joy: 13 So that the people could not discern the noise of the shout of joy from the noise of the weeping of the people: for the people shouted with a loud shout, and the noise was heard afar off.

Fifty years after its destruction in 586 B.C. by the Babylonians, the temple was being rebuilt. Because the new temple was built on the same foundation as the first one, the two structures were similar in size. However, the old structure was vastly more elaborate and ornate. Solomon's temple was the center of a thriving metropolis, while Zerubbabel's temple was

surrounded by ruins. Many of the older people remembered the glory of the first temple and wept because the second temple was far less grandiose.

The celebration, after the laying of the temple's foundation, was marked by a contrast in the people's emotions. Many of the people were relieved that the shame of their destruction as a nation was now over. Yet some of the older exiles remembered Solomon's grander temple and they wept at the new temple.

Those painful emotions were caused by several sad contrasts; the prosperity of the nation when the first temple was begun and the reduced state of the country of the second temple, as well as the beauty and splendor of the first temple compared to the second. Perhaps the main cause of grief was that the second temple would be destitute of those things which formed the great and distinguishing glory of the first, namely, the ark, the *shekinah* (glory cloud), the *Urim* and *Thummim*, etc. Zerubbabel's temple may have been a grand and beautiful structure, but no matter how great its material splendor, it was inferior to that of Solomon's. Among Eastern people, expressions of sorrow are always very loud and vehement. Expressions of both sorrow and joy are often indicated by wailing, the howl of which is sometimes not easily distinguished.

DAILY BIBLE READINGS

M: The People Worship in Jerusalem
Ezra 3:1-5
T: Worship the Lord with Gladness
Psalm 100:1-5
W: The People Build the Foundation
Ezra 3:6-13
T: Adversaries Discourage the People
Ezra 4:1-5
F: Adversaries Write to the Persian King
Ezra 4:6-16
S: The King Orders the Work Stopped
Ezra 4:17-24
S: Your Foundation Shall Be Laid
Isaiah 44:24-28

TEACHING TIPS

June 15
Bible Study Guide 3

1. Words You Should Know

A. Waste—(Haggai 1:4) Total destruction or disintegration.

B. Messenger—(v. 13) A bearer of news.

2. Teacher Preparation

A. To prepare for today's lesson, read the PEOPLE, PLACES, AND TIMES and BACKGROUND sections. Then read the Bible background, the book of Haggai and Ezra 5:1-2.

B. Study the FOCAL VERSES. Read them from several translations and make notes of pertinent differences to help you explain the verses to the class.

C. Read the LESSON AIM and focus your teaching on achieving these goals. Answer the SEARCH THE SCRIPTURES and MAKE IT HAPPEN questions so you can be prepared to assist the students. You may also think of additional questions that address your students' specific needs and concerns.

3. Starting the Lesson

A. Write the LESSON AIM on the chalkboard. List each point separately to help students focus on the various objectives.

B. Open in prayer, asking God to help students understand the word sent to the exiles and how to apply it to their lives.

4. Getting into the Lesson

A. Discuss the "Words You Show Know" with students.

B. Read the FOCAL VERSES and the KEEP IN MIND verse. Use the IN DEPTH section to discuss the meaning of the verses.

C. Answer the SEARCH THE SCRIPTURES and DISCUSS THE MEANING questions as a group.

5. Relating the Lesson to Life

A. Ask a volunteer to read the IN FOCUS sec-

tion. Discuss Attuk's attitude.

B. Give students paper. Ask each one to reflect on his/her life. How do they compare to the exiles in today's lesson? Have they focused more on taking care of their personal agendas than on taking care of God's kingdom? If so, what has been the result of their actions? How can they change things?

C. Have a brief open discussion about their reflections.

D. Reflect on the LESSON IN OUR SOCIETY section.

6. Arousing Action

A. Encourage the class to continue reflecting on their situations by completing the MAKE IT HAPPEN assignment.

B. Close in prayer, lifting up your students' concerns.

GOD'S MESSAGE TO THE EXILES

Bible Background • HAGGAI; Ezra 5:1-2
Printed Text • HAGGAI 1:2-14
Devotional Reading • 1 CORINTHIANS 3:10-17

JUNE 15TH

LESSON AIM

By the end of the lesson, students will be able to state the issues for which God rebuked the returning exiles, learn from their failure, repentance, and success, act on the word of God, and adjust their priorities according to the Word of the Lord.

KEEP IN MIND

"Is it time for you, O ye, to dwell in your ceiled houses, and this house lie waste?" (Haggai 1:4).

FOCAL VERSES

Haggai 1:2 Thus speaketh the LORD of hosts, saying, This people say, The time is not come, the time that the LORD's house should be built.

3 Then came the word of the LORD by Haggai the prophet, saying,

4 Is it time for you, O ye, to dwell in your ceiled houses, and this house lie waste?

5 Now therefore thus saith the LORD of hosts; Consider your ways.

6 Ye have sown much, and bring in little; ye eat, but you have not enough; ye drink, but ye are not filled with drink; ye clothe you, but there is none warm; and he that earneth wages earneth wages to put it into a bag with holes.

7 Thus saith the LORD of hosts; Consider your ways.

8 Go up to the mountain, and bring wood, and build the house; and I will take pleasure in it, and I will be glorified, saith the LORD.

9 Ye looked for much, and, lo, it came to little;

LESSON OVERVIEW

LESSON AIM
KEEP IN MIND
FOCAL VERSES
IN FOCUS
THE PEOPLE, PLACES,
AND TIMES
BACKGROUND
AT-A-GLANCE
IN DEPTH
SEARCH THE SCRIPTURES
DISCUSS THE MEANING
LESSON IN OUR SOCIETY
MAKE IT HAPPEN
FOLLOW THE SPIRIT
REMEMBER YOUR THOUGHTS
MORE LIGHT ON THE TEXT
DAILY BIBLE READINGS

and when ye brought it home, I did blow upon it. Why? Saith the LORD of hosts. Because of mine house that is waste, and ye run every man unto his own house.

10 Therefore the heaven over you is stayed from dew, and the earth is stayed from her fruit.

11 And I called for a drought upon the land, and upon the mountains, and upon the corn, and upon the new wine, and upon the oil, and upon that which the ground bringeth forth, and upon men, and upon cattle, and upon all the labour of the hands.

12 Then Zerubbabel the son of Shealtiel, and Joshua the son of Josedech, the high priest, with all the remnant of the people, obeyed the voice of the LORD their God, and the words of Haggai the prophet, as the LORD their God had sent him, and the people did fear before the LORD.

13 Then spake Haggai the LORD's messenger in the LORD's message unto the people, saying, I am with you, saith the LORD.

14 And the LORD stirred up the spirit of Zerubbabel the son of Shealtiel, governor of Judah, and the spirit of Joshua the son of Josedech, the high priest, the spirit of all the remnant of the people; and they came and did work in the house of the LORD of hosts, their God,

IN FOCUS

Attuk had been alienated from his family since

he was 22. He had a fallen out with his parents about something he could not remember. He had moved without leaving a forwarding address, and he never called. Now, at the age of thirty, he was married with three children who had never seen and seldom heard about their grandparents. However, Attuk's parents never stopped loving him, and they would ask every family friend and acquaintance about him. One day while he was out shopping, a childhood acquaintance saw him and called out his name. "Where have you been?" asked the old acquaintance. "Your parents are concerned about you," the man continued. Attuk was ashamed and then turned to the man and said, "I have been away so long and there are many hurt feelings between me, my parents, and all my old friends." To this the man responded, "You can still come back home." Attuk went on, "I thought that I would come back to my parents when I had accomplished something and made a life for myself. However, when that happened, I told myself that I would come back when I had made enough money; then the Lord blessed me with money. I then said that I would come back when the Lord blessed me with children, but I never came back." Then the man asked him, "Do you think it is right for you to live in a mansion while your parents live in a shack? Do you suppose it is good for you to have your children while your parents lose the opportunity to be with their own child? Do you suppose that it is good for you to have finances while your parents have spent every dime they have looking for you?"

In today's lesson we see a people who, in spite of God's love for them, have created a priority system that is out of touch with the reality of the God who brought them from exile.

THE PEOPLE , PLACES, AND TIMES

Haggai. An Old Testament prophet and author of the Book of Haggai. As God's spokesman he encouraged the captives who had returned to Jerusalem to complete the reconstruction of the temple. This work had started shortly after the first exiles returned from Babylon in 538 B.C. But the building activity was soon abandoned because of discouragement and oppression. Beginning in 520 B.C. Haggai and his fellow prophet,

Zechariah, urged the people to resume the task. The temple was completed four years later, about 516 B.C. (Ezra 5:1; 6:15)

Remnant. The part of a community or nation that remains after a dreadful judgment or devastating calamity, especially those who have escaped and remain to form the nucleus of a new community. The survival of a righteous remnant rests solely on God's providential care for His chosen people and His faithfulness to keep His covenant promises.

Zerubbabel. The temple that Zerubbabel built in Jerusalem in the sixth century b.c. lasted longer than the temples of Solomon and Herod the Great combined. He was placed in charge of the returning Jews and given the title "Governor of Judah."

BACKGROUND

The Lord had provided wondrously for the children of Israel. They had sinned against Him. Yet He had mercy and promised to deliver them from the hands of their captives. He gave careful instruction to them through the prophets on how and when to build the temple. Yet the Lord's house was not rebuilt. God was waiting for Israel to get their act together and prepare and build again. He was also perhaps waiting until they were settled in their own homes (after being held captive for so long, there had to be a period of adjustment). That period of adjustment, however, had long past, and God was waiting for His people to complete the temple.

AT·A·GLANCE

1. The Message of the Prophet Haggai (Haggai 1:2)
2. A Prophetic Challenge (vv. 3-6)
3. God Sends a Second Command to Build (vv. 7-8)
4. Obedience and Transformation (vv. 9 14)

IN DEPTH

1. The Message of the Prophet Haggai (Haggai 1:2)

Haggai is a message to the returned exiles. Even though they have had more than seventy years to learn about the priority of divine things, a few years after returning from exile, they were back to the old pattern of misplaced priorities and misunderstood purposes. As is the manner of God with Israel, the prophet deals with Israel's seeming ingratitude. God brought them back and made it clear, through the pagan King Cyrus, that the reason for the return was to build the house of the Lord again and to make sure that worship resumed in it. The command was clear: "Go rebuild the temple of God." But after the people had received their freedom, they put other priorities before those of God's. The people had an excuse for not doing this task, which is not unlike the excuses we use as we procrastinate about the things of God. The first excuse was that it was not time. What is the rush? It can wait. Is it not amazing how we suddenly acquire the gift of patience when it comes to doing the things that God has commanded us? Why was it not time to build the house of God? The text lets us know that while they had been freed from physical bondage, they were still bound by the tyranny of time. There never seems to be enough time to do the things of God, but we can always find time for whatever else that may suit our fancy.

They could not say that they did not know how to go about the work, for God had given them specific instructions on how to do it. They could not say that they had no money, for God had provided the monies. They could not say that they had no experts, for God had provided skilled workers. In spite of all the providential preparation, they said that it was not time yet. Could it be that there was something more serious going on here than just the lack of time or even the constraint of time?

2. A Prophetic Challenge (vv. 3-6)

In these verses God, through the prophet, responds to the question raised in the previous section. Since they argued that they did not have time, where did they find the time to do all the things that they were doing? Where did they find time to watch "Jerusalem TV" twenty-four hours a week but could not find time to fellowship with God's people? How could they have a question of time as it relates to God's work but find the time to build their houses? They had placed God lower in importance. Their own comfort had become their god. In short, they had become their own god. What they wanted took precedence over what God wanted. Look at the way God poses the question to them in verse 4: "Is it time for you?" This implies that it was not an issue of time but of their view of God's place in their lives.

This kind of attitude calls for self-examination. God has to rebuke His people. He says in verse 5: "Consider your ways." The idea here is that they now need to think clearly about their stance. The very root of their being (figuratively) and the ground of their inferences needed to be examined in light of God's nature and the work that He had done in their lives. This is God's wake-up call. There is also the call to change, to reconsider, and to recommit. They were to take off their disguise and dispose of it for good.

This call to self-examination implies that if they truly weighed things carefully, they would notice their way was not working. According to verse 6, having made God secondary, rather than having victory (which God promised them), they struggled just for the bare minimum. God, having been put on the back shelf, was withholding His blessings. These people were like so many of us; we want the gifts but not the giver. We need to be reminded that God is our source. We must keep in mind that God is the reason we have what we now possess. How soon do we forget?

3. God Sends a Second Command to Build (vv. 7-8)

God has revealed that there was an imbalance in their lives because of their procrastination and disobedience. In verses 7 and 8, He reveals how they can get back on track again. First, "consider your ways." Second, God seems to be saying: reprioritize. You have a way of escape. God says to go and "build the house" (v. 8). Notice that God does not change the command; He merely gives them a second chance. Obedience to God realigns us with the will of God and puts us in the place where we are able to receive from the Lord. God shows them the immediate consequence of their misplaced loyalty (vv. 9-11). If they have been in trouble in this case, they brought it upon themselves. They chose their own houses instead of God's house. The desolation of God's house led to the desolation of their own houses. Everything that happens to them here is directed to something that they have done or refused to do in relating to God. Just like them, our ways and actions determine our future. God is repeating why His people are in the condition they are in. God had provided everything that they needed and yet there was not a house for Him. The law of recompense was in progress—you reap what you sow.

4. Obedience and Transformation (vv. 9-14)

God is pleased when we hear a rebuke and repent. The people repented after Haggai revealed what God was saying to His people. They did just what God said to do and that was to "consider their ways." We need the Lord to speak to us and tell us about ourselves. He needs to tell us how foolish we are sometimes. When you are suffering, you want answers. God's people were struggling. Maybe they did, or didn't, know why. Perhaps they were in denial and needed a spiritual "thump" on the head to get them back on track.

Haggai assured the people of God's presence (vv.13-14) Once the people obeyed, God reassured them. He said, " I am with you." Just in case there was fear in the camp, God reassured His people that He would be there. This reassurance caused the people to complete the work they started. Their spirits were stirred. They were ready to work.

SEARCH THE SCRIPTURES

1. How did Haggai describe the LORD's house to His people? (Haggai 1:4)

2. What does the LORD of hosts tell Israel to do? (v. 5) Explain.

3. How will God be glorified? (v. 8)

DISCUSS THE MEANING

1. Explain the meaning of verse 6.

2. Explain the meaning of verse 9.

3. Why do you think God is so patient with us?

4. Explain the wrath of God in verse 11.

LESSON IN OUR SOCIETY

If we are honest with ourselves, we will discover that many (not all) of the calamities in our lives are a direct result of our disobedience to God's law. God has told us the way to achieve and succeed, and we choose to go our own way. He says left and we say right. He says up and we say down. He says no and we say yes. In today's lesson the Lord of hosts reveals to His people their disobedience, and they acknowledge it. They acknowledged their disobedience and moved on to do great things in the kingdom. Do you have the same attitude as the children of Israel? If you do, try seeking God's help today.

MAKE IT HAPPEN

Make a list of some circumstances in your life that are not going so favorably. Apply the Scriptures to that situation and watch for the results.

FOLLOW THE SPIRIT

What God wants me to do:

_____

_____

REMEMBER YOUR THOUGHTS

Special insights you have learned:

_____

_____

MORE LIGHT ON THE TEXT
Haggai 1:2-14

1:2 Thus speaketh the LORD of hosts, saying, This people say, The time is not come, the time that the LORD's house should be built.

The temple of the LORD was central to the nation of Israel and to the Jewish religious life. Without the temple the Jews had no rallying point to bind them together. Even in their diaspora (or scattering abroad) whenever they prayed, they faced the direction of the temple (1 Kings 8:48; Jonah 2:7). When the exiles arrived in Jerusalem, their primary concern was the rebuilding of the temple. Unfortunately the Samaritans, who had resided in Palestine since the Jews were taken into captivity, attempted to join the Jews in their rebuilding efforts but were rejected.

The rejected Samaritans applied threats and political pressure to bring the temple work to a halt. Finding it easier to stop building than to fight their neighbors, the Jews stopped working on the temple. Their pessimism led to spiritual lethargy, and they soon became preoccupied with building homes. They used opposition as an excuse for neglecting the house of the LORD, claiming the timing wasn't right. Work on the temple ceased in 536 B.C.; sixteen years later in 520 B.C. God called His prophet Haggai to the task of urging the people to complete the temple.

The name Haggai is derived from the Hebrew word *hag* meaning feast or festival, which usually refers to the three pilgrimage feasts of the Jewish religious calendar (Feasts of Unleavened Bread, of Weeks, and of Tabernacles). The prophet may have been born during the celebration of one of these feasts.

The phrase "thus speaketh the LORD of hosts" makes it clear that the words the prophet spoke were not merely his, but God's. A similar phrase "saith the LORD" is constantly repeated throughout the book (1:7, 13; 2:4, 6-9, 11, 14, 23). The point is that Haggai was merely an instrument through whom God spoke.

"The title "LORD of hosts" is a translation of the Hebrew phrase *YHWH Sava* (pronounced **tsah-VAH**), rendered in the Greek Septuagint as *Jehovah Sabaoth* and literally means Lord of armies or hosts. Although *sava* had definite military implications, it points to God's rulership over the entire universe. The "army of the Lord" (Joshua 5:14-15) and the "host of heaven" probably refer to angelic beings.

Haggai's first words to the people attack their excuse for not completing the temple-building project. He begins by addressing the people as "this people" rather than "my people." Since they have neglected *His* service, they do not deserve to be *His people*. The prophet used the same phrase as a term of reproach (Jeremiah 14:10, 11).

"That time" (or the proper time for building

the temple) had not come was the excuse the people used to explain their neglect of God's work. They claimed that the interruption in the work caused by their enemies proved it was not yet the "proper time" to rebuild the temple. However, their real motive was selfish dislike of the trouble, expense, and danger from enemies. Now that Darius, who was sympathetic to their cause, was king, there was no excuse for not beginning the work at once.

3 Then came the word of the LORD by Haggai the prophet, saying, 4 Is it time for you, O ye, to dwell in your ceiled houses, and this house lie waste?

The Lord (Hebrew, *Yahweh*) is God's covenant title, implying His unchangeableness, the guarantee of His faithfulness in keeping His promises to His people. In response to the people saying that it was not the time to build the Lord's house, God asks the people how is it that they make it a good time not only to build but to "dwell" at ease in their own houses?

He says, "O ye" or rather (literally) "you, you"; the repetition shows the shameful contrast between their concern for themselves and their unconcern for God (see 1 Samuel 25:24 and Zechariah 7:5 for similar uses of repetition). The word "ceiled" is from the Hebrew *sapan* (pronounced **sah-FAN**), meaning "paneled," referring to the walls and ceilings of the people's homes, which were not only furnished with comfort but with luxury, in sad contrast to God's house which was not merely unadorned, but the very walls were not raised above the foundations.

5 Now therefore thus saith the LORD of hosts; Consider your ways. 6 Ye have sown much, and bring in little; ye eat, but ye have not enough; ye drink, but ye are not filled with drink; ye clothe you, but there is none warm; and he that earneth wages earneth wages to put it into a bag with holes.

"Consider your ways" translates two Hebrew words: *Siym* (pronounced seem) meaning set, put, or establish, and *lebab* (pronounced **lay-VAHV**), meaning heart (and thus conscience or mind). The phrase is literally, "Set your heart" and so "give careful consideration." The implication is to consider both what you have done and what you have suffered. The plural "ye" implies that all the people had been seeking self above God.

The people would not prosper while neglecting their duty to God. They sought to escape poverty by not building and thus keep their money to themselves. God was not punishing them because they neglected building, but because of their cheating. Instead of cheating God, they had only been cheating themselves.

The verbs are in infinitive form, implying a continuing state of want: "Ye have sown much, and [continually] bring in little; ye eat, but ye [never] have enough; ye drink, but ye are [never] filled with drink; ye clothe you, but there is none [who is ever] warm; and he that earneth wages earneth wages to put it into a bag with holes."

"Wages . . . put . . . into a bag with holes" is a proverbial saying for labor and money spent profitlessly. Because of the high cost of necessities or through foolish spending, those who worked for a day's wages parted with them at once, as though they had put the money into a bag with holes in it.

7 Thus saith the LORD of hosts; Consider your ways. 8 Go up to the mountain, and bring wood, and build the house; and I will take pleasure in it, and I will be glorified, saith the LORD.

"The mountain" is probably a reference to the mountains around Israel, which would now be covered with trees because of the long period of the captivity.

"Wood" was the first necessity to building the temple, though not to the exclusion of other materials, such as stones, which would also be needed.

God declared "I will take pleasure" and "I will be glorified" in the newly built temple. "Pleasure" from the Hebrew *Ratsah* (pronounced **rah-SAH**), denotes "delight in" or "to be pleased with." *Ratsah* frequently describes God's pleasure with His servants. "Glorified" is from *kabed* (pronounced **kah-VADE**), meaning to be honored or renowned. God is saying that He would be favorable to supplicants in the temple and receive the honor due to Him which had been withheld by

neglecting the temple, which is the sign of His presence.

9 Ye looked for much, and, lo, it came to little; and when ye brought it home, I did blow upon it. Why? saith the LORD of hosts. Because of mine house that is waste, and ye run every man unto his own house.

You "looked" so as to turn your eyes to "much." The Hebrew infinitive here expresses continued looking. The people hoped to increase their own possessions by neglecting the temple. But "when ye brought it home, I did blow upon it." Even the little crop the people harvested and stored in their barns God scattered. "I did blow upon it," that is, God scattered and caused it to perish with His mere breath, as with scattered and blighted wheat. Why did God deal so harshly with His people? Because His house was in ruin while the people rushed ("run") to pursue their own selfish interests.

10 Therefore the heaven over you is stayed from dew, and the earth is stayed from her fruit. 11 And I called for a drought upon the land, and upon the mountains, and upon the corn, and upon the new wine, and upon the oil, and upon that which the ground bringeth forth, and upon men, and upon cattle, and upon all the labour of the hands.

The sky (heaven) is stayed or literally "stays itself." Here sky is personified; implying that even inanimate nature (heaven and earth) obeys God's will and withholds its goods from disobedient people. God identifies Himself as the invisible first cause and declares it to be His doing. He "calls for" famine, drought, and poverty as instruments of His wrath. "Drought," from the Hebrew *choreb* (pronounced **KHO-rev**), sounds like *chareeb* (pronounced **khah-RAVE**), meaning "waste," which describes God's house (vv. 4, 9), implying the correspondence between the sin and its punishment. They have let His house "be waste," and He will send "a drought" on all that is theirs. This would affect not only the crops, but also "men" and "cattle." The "labour of the hands" refers to the fruit of lands, gardens, and vineyards obtained by labor of their hands.

12 Then Zerubbabel the son of Shealtiel, and Joshua the son of Josedech, the high priest, with all the remnant of the people, obeyed the voice of the LORD their God, and the words of Haggai the prophet, as the LORD their God had sent him, and the people did fear before the LORD.

Zerubbabel the political leader, Joshua the high priest, and all those who returned from the exile heard Haggai's word and obeyed God's call to complete their divinely appointed task. "Obeyed" translates the Hebrew word *shama* (pronounced **shah-MAH**), which literally means to "hear" and implies to "give undivided attention to." The people heard the message and responded with heartfelt obedience even though the work on the temple had not yet begun. The Hebrew *dabar* (pronounced **dah-VAHR**), in this case refers to the "word of the Lord." The "word of the Lord" is the essential content of God's revelation through His prophets or messengers.

13 Then spake Haggai the LORD's messenger in the LORD's message unto the people, saying, I am with you, saith the LORD.

The Lord's "messenger," Hebrew *malak* (pronounced **mah-LAHK**), generally depicts an ambassador who carries a message or performs some specific commission or serves as a representative of the one who sent him. God's message, delivered by Haggai, was four simple but profound words, "I am with you." It is a promise of God's ever-present empowerment to all those He commissions to service.

The people's attitude had changed and even before they actually set to work, God's tone changes at once from reproving tenderness. He immediately forgets their past unfaithfulness and assures them that their obedience leads to blessing.

14 And the LORD stirred up the spirit of Zerubbabel the son of Shealtiel, governor of Judah, and the spirit of Joshua the son of Josedech, the high priest, and the spirit of all the remnant of the people; and they came and did work in the house of the LORD of hosts, their God.

The "Lord stirred up the spirit," that is, God

blessed them with enthusiasm and perseverance to complete the good work, though they had been slothful. The people eagerly "came and did work" collecting the wood, stones, and other materials for the work.

Zerubbabel ultimately became the Persian governor of Judah under Darius and after much delay succeeded in building the temple (Ezra 3:8-10; Haggai 1:14) Because of the deep. personal interest he took in the temple, it was often called Zerubbabel's temple.

DAILY BIBLE READINGS

M: Time to Rebuild
Haggai 1:1-6
T: God Stirs the People's Spirits
Haggai 1:7-15
W: Take Courage, I Am With You
Haggai 2:1-9
T: They Did Not Stop
Ezra 5:1-5
F: We Are the Servants of God
Ezra 6:6-12
S: From That Time Until Now
Ezra 5:13-17
S: From This Day I Will Bless
Haggai 2:13-23

TEACHING TIPS

June 22
Bible Study Guide 4

1. Words You Should Know

A. Jealous—(Zechariah 8:2) Vigilant in guarding something, envious, desirous.

B. Fury—(v. 2) Violent anger, rage.

C. Residue—(v. 11) The remainder of something after removal of parts or part.

2. Teacher Preparation

A. To prepare for today's lesson, read the PEOPLE, PLACES, AND TIMES and BACKGROUND sections. Then read the Bible background to Zechariah 8.

B. Study the FOCAL VERSES. Read them from several translations and make note of pertinent differences to help you explain the verses to the class.

C. Write down the answers to the SEARCH THE SCRIPTURES and DISCUSS THE MEANING questions and study them.

D. Read and reflect upon the devotional reading.

3. Starting the Lesson

A. Open the class with prayer, asking the Lord to help students to know His will for their lives.

B. Share "Words You Should Know" with students.

C. Read FOCAL VERSES and KEEP IN MIND verses together as a class. Then have each student read two paragraphs of the IN DEPTH section. Discuss the meaning of the verses.

4. Getting into the Lesson

A. Ask a volunteer to read IN FOCUS and ask if the students know of anyone like Mr. Watershaw. Ask them to reflect on how they may be like Mr. Watershaw.

B. Ask students to work together in pairs to answer the questions. Assign each pair a question from the SEARCH THE SCRIPTURES and DISCUSS THE MEANING sections. Have them

answer their respective question and discuss as a class.

5. Relating the Lesson to Life

A. As a group, reflect on the poem in LESSON IN OUR SOCIETY.

B. Ask students to write their own modern-day description of Zechariah 8:4-5. What can they do this week to help bring about this vision?

6. Arousing Action

A. Ask the class to complete the FOLLOW THE SPIRIT and REMEMBER YOUR THOUGHTS sections.

B. Encourage your class to read the DAILY BIBLE READINGS each day and to memorize key Scriptures to hide in their hearts.

C. End the class in prayer.

WORSHIP GUIDE

For the Superintendent or Teacher
Theme: Hope For A New Ear
Theme Song: "Tis So Sweet To Trust In Jesus"
Scripture: Zechariah 8:1-13
Song: "The Only Hope"
Devotional: "Lord, thank You for having great expectations for me. Thank You for loving, restoring, and encouraging me. I appreciate Your love for me. I appreciate Your encouraging me. Teach me how to do the same to my fellow brothers and sisters. Amen."

HOPE FOR A NEW ERA

Bible Background • ZECHARIAH 8
Printed Text • ZECHARIAH 8:1-13
Devotional Reading • PSALM 48:1-14

LESSON AIM

By the end of this lesson, students will be able to articulate Zechariah's vision of the new world, grasp the requirement to participate in it, and appreciate God's plan for believers and walk in that knowledge.

KEEP IN MIND

"I am returned unto Zion, and will dwell in the midst of Jerusalem: and Jerusalem shall be called a city of truth; and the mountain of the LORD of hosts the holy mountain" (Zechariah 8:3).

FOCAL VERSES

Zechariah 8:1 Again the word of the LORD of hosts came to me, saying,

2 Thus saith the LORD of hosts; I was jealous for Zion with great jealousy, and I was jealous for her with great fury.

3 Thus saith the LORD; I am returned unto Zion, and will dwell in the midst of Jerusalem: and Jerusalem shall be called a city of truth; and the mountain of the LORD of hosts the holy mountain.

4 Thus saith the LORD of hosts; There shall yet old men and old women dwell in the streets of Jerusalem, and every man with his staff in his hand for very age.

5 And the streets of the city shall be full of boys and girls playing in the streets thereof.

6 Thus saith the LORD of hosts; If it be marvellous in the eyes of the remnant of this people in these days, should it also be marvellous in mine eyes? saith the LORD of hosts.

JUNE 22ND

7 Thus saith the LORD of hosts; Behold, I will save my people from the east country, and from the west country;

8 And I will bring them, and they shall dwell in the midst of Jerusalem: and they shall be my people, and I will be their God, in truth and in righteousness.

9 Thus saith the LORD of hosts; Let your hands be strong, ye that hear in these days these words by the mouth of the prophets, which were in the day that the foundation of the house of the LORD of hosts was laid, that the temple might be built.

10 For before these days there was no hire for man, nor any hire for beast; neither was there any peace to him that went out or came in because of the affliction: for I set all men every one against his neighbour.

11 But now I will not be unto the residue of this people as in the former days, saith the LORD of hosts.

12 For the seed shall be prosperous; the vine shall give her fruit, and the ground shall give her increase, and the heavens shall give their dew; and I will cause the remnant of this people to possess all these things.

13 And it shall come to pass, that as ye were a curse among the heathen, O house of Judah, and house of Israel; so will I save you, and ye shall be a blessing: fear not, but let your hands be strong.

IN FOCUS

Watershaw considered himself a good father; he worked several jobs to provide for his family. One day while he was coming home from a meeting, he decided to stop at a bar. He had never been a drinker, and subsequently he ended up drunk. To make matters worse, on his way home he had an accident in which a man lost his life. The next day he found himself in the hospital handcuffed, and a policeman was sitting by his bed. He was allowed to make one phone call, and he called home to his wife who had been worried all night. She answered the phone with panic in her voice, "Are you alright?" He answered, "No, I got drunk last night and got into an accident." Shocked, his wife replied, "But you do not drink!" Watershaw replied, "I know, and that's not all; a man is dead." She began to weep. All he could say was: "I am truly sorry." His wife promised to stay with him throughout the process. The family of the dead man sued him, and they had to sell their house to pay the legal fees. Eventually, Watershaw was sentenced to three years in prison. The pressure became so great that his three boys began to fight amongst themselves. In addition, the neighbors began to mock Mrs. Watershaw, telling her that they knew her husband was no good and their children would amount to nothing.

Mrs. Watershaw began to pray and read Zechariah 8. She believed that just as God promised Israel restoration, so too, God would restore her family. After her husband was released they both worked hard to send their children through school. One son is a pastor, the other a dentist, and another is an engineer. God did restore her family, and today the same people who mocked the family now consider them a blessing. Although the family still has problems, they have been transformed by the word of God. This is what God can do and has promised to do for His people, now and in His everlasting kingdom.

THE PEOPLE, PLACES, AND TIMES

Zechariah. One of the twelve minor prophets whose work conclude the Old Testament. Zechariah wanted to motivate the Jews to rebuild the temple after their return from exile in Babylon, but he used a different approach from that of his contemporary Haggai. Prophesying between August and December of 520 B.C., Haggai promised the Jews an end to their crop failures and economic misery. "From this day [on]," the prophet said, quoting God, "I will bless you" (Haggai 2:19). Zechariah, prophesying from 520 B.C. to perhaps 480 B.C., promised them a Messiah and a return to the glorious days of King David.

Lord of Hosts. *Yahweh-tsebaoth,* (pronounced **tsih-vah-OATH**). This name, translated "the Lord-of-hosts," was used in the days of David and the prophets, witnessing to God the Savior who is surrounded by His armies of heavenly power (1 Samuel 1:3).

Curse. A prayer for injury, harm, or misfortune to befall someone. Noah, for instance, pronounced a curse on Canaan (Genesis 9:25). Isaac pronounced a curse on anyone who cursed Jacob (Genesis 27:29). The soothsayer Balaam was hired by Balak, king of Moab, to pronounce a curse on the Israelites (Numbers 24:10). In Bible times a curse was considered to be more than a mere wish that evil would befall one's enemies; it was believed to possess the power to bring about the evil the curser spoke.

BACKGROUND

The setting at the beginning of the Book of Zechariah is the same as the setting of the Book of Haggai. The prophet Haggai spoke directly to the issue of rebuilding the Temple, encouraging those who returned from captivity in Babylon to finish the task. Zechariah spoke to that issue as well. According to Ezra 5:1, Zechariah wished to bring about a complete spiritual renewal through faith and hope in God. He spoke about the nature of God's Law and of the hope which God

---

AT-A-GLANCE

1. The Divine Jealousy for the Land (Zechariah 8:1-2)
2. Divine Jealousy for the People (vv. 4-5)
3. The Power of Divine Jealousy (vv. 6-13)

promised to those who were faithful to Him. There is also a certain eschatological (or end-times) dimension to this passage of Scripture on which this lesson is grounded.

IN DEPTH

1. The Divine Jealousy for the land (Zechariah 8:1-2)

Zechariah the prophet received a word from the Lord concerning Zion. This was a heartfelt word filled with compassion. God is telling His people that He is jealous. He feels desire towards Zion with "great jealousy." The idea here is that God has been provoked to respond because of the treatment of Zion. God says, "My love for Mount Zion is passionate and strong" (v. 2, NIV). Very strong language. The word great, mighty, or immense is used twice in one sentence and "jealous" from the Hebrew *qana* (pronounced kah-NAH) is used three times. Where does this jealousy come from? Here God is not jealous because Israel is worshiping another god; this is an anger about what has been done to the people of God's heritage. Zion has been in the hands of another and has been treated as an unwanted spouse. People have exploited her and treated her with contempt. Those who had authority over her did not know her worth.

This jealousy (or zeal) of God is grounded in the fact that God had betrothed Israel unto Himself. God's heart is moved because, having chastened Israel, she now has become fair game to all the powers that be. This jealousy is combined with anger not at Zion but for her. What great love! This jealousy (or desire) moves God to return to Israel because she had provoked Him to anger, but in verse two God returns also out of jealousy on her behalf. This time God is not returning just to visit but to "dwell in Jerusalem." One reason for God's return is that Jerusalem had gained a reputation for lying and stealing. God's name was joined to the city, and His return would bring back truth and holiness. When God leaves there is disaster; when He returns there are blessings.

2. Divine Jealousy for the People (vv. 4-5)

One of the consequences of the jealousy which

resulted from Israel's disobedience was that old men and women were afraid to sit on the streets. Vandals and hoodlums had taken over the city, resulting in the aged (who should be enjoying the children playing) hiding in their houses afraid to come out. One of the things which we are fast losing is the African and African American tradition of elders sitting outside in the evening and watching the young enjoy the world. God's jealousy here is that though His people had come back from exile, they were not free. There is another implication as well; if the old people could not sit outside, they could not go to worship. If they went to worship, they could not stay and enjoy themselves for fear of danger. The measure of any people's freedom is the extent to which their elders and children are safe within their streets.

What a wonderful picture. The young and old, boys and girls are dwelling peaceably in the streets of Jerusalem. The children are playing and having a good time. They don't have to worry about a stray bullet from a drive-by shooting harming them. They can play hopscotch and baseball without fear of being kidnaped or molested. The elderly can walk without worrying if they will be robbed. This is what God pictured for Jerusalem, a happy and safe place. Rest assured that whatever God says He is going to do, He will do.

3. The Power of Divine Jealousy (vv. 6-13)

The LORD of hosts says that this vision of Jerusalem is marvelous. Divine jealousy in this text results not in judgement, but in compassion. He is going to gather His people from the east and west countries and bring them to Jerusalem. In Jerusalem He is going to be their God, in truth and righteousness. The people whom He loves shall be in one place. God is revealing His love by saying all that He wants to do. He wants to save them. He wants to gather them. He wants to bring them to His choice place.

God wants the hands of His people to be strong because things were about to change. Prior to this, there was no peace because God Himself had set the people against each other. But now He won't act in that way. Their farming is going to be prosperous; the ground will increase, and the drought will cease. God is going to cause His people to possess all things, and they will no longer be cursed.

SEARCH THE SCRIPTURES

1. What type of city shall Jerusalem be called? (Zechariah 8:3)

2. Who will fill the streets in the city of Jerusalem? (vv. 4, 5)

3. Where will the Lord of hosts save His people from? (v. 7)

4. What did God command to be strong? (v. 9)

5. God set all men against his _____. (v. 10)

DISCUSS THE MEANING

1. The Ten Commandments reveal that God is jealous. What does God mean by "I was jealous for Zion" ?

2. What will be marvelous in the eyes of the Lord of Hosts? (v. 6)

3. Explain verse 10.

4. What is meant by "residue"? (v. 11)

LESSON IN OUR SOCIETY

This writer wrote a poem in 1999 inspired from the Holy Scripture of Zechariah 8:5. "And the streets of the city shall be full of boys and girls playing in the streets thereof."

MOVING IN THE STREETS
Can You Hear it?
There Is Movement In The Streets
Little Boys Playing Baseball
Caps Turned Backward
Red, Blue, & White
Sucking On Bright Red Blow Pops
Forming Little Lumps In Their Jaws
Little Girls Playing Jumprope,
Hopscotch
Braided Hair Waving In The Air
1, 2 Buckle My Shoe
3, 4 Shut The Door
Mommas Walking With
Their Babies In Carriages
High Heels, Gym Shoes, No Shoes
Hush, Little Baby, Don't You Cry!
Daddies & Big Brothers Washing Cars

Buicks, Chevrolets, Mercedes, Lincolns
and Cadillacs
Oh Yes, Moving In The Streets
Little Girls & Little Boys & Mommas &
Babies
Daddies & Big Brothers
Unity

Is This Not Marvelous In God's Sight?
The Holy Prophet Zechariah Saw It in
Verses 5 & 6 in Chapter 8

MAKE IT HAPPEN

Zechariah paints a wonderful picture of how Christ desires the streets of the community and the world to be. What are we doing as children of God to keep our streets crime free and drug free? Make a personal commitment today to make your community a picture similar to Zechariah 8:3-5.

FOLLOW THE SPIRIT

What God wants me to do:

_____

_____

REMEMBER YOUR THOUGHTS

Special insights you have learned:

_____

_____

MORE LIGHT ON THE TEXT
Zechariah 8:1-13

1 Again the word of the LORD of hosts came to me, saying, 2 Thus saith the LORD of hosts; I was jealous for Zion with great jealousy, and I was jealous for her with great fury.

Zechariah, meaning "the LORD remembers," is the eleventh of the twelve Minor Prophets. He describes himself as "the son of Berechiah" (1:1). In Ezra 5:1 and 6:14 he is called "the son of Iddo," who was probably his grandfather. Born during the Babylonian captivity, Zechariah was a fairly young man when he returned to Jerusalem with the first group of exiles in 538 B.C.

Zechariah was both a prophet and a priest, and he was a contemporary of Haggai. He delivered his first prophecy two months after Haggai's first prophecy. (Compare Haggai 1:1 and Zechariah

1:1.) Like Haggai, Zechariah encouraged the people to continue rebuilding the temple. Zechariah spoke to the people's apathy in continuing the work and their discouragement over the smaller size of the new temple's foundation.

The first six chapters of Zechariah's book record a series of eight visions succeeding one another in one night. The visions may be regarded as a symbolical history of Israel, intended to furnish consolation to the returned exiles and stir up hope in their minds. The symbolical action, the crowning of Joshua the priest (6:9-15) describes how the kingdoms of the world become the kingdom of God's Christ. Chapters 7 and 8 are an answer to the question whether the days of mourning for the destruction of the city should be kept any longer, plus an encouraging address to the people, assuring them of God's presence and blessing.

"Again" alludes to the fact that the phrase "the word the LORD came to me" or some variation appears eleven times in the Book of Zechariah. On one occasion it was to Zerubbabel, but given

to Zechariah (4:6). In all the other instances the word of the LORD came to Zechariah and was delivered to the people.

There are ten blessings promised in this chapter; each blessing is preceded by the phrase "Thus saith the LORD." The first blessing is God's burning desire towards Jerusalem. Zion refers to Mt. Zion, the hill on which the city of Jerusalem is located. God, being jealous for Zion, expresses His jealousy for the city of Jerusalem. Jealous (Hebrew *qana,* (pronounced **kah-NAH**), is both a warning to Israel that it should be careful not to sin against God's love and its own welfare, plus a pledge of His great desire to do her good and to rescue her from her enemies. God's jealousy for His people is first spoken of at Mt. Sinai at the giving of the Law (Exodus 20:5). His divine love is so great that He tolerates no rivals for its affection (34:14) and prompts His fury on all those who oppose Him. "Fury" is from the Hebrew *hemah* (pronounced **hkay-MAH**), meaning anger or (in this case) God's divine wrath.

3 Thus saith the LORD; I am returned unto Zion, and will dwell in the midst of Jerusalem: and Jerusalem shall be called a city of truth; and the mountain of the LORD of hosts the holy mountain.

God's presence is the key to the second blessing of this chapter. "I am returned unto Zion." God pledges to restore Israel from captivity and to dwell among His people. The temple shall be rebuilt, as will Jerusalem. Instead of being false or unholy, the city will be called the "city of truth" and the temple mount will be referred to as "the holy mountain."

The basis of the full restoration of Israel is God's return to Zion, "the mountain of the Lord." God's "return" from the Hebrew *sub* (pronounced **shoov**), denotes a movement back to a point of departure. The promise of God to Zion looks ahead to the time when Christ will return and establish His reign over all the nations of the earth. The word translated "truth" from the Hebrew *emeth* (pronounced **EH-meh**), suggests the idea of faithfulness. The people of Israel will love the truth and worship God in their hearts and in their conduct. At that time God's presence will make Mt. Zion a holy mountain. This means that Mt. Zion will be set apart for the worship of the one true God.

4 Thus saith the LORD of hosts; There shall yet old men and old women dwell in the streets of Jerusalem, and every man with his staff in his hand for very age. 5 And the streets of the city shall be full of boys and girls playing in the streets thereof.

During periods of turmoil and strife the young, old, and the infirmed are the most likely to suffer and die. These groups are plentiful in this vision. This is a promise of complete peace and prosperity in the new kingdom. Israel shall be tranquil and prosperous. War shall no longer kill people prematurely. Therefore, men and women will reach advanced ages. The promise of long life was esteemed one of the greatest blessings in the Jewish theocracy with its temporal rewards of obedience (Exodus 20:12; Deuteronomy 4:40). "Boys and girls playing" implies both security and an abundant progeny, which was also seen as a leading blessing among the Jews.

6 Thus saith the LORD of hosts; If it be marvellous in the eyes of the remnant of this people in these days, should it also be marvellous in mine eyes? saith the LORD of hosts.

The words of verse six were spoken to those who lacked the faith to receive God's promises. The rhetorical question implies that nothing is too hard for God. The word "marvelous" is a translation of the Hebrew word *pala* (pronounced **pah-LAH**) meaning wondrous or miraculous. The word describes things and events that are beyond the limits of human power and expectation. However impossible these promises may seem to you, they are not so impossible with God. The "remnant" who had returned from the Babylonian captivity saw a desolate city whose walls and houses were in ruins. They could hardly believe what God promised, even though they had experienced His power so marvelously displayed in their restoration.

7 Thus saith the LORD of hosts; Behold, I will save my people from the east country, and from the west country; 8 And I will bring them, and they shall dwell in the midst of Jerusalem: and they shall be my people, and I will be their God, in truth and in righteousness.

God's covenant relationship with His people had been broken by their constant sin. Here Zechariah prophesies a renewal of the relationship as promised in Deuteronomy 30:1-6. God promises a future re-gathering of Jews to the land of Israel. To "save" literally means to rescue, help, or preserve. Here the word denotes the physical deliverance from enemies and hints at everlasting salvation. The name Jesus, from the Hebrew *Yeshuah* (pronounced **YESH-shoo-uh**), is from this root.

"From the east country, and west country" refers to every region on earth. "East" is the rising of the sun and west is literally "the going down of the sun." The dispersion under Nebuchadnezzar was only to the east, that is, to Babylonia. Therefore, the restoration, including God dwelling in their midst, must refer to a future event. "In truth" means in good faith, both on their side and God's. God is always faithful to His everlasting covenant, and His Spirit in them will enable them to be faithful to Him.

9 Thus saith the LORD of hosts; Let your hands be strong, ye that hear in these days these words by the mouth of the prophets, which were in the day that the foundation of the house of the LORD of hosts was laid, that the temple might be built.

After assuring the people of their future, the LORD now returns to their present and encourages the people in their struggles. The phrase "let your hands be strong" is used as an exhortation for the strength and courage necessary for battle (cf. Judges 7:11; 2 Samuel 2:7). The exhortation was addressed to those who "hear in these days" or the returned remnant. "The prophets" here are not Zechariah or Haggai who encouraged completion of the temple after the foundation had been laid. These are unknown prophets who ministered back in the days when the repairs on the temple had first begun.

10 For before these days there was no hire for man, nor any hire for beast; neither was there any peace to him that went out or came in because of the affliction: for I set all men every one against his neighbour.

Verse 10 reflects on the situation in Judah before the work on the temple resumed. "For before these days" is a reference to the time before the people proceeded with the building of the temple, during which the temple was neglected and ignored. During this time there was "no hire for man" which means there was no produce from the field to pay for labor or to feed the livestock (compare Haggai 1:6, 9-10). "Neither was there any peace" declares that no one could safely do business at home or abroad, in the city or in the country, whether going or returning. "Because of the affliction" means being sorely pressed by foes inside and outside the city.

11 But now I will not be unto the residue of this people as in the former days, saith the LORD of hosts. 12 For the seed shall be prosperous; the vine shall give her fruit, and the ground shall give her increase, and the heavens shall give their dew; and I will cause the remnant of this people to possess all these things.

The key words of verse 11 ("but now") indicate a change in tenor from verse 10. Before beginning the work, the people had been subject to the covenant curses (Leviticus 26:14-33). "But now" they enjoy the blessing of their covenant relationship (26:1-13). For the seed shall be prosperous" has a double meaning. First, the people shall be a holy and peaceable people. Secondly, God will pour down His blessing on them. The planted "seed" now yields abundant crop, and the "heavens shall give her dew" or the rainfall so necessary to growing crops.

13 And it shall come to pass, that as ye were a curse among the heathen, O house of Judah, and house of Israel; so will I save you, and ye shall be a blessing: fear not, but let your hands be strong.

Verse 13 summarizes the main thoughts of chapters 1 through 8, contrasting Israel's past with her future. "Curse" is a translation of the Hebrew word *qelalah qelalah* meaning to despise

or vilify (the exact opposite of blessing). The destruction of the country caused Israel to be vilified (seen as vile) among the nations. The heathen had made Israel another name for "a curse." In the future their name would become a formula of blessing, so that people would pronounce blessings on their friends and loved ones by saying, "May your happiness be like Judah's" (Genesis 48:20).

Instead of being despised among the people, they shall be blessed; instead of being reproached, they shall be commended. The Israelites would be a blessing to all the nations round about. All these promises we may expect to be completely fulfilled when the Jews acknowledge their Messiah (Romans 11:26; Revelation 1:7).

The distinct mention of "Judah" and "Israel" proves that the prophecy has not yet had its full accomplishment because the ten tribes of Israel have not yet been restored, though individuals from Israel returned with Judah.

DAILY BIBLE READINGS

M: I Will Return to Zion
Zechariah 8:1-6

T: Let Your Hands Be Strong
Zechariah 8:7-12

W: You Shall Be a Blessing
Zechariah 8:13-17

T: Many People Will Seek the Lord
Zechariah 8:18-23

F: Great Is the Lord
Psalm 48:1-8

S: Let Zion Be Glad
Psalm 48:9-14

S: Sing Praises Among the Nations
Psalm 57:7-11

TEACHING TIPS

June 29
Bible Study Guide 5

1. Words You Should Know

A. Dedication—(Ezra 6:16) To set apart for a deity or for religious purposes.

B. Unleavened Bread—(v. 22) Bread that has no yeast or dough that rises; flat bread like a cracker.

2. Teacher Preparation

A. To prepare for today's lesson, read the PEOPLE, PLACES, AND TIMES and BACKGROUND sections. Then read the Bible background to Ezra 5-6.

B. Study the FOCAL VERSES. Read them from several translations and make notes of pertinent differences to help you explain the verses to the class.

C. Write down the answers to the SEARCH THE SCRIPTURES and DISCUSS THE MEANING questions and study them.

D. Read and reflect upon the devotional reading.

3. Starting the Lesson

A. Open the class with prayer.

B. Share "Words You Should Know" with students.

C. Read FOCAL VERSES and KEEP IN MIND verses together as a class. Then have each student read two paragraphs of the IN DEPTH section and explain the verses.

4. Getting into the Lesson

A. Ask a volunteer to read IN FOCUS and ask students to discuss times they've celebrated a long awaited fulfillment of a promise or prayer request.

B. As a group, answer the SEARCH THE SCRIPTURES and DISCUSS THE MEANING questions.

5. Relating the Lesson to Life

A. Ask students to reflect on the LESSON IN OUR SOCIETY section. Encourage them to make a list of tasks they have been procrastinating. Ask them to develop a realistic timeline and date for completing each task.

B. Continue the reflection by reading the MAKE IT HAPPEN section.

C. Complete the FOLLOW THE SPIRIT and REMEMBER YOUR THOUGHT sections.

6. Arousing Action

A. Encourage your class to read the DAILY BIBLE READINGS each day. Ask them to be prepared to name their favorite verse from this week's reading during the next class session.

B. End the class in prayer.

DEDICATION OF THE TEMPLE

Bible Background • Ezra 5—6
Printed Text • EZRA 6:13-22
Devotional Reading • PSALM 96:1-13

LESSON AIM

By the end of this lesson, students will learn from the joyful celebration of the re-builders of the temple, know that God's care is available for them to complete their work and plan, dedicate their accomplishment to God, and celebrate His grace.

KEEP IN MIND

"And the children of Israel, the priests, and the Levites, and the rest of the children of the captivity, kept the dedication of this house of God with joy" (Ezra 6:16).

FOCAL VERSES

Ezra 6:13 Then Tatnai, governor on this side the river, Shethar-boznai, and their companions, according to that which Darius the king had sent, so they did speedily.

14 And the elders of the Jews builded, and they prospered through the prophesying of Haggai the prophet and Zechariah the son of Iddo. And they builded, and finished it, according to the commandment of the God of Israel, and according to the commandment of Cyrus, and Darius, and Artaxerxes king of Persia.

15 And this house was finished on the third day of the month Adar, which was in the sixth year of the reign of Darius the king.

16 And the children of Israel, the priests, and the Levites, and the rest of the children of the captivity, kept the dedication of this house of God with joy.

17 And offered at the dedication of this house of God an hundred bullocks, two hundred rams, four

LESSON OVERVIEW

LESSON AIM
KEEP IN MIND
FOCAL VERSES
IN FOCUS
THE PEOPLE, PLACES, AND TIMES
BACKGROUND
AT-A-GLANCE
IN DEPTH
SEARCH THE SCRIPTURES
DISCUSS THE MEANING
LESSON IN OUR SOCIETY
MAKE IT HAPPEN
FOLLOW THE SPIRIT
REMEMBER YOUR THOUGHTS
MORE LIGHT ON THE TEXT
DAILY BIBLE READINGS

hundred lambs; and for a sin offering for all of Israel, twelve he goats, according to the number of the tribes of Israel.

18 And they set the priests in their divisions, and the Levites in their courses, for the service of God, which is at Jerusalem; as it is written in the book of Moses.

19 And the children of the captivity kept the passover upon the fourteenth day at the first month.

20 For the priests of the Levites were purified together, all of them were pure, and killed the passover for all the children of the captivity, and for their brethren the priests, and for themselves.

21 And the children of Israel, which were come again out of captivity, and all such as had separated themselves unto them from the filthiness of the heathen of the land, to seek the LORD God of Israel, did eat.

22 And kept the feast of unleavened bread seven days with joy; for the Lord had made them joyful, and turned the heart of the King of Assyria unto them, to strengthen their hands in the work of the house of God, the God of Israel.

IN FOCUS

A pastor in Illinois was called of God to build a church. He had purchased the land with cash and the next step was to build the church. But that process would prove to be difficult. Before any

JUNE
29TH

417

construction could begin, the village had to approve a church building being constructed on the land. After several village meetings the board voted against a church structure being constructed.

There were times when the pastor became discouraged and wondered if God really told him to build a church for His glory. The church would try one more time to get the village to approve the construction of the church building. It was at the last meeting that the village finally approved the building project. The pastor came back to the church with the good news and everyone rejoiced. Even after the village approved the construction, the church faced other obstacles. But the will of God prevailed! Finally, the construction was completed and a dedication service was held. The people rejoiced and God was pleased. In today's lesson we see, after much discouragement and trial, the temple was finally completed.

THE PEOPLE, PLACES, AND TIMES

King Darius. Darius the Great reigned from about 522 to 485 b.c. He was one of the most able Persian kings and is also known as Darius Hystaspes, or Darius, son of Hystaspes.

Darius was an effective organizer and administrator; he developed trade, built a network of roads, established a postal system, standardized a system of coinage, weights, and measures, and initiated fabulous building projects such as Persepolis, Ecbatana, and Babylon.

Darius continued Cyrus the Great's policy of restoring the Jewish people to their homeland. In 520 b.c., Darius's second year as king, the Jews resumed work on the still unfinished temple in Jerusalem. Darius assisted with the project by ordering it to continue and even sending a generous subsidy to help restore worship in the temple. The temple was completed in 515 b.c. in the sixth year of Darius's reign.

Sin Offering. This offering is also known as a guilt offering. It was presented for unintentional or conscious sins for which there was no possible restitution. This offering signified repentance and a search for divine forgiveness. Usually this offering was also accompanied by a fine. If one did not give his servants their due, such a person

could make a sin offering. But in Numbers 15:30 this sin can only be expiated by such an offering only if not done by defiant rebellion against the law of God.

Temple. A building in which a god (or gods) is worshiped. The Old Testament describes temples as some of man's oldest buildings. The Tower of Babel is the first recorded example of a structure that implies the existence of a temple. A temple was thought of as the building where the god manifested his presence, so the place the temple occupied was holy or sacred.

In biblical times three temples were built to the true God on the same site; Solomon's, Zerubbabel's, and Herod's. Solomon's temple was in the shape of a rectangle that ran east and west. It may have stood on a platform and there was an inner and an outer courtyard.

Three main objects were situated in the inner courtyard. First was the bronze altar that was used for burnt offerings. Between that and the porch of the temple stood the bronze laver, or molten sea, that held water for the ritual washings. Twelve bronze oxen, in four groups of three, faced outward toward the four points of the compass, with the bronze laver resting on their backs. It was said to have a bronze platform and porch.

BACKGROUND

The decree had gone forth from King Cyrus for the children of Israel to rebuild the temple after their captivity in Babylon. Unfortunately, the job was not completed under Cyrus's reign. Because of this, when the Jews were trying to complete the Jerusalem temple later on, there were local leaders concerned about who told them to rebuild the temple. These non-Jews were also concerned about whose authority the Jews were rebuilding the temple.

Darius was king at the time, and he issued an order that the archives be searched for the decree made by King Cyrus. The decree was discovered. King Darius in turn issued this decree (Ezra 6:8, NIV) "Moreover, I hereby decree what you are to do for these elders of the Jews in the construction of this house of God."

The expenses of these men were to be fully

paid out of the royal treasury, from the revenues of Trans-Euphrates, so that the work would not stop. Whatever was needed, young bulls, rams, male lambs for burnt offerings to the God of heaven, and wheat, salt, wine, and oil, as requested by the priests in Jerusalem must be given to them daily without fail, so that they may offer sacrifices pleasing to the God of heaven and pray for the well-being of the king and his sons. He continues (in v. 12), "May God, who has caused his Name to dwell there, overthrow any king or people who lifts a hand to change this decree or to destroy this temple in Jerusalem. I Darius have decreed it. Let it be carried out with diligence."

Thus begins today's lesson.

AT-A-GLANCE

1. The People of Judah Finished the Building (Ezra 6:13-15)
2. The People of Israel Rejoice (v. 16)
3. The People of Israel Offer Sacrifices (vv. 17-18)
4. The Passover Celebrated (vv. 19-20)
5. Joyous Celebration (vv. 21-22)

1. The People of Judah Finished the Building (Ezra 6:13-15)

The temple was finally completed! God's people had been through so much. They had endured many obstacles, but the finished product was now visible. They had been held captive by the enemy because of their sins, and God came and delivered them. When He delivered them, He commanded that they rebuild the temple. They didn't immediately lay the foundation, and God had to rebuke them for that. But they got it together and completed the foundation. Once the foundation was laid, it took them some years to complete the project. Praise God, in today's lesson the temple, after much opposition, was finally completed.

2. The People of Israel Rejoice (v. 16)

They rejoiced not because in their own strength they had accomplished something, but because of the favor of the Lord which had been upon them as they sought to honor God by reinstituting the worship. It was a time to celebrate. To start a work and to see it to completion is a sign of the grace of the Most of High. Israel knew this. How many times we complete a task after many struggles and then get it in our head that it is by our own strength that we were able to complete the task. The temple was completed but not by human powers. From the touching of the heart of Cyrus, to the divine sleeplessness which led Darius to command the completion of the work, it was all of God. We can learn from these past people of God. Having completed the building by the power of God, it was logical to dedicate the building back to God. It was God who initiated the project by His Spirit. It was God who guided their hands to its completion. The house belonged to God. All of our victories, all of our accomplishments, all of our celebrative possibilities are because God has favored us. The children of Israel, the priests, and the Levites were excited and filled with joy.

Rebuilding the temple was by no means a small feat. It took unity, hard work and dedicated people to bring it to pass. God had given the word to go forth; now it was their turn to finish the work. And finish it they did! What a great victory! It was time to praise God.

3. The People of Israel Offer Sacrifices (vv. 17-18)

The children of Israel did not just sing and dance and shout; they brought an offering. They could have said: we have already worked. We gave our time and we gave our talent; we do not need to give any more sacrifices. But they went a step further and offered sacrifices not just because God commanded it, but because they were filled with joy and gratitude at the grace of a God who would bring back a band of exiles and then empower them to rebuild from nothing. Hallelujah. What a God!

Because there was work to do did not mean that they forgot the laws of the Lord. Too many times we use work, even church work, as an occasion for hurting each other and disobeying God.

The children of Israel were doing things in order and according to what was written in the books of Moses. During the dedication of the new temple they offered sacrifices. Sacrificial offerings in the Old Testament were a means to atone for human sins and restore people back to God. Jesus, the perfect sacrifice, did away with all of that when He died for us once and for all on the Cross. The children of Israel offered what is called a sin offering. This included the blood from bullocks, rams, lambs, and goats.

4. The Passover Celebrated (vv. 19-20)

In a sense this was a second exodus. The freed captives had just been delivered from the house of exile. The Passover as celebrated by Hebrew people is the archetype (or pattern) of divine intervention in the life of God's people. It is not a coincidence that dedication was during Passover. What better time to declare the glorious grace of the Most High who rescues the lonely and restores those who are accounted for death? It was the fourteenth day of the first month and everyone was ceremonially clean. The Levites slaughtered the Passover lamb for all the exiles, for their brothers, the priests, and for themselves.

5. Joyous Celebration (vv. 21-22)

Joy did not override discipline, for they still kept what God had commanded them. We can learn something from this. How often in our celebrations do we destroy our neighborhood and hurt our brothers and sisters? If we would include God in our celebrations, they could be times, like the Israelites' celebration, to eat and share together. We read that they separated themselves from the unclean practices of their Gentile neighbors in order to seek the LORD, the God of Israel. For seven days they celebrated with joy the Feast of Unleavened Bread because the Lord had filled them with joy by changing the attitude of the king of Assyria, so that he assisted them in the work on the house of God, the God of Israel. When the Lord blesses us to complete a task, rather than go out and get high, may we rather rejoice in hope and rededicate ourselves to God.

SEARCH THE SCRIPTURES

1. Who rebuilt the temple and did they complete it? (Ezra 6:14)
2. Who issued the commandment? (v. 14)
3. When was the temple completed? (v. 15)
4. What was offered during the dedication? (v. 17)
5. What was kept for seven days? (v. 22)

DISCUSS THE MEANING

1. Why do you think the elders prospered?
2. Who was set for the service of the Lord? Explain.
3. Why do you think it was important to keep the Passover?

LESSON IN OUR SOCIETY

So often we start projects and do not complete them in a speedy manner. If God gives us a command, we must complete the job without delay. A lot of obstacles we are confronted with can be avoided if we do things in a timely manner and not procrastinate. In today's lesson we see that the temple was completed, but what obstacles could have been avoided if the elders had moved swiftly after they received the first command from King Cyrus? Are you procrastinating?

MAKE IT HAPPEN

Examine your own life. Think of some projects you are currently working on that you can speed up the process.

FOLLOW THE SPIRIT

What God wants me to do:

_____

_____

REMEMBER YOUR THOUGHTS

Special insights you have learned:

_____

_____

MORE LIGHT ON THE TEXT
Ezra 6:13-22

13 Then Tatnai, governor on this side the river, Shethar-boznai, and their companions, according to that which Darius the king had sent, so they did

speedily. **14 And the elders of the Jews builded, and they prospered through the prophesying of Haggai the prophet and Zechariah the son of Iddo. And they builded, and finished it, according to the commandment of the God of Israel, and according to the commandment of Cyrus, and Darius, and Artaxerxes king of Persia.**

When the Jews originally started work on rebuilding the temple, their Samaritan neighbors opposed them. The Samaritans sent a letter to (then) King Artaxerxes (pronounced **r-tuh-ZURK-seez**) informing him of the supposed danger of allowing the Jews to complete their work. Artaxerxes agreed with the Samaritans and ordered all work to come to an immediate halt. The letter that the Samaritans sent to the king was written in Aramaic (pronounced **air-uh-MAY-ick**, Ezra 4:7). Ezra quotes the letter in the language it was written and continues writing in Aramaic through chapter 6, verse 8. (Aramaic was the language the Jews had picked up in Persia.)

Work on the temple stopped for 16 years until God sent His prophets Haggai and Zechariah, during the second year of the reign of Darius of Persia, to encourage the Jews to resume the rebuilding of the temple (Haggai 1:1-3; Zechariah 1:1). Under the leadership of Zerubbabel (governor) and Jeshua (the high priest), the people immediately went back to work rebuilding the temple (Ezra 5:1-2).

When word of the rebuilding reached Tatnai, the Persian governor west of the Euphrates River, and Shethar-boznai, his aide, they sent a letter to King Darius informing him of the Jewish activities and asking if there was any legal basis for the work. Darius had his officials search the royal archives in Babylon to find Cyrus's original decree without success. The order was finally found in the city of Achmetha (or Ecbatana) in the province of Media (6:1-2). When Darius read the decree, he allowed the rebuilding work to continue and added his own order to it. The Persian officials were not only ordered not to interfere with the Jews but to help finance the operation from their treasury and to supply the Jews with any animals they needed for sacrifice (vv. 8-9).

Tatnai and Shethar-boznai complied with the king's decree, and work on the temple continued and prospered through the prophesying of Haggai and Zechariah. "Prophesying" is a translation of the Aramaic *nebuah* (pronounced nu-vooh-ah), and refers to preaching, teaching, and/or predicting the future. The phrase "through the prophesying" points out that this great and unexpected success was not to be credited to chance or to King Darius's kindness but to God alone. It was God acting through His prophets who had required and encouraged the people to proceed in the work, and it was His mighty power that moved Darius's heart to allow the work to continue.

"According to the commandment" establishes the order of the various decrees to build the temple. Here the writer reviews the different rulers who favored the Jews in their return from captivity and the rebuilding of the temple.

15 And this house was finished on the third day of the month Adar, which was in the sixth year of the reign of Darius the king. 16 And the children of Israel, the priests, and the Levites, and the rest of the children of the captivity, kept the dedication of this house of God with joy,

Four years later, on March 12, 515 B.C. in the sixth year of the reign of Darius, the temple was completed 20 years after the foundation had been laid during the reign of Cyrus. The Ark of the Covenant containing the two tablets of the Law was not in the new temple. The Ark had apparently been lost or destroyed at some unknown time in the past.

When they completed the temple, which became known as Zerabbabel's Temple, it was ninety feet high and ninety feet wide (6:3). This was much smaller and far less grand than Solomon's original temple. However, this temple would stand for 500 years, longer than both Solomon's original temple and Herod's third temple combined.

The Israelites celebrated the dedication of the temple with a great feast similar to the one that Solomon had when he dedicated the original temple (1 Kings 8:23). The reference to the "children of Israel" affirms that there were members of the northern kingdom of Israel who returned from Babylonian captivity along with the vast majority from the southern kingdom of Judah. The priests and the Levites led the temple dedication. Of the twelve tribes, the tribe of Levi, was set aside for ritual religious service. Within the tribe of Levi, only those descended from the bloodline of Aaron could serve as priests. Other families from the tribe were assigned various duties linked with tabernacle or temple worship.

The priesthood was vital to the practice of Old Testament faith. The Hebrew word for priest, *kohen* (pronounced **koh-HANE**), occurs over 700 times in the Old Testament. According to Deuteronomy 33:8-10, the priest had a trifold ministry of (1) watching over and guarding the covenant, (2) teaching God's precepts and law, and (3) offering incense and offerings at God's altar. The high priest had two mediatorial functions that summed up the role of the priesthood. In his vestments the high priest had the Urim and Thummim (Deuteronomy 33:8). God spoke to the people through these twin instruments to provide guidance for His people and to communicate His will. The second function of the high priest involved a unique sacrifice. Once a year on the Day of Atonement the high priest would enter the Holy of Holies in the tabernacle, carrying the blood of the sacrifice and sprinkling it on the cover of the ark. This was done to atone for all the sins of all of God's people (Leviticus 16).

17 And offered at the dedication of this house of God an hundred bullocks, two hundred rams, four hundred lambs; and for a sin offering for all Israel, twelve he goats, according to the number of the tribes of Israel.

The Hebrew/Aramaic word for "dedication" is *hannukkah* (pronounced **HKHAN-uh-kah**). Jews today have a different holiday called Hanukkah. The Old Testament emphasizes the dedication ceremonies that inaugurated the use of something for God's service. The sin offering at the dedication consisted of 100 male bulls, 200 rams, and 400 male lambs. Solomon offered 200 times more animals at the dedication of the original temple, but because of the poor circumstances

the offering was accepted. Their hundreds meant much more to them than Solomon's thousands.

The sin offering (from the Aramaic) is the equivalent of the Hebrew *hatae* (pronounced **chah-TAH**). The sin offering as explained in Leviticus 4:3 was sacrificed for those who committed a sin unintentionally or out of weakness or negligence as opposed to outright rebellion against God.

18 And they set the priests in their divisions, and the Levites in their courses, for the service of God, which is at Jerusalem; as it is written in the book of Moses.

King David divided the descendants of Aaron who served as priests into 24 classes as the basis for rotating priestly duties (1 Chronicles 24:3, 7-19). Some of the classes died out or had to be consolidated with others, and new ones were formed to take their places. In the return from exile only four registered classes were represented (Ezra 2:36-39). By the time of Nehemiah's return 22 classes had been reinstated (Nehemiah 10:2-8). The Levites were also divided into groups, or courses, corresponding to the bloodlines of Gershon, Kohath, and Merari (Exodus 6:16). The duty of the Levites was to assist Aaron's descendants in the service of the temple (Exodus 38:21; Numbers 3:6-7).

19 And the children of the captivity kept the passover upon the fourteenth day of the first month.

The "children of captivity" is a translation of the Hebrew *ben golah* (pronounced **ben go-LAH**). In this case *ben* is used idiomatically to denote children or descendants. *Golah* refers to anyone who has been deported as a slave or taken into captivity. In this case the phrase describes the descendants of those carried into Babylonian captivity.

The Passover is called *pasah* (pronounced **pah-SAHK**), in Hebrew. This Hebrew verb means "to skip or pass over, to grant exemption from penalty or calamity." The Passover is an annual feast that celebrates the day when the Lord selectively passed over the homes of those who put lambs' blood over the door frames of their homes. On that night the firstborn male of every household who did not have the blood over the door frame was killed. This event precipitated Israel's deliverance from Egyptian bondage. The Passover lamb and the blood of the lamb point to Jesus Christ, the Lamb of God, whose blood takes away the sins of the world (John 1:29; 1 Corinthians 5:7).

20 For the priests and the Levites were purified together, all of them were pure, and killed the passover for all the children of the captivity, and for their brethren the priests, and for themselves.

"The Levites were purified together" means that they were all ready at one time to observe the proper rites and ceremonies. There was no need to postpone the celebration as was prescribed by law. If circumstances made it necessary, the Passover could be postponed from the first month to the second (Numbers 9:10-11; cf. 2 Chronicles 30:3).

"Purified" is a translation of the Hebrew *taher* (pronounced **tah-HAYR**), and literally means de-sinned so as to be ceremonially clean. The word is used almost exclusively of ritual or moral purity. Those who were considered unclean were not permitted to participate in temple rituals until they were purified.

21 And the children of Israel, which were come again out of captivity, and all such as had separated themselves unto them from the filthiness of the heathen of the land, to seek the LORD God of Israel, did eat.

Those who had "separated themselves" refers to the proselytes who had embraced the Jewish religion during the time of their captivity in Babylon. The proselytes are proof that the Jewish captives had maintained the principles of their religion. The unbelievers saw it, and they converted to the religion of the one true God.

22 And kept the feast of unleavened bread seven days with joy: for the LORD had made them joyful, and turned the heart of the king of Assyria unto them, to strengthen their hands in the work of the house of God, the God of Israel.

The Feast of Unleavened Bread was closely associated with the Passover. In fact, in preparation for the Passover the man of the house would search through the house for leaven (yeast) and remove it.

God had given the people both causes to rejoice and hearts to rejoice. God is the fountain from which all true joy flows. The Persian king is here called the King of Assyria (two empires back) to emphatically stress the great power and goodness of God in turning the hearts of these present Persian monarchs, whose Assyrian predecessors had formerly been the chief persecutors and cruel oppressors of God's people.

DAILY BIBLE READINGS

M: A Decree to Rebuild
Ezra 6:1-5
T: Adversaries Must Let the Work Alone
Ezra 6:6-12
W: A Joyous Dedication
Ezra 6:13-18
T: Sing to the Lord
Psalm 96:1-6
F: Ascribe to the Lord Glory
Psalm 96:7-13
S: God Has Done Marvelous Things
Psalm 98:1-6
S: Extol the Lord Our God
Psalm 99:1-5

TEACHING TIPS

July 6
Bible Study Guide 6

1. Words You Should Know

A. Sepulchers—(Nehemiah 2:5) A place of burial; the place where ancestors are buried.

B. Reproach—(v. 2:17) A cause or occasion of blame, discredit, or disgrace.

2. Teacher Preparation

A. Read all four lessons for Unit 2 and be prepared to present the unit to the class.

B. It may be helpful to review last week's lesson to see how students related it to their lives. Have a few students share their testimonies and what they learned from their DAILY BIBLE READINGS of the week.

3. Starting the Lesson

A. Begin the class by having a student open in prayer.

B. Have students discuss last week's MAKE IT HAPPEN assignment and if they were able to practice keeping short accounts with God.

C. Have a student read the IN FOCUS of this lesson and briefly discuss it.

4. Getting into the Lesson

A. Read the BACKGROUND section to help the students understand the lesson better.

B. Have a student read the AT-A-GLANCE and if possible write it on a chalkboard or poster to be reviewed if necessary.

C. Have two students read the FOCUS VERSES, dividing the reading according to the division given in the AT-A-GLANCE.

D. Try a little role-playing. Ask two students to role-play the encounter of Nehemiah before the king in Nehemiah 2:4-8. Then read the IN DEPTH section for these verses for further understanding of this encounter.

E. Have a student read the second section of the IN DEPTH. Then answer the questions in SEARCH THE SCRIPTURES together.

5. Relating the Lesson to Life

A. Use the question in DISCUSS THE MEANING to help students see some relationship to Nehemiah's action with our daily actions.

B. Read and discuss the LESSON IN OUR SOCIETY to help the students further apply this lesson to their lives individually.

6. Arousing Action

A. Read the MAKE IT HAPPEN assignment and challenge students to do as it suggests. You may want to challenge the students further by having them share with a partner their plan of action to increase their prayer life in the next week. This will give them a sense of accountability.

B. Close the class by reading Philippians 4:6-7 to the class and praying accordingly.

WORSHIP GUIDE

For the Superintendent or Teacher
Theme: Nehemiah's Work Begins
Theme Song: "Here Am I, Send Me"
Scripture: Nehemiah 1:1-4, 2:4-5, 13, 15-18.
Song: "To the Work!"
Devotional: God, my Father, thank You that You will always guide me to do what you want me to do. Help me to be obedient to Your will that I may always please You. Amen

NEHEMIAH'S WORK BEGINS

Bible Background • NEHEMIAH 1–2
Printed Text • NEHEMIAH 1:1-4; 2:4-5, 13, 16-18
Devotional Reading • ISAIAH 26:1-9

LESSON AIM

By the end of the lesson, students will be able to relate the story of Nehemiah's call to service, understand the importance of interceding both in prayer and in action, and determine to become a part of the solution to problems they see in their churches, homes, or communities.

KEEP IN MIND

"Then I told them of the hand of my God which was good upon me; as also the king's words that he had spoken unto me. And they said, Let us rise up and build. So they strengthened their hands for this good work" (Nehemiah 2:18).

FOCAL VERSES

Nehemiah 1:1 The words of Nehemiah the son of Hachaliah. And it came to pass in the month Chisleu, in the twentieth year, as I was in Shushan the palace,

2 That Hanani, one of my brethren, came, he and certain men of Judah; and I asked them concerning the Jews that had escaped, which were left of the captivity, and concerning Jerusalem.

3 And they said unto me, The remnant that are left of the captivity there in the province are in great affliction and reproach: the wall of Jerusalem also is broken down, and the gates thereof are burned with fire.

4 And it came to pass, when I heard these words, that I sat down and wept, and mourned certain

LESSON OVERVIEW

LESSON AIM
KEEP IN MIND
FOCAL VERSES
IN FOCUS
THE PEOPLE, PLACES, AND TIMES
BACKGROUND
AT-A-GLANCE
IN DEPTH
SEARCH THE SCRIPTURES
DISCUSS THE MEANING
LESSON IN OUR SOCIETY
MAKE IT HAPPEN
FOLLOW THE SPIRIT
REMEMBER YOUR THOUGHTS
MORE LIGHT ON THE TEXT
DAILY BIBLE READINGS

days, and fasted, and prayed before the God of heaven,

2:4 Then the king said unto me, For what dost thou make request? So I prayed to the God of heaven.

5 And I said unto the king, If it please the king, and if thy servant have found favour in thy sight, that thou wouldest send me unto Judah, unto the city of my fathers' sepulchers, that I may build it.

JULY 6TH

13 And I went out by night by the gate of the valley, even before the dragon well, and to the dung port, and viewed the walls of Jerusalem, which were broken down, and the gates thereof were consumed with fire.

16 And the rulers knew not whither I went, or what I did; neither had I as yet told it to the Jews, nor to the priests, nor to the nobles, nor to the rulers, nor to the rest that did the work.

17 Then said I unto them, Ye see the distress that we are in, how Jerusalem lieth waste, and the gates thereof are burned with fire: come, and let us build up the wall of Jerusalem, that we be no more a reproach.

18 Then I told them of the hand of my God which was good upon me; as also the king's words that he had spoken unto me. And they said, Let us rise up and build. So they strengthened their hands for this good work.

IN FOCUS

A preacher and an atheistic barber were once walking through the city slums. The barber said to the preacher, "Look at this place and these people. This is why I cannot believe in a God of love. If God were as kind as you say, He would not allow these rejects of society to be addicted to dope, alcohol, and other life-destroying habits. No, I cannot believe in a God who permits these things to occur in the world."

The minister was silent until they met a man who was especially unkempt and filthy. His hair was running down his neck, and he had a half-inch of stubble on his face. The minister said to the barber, "You can't be a very good barber, or you wouldn't permit a man like this to continue living in this neighborhood without a haircut and shave." Indignantly the barber answered, "Why blame me for the man's condition? I can't help it that he is like that. He has never come into my shop where I could fix him up and make him look like a fine Black gentleman!"

Giving the barber a penetrating look, the minister said, "Then don't blame God for allowing the people to continue in their evil ways, when He is constantly inviting them to enter into a relationship with Him and be saved. If these people turned to God, He could clean up their lives."

It is easy to blame God for many of the ills affecting our communities and our world. However, God does not call us into service to be complainers but to be doers. Nehemiah, the focus of today's lesson, is an excellent example of a God-driven person seeing a problem and interceding both in prayer and in action.

THE PEOPLE, PLACES, AND TIMES

Nehemiah. Our only knowledge of this great builder and statesman comes from the book that bears his name. The man whose name means "God has consoled" was born in exile. But Nehemiah grew up in the faith of his fathers, and he loved Israel. Since no mention is made of a wife, it is likely that he was a eunuch.

As the king's cupbearer, Nehemiah held a high place of honor (Nehemiah 1:11) and had confidential access to the king. After hearing of the desolate state of Jerusalem, Nehemiah obtained permission from the king to go to his native country and was appointed governor. Twelve years after Ezra's return to Judah, Nehemiah and the final group of returned exiles returned to the holy city.

Nehemiah was well qualified for this patriotic task. A true Israelite, he labored for the purity of public worship, the integrity of family life, and the sanctity of the Sabbath. He was a courageous and God-fearing man who labored selflessly and served with an unswerving loyalty to God.

BACKGROUND

The book bearing the author's name is probably Nehemiah's personal memoirs. The writer, whose name means "comfort of Jehovah," records the events involved in the third and final exodus to Jerusalem and the rebuilding of the city's walls.

Nehemiah was a contemporary of Ezra. His book completes the history of the remnants, return from exile and Jerusalem's restoration. While Ezra primarily records the religious restoration of Jerusalem, Nehemiah focuses on the city's political restoration.

The returned exiles had been in Jerusalem for more than ninety years, the temple had been completed, but the city's walls remained in ruins. The condition of the walls left the city, the temple, and the people vulnerable to attack and gave their enemies cause to ridicule.

Although Ezra was an excellent spiritual leader, the people lacked political leadership. They needed someone to motivate them, show them where to begin and to direct their activities. God had just the man for the job. Nehemiah left the comfort of a king's palace to return to his ancient homeland to challenge his countrymen to get busy and reconstruct the walls.

AT-A-GLANCE

1. Call to Action (Nehemiah 1:1-4)
2. Prayer before Action (2:4-5)
3. Action after Prayer (vv. 13, 16-18)

IN DEPTH

1. Call to Action (Nehemiah 1:1-4)

Nehemiah opens his memoirs by simply announcing who he is. He mentions his father, Hachaliah, as a means of distinguishing himself from the two other Nehemiahs mentioned in Ezra 3 and Nehemiah 6. Without fanfare the writer dives directly into his story.

The action begins during the twentieth year of the reign of Artaxerxes, king of Persia. Sometime between mid-November and early December Nehemiah, who served as cupbearer to the king, was at the winter palace in Susa. Hanani and some other men from Jerusalem came up to visit him. Nehemiah describes Hanani as one of his brethren, which could simply mean a fellow Israelite, but a later reference (7:2) makes it more likely that Hanani was a blood relative.

Nehemiah questions Hanani and his companions about the situation in Jerusalem, and the news they give him breaks the cupbearer's heart. Hanani tells Nehemiah that the returned Israelites "who survived the exile and are back in the province are in great trouble and disgrace. The wall of Jerusalem is broken down, and its gates have been burned with fire" (Nehemiah 1:2-3, NIV).

The situation with the walls had left the people disheartened and defeated. Nehemiah was crushed by this news. The cupbearer loved his homeland even though he had been born in captivity and had never seen his homeland. Nehemiah shared the nationalistic fervor of his people. David summed up the Israelite passion for Jerusalem with the words, "If I forget thee, O Jerusalem, let my right hand forget her cunning. If I do not remember thee let my tongue cleave to the roof of my mouth" (Psalm 137:5-6).

The bad news stunned Nehemiah. "When I heard these things, I sat down and wept. For some days I mourned and fasted and prayed before the God of heaven" (Nehemiah 1:4, NIV). The several days was more like four months (see 2:1). However, instead of wallowing in pity, Nehemiah took his heartbreak to the only person who could possibly help him, the God of heaven. He fasted and prayed for many days, until God provided a way to remedy the situation. Notice that

Nehemiah did not just ask God to fix it; he desired to be an instrument in solving the problem (see 1:11). After four months of praying and fasting God finally opened the door for Nehemiah to approach the king with his problem, but in those four months Nehemiah never lost hope. He knew that God would honor his promise if he had the patience to wait.

When you hear of heartbreaking news in the lives of others, how do you respond? Do you pity them? Do you blame God for their situation, or do you discuss the matter with the only person who can fix it? The believer's first reaction to bad news should always be to pray. Then we wait on God to direct our responses. "They that wait upon the Lord shall renew their strength, they shall mount up with wings of eagles" (Isaiah 40:31). Then we make ourselves available to be used by God to help in whatever ways He chooses.

2. Prayer before Action (2:4-5)

Nehemiah knew he had to do something about the city's walls, but what and how? Nehemiah did not sit down and formulate a plan of action, he prayed to God for direction (Nehemiah 1:4). As soon as God opened the door, Nehemiah put his plan into action. As cupbearer, Nehemiah's job was to taste the king's drinks before the king drank them to insure they were not poisoned. This position afforded him a great deal of influence with the king. Yet Nehemiah did not rely on his friends in high places when he needed help. His first impulse was to seek God.

When he served King Artaxerxes his wine, he allowed his distress to show on his face. This was a dangerous action for a palace servant. The king's servants were expected to always display a cheerful appearance before him. Even wearing mourning clothes was forbidden in the palace. The king could execute anyone who displeased him. But Nehemiah had prayed and knew that he had to take the chance.

Instead of being angry the king, who had an obvious fondness for his cupbearer, was concerned and asked, "Why does your face look so sad when you are not ill? This can be nothing but sadness of heart" (Nehemiah 2:2, NIV). The king's question caused Nehemiah to fear for his position at court and more importantly for his life. Instead of giving in to his fear Nehemiah summoned up his courage and took opportunity to present his request. After Nehemiah explained the problem the king asked, "What is it you want?" (2:4 NIV). Nehemiah uttered a brief prayer before answering. He knew that only God could touch the king's heart and cause him to grant the requests.

After his prayer Nehemiah went straight to the point. He requested the king allow him to travel to Jerusalem. Naturally, the king had a couple of questions. "How long will your journey take, and when will you return?" (v. 6, NIV) Nehemiah had no idea of the amount of work before him, but he gave the king a timeframe. The Bible does not record Nehemiah's exact answer, but he stayed in Jerusalem for 12 years (cf. 5:14, 13:6).

The king granted Nehemiah's requests, and Nehemiah pressed on. He asked the king for letters to give to the governors of the land he would cross guaranteeing safe passage. Then he asked for a letter to Asaph, the king's forest keeper, authorizing him to give Nehemiah timber for the walls.

Nehemiah made it a habit to always pray before acting. He spent an extended period praying and fasting before he approached the king. Then he briefly prayed before answering the king. On several other occasions Nehemiah spontaneously called out to God in times of need (5:19; 6:9, 14; 13:14, 22). The key to Nehemiah's success as a leader of his people was his total dependence on God.

3. Action after Prayer (vv. 13, 16-18)

When Nehemiah arrived after a three-month journey, he presented the letters from the king to the territorial governors. The governors immediately opposed the plan. Although he had the full support of the king, Nehemiah did not immediately rush into action or expose his plan to the people (2:11-12). Instead Nehemiah secretly inspected the wall to assess the damage and estimate the work needed to rebuild it. After determining what was needed, Nehemiah was ready to lead the people to action. He began by telling them, "You see the trouble we are in: Jerusalem

lies in ruins, and its gates have been burned with fire. Come, let us rebuild the wall of Jerusalem, and we will no longer be in disgrace" (2:17, NIV).

Nehemiah appealed to the people's pride in Jerusalem as God's holy city. Next, he appealed to their love for God and their desire not to bring shame (reproach) on Him. He acknowledged God and His divine guidance in the plan to rebuild the wall. Then he recounted the conversation between him and King Artaxerxes for them.

Leadership ability is often confirmed by the attitude and actions of one's followers. When Nehemiah completed his brief speech the people exclaimed, "Let us start rebuilding" (v. 18, NIV). Nehemiah challenged and inspired the people, and God strengthened them to complete the work.

SEARCH THE SCRIPTURES

1. Where was Nehemiah when Hanani and the other men brought him the news concerning Jerusalem? (Nehemiah 1:1-2)

2. When King Artexerxes asked Nehemiah to state his request, what did the cupbearer do before answering? (2:4)

3. What two questions did the king ask Nehemiah? (v. 6)

4. Why was the letter to Asaph the forest keeper so necessary? (v. 8)

5. What time of day did Nehemiah secretly visit the walls of the city? (v. 12)

6. What did the people in Jerusalem do to show that they were ready to follow Nehemiah in rebuilding the wall? (v. 18)

DISCUSS THE MEANING

1. Sometimes difficult situations arise without warning and require an immediate response. How are believers supposed to consult God during these times?

2. What did Nehemiah mean by the statement, "If it please the king, and if thy servant have found favour in thy sight?" (2:5) What lesson can we learn from Nehemiah to help us in our relationships with our employers?

LESSON IN OUR SOCIETY

Some inner cities of many American communities are crumbling around the people who live there. Slumlords and people who desert their property account for much of the problem, but cleanliness and maintenance are problems the residents can solve. Should a church's vision for its community include upkeep and maintenance? What are some ways the church can motivate members to clean up and maintain their neighborhoods?

MAKE IT HAPPEN

This week think of some method of ministry that you avoid because of fear of discomfort. Summon up your courage and make it a point to tackle that area of ministry. Remember that God has not given us a spirit of fear but of power, love, and a sound mind.

FOLLOW THE SPIRIT

What God wants me to do:

_____

_____

REMEMBER YOUR THOUGHTS

Special insights you have learned:

_____

_____

MORE LIGHT ON THE TEXT
Nehemiah 1:1-4, 2:4-5, 13, 16-18

The book of Nehemiah is about one man's love, dedication, and faithfulness to both his God and his country. It is a journal of one man's perseverance to make a difference for his people, to rebuild the ruins of the walls of his people's proud city, Jerusalem, in spite of opposition. The book depicts Nehemiah's sacrifice of an enviable position (2:5) for the cause of his people. The story demonstrates God's faithfulness and authority over man's affairs when we put all our problems, our will, and our desires into His hands.

1:1 The words of Nehemiah the son of Hachaliah. And it came to pass in the month Chisleu, in the twentieth year, as I was in Shushan the palace, 2 That Hanani, one of my brethren,

came, he and certain men of Judah; and I asked them concerning the Jews that had escaped, which were left of the captivity, and concerning Jerusalem.

The book begins by introducing its author as "Nehemiah the son of Hachaliah." There is therefore no doubt who wrote this book; it dismisses the argument that another person other than Nehemiah authored the book. The proof of Nehemiah's authorship is further strengthened in the use of the first person in chapters 1-7 and 12:27-43. However, chapters 8:1-10:30 and 12:44-13:3 are written in the third person, which suggests that another person had a part in the writing of this narrative, probably Ezra the scribe. There is a strong argument that probably Ezra and some other scribes in the synagogue took Nehemiah's memoirs and compiled the work into its present form. It should be noted that "Ezra" and "Nehemiah" were originally called "The book of Ezra." Later "Nehemiah" was separated from "Ezra" and was called "The second book of Ezra" until about fourth century a.d. when Jerome gave it its present name.

The phrase "Nehemiah the son of Hachaliah" distinguishes him from others of this same name (3:16; 7:7; Ezra 2:2). It is customary in the Jewish tradition to identify a person by his father's name. However, nothing is further known of his father, neither are we informed of his tribe. The name "Nehemiah" is transliterated from the Hebrew *Nechemyah* (pronounced **Nekh-em-yaw'**) which means consolation of *Jah* or *Jehovah* comforts. He was the cupbearer of Artaxerxes, king of Persia, a royal and an honorable office in the Persian court. Cupbearing is a position of trust. Cupbearers were generally eunuchs, whose duties included being in the presence of the king daily and testing the king's food and wine before they were presented to the king. Solomon had cupbearers who attended to him (1 Kings 10:5; 2 Chronicles 9:4).

The author gives us the precise date and place the event began, which gives the story a historical authenticity. "And it came to pass," or its Hebrew equivalent *hayah* (**haw-yaw**), also interpreted as "it happened" is a Jewish expression commonly used to begin narratives. It is also used to emphasize

leader sent by the Jewish elders to meet Nehemiah. The purpose was probably to solicit help in rebuilding of the walls of their proud city Jerusalem, a continuation of the restoration and rebuilding process, which started in the book of Ezra, including the temple in Jerusalem. After the temple the people probably thought that the next phase was the rebuilding of the walls of Jerusalem. Hence the delegation is sent to Persia. As the delegation approaches him, Nehemiah, without waiting for them to tell their story, and with deep love, concern, and compassion for his dear country, asks them about Jerusalem and the remnant. The answer is clear and precise. They describe the deplorable condition of those left behind in Jerusalem and of the city.

Another probability to this narrative is the account Josephus (a Jewish historian) gives. He writes:

"Nehemiah, being somewhere out of Susa, seeing some strangers, and hearing them converse in the Hebrew tongue, he went near; and finding they were Jews from Jerusalem, he asked them how matters went with their brethren in that city, and what was their state?" And the answer they gave him is, in substance, that recorded in the text, though with several aggravations in Josephus. (Joseph. Ant. lib. xi., c. 5. from *Adam Clarke's Commentary, Electronic Database.* Copyright (c) 1996 by Biblesoft).

3 And they said unto me, The remnant that are left of the captivity there in the province are in great affliction and reproach: the wall of Jerusalem also is broken down, and the gates thereof are burned with fire.

and stress the importance of the story that follows. The story begins while Nehemiah is in "Shushan," the king's court (palace) in Persia in the month of Chisleu, the Jewish ninth month (probably December) in the twentieth year of the reign of King Artaxerxes (Nehemiah 2:2). Certain men from Judah visit Nehemiah, which includes Hanani whom he identifies as his brother. This identity suggests that either Hanani was Nehemiah's actual blood brother (7:2) or a close kin in the tribe of Judah. However, Hanani was trustworthy and reliable, hence he was appointed governor of Jerusalem (7:2). It is believed that Hanani and the "certain men from Judah" were among those of the captivity who had returned to Jerusalem under Ezra and Zerubbabel (Ezra 2:2).

The mention of these people suggests that they were a delegation from Judah with Hanani as its

The delegation tells Nehemiah that "the remnant are in great affliction and reproach." The word "affliction" is the Hebrew adjective *ra* (**rah**), which means bad, evil in the sense of an unpleasant and unhappy condition. The word "reproach" or its Hebrew equivalent *cherpah* (pronounced **kher-paw'**) used here further describes the shameful condition of the remnant left behind. These words describe the suffering and humiliation the people were going through. Added to the suffering of the people is the total desolation and destruction of the walls of Jerusalem, which are "broken down, and the gates thereof burned with fire." The idea here is that while the temple has been rebuilt, as seen in the Book of Ezra, the walls and gates of the city are still in ruins, perhaps from the destruction of the Babylonian invasion of 586 b.c. On hearing the news of the situation back in his own country, Nehemiah is shocked and reacts emotionally and spiritually.

4 And it came to pass, when I heard these words, that I sat down and wept, and mourned certain days, and fasted, and prayed before the God of heaven,

The use of the phrase "and it came to pass" again here (v. 1) not only gives emphasis, but signifies the urgency of Nehemiah's reaction following the news from the delegation. His action was immediate. As soon as he heard them, he grieves over the situation. His first and immediate reaction is emotional—he sits down and weeps and mourns for a number of days. His next reaction is spiritual—he fasts and prays to God for intervention and mercy for his people (see vv. 5-11 for Nehemiah's prayer). The prayer and fasting lasted over four months (2:1), and he prayed "day and night" (1:6) on behalf of his people. It is after the prayer and fasting that he approaches the king in the month of Nisan, also called the month Abib, which is the first month in the Jewish calendar, and the fourth month after the month of Chisleu. Included in his prayer is that God might grant him favor in the sight of the king. Chapter 2:1-3 records how Nehemiah's concern for his country is brought to the king's attention through Nehemiah's sad countenance as he performs his royal duties for the king.

2:4 Then the king said unto me, For what dost thou make request? So I prayed to the God of heaven. 5 And I said unto the king, If it please the king, and if thy servant have found favour in thy sight, that thou wouldest send me unto Judah, unto the city of my fathers' sepulchres, that I may build it.

Nehemiah, without mincing words, tells the king what is troubling him. The king permits him to make his request. Nehemiah prays again to God. He had earlier prayed that God would touch the heart of the monarch to grant him his request (1:11), and now he prays again to "the God of heaven." This must have been a quick and silent prayer. The content of this prayer is not made known to us. But Nehemiah must have solicited for God's assistance and intervention, not only that He might touch the heart of the king so that his request might be granted him, but the boldness to speak to the king. All through the book we see Nehemiah going constantly back to God in prayer (1:5-11; 2:4; 4:4-5; 5:19; 6:9, 14; 13:14, 22, 29, 31).

His request to the king is clear and straightforward, that he might be permitted to return to Jerusalem "unto the city of my fathers' sepulchres, that I may build it" (v. 5). His prayer to God and his request to the king are both answered (vv. 6-8). The brief and silent prayer backed by months of fasting and prayer to the God of heaven (1:4-11) changed the course of history and reversed the royal policy. The king sends him back to Judah with certain building materials to commence his task of rebuilding the Jerusalem walls.

2:13 And I went out by night by the gate of the valley, even before the dragon well, and to the dung port, and viewed the walls of Jerusalem, which were broken down, and the gates thereof were consumed with fire. 16 And the rulers knew not whither I went, or what I did; neither had I as yet told it to the Jews, nor to the priests, nor to the nobles, nor to the rulers, nor to the rest that did the work.

Nehemiah arrives at Judah and goes in the night to view the extent of the destruction. The mention of different areas and sections of the wall in verse 13 indicates that he made a thorough inspection and study of the situation in order to understand the extent of work to be done. He finds the ruins just as the delegate has informed him—the walls of Jerusalem broken and their gates consumed with fire. We learn from verses 12 and 13 that all the while he kept his plans to himself. He did not tell anyone, the rulers, the people, the priests, the nobles, not even the rest of the people, what the Lord had led in his heart and the favor He granted him through the king to rebuild the walls. Why did he keep it a secret? The best reason is to hide it from their enemies (v. 10) until everything is ready and all plans are finalized so they cannot jeopardize the work. The next reason would probably be that he kept them away from the people until everything was in place to avoid discouragement because of the immensity of the job facing them.

17 Then said I unto them, Ye see the distress that we are in, how Jerusalem lieth waste, and the gates thereof are burned with fire: come, and let us build up the wall of Jerusalem, that we be no more a reproach.

Probably after making sure that everything is in place, Nehemiah now calls an assembly and tells the people his plans. He first calls their attention to their plight, reminding them of their suffering, and the deplorable condition of their city. Nehemiah, as an individual, could be excluded from the suffering (being one of the highest positions one could think of at that time, a cupbearer to the most powerful king), however, he identifies with the suffering of his people. He sees himself as a member of the suffering community. He never allowed his personal comfort in the king's palace to blind him to the suffering of his people in Judah or to separate him from the community of his people. Rather he includes himself saying, "Ye see the distress that we are in" reminding them of the humiliation facing them as a result of the desolation of their proud city and "How Jerusalem lieth waste, and the gates thereof are burned with fire." He then challenges them to work. With the imperative "come" yalak (yaw-lak') he summons them to the task ahead saying, "Let us build up the wall of Jerusalem, that we be no more a reproach." In other words, let us by building the walls of Jerusalem and its gates put to an end the destitute condition, which gives our foes the opportunity to reproach or deride us.

18 Then I told them of the hand of my God which was good upon me; as also the king's words that he had spoken unto me. And they said, Let us rise up and build. So they strengthened their hands for this good work.

To assure them of the possibility of the work ahead and gain their support, Nehemiah tells the assembly how God's hand has been with him in the plan, how God has so far provided for him in the project. He informs them also of the king's approval and support, morally and materially (2:8). Challenged by the speech and encouraged by the information of God's providence, which they have hitherto experienced through Ezra's undertaking in the temple building, the people exclaimed with one voice, "Let us rise and build!" The effect is instantaneous and wholehearted for the people who "strengthened their hands for this good work," i.e., they set out to work with vigor.

DAILY BIBLE READINGS

M: Nehemiah Mourns the Ruined Walls
Nehemiah 1:1-4
T: Nehemiah's Prayer of Confession
Nehemiah 1:5-11
W: Nehemiah Asks to Go to Judah
Nehemiah 2:1-5
T: Plans Are Made
Nehemiah 2:6-10
F: Nehemiah Inspects the Walls
Nehemiah 2:11-15
S: Let Us Start Building
Nehemiah 2:16-20
S: He Sets Up Victory Like Walls
Isaiah 26:1-6

TEACHING TIPS

July 13
Bible Study Guide 7

1. Words You Should Know

A. Gates–(Nehemiah 6:1) Hebrew *Sa' ar* An entrance, the place of controlled access to the city. The city gates were where people congregated for business transactions (Ruth 4:11), the administration of justice (Deuteronomy 17:5), and social interaction (2 Kings 9:31).

B. Prayed–(v. 9) Hebrew *palal* To intercede or plead, praying on behalf of someone else.

2. Teacher Preparation

A. Read all four lessons for Unit 2 and be prepared to present the unit to the class.

B. Review last week's lesson to see how students related it to their lives. Have a few students share their testimonies and what they learned from their DAILY BIBLE READINGS of the week.

3. Starting the Lesson

A. Have students silently read the FOCAL VERS-ES. Ask, what are some of the key points in the verses? Is there anything we can see in Barnabas's character that can help us?

B. Use the SEARCH THE SCRIPTURES questions to introduce the lesson.

C. Have a student lead the class in prayer, focusing on the LESSON AIM, as well as thanking God for the opportunity of studying His Word this week.

4. Getting into the Lesson

A. Read the AT-A-GLANCE outline. Assign students to focus on specific aspects and assign the corresponding SEARCH THE SCRIPTURES questions to go along with their part of the discussion.

B. Discuss THE PEOPLE, PLACES, AND TIMES background information that will help students understand why Sanballat was so opposed to Nehemiah's work.

5. Relating the Lesson to Life

A. Share your testimony of the time you needed and received encouragement. Have students think back when they were discouraged and what happened when someone encouraged them. Can they use those examples to do the same with others who may feel hopeless and discouraged? Discuss.

B. Break the class into four groups and assign each group a question from the DISCUSS THE MEANING section. Have each group present their conclusions to the class.

C. The LESSON IN OUR SOCIETY can help students see how the lesson parallels with many present-day situations.

6. Arousing Action

A. The MAKE IT HAPPEN section contains a suggestion of what may be done to implement principles learned. Since it is a suggestion, you will want to tailor the implementations to your own specific needs.

B. Challenge students to read the DAILY BIBLE READINGS for the week. This will help build their faith and biblical knowledge.

C. Close the class with prayer, thanking God for the opportunity to be a source of encouragement to people.

JULY 13TH

WORSHIP GUIDE

For the Superintendent or Teacher
Theme: The Wall Completed
Theme Song: "I'm Encouraged to Serve the Lord"
Scripture: Isaiah 14:13-18
Song: "Thank You Lord"
Devotional: Your word teaches that we are more than conquerors through Christ who strengthens us and that we can accomplish all things through Him. Help me to bear this in mind during my challenges. In Jesus' name. Amen.

THE WALL COMPLETED

Bible Background • NEHEMIAH 6
Printed Text • NEHEMIAH 6:1-9, 15-16
Devotional Reading • ISAIAH 49:13-18

LESSON AIM

By the end of the lesson, students will understand the obstacles faced by Nehemiah and the Israelites in rebuilding the walls of Jerusalem, be able to explain why dedication and commitment are necessary elements to success, and determine to acknowledge God in all their endeavors.

KEEP IN MIND

"When all our enemies heard about this, all the surrounding nations were afraid and lost their self-confidence, because they realized that this work had been done with the help of our God" (Nehemiah 6:16).

FOCAL VERSES

Nehemiah 6:1 When word came to Sanballat, Tobiah, Geshem the Arab and the rest of our enemies that I had rebuilt the wall and not a gap was left in it though up to that time I had not set the doors in the gates

2 Sanballat and Geshem sent me this message: "Come, let us meet together in one of the villages on the plain of Ono." But they were scheming to harm me;

3 So I sent messengers to them with this reply: "I am carrying on a great project and cannot go down. Why should the work stop while I leave it and go down to you?"

4 Four times they sent me the same message, and each time I gave them the same answer.

5 Then, the fifth time, Sanballat sent his aide to me with the same message, and in his hand was an unsealed letter

LESSON OVERVIEW

LESSON AIM
KEEP IN MIND
FOCAL VERSES
IN FOCUS
THE PEOPLE, PLACES, AND TIMES
BACKGROUND
AT-A-GLANCE
IN DEPTH
SEARCH THE SCRIPTURES
DISCUSS THE MEANING
LESSON IN OUR SOCIETY
MAKE IT HAPPEN
FOLLOW THE SPIRIT
REMEMBER YOUR THOUGHTS
MORE LIGHT ON THE TEXT
DAILY BIBLE READINGS

6 In which was written: "It is reported among the nations and Geshem says it is true that you and the Jews are plotting to revolt, and therefore you are building the wall. Moreover, according to these reports you are about to become their king

7 And have even appointed prophets to make this proclamation about you in Jerusalem: 'There is a king in Judah!' Now this report will get back to the king; so come, let us confer together."

8 I sent him this reply: "Nothing like what you are saying is happening; you are just making it up out of your head."

9 They were all trying to frighten us, thinking, "Their hands will get too weak for the work, and it will not be completed." [But I prayed,] "Now strengthen my hands."

15 So the wall was completed on the twenty-fifth of Elul, in fifty-two days.

16 When all our enemies heard about this, all the surrounding nations were afraid and lost their self-confidence, because they realized that this work had been done with the help of our God.

IN FOCUS

There once was a man who had nothing for his family to eat. He had an old rifle and three bullets. So he decided that he would go out and kill something for dinner. As he went down the road, he saw a rabbit. He shot at the rabbit, but he missed it.

Then he saw a squirrel and fired a shot at the squirrel, but he missed it.

As he went further, he saw a wild turkey in the tree. He had only one bullet, but a voice came to him and said, "Pray first, aim high, and stay focused."

However, at the same time, he saw a deer, which was a better kill. He brought the gun down and aimed at the deer. But then he saw a rattlesnake between his legs about to bite him, so he naturally brought the gun farther down to shoot the rattlesnake. Again the voice spoke to him, "I said pray, aim high, and stay focused."

So the man decided to listen to the voice. He prayed, then aimed the gun high up in the tree and shot the wild turkey. The bullet bounced off the turkey and killed the deer. The handle fell off the gun and hit the snake in the head and killed it.

When the gun had gone off, it knocked the hunter into a pond. When he stood to look around, he had fish in all his pockets, a deer, and a turkey to eat, and the snake was dead simply because he listened to God.

In our lesson today, Nehemiah's enemies make several attempts to distract him from his task. However, Nehemiah stays focused on the task at hand and keeps looking to God to deal with his enemies.

THE PEOPLE, PLACES, AND TIMES

Sanballat. In Nehemiah 2:10, 19 he is called the Heronnite, which probably means that he came from a town called Beth-Horon. He was the chief opponent of Nehemiah and leader of the group that included Tobiah and Geshem. These three men were dedicated to stopping the work of rebuilding the walls of Jerusalem. It is generally believed that Sanballat was the governor of Samaria and had designs on controlling Judea as well. Sanballat and his fellow plotters tried to intimidate the Israelite builders, to set Nehemiah up for assassination, to blackmail him, and finally to discredit Judea's governor. All of their plots amounted to nothing since Nehemiah and the Israelites completed their building project in a miraculously short time.

BACKGROUND

We first encounter Sanballat and Tobiah in the second chapter of the Nehemiah. These two men, who are later joined by Geshem, would prove to be a huge thorn in Nehemiah's side. When the Israelites started to work on the walls, Sanballat, Tobiah, and their Samaritan and Arab cohorts ridiculed the work. "They mocked and ridiculed us. 'What is this you are doing?' they asked. "Are you rebelling against the king?'" (Nehemiah 2:19, NIV)? "And in the presence of his associates and the army of Samaria, Sanballat said, 'What are those feeble Jews doing? Will they restore their wall? Will they offer sacrifices? Will they finish in a day? Can they bring the stones back to life from those heaps of rubble burned as they are?' Tobiah the Ammonite, who was at his side, said, 'What they are building if even a fox climbed up on it, he would break down their wall of stones!'" (4:2-3, NIV).

In spite of their taunts, the work continued on the walls and the people put their hearts into the work. In a very short time, the gaps in the wall had been closed and the wall had reached half its original height. When Sanballat and his cohorts heard about the progress on the wall, they became very angry and plotted to stop the work. "Before they know it or see us, we will be right there among them and will kill them and put an end to the work" (v. 11, NIV). Nehemiah found out about the plot and stationed warriors at strategic places along the wall. From that day on, half of Nehemiah's men did the work, while the other half were equipped with spears, shields, bows and armor. The officers posted themselves behind all the people of Judah who were building the wall. Those who carried materials did their work with one hand and held a weapon in the other, and each of the builders wore his sword at his side as he worked" (vv. 16-18, NIV). This eliminated any possibility of a surprise attack.

As the work continued on the walls, internal problems sprang up. The more affluent Israelites were oppressing their needy brethren. The poor people brought their problems to Nehemiah "Although we are of the same flesh and blood as our countrymen and though our sons are as good as theirs, yet we have to subject our sons and daughters to slavery. Some of our daughters have already been enslaved, but we are powerless, because our fields and our vineyards belong to others" (5:5).

Nehemiah was horrified when he heard of what was being done to the poor Israelites by their own people. After giving the matter some thought, he called a meeting of the wealthy Israelites and confronted them: "You are exacting usury from your own countrymen!" (v. 7). He demanded that the nobles restore to the people what they had taken away as well as all the money they had extorted from their brethren. The nobles agreed to Nehemiah's demands and promised to stop charging usury on loans to fellow Israelites.

In spite of the external and internal problems, the Israelites soon completed the rebuilding of the wall. When word of their accomplishment reached Israel's enemies, they knew they would have to devise a more devious method of attack. Rather than concentrating on intimidating the populace, they would try to destroy the people's leader.

AT-A-GLANCE

1. The Plot to Assassinate (Nehemiah 6:1-5)
2. The Plot to Blackmail (vv. 6-9)
3. The Plot's Failure (vv. 15-16)

IN DEPTH

1. The Plot to Assassinate (Nehemiah 6:1-5)

Work progressed on the wall at an astounding pace. In less than two months, the Israelites had almost completely rebuilt the wall. All that remained was to fill in certain gaps and to hang the gates. When word of their progress reached Nehemiah's enemies, Sanballat, Tobiah, and Geshem, the three men plotted to kill Nehemiah before the wall was completed.

Their plan was to lure Nehemiah away from the protection of Jerusalem and assassinate him. Then, with their leader dead, it would be much

easier to intimidate the people and frighten them into stopping the work on the walls. To accomplish this, they sent a messenger to Nehemiah inviting him to a meeting away from the city in a desert plain called Ono.

When Nehemiah received the message, he immediately saw through their ruse. If Sanballat and his friends wanted to negotiate peace, why couldn't they come to Jerusalem like they did when they ridiculed the work at its beginning?

However, rather than let his enemies know that he was on to their plan, Nehemiah sent word back, "I am carrying on a great project and cannot go down. Why should the work stop while I leave it and go down to you?" (Nehemiah 6:3, NIV). Nehemiah's enemies were nothing if not persistent. They sent the same message to Nehemiah four times, and four times Nehemiah answered them in the same manner.

Perhaps Nehemiah's enemies thought they could wear him down by their dogged persistence, or maybe they thought that the governor's desire for a peaceful resolution to the people's problems might persuade him to take a chance. Whatever they thought, Nehemiah would not be drawn away from his God—ordained tasks. Whenever a great work is begun, distractions always follow. One of the secrets of success is to stay focused on the task and not yield to other temptations.

2. The Plot to Blackmail (vv. 6-9)

After they had failed four times to lure Nehemiah away, it finally dawned on the three men that perhaps a new tactic was necessary. So they sent Nehemiah a fifth letter. This time, they sent an unsealed letter to the governor. This was an insult to Nehemiah. Whenever correspondence was sent to people of Nehemiah's position, the letter was sent in a sealed silk bag. Sending an open letter meant that the contents could have been read by anyone. The text may even suggest that the letter was read openly to Nehemiah in front of the people.

The letter was a clear attempt to cause Nehemiah problems among the Israelites and to blackmail him. The letter claimed that Nehemiah had appointed prophets to proclaim him king in

Jerusalem. Only God could appoint true prophets. If Nehemiah had appointed false prophets to make false prophecies, the people would rise up against him.

Secondly, the letter accused the Israelites of building the wall so that they could revolt and issued a final threat. Unless Nehemiah agreed to meet with the men as they had originally asked, they would send their lies to the king.

Nehemiah was very concerned with this latest threat. If word of a budding revolt got back to the king, even Nehemiah's high standing at court may not be enough to appease the king's wrath. However, the great wall builder refused to give in to fear. He knew that the enemy's intent was to frighten the people into quitting the work. "They were all trying to frighten us, thinking, 'Their hands will get too weak for the work, and it will not be completed'" (v. 9, NIV). Instead of giving in to fear, Nehemiah turned to prayer. "But I prayed, 'Now strengthen my hands'" (v. 9, NIV). He then sent word back to Sanballat telling the troublemaker that he was lying and making up fairy tales in his head.

This reply must have really angered Sanballat, Tobiah, and Geshem. If they could not divide the people or kill their leader, they had no hope of stopping the work. They had done their worst, and the people had remained committed to their task. Obstacles can either be an excuse to quit or an evidence of our commitment to success.

3. The Plot's Failure (vv. 15-16)

Nehemiah's enemies would make one more attempt to discredit him. They would have a trusted prophet try to get Nehemiah to take refuge in the temple. Once Nehemiah had taken shelter in the temple, Sanballat would launch his attack on the leaderless people and disgrace Nehemiah and discourage the people (vv. 10-14). Nehemiah once again saw through their plot and refused to hide away. It soon became evident to Sanballat and his cohorts that they would not be able to stop the work from proceeding.

Fifty-two days after the work on the walls had begun, the task was completed. When the discouraged enemies of Israel heard about the comple-

tion in such a short time, even they had to acknowledge that this work was done with the help of God and nothing they could do would stop it.

When God divinely appoints people to assignments, He does not promise success without trials, but He does promise victory. If we remain focused on the task at hand, committed to its completion and submitted to the will of God, there is no job too big and no person too small.

SEARCH THE SCRIPTURES

1. Who were Nehemiah's three main adversaries in rebuilding the walls? (Nehemiah 6:1)

2. Nehemiah's enemies were trying to lure him away from the city to kill him. How many times did they appeal to the governor directly? (v. 4)

3. The fifth time, they sent word to Nehemiah with an open letter. What did the open letter accuse Nehemiah of? (vv. 6, 7)

4. Nehemiah's enemies were trying to frighten him into making a big mistake, but instead of giving in to fear, how did Nehemiah react? (v. 9)

5. The Israelites completed the building of the walls in an astounding fifty-two days. When their enemies became aware of this great feat, what was their reaction? (v. 16)

DISCUSS THE MEANING

1. If you are sure that God has called you to a certain ministry or task, is it safe to assume that He will eliminate all opposition? What can we expect in fulfilling God-ordained assignments?

2. Whenever Nehemiah was faced with difficulties, he always turned to prayer. What lessons can we take from his example?

LESSON IN OUR SOCIETY

There is an old proverb that says evil triumphs when good people do nothing. There are a number of issues facing American society where cultural liberals and hedonists turn out in droves to support their causes while Christians stay at home and bemoan the decline in American morals. What are some ways that believers can ensure that our voices are heard on the moral issues facing our country? What can you do to ensure that your voice is heard in your community?

MAKE IT HAPPEN

At the end of class, spend a few minutes in silent prayer. Ask God what you can do to make your community a better place to live. Things like helping elderly people with their lawns and picking up loose trash are a couple of ideas. After the prayer, list all the things you can think of. From your list, choose a couple of things you can accomplish this week.

FOLLOW THE SPIRIT

What God wants me to do:

_____

_____

REMEMBER YOUR THOUGHTS

Special insights you have learned:

_____

_____

MORE LIGHT ON THE TEXT
Nehemiah 6:1-9, 15-16

The work on the walls of Jerusalem has progressed up to the point of completion despite the open violence and opposition from Sanballat and his associates (Nehemiah 4). Failing to stop the work, Sanballat and his group focus their attack directly on Nehemiah. Sanballat plots to lure Nehemiah into a snare in order to assassinate him. Failing in that plot, he conceives another plan, accusing him of insurrection against the king. Both plots fail, and the walls are completed.

1 Now it came to pass, when Sanballat, and Tobiah, and Geshem the Arabian, and the rest of our enemies, heard that I had builded the wall, and that there was no breach left therein; (though at that time I had not set up the doors upon the gates;) 2 That Sanballat and Geshem sent unto me, saying, Come, let us meet together in some one of the villages in the plain of Ono. But they thought to do me mischief.

The news of the completion of the Jerusalem wall has come to the knowledge of Sanballat, Tobiah, Geshem (an Arabian), and the other enemies of Jerusalem, and they plan to stop the work. Seeing that the work has progressed so swiftly that perhaps attacking the people directly seems unre-

alistic, these enemies attack the leader to take him off the scene. The plot is to lure Nehemiah away from his supporters in Jerusalem to where he would not have protection.

They invite Nehemiah to meet with them in "one of the villages in the plain of Ono." Ono, or *Ownow,* is said to be a village in the territory of Benjamin, about 19 miles from Jerusalem. This seemed to be an obscure place where there would be no suspicion by the people or protection for Nehemiah. In the plot, they pretend to be friendly and only wanted to consult with him. Taking him away from Jerusalem would probably make his assassination easier; it would also facilitate an attack against Jerusalem in his absence. However, their plot fails because Nehemiah becomes aware of the plan.

3 And I sent messengers unto them, saying, I am doing a great work, so that I cannot come down: why should the work cease, whilst I leave it, and come down to you? 4 Yet they sent unto me four times after this sort; and I answered them after the same manner.

Nehemiah sends a message back to them through messengers that he was so busy with the work at hand that he could not leave it to come to them. The phrase, "I am doing a great work" means that he is doing an important work. The word "great" used here is the Hebrew adjective *gadowl,* or (shortened) *gadol* (pronounced **gaw-dole'**), which has various meanings including large (in magnitude and extent) and great in number or importance. Nehemiah tells Sanballat and his group that the work at hand is so important that he cannot leave it to meet with them. As the leader, he knows that his absence would affect the progress of the work. Of course he is quite aware that Sanballat knows this, and this is definitely Sanballat's plan—to stop the building of the walls. Therefore, Nehemiah states his case rhetorically to him thus: "Why should the work cease, whilst I leave it, and come down to you?" This implies that Nehemiah is knowledgeable of their plan, and that it would be foolish to fall for such a plan. Sanballat tries this plan four times, and four times Nehemiah sends Sanballat the same message, thus frustrating him and his plan.

Desperate to do away with Nehemiah so that the work is stopped, Sanballat and his "henchmen" devise another method to entrap Nehemiah in their snare.

5 Then sent Sanballat his servant unto me in like manner the fifth time with an open letter in his hand; 6 Wherein was written, It is reported among the heathen, and Gashmu saith it, that thou and the Jews think to rebel: for which cause thou buildest the wall, that thou mayest be their king, according to these words.

Failing four times to convince Nehemiah to meet with them, Sanballat tries the fifth time. He sends an open letter to Nehemiah, hand delivered through one of his servants. In the letter, Sanballat falsely accuses Nehemiah of subversion against the king by proclaiming himself as king in Judah. This is well understood in the region as treason, which of course carries the death penalty. Sanballat pretends to be on Nehemiah's side by asking him to come so that they can discuss it together and avert this penalty.

In the open letter, Sanballat says that it has been reported among the heathen and confirmed by "Gashmu" that Nehemiah and the Jews are planning to rebell; that is why they are rebuilding the wall. Furthermore, Nehemiah is accused of rebuilding the wall so that he can proclaim himself king. The accusation, according to this letter, states further that not only is Nehemiah planning a rebellion and trying install himself as king, but that he has already appointed (or hired) prophets to preach the same at Jerusalem. The word "preach" is the Hebrew verb *qara'* (pronounced **kaw-raw'**), which means to proclaim, publish, or announce publicly.

The magnitude of Sanballat's treachery is demonstrated in the statement, "And now shall it be reported to the king according to these words. Come now therefore, and let us take counsel together" (6:7). In other words, he seems to say to Nehemiah, "You know how serious this accusation is and its penalty if it is reported to the king. You would not like to be reported to the king, would you?" The obvious answer of course is no. With this assumption, Sanballat extends his "friendly" arm of fellowship to Nehemiah: "Come

now therefore, and let us take counsel together." The word "counsel" is the Hebrew *ya`ats* (pronounced **yaw-ats'**) and means to deliberate or resolve, to consult together, with the idea here being to consult as equals. He makes the letter and the invitation look genuine and well-intented. However, his dishonesty is well understood by Nehemiah, who rejects his invitation just as he did the previous four attempts.

The extent of Sanballat's treachery can been seen in the following gimmicks he uses to entrap Nehemiah. First, he pretends that he wants to save Nehemiah from so-called treason by inviting him to a "peaceful" conference through a letter as if he had Nehemiah's best interests at heart. The idea here is that such a meeting is supposed to be a secret one. The irony is that, instead of keeping the deal secret through a sealed letter, Sanballat sends an open letter with the intent of making the accusation public, thereby causing rebellion among the people. Open letters were usually read publicly, and this act clearly reveals Sanballat's evil motive: to implicate Nehemiah and weaken the hands of the workers, thereby delaying or stopping the work.

Sanballat tries to make the accusation look serious so that on reading the letter Nehemiah will respond immediately. He does this by invoking Nehemiah's religious beliefs in connection with the prophets. He knows that Nehemiah will be worried and will take seriously an accusation of propagating false prophecy. Such an accusation would make Nehemiah respond immediately to their invitation in order to clear himself of such a false accusation. This last attempt fails also.

7 And thou hast also appointed prophets to preach of thee at Jerusalem, saying, There is a king in Judah; and now shall it be reported to the king according to these words. Come now therefore, and let us take counsel together. 8 Then I sent unto him, saying, There are no such things done as thou sayest, but thou feignest them out of thine own heart.

Just as he did with the previous four attempts, Nehemiah sends a message back to Sanballat denying the accusation and accusing him of treachery. He tells Sanballat that he is the one making up the story. There is neither such a plan being hatched, nor is there such a rumor as he purports. Rather, Sanballat is making up the story by himself. Therefore, his invitation is totally rejected. In the phrase "thou feignest them out thine own heart," the word "feign" is the Hebrew word *bada'* (baw-daw'), which means to devise or contrive.

9 For they all made us afraid, saying, Their hands shall be weakened from the work, that it be not done. Now therefore, O God, strengthen my hands.

The accusation of rebellion is to make Nehemiah and his people afraid so that "their hands shall be weakened from the work" and the work eventually stopped. As is his custom (see 1:5-11; 2:4; 4:4-5; 5:19; 6:14; 13:14, 22, 29, 31), Nehemiah resorts to praying to God. He asks God to "strengthen his hands." Failing further in a desperate effort to kill Nehemiah and to get him out of the way in order to stall the completion of the walls of Jerusalem, Sanballat and Tobiah hire some false prophets to lure Nehemiah into the temple to kill him (vv. 10-14). However, Nehemiah also discovers this evil plot through wisdom from God given through prayer.

6:15 So the wall was finished in the twenty and fifth day of the month Elul, in fifty and two days. 16 And it came to pass, that when all our enemies heard thereof, and all the heathen that were about us saw these things, they were much cast down in their own eyes: for they perceived that this work was wrought of our God.

In spite of all the plots against Nehemiah and his people by Sanballat and the enemy nations, the wall is completed in fifty-two days. The narrator gives us the exact time and date the work is completed: the twenty-fifth day of the month of Elul, the sixth month according to Jewish calendar (equivalent to our month September). The purpose of this specificity is probably to emphasize that, despite the opposition that had characterized the project from the beginning, the work is completed in record time—only fifty-two days. The fifty-two days, however, does not include the Sabbath days, which the people had to keep according to the Jewish law. The time of completion of this task looks extremely short, but we should bear in mind that there were thousands of enthusiastic workers who dedicated themselves to the work, who never allowed the opposition from within and without to discourage or stop them from the task. Instead of being discouraged by their enemies' threats, the people were energized by them to work harder to finish the work. It was such a great accomplishment that the enemies were discouraged and humiliated. They realized that it was done only by the power of God.

DAILY BIBLE READINGS

M: The People Had Minds to Work
Nehemiah 4:1-6
T: Enemies Plot against the Workers
Nehemiah 4:7-14
W: A Guard Is Set
Nehemiah 4:15-23
T: O God, Strengthen My Hands
Nehemiah 6:1-9
F: The Wall Is Finished
Nehemiah 6:10-19
S: Gates and People Are Purified
Nehemiah 12:27-31b
S: Jerusalem's Joy Is Heard Far Away
Nehemiah 12:43-47

TEACHING TIPS

July 20
Bible Study Guide 8

1. Words You Should Know

A. Understand (Nehemiah 8:3); Hebrew *biyn* (pronounced **bin**)—Connotes the ability to separate something mentally; the ability to distinguish sense from nonsense; the ability to consider an issue or presentation diligently. It can also mean to be informed.

B. Worship (v. 6); Hebrew *shachah*—To prostrate; specifically used paying homage to God.

C. Grieve (v. 11); from the Hebrew *atsab* (pronounced **aw-tsab'**)—To fabricate or fashion as it relates to working hard; to work oneself up in a bad sense and to worry. It can also mean to feel pain or anger.

2. Teacher Preparation

A. Read the text for the lesson at least twice.

B. Bring a tape with celebration music. Also bring a 3 x 5 index card for each member of the class.

C. Read the Bible Study Guide and prepare your answers for the SEARCH THE SCRIPTURE questions. Read the LESSON IN OUR SOCIETY to see if you can come up with an example. Write out what you will do in the MAKE IT HAPPEN section. Use a Bible dictionary to gain some understanding of who Nehemiah was. Check out the term "scribe" for yourself.

3. Starting the Lesson

A. To set the atmosphere with praise as students arrive, play the music until everyone is seated.

B. Review the LESSON AIM and present the BACKGROUND information for the lesson.

C. Have someone read the FOCAL VERSES. When Nehemiah 8:6 is read, ask the class to enact the same actions taken by the people in this verse.

D. Now divide the class into three sections to discuss the IN DEPTH section.

Ask group 1 the question, "What does it mean to attend to God's law?" Group 2 should discuss the concept of appreciating the Word of God. Group 3 should look at the concept of celebration and understanding.

4. Getting into the Lesson

Bring the class together and discuss the various insights gleaned from the lesson. Discuss the IN FOCUS story and IN DEPTH sections. Allow time to discuss the SEARCH THE SCRIPTURES and DISCUSS THE MEANING questoins.

5. Relating the Lesson to Life

Do not restrict the students only to what is in the text. See what applications they can bring forth.

6. Arousing Action

A. Encourage students to read the MAKE IT HAPPEN section and respond to the questions posed.

B. Challenge students to read the DAILY BIBLE READINGS for the week. This will help build their faith and biblical knowledge so that when they go out to share with other believers they will be well versed in Scripture.

C. Close the class with prayer, thanking God for the opportunity to be a source of encouragement to people.

JULY 20TH

WORSHIP GUIDE

For the Superintendent or Teacher
Theme: Call to Obey the Law
Theme Song: "I Have Decided to Follow Jesus"
Scripture: Nehemiah 8:1, 3, 5, 6, 8, 12
Song: "Yes To Your Will"
Devotional: Heavenly Father, thank You for the opportunity to grow in Your Word on a daily basis. I thank You that Your living Word is a manual that will lead to a victorious life in Christ Jesus. In Jesus' name. Amen.

CALLED TO OBEY THE LAW

Bible Background • NEHEMIAH 8
Printed Text • NEHEMIAH 8:1-3, 5-6, 8-12
Devotional Reading • PSALM 119:33-40

LESSON AIM

By the end of this lesson, students will know the importance of the Word of God for the exiles, appreciate the need for public reading of the Word of God, and decide to celebrate the Word of God by sharing with others.

KEEP IN MIND

"So they read in the book in the law of God distinctly, and gave the sense, and caused them to understand the reading" (Nehemiah 8:8)

FOCAL VERSES

Nehemiah 8:1 And all the people gathered themselves together as one man into the street that was before the water gate; and they spake unto Ezra the scribe to bring the book of the law of Moses, which the LORD had commanded to Israel.

2 And Ezra the priest brought the law before the congregation both of men and women, and all that could hear with understanding, upon the first day of the seventh month.

3 And he read therein before the street that was before the water gate from the morning until midday, before the men and the women, and those that could understand; and the ears of all the people were attentive unto the book of the law.

5 And Ezra opened the book in the sight of all the people; (for he was above all the people;) and when he opened it, all the people stood up:

6 And Ezra blessed the LORD, the great God. And all the people answered, Amen, Amen, with

LESSON OVERVIEW

LESSON AIM
KEEP IN MIND
FOCAL VERSES
IN FOCUS
THE PEOPLE, PLACES, AND TIMES
BACKGROUND
AT-A-GLANCE
IN DEPTH
SEARCH THE SCRIPTURES
DISCUSS THE MEANING
LESSON IN OUR SOCIETY
MAKE IT HAPPEN
FOLLOW THE SPIRIT
REMEMBER YOUR THOUGHTS
MORE LIGHT ON THE TEXT
DAILY BIBLE READINGS

lifting up their hands: and they bowed their heads, and worshipped the LORD with their faces to the ground.

8 So they read in the book in the law of God distinctly, and gave the sense, and caused them to understand the reading.

9 And Nehemiah, which is the Tirshatha, and Ezra the priest the scribe, and the Levites that taught the people, said unto all the people, This day is holy unto the LORD your God; mourn not, nor weep. For all the people wept, when they heard the words of the law.

10 Then he said unto them, Go your way, eat the fat, and drink the sweet, and send portions unto them for whom nothing is prepared: for this day is holy unto our Lord: neither be ye sorry; for the joy of the LORD is your strength.

11 So the Levites stilled all the people, saying, Hold your peace, for the day is holy; neither be ye grieved.

12 And all the people went their way to eat, and to drink, and to send portions, and to make great mirth, because they had understood the words that were declared unto them.

IN FOCUS

Three years ago, Brother Utim bought an expensive car. Because the car ran well, he did not bother to check out the manual; his feeling was he could always take it to a mechanic. As a matter of fact, the car ran so well that he bought a similar one for his spouse. Again, being the man that he was, he did not read the manual. After five years of owning both vehicles, his car began to experience a variety of minor mechanical problems.

One day Brother Utim parked the car, locked it with his remote, and left for two hours. Upon his return he attempted to start the car; however, it would not respond. Automatically he knew that the parking brake was on. He tried to release the brake but could not find the release handle. He looked all around the inside of the car trying to find a way to release the brake. He got out and walked around outside the car several times wondering how to release the brake. Being a proud man, he did not want to call and ask anyone how to release the brake. So he looked for the manual. Although he searched the car throughly, he could not find the owner's manual (remember, he had not seen the manual since he bought the car). Eventually he gave up and decided to call home and ask his wife to come pick him up. Much to his dismay, no one was home. So he decided to walk home. On the way home he saw his wife, who picked him up and took him to the location of his car. Thank God, he thought, she has her manual. Immediately he took the manual, opened it, and read the first sentence: "Always keep this manual near." As it turned out, all he needed to do was press his foot on the accelerator pedal to release the brake. If only he had read the manual he would have known what to do.

The Bible, the living Word of God, can be viewed as a manual on how to live our daily lives. Today's lesson is about getting acquainted with the manual, God's Word. One cannot obey what one does not know. Therefore, as Christians, we are admonished to read the manual.

THE PEOPLE, PLACES, AND TIMES

In 538 B.C., seventy years after Israel had gone into exile, the first group returned to Judah under the leadership of Zerubbabel. Over several years of opposition from the Samaritans, the returnees eventually rebuilt the temple in 515 B.C.

A number of years later, in 458 B.C., under the leadership of Ezra, a second group returned. Under Ezra's faithful teaching most of these people turned from their sins and to the Lord, agreeing to follow God's will for their lives.

In 444 B.C., 14 years after Ezra, Nehemiah also returned and succeeded in rebuilding the walls. The book of Nehemiah chronicles this man's remarkable achievements.

BACKGROUND

Israel had gone into exile for nearly 150 years and Judah for 70 years. When Judah was conquered, the Babylonians took all the scrolls from the temple and the temple artifacts. As is usually the case such domination with only a few of them were allowed to read and write. These select people included Daniel and his three friends. While many of the people of Israel were taken to Babylon, many others went into Africa and were dispersed throughout the continent. The group that was led by Nehemiah were mostly from Babylon. In the background to this text is not only the servitude of Jews to Babylonians but also prophetic utterances given by the prophet Jeremiah that God would bring them back. Isaiah, of course, speaks of the remnant that would return.

AT-A-GLANCE

1. Attending to the Law of God
(Nehemiah 8:1-3)
2. Appreciating the Law (vv. 5-6)
3. Celebrating the Law (vv. 8-12)

IN DEPTH

1. Attending to the Law of God
(Nehemiah 8:1-3)

After the returned exiles were settled in their towns, all the people gathered in the square before the Water Gate in Jerusalem and asked Ezra to bring the book of the law of Moses (vv. 1-

2). As they gathered there from morning to midday, Ezra read the book to all who could understand, and they listened attentively (v. 3). This is a sign that these exiles took the Word of God seriously. When the term "the law of God" is used, we usually think of the Decalogue or the Ten Commandments. But the word used to describe the law here is "Torah," referring to the Word which God gave to Moses. Attending to the law of God, then, is not just paying attention to the dos and don'ts, but giving oneself completely and totally to the Word of God.

These returning exiles had many things to which they had to attend. There was the matter of their having just arrived in Canaan and all the logistics of settling into a new place. They could have attended to their own houses, for the houses of their ancestors had been burnt and destroyed by their enemies. They could have attended to matters pertaining to their safety. Looking at all the danger surrounding them, they could have chosen to stay at home and worship the Lord alone. But paying attention to all of these things would not have satisfied their need for security and belonging. Attending to the law of the Lord provided them with the opportunity to enter into the sphere of the covenant which God made with their ancestors. Why is it important to attend to the law in this context? Because without the law they would not grasp the breach which had caused them to be exiles in the first place. They had been in exile so long, and now that they were in the Promised land, they needed to cleanse themselves from the reproach of Babylon.

How do we give attention to the law of the Lord? In this text, the people found the Word, which suggests that they were searching for it. Searching, implies desire and we tend to search for what we desire. Jesus was clear when He said, "Where your treasure is, there will your heart be also" (Matthew 6:21). We attend to God's Word by listening to and understanding it.

The depth of our attending to the Word of the Lord is also seen in the amount of time we put into it. We read here the words, "from early morning until midday." There is no intimation that the people were agitated because Ezra was reading the Scriptures too long. Attending to the Word of God requires that we listen, not just for ourselves, but for the sake of those who cannot grasp the Word at the level at which is being proclaimed. The concept of attending to anything requires our time, respect, resources, and our presence. Attending to the Word of the Lord begins through prayer and disciplined acquaintance with the word. It is having such a posture that we begin to appreciate the Word as it flows from the Holy Spirit to us.

2. Appreciating the Law (vv. 5-6)

These people appreciated the Word of God. Who knows how long it had been since they had heard the Word read? From the context, it would seem that many of them had never heard the Word read and could not understand it. Their appreciation is shown by the fact that they stood. "The people stood when Ezra began to read." This standing is really a sign of reverence for the Word. One could infer that the standing suggests they were taking a posture of readiness for action to move based on what they heard. Whenever a dignitary enters the room, people will rise as a way to honor that person. Standing is not required when the Word is read, but indicates reverence for the Word.

Further, appreciation is seen in what is said: "Ezra blessed the Lord, the great God." This blessing is specifically directed to God for giving the Word. The people then respond, "Amen, amen." This verbal appreciation is powerful in this context because it distinguishes the Lord from other gods. This Lord is the great God. Our verbal acknowledgment of the Word of God is important, especially when we have in our midst persons who may not believe the efficacy of the Word. The appreciation of the people is seen in their verbal response to Ezra's blessing. Appreciation of the Word flows out in our praise and thanksgiving for divine blessings. How could they not respond with outbursts of praise, knowing that, "the Lord, the great God" had chosen to speak a word into their situation of despair? Therefore, the appreciation is not just for the mere letter of the law, but to the God who gives it and to the power it brings with it as it enters into our souls.

We read further that they lifted up their hands. Lifting up of the hands is both a sign of praise and a sign of surrender. This appreciation also arises from the fact that God had brought them back to the land of their fathers and mothers. Appreciation is something that happens in the human consciousness when it has been touched by the value of a concept or act. It flows out in gratitude, which inturn leads to action and finally to worship (v. 6).

3. Celebrating the Law (vv. 8-12)

Having become reacquainted with the Word, the people were now ready to celebrate. While interpretation of the Word does not necessarily have to precede celebration, an understanding of the God who gives the Word is (v. 8). In fact, such understanding is vital for a genuine celebration.

The Scripture says, "The people wept when they heard the words." Hearing the Word caused the shedding of tears. God does not give the Word merely to cause us sadness. Rather, the Word is meant to lead us to repentance and forgiveness and to propel us to joyful celebration. The leaders of the people knew this, so they instructed them to rejoice. Why? Because the day was holy to the Lord. Why was the day holy? The Word of God had sanctified the day. How? It brought light to their lives and showed them what was required of them. The Word revealed to them their sins, but the same Word revealed their divine destiny. They ought to rejoice because the words declared to them were not merely words of judgment but words of comfort (v. 12). Though we are convicted by the Word of God, it is not just so we can sit around and feel sorry for ourselves. It is so we will be led to salvation and thus enter into the joy of the Lord.

Celebratory worship leads to sharing. Such celebration reveals that God has shared His divine resources with His people. We are called to cele-

brate based on the fact that we have heard and understood the Word. We should seek to grasp the Word and our celebration should stem from being grounded in the Word of God.

There is a great danger in the church when emotions are given more prominence than understanding the Word of God. Thus much of what we call celebration fails to be seasoned by the salt of the Word. Let celebration grow out of genuine appreciation for the Word and a deep spiritual attentiveness to the precepts of the Lord.

SEARCH THE SCRIPTURES

1. Who read the law to the returning exiles? (Nehemiah 8:1)

2. What is the law of Moses? (v. 2)

3. How long did Ezra read the word for the exiles? (v. 3)

4. What did the people do when Ezra read the word? (v. 5)

5. After the word had been read, what three things did God's people do? (v. 10)

6. What are the two emotional responses of the people to the word? (vv. 6-9)

DISCUSS THE MEANING

1. How do you see this text relating to the concept of obeying the law?

2. What did the priest mean by "this day is holy?"

3. Is a holiday necessarily a day of celebration?

4. How important is the hearing of the Word of God in the context of celebration?

5. How important is it that people understand the reading of the Word of God?

LESSON IN OUR SOCIETY

There is a rise of celebrative worship in the church today. What a wonderful thing it is that we now praise and worship, allowing our emotions to be involved. However, there is some concern that this bent to "feel good" has taken center stage away from the Word of God. Today it seems that believers are attuned to emotional involvement in worship, but are not always grounded in the Word. Understanding the Word of God has become increasingly more important as entertainment has crept into the church. Content must give rise to celebration, and celebration must give rise to a deeper understanding of the Word.

MAKE IN HAPPEN

The next time you are in church, determine to grasp the truth of the word spoken by the pastor before giving expression to your emotions. See if you are responding to the Word of God or just to your emotions. Also, allow every celebration to be an opportunity to share your blessings with others.

FOLLOW THE SPIRIT

What God wants me to do:

_____

_____

REMEMBER YOUR THOUGHTS

Special insights you have learned:

_____

_____

MORE LIGHT ON THE TEXT
Nehemiah 8:1-3, 5-6, 8-12

The temple has been restored (see the Book of Ezra), and the walls of Jerusalem have been rebuilt and restored (Nehemiah 6:15ff). The people have been resettled in their lands (Chapter 7). Now the people embark on spiritual revival and restoration of the worship of the Lord beginning with the reading of the Law under the leadership and priesthood of Ezra.

8:1 And all the people gathered themselves together as one man into the street that was before the water gate; and they spake unto Ezra the scribe to bring the book of the law of Moses, which the LORD had commanded to Israel.

The people themselves initiate the spiritual revival that takes place. They assemble themselves "as one man into the street" before "the water gate." The word "street" here does not mean street in the modern sense of a narrow road with houses arranged on both sides where cars drive

through or where people and other road users go through. Rather, it a spacious open area, containing a large number of people who gather for important meetings or events. The word is a translation of the Hebrew word *rechob*, or *rechowb* (pronounced **rekh-obe'**), which means a broad or open space, or plaza. It is like a town center or town square as in African traditions, especially among the Igbo culture of Nigeria. For example, in the Igbo culture the town square was where important events took place, such as festivities, sports events, or very important meetings that concerned the whole village. Everyone was expected to attend; hence, the place was spacious to accommodate everyone. In western culture it can be called a stadium. In recent years such arenas have been used not only for sporting events, but also for religious and evangelistic meetings and crusades.

The author writes that the people assembled together "as one man" in the open space, or more appropriately, in the town center or village square. The phrase "as one man" speaks of the unity and cooperative "hunger" the people have for the Word of God. Therefore, they call all the people together for open-space worship; everyone is involved and no one is left out, except children and those unable to understand what is being read (see v. 2). The oneness also carries the idea that the people gather voluntarily by common agreement and that no one is compelled to attend.

The assembly is held before the "water gate," probably one of the gates in the recently rebuilt wall of Jerusalem (see Chapter 6). The Bible speaks of many gates, e.g., gates of Jerusalem (3:13, 26; 12:39; 2 Kings 14:13; 2 Chronicles 25:23) and gates of cities or towns as places for business (Genesis 23:10; 34:20; Deuteronomy 16:18; 21:19; Joshua 20:4; Ruth 4:1). Punishment of criminals took place outside the gates (Deuteronomy 17:5; Jeremiah 20:2; Hebrews 13:12). As the people gather in the "town square," they call on Ezra "the scribe" to bring along with him the book of the Law of Moses. A "scribe," from the Hebrew *caphar* (pronounced **saw-far'**) in the Jewish sense can be a writer or transcriber of the law, a king's secretary, or an instructor of the Law. Scribes are usually custodians of the Law as Ezra is here, people who not only copy and keep the Scriptures, but also interpret them and keep records for the king and the people. Scribes are mentioned in many places in both the Old and New Testaments (see 2 Samuel 8:17; 2 Kings 18:18; Ezra 7:6; Jeremiah 8:8). In New Testament times the scribes were among the ruling class or members of the Sanhedrin. Jesus had numerous encounters with them during His earthly ministry (Matthew 5:20; 9:3; 16:21; 17:10; Mark 12:38; Luke 5:21; 20:46; John 8:3). Here it seems that Ezra is now the custodian of "the Law of Moses" (i.e., the Jewish Bible, comprising the first five books of the Bible). The people ask him to bring the book to the square.

2 And Ezra the priest brought the law before the congregation both of men and women, and all that could hear with understanding, upon the first day of the seventh month.

While in verse 1 Ezra is called "the scribe," in verse 2 we learn that he is referred to as "the priest." This means he was also a Levite since priests came only from the tribe of Levi. Ezra brings the book of the Law before the congregation, which consisted of all the people, male and female, young and old, even strangers (Deuteronomy 31:12). Everyone who was able to understand what was being read and taught came. The gathering took place on the first day of the seventh month, probably in obedience to the commandment that Moses gave them (Deuteronomy 31:9-12). This is also in keeping with the Feast of Trumpets instituted by God (Leviticus 23:23-25), which took place on the first day of the seventh month. In Jewish law it is the duty of the priest to teach the people the Word of God (Deuteronomy 17:9-12; 33:10; Malachi 2:7).

3 And he read therein before the street that was before the water gate from the morning until midday, before the men and the women, and those that could understand; and the ears of all the people

were attentive unto the book of the law.

Verse 3 gives a summary of the reading of the book before the people, while verses 4 and following tend to give an account of the process. The reading of the Law lasts from morning until midday, from daylight to noon—probably over six hours of worship. Here the writer mentions the people involved in the worship: "the men and the women, and those that could understand." The statement "the ears of all the people were attentive unto the book of the Law" means that the people paid close attention to the reading of the book; it also gives the idea of solemnity and respect for the Word of God. This solemnity and reverence is further emphasized in the next verse, where the people stand up at the reading of the Word.

8:5 And Ezra opened the book in the sight of all the people; (for he was above all the people;) and when he opened it, all the people stood up: 6 And Ezra blessed the LORD, the great God. And all the people answered, Amen, Amen, with lifting up their hands: and they bowed their heads, and worshipped the LORD with their faces to the ground.

As mentioned above, verses 4–6 give us the details of how the meeting progresses. In verse 5, Ezra steps to the pulpit (or podium), a wooden stand made for such a purpose; he is flanked on both sides by thirteen other priests (six on his right and seven on his left) while he reads the Word of God to the people. In verse 4, we can picture Ezra walking to the podium with the priests and with the scroll, which he places on the pulpit. As he opens "the book in the sight of all the people," the people all stand on their feet in reverence to God's Word. This respect for the Lord is further demonstrated as Ezra blesses the Lord and the people shout "Amen, Amen" while lifting up of "their hands" to the Lord. The phrase "Ezra blessed" the Lord means that he praised and thanked the Lord. "Blessed" is from the Hebrew verb *barak* (pronounced **baw-rak'**), which means to praise, salute, or thank and often involves kneeling as an act of adoration. Simply put, Ezra opens the meeting with a prayer of thanksgiving and eulogy to the Lord, and the people respond with a resounding "Amen, Amen." "Amen" is a direct rendering of the Hebrew *'amen* (**aw-mane'**), meaning "so be it." This is one way the people participate in the public worship. The act of worship is also shown by lifting up their hands and bowing down their heads with their faces to the ground. The word "worship," or in Hebrew *shachah* (pronounced **shaw-khaw'**), means to prostrate or pay homage to royalty or God; it is to stoop or fall down in reverence to a superior or to God.

8 So they read in the book in the law of God distinctly, and gave the sense, and caused them to understand the reading. 9 And Nehemiah, which is the Tirshatha, and Ezra the priest the scribe, and the Levites that taught the people, said unto all the people, This day is holy unto the LORD your God; mourn not, nor weep. For all the people wept, when they heard the words of the law.

In verse 7 we read there were other people who accompanied Ezra to the pulpit; they assisted Ezra in reading and explaining the Word of the Lord to the people. The priests and the teachers of the Law, including Nehemiah and the Levites (v. 9), explain the Word of God "distinctly" (Hebrew *parash*, pronounced **paw-rash'**), i.e., they clarify the Word by declaring the truth of the Word. They did not give personal interpretations, but rather emphasized what is written in the Law. As the teachers of the Word explain the Scriptures, all the people are touched in their hearts or probably convicted of their wrongdoing as they remember the past and their former relationship with God. They begin to weep. But Nehemiah, Ezra the priest and scribe, and the Levites encourage the people to stop weeping, because it is not a day for weeping. It is a holy day unto the Lord, a Sabbath (Leviticus 23:24), thus a day of rejoicing. The weeping of repentance is to be changed to rejoicing and celebration because their sins are forgiven, and the Word is to be obeyed.

Nehemiah at the time of this spiritual revival was the Tirshatha, which means governor, a title used by the Persian governor in Judea. It is believed that Ezra was an old man by this time (about ninety years old), having brought exiles with him from Babylonia about sixty-nine or seventy years before (Ezra 8). Therefore he was the spiritual leader and called on the people to celebrate the Lord by praising Him instead of mourning.

10 Then he said unto them, Go your way, eat the fat, and drink the sweet, and send portions unto them for whom nothing is prepared: for this day is holy unto our Lord: neither be ye sorry; for the joy of the LORD is your strength.

The pronoun "he" in verse 10 seems to refer to Nehemiah as the governor and community head but does not exclude Ezra and the Levites. He calls on the people, probably at the end of the day's celebration as he dismisses them to their homes to continue with the festival. He says to them, "Go your way, eat the fat, and drink the sweet, and send unto them for whom nothing is prepared." The word "fat" is translated from the Hebrew *mashman* (pronounced **mash-mawn'**), which literally means fatness but figuratively means a rich dish or fertile field. Here, with the accompanying phrase "and drink the sweet," it conveys the idea of a spirit of festivity, enjoyment, and merriment. Such celebrations were usually accompanied by a lot of eating and drinking, exchanging gifts, and alms-giving to the poor (Esther 9:19, 22). Farmers selected the best (the fatted cow or sheep) from their flock and killed it for the celebration and merriment. Jesus alluded to this idea in His parable of the prodigal son. When the son returned, his father ordered his servants to "bring hither the fatted calf, and kill it; and let us eat, and be merry" (Luke 15:23). It was also customary with the Israelites that during such festivities the people would send portions of food and drink to the poor so that they could participate in the joy of the day.

This practice has not changed; it is continued in our present culture during Christmas or Thanksgiving. During this time, people are more generous in their giving to the poor, either directly to the needy or through different agencies such as the "Food Bank" in Canada, the Salvation Army, and other not-for-profit agencies. Growing up I remember my parents sending food and jars of "palm wine" to various homes in our neighborhood or to another village during important festivals such as Christmas or "New Yam harvest festivals." All this signifies a joyous mood. Hence, Nehemiah and the rest of the leaders call on the people to cease from their weeping and sorrow; they should not continue to be sorry (for their sins), but to rejoice and share with others. First, they should rejoice because their sins have been forgiven. Second, they should rejoice because "this day is holy unto the Lord," and therefore it does not call for mourning but for joy and an extension of mercy to others. Third, and most significant they should rejoice becaue they had been reconciled with their God, and the joy of the LORD" is their strength. The *chedvah* (**khed-vaw'**) of Yahweh is the "joy" that is grounded in the feeling of deep relationship and communion with the Lord, the God who is loving and forgiving, who abounds in long-suffering, grace, and truth (Exodus 34:6-7a). This joy will be *ma` owz* (pronounced **maw-oze'**), a "strength," a place of refuge or safety for them. It is their stronghold because the everlasting Lord is their refuge (Jeremiah 16:19).

11 So the Levites stilled all the people, saying, Hold your peace, for the day is holy; neither be ye grieved. 12 And all the people went their way to eat, and to drink, and to send portions, and to make great mirth, because they had understood the words that were declared unto them.

It seems that the weeping and wailing were unabated and uncontrollable (in spite of the encouragement from Nehemiah, Ezra, and the officiating priests), so the Levites step in to help. They try to pacify the people by calling on them to "hold your peace," and they reiterate the same instructions previously given to them by Nehemiah and Ezra. They say to the people, *hacah!* (**haw-saw'**), "hold your peace," i.e., "hush,"

or keep silent and stop weeping because "the day is holy" to the Lord. It is a sacred or *qadowsh* (**kaw-doshe'**) day, and it should be a day for rejoicing rather than a day for "grieving," or `*atsab* (**aw-tsab'**), meaning pain. This appeal has an effect. The people retire to their homes celebrating, eating, drinking, and giving portions to the poor as they were instructed. They make great "mirth," not because of the eating and drinking, but "because they had understood the words that were declared unto them." It is amazing how remorseful and sorrowful we feel when we hear and understand the convicting words of God. Immediately following our repentance and confession that sorrow and weeping turns into inexplicable joy and gladness the moment we know our sins are forgiven. We are in communion and right relationship with the Lord. What follows is celebration and reaching out to others because we have been transformed from darkness into Hiw marvelous light (1 Peter 2:9) through God's Word.

DAILY BIBLE READINGS

M: The People Gather
Nehemiah 7:66—8:1
T: Ezra Reads from the Law
Nehemiah 8:2-6
W: This Day Is Holy
Nehemiah 8:7-12
T: The Study of the Law Continues
Nehemiah 8:13-18
F: Teach Me Your Statutes
Psalm 119:33-40
S: Your Commandment Makes Me Wise
Psalm 119:97-104
S: I Long for Your Commandments
Psalm 119:129-136

TEACHING TIPS

July 27
Bible Study Guide 9

1. Words You Should Know

A. Separated themselves—(Nehemiah 10:28), Hebrew *badal*—To separate or divide; to select out of a gross; to exclude or make a difference.

B. Observe—(v. 29), Hebrew *asah* —To obey; the word carries the connotation of ethical obligation.

2. Teacher Preparation

A. Begin preparing for this lesson by reading the DEVOTIONAL READING and the BIBLE BACKGROUND.

B. Materials needed: bible, chalkboard or white board, chalk, or a marker.

3. Starting the Lesson

A. Open the class to a wider discussion, using the FOCAL VERSES as the foundation of the discussion. Keep the discussion as focused as possible on Stephen and his connection with the Lord.

B. Have a student read the BACKGROUND section.

C. Have students discuss the SEARCH THE SCRIPTURES questions in pairs, or if your class is large, assign a group of people to answer specific questions. Give them time to find the answers, and then ask for responses.

D. Discuss THE PEOPLE, PLACES, AND TIMES to help students understand the setting for today's text.

4. Getting into the Lesson

A. Have students answer the DISCUSS THE MEANING questions. This will help students to determine how the lesson applies to their own lives. Open the discussion so the students can ask whatever questions may be appropriate to the Scriptures.

B. Select three students and have them share the most significant point they have learned from this lesson.

C. Use the LESSON IN OUR SOCIETY exercise to help students connect the biblical significance of this lesson with their social context.

D. Ask several students what they have learned from today's lesson and see how close the class came to achieving the LESSON AIM.

5. Relating the Lesson to Life

A. Encourage students to read the DAILY BIBLE READINGS for the week to help reinforce the lesson's principles. Challenge students to develop good study habits by reading God's Word and applying it to their daily lives.

B. Thank God for the opportunity to learn the Word of God today so that we can go out and share with others who may not know that God is still moving by His Spirit.

6. Arousing Action

A. Before the end of the class, share your testimony that you wrote during the week.

B. The MAKE IT HAPPEN section suggests that the students write or type their testimonies and share them with someone else this week. Encourage the students to carry out this suggestion and be prepared to share their experiences and their testimonies with the class next week.

C. Close the class in prayer.

WORSHIP GUIDE

For the Superintendent or Teacher
Theme: Revive Us Again
Theme Song: "Lord, I'm Available
to You"
Scripture: Psalm 66:8-20
Song: "Revive Us Again"
Words of Faith: Dear God, thank You for
the New Covenant signed with the blood
of Your only begotten Son. Although the
covenant is unconditional, I desire to live
a life that pleases You and brings glory to
Your name.

RENEWAL OF THE COVENANT

Bible Background • NEHEMIAH 10:28-39
Printed Text • NEHEMIAH 10:28-33, 35-38
Devotional Reading • PSALM 66:8-20

LESSON AIM

By the end of the lesson, students will be able to explain the details of the returned Israelites' oath to God, understand the privilege of honoring the Sabbath and giving of their time and resources to support God's work, and determine to give of themselves and honor God with their tithes and offerings.

KEEP IN MIND

"And because of all this we make a sure covenant, and write it; and our princes, Levites, and priests, seal unto it" (Nehemiah 9:38).

FOCAL VERSES

Nehemiah 10:28 And the rest of the people, the priests, the Levites, the porters, the singers, the Nethinims, and all they that had separated themselves from the people of the lands unto the law of God, their wives, their sons, and their daughters, every one having knowledge, and having understanding;

29 They clave to their brethren, their nobles, and entered into a curse, and into an oath, to walk in God's law, which was given by Moses the servant of God, and to observe and do all the commandments of the LORD our Lord, and his judgments and his statutes;

30 And that we would not give our daughters unto the people of the land, nor take their daughters for our sons:

31 And if the people of the land bring ware or any victuals on the sabbath day to sell, that we would not buy it of them on the sabbath, or on the holy day: and that we would leave the seventh year, and the exaction of every debt.

32 Also we made ordinances for us, to charge ourselves yearly with the third part of a shekel for the service of the house of our God;

33 For the showbread, and for the continual meat offering, and for the continual burnt offering, of the sabbaths, of the new moons, for the set feasts, and for the holy things, and for the sin offerings to make an atonement for Israel, and for all the work of the house of our God.

35 And to bring the firstfruits of our ground, and the firstfruits of all fruit of all trees, year by year, unto the house of the LORD:

36 Also the firstborn of our sons, and of our cattle, as it is written in the law, and the firstlings of our herds and of our flocks, to bring to the house of our God, unto the priests that minister in the house of our God:

37 And that we should bring the firstfruits of our dough, and our offerings, and the fruit of all manner of trees, of wine and of oil, unto the priests, to the chambers of the house of our God; and the tithes of our ground unto the Levites, that the same Levites might have the tithes in all the cities of our tillage.

38 And the priest the son of Aaron shall be with the Levites, when the Levites take tithes: and the Levites shall bring up the tithe of the tithes unto the house of our God, to the chambers, into the treasure house.

JULY 27TH

IN FOCUS

In most western movies Native Americans are portrayed as savages who burn, pillage, and rape defenseless white women and take scalps. The culture of these

451

once proud people has been destroyed, and even today they are ridiculed as emblems for various sports teams.

However, the truth is far from what we have been led to believe. Far from their being inherently hostile, history has shown Native Americans to be a giving people. The first European settlers in America would have starved to death if the Native Americans had not shared their resources and taught the settlers farming and survival skills.

These gracious Native Americans were perfectly willing to share their land with the European newcomers. They entered into treaties that allowed the newcomers a portion of the land they had absolutely no legal right to. To the Native Americans, these treaties were blood oaths and therefore unbreakable. To the Europeans, the treaties were nothing more than words on paper. Eventually the newcomers devised a plan called "Manifest Destiny," which decreed the European right to all the land in America from sea to shining sea.

The European greed for land put the Native Americans in a precarious position. The only way to nullify a blood oath was for someone to die. So the Native Americans went to war. They were outnumbered, vastly outgunned, and eventually they died as a nation.

Today's lesson resumes the story of a nation brought back to life. After recounting their blessings in a prayer of gratitude, the returned Israelites entered into an oath with their creator and redeemer. To violate this oath would mean their death as a nation.

THE PEOPLE, PLACES, AND TIMES

Sabbath. Scripture affirms that one day in seven shall be set apart as a day holy to God. God Himself set the example for the Sabbath in creation. The work of creation took six days, and on the seventh day God rested from His labors.

The fourth commandment directs the observance of the Sabbath. The Sabbath is presented as a gift from God to benefit his people.

The Sabbath does not benefit God in any way, but we are restored and refreshed physically and spiritually when we set aside time to rest and focus our attention on God. Because Jesus, the

"Lord of the Sabbath," rose from the grave on Sunday, the first day of the week, Christians set this day apart as the Sabbath. This is a day that should be holy to God and not a day to spend in activities that have nothing to do with our worship of God.

BACKGROUND

After the building of the walls was completed, which provided for the nation's security, the people are now ready to rededicate themselves and their nation to the Lord. The first week of the seventh month was set aside to observe the Feast of Trumpets (Numbers 29:1-6). This feast was a time when the people would humble themselves and confess their sins of arrogance. On the first day of this feast, all the returned exiles gathered themselves together, and Ezra read the book of the law to them from daybreak until noon. Because most of the people had forgotten their native tongue, the Levites translated the reading from Hebrew to Aramaic (Nehemiah 8:1-17).

On the twenty-fourth day of the same month, the people came together again to seek the Lord through fasting and humbling themselves. The people separated themselves from all foreigners and gathered together to hear the Word of the Lord, confess their sins, and commit themselves to keeping the statutes of the covenant. The people prayed a very long prayer that recapped the deliverance of their ancestors from Egyptian bondage (9:18-37). Rehashing all that God had done for their ancestors assured the people of God's faithfulness and encouraged the people that He would perform miraculous feats to affirm His promises. At the end of the prayer, all the people agreed to an oath to the Lord: "In view of all this, we are making a binding agreement, putting it in writing, and our leaders, our Levites and our priests are affixing their seals to it (v. 38, NIV). The oath was put in writing and sealed by the signatures of the nation's leaders: Nehemiah, the political leader, and the Levites and priests, who served as religious leaders.

The binding oath contained six basic provisions. The people agreed not to marry foreigners, to observe the Sabbath and the Sabbath year, and to provide for the upkeep and maintenance of the temple.

IN DEPTH

1. Promise to God (Nehemiah 10:28-30)

The revival that took place in the seventh month was one the greatest revivals in Old Testament history. The revival resulted in a renewed commitment to serve the Lord and a separation from ungodly influences. As a result, the people felt it necessary to separate themselves from the neighboring people in order to purify and consecrate themselves. All the returned exiles joined together, from the humblest farmer to the greatest leader, along with their wives and the children who had reached the age of understanding, and renewed the covenant with God.

The oath was the same covenant given to the people in the time of Moses. If the people abided by the promise, God would bless them: "If you fully obey the Lord your God and carefully follow all his commands I give you today, the Lord your God will set you high above all the nations of the earth. All these blessings will come upon you and accompany you if you obey the Lord your God" (Deuteronomy 28:1-2, NIV). On the other hand, if the people were not faithful to the covenant they would be cursed: "However, if you do not obey the Lord your God and carefully follow all his commands and decrees I am giving you today, all these curses will come upon you and overtake you" (v. 15, NIV).

When the remnant entered into the oath with God, the first thing they did was to separate themselves from their pagan neighbors. This action was not taken because the Israelites felt superior or better than their neighbors but as a means of separating themselves from ungodly influences. The people agreed to end the practice of marrying women from among their pagan neighbors. If the Israelites were going to be a separated people witnessing to God's glory, it was essential that they avoid the temptation to worship the gods of their neighbors. That is why God prohibited them from intermarriage (Deuteronomy 7:3-4).

No matter how good our intentions, it is always best for those in a covenant relationship with God to separate themselves from ungodly influences. This is why Scripture commands us, "Do not be yoked together with unbelievers" (2 Corinthians 6:14, NIV). Believers have a responsibility to allow God to shape and mold them into the image of Christ. This means we must control our environment, our entertainment, and our social and marital relationships.

2. Promoting the Sabbath (vv. 31-32)

The next thing the people promised was a recommitment to honor the Sabbath and to keep it holy. God at the beginning of creation established a Sabbath day's rest (see Genesis 2:2-3). It was confirmed in the Old Covenant: "Remember the Sabbath day by keeping it holy. Six days you shall labor, but the seventh day is a Sabbath to the Lord your God" (Exodus 20:8-10, NIV). The Sabbath was a sign that the Israelites belonged to God. Honoring the Sabbath meant setting apart one day from all the others. On this day, people would cease from their work to rest and honor God.

God knew that the greatest temptation to dishonor the Sabbath would be in the love of money. So the people agreed to prohibit trade with their neighbors on the Sabbath. By refusing to conduct business on the Sabbath, the Israelites affirmed that money would not become their God.

The Old Testament Sabbath also included a Sabbath year. Every seventh year was also set apart to honor God. Every seventh year, the cultivated land was to rest: "For six years you are to sow your fields and harvest the crops, but during the seventh year let the land lie unplowed and unused (20:10). All debts acquired from fellow Israelites during the previous six years were forgiven in the seventh year: "At the end of every seven years you must cancel debts. This is how it is to be done: Every creditor shall cancel the loan he made to his fellow Israelite or brother because the Lord's time for canceling debts has been proclaimed" (Deuteronomy 15:1-2).

Not only were the people prohibited from doing business on the Sabbath day, but also all debt was to be forgiven during the Sabbath year. God knows that money is one of the greatest lures the devil has to tempt God's people. Wealth can easily lead one into sin. Money itself is not evil, but to serve money rather than have money serve you is idolatry. That is why Scripture adamantly teaches, "You cannot serve both God and money" (Luke 16:13).

The oath the Israelites agreed to required a time and financial sacrifice. The greatest sacrifice we can make to God is that of our time and our resources.

3. Provision for Temple (vv. 35-37)

The final part of the oath concerned the upkeep and maintenance of the temple that had been built under the leadership of Ezra the priest about seventy years earlier (Ezra 6:14-15). To cover the cost of maintaining the temple, an annual temple tax was imposed on every male twenty years and older. The tax was one shekel, or about 1/8 ounce of silver (Nehemiah 10:32; cf. Deuteronomy 30:11-16).

The people also agreed to provide the ingredients for the "Bread of the Presence." This was bread that was baked on the Sabbath and placed in the holy place in the temple (Leviticus 24:6). They would also provide the daily grain offering and animals to be sacrifices for the daily offering as well as animals for the special holy days.

Finally, the people agreed to give the firstfruits of the annual harvest and the firstborn calves of their cattle and flocks. The practice of offering the firstfruits was instituted at the time of the Israelite Exodus from Egypt (Exodus 13:12-14). The offering of the firstfruit acknowledged God as the ultimate owner of the land and provider of life.

The practice of offering firstfruit was not carried over into the New Testament, but the practice of giving God the first portion of our time and resources is still a valid means of demonstrating trust in and obedience to God.

Finally, the people agreed to bring a tenth of their produce to the temple for the support of the Levites who took care of the temple. The Levites gave a tenth of what they collected to the priests for their support. The principle of giving and tithing was given to ensure the support of the house of God and of those He appoints to service.

The New Covenant is an oath that Christians have entered into with God. This covenant is ratified by the blood of Jesus. Unlike the Old Covenant, which was conditional, the New Covenant is unconditional. It is purely a product of God's grace. However, our love for God and appreciation for all He has done for us compels us to promise Him to live our lives to please Him and glorify His name in all the earth. We glorify God when we give freely of our time, our possessions, and our resources to accomplish His work, build His church and encourage His people.

SEARCH THE SCRIPTURES

1. What was the only limitation placed on those who entered into a covenant relationship with God? (Nehemiah 10:28)

2. How did Nehemiah sum up the oath the people agreed to? (v. 29)

3. To whom would the Israelites not give their daughters in marriage? (v. 30)

4. What were the people supposed to bring annually to the house of the Lord? (v. 35)

5. How much of their produce were the Israelites required to bring to the storerooms of the house of God? (v. 37)

DISCUSS THE MEANING

1. Is it necessary for Christians to separate themselves from non-Christian friends and relatives in order to live holy lives? What are some ways that association with non-believers can negatively impact our walk with Christ? How can Christians positively impact the lives of non-Christians?

2. Old Testament believers celebrated the Sabbath on the seventh day. Christians celebrate the Sabbath on the first day of the week. What does the first day commemorate? Does God care which day is set aside or the fact that one day per week *is* set aside to rest and worship?

LESSON IN SOCIETY

In today's society, many contracts are not worth the paper they are written on. Athletes sign multi-year contracts for millions of dollars, then demand to renegotiate before the ink is dry. Consumers buy on credit and think nothing of filing bankruptcy to get out of debt. Lying politicians are treated as the norm. When believers give their word or enter into a contractual agreement, it is imperative that we do our utmost to live up to our agreements. What effect do you think believers who are faithful to their word can have on their communities?

MAKE IT HAPPEN

This is a good time to review your giving habits. Spend some time in prayer and ask God to reveal areas of giving in which you could improve. The question is not only whether you faithfully tithe, but whether you give to the best of your ability of both your resources and yourself. Also, examine your attitude and motivation in giving.

FOLLOW THE SPIRIT

What God wants me to do:

_____

_____

REMEMBER YOUR THOUGHTS

Special insights you have learned:

_____

_____

MORE LIGHT ON THE TEXT
Nehemiah 10:28-33, 35-37

The revival convention, which started on the first day of the seventh month (Nehemiah 8:2), continues to the twenty-fourth day (9:2). Having heard the Law of Moses read, preached, and explained thoroughly to their understanding, the people begin fasting and praying. They repent and confess their sins. The rest of Chapter 9 contains the full content of their prayer. In it they confess God's manifold goodness and their own wickedness; they reiterate how God has been dealing with them from the time of their forefathers until the present; how, in spite of all their wrongdoing, God has been gracious and merciful to them. In keeping with their repentance and confession, the people resolve to return to their God and renew their covenant with Him. The convention climaxes with the sealing (signing) of the written covenant by the princes, Levites, and priests (9:38). Their names are recorded in the

first twenty-seven verses of Chapter 10, including that of Nehemiah the governor. Verses 28 and following contain some of the terms of the covenant.

28 And the rest of the people, the priests, the Levites, the porters, the singers, the Nethinims, and all they that had separated themselves from the people of the lands unto the law of God, their wives, their sons, and their daughters, every one having knowledge, and having understanding;

Among the terms of the covenant is their commitment to follow the commandment of the Lord their God according to the Law which Moses gave to them. The commitment starts with their separation from the people of the land. One of God's important covenant agreements with Israel is that they should not have any union, either in marriage, or in fellowship with the heathen nations as they live in the land which He promised to give to their fathers (Exodus 33:16; Leviticus 20:26; Numbers 23:9; Deuteronomy 7:2). Joshua instructs the people, "That ye come not among these nations, these that remain among you; neither make mention of the name of their gods, nor cause to swear by them, neither serve them, nor bow yourselves unto them" (Joshua 23:7). Keeping away from the people of the heathen nations is a major part of keeping "all that is written in the Law of Moses" according to Joshua (23:6; see also Judges 2:2). Evidently, one of Israel's acts of rebellion and disobedience that led them to greater sins and consequently God's anger and punishment was their abandonment of this law. As a demonstration of their repentance and change of heart (and resolve to return to their God), they pledge to separate themselves from the heathen nations. Verse 28 lists the group of people who committed themselves to following the Lord. The list includes "the priests, the Levites, the porters, the singers, the Nethinims, and all they that had separated themselves from the people of the lands." This inclusion shows the total commitment of every stratum of society. The clause "and all they that had separated themselves from the people of the land" implies that many of the people had already separated themselves from their foreign wives as indicated in Ezra 9-10.

29 They clave to their brethren, their nobles, and entered into a curse, and into an oath, to walk in God's law, which was given by Moses the servant of God, and to observe and do all the commandments of the LORD our Lord, and his judgments and his statutes;

Having understood the law and having resolved to change their ways, the people enter into a covenant with one another, including all the nobles and other officials, to obey the Law and to observe all the commandments of the Lord and keep His statutes. The phrase, "they clave to their brethren" means that the people "bonded together with the brethren," i.e., they were united in their resolution. "They clave" is the Hebrew *machaziyqiym*, from *chazaq* (pronounced **khaw-zak'**), which means to fasten upon, to bind, or to cleave. The author describes this covenant by using two synonymous Hebrew nouns: *'alah* (pronounced **aw-law'**), and *shebuw ah* (pronounced **sheb-oo-aw'**), meaning "something sworn," e.g., an oath or a curse. The word *'alah* seems to imply that failure to keep the covenant would bring a grievous punishment, while *shebuw` ah* implies a promissory oath to live in conformity with the law of the Lord. The use of both synonyms indicates the importance of the covenant and the people's resolve to obey the law. The terms of the covenant are detailed in the rest of this chapter. The covenant is summed up in the following statement: "To walk in God's law, which was given by Moses the servant of God, and to observe and do all the commandments of the LORD our Lord, and his judgments and his statutes."

30 And that we would not give our daughters unto the people of the land, nor take their daughters for our sons: 31 And if the people of the land bring ware or any victuals on the sabbath day to sell, that we would not buy it of them on the sabbath, or on the holy day: and that we would leave the seventh year, and the exaction of every debt.

Since union with the heathen, especially through intermarriage, usually resulted in failure to keep the precepts of the Lord, the first resolution of the people is to break every tie with the people of the land (see v. 28). They resolve never inter-marry with the people of the land (Deuteronomy 7:3). They resolve to keep the Sabbath and the holy day by not trading with heathen nations on those days (Amos 8:5) and to keep the seventh year as a sabbatical year. The seventh–year Sabbath deals with sanctification of the land, which is left fallow and untilled (Exodus 23:10-11; Leviticus 25; Deuteronomy 15:1-2). They would not severely exact their debts but would observe the seventh year as a year of release in keeping with the precepts of the law, a law which they had failed to keep in the past (see Chapter 5). Releasing the poor and the oppressed is what the Lord prescribes as the type of fast that He approves (Isaiah 58:6). This seventh–year Sabbath is also known as the year of jubilee.

32 Also we made ordinances for us, to charge ourselves yearly with the third part of a shekel for the service of the house of our God; 33 For the shewbread, and for the continual meat offering, and for the continual burnt offering, of the sabbaths, of the new moons, for the set feasts, and for the holy things, and for the sin offerings to make an atonement for Israel, and for all the work of the house of our God.

The people covenanted not only to repent from sins but also to do good by restoring the temple service and worship. Part of this service is to pay dues of "the third part of a shekel for the service of the house of God." This is a revival of the Mosaic law, which stipulates that every man who had attained to the age of twenty-one had to contribute half a shekel for the support of the tabernacle (Exodus 30:13ff.; cf. Matthew 17:24). The change to a lesser amount (one–third of a shekel) is probably because of the poverty that was prevalent among the people at this time. The peope also resolve to reinstate the different temple offerings and feasts. These include the supply of the "shewbread" and other necessities to perpetuate the various services and offerings, such as the "meat offering . . . burnt offering . . . the Sabbaths . . . the new moons . . . the holy things . . . the sin offerings" for making "atonement for (the people) of Israel." In the past it was the rich kings, such as Hezekiah, who provided for these services and festivals (2 Chronicles 31:3), or defrayed the costs out of the treasury of the temple (1 Chronicles 26:20). But the people do not have rich kings anymore. The treasury is empty, and the priests and the nobles could not contribute for these things. The people, therefore, decided to voluntarily contribute one–third of a shekel yearly to keep up with these temple expenses. It should be noted that the *tirshatha* (or governor) never imposed these contributions on the people; rather, the people made the "ordinances" for themselves and charged themselves for this task.

35 And to bring the firstfruits of our ground, and the firstfruits of all fruit of all trees, year by year, unto the house of the LORD: 36 Also the firstborn of our sons, and of our cattle, as it is written in the law, and the firstlings of our herds and of our flocks, to bring to the house of our God, unto the priests that minister in the house of our God:

In addition to contributing to the maintenance of the temple worship and services, the people obliged themselves to bring the firstfruits of their labor into the temple for the upkeep of the temple work and its workers, (i.e., the priests and Levites). This is in accordance with the Law of Moses. Verses 35–37 list in detail the firstfruits. These include the firstfruits of the ground (Exodus 23:19; 34:26; Deuteronomy 26:2), which probably means crop fruits; the firstfruits of all fruit trees (Numbers 18:13; Leviticus 19:23); and the first-born of their sons (Numbers 18:16) and of their cattle (Exodus 13:12ff; Numbers 18:15). The list also includes the firstlings of their herds and flocks (Numbers 18:17). These are to be brought into the house of the Lord their God and to the priests who serve in the house of the Lord.

37 And that we should bring the firstfruits of our dough, and our offerings, and the fruit of all manner of trees, of wine and of oil, unto the priests, to the chambers of the house of our God; and the tithes of our ground unto the Levites, that the same Levites might have the tithes in all the cities of our tillage.

They also pledged to bring into the house of the Lord the firstfruits of the "dough" (Hebrew `ariycah*, pronounced **ar-ee-saw'**), or meal, referring to baked foods of all types, such as cake (Numbers 15:20). They resolved to bring their offerings; the fruits of all manner of trees and of wine and oil (Numbers 18:12). These were to be brought into the chambers of the house of God, where they would be stored and distributed to the priests. The people also promised to pay "the tithes" of their ground unto the Levites, so that they (the priests and Levites) would have the tithes, i.e., one-tenth of the land, according to God's ordinance which He made with their forefathers (Leviticus 27:30; Numbers 18:21; Deuteronomy 12:6; 14:28; 26:12). The climax of the convention was the renewal of the covenant with their Lord and their obedience to the Law and its precepts and their engagement to some specific duties.

TEACHING TIPS

1. Words You Should Know

A. Edom—(Obadiah 1:1) The name for the descendants of Esau, the twin brother of Jacob; both were later known as Edom and Israel, respectively.

B. Sela—Hebrew word meaning "rock."

C. Ally—A friend. Edom and Israel could have benefitted from their close kindred relationship by helping to defend each other from their enemies.

D. Adonai—Hebrew from the word *adonAy*, translated Lord and signifying, from its derivation, "sovereignty." Lord GOD and Sovereign LORD are two words that generally appear side by side in the Hebrew text.

2. Teacher Preparation

A. Prepare for today's lesson by reading the DAILY BIBLE READINGS each day of the week leading up to the lesson. Examine the FOCAL VERSES. Look up the meaning of new words in a Bible dictionary. Read the IN DEPTH study of each Scripture.

B. Materials needed: Bible, chalkboard or white board, chalk, and a magic marker.

3. Starting the Lesson

A. Prior to the arrival of students, draw a family tree diagram on the board and write the words ALLY and FAMILY.

B. Open the class with prayer. Ask the class to identify close family members. Depict the family members on a family tree. Discuss the meaning of family and the ways in which family members can act as allies to each other.

C. Ask the class to identify the allies that surround their local church. Name the nearby churches and family homes in the neighborhood. Are the the students able to call each neighbor by name? Ask the class to name ways in which the local congregation can be of assistance as a good neighbor to other members of the community, including families, local stores, and other churches.

D. Read the IN FOCUS story and ask students to take turns reading the Scripture verses in today's lesson.

4. Getting into the Lesson

A. Ask the students to read BACKGROUND and THE PEOPLE, PLACES, AND TIMES.

B. Permit the students to discuss the meaning of the today's Scripture texts verse by verse. Be sure to answer the questions in the DISCUSS THE MEANING section.

5. Relating the Lesson to Life

Ask students to list instances in which they see allies forming in their families, community, school environment, and job setting.

6. Arousing Action

A. The MAKE IT HAPPEN exercise urges students to think of examples of covenant and breach of covenant. Read together the suggested Scripture in Obadiah 1:7. Now give the students the opportunity to write down and discuss the suggestion.

B. Adjourn with a closing prayer, using a student volunteer from the class to offer the prayer to MAKE IT HAPPEN.

WORSHIP GUIDE

For the Superintendent or Teacher
Theme: Edom's Condemnation
Scripture: Obadiah 1
Song: "What a Friend We Have in Jesus"
Devotional Thought: Lord of power and might, thank You for placing me in the lives of others, and for placing others in my life, so that we may show Your good and perfect love.

EDOM'S CONDEMNATION

Bible Background • OBADIAH
Printed Text • OBADIAH 1-4, 10-11, 15, 21
Devotional Reading • ISAIAH 43:1-7

LESSON AIM

By the end of the lesson, students will look for opportunities to serve God. They will be able to understand God's expectation of His people for mutual love, aid in times of trouble, and intervention, even fighting each other's battles as protection against the enemy.

KEEP IN MIND

"As thou hast done, it shall be done unto thee: thy reward shall return upon thine own head" (Obadiah 15).

FOCAL VERSES

Obadiah 1 The vision of Obadiah. Thus saith the Lord GOD concerning Edom; We have heard a rumour from the LORD, and an ambassador is sent among the heathen, Arise ye, and let us rise up against her in battle.

2 Behold, I have made thee small among the heathen: thou art greatly despised.

3 The pride of thine heart hath deceived thee, thou that dwellest in the clefts of the rock, whose habitation is high; that saith in his heart, Who shall bring me down to the ground?

4 Though thou exalt thyself as the eagle, and though thou set thy nest among the stars, thence will I bring thee down, saith the LORD.

10 For thy violence against thy brother Jacob shame shall cover thee, and thou shalt be cut off for ever.

11 In the day that thou stoodest on the other side, in the day that the strangers carried away captive his forces, and foreigners entered into his

LESSON OVERVIEW

LESSON AIM
KEEP IN MIND
FOCAL VERSES
IN FOCUS
THE PEOPLE, PLACES, AND TIMES
BACKGROUND
AT-A-GLANCE
IN DEPTH
SEARCH THE SCRIPTURES
DISCUSS THE MEANING
LESSON IN OUR SOCIETY
MAKE IT HAPPEN
FOLLOW THE SPIRIT
REMEMBER YOUR THOUGHTS
MORE LIGHT ON THE TEXT
DAILY BIBLE READINGS

gates, and cast lots upon Jerusalem, even thou wast as one of them.

15 For the day of the LORD is near upon all the heathen: as thou hast done, it shall be done unto thee: thy reward shall return upon thine own head.

21 And saviours shall come up on mount Zion to judge the mount of Esau; and the kingdom shall be the LORD's.

IN FOCUS

As a child Reginald was charged with the responsibility of protecting his sister Jacque. On many days when Reginald was plaing with his friends or just talking on the telephone with his cute childhood girlfriend (whom he married as soon as he achieved the age of maturity) his parents would disturb his fun by requesting that he walk his sister to her music teacher's house for her weekly piano lesson. As they left the house his mother would say, "Oh, and wait for her to finish her lessons, too, my son." "Darn it," Reginald exclaimed. "That music lesson could take fifty minutes or more. By the time it is over and I walk her back home, it will be dark. All of my friends will be finished playing ball and gone back to their homes. My girlfriend can't wait until I walk this stupid little kid around the neighborhood. What's so special about her that she needs to be protected? Who wants her anyway?" Reginald argued every angle. His personal life and recreational time were wasted. "This is really putting a crimp in my basketball game. How will I

AUG 3RD

ever get good enough to be a starter on the varsity team if I don't practice with the boys?" he complained.

Another time after she returned home from her music lesson, Jacque remembered that she needed to go to the library about five blocks away to return a book. Again Reginald was called to go with her. This time he was furious. So he decided not to shepherd his sister all of the way to the library. He turned back and headed for the gym after walking with Jacque only a few blocks. When their mother and father found out that he had deserted his sister, they were livid! Reginald's father said, "Son, you will be punished for refusing to protect your sister. You only have one sister. Protect her as long as you can." "But . . . but . . . but," said Reginald, "Walking her to the library conflicted with my time at the gym with my friends." To which his father responded, "You'll always be able to meet new basketball buddies and have other friends, but if you lose your sister, you can never replace her."

One week later at school, a student opened his locker, took out a high-powered rifle, and began to shoot students as he patrolled the high school hallways. Jacque heard the gunshots and hurriedly found her brother, Reginald, in French class. She quietly took him by the hand, and led him safely through a back door leading to the streets. Together, the two siblings ran home. By school dismissal, four students had been killed and eighteen wounded in the senseless bloodbath.

THE PEOPLE, PLACES, AND TIMES

The prophetic book of Obadiah is a solitary prophecy about the relationship and attitude that Edom had demonstrated toward God's chosen people, Judah. The story told by the messenger in the Book of Obadiah is a vision of doom for Edom as Yahweh declares war on Edom. The Moabites, Ammonites, and desert Bedouins were all allies of Edom. Edom, we recall, was a descendant of Esau, the twin brother of Israel. Thus, the tribes of Edom and Israel originated as close siblings. Other tribes related to Israel included Lot's descendants, the Moabites and the Ammonites, Semitic peoples living northeast of the Dead Sea in the area surrounding Rabbah, their capital.

But these tribes often battled with the Israelites for possession of the fertile Gilead. The smaller kingdom of Judah consisted of only two of the twelve tribes of Israel. Geographically, Judah was situated close to Edom.

The Book of Obadiah provides no time frame nor does it identify the ancestors or other family members of Obadiah. Because of the events surrounding the exile, we must construe the period as post 586 B.C. and subsequent to the destruction of Jerusalem.

BACKGROUND

Obadiah is the shortest book of the Hebrew text (Old Testament), containing only one chapter, and Obadiah is one of the twelve minor prophets. Little is known about the writer of the book or the person of Obadiah. The name Obadiah means "servant of Yahweh." The book begins with God calling Obadiah to experience a vision. The vision describes a condemning judgment against Edom due to its relationship with Judah.

Its central message concerns the destruction of Jerusalem, which had been carried out by the Babylonians in 586 B.C. The Edomites played a pivotal part in the tragedy. Located south of the Dead Sea, the Edomites resided in proximity to Judah and could have provided a strategic advantage as protector. Situated to the southeast of Judah, and notwithstanding its relationship as a brother to Judah, Edom refused to come to

AT-A-GLANCE

1. A Message from God to the Disobedient People (Obadiah 1:1)
2. Edom's Misplaced Pride Is a Disease of the Heart (v. 2)
3. God's Expectations for Humanity (vv. 10-11)
4. God's Punishment of Edom; They Reap Just What They Sowed (v. 15)
5. Victory in the End; the Day of the Lord (v. 21)

Judah's assistance during the siege and even assisted Babylon by ravaging Jerusalem and many of its people as refugees.

IN DEPTH

1. A Message from God to the Disobedient People (Obadiah 1:1)

The announcement of Obadiah's vision focuses upon God as the divine giver of the vision. This vision is a prophetic revelation received from God against Edom. God will rise in battle against Edom and utterly destroy it because of its rejection of Israel and its subsequent destruction of the enemies.

2. Edom's Misplaced Pride Is a Disease of the Heart (v. 2)

The capital city of Edom was Sela. Sela is the Hebrew word for rock. It is to this capital city that God refers in the phrase, "live in the clefts of the rock." These rocks were believed to be impregnable, with a long narrow path through the mountains being the only entrance and exit to and from Edom. Edom found refuge in its wonderful geographic location, high atop fortified hills on a plain. The "nest" is situated in a hidden and inaccessible place. The "nest among the stars" constitutes an exaggerated image of the height of the mountain against the stars of the sky and refers to the stardom of Edom itself. Very important in this scheme is the power and authoritative voice of God, a power that is far greater that that of Edom. Thus, God declares that He is the one who has spoken this prophecy to the people to differentiate the Prophet Obadiah's words from the message of the Lord.

Edom turned against Judah in her time of need as she battled against the Babylonian siege on the brink of exile. God's plan would be that the strength and strategic positioning of Edom would be helpful to Judah against her enemies. It was the overwhelming pride of Edom that caused it to sin. The statement, "your proud heart has deceived you" translates the Hebrew meaning concerning Edom's heart and its pride about its military might. Edom doubted that its armies could be defeated in battle. It paraded its military independence and power.

3. God's Expectations for Humanity (vv. 10-11)

The brotherly relationship of Edom and Judah is based on the patriarchal accounts of Genesis 25–29 and 32. Esau and Jacob were blood brothers. However, tensions ran high between Edom and Judah from the early days of the rivalry between the twin brothers, Jacob and Esau. Other texts throughout the Old Testament testify to Edom's rejoicing at the pitiful state and weakness of Judah. Instead of helping Judah, Edom stood by and watched her defeat and pillage by her enemies. Edom even assisted in the pillaging of the nation. It was always God's plan that the two nations would love each other. Deuteronomy 23:7 clearly states: "You shall not abhor any of the Edomites, for they are your kin" ["brother"]. Even though the relationship between these peoples involved varying levels of hostility, their fraternity presupposes a moral obligation of solidarity that should not be ignored.

4. God's Punishment of Edom; They Reap Just What They Sowed (v. 15)

The nation's suffering will be complete, its destruction total and severe. The prediction is a haunting threat. The timing of the destruction is unknown, but it is still promised, "Oh, what a disaster awaits you." The God of enviable lavishness and promise to Israel could have been a blessing to Edom's future. Instead, because of its jealousy of and failure to protect Israel, this curse looms over its future.

God sends Obadiah with a vision of Edom's own suffering. Edom will be plundered by enemies and betrayed by its allies in the same manner that Edom had just treated Judah. Edom's former mammoth strength will be watered down to the extent that it will not be able to save itself. Even the other nations formerly friendly to Edom will plunder it. Edom will be expelled from its own homeland. Eventually Edom was driven out of its homeland, westward to the Negeb.

5. Victory in the End; The Day of the Lord (v. 21)

The day of the LORD is the time of Christ's second coming and of the judgments on all the nations that accompany that event. Edom's pun-

ishment, however, does not await that future time but has already been carried out.

The day of the Lord is God's eschatological statement describing the end times. God will deploy saviors, most likely judges who will help rule in the millennial kingdom.

SEARCH THE SCRIPTURES

1. How was Edom related to Judah? (v. 10)

2. What did Edom do to cause God's condemnation and prophecy of destruction? (vv. 3, 10-11)

3. What punishment did God promise to Edom? (v. 15)

DISCUSS THE MEANING

1. What does it mean for a Christian to be a brother or sister to another person?

2. What is the "day of the Lord"? (vv. 15–16)

3. In this age when self-pride and self-esteem are major foundations of positive living, when and how is pride destructive? (vv. 3-4)

LESSON IN OUR SOCIETY

A unifying presence is needed in our world. The kindred relationship between people is blurred by the many distinctions that we allow to set us apart. The differences between nations, continents, races, various ethnic groups, male and female, homosexuals and heterosexuals, and the rich and the poor are actually far smaller than the commonalities. The world is richly diverse. The opportunity is ample for all to respond to God's call, for each of us to act as the sisters and brothers that we are. Archaeology and history confirm the biblical truth that each of us originates from a single ancestor and heritage. Yet rather than display solidarity, the world is separated because of its diversity. Evil is persistent as each faction endeavors to dominate the others. Yet God is a God of second chances. Over and over again, we have seen the mercy and power of God in our lives, working through people who act in brotherly and sisterly love in times of trouble for our families and communities.

MAKE IT HAPPEN

Read Obadiah 1:7. How many communities in your city have neighborhood covenants that govern their residents? Do any of these covenants impart a view of the beloved community in which neighbors show love and protect and preserve the lives, emotions, and the well-being of its residents? What about the churches? Does each church shepherd its own, or is it in competition for the same members? In your church does each member actively seek to perform deeds of goodness and protection for fellow members and visitors? Can you envision what your community would be like if it had such intentional caring and protection for its brothers and sisters? Share with the members of your class the ways in which specific groups and individuals can restore the family God created by performng intentional acts of caring and protection for one another.

FOLLOW THE SPIRIT

What God wants me to do:

_____

_____

REMEMBER YOUR THOUGHTS

Special insights you have learned:

_____

_____

MORE LIGHT ON THE TEXT
Obadiah 1-4, 10-11, 15, 21

1:1 The vision of Obadiah. Thus saith the Lord GOD concerning Edom; We have heard a rumour from the LORD, and an ambassador is sent among the heathen, Arise ye, and let us rise up against her in battle.

Obadiah receives the prophetic instruction from an unspecified divine council. Acting on a rumor from God, the council condemns the decision of Edom to contribute to the detrimental siege against Israel. God, identified as this divine council, has announced an impending judgment on the people of Edom. The name of "the LORD" in Hebrew, *Yehovah*, is the Jewish national name of God—Jehovah, the Lord, the self-existent or eternal One. It is not altogether clear to whom in Edom Obadiah delivered this message.

"Battle" is the Hebrew word *milchamah* that means, and refers to engagement in a battle, warfare, or fighting. God calls several nations to war against Edom.

2 Behold, I have made thee small among the heathen: thou art greatly despised.

The prophetic message is structured as if it were being addressed directly to the Edomites. This strategy lets the people of Israel know that God is about to punish their traditional enemies. God vows to reduce this puffed–up nation, affirming in this text that "I will surely make you least or small among the nations" since Edom proved itself to be Judah's enemy. The Hebrew word for "small," *qatan* or *qaton,* is a diminutive, literally meaning small in quantity, size, number, age, or importance. God vows to make Edom the least, lesser, and little one. Because Edom stood idly by and watched the siege upon Judah, it was just as bad as if they had attacked Judah themselves. The Hebrew word *bazah* is used, meaning to disesteem, despise, disdain, show contempt for, or scorn. The size, the might, even the power and authority of Edom will be diminished.

3 The pride of thine heart hath deceived thee, thou that dwellest in the clefts of the rock, whose habitation is high; that saith in his heart, Who shall bring me down to the ground?

The statement, "Your proud heart has deceived you" refers to Edom's huge military entity. Its pride in its military might have produced a false comfort level in the belief that it could never be defeated. This foolish pride is the source of its sin against Judah. Edom withheld its powerful helping hand from its sister Judah at the time of Judah's vulnerability to the invasion of Babylon.

The positioning of the city on a plain atop a series of mountains gave it a fortress-like, strategic advantage over other communities. It was both a strength and a weakness that the city was accessible from only one direction. Yet the condition of the heart was the issue with God concerning Edom. The expression, "you say in your heart" referred to Edom convincing itself of its safety from the attack of enemies because of its power. The word *zadown* describes Edom's arrogance, presumptuous, and pride. In its heart, Edom affirms its superiority: "Who will bring me down to the ground?" The place in the rock where Edom dwells is described with the word *shakan*, which carries with it the idea of lodging, to reside or permanently stay, abide, continue, inhabit, remain, and be able to rest.

4 Though thou exalt thyself as the eagle, and though thou set thy nest among the stars, thence will I bring thee down, saith the LORD.

The Prophet Obadiah personifies the pride, majesty and strength of Edom with the imagery of a proud eagle. The eagle is enormous.

From the tip of one wing to the tip of the other, the wingspan of the bird is six to eight feet. It is the pride of the sky. Eagles represent prestige, with an enormous wing span and grace during very high flight they build nests in insular places. Its ability to gracefully fly the skies is the source of its strength as a bird of prey.

Edom's predatory strike against Israel in its time of weakness and vulnerability was a disgrace. Yet Israel protected itself by building a nest in a secluded place. Because of Edom's betrayal, Israel, with all of its strength and might, become vulnerable to God's promises to disempower it. The issue of pride is often stressed in the prophetic oracles against the nations (see in Isaiah 10:5-15; Jeremiah 50:31-32). In Obadiah's prophecy, God brings down even the prideful saying, "You soar . . . [but] I will bring you down."

10 For thy violence against thy brother Jacob shame shall cover thee, and thou shalt be cut off for ever.

The cause of the ruin of the Edomites (Esau) is their wickedness towards their brother nation Judah (Jacob). The Hebrew *chamac* means violence, wrong, unjust gain, cruelty, or damage. The unrighteous violence was an assault against God. God's expectation concerning Edom and Judah was solidarity between the two nations that were brothers from the same womb (Rebecca). The brotherly relationship mentioned in the text is based on the patriarchal accounts (Genesis 25–29, 32). Additionally, Deuteronomy 23:7 clearly states, "You shall not abhor any of the Edomites,

for they are your kin" ["brother"]. Even though the relationship between these peoples involved varying levels of hostility, their fraternity presupposes a moral obligation of solidarity that should not be ignored. Although Esau and Jacob were blood brothers, for the future generations reading about the struggles between these two brothers, the term "brother" is not to be taken literally. The word conveys the notion of kinship as well as that of a covenant partner.

God enters the charges against Edom into evidence. The violence was Edom's failure to protect Israel and to respect the human rights of the Israelites. The punishment will be the destruction and humiliation of the nation of Edom. Edom took advantage of Judah's misfortune to vent its resentment and hostility toward her. Edom will be "cut off" (*karath*, meaning cut down or asunder, destroyed or consumed) "forever" (*owlam* meaning to the vanishing point, time out of mind, until practically eternity).

11 In the day that thou stoodest on the other side, in the day that the strangers carried away captive his forces, and foreigners entered into his gates, and cast lots upon Jerusalem, even thou wast as one of them.

The indictment is pronounced against Edom with explicit details describing its sin. "Stoodest on the other side" recounts how Edom stood on its own mountain without lifting a finger, and inhumanely watched the slaughter and defeat of Judah. These were Obadiah's charges. Judah was carried into captivity. Edom acted as an enemy by allying itself with Judah's invaders: "Even thou wast one of them." The result of the enemy's attack on Judah was that "strangers carried off his wealth" and "foreigners entered his gates, and cast lots for Jerusalem." In the midst of this disaster, even the Edomites took part in the plundering and violence against Judah. The Hebrew word *echad* describes how Edom was united "as one of them." In the siege Edom's involvement to destroy Judah was as if it were one of the enemy captors.

15 For the day of the LORD is near upon all the heathen: as thou hast done, it shall be done unto thee: thy reward shall return upon thine own head.

The prophet begins his message by announcing judgment "against all the nations." The "day" of divine judgment is God's response to Edom's behavior after the devastation of Jerusalem in 587 and 586 B.C. The word "day" refers to the eschatological day of God's final judgment. This "day" in Hebrew is *yowm* (pronounced **yome**), from an unused root meaning to be hot, the warm hours, or can be understood figuratively as the space of time defined as an age chronicles, continually full, life, outlived. The timing of God's day is *qarowb*, which means near, or at hand, or to occur shortly. God ensures that Edom's disgraceful conduct as an ally with Babylon against Israel is directly related to a day of divine judgment at an undisclosed future time. In this future day the victory will belong to Judah. Judah will then be vindicated.

God's victory over Edom is a foretaste of His victory and sovereignty over competing human powers of the world. In effect, Edom accomplished evil and would receive its "reward," understood in the Hebrew word *'asah*, meaning to do or to make, accomplish, advance, or appoint. The punishment of God in the day of the Lord will return upon their own head, and the Hebrew word *ro'sh* (**roshe**) gives an understanding of this punishment as meaning to shake the head, the captain, chief place.

21 And saviours shall come up on mount Zion to judge the mount of Esau; and the kingdom shall be the LORD'S.

The concluding message of the prophet Obadiah is God's victory. The final aspect of the prophecy is the gracious act of God granting salvation by restoring Israel to its home on Mount Zion. Israel shall conquer its enemy, the Canaanite nations: "Deliverers will go up on Mount Zion to govern the mountains of Esau. And the kingdom will be the LORD'S" (v. 21, NIV). God will save Israel, who in turn, will judge Edom, but the victory over the kingdoms shall belong to God. The Hebrew word *yasha'* describes the salvation to be open wide or free and implies safety, freedom, or succor. God will avenge, defend, deliver, help, preserve, rescue, bring salvation, and get the victory. Esau will represent the heathen world in its defeated state, conquered by God. But Mount Zion will represent God's kingdom, and it shall belong to the Lord. *Siyown* is the same as *Tsijon*, the permanent capital and the mountain of Jerus or Zion.

The Israelites arrived at Mount Zion to rule over the Edomites, who in this verse are again called Mount Esau (vv. 8, 19). The Hebrew word *misa* (*am*) means "deliverers" or "those who have been saved." Ultimately, the victory and salvation pronounced in Obadiah is a bold affirmation that in the end (*eschaton*) "the kingdom will be the Lord's." Edom will finally recognize the kingdom of God.

DAILY BIBLE READINGS

M: A Report from the Lord
Obadiah 1-9

T: You Should Not Have Rejoiced
Obadiah 10-16

W: Israel Shall Take Possession
Obadiah 17-21

T: I Will Say, "Give Them Up"
Isaiah 43:1-7

F: God Is Israel's Savior
Isaiah 43:8-13

S: Israel Will Be the Lord's
Isaiah 44:1-8

S: God Will Comfort Israel
Isaiah 66:10-14

TEACHING TIPS

August 10
Bible Study Guide 11

1. Words You Should Know

A. Trumpet–(Joel 2:1); Hebrew *sìpAr;* A war trumpet of Israel. It is made of a hollowed horn of a ram and is used to sound a warning to the people.

B. Theophany—An appearance of the Lord, usually to some human, with a message or a sign of affirmation.

C. Gracious —(v. 13); Hebrew *hannñn;* The total goodwill of a superior to an inferior.

D. Slow to anger —(v. 13); Hebrew *apayim;* God's attribute of resisting immediate punishment of the people for their sins, but wait patiently for repentance and turning.

E. Steadfast love —(*hesed*); God's faithfulness to His covenant with the people.

2. Teacher Preparation

A. Prepare for today's lesson by reading the DAILY BIBLE READINGS throughout the week. Examine the FOCAL VERSES. Look up the meaning of new words in a Bible dictionary. Study Hebrew words for deeper meaning in a Hebrew concordance. Read the IN DEPTH study of each Scripture.

B. Materials needed: Bible, chalkboard or white board, chalk, magic marker.

3. Starting the Lesson

A. Prior to the arrival of students, place the words "Repent" and "Prophecy" on the chalkboard.

B. After the students arrive, open the class with prayer. Ask students to reflect upon the words on the chalkboard and contrast their meaning and their relevance in the time of the text and today.

C. Read the IN FOCUS story and ask students to take turns reading the Scripture verses in today's lesson.

4. Getting into the Lesson

A. Ask the students to read the BACKGROUND THE PEOPLE, PLACES, AND TIMES sections.

B. Permit the students to discuss the meaning of today's Scripture text verse by verse. Be sure to answer the questions in DISCUSS THE MEANING.

5. Relating the Lesson to Life

A. Have a student read LESSON IN OUR SOCIETY aloud.

B. Describe the life God originally designed for us as a way of moving into the future in accordance with His will.

6. Arousing Action

A. The MAKE IT HAPPEN exercise challenges students to critically make observations of the world and of their own lives in the context of righteousness. Read together the suggested Scripture in Joel. Now ask the students to write on an index card the action and reaction of God concerning the deeds they've observed.

B. Adjourn with a closing prayer, using a student volunteer from the class to offer a prayer for students to take action to change their lives.

466

CALL TO REPENTANCE

Bible Background • JOEL 1—2
Printed Text • JOEL 2:1-2, 12-14, 28-29
Devotional Reading • ACTS 2:14, 23, 32-33

LESSON AIM

By the end of the lesson, students will be able to summarize the changes in the heart of the believer and the behavior required of a believer in response to knowing God's plan of salvation. Participants will become aware of God's certain imposition of punishment as a consequence of sin and His reward for righteousness.

KEEP IN MIND

"Therefore also now, saith the LORD, turn ye even to me with all your heart, and with fasting, and with weeping, and with mourning: And rend your heart, and not your garments, and turn unto the LORD your God: for he is gracious and merciful, slow to anger, and of great kindness, and repenteth him of the evil" (Joel 2:12, 13).

FOCAL VERSES

Joel 2:1 Blow ye the trumpet in Zion, and sound an alarm in my holy mountain: let all the inhabitants of the land tremble: for the day of the LORD cometh, for it is nigh at hand;

2 A day of darkness and of gloominess, a day of clouds and of thick darkness, as the morning spread upon the mountains: a great people and a strong; there hath not been ever the like, neither shall be any more after it, even to the years of many generations.

12 Therefore also now, saith the LORD, turn ye even to me with all your heart, and with fasting, and with weeping, and with mourning:

13 And rend your heart, and not your garments,

LESSON OVERVIEW

LESSON AIM
KEEP IN MIND
FOCAL VERSES
IN FOCUS
THE PEOPLE, PLACES,
AND TIMES
BACKGROUND
AT-A-GLANCE
IN DEPTH
SEARCH THE SCRIPTURES
DISCUSS THE MEANING
LESSON IN OUR SOCIETY
MAKE IT HAPPEN
FOLLOW THE SPIRIT
REMEMBER YOUR THOUGHTS
MORE LIGHT ON THE TEXT
DAILY BIBLE READINGS

and turn unto the LORD your God: for He is gracious and merciful, slow to anger, and of great kindness, and repenteth him of the evil.

14 Who knoweth if he will return and repent, and leave a blessing behind him; even a meat offering and a drink offering unto the LORD your God?

28 And it shall come to pass afterward, that I will pour out my spirit upon all flesh; and your sons and your daughters shall prophesy, your old men shall dream dreams, your young men shall see visions:

29 And also upon the servants and upon the handmaids in those days will I pour out my spirit.

IN FOCUS

Darlique has the ability to charm even the most rigid and stoic rationalists around her. All of her life she has manipulated people to get her way. Now she has the most envied position among college coeds: dating the college football quarterback. Having her choice of being a cheerleader or a majorette, she achieved even one better: she tried out and was selected as a drum major. She travels the country with the team during football season staying in posh hotels overnight—life is great for her.

Only a handful of freshmen are fortunate enough to drive their own cars on campus. Even at that, Darlique's is the only one that is a sparkling new two-seater. Her parents warned her that the car, the sports activities, and all of the travel must

AUG 10TH

end if her grades suffer. More than anything else, Darlique's parents wanted the best for her. They loved her deeply. She convinced her parents that she was doing okay in school, and that for them to fly to Atlanta to visit her on campus would be a waste of their money. She was managing campus life quite fine. Life was good.

During her visit back home at Christmas break, just as Darlique returned from the doctor's office for her annual physical, Darlique's grades arrived by mail at her parents' home. Her parents learn that Darlique's medical tests reveal she has contracted a sexually transmitted disease (STD), and her first semester grades are totally disgusting. Her parents ground her and take her car keys. She has played a game of deception to cover her lack of attention to schoolwork and her reckless dating.

Returning back to campus in January, Darlique finds her boyfriend is dating another cute coed from his hometown. The medical test results, bad grades, faltering popularity, and loss of her boyfriend are four events sounding a wake-up call for her. She learns that goals supported by a sound value system, a spiritual reliance upon God to sustain her, and respect for other people around her are most important in her pursuit of life. Darlique's parents had taught her to use her powerful gifts and graces for the Lord, but she totally ignored them. She used her gifts selfishly. Darlique woke up that Sunday morning, and hurried to chapel service, where sat in the back row of the sanctuary very quietly as if she needed to hear a word from the Lord.

THE PEOPLE, PLACES, AND TIMES

Joel's name means "whose God is Jehovah." The time of the writing of the Book of Joel is debated, and scholars are divided. Some believe it could have been written as early as the ninth century B.C., while others support a pre-exilic date. Most now have arrived at a date between 500 and 350 B.C. The time is after the Babylonian exile, subsequent to the building of the second temple and the rebuilding of the walls of Jerusalem. Far more important than the time of the prophecy is the content of the message. Judah had previously been taken into Babylonian captivity. Upon

release, some of the people decided to return to their homeland, while others decided to remain in Babylon. The temple has been rebuilt, according to Joel 1:2–2:27, and the walls of Jerusalem have been reconstructed. This message from God, delivered by Joel, will impact many future generations

BACKGROUND

The Old Testament promise of the coming of the Holy Spirit in this passage in Joel is fulfilled at Pentecost in the New Testament (Acts 2). Clearly, the content of the Apostle Peter's sermon in Acts is a direct interpretation of the prophecy in Joel 2. Judah is a small province under the hegemony of the Persian Empire. As we recall, during a prior period of unification, Judah was the southern kingdom, composed of two of the twelve tribes of Israel, with its capital at Jerusalem (1 Kings 12; 2 Kings 25). Joel's message comes to Judah as a matter of urgency. It will mean life or death for Judah and all future generations. Chapter 2 of Joel is a prophecy from God. Eschatological in nature, dealing with the end times, it tells Judah how God would move Judah into the future from her present condition.

For Christians the prophecy of Joel applies to us and to Christ's church even today. The Apostle Peter in Acts 2, delivers a sermon with the exact prophetic words from Joel 2. Prophecy functions to teach us God's desires for our lives. It is a warning, a teaching, and a call to action. The prophet must deliver the message to the people, notwithstanding any of their own internal conflicts and hesitations. All of the attention resulting from a prophecy is to be focused upon God. The responsibility of the hearer of the prophecy is to take heed, transform his or her life, and spread the word to those who are unaware of it.

The prophecies found in the Book of Joel have impact upon the New Testament, and therefore upon Christianity. Inner repentance, moral control, and faithfulness to God are of utmost importance as the primary goals of humanity, according to God's purposes. Our ultimate path away from God's wrath is through repentance and faith (Joel 2:12-17). Our capacity to have ultimate faith and our ability to interpret the will of God are made possible by the outpouring of God's Spirit on all flesh. God's merciful offering of the Holy Spirit to us is for a purpose. It is to spread the word of God as God's "witnesses" to all the earth. Thus, we are to be examples of the power of the Gospel.

AT-A-GLANCE

1. God's Plague in Judah and the Prophetic Messenger's Warning (Joel 2:1-2)
2. God Uses Symbols to Turn His People Back to Him (vv. 12-14)
3. God's Ultimate Blessing: God's Spirit Poured Upon All Flesh (vv. 28-29)

IN DEPTH

1. God's Plague in Judah and the Prophetic Messenger's Warning (Joel 2:1-2)

Since a locust plague and a drought in Judah have afflicted its people so dramatically, relief from these natural disasters is a sign of a relenting God. Yearning for restoration from this extraordinary ravaging of Judah, Joel addresses Judah with the herald of the trumpet. This sound is of a war trumpet. The message was meant to be loud for all of Judah's guards stationed as lookouts to hear. The warning is then communicated to all of Judah. It is to be enunciated clearly that the day of the Lord is near. The war is being waged by the mighty army of God.

The horn is to be sounded to notify Zion to gather for worship and to sanctify themselves with a fast. To sanctify oneself is to be set aside for God's purpose. Old and young are urgently called to be numbered in this congregation to worship God. The priests and ministers of great faith in God are to be consecrated. In worship to God, the clergy will intercede with prayer and weeping for the people's redemption. On behalf of the people, the priests and ministers ask God to show mercy upon His chosen people. The people's worship is in the presence of others who observe and wait to mock the futile results of their faith should the Lord decide to publicly punish Judah.

2. God Uses Symbols to Turn His People Back to Him (vv. 12-14)

The Prophet Joel describes an awesome devastation of Judah by locusts and scorching heat. It is the judgment Yahweh inflicts upon the people. At this terrible event, the people of God from all social strata are to observe a general day of penitence, fasting, and prayer. The place for these activities is to be in the sanctuary upon Zion. The Lord God will observe the worship of the people and have compassion upon Israel.

The prophet answers the question, Who can endure this judgment of the Lord when it happens? The only way one can expect to endure it is to repent, which simply means to turn to God and away from evil. God only wants His people to repent, but this repentance must be a complete change of heart. To repent is to turn towards God and turn away from their current direction of sin. The traditional signs of remorse and penitence are prescribed in God's word as sacrifice through fasting. To sacrifice is to deny oneself. God wants to witness the people's contrite hearts, depicted by weeping, sorrow, and a change in the ways of Judah. This turnabout is a change in the heart with mental anguish and feelings of grief in response to God's disappointment.

The prophet leaves open the possibility that, as their hearts change, the Lord has the capacity to relent from inflicting horrific consequences upon them because of His compassion. Joel asks the question, "Who knows whether God will change from the pronounced judgment?" God is sovereign with the infinite ability to do whatever He wishes. This unpredictable nature of God is not a cause for us to doubt His promises. When God pronounces goodwill, we can count upon His word. That is the compassion of God, the ability to suffer with us and to feel sorrow for us that He has shown repeatedly in Israel's history. God will relent from punishing us if He desires to do so. We are required to relent, repent, and change to move our hearts in the direction of God.

God has the capacity to deal with us according to His love and compassion rather than according to our sin and iniquity. A sacrificial worship becomes central to Judah's relationship with God. An offering of sufficiency, either meat or drink, can be persuasive to God. Judah remembers God's mercy, love, and kindness.

3. God's Ultimate Blessing: God's Spirit Poured Upon All Flesh (vv. 28-29)

Finally, after the prediction of destruction through the mighty army of God, there is a word of hope and promise. After the beatitude of verse 26, a blessing of plenty for Judah's consumption, comes a promise. The New Revised Standard Version renders verse 26 this way, "You shall eat in plenty and be satisfied, and praise the name of the LORD your God, who has dealt wondrously with you. And my people shall never again be put to shame." God promises grace upon Judah for its restoration. God's people are once again a covenant people. The fear of public shame for their destruction is over.

The prophet then states the benefits of being God's people; the outpouring of God's spirit will come "afterward," meaning after the day of the coming of the Lord. This gift is from God, but it is not limited to a select few who are privileged by some materialistic stratification. The operative word "all" flesh clearly indicates that God is no respecter of persons, be they rich, elite, powerful, woman, or man. Verse 29 specifically mentions the lowly who are included and will receive God's spirit. These handmaids and servants represent the women and men who are the poor, the down-trodden, the oppressed, and those who labor as service workers—it those who are included in "all" flesh (or humans) and will receive God's spirit. Truly the last shall be first.

The specific role of the Spirit of God given to the people would be that of revealing the will of God. Their mortal's limitations are numerous prior to this outpouring of the Spirit of God. But now the power to become infinitely enhanced with this new gift provides prophetic vision, and dreams that bear strong truths become a reality.

SEARCH THE SCRIPTURES

1. What is the role of the prophet? (Joel 2:1)
2. What was the reason that God sent Joel to prophesy to Judah? (2:27 and 3:17)
3. What would make Joel so effective and convincing at delivering this prophecy? (1:5-6)
4. What is the responsibility of Judah as hearers of the prophetic word? (2:12, 14)
5. What happens at the coming of the day of the Lord? (vv. 2:28-29)

DISCUSS THE MEANING

1. What response did God desire from Judah? (Joel 2:12)
2. Discuss why God wanted the people of Judah to tear their hearts and not their garments? (v. 13)
3. Who were the soldiers of the great army of God? (vv. 1-2, 25)
4. What was the role of priests? (v. 17)
5. What does it mean to receive the Spirit of God? (vv. 28-29)

LESSON IN OUR SOCIETY

It is no secret that society's preoccupation is primarily fixed on the pursuit of wealth, power, and domination of one race over another. The sin of the world is consistently against the will of God. A major sin is our disregard for God and His plan for the love and coexistence of humanity. With a spirit of independence, we have taken what God has given us and left Him behind. Yet, God is a God of second chances. Over and over again, we have seen the mercy of God in our lives, and His power in times of trouble. It will be God's Spirit who will guide us in our daily living and in our interaction with each other according to His will. This same spirit will be the basis for our witness and prophetic voice warning others to heed the Lord our God.

MAKE IT HAPPEN

Read Joel 2:1–2, 12–13. Do you constantly witness sin, disobedience, and lack of care for humanity and God in our world? Permit the prophecy given to Joel to infuse your thoughts. Can you see how God's Word can be made manifest in your own life and in the disobedient world around you? Share with your class members the ways in which specific groups and individuals can advance God's kingdom by making a change in their direction and in their ways.

FOLLOW THE SPIRIT

What God wants me to do:

_____

_____

REMEMBER YOUR THOUGHTS

Special insights you have learned:

_____

_____

MORE LIGHT ON THE TEXT
Joel 2:1-2, 12-14, 28-29

Joel 2:1 Blow ye the trumpet in Zion, and sound an alarm in my holy mountain: let all the inhabitants of the land tremble: for the day of the LORD cometh, for it is nigh at hand;

The multivalent images Joel uses predominate in this picture of the day of the Lord. The first image is the military battle. God commands the prophet to sound the alarm of the "trumpet" using the familiar war trumpet of Israel, the *sipAr.* This is a cornet intended to give a clear sound and is actually a curved horn or hollowed-out ram's horn. The purpose of its use is to warn the people of the coming enemy (cf. Jeremiah 6:1; Hosea 5:8; 8:1). The "sound" is also the Hebrew *ruwa',* figuratively meaning to split the ears with sound, to shout for alarm or joy. The warning is reminiscent of the guards who were also lookouts, positioned on the fortified walls of the city of Jerusalem. Their function was to sound the alarm and to spread the word all over the city to gather the people for safety within the city walls.

2 A day of darkness and of gloominess, a day of clouds and of thick darkness, as the morning spread upon the mountains: a great people and a strong; there hath not been ever the like, neither shall be any more after it, even to the years of many generations.

The second image used is that of an army, swarming and infesting the city with the locust plague. The army spreads upon the "mountains," or *har,* a mountain or range of hills and hill country. The onset of this army of locusts is importune, steady and overpowering as Israel's enemy overruns the city walls and houses, leaving desolation behind it. The "darkness" is the *choshek,* literally, darkness, and figuratively misery, destruction, death, ignorance, sorrow, wickedness, and obscurity. The day of the Lord brings darkness and gloom, familiar from other Old Testament passages including Zephaniah 1:14-15 ("near," "darkness and gloom," "clouds and thick darkness"). The anguish and darkness overpower the people (Nahum 2:10 and Isaiah 13:8) who are inflicted by this "great and powerful" army, or *'atsuwm,* which is powerful by being numerous, great,

mighty, and strong, as remarked in Malachi 3:2, 4.

"Who can endure" this "great and terrible day"? These descriptions of the day of the Lord represent imagery of a theophany of God, or an appearance depicted as a cosmic disturbance.

12 Therefore also now, saith the LORD, turn ye even to me with all your heart, and with fasting, and with weeping, and with mourning:

God, *Yehovah,* is the self-existent or eternal Jehovah. It is this Lord who sends this enemy from the north (2:20; Jeremiah 1:14; 4:6; 6:1), causing all of the city dwellers, the Judeans, and everyone else to finally turn towards God with their hearts. To repent is to turn in the direction of God, "turning around" completely with all of one's heart in the opposite direction. In Hebrew "all of" is the word *gam,* from an unused root meaning to gather, assemble, or corral. Thus, one lives his or her life totally different than before.

This army that had been sent by God threatens to destroy His enemies (Amos 5:18-20; 9:1; Zephaniah 1:18). Ultimately, the seriousness of the people and the dedication of their hearts in fasting, weeping, and mourning will anticipate the day of God's final judgment of the world, in which the Son of Man will return to set up his kingdom on earth. The actions God requires us to "fast" (*tsowm*), "weep," (*bekiy*); by analogy, a dripping, overflowing, and "mourn," (*micped*), a lamentation, or wailing. God is faithful to give the people an opportunity to repent and to return to Him. Marking their sincere repentance and adherence to God, Joel directs the people to remorseful fasting for the mercy of God.

13 And rend your heart, and not your garments, and turn unto the LORD your God: for he is gracious and merciful, slow to anger, and of great kindness, and repenteth him of the evil.

God calls upon the Judeans to turn to Him, to worship with all their hearts and to rend (split, tear, or rip) their hearts. God specifically instructs the people not to tear their garments. The tearing of garments in lamentation is an expression of grief in the presence of misfortune (see Genesis 37:29, 34; Numbers 14:6; 2 Samuel 3:31; 1 Kings 21:27; Ezra 9:3). In this text, tearing of garments is a means of "sanctifying" (*qiddes*, meaning to set apart) for God's purposes in preparation for worship.

Repentance must be in Judah's heart. The "heart" in Hebrew symbolizes the human will and intellect. God is gracious (Hebrew *hannñn*), merciful (*rahñm*), and slow to anger (*apayim*). He imparts the kind of love a mother has for her child. He does not immediately punish, but rather always patiently provides an opportunity for people to repent and turn back to Him.

14 Who knoweth if he will return and repent, and leave a blessing behind him; even a meat offering and a drink offering unto the LORD your God?

The Hebrew translation for the word "return" or "turn" is *shuwb*, signifying to turn back, hence, away. In other words, to literally or figuratively retreat, but not necessarily with the idea of returning to the starting point. Assuming that the fast of repentance has taken place (with all of the requisite prayers, fasting, and lamentation), the physical sacrifice of an offering of meat and drink accompanies the worshipful action of the people. The "offering" is *minchah*, meaning to bestow a donation or a tribute (especially a sacrificial offering). It is usually bloodless and a voluntary gift or oblation. It can also be a meat offering, present, or sacrifice. God then responds in saving action to that repentance. We are not told the people's response. Thus, we are left to assume that in this awesome day of the Lord the people responded. The promise of God is that if Judah repents, He will respond in salvation.

28 And it shall come to pass afterward, that I will pour out my spirit upon all flesh; and your sons and your daughters shall prophesy, your old men shall dream dreams, your young men shall see visions:

The manifestation of certain powerful signs of the fulfillment of God's promise is evident. God will then pour out the Spirit on "all flesh," much like one pours out a fluid. The action to "pour out" is the Hebrew *shaphak*, meaning to spill forth blood, a libation, liquid metal, or even a solid. Figuratively, it also means to expend life, to

sprawl, or to gush out. The Spirit of God is always depicted as a gift of power given to enable the recipient to fulfill a specific role for God (see Exodus 31:2-5; Judges 6:34; Micah 3:8; Haggai 1:14). The Hebrew word for spirit is *ra'ah*, which both literally and figuratively has numerous meanings including to advise, appear, approve, behold, discern, or make to enjoy.

The parallel for this text in Joel is found in the New Testament in Acts 2:4. Therein the newly appointed Apostle Peter declares the outpouring of the Spirit upon the disciples, enabling them to become effective witnesses for Christ "to the ends of the earth" (Acts 1:8; 2:4).

29 And also upon the servants and upon the handmaids in those days will I pour out my spirit.

God promises that the gift of the Spirit extends to all flesh. The "bond" person, *'ebed*, is a servant. The "female servants" are *shiphchah*, from an unused root meaning to spread out as a family, a female slave as a member of the household, a maiden servant, or a woman servant. Those who call on the name of the Lord will be saved on the final day of judgment.

DAILY BIBLE READINGS

M: Sound the Alarm
Joel 2:1-11
T: Return to the Lord
Joel 2:12-17
W: God Had Pity on the People
Joel 2:18-22
T: I Will Pour Out My Spirit
Joel 2:23-29
F: God Is a Stronghold
Joel 3:16-21
S: The Day of Pentecost
Acts 2:14-23
S: God Has Made Jesus Lord
Acts 2:29-36

TEACHING TIPS

August 17
Bible Study Guide 12

1. Words You Should Know

A. Eschaton—Literally, "discourse about the last things." Eschatology is the doctrine concerning the end times, the return of the Lord, life after death, and the final stage of the world.

B. Messenger—(Malachi 3:1); Hebrew *malak* or *malakhi*— An individual sent from the Lord with a specific message or series of messages over a period of time to be delivered to humans.

C. Mispat—The day of the coming of the Lord to demonstrate God's justice and judgment.

D. Root and branch—(4:1) Tree: imagery used to represent the mass of ungodly people.

2. Teacher Preparation

A. Prepare for today's lesson by reading the DAILY BIBLE READINGS throughout the week. Examine the FOCAL VERSES. Look up the meaning of new words in a Bible dictionary. Study Hebrew words for deeper meaning in a Hebrew concordance. Read the IN DEPTH study of each Scripture.

B. Materials needed: Bible, chalkboard or white board, chalk, magic marker.

3. Starting the Lesson

A. After the students arrive, open the class with prayer. Ask students to take turns reading alternate verses of the Scripture lesson until each student has had an opportunity to read. This way there will be a two-way discussion between them to reflect the question–and–answer style that Malachi employs.

B. Discuss the meaning and expectation of the *eschaton* or end times as discussed in the text.

C. Read THE PEOPLE, PLACES, AND TIMES and BACKGROUND sections.

4. Getting into the Lesson

A. Permit the students to discuss the meaning of the today's Scripture texts verse by verse. Be sure to answer the questions in DISCUSS THE MEANING.

5. Relating the Lesson to Life

Engage students in a discussion to illicit their response to the last days. Describe a typical day in the life of a Christian on just one day at the end.

6. Arousing Action

A. The MAKE IT HAPPEN exercise urges the students to think of situations in their experience of covenant and breach of covenant. Read together the suggested Scripture in Malachi Chapter 3. Students are then requested to name the prophetic warnings of prominent messengers of our time. Write on the board the prophecies that are really affecting changes in how people live.

B. Ask a student volunteer to close the class in prayer.

A PROMISE TO THE FAITHFUL

Bible Background • MALACHI 3—4
Printed Text • Malachi 3:1-4, 16-18; 4:1-3
Devotional Reading • Psalm 90:1-17

LESSON AIM

By the end of the lesson, should know that God confronts the believer about sin. Even as God judges, an integral part of His intense love for us is that He prepares us for restoration.

KEEP IN MIND

"Then shall ye return, and discern between the righteous and the wicked, between him that serveth God and him that serveth him not" (Malachi 3:18).

FOCAL VERSES

Malachi 3:1 Behold, I will send my messenger, and he shall prepare the way before me: and the Lord, whom ye seek, shall suddenly come to his temple, even the messenger of the covenant, whom ye delight in: behold, he shall come, saith the LORD of hosts.

2 But who may abide the day of his coming? and who shall stand when he appeareth? for he is like a refiner's fire, and like fullers' soap:

3 And he shall sit as a refiner and purifier of silver: and he shall purify the sons of Levi, and purge them as gold and silver, that they may offer unto the LORD an offering in righteousness.

4 Then shall the offering of Judah and Jerusalem be pleasant unto the LORD, as in the days of old, and as in former years.

16 Then they that feared the LORD spake often one to another: and the LORD hearkened, and heard it, and a book of remembrance was written before him for them that feared the LORD, and that thought upon his name.

LESSON OVERVIEW

LESSON AIM
KEEP IN MIND
FOCAL VERSES
IN FOCUS
THE PEOPLE, PLACES,
AND TIMES
BACKGROUND
AT-A-GLANCE
IN DEPTH
SEARCH THE SCRIPTURES
DISCUSS THE MEANING
LESSON IN OUR SOCIETY
MAKE IT HAPPEN
FOLLOW THE SPIRIT
REMEMBER YOUR THOUGHTS
MORE LIGHT ON THE TEXT
DAILY BIBLE READINGS

17 And they shall be mine, saith the LORD of hosts, in that day when I make up my jewels; and I will spare them, as a man spareth his own son that serveth him.

18 Then shall ye return, and discern between the righteous and the wicked, between him that serveth God and him that serveth him not.

4:1 For, behold, the day cometh, that shall burn as an oven; and all the proud, yea, and all that do wickedly, shall be stubble: and the day that cometh shall burn them up, saith the LORD of hosts, that it shall leave them neither root nor branch.

2 But unto you that fear my name shall the Son of righteousness arise with healing in his wings; and ye shall go forth, and grow up as calves of the stall.

3 And ye shall tread down the wicked; for they shall be ashes under the soles of your feet in the day that I shall do this, saith the LORD of hosts.

IN FOCUS

Devon painstakingly constructed his snowman during his winter holiday from school, while day after day he deferred the task of cleaning his room. He relished his first winter living in a northern state, far from the sunbelt where he was born. For years he watched cartoons and home movies in which children played in the snow, sledding, enjoying snowball fights, and practicing the fine art of designing and building a snowman.

Devon's mother warned him of the fragility of

the snowman. Certainly child's play is fun, but it never lasts. The snowman would melt on the first sunny day when the temperature rose above freezing, and there were other more solid pursuits that could be much more fun. But, Devon used every engineering scheme he could think of to foil the inevitable meltdown. He found a cool place on the shady side of the yard to build the snowman. He monitored the temperature with his grandfather's old outdoor thermometer and used the northern wind to his advantage. Along with this, he carefully crafted his snowman with a mixture of large, solid frozen ice chunks as the snowman's foundation, expecting that this ice would endure the heat longer than mere fragile snowflakes, thereby keeping it frozen.

Day after day, Devon invested all of his time and the best known scientific principles in his engineering feat. On the final day of his school break, after he awakened from sleeping in late, Devon peered out of the window, only to find the fidelity of his mother's warning. His snowman was melting just as fast as any other in the neighborhood. As his mother predicted, even in competition with normal snowmen made without the fancy designs that he used, nothing could withstand the heat of the sun.

THE PEOPLE, PLACES, AND TIMES

Malachi. The Hebrew meaning of the name Malachi is "my messenger." This name appears in the first verse of today's text in Chapter 3. Malachi concludes the entire prophetic section of the Bible and is the final book of the Old Testament. Malachi's prophecy functions to close the twelve minor prophets, Hosea through Malachi, and the major prophets starting with Isaiah. At the same time, it provides a perfect starting place for and segue into the New Testament. Malachi is the last prophecy to be heard. The phrase "minor prophet" describes the brevity of the period over which these prophets delivered their prophetic message. "Minor" in no way reflects the significance of their warnings. In addition, the word "minor" usually indicates a single prophecy or a small number of prophecies delivered. Even in the Hebrew canon, Malachi is respected as an important prophecy.

Although Malachi provides no dates and only refers to unnamed individuals, it is an historical account. Yet, some scholars have speculated that the prophecy is a post-exilic account given during the period between 520 B.C. (after the rebuilding of the temple) and 400 B.C.

BACKGROUND

Malachi delivers six prophecies within its four short chapters. Malachi describes the love of God, the permissive sins of the priests, unfaithfulness, God's justice, the requirement that God's people give high–quality offerings (tithe) to God, and finally, the future of both righteous and sinful people. It is in the fifth prophecy that God's requirement for obedience is stressed. The people have enjoyed God's lavish blessings but are now plagued with crop failure. Final judgment is imminent. There is a definate relationship between disobedience and judgment. Malachi uses the dialectic literary style of questions and answers between God and His people.

AT-A-GLANCE

1. God Sends a Faithful Messenger (Malachi 3:1-3)
2. The Righteous after Being Purged of Unrighteousness (vv. 4-6)
3. God's Own Precious People Serve Him (v. 17)
4. The Righteous Will Have a Special Place of Remembrance to God (vv. 3:18; 4:3)

IN DEPTH

1. God Sends a Faithful Messenger (Malachi 3:1-3)

In Malachi is the announcement of the coming of a king who is superior to all other kings. God will send a messenger to precede the Lord whose specific role is to prepare for the entrance of the great king, attended by a royal processional. The most important function of the Lord after His coming is to reign. The role of judge is a primary role of the king. The temple is the place of this appearance of God, or theophany.

The priests are required to bring an offering of righteousness. First, though, the priests must be prepared for this service by a purification rite. The purification is signified by the imagery of a refiner's fire and fullers' soap. The ministers are the priests, the sons of Levi. God comes to purify the priests and to restore the blessing through offerings. The day of the coming of the Lord is both sudden and is a radical change in the present reality and world order.

2. The Righteous after Being Purged of Unrighteousness (v. 4-6)

After being purged from all sin, the priests shall present themselves as an acceptable sacrfice. This is the offering that God really wants. Such an offering refers to the righteousness of the ones who serve and obey the Lord. The righteous fear God and in recognition of His power, they have the faith to call upon His name.

3. God's Own Precious People Serve Him (v. 17)

Each covenant that God made with Israel, both before and after the famous covenant of Exodus 19:5, urgently focuses upon God's desire for the people to belong to Him. The covenants make God's people vassals, property owned by Him, just as if He had won them as the award of the victor in war. God is generous. The concept of the covenant all along is of the valued possession of those who are righteous and who belong to God. Jewels are precious items used for adornment. God will save His own children. The Lord will spare them in the judgment as a father or mother spares his or her own son. The criterion for salvation is service to God that comes from belief in Him. To spare the righteous is to save them for God's very own and to extract them from among the ones to be punished.

4. The Righteous Will Have a Special Place of Remembrance to God (vv. 3:18; 4:3)

A record of the righteous will be kept by God and written in "the book of remembrance." The concept of this book of remembrance would not be unfamiliar to Israel. People whose names are written in such a book are commended with the reward celebrating the merits of their deeds. These are the faithful who fear the name of the Lord. God predicts the coming of the Son of righteousness, who will heal.

These are the events of the end times, also known as the *eschaton*. The righteous have a rich and comfortable reward. Eschatology is the study of the events, descriptions, and discourse about the last things. The end times will accompany the events of the return of the Lord. Yet no prediction is made as to when God will appear. The events bring forth a physical life after death which occurs at the final stage of the world.

SEARCH THE SCRIPTURES

1. God promised to send a messenger for the purpose of _____. (Malachi 3:1)

2. God desired that the people present the Lord_____. (v. 2)

3. The righteous ones' names are written in a _____. (v. 16)

4. The righteous is the one that _____ God. (v. 18)

DISCUSS THE MEANING

1. What is meant by a "book of remembrance"? (Malachi 3:16)

2. How are the righteous selected? (v. 17)

2. What shall be the fate of the wicked? (Malachi 4:1)

LESSON IN OUR SOCIETY

Learning of one's own significant deficiencies is an important call to action for correction. Changes are required that transform one's thinking, actions, and reason for being in the world. Everything we are is made possible only because God has already first given to us a treasury of life and resources from which to respond. What can we learn from today's lesson for application in our lives about our consistency in meeting God's expectations of us to avoid disappointing Him? What changes would be required of us in our habits to measure up to God's expectation? The

Lord expects sacrificial self-giving to God of one's life of righteousness and reverence. How has the knowledge that God will come to judge and reign changed our larger community and world?

MAKE IT HAPPEN

Read the FOCAL VERSES of today's lesson from Malachi. Do you feel the challenges of competing messages exclaimed by prophets in our own day of a future reality? What is the content of messages about the end times? Who are the messengers? Do these messengers represent the messenger of the covenant, the forerunner of the Lord? Are we warned to make preparation? How important is the revelation to us to have knowledge of the timing of the day of the Lord? Life presents each of us with internal conflicts that cause us to choose. Can you see how God's Word can be made manifest in your own life and in the disobedient world around you? Share with your class members the ways in which specific groups and individuals can advance God's kingdom by making a change in the direction of their ways.

FOLLOW THE SPIRIT

What God wants me to do:

_____

_____

REMEMBER YOUR THOUGHTS

Special insights you have learned:

_____

_____

MORE LIGHT ON THE TEXT
Malachi 3:1-4, 16-18; 4:1-3

3:1 Behold, I will send my messenger, and he shall prepare the way before me: and the Lord, whom ye seek, shall suddenly come to his temple, even the messenger of the covenant, whom ye delight in: behold, he shall come, saith the LORD of hosts.

The narrator is God, speaking in the first person. God foretells the arrival of God's messenger, the Hebrew *malak* or *malakhi,* meaning one who is dispatched as a deputy or messenger, specifically for God. The messenger is a prophet, priest, or teacher, an ambassador, a messenger to be placed

in the forefront and in the midst of the people. This messenger will have a specific role. This messenger will prepare the way of God. The identity of the messenger is unknown but is presumed to be Malachi. Two possibilities exist for the timing of the imminent entrance of the messenger, supporting both an immediate and a long-delayed coming. Three persons are mentioned in verse 1, including the messenger, the Lord, and the messenger of the covenant. This manifestation of the messenger shall take place in the temple.

God will make a "covenant" (Hebrew *beriyth*) The covenant will be made with the ones in whom God "delights" *haphet* (i.e., is pleased with, delights in, desires, favors). These have pleased God, and He is willing to make with them a covenant.

2 But who may abide the day of his coming? and who shall stand when he appeareth? for he is like a refiner's fire, and like fullers' soap:

Even before the danger is described, concern surrounds any possible ability to "abide," to keep in, to maintain, or to bear it. The Hebrew word *kuwl* also means to comprehend, to contain, to hold, remain present, or sustain.

God describes a purifying fire directed against the descendants of Levi. The "refiner" (Hebrew *tsaraph),* means to fuse as in metal, or a founder or goldsmith who melts, makes pure, and purges. This trial comes in the day of God. Typically this picture is associated with the reference in the Gospel of Luke to the baptism of "fire" that will come to all the people. It is, however, the "unquenchable fire"; *'esh* is a burning, fiery, flaming fire that will destroy the wicked on the day of eschatological judgment. That day shall bring turmoil and fear. But the question is asked, who will be able to stay and withstand this awesome day of His coming?

3 And he shall sit as a refiner and purifier of silver: and he shall purify the sons of Levi, and purge them as gold and silver, that they may offer unto the LORD an offering in righteousness.

The role of God in His coming is expressed by the Hebrew word *mispat,* to judge. This role of the

Lord in this announced coming will be to cleanse and to judge. The Lord's coming will shape, bend, draw, and hammer out everything and everyone that is pliable as a refiner uses fire, removing all impurities as in the process of preparing a precious metal. The Levites, attached to Levi, a son of Jacob, will become purified, just as do the precious metals of gold and silver in the refining process. Righteousness in Old Testament terms is obedience to the Law of God. It is the righteous fear and reverence of God with compliance to His will. Righteousness is the manner in which the relationship between God and an individual believer is made right. The word "righteous" in Hebrew is *tsedaqah,* which means rightness, rectitude, justice, virtue, or, figuratively, prosperity and justice. That relationship is a trust in God and a deliberate distancing of oneself from sin.

4 Then shall the offering of Judah and Jerusalem be pleasant unto the LORD, as in the days of old, and as in former years.

Jerusalem, the capital city of the nation, means peaceful. The relinquishing of all sin from Judah shall be the offering to God that He has expected. This "offering" refers to the righteousness of the ones who serve and obey the Lord. This type of offering means to bestow, a donation; (Hebrew *euphem),* a tribute or a sacrificial offering in this case, a bloodless and voluntary gift, oblation, of a sacrificial nature. This offering is ultimately acceptable to God. They "please" God as indicated by the use of the the Hebrew word *'areb,* meaning to be agreeable, pleasant, take pleasure in, or to be sweet. The righteous fear God. In recognition of God's power, they have the faith to call upon His name.

16 Then they that feared the LORD spake often one to another: and the LORD hearkened, and heard it, and a book of remembrance was written before him for them that feared the LORD, and that thought upon his name.

The secret of wisdom, according to Proverbs 1:7, is that the "fear of the Lord is the beginning of knowledge." Likewise, in this text, the ones who feared Jehovah were noticed by the Almighty. This became a model that the whole nation of Israel could emulate. A record of their dialog with one another was recorded in the book of remembrance. The concept of this book of remembrance would not be unfamiliar to Israel. People in the Persian culture had occasion to be named in a book, with the reward being a citation from the king celebrating their merits (see Esther 6:1).

17 And they shall be mine, saith the LORD of hosts, in that day when I make up my jewels; and I will spare them, as a man spareth his own son that serveth him.

Originally, in the covenant God made with Israel, Exodus 19:5 records God's desire for Israel to be His people. The concept of the covenant all along is of the valued possession who are the righteous and who belong to God. Jewels are precious items used for adornment. God will save His own children. The Lord will spare them in the judgment as a father or mother spares his or her own son. The criterion for salvation is service to God. To spare the righteous is to save them for God's very own and to extract them from among the ones to be punished.

8 Then shall ye return, and discern between the righteous and the wicked, between him that serveth God and him that serveth him not.

The elect will be the ones of whom God says, "they will be mine" and "my special possession" (cf. Exodus 19:5; Deuteronomy 7:6; 14:2; 26:18; Psalm 135:4). Not all of Israel will qualify but only the righteous. In Egypt the Lord had caused a separation to be made (Exodus 11:7). The words do not imply that the persons addressed had previously stood in a different relation from that in which they were standing.

4:1 For, behold, the day cometh, that shall burn as an oven; and all the proud, yea, and all that do wickedly, shall be stubble: and the day that cometh shall burn them up, saith the LORD of

hosts, that it shall leave them neither root nor branch.

The fire will consume the ones who are identified as part of the complaining, jealous, or murmuring nation as stubble is burned up, and indeed all who do wickedness. The proud and the disobedient against God's word are themselves chosen for this fiery fate. The "root and branch" is borrowed from tree imagery, representing the ungodly masses of the people (cf. Amos 2:9). It denotes total destruction of both the ancestors and the generations, so that nothing will be left of them.

2 But unto you that fear my name shall the Sun of righteousness arise with healing in his wings; and ye shall go forth, and grow up as calves of the stall.

The end times, the *eschaton,* is comfort to the righteous one. Eschatology is literally the "discourse about the last things." Eschatology is the doctrine concerning the end times, the return of the Lord, life after death, and the final stage of the world. This doctrine dates from the original concepts of humanity and immortality. "Healing wings" refer to the restoration of the body to its wholeness and the eradication of the maladies that may have caused physical death. This concept of the end times has progressed in religious development, and "things to come" now includes more than the physical or bodily determination of the person. Since it is not limited to the fate of the individual, the broader thought includes the actions of God in the end to judge according to His perfect justice.

3 And ye shall tread down the wicked; for they shall be ashes under the soles of your feet in the day that I shall do this, saith the LORD of hosts.

The great day of the Lord to come is a day of punishment for the wicked and salvation for the righteous. God paints a grim picture for the unrighteous, which is a picture of doom and destruction. In fact, in that final day, it is the righteous whom God will set over the unrighteous. The vivid image of the doom of the wicked

and unrighteous is depicted in defeat and destruction, and the righteous deliver the punishment, which is referred to in the phrase, "under the soles of your feet." The wicked are lowered and debilitated. Judah will be the victor over the wicked. God's signature ends the prophecy of doom, leaving no doubt in our minds that God acts to punish.

DAILY BIBLE READINGS

M: A Priest Should Guard Knowledge
Malachi 2:1-9
T: The Lord's Messenger Will Refine
Malachi 3:1-5
W: Return to Me
Malachi 3:6-12
T: The Lord's Special Possession
Malachi 3:13-18
F: The Sun of Righteous Shall Rise
Malachi 4:1-6
S: God's Steadfast Love
Psalm 89:19-29
S: God Will Keep His Covenant
Psalm 89:30-37

TEACHING TIPS

August 24
Bible Study Guide 13

1. Words You Should Know

A. Mekhashshephim–The *kesheph* is the term used for a sorcerer; individuals who chant or use incantations.

B. Chaldean–The term for the caste of wise persons. Nabopolassar founded the Chaldean dynasty including all of Babylonia, Assyria and Syria-Palestine. Nabopolassar was the father of Nebuchadnezzar II.

C. The Greek Apocalypses–A biblical term used to describe a type of biblical literature (revelation).

D. Shallot—One having the authority to command and control, as a king.

2. Teacher Preparation

A. Prepare for today's lesson by reading theDAILY BIBLE READINGS throughout the week. Examine the FOCAL VERSES. Look up the meaning of new words in a Bible dictionary. Study Hebrew words for deeper meaning in a Hebrew concordance. Read the IN DEPTH study of each Scripture.

B. Materials needed: Bible, chalkboard or white board, chalk, magic marker.

3. Starting the Lesson

A. After the students arrive, open the class with prayer. Ask them to reflect upon the words TRANSFORMATION and PROPHECY and to discuss their meaning and relevance at the time of this week's text and today.

B. Read the IN FOCUS story and ask students to take turns reading the Scripture verses in today's lesson.

4. Getting into the Lesson

A. Ask the students to read BACKGROUND and THE PEOPLE, PLACES, AND TIMES.

B. Permit the students to discuss the meaning of today's Scripture texts verse by verse. Be sure to answer the questions in DISCUSS THE MEANING.

5. Relating the Lesson to Life

Ask students to list instances in which they see the situation in the text (i.e., powerful rulers being overcome by the oppressed). In what instances have students observed wicked, hardened rulers become genuinely ethical and led by God?

6. Arousing Action

A. The MAKE IT HAPPEN exercise urges the students to think of situations in their experience regarding a covenant and breach of covenant. Read together the suggested Scripture in Daniel 2:44. Now give the students the opportunity to write on cards the visions of Daniel that point to the kingdom of God in the end times.

B. Adjourn with a closing prayer, using a student volunteer from the class to offer the prayer to MAKE IT HAPPEN.

AN ETERNAL REIGN

Bible Background • DANIEL 2
Printed Text • DANIEL 2:26, 36-45
Devotional Reading • REVELATION 21:1-7

LESSON AIM

By the end of the lesson, students will be able to summarize the difference between an indestructible kingdom of God over all of earth, His kingdom in the hearts of believers, and a physical kingdom in the land.

KEEP IN MIND

"And in the days of these kings shall the God of heaven set up a kingdom, which shall never be destroyed: and the kingdom shall not be left to other people, but it shall break in pieces and consume all these kingdoms, and it shall stand for ever" (Daniel 2:44).

FOCAL VERSES

Daniel 2:26 The king answered and said to Daniel, whose name was Belteshazzar, Art thou able to make known unto me the dream which I have seen, and the interpretation thereof?

36 This is the dream; and we will tell the interpretation thereof before the king.

37 Thou, O king, art a king of kings: for the God of heaven hath given thee a kingdom, power, and strength, and glory.

38 And wheresoever the children of men dwell, the beasts of the field and the fowls of the heaven hath he given into thine hand, and hath made thee ruler over them all. Thou art this head of gold.

39 And after thee shall arise another kingdom inferior to thee, and another third kingdom of brass, which shall bear rule over all the earth.

40 And the fourth kingdom shall be strong as iron: forasmuch as iron breaketh in pieces and subdueth all things: and as that breaketh all these, shall it break in pieces and bruise.

41 And whereas thou sawest the feet and toes, part of potters' clay, and part of iron, the kingdom shall be divided; but there shall be in it of the strength of the iron, forasmuch as thou sawest the iron mixed with miry clay.

42 And as the toes of the feet were part of iron, and part of clay, so the kingdom shall be partly strong, and partly broken.

43 And whereas thou sawest iron mixed with miry clay, they shall mingle themselves with the seed of men: but they shall not cleave one to another, even as iron is not mixed with clay.

44 And in the days of these kings shall the God of heaven set up a kingdom, which shall never be destroyed: and the kingdom shall not be left to other people, but it shall break in pieces and consume all these kingdoms, and it shall stand for ever.

45 Forasmuch as thou sawest that the stone was cut out of the mountain without hands, and that it brake in pieces the iron, the brass, the clay, the silver, and the gold; the great God hath made known to the king what shall come to pass hereafter: and the dream is certain, and the interpretation thereof sure.

LESSON OVERVIEW

LESSON AIM
KEEP IN MIND
FOCAL VERSES
IN FOCUS
THE PEOPLE, PLACES, AND TIMES
BACKGROUND
AT-A-GLANCE
IN DEPTH
SEARCH THE SCRIPTURES
DISCUSS THE MEANING
LESSON IN OUR SOCIETY
MAKE IT HAPPEN
FOLLOW THE SPIRIT
REMEMBER YOUR THOUGHTS
MORE LIGHT ON THE TEXT
DAILY BIBLE READINGS

IN FOCUS

Year after year, one governor after the next was elected by the people in this one southern state. The prevailing ideal of life was the oppression of disempowered people for economic and political gain by the majority. Finally, the most eloquent governor of all, supporting unjust ideals, took

AUG 24TH

481

the oath of office. His ability to articulate the oppressive ideology of the dominant class propelled his political career. Before long his reputation and power gained national attention. It was a slice in time when the powerful robbed the meager rights and possessions of the powerless. This power was used to dominate and to undermine justice. The governor was a student of the law and a member of the state bar association, having once served as a district court judge.

Messengers brought clear word to him of the future to come, that an end to such rule would be near. Finally, a would-be assassin lodged a crippling bullet in the spine of the governor's body and in the backbone of the cruel, racist ideology. The reign of terror for the social and racial underclass would begin to come to an end. The attempted murderer's bullet, though caused by an illegal act, became transformative to rid the world of another illegal system. Transformation was thorough because, in time, this governor's heart was moved to restore the lives of the very people that he had formerly violated. He elected appointed statewide commissioners and made other gubernatorial appointments, all stemming from his renewed heart.

THE PEOPLE, PLACES, AND TIMES

The second chapter of Daniel is written in a mixture of the familiar languages of the Jews (Aramaic and Hebrew), causing us to focus on the influence of foreign or Babylonian rule that day. The writings are often called Diaspora novella stories, court stories, and contest/conflict stories. The times were those of the Jewish Diaspora after Israel's exile in 587 B.C. The period extends to the victorious Maccabean revolt of the Jews over the Hellenizing forces in response to their domination. Eventually the advocacy and socialization of captive Jews was forced, requiring a change in their native language to Greek from their Aramaic dialect and Hebrew. In addition, there were forced changes in their culture and way of life. The time is the second year of the reign of King Nebuchadnezzar.

BACKGROUND

In the Hebrew Bible, the Book of Daniel contains the only Old Testament biblical example of apocalypses, or revelations. However, many other examples of prophetic texts were written during and after the Babylonian exile. Recall that Jesus' long discourse in the New Testament and a great majority of the book of Revelation are apocalyptic, or literature of revelation intended to interpret mysteries. It is a genre of revelatory literature with a narrative framework presented to a human, disclosing transcendent reality that is often eschatological and salvific. Often apocalyptic literature interprets present events and conditions in view of the supernatural for the purpose of enhancing understanding of divine will.

In the Book of Daniel, both a collection of stories and a series of Daniel's visions unfold. Daniel was victoriously rewarded for the role he played in interpreting visions for the king and ultimately for his divinely given prophecies. Daniel had the ability to interpret dreams because he was enabled by his requests to God to make such abstract visions known to him. The settings in Daniel are the king's courts of the Babylonian, Median, and Persian empires. The northern kingdom of Israel was conquered by the Assyrians in 722 B.C. The southern kingdom of Judah was conquered by the Babylonians in of 587 B.C.

Ultimately, even the powerful non-Israelite rulers were influenced to worship and to abide by the will of Israel's God. These rulers were influenced by their observation of disempowered Jewish exiles who demonstrated tremendous faith in a powerful almighty God in the midst of powerful ruling kings and military forces. The Israelite exiles' ability to call on a God who was more powerful than the political powers of day was so impressive that it influenced the beliefs of the later rulers, especially Darius and Cyrus, who, because they were moved by God, freed

AT-A-GLANCE

1. Make Known the Meaning of the Dream (Daniel 2:26, 36)
2. God of Heaven Gives Kingdoms but Retains Ultimate Kingdoms, Power, and Strength, and Glory (vv. 37-44)
3. The Meaning of God's Kingdom (v. 45)

IN DEPTH

1. Make Known the Meaning of the Dream (Daniel 2:26, 36)

The exile was Israel's experience of military defeat, deportation, and oppression in a foreign land. Nebuchadnezzar's invasion of Jerusalem, its temple, and the possessions of Israel are devastating to the Jews (2 Kings 25). Later, King Nebuchadnezzar, in the second year of his reign, had a dream that tormented his spirit. So troubled was he that he desperately sought an interpretation of the dream. None of the wise men, astrologers, or Chaldeans could interpret the dream. The king sent for Daniel, who prayed to the Lord and received a revelation of the meaning of the dream.

Daniel prayed to God, and God gave him the revelation of the meaning of the king's dream. Daniel saved the lives of the unsuccessful interpreters who had preceded him by halting their execution in exchange for the dream's interpretation. Believing that they were somehow withholding the real meaning of the dream, the king had ordered the other fortunetellers killed as they tried and failed to make known to the king its significance. Daniel is now prepared to explain the dream to the king.

2. God of Heaven Gives Kingdoms but Retains Ultimate Kingdoms, Power, and Strength, and Glory (vv. 37-44)

Daniel starts his discourse by praising the king and appeasing him for the power he has. Daniel informs the king that this power comes from the Lord God. God has permitted the king to have riches and to rule. Daniel's discourse was a calming move whereby he provided a cushion for the king to soften the blow of the hard message that he was about to deliver.

God has given power to the king to rule over the people of the kingdom and the animals only for a time. Daniel emphasizes thatthe source of true power is God. This mighty one claims power and authority over Babylon but is actually given authority only by the permission of God. In 1 Chronicles 29:11-12, similar statements are made: "Riches and honor come from you, and you rule over all. In your hand are power and might" (cf. 2 Chronicles 20:6). A succession of kings will replace Nebuchadnezzar. The very next king will be one with less grandeur. The kingdoms decline in significance from gold to bronze to iron mixed with clay. The statue's feet and the mixture of iron and clay suggest the lesser power of these kingdoms, which will decline to worthlessness. Yet, the third king will have a power over all of the earth. Daniel confirmed God as the source of the king's assignment as king and earthly power. The beasts of the fields represent the earthly creatures over which the king rules in the kingdom of Babylon, and the head of gold depicts his kingship.

Daniel continues to reveal a vision of four kingdoms that will be established. The Babylonian kingdom, under the rule of King Nebuchadnezzar was the first kingdom (symbolized by gold). Following his rule is Darius' and Cyrus' leadership over the Medo-Persian kingdom after the fall of Babylon (Daniel 5:31; 9:1; 11:1). The Medo-Persian kingdom, symbolized by silver would be inferior to Nebuchadnezzar's Babylonian kingdom . The third kingdom is Alexander's Greek empire and is characterized by the lesser metal of brass. The fourth kingdom is the Roman empire, symbolized by iron. During the Roman empire, which began in 63 B.C. God establishes His kingdom which will never pass away. It was during the Roman empire that Jesus Christ was born and announced that the kingdom of God was at hand (cf. Matthew 4:17, Mark 1:14-15).

The kingdom of the Lord God will cause these earthly establishments to break into pieces when He comes and exerts His violent force to terminate these kingdoms. God shall be the ultimate ruler whose control will never end; He will establish a kingdom that is indestructible. That God's kingdom will be manifest in the near term is implied in the phrase "days of these kings." This kingdom will make obsolete all existing established human kingdoms. God's reign will be everlasting and just.

3. The Meaning of God's Kingdom (v. 45)

The interpretation of the dream is increasingly detailed. The phrase, "you saw the stone was cut out of the mountain" refers to God establishing a kingdom. "Without hands" means that humans will not establish the kingdom. "It brake in pieces the iron, the brass, the clay, the silver and the gold" means that the kingdom God makes will destroy all other kingdoms. It will tumble the strong kingdoms of iron and gold and the weaker one of brass. The uncut stone, however, represents a kingdom that has a superior value than one that is mined and put in place by a human. Until it is mined or cut and becomes accesible, this stone cannot be used as purchasing power. But this stone is in the hand of God, and its destruction of the human pretense to power is total. God will not pass on the power and reign of the kingdom to any other earthly entity. the chronological frame of the reign of god shall be forever. the territorial space of control shall encompass everything. God's kingdom power will encompass Babylon, Persia, the Medes, and the rest of the world. God's reign shall be eternal, infinate, and unchallenged.

Uniquely powerful is God's action in using Daniel to cause the conversion of the foreign kings who, in the end, affirm God. In Daniel, kings are transformed just enough to be useful and positive forces to further the will of God. This includes releasing Israel to its homeland. Nebuchadnezzar was converted as he realized the limitation of his own power and the unlimited power of God.

God's stone, which turns into a mountain, reminds us of the repetitive use of stones in the Bible as symbols of strength and power against human authority. The image of uncut stones means that there shall be no human authority and that the power is that of God, who made the mountains and the stones. The stone "not cut by human hands" means that God is directly involved in the sovereignty over the world and any human power. God will put an end to oppression and deliver the people of God.

SEARCH THE SCRIPTURES

1. Why was Daniel summoned to interpret Nebachadnezzar's dream? (v. 26)

2. From whom did Nebuchadnezzar receive power to rule? (v. 37)

3. In Daniel's interpretation, who was the head of gold? (v. 38)

4. How many kingdoms would follow the Babylonian kingdom? (vv. 39-40)

5. During which kingdom would God establish His kingdom that will never pass away? (v. 44)

DISCUSS THE MEANING

1. What proof can we cite that God's kingdom was greater than any of the prior kingdoms? (Daniel 2:46)

2. Discuss the character of Daniel. (Daniel 2:24)

3. By what power was Daniel's authority made manifest? (Daniel 2:18, 23)

LESSON IN OUR SOCIETY

It is rather uncommon today to observe individuals who hold themselves out as interpreters of the visions of others. Yet, frequently, people attempt to interpret the many world events and the meanings of signs in apocalyptic terms. Is there any evidence that the dream of the social underclass is the same as that of the rich and powerful? What have you observed over the past fifty years of the predictions of these foretellers of the future? Name the succession of apocalyptic foretellers in the United States and note any successful or failed interpretative attempts in the history of the world.

MAKE IT HAPPEN

Read Daniel 2:44. Can you see how God's reign has become the ultimate entity of authority and power? Do you see God's full reign in place and in effect right now? What changes in belief in God and religious practice should you or the people in your community accept that will influence the diminishing trend of human predictions and self-proclaimed apocalyptics?

FOLLOW THE SPIRIT

What God wants me to do:

_____

_____

REMEMBER YOUR THOUGHTS

Special insights you have learned:

_____

_____

MORE LIGHT ON THE TEXT
Daniel 2:26, 36-45

2:26 The king answered and said to Daniel, whose name was Belteshazzar, Art thou able to make known

unto me the dream which I have seen, and the interpretation thereof?

Upon the failure of many others to satisfy his request, King Nebuchadnezzar summons one of his captives of the exile, Daniel, to take a stab at revealing the meaning of his troubling dream. *Beltesha'tstsar* was the Chaldean name for Daniel. The original text records that Daniel was "commanded" to reveal the vision using the Chaldean word *amar,* which means to command, to declare, to speak, or to tell. By now the king is desperate because he is unable to rest, appalled at the tormenting vision he has received.

36 This is the dream; and we will tell the interpretation thereof before the king.

Daniel, after being summoned by King Nebuchadnezzar, has an awesome opportunity to assert his ability to "interpret" (*peshar* Chaldean) the dream. It is with great danger and guardedness that anyone is engaged directly with the king. The predecessors in this endeavor to interpret the dream failed, and a terrible punishment was ordered. The "dream" is *helem,* from a root word corresponding to a dream. Daniel takes an opportunity to distinguish his ability to explain the meaning of the dream in comparison to the failure of the former sorcerers who had been commissioned.

37 Thou, O king, art a king of kings: for the God of heaven hath given thee a kingdom, power, and strength, and glory.

Daniel calls out three variations for the noun "king" (Hebrew *melek*). Daniel attributes his ability to know the meaning of the vision to the power of God. The nouns for "king" are expanded in the original language: "power," *checen;* "might," *teqoph;* and "glory," *yeqar;* but these characteristics are not higher than the powerful characteristics of God. The sentiments are honorable and respectful, flowery compliments to the earthly king. These praises to the king are made possible by and granted by God.

38 And wheresoever the children of men dwell, the beasts of the field and the fowls of the heaven hath he given into thine hand, and hath made thee ruler over them all. Thou art this head of gold.

Nebuchadnezzar will have dominion over beasts, birds, and the mineral resources of the earth. We are reminded of the Genesis account when God commanded to have dominion over the earth. Likewise, Nebuchadnezzar's will dominate, *re'sh* (Chaldean), and head material "things" of the world. Yet, these are temporary, having both a determinable beginning and an end.

39 And after thee shall arise another kingdom inferior to thee, and another third kingdom of brass, which shall bear rule over all the earth.

Daniel reveals the coming kingdoms. These kingdoms shall "arise", (Hebrew *quwm* meaning to be appointed, established, or raise up self, be made to stand). The first one after King Nebuchadnezzar will be "inferior" to his. These kingdoms shall rise and fall; they will be both powerful and very weak. Yet none shall overwhelm the power of the coming Lord's kingdom, which shall have infinite rule over all of the earth and shall not end.

40 And the fourth kingdom shall be strong as iron: forasmuch as iron breaketh in pieces and subdueth all things: and as iron that breaketh all these, shall it break in pieces and bruise.

Nebuchadnezzar will not have the ultimate power on earth. God does not relinquish complete control. Future kingdoms will rise, Nebuchadnezzar's kingdom will diminish from gold, and these other kingdoms will be inferior (i.e., silver, brass , and iron) but still very strong.

41 And whereas thou sawest the feet and toes, part of potters' clay, and part of iron, the kingdom shall be divided; but there shall be in it of the strength of the iron, forasmuch as thou sawest the iron mixed with miry clay.

The imagery of the mixing of iron and clay represents the attempts of the Roman empire to unite the known world into one entity under one imperial rule.

42 And as the toes of the feet were part of iron, and part of clay, so the kingdom shall be partly strong, and partly broken. 43 And whereas thou

sawest iron mixed with miry clay, they shall mingle themselves with the seed of men: but they shall not cleave one to another, even as iron is not mixed with clay.

The references to the feet and the mixed iron and clay is an indication of the Hellenistic/ Roman period in which colonization and cultural influence become prevalent. The divided kingdom will exhibit the inherent characteristic strength of iron. The clay, a weaker material of much lower value, will not bond to the iron.

44 And in the days of these kings shall the God of heaven set up a kingdom, which shall never be destroyed: and the kingdom shall not be left to other people, but it shall break in pieces and consume all these kingdoms, and it shall stand for ever.

During the Roman empire, God established His kingdom through Jesus Christ. Although today Christ is Lord of the church and rules in the hearts of believers, one day He will return to claim His earthly throne and rule forever.

The Hebrew word for "days" is the *yowm*, meaning day–by–day, or in time. The "kings" (*melek*, a king, or royal God), will establish the kingdom. The strength of this kingdom that God has established consists of God's people and the created world and everything in it. Even though the Jews are now mixed after being Hellenized, the nation shall still stand strong and indestructible. God shall rule over it all, so that "the kingdom shall not be 'left' (*shebaq*, to quit, i.e., allow to remain, leave, let alone) to other people." Other kingdoms will be powerless against what God establishes.

45 Forasmuch as thou sawest that the stone was cut out of the mountain without hands, and that it brake in pieces the iron, the brass, the clay, the silver, and the gold; the great God hath made known to the king what shall come to pass hereafter: and the dream is certain, and the interpretation thereof sure.

The mountain as imagery symbolizes the dominance of God. It is God (*'elahh*) who "makes known" (*yeda'*, meaning to certify, know, make

known, or teach) to the king the ultimate future and all authority belong to him. The "dream" is from the Hebrew word *chaza'* meaning to gaze upon or to dream mentally. Daniel's prophecy later proved true. In the story the future kings bow to the higher, ultimate power of God. They do God's will in releasing Daniel and ultimately in releasing the Israelites to return to their homeland.

DAILY BIBLE READINGS

M: The King Has a Dream
Daniel 1:18—2:6
T: Daniel Agrees to Interpret
Daniel 2:7-16
W: Daniel Prays for Wisdom
Daniel 2:17-23
T: God Reveals Mysteries
Daniel 2:24-28
F: Daniel Tells the Dream
Daniel 2:29-35
S: This Kingdom Will Last Forever
Daniel 2:36-45
S: The Alpha and Omega
Revelation 21:1-7

TEACHING TIPS

August 31
Bible Study Guide 14

1. Words You Should Know

A. Book of names —Used in Daniel's vision of the end times; contains the names of the righteous and of the evil who will be judged.

B. Resurrection—The awakening of the dead who, in wisdom, lived in righteousness.

C. Eschaton —The end times; the return of Jesus and the judgment of God.

D. Hellenism —The impact of Greek culture–particularly on Jewish communities. Hellenism included professional contacts, mixed populations, and adoption of Greek culture, religion, and language.

E. Everlasting life –That quality of life including the promise of resurrection and life with God.

F. Everlasting contempt—A protracted, continual, and unending judgment. It is a punishment for wrongdoing and evil.

G. Righteous –Refers to a positive relationship between God and a person. It is reflective of a person's love of God, the fulfillment of the terms of a covenant between God and humanity.

2. Teacher Preparation

A. Prepare for today's lesson by reading the DAILY BIBLE READINGS throughout the week. Examine the FOCAL VERSES. Look up the meaning of new words in a Bible dictionary. Study Hebrew words for deeper meaning in a Hebrew concordance. Read the IN DEPTH study of each Scripture.

B. Materials needed: Bible, chalkboard or white board, chalk, magic marker.

3. Starting the Lesson

A. Prior to the arrival of students, write the words TITHE, OFFERING, and CURSE on the chalkboard.

B. After the students arrive, open the class with prayer. Ask them to reflect on the words and to discuss their meaning and relevance at the time of this week's text and today.

C. Read the IN FOCUS story and ask students to take turns reading the Scripture verses in today's lesson.

4. Getting into the Lesson

A. Ask the students to read BACKGROUND and THE PEOPLE, PLACES, AND TIMES sections.

B. Permit the students to discuss the meaning of today's Scripture texts verse by verse. Be sure to answer the questions in DISCUSS THE MEANING.

5. Relating the Lesson to Life

Ask students to list instances when they have seen people fully invested in living a life of the righteousness before God.

6. Arousing Action

A. Read together the suggested Scripture in Daniel 12:2. Now give the students the opportunity to write down and discuss the suggestion. Think about how your life might change today so that you are resurrected in the day of the Lord.

B. Adjourn with a closing prayer, using a student volunteer from the class to offer the prayer to take action to change their lives.

WORSHIP GUIDE

For the Superintendent or Teacher
Theme: The End Days
Scripture: Daniel 12
Song: "When We All Get to Heaven"
Devotional Thought: Lord of infinite wisdom and power, I thank You for the wisdom that You impart to us, so that we may seek life with You in that great day of resurrection, in which there is no sunset or dawning.

THE END OF THE DAYS

Bible Background • DANIEL 12
Printed Text • DANIEL 12:1-9
Devotional Reading • REVELATION 7:9-17

LESSON AIM

By the end of the lesson, students will be able to trace the roots of resurrection through the Old Testament and understand its meaning in relationship to life today and the imminent coming of Jesus. Students will learn the concept of resurrection and everlasting life in relation to those whose names are written in the Lamb's Book of Life.

KEEP IN MIND

"And many of them that sleep in the dust of the earth shall awake, some to everlasting life, and some to shame and everlasting contempt" (Daniel 12:2).

FOCAL VERSES

Daniel 12:1 And at that time shall Michael stand up, the great prince which standeth for the children of thy people: and there shall be a time of trouble, such as never was since there was a nation even to that same time: and at that time thy people shall be delivered, every one that shall be found written in the book.

2 And many of them that sleep in the dust of the earth shall awake, some to everlasting life, and some to shame and everlasting contempt.

3 And they that be wise shall shine as the brightness of the firmament; and they that turn many to righteousness as the stars for ever and ever.

4 But thou, O Daniel, shut up the words, and seal the book, even to the time of the end: many shall run to and fro, and knowledge shall be increased.

LESSON OVERVIEW

LESSON AIM
KEEP IN MIND
FOCAL VERSES
IN FOCUS
THE PEOPLE, PLACES, AND TIMES
BACKGROUND
AT-A-GLANCE
IN DEPTH
SEARCH THE SCRIPTURES
DISCUSS THE MEANING
LESSON IN OUR SOCIETY
MAKE IT HAPPEN
FOLLOW THE SPIRIT
REMEMBER YOUR THOUGHTS
MORE LIGHT ON THE TEXT
DAILY BIBLE READINGS

5 Then I Daniel looked, and, behold, there stood other two, the one on this side of the bank of the river, and the other on that side of the bank of the river.

6 And one said to the man clothed in linen, which was upon the waters of the river, How long shall it be to the end of these wonders?

7 And I heard the man clothed in linen, which was upon the waters of the river, when he held up his right hand and his left hand unto heaven, and sware by him that liveth for ever that it shall be for a time, times, and an half; and when he shall have accomplished to scatter the power of the holy people, all these things shall be finished.

8 And I heard, but I understood not: then said I, O my Lord, what shall be the end of these things?

9 And he said, Go thy way, Daniel: for the words are closed up and sealed till the time of the end.

IN FOCUS

Whenever war flares up in northwest Africa (the Middle East) between the Palestinians and modern Israel, students of the Bible ask themselves whether or not the events are related to the end times as described in the Bible. Where will it lead? Who can tell? One truth is certain, however: God in any age is concerned for justice and righteousness for all people. As these two groups battle, we are reminded of the eschatological events described in our Bible text taken from the prophecies of Daniel found in the book that bears his name.

THE PEOPLE, PLACES, AND TIMES

The Southern Kingdom of Israel went into captivity in 586 B.C. They remained in captivity for 70 years. By 536 B.C., they had returned to their land because of the favor of Cyrus, the Medo-Persian king. Daniel never returned, perhaps because of his age. Daniel is concerned about the future of his people, so God sends an angel to inform him (Daniel 10).

The angel tells Daniel that the Persian leadership would be followed by four rulers (11:2): Cyrus's son Cambyses (530 B.C.), Pseudo-Smerdie (522 B.C.), Darisu I Hystaspes (521 B.C.), and Xerxes or Ahasuerus (485 B.C.).

Eventually, a "mighty king" would arise from the west (Alexander the Great). He ruled from 333 B.C. until 323 B.C. When he died, his empire was divided among his four generals. One general, Ptolemy, became the ruler of the southern region (Egypt). Another general, Seleucus, became ruler of the northern region, which included Syria. These two dynasties fought back and forth for several hundred years. Israel, located in between them, was always caught in the middle. Daniel is assured that even though his nation would experience trouble because of this fighting, in the end Israel would be delivered.

Daniel Chapter 12 describes what to expect after the fulfillment of the events described in Chapter 11.

BACKGROUND

Unlike the first six chapters of the book in which Daniel and his companions were woven into Diaspora novella-stories that describe the life and lifestyle of Judah in Babylonian exile, the final six chapters are a unique blend of apocalyptic literature. The "apocalypse" is a genre of literary works of revelation interlaced in a narrative. Often a supernatural being speaks to a human being, disclosing information relating to a human situation with an interpretation that relates to the future and brings deliverance. With its goal being to influence both the understanding and the behavior of the observer/reader, the apocalypse is intended to interpret present earthly circumstances in the light of supernatural statements about the future.

In the first year of Darius's rule, Gabriel, an advocate of God, supported Michael in his struggle against King Darius. Three kings of Persia are Cyrus (560–530 B.C.), Xerxes (486–465 B.C.), and Artaxerxes (465–424 B.C.). The Seleucid king, Antiochus IV Epiphanes, attacked the Jews in Jerusalem because of his own imperialism and due to the Hellenizing of the Jewish community. Jews benefited economically from cooperating with the Hellenists.

Most of the prophecy in this text occurs during the reign of Antiochus IV Epiphanes and foretell his death. Because the visions do not accurately describe his death, they probably were written just prior to his demise. God will destroy all evil. God's people who are faithful until the end will be victorious.

AT-A-GLANCE

1. The People's Deeds Found Written in the Book and the Consequences of It (Daniel 12:1-3)
2. Partially Disclosed and Partially Hidden Meaning (v. 4)
3. The Vision of Figures at the Bank of the River (vv. 5-8)
4. Daniel Is Sent Away at the End of the Prophecy (v. 9)

IN DEPTH

1. The People's Deeds Found Written in the Book and the Consequences of It (Daniel 12:1-3)

Michael is reintroduced into the text. We remember him from Chapter 10, where he fought his enemies, both Persian and Greek (10:21—11:1). In the midst of trouble for God's people Israel, Michael stands as an agent of deliverance from their distress. Israel, in the end, is delivered from its suffering. One of the oldest religious concepts of judgment is mentioned in this verse. This thought is that the names of individuals who will be saved will be "found written in the book." For Christians, this book is familiar in Revelation. Psalm 69:28 and Isaiah 4:3 also mention this book as a tool used at the divine judgment.

A biblical and theological basis is presented for the expectation of a life after death. For many of the ones sleeping in the dust will awaken. Resurrection is for the wise who were righteous; they will receive everlasting life. Daniel also cites resurrection as the fate of those who will be judged and suffer everlasting punishment and contempt. The resurrection theme was strongly supported by Jesus in the New Testament when he talked to Martha in the Gospel of John just prior to Lazurus' death. The tone of the text, however, is not resurrection alone. There is a necessary process of judgment of the righteous and the unrighteous as evidenced in the Gospel of Matthew with the separation of sheep and goats.

Everlasting life refers to the quality of life and includes a human's eventual physical resurrection, enabled by God on behalf of the righteous who believe in the Lord. For Christians, the basis for resurrection is our belief in Jesus as the Christ. Everlasting life is a quality of life unbound by physical death. Although physical death is a reality, everlasting life is a joyful existence that is without end. The quality of life is more important than the duration of life. Quality of life is a life enjoyed with the knowledge of God, revival of life, and the ability to overcome sin and evil.

Everlasting punishment is a protracted, continual, and eternal period of judgment. The word "everlasting" is infinite at the end of time. Punishment introduces the concept of Israel's wrongdoing and evil; justice will be dispensed to the righteous and just payment to the unrighteous.

The quality of the reward for the righteous is defined. The writer links the "wise" or wisdom with the reward of the brightness of the firmament. Proverbs commends wisdom, describing its

attribute as the fear of the Lord. The prophecy does not stop there, however. Those who evangelize others, leading them to the way of the Lord, causing them to make a decision to turn their lives toward God's righteousness, also win elevation as "stars forever."

The wise made a good choice for righteousness and are now affirmed and glorified. The brightness imagery is reminiscent of righteousness. In John Chapter 1, light as righteous is contrasted with darkness representing evil. Daniel's prophecy uses this imagery for the righteous.

2. Partially Disclosed and Partially Hidden Meaning (v. 4)

The writer calls Daniel by name in a dialogue between Daniel and God. In the end times the knowledge will be revealed. The book containing the information on the righteous and the evil will be kept until that time. Daniel is charged to keep the information. The search of humanity ("run to and fro") to know the content of the knowledge is desperate. Yet those who are wise will receive the inner comfort necessary to wait because these know they have tried to be righteous.

3. The Vision of Figures at the Bank of the River (vv. 5-8)

Daniel is witness to four figures on a riverbank. Two figures stand on opposite banks of the river. These pursue the timing of the end time. The linen garment represents holiness. Gabriel often appears clothed in linen. Daniel has the ability to provide the information to the figure clothed in linen, presumably Gabriel, who is making the query.

The answer comes that the end time will be "a time, and a time, and a half time." Still the response is incomprehensible and left undisclosed. When will the righteous and the wicked be sorted out and the consequences meted? The wise await the crucial time as imminent and unknown; thus, it is wise to remain righteous.

The power of the oppressors will be "shattered." The holy people of God will have endured but will have suffered in the process. The righteous of Israel will see their oppressors' power come to an end. This time will mark the conclusion of the persecution by Antiochus IV.

Although Daniel has seen a lot and knows the contents of the book that has been shut up, he is still without a clue about certain key information. Daniel speaks to the one clothed in linen. Even Daniel wants to know the exact time of the end. In this regard, only God is the possessor of infinite knowledge, capable of answering the questions of who, what, where, when, and even how the end shall be. Notwithstanding the descriptive vision of Daniel, only God really knows.

4. Daniel Is Sent Away at the End of the Prophecy (v. 9)

Even Daniel is not privileged to receive the date of the actualization of the commanding event. He is told to go his way, and there the prophecy ends. The words of the prophecy are closed using the Hebrew words "closed" (*sputum*) and "sealed" (*atomism*), which provide consistency to the prophecy that it is confidential and not fully interpreted as a revelation as apocalyptic vision.

SEARCH THE SCRIPTURES

1. Who will be able to experience the positive rewards of righteousness? (Daniel 12:1)

2. What outcome in the end of time can the righteous of God expect? (12:2)

3. How long shall it be to the end of these wonders? (12:17)

DISCUSS THE MEANING

1. What does the brightness imagery symbolize in the Old Testament? (Daniel 12:3)

2. What does the linen clothing of the figure at the riverside symbolize? (12:6)

3. Whose will be the final reign over the kingdoms of the world? (12:17)

LESSON IN OUR SOCIETY

In our world, there exists a persistent personal and institutional necessity to separate people into categories or to stratify society based on artificial criteria of gender, race, and economic and societal classes. Once this stratification has taken place, the tendency to dominate the weak and overcome the disadvantaged has been consistent. God is on the side of the oppressed. Somehow the oppressed in our society, those who are poor and disadvantaged, have a special understanding, a unique ability to know God, and are wise enough to do the will of God. This wisdom, this unique knowing of God, leads to righteousness. Often power distances people from this spiritual ability to discern.

MAKE IT HAPPEN

Read Daniel 12:2. Think about your own deeds of good and assistance to others in the world, your personal power and wealth, and how you utilize it in society. Make a list of and discuss with your class the oppressive rules you observe today. Think of the consequences of this oppression in the *eschaton*.

FOLLOW THE SPIRIT

What God wants me to do:

_____

_____

REMEMBER YOUR THOUGHTS

Special insights you have learned:

_____

_____

MORE LIGHT ON THE TEXT
Daniel 12:1-9

1 And at that time shall Michael stand up, the great prince which standeth for the children of thy people: and there shall be a time of trouble, such as never was since there was a nation even to that same time: and at that time thy people shall be delivered, every one that shall be found written in the book.

Michael comes on the scene as the agent of deliverance, who we recall was in the battle with the Persian and Greek forces in Daniel 10:21—11:1. Michael will arise and be present before a judicial trial in which the judgment scene follows. Michael is the calming and consoling presence in the midst of this time of great distress for the people. He is the "protector" and the agent of deliverance of God's people from the physical turmoil imposed by their enemies in battle. The "people" (Hebrew *am*) can be a congregated unit, a tribe as those of Israel, ones who are collected troops or a flock of women and men of nation. God's people emerge relatively unscathed since they are protected by Him from the danger. The certain "time," *eth*, is now always continually due season. The purpose of God in delivering this remnant, or reserve of people, is not an end in itself. Based on their deeds of righteousness or evil, their names are written in a book. This "book," *cepher*, is a writing as in the art of writing a document, a book, letter, register, or scroll.

Those who were righteous served God day and night. As their highest and first priority they kept God's covenant. Righteousness is not an attribute of human ability alone, to do everything right and good. Yet it is based on the depth of the dependence of the believer on God. The righteous choose God's way in faith.

2 And many of them that sleep in the dust of the earth shall awake, some to everlasting life, and some to shame and everlasting contempt.

The ones who sleep are physically dead. "Sleep" in the Hebrew, *yashen*, means sleepy, asleep. All of these people will be resurrected, but there will be a separation of the group into two groups with different destinations. To become resurrected is to "awake," *quwts*, which carries the idea of abruptness in starting up from sleep, to awake, literally and figuratively to arise, to watch. Eternal life and eternal contempt represent the polarities.

3 And they that be wise shall shine as the brightness of the firmament; and they that turn many to righteousness as the stars for ever and ever.

The word "wise" in Hebrew is *sakal* and means to make or act circumspectly and hence intelligently, to consider, expertly instruct, prosper, or to deal prudently, skillfully. The reward awaiting the righteous is an existence of "brightness" in glory. The "brightness," *zahar*, is to gleam, to enlighten by caution, admonish, shine, to teach, and to warn. The light images in the book of Daniel are used as the main symbol of righteousness. This reward of brightness awaits those who are righteous, and the symbol of the "stars" is also associated with those righteous who lead others to turn to righteousness. This text is a clarion call to the righteous believer to move past the accomplishment of a personal salvation to involve others, that is, going forth to make more disciples.

4 But thou, O Daniel, shut up the words, and seal the book, even to the time of the end: many shall run to and fro, and knowledge shall be increased.

As the content and value of the great vision is concluded, Daniel must keep confidential the information that he has seen, heard, and understood. The information must be guarded, as people will become harried to obtain the knowledge and forms of evil will escalate. Thus, knowledge of the events to come is positive in the hands of the righteous who will lead others to righteous. At the same time, knowledge in the hands of the evil will be used destructively as they are agents of confusion. Evil will even "increase," *rabah*, to bring in abundance, to be in authority, or to bring up.

5 Then I Daniel looked, and, behold, there stood other two, the one on this side of the bank of the river, and the other on that side of the bank of the river.

On being admonished to keep secret the content of the vision, Daniel is in the midst of a setting on a riverbank. The entry of two additional figures standing on opposite sides of the river's banks is clear. This "river" is *ye'or*, a channel, a canal, a shaft, specifically the Nile, as the one river of Egypt, including its trenches; also the Tigris, as the main river of Assyria, like a brook, flood, river, or stream. The test of confidence now comes with inquiry by the first figure who asks about the timing of the events. The figure wears a

linen garment, the symbol of holiness traditionally worn by one known as Gabriel.

6 And one said to the man clothed in linen, which was upon the waters of the river, How long shall it be to the end of these wonders? 7 And I heard the man clothed in linen, which was upon the waters of the river, when he held up his right hand and his left hand unto heaven, and sware by him that liveth for ever that it shall be for a time, times, and an half; and when he shall have accomplished to scatter the power of the holy people, all these things shall be finished.

The response is not definitely known to or understood by most.The view of time is probably both God's quantity of time but incomprehensable to humans; yet this time is also the quality of time, as in "the right time." Similar portions of this response were the words written on the wall for King Belshazzar, which Daniel interpreted as *mene, mene, parsin.* The two phrases are not equivalent, however. The power of God's own people is challenged to shattering proportions. The times are marked y turmoil and suffering for God's people, when Michael interceded as God's agent of comfort. God "accomplishes," *kalah,* from the prime root, to end, to cease, to be finished, to perish, or to complete. Yet it also means to consume away, to utterly destroy, and to cause to expire.

8 And I heard, but I understood not: then said I, O my Lord, what shall be the end of these things?

The "outcome" of God's action is the Hebrew *'achariyth,* meaning the last or end, hence the future; also posterity, the remnant, residue, or reward. There will be a period of suffering that will include the suffering of God's people and a decrease in human power. The end times will bring about general suffering. The close of this final prophecy of Daniel covers a period described in Chapters 10-12, and the turmoil that has been characteristic of these times. There will be an end to persistent persecution of Judah by the ruler Antiochus IV. Gabriel is often viewed as the linen-clothed figure. As Daniel speaks to this figure draped in linen requesting the exact timing of the end, the secrecy is confirmed by the lack of a response.

9 And he said, Go thy way, Daniel: for the words are closed up and sealed till the time of the end.

As Daniel is sent his way, the prophetic vision is ended, and the other worldly communication ends. "Go your way" in the Hebrew is *yalak,* meaning to walk, to carry again away, or to depart on one's way. God tells Daniel to go on his way, *'amar,* to answer, appoint, certify, challenge, and to charge or to demand Daniel's action. The words are closed and sealed as seen in the Hebrew "closed" (*sutumâm*) and "sealed" (*hatumâm*). A similar word that describes the confidential character of this apocalyptic secrecy is *katham,* meaning to close up, to seal, to make an end, or to stop. The future of both the righteous and the wicked is known. The wisdom of the righteous enables their faith to sustain them until the unknown time of the events that have been described, and they attend to this partial understanding to be both watchful and faithful.

DAILY BIBLE READINGS

M: The Sealed Book
Daniel 12:1-7
T: Happy Are Those Who Persevere
Daniel 12:8-13
W: I Will Make You a Pillar
Revelation 3:7-13
T: Inherit the Imperishable
1 Corinthians 15:50-56
F: The Multitude before God's Throne
Revelation 7:9-17
S: The Lord Will Be Their Light
Revelation 22:1-7
S: Come, Inherit the Kingdom
Matthew 25:31-40

The Word is Alive

The *Precepts for Living* free CD-ROM is the perfect tool to help bring the word of God to life. With new enhanced interactivity, you can delve deeper into the content than ever before.

UMI connects you to online lesson discussions with other serious students, accessible right from your CD-ROM. Plus you can take advantage of great learning tools such as the comprehensive word and topic searches and the complete Bible in the New Living translation and the traditional King James version.

Revelation is only a click away.
Simply load the CD to begin your expansive biblical exploration.

Minimum requirements:

• Windows 98 or above.
• 40 megabytes of hard drive space
• 32 megabytes of random access memory for Windows 98/ME
• 64 megabytes of random access memory for Windows 2000/XP
• Capable of 800x600 video resolution with high color
• Certain features require modem or Internet connection
• CD or DVD drive required

NOTES

NOTES

NOTES

NOTES

NOTES